The World Bank Legal Review

Law and Justice for Development

Volume 1

The World Bank Legal Review
Law and Justice for Development

The World Bank Legal Review: Law and Justice for Development is a publication for policy makers and their advisers, attorneys, and other professionals engaged in the field of international development. It offers a combination of legal scholarship, lessons from experience, legal developments, and recent research on the many ways in which the application of law and the improvement of justice systems promote poverty reduction, economic development, and the rule of law.

The World Bank Legal Review: Law and Justice for Development is produced by the Legal Vice Presidency of the World Bank in collaboration with the legal departments of the International Finance Corporation and the Multilateral Investment Guarantee Agency. It will be published on an annual basis.

The World Bank Legal Review

Law and Justice for Development

Volume 1

THE WORLD BANK

KLUWER LAW INTERNATIONAL
THE HAGUE / LONDON / NEW YORK

Cite as: World Bank Leg. Rev.

ISBN 90-411-2001-7 (hard cover)
0-8213-5064-1 (paperback)

Rights and Permissions

The World Bank Legal Review

Law and Justice for Development

Volume 1

* Editorial Board member through March 30, 2002.

CONTENTS

Recent Reports

NOTE FROM THE EDITOR IN CHIEF

KO-YUNG TUNG
Vice President and General Counsel, The World Bank

The World Bank's mission is to promote economic growth and reduce poverty. Economic growth and poverty reduction can be neither sustainable nor equitable in the absence of the rule of law.

Modern economic systems rely on legal frameworks that facilitate market transactions and promote efficiency while safeguarding important social interests. The dynamism of the business world continually forces renewal and adaptation. New laws need to be written and old ones repealed. And institutions have to be created or modified to direct, implement, and enforce the new ways. While laws and legal institutions need to adapt and change, certain principles must remain at the core: equity, transparency, predictability, impartial application, and access to justice.

Well-functioning market mechanisms alone are not enough. There can be no sustainable development without protection of the environment and natural resources. There can be no lasting social harmony without support for the voiceless and the vulnerable, and without their inclusion in progress.

The critical role of law in shaping and accomplishing these transformations is all pervasive. The manner in which laws are written and the quality of the institutions that guide their implementation determine their effectiveness in accomplishing change. But laws and rules mean very little without the underpinning of an accessible, fair, competent, and effective judicial system. A respected and well-functioning judiciary is indispensable to ensuring respect for constitutional values and the rule of law.

It is hard work for governments to accord to their citizens the fruits of development and the reality of a better life, but the efforts of leaders cannot be confined to their countries' borders. There are daunting threats to international welfare: communicable diseases, attacks on the environmental commons, a growing digital divide, and transnational economic crimes. At the same time, increased world trade and investment, electronic commerce, and economic integration offer new opportunities for growth. Arrangements for international cooperation are more

The World Bank Legal Review: Law and Justice for Development: ix-x.

Printed in the Netherlands.

necessary than ever if we are to enjoy increased well-being and peace on our precious planet.

The World Bank Legal Review is devoted to issues of law and justice for development. Legal scholarship, lessons from experience, important legal developments, and the results of recent research in any of these areas will find a home in this new publication. The Legal Vice Presidency of the World Bank is pleased to contribute in this manner to building capacity for better legal frameworks and greater justice the world over.

FOREWORD

JAMES D. WOLFENSOHN
President, The World Bank

Law plays a critical and all-pervasive role in development. Indeed, when in January 1999 I introduced the Comprehensive Development Framework as a tool for ensuring that the structural, social, and human aspects of development would be addressed in a systematic and holistic fashion alongside the macroeconomic dimension, I listed an effective law and justice system as one of the key structural pillars of development. Laws and regulations are indispensable instruments through which societies express their order and, indeed, their aspirations. Social peace and equity, without which no lasting progress can be achieved, require a culture of respect for the rule of law, and an effective and impartial judiciary to ensure that both government and citizens stay the course.

We come to this issue on the basis of the challenge of development. This is a challenge that faces us globally, with half of the six billion people on our planet living on less than two dollars a day and a fifth living on less than one dollar a day. It is an even more difficult issue as we look forward. We know that in 25 years our planet will have eight billion people and that nearly 98% of the additional two billion people will join the developing countries and countries with economies in transition.

This very real challenge faces us all.

Bringing about equitable growth necessitates confronting the issue of poverty. To do that we must take into account various aspects of the development process at the same time. We have learned that just pouring money into a country to help it develop or that trying to impose programs from Washington, London, or Paris simply does not work. We have also learned that development plans are useless unless they have a foundation in sound economic, political, and legal systems.

The first key contributor to equitable growth and sustainable development is an effective government framework. This means properly trained and equipped officials, suitably remunerated and absolutely committed to clean government, and a transparent legislative and regulatory system, so that the instruments of govern-

The World Bank Legal Review: Law and Justice for Development: xi-xiv.

Printed in the Netherlands.

ment can work. The second component, which is equally critical, is an accessible, fair, transparent, and honest legal and judicial system – without it, there can be no equitable development. Third, a sound and transparent financial system is needed; it must be honest and available to all people.

As Amartya Sen, the Nobel Prize-winning economist, has repeatedly pointed out, social development and economic development, and, may I say, legal and judicial development, cannot be looked at separately. The issue is development. Segmentation is not appropriate because there is a close interconnection between the political, economic, social, and legal spheres.

We have seen many changes.

First, the world is moving towards increased democracy, and many countries are trying to find their way as they work to establish better governance and legal systems. At the same time, they are trying to strengthen their governments and their social and political awareness.

Globalization is another major change. One of the positive aspects of globalization is that individual states are able to form consensuses on internationally accepted principles. Some of these principles are enshrined in agreements, and others are highlighted through U.N. resolutions and declarations. The emerging global consensus was eloquently embodied in the U.N. Millennium Declaration, which encompassed the fundamental values that we all hold dear: peace and security, development and poverty eradication, environment, human rights, democracy, rule of law, and good governance. While states are certainly separate and individual, there is also an overriding influence, often a moral influence, which encourages nations to learn to live together.

In addition to these changes, two things should be made clear. First, development does not happen overnight. It is a process that takes time. Second, we need to understand the many forms of development and accept as fact that they need to be built on local cultures, local mores, local habits, local traditions, and local systems.

This is the background against which we are working and helping countries to establish the rule not of individuals, but rather the rule of law. By this I mean a system in which the government is accountable to the law, in which everyone is equal before the law and has access to the protection of the law, and in which there is a core of individual rights which are respected, including human and property rights.

Why do I mention this in terms of poverty? We have moved in our considerations of poverty well beyond the question of living on one or two dollars a day. What we are talking about is quite different in terms of tone and substance. We are talking about human beings and the way they live.

We have recently completed a study in which we interviewed 60,000 poor people in 60 countries. What we have learned is that people in poverty do not start immediately talking about money or even baskets of goods. What they start talking about is voice, access, integrity, the ability to live peacefully and to provide their children with opportunities, and for women in particular, freedom from violence and discrimination. It is also the ability to live protected under the law. They also speak of having a job and earning some money. The results of this study were enormously interesting and moving.[1]

For example, the study cites a woman in Ecuador who said, in speaking about the municipal administration: "Some receive us and others don't. It's awful. They are abusive. They treat us like dogs. The municipality only serves the high-born." A woman in Brazil reported, "I don't know who to trust, the police or the criminals. We work and we hide indoors." In Uganda, a woman told us, "If a woman is given a chicken or a goat by her parents, she cannot own it. It belongs to her husband. A wife may work hard and get a chicken. If it lays eggs, they belong to the husband." A woman, a parent, living in Ghana said, "We watch the children die because we cannot pay hospital bills and we cannot get access to government services."

What does a country's legal and justice system have to do with this? Everything. It has to do with the protection of rights. It has to do with equity. It has to do with access. It has to do with voice. And, ultimately, it has to do with the most important thing of all: it has to do with peace. Because if there is poverty, and if there is expanded poverty, the simple fact is there will be no peace. We know all too well that poverty and hopelessness can lead to exclusion and anger, and can provide a breeding ground for the ideas and actions of those who seek conflict and violence.

There is no best practice that applies everywhere. We must recognize that we need to start on the ground, look at the multiple layers of the informal systems, and then build on them as we develop a sound system based on the leadership of the governments and democratic procedures.

Establishing a legal system is a long-term challenge. We know from our work in the Bank over many years that there is no endpoint at which you can tick it off and

---

[1] The study was published in a three-volume series entitled *Voices of the Poor*. Deepa Narayan et al., *Can Anyone Hear Us?* (World Bank 2000); Deepa Narayan et al., *Crying Out for Change* (World Bank 2000); Deepa Narayan & Patti Petesh, *From Many Lands* (World Bank 2002).

say you now have done it. What is needed is the capacity to grow, to develop, to change, and to adapt to new conditions. But what is critical is that we do not change the fundamentals – that we do not put the laws back in the hands of a potentate. Respect for the rule of law must lie at the base of any changes that might be made.

I am pleased that the Legal Vice Presidency of the World Bank, in collaboration with the legal departments of IFC and MIGA, has decided to launch *The World Bank Legal Review: Law and Justice for Development*. It is intended to meet the needs of government policy makers and their advisers, business entities and their attorneys, and all those in civil society who are committed to the joint effort to uplift the lives of people around the world. I am convinced that *The World Bank Legal Review*, by sharing our knowledge on legal aspects of development, will make a significant contribution in the difficult struggle against poverty.

ARTICLES

LEGAL AND REGULATORY ASPECTS OF E-COMMERCE AND THE INTERNET

HANK INTVEN, RICHARD PFOHL,
CHERYL SLUSARCHUK AND BARRY SOOKMAN*

An "e-friendly", "e-ready" enabling legal and regulatory framework is indispensable if a country is to reap the economic and social benefits of electronic commerce and the Internet. While much of the experience in creating such an enabling legal and regulatory framework on a national level is found in and derives from the industrialized countries, the issues explored in this article raise particular challenges for policy makers in the developing world, and have implications for development of the global web-based economy. Much of the international experience points to certain advantages in harmonizing legislation. Yet there is also strong demonstration that in certain areas, particular national requirements must also be taken into account. The variety of issues and requirements dealt with in this article for the elaboration of the legal and regulatory infrastructure for e-commerce and the Internet highlights the necessity of a comprehensive approach. The evolving nature of e-commerce and the Internet and the legal issues surrounding that evolution, dictate the focus taken in this overview on the underlying essential legal infrastructure. The authors, specialists in the law of telecommunications, e-commerce, Internet, intellectual property rights, and technology, combine their experience to provide a practical overview of how the attendant legal and regulatory issues have been treated at the international and national levels in a variety of jurisdictions.

---

* The authors are members of the Toronto and Vancouver offices of the law firm McCarthy Tétrault, www.mccarthy.ca. The authors wish to thank their colleagues who provided valuable input, comments, and assistance in the preparation of this article, including Cappone D'Angelo, Sandra Draibye, Brent Kerr, Navin Khanna, and Gabrielle Richards, and express special appreciation to Karen Gilmore who provided invaluable assistance in developing, reviewing, and revising the article. Without further attribution, portions of the article draw on extracts from *Sookman*: *Computer, Internet and Electronic Commerce Law* (Carswell 1989), in some cases paraphrasing text and related footnotes.

The World Bank Legal Review: Law and Justice for Development: 3-159.

Printed in the Netherlands.

Contents

Hank Intven is a partner in the firm's business law practice group in Toronto. His practice focuses on regulatory and commercial matters involving the communications industries. He is the former executive director of telecommunications at the Canadian Radio-Television and Telecommunications Commission (CRTC). He is editor and co-author of the *Telecommunications Regulation Handbook*, published in 2001 by the World Bank, with the support of the International Telecommunications Union. He holds an LL.B. from Osgoode Hall Law School (1974) and a B.A. from the University of Western Ontario (1971).

Richard T. Pfohl is counsel in the firm's business law practice group in Toronto, practicing in the Internet and electronic commerce, technology, and intellectual property law groups. He has taught Internet and e-commerce law as an adjunct faculty member of the University of Toronto Faculty of Law and lectured in the law school and e-business LL.M. program at Osgoode Hall Law School. Mr. Pfohl previously served as counsel to the United States Senate Judiciary Committee, Subcommittee on Technology and Government Information. He holds a J.D. from Harvard Law School (*cum laude,* 1993) and an A.B. degree from Princeton University (1986).

Cheryl Slusarchuk is a partner in the firm's Technology Law group in Vancouver. She practices in the areas of U.S. and international e-commerce, as well as commercial and corporate transactions. Prior to joining the firm, Ms. Slusarchuk lived for several years in the United States, where she was a partner in the technology/e-commerce group at a large international law firm and, previously, general counsel of a NASDAQ-listed technology company. She holds an LL.B. degree from McGill University (1991) and a J.D. from Chicago-Kent College of Law (2000). Ms. Slusarchuk is admitted in British Columbia, Canada; New South Wales, Australia; and Colorado and Illinois, United States.

3.2 Authorization Laws and Policies
3.3 Competition Law and Policy
3.4 Interconnection
3.5 Tariff Regulation
3.6 Universal Access
3.7 International Trade Law

4. The Domain Name System
4.1 Overview
4.2 gTLDs
4.3 ccTLDs
4.4 Domain Name Dispute Resolution

5. Electronic Contracting
5.1 Overview
5.2 Formality Requirements
5.3 Legislative Approaches to Meeting Formalities Electronically
5.4 Electronic Authentication
5.5 Public Key Infrastructures
5.6 Balancing Confidence against Cost and Complexity

6. Consumer Protection
6.1 Overview
6.2 Policy Considerations

7. Privacy
7.1 Introduction
7.2 Core Information Privacy Principles
7.2.1 OECD Guidelines

Barry B. Sookman is the chair of the firm's internet and electronic commerce law practice group in Toronto. He is the author of the three-volume text *Sookman: Computer Law: Acquiring and Protecting Information Technology* (Carswell 1989), the four-volume text *Sookman: Computer, Internet and Electronic Commerce Law* (Carswell Apr. 2000), and *Computer, Internet and Electronic Commerce Terms: Judicial, Legislative and Technical Definitions* (Carswell 2001). He regularly advises on a wide range of issues related to computer, electronic commerce, and Internet law. He is a director of the Canadian IT Law Association and a member of the Advisory Board of the University of Toronto Faculty of Law's Centre for Innovation. Mr. Sookman holds an LL.B. from Osgoode Hall Law School (1980), a M.E.S. from the University of York (1980), and a B.A. from Concordia University (1976).

1. Introduction

This article considers certain fundamental issues related to the creation of a legal and regulatory enabling framework for e-commerce, and generally for Internet information services.[1] The article draws upon the experience of a range of countries and international organizations that have worked, over the past decade, to devise laws and policies to meet the challenges posed by these new and truly transnational phenomena.

As will be evident to readers, the article describes a work in progress. Like the Internet and e-commerce, the laws and policies governing them are in a state of evolution. While there are signs that the Internet and e-commerce are maturing, new uses – and abuses – of the Internet continue to develop. Many industrialized countries, and many more with emerging economies, are still constructing the legal and regulatory framework for the Internet and e-commerce. It is hoped that the review of the issues addressed in this article will provide a useful basis for the development of policies and laws that promote robust development of e-commerce and the Internet in other countries.

E-commerce is defined in different ways.[2] Table 1 sets out a standard classification of e-commerce and related Internet and electronic information-related activities.

Financially, the greatest promise of e-commerce lies in the business-to-business or B2B marketplace and, to a lesser but still important extent, the business-to-consumer or B2C marketplace. The worldwide B2B marketplace is projected to be valued at between U.S.$ 100 billion and U.S.$ 5 trillion by 2004.[3] The B2C

---

1 By necessity, this article does not attempt to address all legal or regulatory issues related to e-commerce or the Internet, but rather focuses on those key issues that international experience has demonstrated are necessary for creating an enabling environment – the legal and regulatory infrastructure for e-commerce necessary for the transmission of data information – without focusing on the legal framework of any particular application such as e-finance (e.g. banking, financial sector law or regulations, or anti-moneylaundering, currency or exchange controls, e-ducation, e-government, etc.)

2 *See e.g.* United Nations Committee on Trade and Development (UNCTAD), *Building Confidence* 13 (UNCTAD E-Commerce and Development Report 2001).

3 The range in estimates depends on many factors, an important one of which is whether Electronic Data Interchange (known as EDI) is included as e-commerce. The Boston Consulting Group includes private EDI and accordingly its estimates are among the highest, *see* <http://www.bcg.com>. IDC excludes private EDI transactions and expects B2B e-commerce through marketplaces to be just over 100 billion in 2004. *See* <http://

Table 1. Types of E-commerce and Related Internet Activities[4]

	Government ("G")	Business ("B")	Consumer ("C")
Government	G2G – coordination	G2B – information	G2C – information
Business	B2G – government procurement	B2B-e-commerce between businesses	B2C – e-commerce in consumer markets
Consumer	C2G – e.g., tax compliance	C2B – price & other comparisons	C2C – auction markets

marketplace has been valued at 20% of the B2B marketplace.[5] This article discusses issues of concern to all types of e-commerce and Internet information-related activities conducted over open networks such those listed in the table.

---

www.idc.com> and the chart at <http://www.idc.com/ebusinesstrends/images/issues/ebt20001116g1.gif>. *See also B-to-B Buying Picks Up!*, The Industry Standard (Oct. 2000) <http://www.thestandard.com>. For similar statistics on e-commerce in Canada, *see Statistics Canada, E-commerce and Technology*, The Daily (Apr. 3, 2001) <http://www.statcan.ca/daily/english/010403/d010403a.htm>.

4 This table is extracted from Jonathan Coppel, *E-Commerce: Impacts and Policy Challenges* 4 (OECD Economic Department Working Paper No. 252, June 23, 2000).

5 For a discussion of B2C e-commerce statistics in the OECD including the types of online consumer purchases most visited websites and value of online transactions, *see generally* Directorate for Science, Technology, and Industry, *Business-to-Consumer E-Commerce Statistics*, OECD, Consumers in the Online Marketplace OECD Workshop on the Guidelines: One Year Later, available at <http://www1.oecd.org/dsti/sti/it/secur/act/Berlin/Berlin_workshop.htm> (Berlin, Mar. 13-14, 2001). *See also* Australian Bureau of Statistics, *Use of the Internet by Householders,* cat. no. 8147.0 (2000). <http://www.noie.gov.au/projects/information_economy/researchofanalysis/ie_Stats/StateofPlayNov2000/index.htm>; Australian National Office for the Information Economy NOIE, *Current State of Play*, (November 2000). <http://www.noie.gov.au/projects/information_economy/ecommerce_analysis/index.htm>; National Computerization Agency and Ministry of Information and Communication, *2000 Korea Internet White Paper* (Oct. 2000);

Market size alone does not explain the attention paid by government policy and lawmakers to e-commerce and Internet information markets. E-commerce is widely seen as a tool to improve economic performance, in both industrialized and developing markets. It is seen as a new means to enable small- and medium-sized enterprises to compete in regional and global markets. It also has significant potential to assist enterprises in developing countries in reducing their economic disparity with industrialized countries.[6]

A recent World Bank report on the global economic prospects for developing countries arrived at four broad conclusions.[7]

(1) Businesses in developing countries should enjoy productivity gains and increased demand as a result of the Internet and e-commerce.

National (U.S.) Retail Federation and Forrester Research, *Online Retail Index* (2001) <http://www.forrester.com/NRF/1,283,0,00.html>; OECD, *Information Technology Outlook 2000*; Retail Council of Canada, *The Canadian Online Retailing Report* 2000 <http://www.retailcouncil.orga/rcc/online.pdf>; Statistics Canada, *Internet Commerce Statistics Summary – Revenue and projections* (2000) <http://strategis.ic.gc.ca/pics/ss/reuproj.pdf>; U.S. Department of Commerce, *E-Stats, March 2001* <http://www.census.gov/estats>. For a discussion of the methodologies used to determine the size of the B2C marketplace, *see Business-to-Consumer E-commerce Statistics* referred to at n.4, and the Annex to the document entitled *Indicators for measuring B2C E-Commerce* <http://www1.oecd.org/dsti/sti/it/secur/act/Berlin/roomdoc_stats.pdf>. The B2C marketplace is estimated based on the following four factors: 1. Transactions: Focuses on the transaction itself including identifying type of product being purchased, average value of transactions and whether payment was online or off-line. 2. Consumers: Focuses on the consumer including socioeconomic purchasing differences, frequency of online purchase, time spent online to make purchase and perceived benefits and barriers. 3. Businesses: Focuses on the supply-side of online retailing including number of businesses engaged in e-commerce, business sectors predominately engaged in e-commerce and barriers to adoption. 4. Readiness Indicators: Focuses on readiness of countries/businesses/consumers to engage in e-commerce including percentage of households with PCs, number of Internet users and hosts and Internet access costs.

6 Economic Commission for Africa, *Business-Government Forum on E-commerce, Maximising the Digital Opportunities, ECA's e-initiatives* (Dubai, Jan. 15-17, 2001) <http://www.oecd.org.dsti/sti/it/ec/act/dubai_ec/ECA-initiatives.pdf>.

7 World Bank, *The World Bank Report, Global Economic Prospects and the Developing Countries* ch. 4 (World Bank 2000) <http://www.wds.worldbank.org/pdf_content/0000949460101100548509/multi_page.pdf>.

(2) Consumers will benefit from increased competition and transparency, but the benefits to businesses will vary greatly depending on the industry sector, degree of product differentiation, and level of technological sophistication.

(3) Government action is critical to removing impediments to e-commerce.

(4) The gap in Internet access between industrial and developing countries, and within countries, will persist through the next decade. This disparity is a significant component of what is known as the "digital divide" or "digital opportunity."[8]

Many governments and multilateral organizations are developing and implementing policies to promote e-commerce as a tool for economic growth and human

---

[8] An important component of access to and deployment of e-commerce is use of the Internet and related technologies by a critical mass of people. Mass use of e-commerce is hampered by what has become known as the "digital divide." Broadly speaking this concept refers to the disparity of access to information and communications technology. This digital divide occurs at both national and international levels. Just as there are differences within nations there are differences between nations. There are physical barriers to access, such as a lack of access to a computer or telecommunications infrastructure. In this instance the digital divide is just a symptom of economic disparity and there is little that can be done to address it without first addressing the underlying economic disparity. If the digital divide is merely that some people lack access to the physical components (computers, Internet connections, etc.) of telephony, then the best approach is to develop strategies to deliver these products at price points accessible to a broad range of consumers. In the early days of television there was a "television divide" because (among other things) television sets were, for many people, prohibitively expensive. However as time passed, prices dropped and the technology saw mass adoption. Systemic barriers to access, however, go beyond the problem of physical access. There are a number of systemic barriers that prevent people from taking full advantage of information and communication technologies. For example there are literacy barriers that include an inability to read and write in any language. This is exacerbated by the fact that the resources on the Internet are predominantly in English. There is also computer literacy and knowing how to use computers and the Internet. To date, there has been no definitive means or approach by which to bridge the digital divide. For a discussion of these issues *see The New Economy: Beyond the Hype, Final Report on the OECD Project* (OECD 2001); Pippa Norris, *Digital Divide: Civic Engagement, Information Poverty and the Internet Worldwide* (Cambridge U. Press 2001). For a discussion of the digital divide related to the DNS, *see Second WIPO Internet Domain Name Processes* (Sept. 3, 2001) <http://WIP02.WIPO.int/process2/index.html>.

development.[9] However, governments have taken different policy approaches. For example, the U.S. government has articulated a non-regulatory, market-oriented approach to e-commerce.[10] Singapore has adopted an "Electronic Master Plan" that requires government and business to collectively focus on developing an

---

[9] The World Trade Organization (WTO) released a key study in 1998 titled *E-commerce and the Role of the WTO* and issued a *Declaration on Global E-commerce*. The study examined the potential trade gains from e-commerce and outlined the complexities and benefits of trade via the Internet. The study was intended to provide background information to WTO members who are developing policy responses to e-commerce. Among the policy issues identified in the study are the legal and regulatory framework for Internet transactions, security and privacy questions, taxation, access to the Internet, market access for suppliers over the Internet, trade facilitation, public procurement, intellectual property questions, and regulation of content. The joint declaration entrusted the general council to establish a comprehensive work program to examine all trade-related issues relating to global e-commerce, taking into account the economic, financial, and development needs of developing countries. The work program is intended to focus on the treatment of e-commerce within the framework of the General Agreement on Trade in Services, known as GATS. Also included in the work program are: principle of most favored nation, the doctrine of transparency (of national laws and regulation), competition law issues, and protection of privacy and customs duties. *See* <http://www.wto.org>. The OECD is also dealing with this issue. For example, the Development Centre of the OECD released a document titled *E-Commerce for Development: Prospects and policy issues* by Andrea Goldstein and David O'Connor <http://www.oecd.org/dev/ENGLISH/NEW/documents/tokyo2.pdf>; *see also* OECD, Economic Commission for Africa, *Business-Government Forum on E-commerce, Maximising the Digital Opportunities, ECA's e-initiatives* (Dubai, Jan. 15-17, 2001) <http://www.oecd.org.dsti/sti/it/ec/act/dubai_ec/ECA-initiatives.pdf>; APEC E-commerce Steering Group, *Statement of the Role of Governments to Promote and Facilitate e-commerce* <http://www.its.doc.gov/td/industry/otea/ecommerce/apec/blueprint.html>; and APEC Secretariat <http://www.apecsec.org.sg>. The ICC also has developed a policy statement regarding the role of regulation to promote the development of e-commerce which is available at <http://www.iccwbo.org/home/statements_rules/statements/2001/trade_related_aspects.asp>. In the United States, William J. Clinton and Albert Gore Jr. released *A Framework for Global E-commerce* (1997) <http://www.iitf.nist.gov/eleccomm/ecomm.htm> and <http://www.ecommerce.gov/internat.htm> which is a website maintained by the U.S. government for links to a number of regional organizations and country websites which focus on e-commerce and policy issues. Singapore has an electronic Master Plan which is available at <http://www.ec.gov.sg/singapore/timeline/ecmasterplan.html>.

[10] Clinton & Gore Jr., *supra* n. 9.

internationally linked e-commerce infrastructure, using e-commerce in the operations of business and government and promoting harmonized e-commerce laws and policies.[11]

Agencies in countries with emerging markets have stressed development objectives. For example, the Economic Commission for Africa has advocated the use of information and communication technologies by small- and medium- sized enterprises, government, and educational institutions. The goal is to allow developing regions to take advantage of the technology revolution and close the gap between developed and developing countries. This commission has suggested a focus on the areas of: e-education, e-health, e-business, and information and communication technology policies and infrastructure building.[12]

A variety of factors will determine the ability of countries to obtain the economic and social benefits promised by e-commerce and the Internet. A strategic focus by governments on their high-technology industries and Internet access is a starting point. Presence of an educated work force and sufficient consumer spending capacity are clearly important. However, a supportive legal and regulatory framework is also essential to establishing "e-readiness."[13] Recent studies and rankings of e-readiness provide evidence that supportive government policies and legal frameworks are significant factors in promoting e-commerce.[14]

How can a country's legal and regulatory framework promote e-commerce and the Internet development? The discussion in the subsequent sections of the article suggests that there is a wide range of answers to this question. A few key themes emerge:

(1) *Make it Easy*: An ideal legal and regulatory framework should facilitate development of a "frictionless" marketplace, with as few barriers as possi-

---

[11] Singapore, E-commerce Master Plan, *supra* n. 9.

[12] Economic Commission for Africa, *supra* n. 9.

[13] "E-readiness" is a term that has many different meanings ranging from a very specific set of activities to a short-hand for a general concept related to Internet-related activities. *See e.g.* OECD Consumer Policy Committee, *Business-to-consumer E-commerce Statistics*, *supra* n. 5, at Annex 1 where "e-readiness" is used to determine the size of the potential B2C marketplace. Another example is the Netherlands government's use of the concept of "e-business readiness" to promote foreign investment and business in the Netherlands, *see* <http://www.nfia.com/html/solution/ebiz_europe.html>.

[14] *See generally The Economist Intelligence Unit and Pyramid Research E-readiness Rankings* <http://www.eiu.com>.

ble to prevent consumers and businesses from finding each other, exchanging information, selling goods and services, making payments and carrying on other legitimate commercial activities, all using the Internet or other electronic networks.

(2) *Increase Access*: Businesses, consumers, and governments must have access to the Internet through widespread availability of information and communications technologies, including adequate telecommunications infrastructure.

(3) *Promote Trust and Confidence*: A key goal of the legal framework for e-commerce is to increase public confidence in e-commerce. The importance of this goal is underlined by research indicating that many people are still reluctant to conduct business online.[15]

(4) *Harmonization*: The Internet and e-commerce are truly borderless phenomena. Governments must recognize this and work to harmonize business practices, technical standards,[16] laws and regulations with the goals of achieving both national and international consistency.

(5) *Neutrality*: The legal framework should be neutral between e-commerce and conventional commerce.

(6) *Protect Intellectual Property Rights*: The legal framework must protect basic property rights, including copyright, that are essential to trade and wealth generation for all creators and businesses in the "new economy."

(7) *Protect Basic Consumer Rights, Human Rights and Security*: Last, but not least, the advent of the Internet did not signal the end of civilized commerce or society. Generally accepted legal norms relating to fraud and other crimes, consumer protection, privacy, hate speech, money-laundering and terrorism should also apply to e-commerce and the Internet, with any necessary modifications to recognize the realities of "cyberspace."[17]

---

15 *See* Ipsos-Reid, *Why Aren't More People Online?* (June 13, 2001) and Ipsos-Reid, *As the Internet moves into post-revolutionary phase America's share of global users declines* (May 14, 2001) <http://www.ipsosreid.com/media/content>.

16 *See* <http://www.diffuse.org> for information on emerging business and technical standards to facilitate electronic exchange of information.

17 The term "cyberspace" was coined by author William Gibson to mean a parallel universe created and sustained by the world's computers (*see* <http://www.ibiblio.org/cmc/mag/1995/sep/doherty.html>). It has also been described as a non-physical terrain

The discussion in the balance of this article is broadly divided into four areas. First is a general discussion of the issues of jurisdiction over the Internet and e-commerce. The second area, covered in chapters 3 and 4, deals with the basic information infrastructure that carries the Internet, and the domain names system that permits traffic to be directed around the Internet. The third broad area relates to e-commerce transactions. Chapter 5 deals with electronic contracting, chapter 6 with consumer protection, chapter 7 with privacy, and chapter 8 with taxation. Finally the fourth broad area deals with the content carried over the Internet. Chapter 9 covers copyright issues, and chapter 10 deals with the regulation of content and criminal activities, both content-related activities and others, such as those dealing with viruses, hacking, and other interference with computer networks.

2. Jurisdiction

2.1. Overview

Most legal systems are premised on the tenet that sovereign states exercise exclusive jurisdiction within their own territories.[18] This tenet is reflected in the public international law principle that each state has jurisdiction to make and apply its own laws within its territorial boundaries.

Geography, however, is a virtually meaningless construct on the Internet. Internet communications and e-commerce transactions can take place in or have consequences in multiple jurisdictions without the parties ever being physically present, or even aware that they are transacting in or affecting, the respective jurisdictions. The traditional physical boundaries, which have also framed legal boundaries, do not provide signposts to warn people that they may be required to abide by

---

created by computer systems (*see* <http://webopedia.lycos.com/TERM/c/cyberspace.html>) and as "an artificial world formed by the display of data as an artificial three-dimensional space, which the user can manipulate and "move through" by issuing commands to the computer" (*see* <http://www.academicpress.com/inscight/10191998/cybersp1.htm>). While not attempting to define "cyberspace" in this article, the term is used in the broadest sense as understood in common usage, reflecting the constantly evolving nature of the connected world.

[18] For a brief discussion of jurisdictional issues, *see* UNCTAD E-commerce Report, *supra* n. 2, at 39.

different rules or become subject to the jurisdiction of a separate sovereign after crossing legal boundaries.[19] This unique nature of the Internet highlights the likelihood that a single actor might be subject to haphazard, uncoordinated, and even outright contradictory regulation and prosecution by, and liability within, states that the actor never intended to reach and possibly was unaware were being accessed.[20]

Multi-jurisdictional Internet communications or e-commerce transactions raise the following two core jurisdictional questions:

(1) *Prescriptive jurisdiction*: Whether a particular country (or political subdivision)[21] can regulate the actions of a particular actor, referred to as prescriptive or regulatory jurisdiction; and

(2) *Personal jurisdiction*: Whether a particular court can decide a dispute concerning an actor, referred to as personal jurisdiction.[22] Similarly, the issue of enforcement jurisdiction concerns whether a judgment rendered by a court will be recognized by a foreign country for the purpose of enforcement.

In respect of any given transaction, at least one country or jurisdiction must have the ability to regulate, adjudicate, and enforce (or procure the enforcement of) the laws that pertain to the transaction and the actions of the participants involved in the transaction.[23] However, if more than one country exercises such jurisdiction, the cost of doing business online may prove to be prohibitive.

---

[19] *Digital Equipment Corp. v. Altavista Technology, Inc.*, 960 F. Supp. 456 (D. Mass. 1997).

[20] *American Libraries Association v. Pataki*, 969 F. Supp. 160 (S.D.N.Y. 1997).

[21] For countries with a federal system, such as the United States, Australia, and Canada, this may include determining not only whether federal laws apply, but also which, if any, state or provincial laws apply.

[22] Besides personal jurisdiction, which is discussed in this section, courts will also require subject matter jurisdiction, that is, the authority to adjudicate a particular type of dispute, in order to assert jurisdiction in the case of a particular dispute. This section does not address the issue of subject matter jurisdiction, which is a matter of common law, civil law, and statute in each country, state, or province.

[23] *Achieving Legal and Business Order in Cyberspace: A Report on Global Jurisdiction Issues Created by the Internet*, ABA Global Cyperspace Jurisdiction Report 7, 14-26, 28-33 (ABA Annual Meeting, London, July 17, 2000) <http://www.abanet.org/buslaw/cyber/initiatives/draft.rtf>.

The following hypothetical scenario illustrates the range of prescriptive and personal jurisdiction issues that can arise as a result of e-commerce activities.

A website owned and operated by a Canadian merchant but hosted on a server based in the United States sells electronic replicas of Canadian flags. The site is in both English and French and may be viewed by anyone in the world who has access to the Internet and can read English or French. Suppose the Canadian-based merchant sells 100 replica flags to consumers all over the world who electronically download the replica flag and pay for it with a credit card. If a consumer is unhappy with the quality of the flag, can the consumer have the complaint dealt with in the consumer's home country or must the complaint be filed in Canada? If the merchant misrepresented that the replica was authorized by the Canadian government, can the consumer or a government agency seek penalties in or seek to stop the misrepresentations in the consumer's home country? In Canada? In the United States? If a logo on the flag is illegal in another country, could the display of the flag on the Internet or its sale abroad be restrained? Are income taxes payable on the sale of 100 replica flags and, if so, is the tax payable to the Canadian government, to the government where the consumer resides or to the government where the server resides?

The answers to the above questions vary from country to country, and even within countries if provinces or states develop different jurisdictional rules. Also, the approach to jurisdiction issues may vary depending on the matter at issue. If the issue is likely to be considered a matter of public policy,[24] it is more likely that a state will assert jurisdiction.

---

[24] For example, the Tribunal de Grande Justice de Paris ruled in November 2000 that the auctioning of Nazi memorabilia on the California-based Yahoo! Website was illegal under French hate crimes laws. *Ligue Contre le Racisme et L'Antisémitisme v. Yahoo! Inc.*, RG: 00/05308, T.G. (Paris, Nov. 20, 2000) <http://www.juriscom.net/txt/jurisfr/cti/tgiparis20001120.pdf>. The German Federal Court of Justice held in *Gegen Gerald Fredrick Toben*, Landgericht Manheim 503 Js 9551/99 available at <http://www.netlaw.dc/urteile/bgh_4.htm> that German hate laws apply to foreigners who post content on the web in other countries, if the content is accessible in Germany. The complaint alleged that Dr. F. Toben, a former German national, living in Australia, had posted content on an Australian-based website disputing the existence of the holocaust.

2.2. Prescriptive Jurisdiction

Prescriptive jurisdiction concerns the authority of a state to apply its laws to regulate conduct or activities. It differs from personal jurisdiction and subject matter jurisdiction, which concern whether the courts of a particular jurisdiction have the authority to adjudicate a dispute or enforce a judgment.

In the Internet environment, where the location of the activity is potentially everywhere where there is Internet access, determining whether the activity implicates the laws of foreign jurisdictions raises significant factual, legal, and policy considerations.

As is discussed elsewhere in this section, states are increasingly adopting Internet and e-commerce specific laws and regulations to address perceived concerns. Laws and regulations need not, however, expressly target Internet communications or e-commerce transactions in order to apply to such activities.

A panoply of private and public law applies to traditional offline commerce. Many of these laws and regulations will apply to Internet communications and electronic commerce transactions. They will be applied by countries, provinces, and states in which parties, through electronic and other contacts, carry on business or have sufficient connections to become subject to the laws and regulations of the jurisdiction. Even if parties specify in a contract which law will govern the adjudication of disputes as between them (choice of law) and the venue where their disputes may be heard (collectively, personal jurisdiction), that contractual clause may not necessarily determine the laws that regulate their activities.

The following list, while by no means exhaustive, illustrates the range of laws, regulations and rules that may apply to online activities:

(1) *Advertising regulation* and self-regulatory codes (governing, e.g., fraudulent or deceptive advertising, disclosure requirements, comparative advertising, advertising to children, offensive or obscene messages or images, racial or ethnic slurs, restrictions on advertising particular products such as alcoholic beverages, warning notices for products such as tobacco and pharmaceuticals);

(2) *Privacy and data protection laws*, including European "omnibus" data privacy laws, anti-"spam" laws regulating unsolicited commercial messages by e-mail, restrictions on selling mailing lists or using credit card transaction data, children's privacy protection, and the enforcement of a website operator's announced policies regarding the collection, use, and disclosure of personal information;

(3) *Contract law*, including mandatory elements of contracts, writing and signature requirements, notarial and other formalities, doctrines of contract interpretation, and concepts of good faith and fair dealing;

(4) *Broadcasting and telecommunications regulations*;

(5) *Public order laws* prohibiting or regulating, for example, gambling and lotteries (which may apply to promotional or fundraising contests and sweepstakes as well as to gaming websites), obscenity and pornography (often especially strict with respect to depictions of children or violence), contracts for illegal acts;

(6) *Antitrust/competition law and fair trade practices laws*, typically designed to protect businesses as well as consumers, may govern aspects of advertising, distributorship, pricing, joint ventures, business-to-business exchanges and a variety of acts that might be characterized as attempts to monopolize a market or abuse a dominant position in a market;

(7) *Franchise or distributorship laws*, specifically designed to define the rights and obligations of intermediaries in distribution channels, which may be implicated in establishing online direct marketing and sales channels;

(8) *Tax laws*, including transaction taxes (sales, use, goods and services, value-added), income taxes (which may be imposed on either a "source" or "residence" basis), and special taxes imposed on Internet or telecommunications usage or on the transaction of business over networks;

(9) *Customs duties and documentation* for the import or export of goods, often ambiguous in the context of electronic delivery or the characterization of online products as goods or services;

(10) *Consumer protection laws*, including obligatory contractual disclosures, labeling requirements for contents and safety, prohibited unfair terms, rights of rescission and return, warranties, rules on limitation of liability, language of the contract, restrictions on debt collection practices, and special or sectoral requirements, for example, distance sales, telemarketing, package travel, automobiles, time-share condominiums, medicinal and health products;

(11) *Insurance regulation*, which may apply not only to traditional insurance products but also to some warranty and after-sales service contracts;

(12) *Securities (investment) regulation*, including licensing requirements, restrictions on solicitation and investment, obligatory adherence to self-regulatory codes and discipline, regulation of communications with investors by e-mail or through a company's or broker's website, and the application of

broker and exchange rules to online facilities for discussing and trading in securities;

(13) *Banking, lending, and credit regulations*, including, for example, licensing and insurance requirements, obligatory disclosures and accounting methods and terms, limits on interest rates and administrative fees, and obligations regarding disputed charges;

(14) *Consumer credit reporting* and credit checking regulations, including obligatory disclosures and postings, rights and restrictions on access to information, and requirements to investigate complaints and objections;

(15) *Regulated professions*, such as law, medicine, pharmacy, accounting, engineering, and architecture, which are typically subject to their own licensing, advertising, and ethical rules;

(16) *Tort law* (delictual offenses), especially doctrines of fraud, commercial libel, negligence, and strict liability for defective or injurious products and services; and

(17) *Restrictions on the import, export, or use of strong encryption algorithms*, which are often used to ensure the security or privacy of online transactions.[25]

Public international law recognizes limits on a government's prescriptive jurisdiction. There must be a legitimate interest in regulating foreign conduct or activity. Conduct that occurs within a country or that has material effects within a country is properly subject to the country's prescriptive jurisdiction. In Canada, for example, the leading approach is to ask whether there is a "real and substantial link" between the subject matter of the proceeding and this country, a test well known in public and private international law. In the United States, five acknowledged bases for the exercise of prescriptive jurisdiction are: conduct within a nation's territory, nationality, effect within a nation's territory, "protective" jurisdiction (jurisdiction of state to punish a limited number of offenses directed against the security or integrity of a state), and universal jurisdiction, such as over piracy.[26] The most controversial of these grounds relates to conduct occurring outside a country that has effects within the country asserting jurisdiction. The U.S. Restatement of

---

[25] International Chamber of Commerce Policy Statement, *Jurisdiction and Applicable Law in E-Commerce, Task Force Discussion Report* (Oct. 15, 1999).

[26] *Restatement (Third) of the Foreign Relations Law of the United States*, sec 402.

Foreign Relations Law precludes assertion of jurisdiction if its exercise would be "unreasonable."

Conflict may arise when more than one country is entitled to assert prescriptive jurisdiction.[27] For example, where a foreign merchant sells goods over the Internet to a consumer, both the merchant's government and the consumer's government might have a legitimate interest in regulating the commercial communications and representations by the merchant.

The development of the Internet and e-commerce requires that users be able to predict the results of their Internet use with some degree of assurance. Haphazard and uncoordinated regulation of the Internet internationally can only frustrate the growth of cyberspace.[28] However, it is also troublesome to allow those who conduct business on the Internet to insulate themselves from the laws and jurisdiction of every territory, except the territory where they or their computer servers are physically located.[29] These considerations strongly militate in favor of a solution which will require national, and more likely global, cooperation.

2.3. Personal Jurisdiction and Enforcement Jurisdiction

The use of the Internet to communicate or conduct electronic commerce raises the complex question of when a foreign court will assume jurisdiction over a person not residing within its territorial boundaries. Personal jurisdiction concerns the authority of a court to assert jurisdiction over the person of the defendant, with the result that the court can determine the dispute. The resolution of these issues will often entail an analysis of the long-arm statutes and rules of civil procedure in the forum state in which an action is brought, and the connections between the cause of action, the parties to the suit, and the forum in which the suit is brought.

Each country has rules for determining the circumstances under which its courts can decide matters involving a foreign defendant. For example, Japan's Code of Civil Procedure provides for personal jurisdiction where the defendant's contractual obligation is to be performed or where the defendant's tortious act took place

---

[27] However, through the doctrine of *forum non conveniens*, a court may exercise its discretionary power to decline jurisdiction when convenience of the parties and ends of justice would be better served if the action were brought and tried in another forum.

[28] *American Libraries Association v. Pataki,* 969 F. Supp. 160 (S.D.N.Y. 1997).

[29] *Supra* n. 19.

in Japan.[30] Courts will typically consider the actions of the non-resident party to justify asserting jurisdiction over that person or entity and whether assertion of jurisdiction is necessary to protect that country's nationals.[31]

Similarly, the primary basis of criminal jurisdiction is territorial. However, states have an interest in applying the provisions of their criminal laws to offenses that have real and substantive connections to the state. Some states have already applied their laws to activities taking place over the Internet.[32] Jurisdictions may have criminal laws or impose sanctions for the commission of criminal offenses that are vastly different from those in other jurisdictions.[33]

As Internet contacts grow and as e-commerce transactions expand, it is increasingly likely that residents of a particular jurisdiction will be sued and judgments will be obtained outside of the jurisdiction where the defendant carries on business. To enforce a judgment of a foreign court, the first step is to obtain recognition of the judgment.[34]

Enforcement jurisdiction concerns the authority to enforce judgments against defendants. In order to enforce a judgment, a court must have the ability to seize assets belonging to a defendant in order to compensate the plaintiff for the loss.

---

[30] Japan, Code of Civil Procedure, arts. 4-7; *see generally* Zentaro Kitagawa, 7 Doing Business in Japan sec. 1.02 (1997); Hiroshi Oda, Japanese Law (2d ed., Oxford U. Press 1999). However, in transnational disputes Japanese courts may take into account "exceptional circumstances" that overcome a general presumption of jurisdiction whenever authorized by the Code. *Id.* at 447-48. *See also* Hideyuki Kobayashi, *Products Liability Act and Transnational Litigation in Japan,* 34 Tex. Int'l L.J. 83 (1999).

[31] For example, Italy provides that a choice of any forum other than the consumer's domicile is deemed unfair and unenforceable, unless the merchant can prove it was freely negotiated, and a choice of law of a non-EU country is void if the protection is less favorable to the Italian consumer and the contract's closest connection is with an EU country. *See* Italy, Civil Code, Law No. 185, sec. 1469 bis et seq. (May 22, 1999).

[32] *See U.S. v. Thomas*, 74 F.3d 701 (6th Cir. 1996); *People v. World Interactive Gaming Corp.* 714 N.Y.S. 2d 844 (1999); *U.S. v. Thomas*, 74 F.3d 701 (6th Cir. 1996).

[33] *See* e.g. *Court Upholds Hackers' Death Sentence*, Reuters (Dec. 3, 1999) <http://www.zdnet.com/zdnn/stories/news/1,4586,2404321,00.html>. (A Chinese court imposed death sentences on two men who hacked into a computer system of a state bank to steal money.)

[34] In some states, conventions may apply to assist in the recognition of foreign judgments. *See e.g. Brussels Convention on Jurisdiction and The Enforcement of Judgements in Civil and Commercial Matters* (1968, as amended, including by regulation) <http://www.law.berkeley.edu/faculty/ddcaron/courses/rpid/rp04/006.htm>.

Difficulties can arise if the assets of the defendant are situated in a foreign country. In such a situation, the adjudicating court requires the assistance of the courts of the foreign country to seize the defendant's assets. International treaties exist to address this issue. In general, a foreign court's judgment will be recognized under the principle of comity in the jurisdiction of the defendant's assets. Exceptions may arise in the case of a violation of procedural due process, an absence of personal jurisdiction or a breach of the public policy of the defendant's state.

A recent decision of the U.S. District Court in California illustrates this point. In *La Ligue Contre Le Racisme et L'Antisémitisme, et al v. Yahoo!, Inc.*,[35] the Tribunal de Grande Justice de Paris ordered California-based Yahoo Inc. to censor Nazi-related auction items on its United States-based websites so that French users who access the sites are not exposed to materials that are illegal in France. Yahoo had argued, among other things, that because it lacks the technology to block people in France from viewing the Yahoo auction site, it could not comply with the order without banning all Nazi-related material from its worldwide services. The court imposed a daily fine of 100,000 francs for each day after the end of February 2001 that Yahoo did not comply with the judgment. However, a U.S. District Court ruled that the French court's order would be repugnant to Yahoo's constitutional rights to sell or display artifacts or expression of viewpoints associated with a particular political viewpoint, including Nazism and anti-Semitism, and refused to enforce the order against Yahoo.[36]

2.4. Online Commercial Transactions

The law that applies to a contract is called the "governing law." A clause in a contract that selects the governing law is often called a "choice of law" clause. A clause in a contract that selects the jurisdiction in which courts can hear a dispute is called a "choice of jurisdiction" or forum selection clause. The choice of law and choice of jurisdiction need not be the same. Because merchants generally draft the terms and conditions of the purchase contract, the sales agreement will often provide for the governing law and jurisdiction to be that of the merchant's home. The question then is whether such a clause will be enforced.

---

35 *Supra* n. 24.

36 *Yahoo Inc. v. La Ligue Contre Le Racisme et L'Antisémitisme,* 145 F. Supp. 2d 1168 (N.D. Cal. 2001).

Most jurisdictions give effect to a valid choice of law clause in a contract, subject to public policy concerns such as consumer protection. For example, assume a purchase agreement specifies New York law, and a consumer brings an action in a German court. Generally, the German court will enforce the purchase contract in accordance with New York law, but subject to German public policy and any mandatory German laws.[37] In most jurisdictions, consumer protection laws are mandatory. Therefore, the German consumer, in a court action in Germany will obtain the protection of German consumer protection laws.

The tension between the merchant and the consumer arises most directly with the choice of jurisdiction clause. The merchant does not want to have the expense of defending itself in numerous courts around the world. However, to continue the above example, if a German consumer must bring his or her complaint in New York, then the German consumer effectively does not have a remedy. The expense of commencing such an action would be prohibitive and is likely higher than the cost of the purchased goods.

Prior to the Internet, merchants generally had to have some physical presence in a jurisdiction before they could make sales in that jurisdiction. Therefore, it was not such a disadvantage to force a merchant to defend itself in that jurisdiction. However, if an online merchant of books located only in England is forced to defend itself in every jurisdiction to which it ships books, the associated cost may force the online merchant to restrict sales to only countries in the community of EU member states.

In determining whether to enforce a choice of law or jurisdiction provision, courts have typically taken a different legal approach with respect to business-to-business ("B2B") commercial transactions than with respect to business-to-consumer ("B2C") commercial transactions.[38]

---

[37] Mandatory laws are laws that parties to a contract may not contract out of or deviate from what is provided in a nation's law.

[38] The future Hague Convention on International Jurisdiction and Foreign Judgements in Civil and Commercial Matters, resulting from the October 1999 and June 2001 Conferences draft agreement [hereinafter Hague Draft Convention] distinguishes between B2B and B2C by providing that choice of forum clauses in B2B are enforceable whereas such clauses may not be enforceable in a B2C contracts <http://www.hcch.net/e/workprog/jdgm.html>. For a contrary view on the benefits of distinguishing between B2B and B2C, *see generally* the website of the Consumer Project on Technology <http://www.cptech.org>.

2.4.1. Business-to-Business

In B2B transactions, absent fraud or other such abuses, the generally accepted guiding principle is "party autonomy." The parties often agree on the governing law, forum, and method and rules of dispute resolution. The parties to a B2B transaction are presumed to be relatively sophisticated and equals. Consequently, under the general principle of freedom of contract, most legal systems will respect and enforce such choices.[39]

Accordingly, states have generally taken a hands-off[40] approach to jurisdiction in the B2B context. Legislative provisions ensure primarily that courts will recognize and enforce awards in respect of arbitral proceedings to which the parties have agreed to submit their commercial disputes. Specifically, signatories to the New York Convention[41] have agreed to enact (and have for the most part enacted) legislation that:

(1) allows parties to an agreement to specify arbitration of disputes relating to the agreement instead of litigation in the court system. The exception is for matters of national public policy; and

(2) provides that the courts of the jurisdiction of the signatory shall recognize and assist in the enforcement of awards made by such arbitral tribunals. Further, where parties have submitted their dispute to arbitration, the arbitrator will apply the choice of law as agreed by the parties. The choice of law can be made specifically in the contract terms or in accordance with the applicable arbitration rules.

As a result, businesses have been able to devise market solutions to jurisdictional issues. There is a minimal, but important legislative framework, which provides certainty not only as to forum, but also as to governing law. This approach pro-

---

39 ABA Jurisdiction Report, *supra* n. 23, at 18-21. *See also* sec. 6.2 of this article.

40 However, where the parties have not agreed as to jurisdiction, default rules may apply. In the EU, for example, the Brussels Convention provides that a defendant may be sued only in his country of domicile (the "country-of-origin" approach), though a plaintiff may commence proceedings in another forum (i) in contract cases (the forum where the contractual obligation is performed) and (ii) in tort cases (where the tortious act occurred).

41 *United Nations Convention on the Recognition and Enforcement of Foreign Arbitral Awards*, 7 June 1959, 330 U.N.T.S. 38.

vides both certainty and flexibility: certainty in which jurisdiction(s) proceedings may be commenced, and flexibility in choice of jurisdiction.

2.4.2. Business-to-Consumer

In contrast to B2B transactions, B2C transactions by their nature typically involve parties of unequal sophistication and bargaining power. Accordingly, legislators and courts have not afforded parties to consumer transactions the same deference regarding choice of jurisdiction as is afforded to parties to B2B transactions. A standard form contract prepared by the merchant will typically contain a choice of jurisdiction clause. However, a merchant generally cannot escape the jurisdiction of the courts of the consumer's domicile in respect of matters of consumer protection legislation or where the court otherwise determines that public policy requires the exercise of jurisdiction. Accordingly, addressing the issue of jurisdiction in the B2C context involves balancing the interests of merchants in creating commercial certainty (as well as minimizing risk and cost) against the country's interest in protecting resident consumers.

EU Approach

In the EU, legislation has taken an expansive approach to personal jurisdiction in the context of consumer transactions. The Brussels Convention[42] and the Rome Convention[43] provide that a contractual choice of forum or of applicable law, respectively, cannot deprive a consumer of the benefit of mandatory consumer protection laws in the consumer's place of habitual residence provided the consumer was solicited there or entered into the contract there. A foreign merchant continues to be subject to consumer protection laws of the consumer's home country. Further, the Brussels Convention permits a consumer to commence proceedings in the consumer's own country with respect to credit contracts, contracts with a merchant that maintains a branch, agency or other establishment in the consumer's home country, or contracts where the consumer was targeted by way of specific solicitation, invitation or advertising. The Brussels Convention reflects a "country-of-destination" approach to B2C transactions.

Recent amendments to the Brussels Convention (in the form of the Brussels Regulation) extend the country-of-destination rule further. The rule applies to any

---

42 *Supra* n. 34, art. 3.

43 Rome Convention, *infra* n. 60, art. 3.

merchant whose website is accessible by the consumer from the consumer's home country, regardless of whether the merchant actually targets the foreign consumer. As well, the Brussels Regulation will remove obligations that consumers were previously required to satisfy before commencing an action outside the merchant's home jurisdiction. Similarly, in the Hague Conference draft Convention on Jurisdiction,[44] the European Union is advocating for a "country-of-destination" approach for online consumer contracts, thereby making online merchants subject to the jurisdiction of the consumer's domicile.

As intra-European rules for the recognition and enforcement of judgments evolve, consumers will face increasingly fewer barriers in enforcing domestic awards against foreign merchants.

The expansive approach to personal jurisdiction is balanced by the "county-of-origin" approach for prescriptive jurisdiction.[45] Under the country-of-origin approach, an EU-resident merchant need only comply with the substantive laws of its country of residence, subject to certain classes of permitted exemptions. Accordingly, the EU-resident merchant need not comply with all substantive laws of each EU member state in which consumers of its products or services may reside. The effectiveness of this balancing of interests depends, in large part, on the fact that EU member states have made significant steps forward in harmonizing and coordinating their substantive law. However, such a scheme may not be viable as between jurisdictions that have yet to significantly harmonize their substantive laws.

U.S. Approach

In contrast to the EU and most civil law jurisdictions, where the approach to jurisdiction has been developed by legislation, the U.S. approach has developed primarily through case law.

The approach of U.S. courts has been to focus on the concept of personal jurisdiction in the context of traditional commerce, then modify it to accommodate the realities of e-commerce and the Internet. Historically, the U.S. approach requires

---

44 In October 1999, delegates to the conference agreed on the text of a draft convention on the Brussels Convention which is referred to as the Hague Conference draft Convention on Jurisdiction <http://www.hcch.net/e/conventions/draft36e.html>.

45 EU Directive 2000/31/EC on Certain Legal Aspects of Information Society Services, in Particular E-commerce, in the Internal Market, 2000 O.J. (L 178) 1, art. 3 [hereinafter *EU E-Commerce Directive*].

that the defendant have some minimum contact with the foreign state that may be characterized as an act of the defendant to "purposefully avail" itself of the privileges of conducting activities within the foreign state. This approach also requires that the assertion of jurisdiction by the foreign state not offend traditional notions of fair play and substantial justice.[46]

Some merchants maintain a website presence that merely provides the potential consumer with general information. For example, contact details for ordering products by telephone or facsimile rather than by e-mail or the Internet. Such sites are characterized as "passive" websites because they provide no interactivity with potential consumers and serve as nothing more than "brochureware." Generally, a "passive" website or the mere accessibility of a website is in itself not sufficient to form a basis for personal jurisdiction over a non-resident.[47]

There exists substantial U.S. case law and discussion regarding the factors that may be considered by a court in determining the active or passive nature of a website.[48] However, in most recent cases, courts in the United States have focused on whether and to what extent a website indicates that the merchant is purposely targeting residents of the foreign state.

Targeting of potential consumers is a concept used in the United States to distinguish between inadvertent contact with persons in another jurisdiction and systematic efforts to reach consumers in another jurisdiction. When there is inadvertent contact, it is generally not appropriate for such person's state to regulate conduct. When there are systematic efforts made to target consumers, it may be appropriate for the consumer's state to regulate the conduct.[49]

---

[46] *International Shoe Co. v. Washington*, 326 U.S. 310 (1045); *Hanson v. Denckla*, 357 U.S. 235, 253 (1958).

[47] *See* ABA Jurisdiction Report, *supra* n. 23, at 60-62 which discuss this aspect.

[48] In the United States, the analytical framework in determining whether jurisdiction should be asserted over a non-resident website operator should depend on the nature and quality of the commercial activities conducted over the Internet, set out by the court in *Zippo Manufacturing Co. v. Zippo Dot Com, Inc.* 952 F. Supp. 1119 (W.D. Pa. 1997). The contention that a mere passive website did not constitute sufficient commercial activities in a jurisdiction to justify exercising jurisdiction over the non-resident website operator was confirmed in *Cybersell, Inc v. Cybersell, Inc*, 130 F.3d 414 (9th Cir. 1997).

[49] United Kingdom courts have taken a similar approach, *see* 800 Flowers Trademark, [2000] F.S.R. 697 (Ch.D.) aff'd Eng. C.A. (17 May 2001) *Euromarket Designs Incorporated v. Peters Eng*. Ch.D (25 July 2000) (unreported).

The following are examples of activities indicating whether a merchant is targeting consumers in a certain jurisdiction.[50]

(1) *Specific transactions directed to persons in the jurisdiction*: For example, promoting a beach vacation during the winter to persons living in a cold climate, or promoting that U.S. residents receive favorable tax treatment in respect of a proposed investment.

(2) *Push technology*: The use of technology or electronic agents to "push" information about the merchant's products or services to consumers of a particular state, with the hope of increasing sales.

(3) *Language and currency*: Use of a jurisdiction's language and/or currency, particularly where a language other than English or a currency other than U.S. dollars is chosen.

(4) *Screening and disclaimers*: A merchant can try to avoid jurisdictions either by posting a disclaimer that residents of certain jurisdictions are prohibited from accessing the website or by physically blocking access to certain portions of the website.[51]

2.5. Consensus, Harmonization, and Coordination

Jurisdictional questions are difficult to address from a legal perspective because legal systems are based on the concept that a sovereign state has exclusive jurisdiction within its borders. In addition, due to the multi-jurisdictional consequences of Internet activities, almost every answer to a jurisdiction question will create an inconvenience or cost for one of the participants in such activities. The key to resolving these jurisdictional issues in a coherent fashion is regional and international consensus, harmonization, and coordination.

Numerous organizations and initiatives are aimed at harmonizing these issues and developing a consistent set of approaches to jurisdiction. These include the

---

[50] Recommendations of the OECD Council Concerning Guidelines for Consumer Protection in the Context of E-commerce 4-5 (Dec. 9, 1999) <http://www.oecd.org/dsti/sti/it/consumer/prod/guidelines.htm>. *See also* State Bar of California, Business Law Section, Dennis T. Rice, *Jurisdiction in Cyberspace 2001: Trying to pour new wine into old flasks* (Education Institute 2001) <http://www.calbar.org/2sec/3bus/4cyber>.

[51] It is not possible to know where a website user is physically located, unless the website user is asked about his or her location and answers accurately.

Global Business Dialogue on Electronic Commerce,[52] the Hague Conference on Private International Law,[53] the European Commission,[54] the International Chamber of Commerce,[55] the American Bar Association,[56] the United Nations Commission on International Trade Laws,[57] the World Intellectual Property Organization[58] and the World Trade Organization.[59] Within the European Union alone, numerous conventions,[60] directives, and regulations[61] address jurisdiction issues.

---

52 *See generally* the Global Business Dialogue on Electronic Commerce (GBD) website <http://www.gbd.org>.

53 The Hague Conference is an intergovernmental organization, the purpose of which is to work for the progressive unification of the rules of private international law. *See generally* <http://www.hcch.net>. The Hague Conference has 54 member states.

54 EC Regulation No 44/2001 of 22 December 2000 on Jurisdiction and the Recognition and Enforcement of Judgements in Civil and Commercial Matters, 2001 O.J. (L012) 1.

55 International Chamber of Commerce, E-commerce Project Ad Hoc Task Force, *Jurisdiction and Applicable Law in E-commerce* (June 6, 2001) <http://www.iccwbo.org/statements_rules/statements/2001/jurisdiction_and_applicable_law.html>.

56 ABA Jurisdiction Report, *supra* n. 23.

57 *See generally* UNCITRAL website <http://www.uncitral.org/en-index.htm>.

58 *See generally* WIPO website <http://www.wipo.org>.

59 *See generally E-commerce* on the WTO website <http:// www.wto.org>.

60 *See e.g.* the Brussels Convention, *supra* n. 34 (which addresses jurisdictional and enforcement issues with respect to member states of the EU); the 1988 Lugano Convention on Jurisdiction and the Enforcement of Judgements in Civil and Commercial Matters (which largely mirrors the Brussels Convention but with respect to member states of the European Free Trade Association (EFTA)); the 1980 Rome Convention on the Law Applicable to Contractual Obligations arts. 5, 7 (which addresses, for EU member states (but not EFTA states), choice-of-law issues in connection with certain contracts for the sale of goods or services) <http://www.jus.vio.no/lm/ec.applicable.law.contracts.1980/doc.html>; the 1955 Hague Convention on the Law Applicable to the International Sale of Goods (which addresses, for potentially all states, 32 choice-of-law matters relating to certain contracts for the sale of goods) <http://www.jus.uio.no/lm/hcpil.applicable.law.sog.convention.1995/>; and the 1980 United Nations Convention on contracts for the International Sale of Goods (CISG) (which again addresses, for potentially all states – currently, over fifty states both within and outside Europe have ratified or acceded to the Convention and, of EU member states, only Greece, Ireland, Portugal and the United Kingdom have not done so – 33 choice-of-law matters in relation to certain contracts

As is discussed above, specific jurisdiction issues are being addressed by a number of countries in the context of both B2B and B2C online commercial transactions. Such international co-ordination is the key to developing efficient and effective means of addressing jurisdiction issues in the future.

2.6. Alternative Approaches

In addition to the approaches discussed above, alternative approaches to resolving jurisdiction conflicts have been suggested. For example, the American Bar Association's report on jurisdiction proposes the following alternatives:[62]

(1) Creating a multinational global online standards commission to study jurisdiction issues and to develop uniform principles and global protocol, working in conjunction with other international bodies considering similar issues.

(2) Encouraging global regulatory authorities of highly regulated industries, such as banking and securities, to reach agreement regarding the uniform application of laws, rules, and regulations to the provision of such products and services, or to develop rules as to whose laws will be applied in an electronic environment.

(3) Developing new forms of dispute resolution designed to reduce transaction costs for small value disputes, and implementing structures that work well across national boundaries.[63] An example is the dispute resolution process established under ICANN[64] to resolve trademark/domain name disputes.[65]

---

for the sale of goods <http://www.jus.vio.no/lm/ec.applicable.law.contracts.1980/doc.html>.

61 EC Regulation No 44/2001, *supra* n. 54.

62 ABA Jurisdiction Report, *supra* n. 23, at 22-23, 85-165.

63 This form of alternative dispute resolution, in lieu of subjecting merchants to the jurisdiction of each of its world-wide consumer's domiciles, is supported by the International Chamber of Commerce (ICC).

64 Internet Corporation for Assigned Names and Numbers. *See* the ICANN website at <http://www.icann.org>.

65 *See* sec. 4.4 of this article for a summary of the ICANN Uniform Dispute Resolution Process.

(4) Implementing "safe harbor" agreements, as a model for the resolution of e-commerce jurisdictional conflicts. Such a model could include a public law framework of minimum standards, back-up governmental enforcement and the opportunity for a multiplicity of private, self-regulatory regimes that can establish their own distinctive dispute resolution and enforcement rules. An example is the safe harbor agreement negotiated between the United States and the European Commission in the context of personal data protection.[66]

(5) Using good faith efforts to prevent access by users to a site or service through the use of disclosures and disclaimers and through the use of screening mechanisms. For example, a merchant may post notices on the website stating that the merchant will ship product only to specific jurisdictions. Or a merchant may require the consumer to confirm whether the consumer is in fact located in such jurisdiction.[67]

3. Regulation of Information Infrastructure

3.1. Overview

Development of e-commerce, and of the Internet generally, is highly dependent on the availability and quality of telecommunications infrastructure (or "information" infrastructure as it is increasingly called). Efficient e-commerce markets require reasonably priced access to reliable high-speed telecommunications services and facilities. Lack of, or restricted access to, such infrastructure has retarded e-commerce development in many markets, especially in transitional and developing countries.

In many countries, the legal framework governing the national information infrastructure includes a combination of telecommunications law, radio spectrum licensing law, competition law, and broadcasting law. In addition, international treaties and laws, such as those developed by the World Trade Organization, have an increasingly significant impact on the development of the information infrastructure in many countries.

---

[66] *See* sec. 7.3.1 of this article for a summary of the safe harbour agreement.

[67] ABA Jurisdiction Report, *supra* n. 23, at 19-22, 78-81, 141-145, 153-160.

Telecommunications law and regulation is a large subject, and this chapter will only highlight some key issues related to the development of e-commerce.

As a general approach, many governments and multilateral development agencies, such as the World Bank, have promoted legal reforms that establish an open, flexible, and facilitative regulatory regime for information infrastructure e-commerce. An example of this approach can be found in the *Internet Toolkit* developed for African policy makers under the auspices of World Bank's *info*Dev program.[68] It proposes the following general principles for government policy related to the Internet.

1. *Think differently and stress openness*: Governments need to treat the Internet as a new technology and not a mere addition to the existing telecommunications or broadcasting regimes. Policies and regulation need to be open and flexible, to adjust to new environments.
2. *Promote competition*: Governments should work to encourage competition at all levels, a tested tool for increasing efficiency and lowering costs.
3. *Avoid unnecessary regulation*: Governments need to work to avoid unnecessary interference with the Internet's development. The Internet has grown so rapidly primarily because it has been allowed the freedom to do so.

The general approach suggested by principles such as these is deregulatory. However, government or regulatory action to implement the principles has sometimes been quite interventionist. One example involves the legal and regulatory measures that have been taken in many countries to promote competition in telecommunications infrastructure, in part to promote e-commerce. Other examples, such as tariff regulation to reduce leased line rates and Internet access rates, are discussed below.

3.2. Authorization Laws and Policies

A variety of approaches are taken in different countries to authorize telecommunications networks and services, including Internet and e-commerce services.[69] These

---

[68] Africa Internet Forum, UNECA & *info*Dev, *Economic Internet Toolkit for African Policy Makers* (World Bank 1999), available at *info*Dev website through <http://www.worldbank.org> [hereinafter *Internet Toolkit*].

[69] For a review of the approaches used to authorize telecommunications services, *see 2000 Telecommunications Regulation Handbook* (Hank Intven ed., McCarthy Tétrault LLP

approaches are normally set out in telecommunications laws or regulations, many of which have been updated as part of regulatory reform programs implemented over the last few years. In general, there are three approaches to authorizing telecommunications networks and services:

1. licensing of individual service providers;
2. general authorizations; and
3. no licensing requirements (i.e., open entry).

The trend is toward liberalization of authorization regimes for all types of telecommunications services. A good example can be found in the proposed European Union directive on the authorization of electronic communications networks and services.[70] The proposed directive is intended to replace the current Directive 97/13/EC on a common framework for general authorizations and individual licenses in the field of telecommunications services which was adopted by the European Parliament and by the Council on 10 April 1997.[71] The new directive takes into account concerns about the complex and burdensome nature of licensing of telecommunications networks and services in many EU member states.

The explanatory memorandum for the proposed directive points out that different member states have created between two to eighteen different license categories for such networks and services, each with its own conditions, procedures, charges, and fees attached. To implement the differentiation between these license categories, member states require many different kinds of information from service providers ranging from nothing at all under the lightest regime, to 49 items under one of the heaviest licensing schemes. The memorandum points out that, as a consequence, the regulatory workload involved in managing the authorization and licensing regime can be extremely heavy and that excessive administrative

---

2000) <http://www.infodev.org/projects/314regulationhandbook> *see* Module 2, Licensing Telecommunications Services.

[70] Commission of the European Communities, 2000 *Proposal for a Directive of the European Parliament and The Council on the Authorization of Electronic Communications Networks and Services* COM(2000)386 (12 July 2000). The European Parliament has recently completed its second reading of this proposed directive; *see* <http://www.europa.eu.int/information society/topics/telecom/regulatory/newrf/index_en.htm>) and it is expected to be adopted as a final text soon.

[71] 1997 O.J. (L 117) 15.

charges are imposed on some operators. A similar situation prevails in a number of developing and transitional countries around the world.

The approach of the proposed EU directive is to cut the red tape. The new directive will limit the use of specific licenses to the assignment of radio frequencies and numbers assigned under national telephone numbering plans. All other electronic communication services and networks would be permitted to operate under a general authorization. No specific licenses would be required to start up a new service or network. The proposed directive would also limit the number of conditions which may be imposed on service providers and requires a strict separation between conditions under general law, applicable to all undertakings, conditions under the general authorization and conditions attached to rights of use for radio frequencies and numbers. It specifies that withdrawing the authorization to provide services or networks shall only be used as an ultimate sanction but not as a permanent threat for any form of noncompliance with any applicable condition. Authorization procedures and information requirements are also simplified under the new directive, and authorization fees are to be reduced to a level that does not exceed associated administrative costs.

The authorization approach of the proposed EU directive is aimed at increasing the ease of entry into European telecommunications markets, and generally improving the competitiveness of those markets. Similar "general authorization" or "open entry" approaches already exist in telecommunications markets in North America and some other jurisdictions. Such approaches can be expected to be introduced in an increasing number of other countries over the coming decade.

The authorization of an increasing number of infrastructure providers has resulted in substantial telecommunications price reductions for e-commerce dependent businesses in North America and, to a lesser extent, in other OECD countries.[72] As a rule, there is still far less competition in telecommunications network service markets in developing countries, and the higher prices in those markets act as a barrier to the adoption of e-commerce.

There are other ways in which the authorization process for telecommunications service providers has been used to promote Internet access and, less directly, e-commerce. In many cases, in developing countries, individual licenses have been

---

[72] The OECD is an intergovernmental organization comprised of 29 member countries. The goal of the OECD is to provide a forum for the governments of the member countries to discuss economic and social policy in order to facilitate growth, jobs, trade and development.

issued to telecommunications service providers subject to conditions requiring network expansion, for example, to cover certain unserved areas, to provide certain high-speed facilities, or to establish public access telephone and Internet centers. In other cases, proceeds from the "sale" of individual licenses or spectrum rights are used to finance telecommunications network or Internet connectivity through a universal access fund.

In some cases, governments that are unwilling or legally unable to license competitive international telecom service providers in the voice telephone market, have nevertheless authorized direct international data links for Internet services. A common approach is to permit Internet service providers (ISPs) to use VSAT (very small aperture terminal) satellite services to bypass the normal international service networks used by the dominant telecommunications operator.[73] Thus, even where legal monopolies are retained for revenue-generation purposes in the international voice market, the licensing of satellite bypass networks can reduce the negative impacts of such monopolies on the Internet and e-commerce markets.

Approaches to authorization of Internet and e-commerce services have generally been more open than for authorization of telecommunications infrastructure services. In most countries, Internet Access Services (usually referred to as Internet Service Providers or ISPs), Internet information services and e-commerce services have been classified as "value added telecommunications services," and subject to lighter-handed or no entry regulation. In a relatively small number of countries, ISP services remain the monopoly preserve of an incumbent telecommunications carrier, sometimes a state-owned Post, Telegraph, and Telecommunications (PTT) Administration. However, this situation is becoming increasingly rare, and is generally regarded to create a significant barrier to the spread of e-commerce services. In more countries, some form of individual license or general authorization is required to provide some Internet services, such as ISP services.

In an increasing number of countries however, the provision of Internet and e-commerce services is liberalized, so that, at most, there is a "notification" requirement. Such a requirement typically requires a service provider to provide its name and legal status, address, contact names, and a brief description of the service provided. Often nothing more is required to start up an Internet or e-commerce business.

---

73 For example, in Ghana, Network Computer Systems (NCS) was given a special license to bypass the Ghana Telecom international network by means of a 2Mbps satellite link to MAE-EAST in Virginia. *See Internet Toolkit*, *supra* n. 68, at 3.

3.3. Competition Law and Policy

Telecommunications, Internet, and e-commerce markets raise unique challenges for the application of competition law and policy.[74] Network-based service markets, such as telecommunications markets, are generally more complex than many product markets, and specific applications of competition policy have evolved to deal with them. In general, these applications or competition law are most relevant insofar as they facilitate entry of various electronic businesses and prevent dominant service providers, such as incumbent telecommunications operators, from establishing or maintaining unnecessary barriers to entry.

Telecommunications operators that are dominant in their markets are usually subject to a greater degree of regulatory control and oversight, in order to ensure that they do not abuse their dominant position and reduce the level of competition in electronic service markets. A frequently cited definition of market dominance is the one adopted by the European Commission in the *United Brands* case:

> A position of economic strength enjoyed by an undertaking which enables it to prevent effective competition being maintained in the relevant market by affording it the power to behave, to an appreciable extent, independently of its competitors, customers and ultimate consumers.[75]

Many telecommunications regulators, including those in the United States, Canada, and the European Union, are implicitly or explicitly authorized by law to determine which telecommunications service providers enjoy market dominance in specific markets. Such a determination is generally a prerequisite for increased regulatory oversight and restrictions against potentially abusive conduct. For example, telecommunications tariffs of dominant operators are generally regulated in the markets where they are dominant, while other telecommunications tariffs are increasingly deregulated. As discussed below, dominant operators are also generally subject to mandatory network interconnection requirements that usually do not apply to nondominant operators.

In some countries, dominant telecommunications operators also participate actively in Internet and e-commerce businesses. For example, they frequently own ISP businesses and operate web portals. In these circumstances, competitive ISPs

---

[74] For a general discussion of the application of competition policy in telecommunications markets, *see Telecommunications Regulation Handbook*, *supra* n. 69, module 5.

[75] *United Brands v. Commission*, ECR 207.

and other e-commerce service providers frequently express concerns that the dominant operators will lever their dominance in the telecommunications infrastructure markets into the adjacent Internet and e-commerce markets. This may be done, for example, through discriminatory pricing or interconnection arrangements, providing confidential customer information from competitors to affiliates, and through a variety of other forms of "abuse" of the network operators' dominant position.

There are essentially two approaches under national law to prevent abuse of dominance by telecommunications operators from undermining competition in Internet and e-commerce markets. One approach, most commonly used by national competition authorities, is an "*ex post*" approach, in which the authority responds to complaints from users and information from its own investigations to punish or prevent recurrence of past anti-competitive conduct. Another approach, more often adopted by telecommunications regulatory authorities, is an "*ex ante*" approach in which rules or guidelines are published in advance, to prevent types of anti-competitive conduct that can be anticipated based on experience in domestic or international telecommunications markets.

Telecommunications regulatory authorities are usually better equipped than competition authorities to develop *ex ante* rules specifically applicable to telecommunications markets, because of their greater experience with the specific operation of telecommunications networks and markets. However, competition authorities have also issued *ex ante* guidances of general application to telecommunications and other markets, for example those describing rules for determining anti-competitive mergers, or what constitutes abuse of dominance.[76] *Ex ante* approaches are sometimes criticized as being unnecessarily interventionist. On the other hand, *ex post* approaches have been criticized as "closing the barn door after the horse has escaped," or, more precisely, after a competitor has been ruined, or a market segment permanently undermined, by anti-competitive behavior.

Lawmakers and regulators have also worked to ensure that dominant telecommunications operators provide access to their "essential facilities" by new entrants in telecommunications markets. The competition law concept of an essential facility is generally defined, in the context of telecommunications markets, as one that:

(1) is supplied on a monopoly basis, or subject to some degree of monopolistic control;

---

[76] For example, the Canadian Competition Bureau issued the *Enforcement Guidelines on the Abuse of Dominance Provisions* <http://www.strategis.ic.gc.ca/SSG/ct02.09e.html>.

(2) is required by competitors (e.g. interconnecting telecommunications service providers) in order to compete; and

(3) cannot practically be duplicated by competitors for technical or economic reasons.

There has been a great deal of debate in recent years regarding the classification of local loops as essential facilities, and regarding the resulting requirement that dominant telecommunications operators make these loops available to competitors, such as ISPs and DSL providers. Local loops are the so-called "last mile" wire connections between end customers and the local telecommunications switches of telephone companies. In Europe particularly, there has been a concern about the slow speed of introduction of high speed Internet access services. Providing access to so-called "unbundled" local loops of the dominant telephone companies has been viewed as an essential initiative to prevent Europe from falling further behind the United States in terms of Internet penetration and e-commerce generally. As a result, the European Union recently adopted a new regulation on unbundled access to the local loop.[77] Unbundled loop access is also mandatory in the United States, Canada, and certain other markets, as a pro-competitive measure aimed at improving penetration of high-speed Internet services.

3.4. Interconnection

Interconnection of telecommunications networks and services is essential for the efficient development of national and global e-commerce markets. In most countries, dominant operators of local access networks continue to control access to the vast majority of, if not all, residential customers. They also continue to control access to the majority of business customers, although business access markets have become considerably more competitive in OECD countries. In developing countries, dominant operators are frequently the only providers of local access to customers, and are sometimes the sole providers of national and international service networks as well. Without efficient interconnection arrangements, local and international service providers will be severely hampered providing or expanding services.

Not surprisingly, incumbent telecommunications operators have not always opened their markets voluntarily to competitors by making interconnection simple

---

77 EU Regulation of 2887/2000 of December 18 2000 on Unbundled Access to the Local Loop, 2000 O.J. (L336) 4 <http://www.icp.pt/oll/iniciativa.1_2887uk.pdf>.

and inexpensive. Resolution of interconnection problems is often cited as the number one regulatory priority for national regulatory authorities.[78]

Significant harm can be caused to telecommunications and Internet markets by delays in interconnection. Accordingly, regulators, policy makers, and international trade organizations have taken steps to expedite the conclusion of interconnection arrangements. Many regulators have required dominant local telecommunications operators to publish their interconnection agreements or provide "reference interconnection offers" so that each operator will not have to commence interconnection negotiations anew. This approach was adopted in the Telecommunications Regulation Reference Paper adopted by most signatories to the 1998 World Trade Organization (WTO) Agreement on Basic Telecommunications.[79] The Reference Paper requires dominant telecommunications network operators, described in the paper as "major suppliers," to make publicly available either interconnection agreements or a reference interconnection offer.[80]

3.5. Tariff Regulation

Tariff regulation of telecommunications services can have a significant impact on the growth of e-commerce and Internet use generally. High telecommunications tariffs can stifle Internet usage and demand. High tariffs have been particularly problematic in some countries where Internet usage is seen as a prerogative of business customers and wealthy individuals. In those countries, high tariffs have been established with the approval of governments or regulators, without sufficient regard to the negative economic impact that results from depressed levels of Internet usage. Regulators and dominant telecommunications service providers in such countries are now realizing that high Internet-related telecommunications tariffs can significantly impair a country's international competitiveness.

In recent years, tariffs for two telecommunications services have been the focus of considerable debate in the context of promoting e-commerce. One debate involves the issue of unmetered Internet access tariffs, the other involves leased

---

[78] *See e.g.* International Telecommunications Union, *Trends in Telecommunications Reform* (1999) (2000).

[79] *Annex to the Fourth Protocol to the GATS Agreement.*

[80] A good discussion of interconnection issues related to the Internet and to telecommunications networks generally is included in the 2000/1 issue of the ITU, *supra* n. 78, which is devoted to interconnection issues. Interconnection issues are also canvassed in detail in Module 3 of the *Telecommunications Regulation Handbook*, *supra* n. 69.

line tariffs. Both issues have been canvassed extensively in the EU and other jurisdictions.

The issue of unmetered Internet access tariffs will be considered first. Most Internet users dial up through the public telecommunications networks to connect to their ISP. In Europe and most countries, dial-up users pay metered local access charges, based on the time they remain online. However, this is not the case in several countries, notably Australia, Canada, New Zealand, and the United States, where flat or unmetered local telecommunications tariffs apply. A landmark study by the OECD in 2000 on *Local Access Pricing and E-commerce* demonstrated that there are marked differences in the growth of the Internet in metered and unmetered markets.[81] The OECD study indicated that:

(1) the difference in the penetration of Internet hosts, between countries with metered and unmetered local telecommunication charges to access the Internet, is a multiple of 6.1; and

(2) the difference in the penetration of secure servers, between countries with metered and unmetered local telecommunication charges to access the Internet, is a multiple of 5.8.[82]

Market research supports the importance of the impact of high metered telecommunications tariffs on Internet usage. A February 2000 study, based on interviews with users in 4000 residential homes in the United Kingdom, indicates that users would make greater use of the Internet if they had unmetered access tariffs. It suggested that residential Internet users would increase the frequency of their Internet access by 46% and the duration of their Internet sessions by over 100% if they had the option of unmetered access. According to the study, such increases in usage would lift the average Internet use in the United Kingdom from 11 hours per month to 32 hours per month. The study concluded that the U.K. Internet economy was being "dramatically" held back by the absence of unmetered Internet access.[83]

This newfound support for unmetered local access tariffs is interesting, since for many years telecommunications economists have promoted metered tariffs as

---

[81] OECD, Working Party on Telecommunication and Information Services Policies, *Local Access Pricing and E-Commerce*, DSTI/ICCP/TISP(2000)1/FINAL (July 2000), <http://www.olis.oecd.org/olis/2000doc.nsf/linkto/dsti-iccp-tisp(2000)\final>.

[82] OECD, *supra* n. 81, at 30.

[83] *Id.*, citing Durlacher (Feb. 14, 2000). The Executive Summary of the Durlacher report is available at <http://www.durlacher.com/research/res-iqreportsq499execsummary.asp>.

a more efficient means of recovering the underlying costs of telecommunications services, and of reducing wasteful consumption of telecommunications services. However, it is clear that international competitiveness has become the watchword. In its report "E-commerce@its.best.uk", the Performance and Innovation Unit of the U.K. Cabinet Office recommended that a wider range of tariff options should be available to increase penetration of electronic commerce. The report stated that tariff structures in the United Kingdom "... should not create inappropriate disincentives for spending online time relative to international rivals."[84]

It is clear that metered local access tariffs do have some benefits, and that factors other than these tariffs can explain some of the differences between e-commerce penetration in different markets. The OECD report on *Local Access Pricing and E-commerce* did not treat flat local tariffs as a panacea for lower Internet penetration in some countries. However, the report's conclusions make it clear that tariff reform, among other issues, should be included in a regulatory framework to promote e-commerce:

> The level and structure, of pricing for Internet access is one of the major constraints facing users and potential users. This report has reviewed new pricing structures that are emerging to facilitate increasing access and use of the Internet, and concludes that the key to greater tariff innovation to support electronic commerce is increased competition, including appropriate regulation of incumbent carriers. In those countries where competition is most advanced, at the local level, the benefits of pricing innovation are increasingly evident. By way of contrast, the growing international digital divide, across the OECD, will further widen in the absence of competition in local markets in other countries.
>
> For policy makers or regulators the preferable response to the challenges of the international digital divide, is not to mandate particular tariff structures *(e.g.* unmetered access), even if the evidence is mounting that they are more appropriate for electronic commerce. This would be a retrograde step in that it would return policy makers to setting telecommunication tariffs. Rather the report highlights other policy options which are available, including:
>
> (1) High level policy support for a greater range of tariff options, in particular pricing favourable to 'always-on' capabilities necessary to support electronic commerce;

[84] e-commerce@its.best.uk, *Performance and Innovation Unit Report* 53 (Sept. 1999) <http://www.cabinet-office.gov.uk/innovation/1999/ecommerce/index.htm>.

(2) Policy support for infrastructure competition;

(3) Policy support for unbundling local loops;

(4) Policy support for the competitive development of high-speed access options.[85]

A case study of Internet development in Argentina provides strong corroboration for the view that tariff regulation, and particularly lowering of local access and leased line tariffs, can have a strongly positive impact on Internet penetration.[86] This study indicates that, in 1993, Argentina had very low Internet penetration compared to neighboring countries. Specifically, it had only 0.05 Internet hosts per 10,000 people, compared to Chile with 1.01, Brazil 0.27, Mexico 0.4 and Venezuela 0.23.

By 1999, however the situation had changed dramatically. In July 1999, the study reports that Argentina had 39 hosts per 10,000 people, compared to only 25 per 10,000 in Chile and Brazil. The number of estimated Internet users in Argentina increased from about 70,000 in late 1996 to about 900,000 in mid 1999. The authors of the study attribute this significant increase in Internet penetration to two main factors. One was the lowering of tariffs for local access to the Internet. Argentina achieved this, not by moving to unmetered tariffs, as exist in the United States and Canada, but by establishing a special dialing code (0610) to access ISPs. Tariffs for Internet access via that code were reduced by as much as 58% relative to the tariffs for local telephone access.

The second factor cited by the authors as causes for the increased Internet penetration level was a reduction in the tariffs for leased lines used for Internet backbone circuits. The low leased line prices that exist in the highly competitive North American telecommunications markets are often cited as a reason for high Internet penetration levels there. For example, a 1999 OECD study[87] indicates that, on average, tariffs for 2 Mbps leased lines in Europe were five times higher than in North America. The Argentina case study indicated that, in 1997, the price for a

---

[85] *Supra* n. 81, at 58.

[86] B. A. Petrazzini & A. Guerero, *Promoting Internet Development: The Case of Argentina*, 24 Telecom Policy (2000).

[87] OECD, Working Party on Telecommunication and Information Services Policies, *Building Infrastructure Capacity for Electronic Commerce Leased Line Developments and Pricing*, DSTI/ICCP/TISP(99)4/FINAL (Aug. 1999).

1.5 Mbps link from the United States to Argentina was U.S.$1,500. At the same time, the same speed link from Argentina back to the United States was more than 10 times that price. Recognizing the negative impact on e-commerce, the Argentine government passed a decree lowering leased line rates by an estimated 45%.

3.6. Universal Access

Many developing countries continue to be hampered by low levels of access to telecommunications networks, a factor that significantly retards the potential for e-commerce there. A variety of approaches have been adopted in telecommunications laws and policies to expand access. These include:

(1) *Market-Based Reforms*: especially privatization, competition, and cost-based pricing;

(2) *Mandatory Service Obligations*: imposed by license conditions or other regulatory measures;

(3) *Cross Subsidies*: between or within services provided by incumbent operators;

(4) *Access Deficit Charges*: paid by telecommunications operators to subsidize the access deficit of incumbent operators; and

(5) *Universality Funds*: independently administered funds that collect revenues from various sources and provide targeted subsidies to implement universality programs.[88]

The latter approach, which is sometimes referred to as involving "output-based subsidies," is particularly apt in expanding services to areas that are uneconomic to serve. A one-time or periodic subsidy can often enable installation of a network. Once the initial capital costs are covered, ongoing revenues can often be sufficient to fund ongoing operating costs. The World Bank and other development agencies are becoming increasingly interested in output-based subsidy programs as a means to reduce the "digital divide" in the world. A common requirement for network expansion programs that are financed by such universality funds is the establishment of community telecenters that permit access to the Internet by people without individual telephone lines or computers. Such approaches to shared access to

---

[88] These approaches are discussed in detail in Module 6 of the *Telecommunications Regulation Handbook*, *supra* n. 69.

the Internet could significantly increase the uptake of e-commerce in developing countries.

3.7. International Trade Law

The WTO provides the institutional and legal foundation for the multilateral trading system. The WTO came into force on January 1, 1995. It was established by a short agreement of sixteen articles. However, four annexes to the agreement contain all the other agreements reached in the Uruguay Round of the WTO's predecessor, the General Agreement on Tariffs and Trade (GATT), as well as the earlier GATT provisions and understandings that have been carried over to the new system of multilateral trade relations.

All WTO member states are bound by the general obligations and disciplines of the General Agreement on Trade in Services (GATS). Several of these are directly relevant to the legal framework for telecommunications and e-commerce services in member states. These include the requirement for Most-Favored-Nation Treatment[89] which requires telecommunications regulatory regimes to treat service providers from other WTO member countries on terms that are no less favorable than those applicable to providers from any other country.

Another key obligation is the transparency requirement,[90] which requires all laws and rules affecting trade in services to be published. The Telecommunications Annex to the GATS specifically requires the publication of, among other things, all notification, registration and licensing requirements, if any, as well as any other forms of recognition and approval needed by foreign service providers. Article VI of the GATS specifically provides that licensing requirements may not constitute unnecessary barriers to trade.

The 1998 WTO Agreement on Basic Telecommunications, adopted as the *Fourth Protocol to the GATS Agreement* contains specific commitments by individual member countries regarding increased access by competitive suppliers to their telecommunications markets.

These commitments, by countries representing well over 90% of the global telecommunications market, constitute an unprecedented initiative to open this market to competition and increased international trade. In addition to the individual commitments, most signatories to the *Fourth Protocol* have agreed to

---

[89] GATS, art. II.

[90] GATS, art III.

adhere to specific regulatory principles set out in the regulation reference paper annexed to the protocol. The regulatory principles deal with the following topics:

(1) competitive safeguards;
(2) interconnection;
(3) universal service;
(4) public availability of licensing criteria;
(5) independent regulators; and
(6) allocation and use of scarce resources.

The general principles set out in the reference paper are being adopted in the laws, regulations, and other regulatory instruments applicable to telecommunications markets around the world. The WTO has continued to promote liberalized trade rules for e-commerce in ministerial conferences that have followed adoption of the *Fourth Protocol*.[91]

4. The Domain Name System

4.1. Overview

As anyone who has surfed the web knows, domain names provide a quick and easy means for consumers and businesses to locate and access websites. The smooth functioning of the Domain Name System (DNS) is essential to the operation of e-commerce and the Internet.

The growth of e-commerce has led to a proliferation of domain names. As of October 18, 2001, the number of Internet domain names registered was 36,129,180.[92] E-commerce has also led to an increase in the value of some names. The value of many major domain names is now over U.S.$ 1,000,000.[93] With the increase in registrations and their associated values, there has also been an increase in disputes over the use of names. As of October 18, 2001, 4,595 disputes had been

---

91 *See also supra* n. 9; and *cf* text accompanying *infra* n. 198. However, treatment of e-commerce by the WTO is under discussion as of the time of this writing, and is an area to be watched.

92 Statistics available at <http://www.domainstats.com>.

93 *See* <http://www.submerged-ideas.com/valuation/topdomainsales.htm>.

filed under the Uniform Dispute Resolution Process, in respect of 7,922 domain names.[94]

4.2. gTLDs

A domain name is a simple alphanumeric "label" that is associated with one or more Internet Protocol (IP) addresses. IP addresses consist of a series of numbers that are used by Internet routers and networks to identify points of origin and destinations for Internet traffic.

Top-level domains are the suffixes of domain names that are located to the right side of the "dot" or ".". The best known top level domain in e-commerce is, of course "dot.com" or ".com". Top level domains are classified as either generic top-level domains ("gTLDs")[95] such as ".com", ".gov", and ".org", or country-code top-level domains ("ccTLDs") such as ".uk".

The domain name system and its governance structure originated from, and largely remains subject to, rules established by the government and the courts[96] of the United States. This remains the case today, although the DNS facilitates communication among Internet users and domain name registrants throughout the world. As of November 25, 1998, the U.S. Department of Commerce contracted the administration of gTLDs to the Internet Corporation for Assigned Names and Numbers (ICANN), a California non-profit corporation.[97] ICANN, in turn, has delegated

---

[94] *Statistical Summary of Proceedings under Uniform Domain Name Dispute Resolution* Policy <http://www.icann.org/udrp/proceedings-stat.htm>.

[95] Currently, the operational gTLDs include .com, .org, and .net (which are open for use by any person), .edu and .int. (which are restricted for use by qualifying educational institutions and by qualifying international organizations, respectively), and .gov, and .mil (which are restricted for use by the U.S. Government). On November 26, 2000, ICANN approved the addition of .biz, .info, .pro, .name, .coop, .aero, and .museum gTLDs to the DNS.

[96] Although the DNS is maintained pursuant to a shared registry system whereby registrars of domain names collectively administer a list of domain names that permits computers to "find" the URL that is typed or linked to by the user, the master computer server from which the entire DNS routes Internet traffic is maintained by VeriSign, Inc. and is located in Herndon, Virginia. Accordingly, the courts of the United States are capable of exercising jurisdiction over most disputes related to the DNS.

[97] Pursuant to a Memorandum of Understanding between ICANN and the U.S. Department of Commerce (25 November 1998) as amended, *see* <http://www.icann.org/general/icann-mou-25nov98.htm>.

the task of registration of individual domain names to registrars that have been certified by ICANN in accordance with its Registrar Accreditation Agreement.[98]

The increasingly global nature of the DNS and the domestic policies and legislation of individual countries have impacted on, and likely will continue to influence the administration of, the DNS. For example, VeriSign's recent introduction of non-English character domain names has raised questions regarding the role of countries other than the United States in administering the DNS. VeriSign is the U.S.-based domain name registrar that is currently charged with administering the .com, .net, and .org gTLDs. In response to VeriSign's initiative, officials from the China Internet Network Information Centre, an agency of the Ministry of Information Industry of the Peoples Republic of China that administers the .cn ccTLD, expressed the view that Chinese character domain names within the gTLD should be under the mandate of the "Chinese people."[99]

Concerns have also been expressed about the extent to which the legal system of one country, the United States, is used to determine the legal rights to the registration and use of domain names, when the intellectual property rights of another country's nationals are at stake. For example, the United States has enacted the *Anti-Cybersquatting Consumer Protection Act* (U.S. ACPA).[100] The U.S. ACPA provides remedies for owners of U.S. trademarks (regardless of whether the owner is otherwise connected to the United States) against persons (again, regardless of connection to the United States) who have in bad faith registered a domain name that is the same as or confusingly similar to the trade mark of a complainant. The U.S. ACPA provides *in rem* jurisdiction against the domain name itself. VeriSign's server, the central domain name registry for the .com, .net and .org gTLDs, is physically situated in the state of Virginia. On this basis, U.S. courts have ruled that they have jurisdiction in U.S. ACPA proceedings relating to these gTLDs, regardless of the country where a domain name's registrant is domiciled.[101]

---

[98] Agreement dated 17 May 2001, *see* <http://www.icann.org/registrars/ra-agreement-17may01.htm>.

[99] *See Row over Chinese domain names deepens*, The Indian Express (November 4, 2001) <http://www.indian-express.com/ie/daily/20001205/iin05013.html>. *See also Asia's multilingual mess on the Net*, CNN (February 20, 2001) <http://asia.cnn.com/2001/WORLD/asiapcf/southeast/02/18/sing.multinet>.

[100] 15 U.S.C. § 1125(d).

[101] *See Heathmount A.E. Corp. v. Technidome.com* 55 U.S.P.Q. (2d) 1735 (E.D. Va. 2000) and further opinion, case No. CA-00-00 714-A (E.D. Va. Dec. 29, 2000)

The increasing globalization of the Internet is likely to lead to continued pressures for international input into the administration of the gTLD system.

4.3. ccTLDs

Country code top-level domains consist of two-letter country codes maintained by the International Organization for Standardization (ISO) in the form of the ISO 3166-1 list.[102] Examples of top level ccTLDs include .de for Germany, .jp for Japan and the recently added .ps[103] for the Palestinian Territories. Decisions regarding the allocation of ccTLDs are made by the Internet Assigned Numbers Authority (IANA). Administrative authority over the ccTLDs has been delegated by IANA to organizations domiciled in each country in accordance with the guidelines of IANA documents RFC 1591[104] and ICP-1.[105]

The IANA documents governing the ccTLD system expressly contemplate the participation of individual countries in administering their respective ccTLDs. In practice, however, few governments have actively participated in administration of the ccTLD system. In the absence of pressure from their local Internet communities, most governments have been content to forego direct regulation of or participation in the administration of their ccTLDs. Therefore, in most cases, ccTLD registration and administration duties remain with the person or organization to which such duties were initially delegated by IANA.[106]

---

102 *See* <http://www.din.de/gremien/nas/nabd/iso3166ma/codlstp1/en_listp1.html>.

103 *See* Internet Assigned Numbers Authority (IANA), *Report on Request for Delegation of the .ps Top-Level Domain* <http://www.iana.org/cctld/reports/ps-report-22mar00.htm>.

104 Internet Assigned Numbers Authority (IANA), Document no. RFC 1591, <http://www.isi.edu/in-n.s/rfc1591.txt>.

105 Internet Assigned Numbers Authority (IANA), Document no. ICP-1, <http://www.iana.org/cctld/icp1.htm>.

106 However, governments of some countries have expressed frustration with the practices of ccTLD registrars, for example, in relation to the fairness and transparency with which country-level domain names are issued. In some cases, delays or disparate pricing schemes have resulted in bottlenecks in the development of web-based services businesses. Overcoming these bottlenecks implies a role for legal and regulatory solutions in dealing with "hidden" barriers to trade and investment, perhaps through the application of general competition principles. Other solutions, such as undertaken by South Africa, have seen the introduction of competition in the registration of certain ".za" domain names (*see ZA domain registration goes competitive* (Aug. 22, 2001) <http://www.itweb.co.za>.)

There have been recent instances in which IANA has redelegated administration of ccTLDs at the request of a government. It is clear that governments will be able to significantly influence, if not determine, the redelegation and subsequent administration of their corresponding ccTLD, whether the original registrar agrees to transfer authority[107] or not.[108]

Models for administration of ccTLDs may be categorized as either "open" or "closed." Registration of open ccTLDs is typically unrestricted, and registrar functions for open ccTLDs are typically delegated to commercial domain name registrars who subsequently offer the domain names to the entire Internet community. Open ccTLDs include .to (Tongo), .tv (Tuvalu), .ws (Western Samoa), .cc (Cocos Islands), .mu (Mauritius), .md (Moldova), .am (Armenia), and .fm (Micronesia). Registration of closed ccTLDs, on the other hand, is typically limited to individuals or organizations domiciled in or otherwise connected to the respective country.[109] Closed ccTLDs include .us (United States)[110] and .ca (Canada).[111]

By restricting the registration of domain names to resident individuals or organizations, closed ccTLD models address the public policy objective of providing a domestic DNS for the domestic Internet community. A closed model can "reserve" the finite number of the country's ccTLDs for use by domestic individuals and organizations. It can also ensure that the country's ccTLD serves as an indicator of country of origin.

---

[107] In Canada, for example, the administration of the .ca domain was recently transferred from the University of British Columbia to a newly incorporated not-for-profit corporation, the Canadian Internet Registration Authority (CIRA). *See* <http://www.cira.ca/en/cat_Cira.html>, which includes copies of letters from the Government of Canada to ICANN requesting the redelegation of administration of the .ca domain.

[108] *See e.g.* IANA, *Report on Request for Redelegation of the .au Top-Level Domain* <http://www.iana.org/reports/au-report-31aug01.htm>; *see also* Michael Froomkin, *How ICANN Policy Is Made* (II) <http://www.icannwatch.org/essays/dotau.htm>, for a critical account of the decision of IANA to re-delegate the .au domain.

[109] How to circumscribe the persons entitled to obtain a ccTLD involves difficult policy questions.

[110] For a critical review of proposed changes to the .us ccTLD, *see* Peter Maggs, *The ".us" Internet Domain* (Law and Economics Working Paper Series No. 00-27, 2001) <http://papers.ssrn.com/sol3/papers.cfm?abstract_id=283908>.

[111] The Canadian Presence Requirements are available at <http://cira.ca>.

The open model, by contrast, seeks to transform a ccTLD into a gTLD by allowing registration of a domain name by any person. Open ccTLDs are typically marketed as an alternative to seemingly scarce .com domain names or for their value as acronyms (such as .ws for "website" or .tv for "television"), and have, in a few cases, provided an economic windfall for countries with little domestic market for domain names. For example, the fees paid by the .tv Corporation to the island of Tuvalu for the right to administer the .tv ccTLD nearly doubled the annual GDP of the country.[112]

4.4. Domain Name Dispute Resolution

Disputes have often arisen between owners of trademarks and individuals or entities that have registered Internet domain names that are the same as, or confusing with the trademark. Disputes arise for a number of reasons, often because of bona fide disputes over trademarks outside of the Internet realm. However, some disputes result from the actions of "cybersquatters" who have made such domain name registrations that are clearly similar to existing trade marks.

To respond to conflicts related to the abuse of domain name registrations, ICANN has adopted a uniform domain name dispute resolution policy.[113] The ICANN policy (ICANN UDRP) establishes a legal framework for the resolution of disputes between domain name registrants and third parties over abusive registration and use of an Internet domain name. The ICANN UDRP is based largely on the recommendations in the report of the WIPO Internet Domain Name Process as well as other comments submitted by registrars and other interested parties.

All registrars accredited to register names in the .biz, .com, .info, .name, .net, and .org top-level domains have agreed to abide by and implement the ICANN UDRP. In turn, any person or entity wishing to register a domain name in the .com, .net and .org top-level domains is required to consent to the terms and conditions of the ICANN UDRP. A registrant's agreement to the ICANN UDRP is obtained by incorporating that policy into the domain name registration agreement. To this end, paragraph 1 of the ICANN UDRP provides that:

---

[112] *See* Suh-kyung Yoon, *Dots on the Map*, Far Eastern Economic Review (Sept. 14, 2000) <http://www.globalpolicy.org/nations/micro/0523net.htm>; *see also* Mark Grossman & Andrew Chulock, *How to Manage "Country-Code" Domain Names in a ".com" World* (Aug. 2000) <http://www.gigalaw.com/articles/grossman-2000-08a-p1.html>.

[113] Uniform Domain Name Dispute Resolution Policy (UDRP). The policy is available at <http://www.icann.org/udrp/udrp-policy-24oct99.htm>.

> 1. *Purpose*. This Uniform Domain Name Dispute Resolution Policy (the "Policy") has been adopted by the Internet Corporation for Assigned Names and Numbers ("ICANN"), is incorporated by reference into your Registration Agreement, and sets forth the terms and conditions in connection with a dispute between you and any party other than us (the registrar) over the registration and use of an Internet domain name registered by you. Proceedings under Paragraph 4 of this Policy will be conducted according to the Rules for Uniform Domain Name Dispute Resolution Policy (the "Rules of Procedure"), which are available at www.icann.org/udrp/udrp-rules-24oct99.htm, and the selected administrative-dispute-resolution service provider's supplemental rules.[114]

Under the ICANN UDRP, registrants must make certain representations and warranties with respect to statements made in the Registration Agreement and with respect to the use and non-infringement of domain names applied for. The representations are set out in the following paragraph:

> 2. *Your Representations*. By applying to register a domain name, or by asking us to maintain or renew a domain name registration, you hereby represent and warrant to us that (a) the statements that you made in your Registration Agreement are complete and accurate; (b) to your knowledge, the registration of the domain name will not infringe upon or otherwise violate the rights of any third party; (c) you are not registering the domain name for an unlawful purpose; and (d) you will not knowingly use the domain name in violation of any applicable laws or regulations. It is your responsibility to determine whether your domain name registration infringes or violates someone else's rights.[115]

Registrars reserve the right to cancel, transfer or otherwise make changes to domain name registrations in the following circumstances: (a) their receipt of written or appropriate electronic instructions from the applicant or its agent to take such action; (b) the receipt of an order or arbitral tribunal requiring such action; and/or (c) the receipt of a decision of an administrative panel requiring such action in any administrative proceeding to which the applicant is a party and which is conducted under the policy or a later version of the policy adopted by ICANN. They also reserve the right to cancel, transfer or otherwise make changes to a domain name

---

[114] UDRP, *supra* n. 113, at 1.

[115] *Id.*

registration in accordance with the terms of the registration agreement or other legal requirements.

In the case of some types of disputes, applicants are required to submit to a mandatory administrative dispute-resolution process. Dispute resolution service providers are approved by ICANN. The dispute-resolution procedure only applies to disputes concerning an alleged abusive registration of a domain name; that is, one which meets the following criteria:

(i) the domain name registered by the domain name registrant is identical or confusingly similar to a trademark or service mark in which the complainant (the person or entity bringing the complaint) has rights;

(ii) the domain name registrant has no rights or legitimate interests in respect of the domain name in question; and

(iii) the domain name has been registered and is being used in bad faith.

The ICANN UDRP sets out examples of circumstances that will be considered by a dispute-resolution panel to be evidence of bad faith registration and use of a domain name. These examples are not intended to be exclusive and other circumstances may be considered by the panel to determine that the registration and use of a domain name were done in bad faith.

The policy also sets out a nonexclusive list of circumstances that the administrative panel may use as evidence to demonstrate the domain name registrant's rights or legitimate interest in the domain name.

The administrative procedure established under the ICANN UDRP provides a quicker and more cost-effective means than court litigation to resolve domain name registrations. The procedures are also less formal than litigation and more attuned to the requirements of the Internet, since the administrative decision makers are experts in the relevant areas. Another benefit is that the procedure has international scope. It provides a single procedure for resolving domain name disputes regardless of where the registrar or the domain name holder or the complainant are located.[116]

ICANN has developed rules to govern the administrative proceedings.[117] It should be noted that the ICANN UDRP does not prevent domain name registrants or

---

[116] For a further discussion of domain name dispute resolution procedures, see *WIPO Guide to Domain Name Dispute Resolution* <http://www.arbiter.wipo.int>.

[117] *See* <http://www.icann.org/udrp/udrp-schedule.htm>.

complainants from submitting disputes to the courts. A party may commence an action before an administrative proceeding is commenced or even after the proceeding has been concluded, if it is not satisfied with the outcome.[118]

A number of registrars of ccTLDs have also established or are in the process of establishing dispute resolution procedures.[119] For example, the authority responsible for administering Singapore's country-code top-level domain names, Singapore Network Information Centre, has launched a new dispute resolution service for ".sg" domains – the Singapore Domain Name Dispute Resolution Policy (SDRP).[120] The SDRP is generally modeled on the ICANN UDRP, but there are differences. These include the possibility of optional mediation before a decision of a dispute-resolution panel, and a different test for successfully challenging a domain name registration.

Two Singapore-based mediation organizations have been appointed by the Singapore Network Information Centre to provide SDRP dispute resolution services. The Singapore dispute resolution process was designed to be fast and inexpensive – reportedly taking about a month and costing as little as S$2,750.

5. Electronic Contracting

5.1. Overview

In order to facilitate electronic commerce, national legal frameworks and international treaties must provide for certainty in electronic contracting.[121] Just as in traditional commerce, clear and consistent guidance must be provided for determining whether a contract has been formed; what are the terms of the contract; and where the contract can be enforced.

---

[118] *Broad Bridge Media L.L.C. v. Hypercd.com*, 55 U.S.P.Q. 2d 1426 (S.D.N.Y. 2000)

[119] Canada has published a draft set of dispute resolution processes. *See* <http://www.circ.ca>.

[120] Available at <http://www.nic.net.sg/pdf/SDRP.pdf>.

[121] Currently under consideration by the e-commerce working group of UNCITRAL is a draft convention on electronic contracting. Issues such as the applicability and relationship of the U.N. Convention on Contracts for the International Sale of Goods (*see* text accompanying n. 139 *infra*) to the draft convention on electronic contracting are being considered by the working group.

Until recently, businesses engaging in electronic commerce did so over closed networks such as those used in electronic data interchange (EDI). In a "closed" or "dedicated" system, such as EDI, participants must meet certain standards or obligations (including typically the execution of a written agreement) prior to participating.[122] EDI represented an important first step towards overcoming the traditional physical barriers to a seamless and efficient global trading system.[123] Through closed network communications systems, two parties can directly exchange information electronically, reducing and in some cases eliminating the use of paper. Further, trading through closed network communications systems permits businesses to agree in trading partner agreements upon the legal effect and the allocation of risks posed by this form of electronic trading.[124]

Electronic commerce over open networks such as the Internet poses the challenges of addressing legal, business, and security aspects of "many-to-many" information exchanges. With the expanding use of the Internet to effect information exchanges between geographically dispersed locations, there is much greater difficulty in obtaining assurances of the identity and authority of the transacting parties. Trading partner agreements used to structure transacting parties' electronic

---

[122] *See* Jane K. Winn & Benjamin Wright, *Law of E-commerce* 5-61 (Aspen Law and Business ed., 4th ed. 2001); Barry B. Sookman, *Computer, Internet and E-commerce Law*, at 10-2 (Carswell ed., perm. Ed. Rev. 2001).

[123] International Chamber of Commerce, *General Usage for International Digitally Insured Commerce* (1997).

[124] Numerous business, audit, and legal issues exist in conducting business electronically even in EDI transactions. *See e.g.* Benjamin Wright *et al.*, *The Law of Electronic Commerce* (Aspen Law and Business, 3rd ed., 1999); Hans Thomsen *et al.*, *Trading With EDI: The Legal Issues* (IBC Financial Books Ltd. 1989); *EDI and the Law* (Ian Walden ed., Blenheim Online Publications 1989); Hans Thomsen *et al.*, *EDI for Managers and Auditors* (Electronic Data Interchange Council of Canada 1991); Hans Thomsen *et al.*, *EDI for Managers and Auditors* (2nd ed., The Canadian Institute of Chartered Accountants 1993); ABA Electronic Messaging Services Task Force, *The Commercial Use of Electronic Data Interchange A Report*, 44 *Business Law* (1990); International Chamber of Commerce, *Electronic Data Interchange Agreement: A Guide and Source Book* (1993). Substantial efforts have been made to develop model electronic data interchange trading partner agreements to assist parties in conducting business through the use of EDI. *See e.g.* the model form of agreements proposed by the EDI Council of Canada, the European Commission in the framework of the TEDIS Program MME and the United Nations Commission on International Trade Law.

communications relationships often do not exist. Similarly, agreements are seldom reached on closed network security procedures. Therefore, there are greater risks of unauthorized access to communications systems and opportunities for fraud.

Electronic signatures,[125] including digital signatures,[126] are increasingly being relied upon to provide assurances of message integrity (that the content of the message received is the same as that sent), confidentiality (to protect information from being viewed in transit or being transmitted to the wrong person), authentication (to provide assurances that an asserted identity is valid for a given person or computer system), and non-repudiation (holding the sender to his/her communication). Trusted third parties, sometimes referred to as certification authorities or certification service providers, are being used to certify the authenticity of users.

Use of digital communications to transact business raises some key questions: What significance will electronic documents have? Will electronic messages be functionally equivalent to written documents so as to achieve at least the same level of certainty and legal efficiency? What legal significance should be accorded electronic signatures? In what circumstances should a signature or message be attributed in law to a party to a communication? What obligations should certification authorities, subscribers, and relying parties have in connection with the issuance and use of digital certificates? Legal systems can provide answers to these questions and consequently, the certainty necessary to facilitate electronic commerce.

Barriers to Electronic Contracting

Principal potential barriers to electronic contracting include the following:

(1) *Functional equivalence*: concerns that electronic contracts and electronic signatures do not have the same legal effect as paper contracts and handwritten signatures.

(2) *Repudiation of identity*: claims by parties to a contract that they did not enter into an agreement and that someone else did so in their name.

---

[125] An electronic signature is a generic, technology-neutral term that refers to the methods by which one can "sign" an electronic record. Although electronic signatures are represented digitally, they can take many forms and be created by many different technologies.

[126] A digital signature is a particular type of electronic signature that is based on public/private key encryption. For a more detailed discussion of public key infrastructure, *see* § 5.5 *infra*.

(3) *Repudiation of receipt*: claims by parties they did not receive the communication.
(4) *Identification or authentication*: concerns relating to proving a contracting party's identity and the genuineness of documents and signatures.
(5) *Integrity of electronic contract terms*: ensuring that electronic communications are protected from tampering and changes to the terms of contracts.
(6) *Confidentiality*: concerns relating to the confidentiality of electronic transmissions.

Each of these concerns affects the level of confidence in electronic transactions. Dealing with these issues is a necessary first step in creating the trust and confidence necessary for parties to engage in electronic commerce. Legal systems can address directly the issue of functional equivalence and can provide a framework for apportioning liability and facilitating the construction of technological means of addressing the remaining concerns.

Removing Barriers to Electronic Commerce

Since the widespread adoption of the Internet as a medium for communicating and transacting business, an increasing number of states and international organizations have endeavored to construct legal frameworks to facilitate and encourage electronic contracting via the Internet. Unlike a closed system such as EDI, in which parties may largely create their own rules for particular transactions, the open nature of Internet transactions requires a legal framework to provide certainty regarding the legal recognition of electronic communications.

Governments around the world have recognized the importance of their role in removing barriers to and in enabling electronic commerce.[127] The approaches taken

[127] *See e.g.* Argentina, *Presidential Decree no. 427/98*; Australia, *Electronic Transactions* (1999) (Commonwealth), which has been enacted in the following states and territories: New South Wales (to commence by proclamation), Victoria, Tasmania and Northern Territories; Bermuda, *Electronic Transactions Act of 1999*; Canada, *Electronic Transactions Act* (*Canada UECA*)(the Uniform Law Conference of Canada adopted the *Uniform E-commerce Act*)(UECA) and provincial legislation based on UECA such as in Saskatchewan, *The Electronic Information and Documents Act* 2000, c. E-7; Ontario, *Electronic Commerce Act,* S.O. 2000, c. 17; Manitoba, *E-commerce and Information Act,* S.M. 2000, c. E-55*;* Quebec, *An Act to Establish a Legal Framework for Information Technology*, S.Q. 2001 c. 32 (In force on dates to be fixed by the government); France, *Electronic Signature Bill*; Hong Kong, *Electronic Transactions Ordinance*;

by governments generally fall into two categories:[128]

(1) *Facilitative laws*: such as those to make an electronic record as legally effective as a written record and an electronically authenticated record as legally effective as a signed record;[129] and

---

India, *Information Technology Act 2000*; Ireland, *E-commerce Act 2000;* Mexico, May 29, 2000, Civil and Commercial Codes amended, *see* n. 144; New Zealand, *Electronic Transactions Bill* (as of October 18, 2001 this bill was awaiting for second reading); Philippines, *E-commerce Act of 2000, Republic Act 8792 (2000 Senate Bill 1902)*; Republic of Korea, *E-commerce Basic Law* and *Digital Signature Law*; Singapore, *Electronic Transactions Act of 1998*; Slovenia, *E-commerce and Electronic Signature Act*; in the United States, the United States National Conference of Commissioners on the Uniform State Laws adopted the *Uniform Electronic Transactions Act* (U.S. UETA) which has been enacted in the states of Alabama, Arizona, Arkansas, California, Delaware, District of Columbia, Florida, Hawaii, Idaho, Indiana, Iowa, Kansas, Kentucky, Louisiana, Maine, Maryland, Michigan, Minnesota, Mississippi, Montana, Nebraska, Nevada, New Hampshire, New Mexico, North Carolina, North Dakota, Ohio, Oklahoma, Oregon, Pennsylvania, Rhode Island, South Dakota, Tennessee, Utah, Virginia, West Virginia, and Wyoming; the United States National Conference of Commissioners on the Uniform State Laws adopted the *Uniform Computer Information Transaction Act* (U.S. UCITA) which has been enacted in the states of Maryland and Virginia, and the *United States Federal Electronic Signatures in Global and National Commerce Act* (U.S. E-SIGN). For a survey of international legislative initiatives *see* Simone van der Hof, *Digital Signature Law Survey* <http://cwis.kub.nl/frw/people/hof/ds-lawsu.htm>; McBride, Baker & Coles, *Summary of Electronic Commerce and Digital Signature Legislation* <http://www.mbc.com/ds_sum.html>.

[128] Barry B. Sookman, *Legal Framework for E-Commerce Transactions*, 4 C.T.L.R., 85 (2001), where three categories are listed. The third category is "to enact laws that extend or adapt existing regulation of transactions to cover electronic transactions."

[129] For example, Australia, *supra* n. 127; Canada, *supra* n. 127; Chile, *Law on Digital Signature & Accreditation of Certification* is under review in Congress and passage is anticipated; China, *Contract Law of the People's Republic of China* (1999) recognizes data-telex including telegram, telex, fax, EDI, and e-mail; Taiwan (China), *Electronic Signature Law* is under review in the Legislative Yuan and passage is anticipated; Hong Kong, *supra* n. 127; Japan, *Electronic Signature and Electronic Signature Certification Business Law*; Singapore, *supra* n. 127; United States, *supra* n. 127; *see* Mark Sneddon, *Legislating to Facilitate Electronic Signatures and Records: Exceptions, Standards and the Impact on the Statute Book* <http://www.law.unsw.edu.au/publications/journals/unswlj/ecommerce/sneddon.html>; Albert Gidari et al., *Survey of Electronic and Digital Signature Legislative Initiatives in the United States*, Paper, *Internet Law and Policy*

(2) *Prescriptive laws*: such as those regulating particular authentication technologies or authorities.[130]

Facilitative laws generally provide that an electronic communication will be considered as legally effective as a paper-based document. The current focus of most e-commerce law reform initiatives relate to these kinds of laws. Such facilitative laws may not, in themselves, be sufficient to solve issues of confidence, such as confirming the identity of the parties. Prescriptive laws can address the confidence issues of authentication and integrity. However, complying with prescriptive laws can make electronic transactions more expensive and complicated to execute. This can make it impracticable for smaller transactions such as many B2C contracts. Any legislation in this area must balance the need to address confidence issues with the need to maintain cost effectiveness.

Forum (Sept. 12, 1997); OECD, *Inventory of Approaches to Authentication and Certification in a Global Networked Society* (Sept. 30, 1998) available at <http://www.andreamonti.net/doc/reg>; Babette P. Aalberts & Simone Van Der Hof, *Digital Signature Blindness, Analysis of Legislative Approaches toward Electronic Authentication* (Nov. 1999) <http://rechten.kub.nl/simone/ds-fr.htm>.

[130] Germany, *Act on Electronic Signatures* ("Signaturgesetz"); Utah, *Utah Digital Signature Act* (Utah Code Annotated §46-3-101 to 504), is a technology specific state legislation which attempts to promote the use of one specific digital-signature technology. The starting point of the Utah statute is the certification of authorities. Mainly, if an electronic record has been digitally signed and the signature has been validated with a public key certified by a licensed certification authority, then the party enjoys a presumption that the signature is that of the owner of the private key. There were four certification authorities licensed under the Utah statute by September 1994; California, *Electronic Transactions Act*, is the first jurisdiction to enact the U.S. UETA, *supra* n. 127, with a few exceptions covering consumer protection and specific statutes such as wills and trusts; Illinois, *Illinois E-commerce Act* – distinguishes electronic signatures and digital signatures. Mainly, the statute attempts to find a middle ground between technology-specific and media-neutral e-commerce legislation; New Jersey, *Final Report Relating to E-commerce and Signatures of New Jersey Law Revision Commission* <http://www.lawewv.state.nj.us/sig/frpt.pdf>, recommended against following the example of other states or the U.S. UETA, *supra* n. 127. Instead, the Commission recommended giving executive agencies expanded authority to revise regulations within their regulatory competence. For further discussion on the U.S. statutes, *see* Sookman, *supra* n. 122, at 5.7.

5.2. Formality Requirements

One of the key roles for electronic commerce legislation is to establish the means by which traditional formalities associated with paper documents such as legal requirements for writings, signatures, notarization, and original documents, can be met electronically.

Signature Requirements

A traditional signature has different roles and legal effects. In the commercial context, a signature is a mark or symbol made by a person with the intent to authenticate a document.[131] Its essential function is to link a person with a document. In some circumstances, in addition to the signatory intending to give legal effect to a signature, the law requires a written signature. This is usually the case, for example, for transfers of land.[132]

Common law courts have developed a functional approach to signature requirements. They accept a variety of marks, including typewritten names and marks made by rubber stamps, as signatures, in the case of paper documents, as long as they provide evidence:

(1) of the identity of the signatory;

(2) that the signatory intended the "signature" to be his or her signature; and

(3) that the signatory approves of and agrees with the contents of the document.[133]

As is discussed below, e-commerce enabling legislation has generally taken a "functional equivalency" test: giving electronic signatures the same weight as signatures made on paper documents when they are capable of fulfilling the same functions.

---

[131] Sookman, *supra* n. 122, at 10-61; UNCITRAL *Model Law on Electronic Signatures* art. 8, 9, 11 (2001), available at <http://www.uncitral.org>.

[132] For examples of common and civil law formality requirements *see* UNCITRAL *Model Law on Electronic Signatures supra* n. 131, art. 6.

[133] Chris Reed, *What is a Signature?*, 3 The Journal of Information, Law and Technology (2000) <http://www.elj.warwick.ac.uk/jilt/00-3/reed.html>.

Writing Requirements

Many countries require certain types of agreements to be in writing[134] in order to form an enforceable contract.[135] A contract may be required to be in writing in order to be admissible as evidence in a court. Information disclosures may also be required to be in writing.[136] Written notice requirements are also common in highly regulated areas of commerce, such as the financial services industry.[137] Mandatory record-keeping or retention requirements may also exist.[138]

For contracts involving the international sale of goods to which the United Nations Convention on Contracts for the International Sale of Goods (1980) applies, no writing or other formalities are required for an enforceable contract.[139] However, that rule, and related provisions dispensing with writing requirements related to the modification of agreements, offers, acceptances, and notices, is expressly

---

[134] Although many jurisdictions interpret "writing" broadly to include different ways of presenting words in visual form (such as typing, printing, photocopying, or photography), traditionally these have not included digital documents, which are not visible. Jens Wener, *E-commerce Co. Inc.- Local Rules in a Global Net: Online Business Transactions and the Applicability of Traditional English Contract Law Rules*, 6 International J. of Communications Law and Policy (2001) (available at <http://www.ijclp.org>).

[135] For example, many common law jurisdictions have enacted legislation similar to the English *Statute of Frauds* requiring written contracts for certain classes of transactions such as land transfers, guarantees or sale of goods over a specified amount. *See* Canada, *Copyright Act*, R.S.C. 1985, ch. C-42, sec. 63; Canada, *Patent Act*, R.S.C. 1985, ch. P-4, sec.50; New South Wales, Australia, *Conveyancing Act* 1919 sec. 54A(1); Ontario, Canada, *Statute of Frauds*, R.S.O. 1990, ch. S.19; US, *Uniform Commercial Code* sec. 2-201(1); United Kingdom, *Statute of Frauds* 1677 (Imp) 29 Car II c3.

[136] For example, consumer protection laws often require disclosure in writing of certain rights or obligations, such as a written notice to consumers that they may return goods without charge for 30 days after purchase.

[137] For example, credit application forms in many jurisdictions are required to provide borrowers written notice of the interest rate and the manner in which the interest rate is calculated.

[138] For example, many taxing authorities require taxpayers to retain contract-related documents for a specified number of years in order to facilitate audits.

[139] U.N. Convention on Contracts for the International Sale of Goods (1980), art. 11.

made subject to the right of a contracting state to opt out of the abolition of writing requirements if domestic law does require a writing.[140]

Requirements for Original Documents

The requirement that a document be an "original" occurs in a variety of contexts for a variety of reasons. In many situations, it is essential that documents be transmitted in their "original" form unchanged so that other parties may have confidence in their contents. Examples of documents where an "original" is often required include trade documents such as weight certificates, agricultural certificates, quality/quantity certificates, inspection reports, insurance certificates, and non-business related documents such as birth certificates and death certificates.[141] Documents of title and negotiable instruments, in which the notion of uniqueness of an original is particularly relevant, pose a particular problem for electronic records.

5.3. Legislative Approaches to Meeting Formalities Electronically

The UNCITRAL Model Law of Electronic Commerce (1996)

E-commerce legislation adopted in many countries provides the means for electronic documents or communications to meet formality requirements such as those for signatures, writings, and original documents. Much of this legislation is based upon or similar in approach to the UNCITRAL Model Law of Electronic Commerce (Model Law).[142]

The Model Law provides primarily for the functional equivalence of electronic and paper contracts. The Model Law was intended to serve as a model for a set of internationally acceptable rules for e-commerce.[143] It is one of the most influential

---

[140] U.N. Convention, *supra* n. 139, at art. 96. Not many states have elected to opt out of the wording requirement even though entitled to do so.

[141] *Guide to Enactment to the UNCITRAL Model Law* para. 63 <http://www.uncitral.org>.

[142] UNCITRAL *Model Law on E-commerce* (1996) <http://www.uncitral.org>.

[143] *E.g.* Argentina, P.D. 427/98; Australia, *supra* n. 127; Canada, *supra* n. 127; France, *supra* n. 127; Hong-Kong, *supra* n. 127; Mexico on May 29, 2000 amended the Civil and Commercial Codes to permit parties to enter into binding electronic contracts subject to evidentiary requirements: Method used to generate, communicate, receive or achieve the electronic contract is reliable, Message or information expressing consent can be attributed to its supposed originator, and message or information can be later retrieved; New Zealand, *supra* n. 127; Singapore, *supra* n. 127; United States, U.S. E-SIGN *supra* n. 127, U.S. UCITA, U.S. UETA, *supra* n. 127.

efforts in providing guidance to national policy makers and legislators on how to approach removing barriers to and facilitating e-commerce.

The Model Law was developed after an analysis of the purposes and functions of traditional contract formality requirements, in order to prescribe how those purposes or functions can be fulfilled through electronic techniques.[144] Because it was completed in 1996 when Internet-based e-commerce was less common, the Model Law does not take into account all of the challenges involved in facilitating electronic transactions over the Internet.

The Model Law provides that an electronic document should not be denied legal effectiveness simply because it is in electronic format.[145] It also provides for functional equivalence of electronic records and signatures with written records and handwritten signatures.[146] It does not supersede other national laws such as consumer protection laws,[147] and it permits parties to contract out of Model Law rules.[148]

Meeting Signature Requirements Electronically

The Model Law provides, in very general terms, for the functional equivalence of an electronic signature with a hand-written signature.[149] The UNCITRAL Model Law on Electronic Signatures (E-signature Model Law)[150] completed in 2001, builds on this principle and provides additional guidance on requirements for electronic signatures. This uniform law, and similar national laws, are discussed in greater detail below.

---

[144] *See* Guide to Model Law, *supra* n. 141, paras. 15-18.

[145] UNCITRAL (E-commerce), *supra* n. 142, art. 5.

[146] *See* UNCITRAL (E-commerce), *supra* n. 142, arts. 5-15; Guide to Model Law, *supra* n. 141, paras. 15-18.

[147] UNCITRAL (E-commerce), *supra* n. 142, states that " This Law does not override any rule of law intended for the protection of consumers". *See* Guide to Model Law, *supra* n. 141, paras. 27 and 46-7.

[148] *See* Guide to Model Law, *supra* n. 141, at paras. 19-21; UNCITRAL (E-commerce) *supra* n. 142, art. 4.

[149] UNCITRAL (E-commerce), *supra*, n. 142, art 7. Article 7 (the minimalist approach on electronic signatures) of the Model Law has been expanded on by the E-Signature Model Law, *supra* n. 131 (which has a two-tier approach).

[150] *Id.*

Meeting Writing Requirements Electronically

Under the Model Law, electronic documents may satisfy a requirement of "writing" if the information in them can be reproduced and read.[151] This focus on "readability" places less emphasis on other functions of written documents, such as document integrity. Many national laws now define "document" to include a record kept on or by means of a computer.[152]

In some cases, the benefits of paper contracts with written signatures are more important than the desire for the cost effectiveness and efficiency associated with e-commerce. Accordingly, countries that have enacted electronic commerce or signature laws have typically exempted certain types of transactions from such laws. The most common examples are documents relating to transfers of land, wills or testamentary documents, and documents creating or recording security interests.[153]

Meeting Requirements for Original Documents Electronically

The Model Law sets out the minimum acceptable form requirement to be met by a data message for it to be regarded as the functional equivalent of an original.[154] The Model Law emphasizes the importance of the integrity of the information for its originality and sets out criteria to be taken into account when assessing message integrity. It links the concept of originality to a method of authentication and puts the focus on the method of authentication to be followed in order to meet the requirement.[155]

5.4. Electronic Authentication

As discussed above, one function of signatures is to provide greater confidence in the identity of the parties to a transaction. Because of the nature of electronic communications, new methods are required to authenticate the identity of a party. Techniques for authentication can take many forms, ranging from technical

---

[151] *Id.*

[152] U.S. UETA, *supra* n. 127; U.S. E-Sign; *supra* n. 127; UECA, *supra* n. 127; Ontario ECA, *supra* n. 21.

[153] *E.g.* U.S. UETA, *supra* n. 127; U.S. E-SIGN, *supra* n. 127; Canada UECA, *supra* n. 127.

[154] UNCITRAL (Electronic Signatures), *supra* n. 131, art. 8.

[155] Guide to the Model Law, *supra* n. 141, para. 65.

standards, to business processes, to legal approaches. Some are simple, such as Personal Identification Numbers (PIN) used for consumer banking transactions,[156] and others are more complex, such as biological identification techniques such as retinal data or genetic code scans.

Establishing the validity of an electronic signature is important because it increases confidence in e-commerce transactions. Linking a signature to a person in an electronic document is also important for evidentiary purposes in order to hold a person to his/her communication. Different types of electronic signatures provide a range of certainty in the identity of the signer and the connection of the signer to the document. The different types of electronic signatures are described below.

Electronic Signature

An electronic signature is a generic, technology-neutral term that refers to the universe of all of the various methods by which one can "sign" an electronic record.[157] Although all electronic signatures are represented digitally (i.e., as a series of ones and zeros), they can assume many forms and can be created by different technological means. Definitions can encompass a range of acts, from clicking a mouse on an "I Accept" button on a website,[158] to a digital signature using a prescribed technology.[159]

A number of statutes, proposed legislation and uniform legislation use the term "electronic signature" to include a broad range of methods of authenticating records electronically.[160] An example of this technologically neutral approach is reflected in the *Uniform Electronic Commerce Act* (UECA). "Electronic signature" as defined in the UECA means "information in electronic form that a person has created or adopted in order to sign a document and that is in, attached to or associated with

---

[156] *See generally* Sookman, *supra* n. 128, at 10-77 – 10-79.

[157] Thomas J. Smedinghoff & Ruth Bro, *Moving with Change: Electronic Signature Legislation as a Vehicle for Advancing E-Commerce*, 3 John Marshall J. of Computer and Information Law 723 (Spring 1999).

[158] UECA, *supra* n. 127.

[159] *Utah Code Ann.*, *supra* n. 130, at sec. 46-3-101 et seq.

[160] For a survey of the different statutory definitions of "electronic signature" *see* the tables prepared by McBride, Baker & Coles of the definitions of the term "electronic signature" available at <http://www.mbc.com/ecommerce/legislative.asp>.

the document."[161] In some cases, the term "electronic signature" is defined in terms of a particular form of a secure electronic signature, such as a "digital signature."[162]

Secure Electronic Signatures

The term "electronic signature" is sometimes used to connote a signature in digital form which, when used, will satisfy the desired goals of authenticity, integrity, and non-repudiation. These types of electronic signatures are sometimes referred to as a "secure electronic signature," or an "enhanced electronic signature." "Secure electronic signatures" and "enhanced electronic signatures" generally contain certain authentication attributes specified by legislation. These attributes typically include requirements that the signature be: (1) unique to the person using it; (2) capable of verification; (3) under the sole control of the person using it; and (4) linked to data in such a manner that if the data is changed, the electronic signature is invalidated. This type of usage of the term "electronic signature" can be found, for example, in the *European Parliament Electronic Signature Directive*.

Digital Signature

Although the technical functions of digital signatures are well known, the legal meaning of the term, particularly as it appears in legislation, varies with the context in which it is used. For example, the term "digital signature" is sometimes used to refer to electronic signatures generally and not to electronic signatures based upon public key cryptography.[163] In some cases, the term "digital signature" refers to a secure electronic signature or an enhanced electronic signature without definitionally requiring the use of public key cryptography to effect the signature. Digital signatures are, however, most frequently understood as a type of electronic

---

[161] Sec. 1.

[162] For example, the *British Columbia Land Title Amendment Act*, 1999 requires an "electronic signature" to be in a format that is created by a subscriber using a private cryptographic key under the control of the subscriber that corresponds to a public cryptographic key contained in a certificate.

[163] For example, in the California Government Code at sec. 16.5, the term "digital signature" is defined to mean "an electronic identifier, created by computer, intended by the party using it to have the same force and effect as a manual signature."

signature that is based on public key cryptography.[164] This technology can address concerns related to authenticity, integrity, and confidentiality.

Legislative Reform Related to Electronic Signatures

A tremendous amount of law reform has occurred in the area of electronic signatures. For example, almost every state in the United States, and many governments around the world have enacted or are currently considering some form of electronic signature legislation.[165] The European Commission has adopted a Directive on a Community Framework For Electronic Signatures for the European Union.[166] A principal reason for the directive was a need for a harmonized legal framework at the European level resulting from increasing legislative activity by member states.[167]

Three main approaches have been taken to electronic signature regimes.[168]

(1) *Prescriptive Approach*: Under the prescriptive approach, legislation may either mandate or assume the use of a digital signature and a Public Key Infrastructure (PKI) regime.[169] This was the approach used for the original electronic signature regimes.

---

[164] *See generally* American Bar Association Information Security Committee, *Digital Signature Guidelines*: *Legal Infrastructure for Certification Authorities and Secure E-commerce* (Aug. 1, 1996) <http:www.abanet.org/scitech/ec/isc/dsgfree.html>.

[165] *See* McBride, Baker & Coles, *Summary of Electronic Commerce and Digital Signature Legislation* <http://www.mbc.com/ds_sum.html>; Internet Law and Policy Forum, available at <http://www.ilpf.org>.

[166] *Directive 1999/93 EC of the European Parliament and of the Council of 13 December 1999 on a Community Framework for Electronic Signatures*, 1999 O.J. (L13) 12 (EU Signatures Directive)

[167] *See Summary of Electronic Commerce and Digital Signature Legislation*, prepared by McBride, Baker & Coles, available at <http://www.mbc.com/ds_sum.html> for a summary of this legislation.

[168] Sookman, *supra* n. 128; Smedinghoff and Bro, *supra* n. 157, ch. III(B).

[169] For example the following countries and states enacted legislation adopting the prescriptive approach in the specified years: Argentina (1998), Italy (1997), Malaysia (1998) and in the United States: Minnesota (1999), Missouri (1998), Utah (1995), Washington (1996).

(2) *Two-Tiered Approach*: Under the two-tiered approach, legislation accepts most forms of electronic signatures and provides certain legal presumptions for advanced electronic signatures.[170] There are normally presumptions of integrity and of identity.[171]

(3) *Technology-Neutral Approach*: Under the technology-neutral approach, signature requirements are described in terms of the function they fulfill rather than the mechanism or procedure for achieving that requirement. Legislation does not mandate a particular technological type of electronic signature, but simply recognizes that such a signature may be given the same effect as a hand-written signature where appropriate.

Educational Approaches

Governments and business associations have devoted significant resources to developing digital and electronic signature policies and enabling laws. Passage of laws is not, however, sufficient in itself. Businesses and consumers must understand the concept of electronic signatures, in order to trust them. Some governments have been active in education programs related to electronic signatures.

In early 2001, after the implementation of the 1998 Singapore *Electronic Transactions Act*,[172] the Singapore government published a report identifying merchant and consumer awareness and education as the next critical steps to successful implementation and use of the electronic signatures and techniques recognized by the law.[173] The Japanese statute dealing with electronic signatures also recognizes the importance of education and awareness to the acceptance of e-commerce, and

---

[170] UNCITRAL (Electronic Signatures), *supra* n. 131; EU E-Signatures Directive, *supra* n. 166; Singapore – Singapore ETAS, *supra* n. 127; India – *E-commerce Act* 1998, Part III and Part IV, available at <http://www.commin.nic.in/doc/ecact.htm>.

[171] The EU E-Signature Directive, *supra* n. 166, also provides for a two-tier approach. The Singapore ETAS, *supra* n. 127 provides that if the "electronic signature" satisfies the requirements for a secure electronic signature, then the person challenging the electronic contract must prove that the electronic signature imputed to them was not affixed by them.

[172] Singapore ETAS, *supra* n. 127.

[173] Infocomm Development Authority of Singapore, *A Framework on Building Trust and Confidence in Electronic Commerce*, February 21, 2001.

accordingly provides that the government "shall strive to deepen the citizens' understanding of electronic signatures and certification services."[174]

5.5. Public Key Infrastructures

One method of addressing the concerns of confidence in electronic transactions and other sensitive Internet communications is use of a Public Key Infrastructure (PKI). A PKI is a cryptographic key and certificate delivery system that enables secure electronic transactions and exchanges of sensitive information between relative strangers. A PKI is intended to provide privacy, access control, integrity, authentication, and non-repudiation support to information technology applications and electronic commerce transactions.[175] A PKI provides a high degree of confidence that in the use of public key cryptography, private keys are kept secure, specific public keys are truly linked to specific private keys, and the party holding a public/private key pair is who the party purports to be.[176]

PKIs[177] involve two components: (i) a certificate delivery system that includes an independent third party (generally known as a certification authority or CA), and (ii) cryptographic keys.[178] Information is coded or "encrypted" by using two mathematically related keys: one is kept confidential by the sender, the other is made public. The private key cannot be determined from the public key. When a recipient receives the digitally signed communication, the sender's public key is used to decrypt the digital signature. If the sender's public key is able to decrypt the digital signature, then the recipient knows it came from the sender. This confirms identity, because only the sender's public key could decrypt what was encrypted using the sender's private key.

---

[174] Japan, *Law Concerning Electronic Signatures and Certification Services* (2001); Hong Kong – *Electronic Transactions Ordinance* (2000).

[175] Treasury Board of Canada Secretariat, *Public Key Infrastructure Management in the Government of Canada* (May 27, 1999) <http://www.tbs-sct.gc.ca/pubs_pol/ciopubs/PKI/pki1_e.html>.

[176] Government of Canada, CSE PKI Project Office, *Information Technology Security.*

[177] *See* <http://www.pkiforum.org/resources.html> for online resources on the business and technical issues associated with PKI, as well as links to PKI providers and certification authorities by geographic region.

[178] *See* Sookman, *supra* n. 118, at 10-97, 10-98; Treasury Board of Canada Secretariat, *Policy for Public Key Infrastructure Management in the Government of Canada* (May 27, 1999) <http://www.tbs-sct.gc.ca/pubs_pol/ciopubs/PKI/pki1_e.html>.

A message digest is then created, including the date and message. If the new message digest matches the decrypted message digest received by the recipient, then the recipient knows that the communication has not been tampered with.

Role of Certification Authorities in PKIs

Any system of digital signatures requires a means for recipients of digitally signed communications to judge whether to rely upon the digital signature as evidence of identity (of the sender) and integrity (of the document). One way for recipients to gain confidence in such signatures is to rely on the assurances of a certification authority (CA).

A CA is an independent trusted entity that provides a service of establishing that the holders of public keys used in public key cryptography are who they purport to be. In transactions over open systems, such as the Internet, parties must find a way to obtain confidence in the public and private keys being issued. A solution to these problems is the use of a trusted party, the CA, to associate an identified signor or the signor's name with a specific public key.

The role of the CA is twofold. The first is to ascertain the identity of the person subscribing for or holding the digital signature (the subscriber). It typically does so by checking traditional means of providing identity, such as passports. Second, to certify that the public key (or the private key/public key pair) used to create the digital signature belongs to the subscriber.

To associate a key pair with the subscriber, the CA issues a certificate. A certificate is an electronic record that lists a public key together with the name of the certificate subscriber as the subject of the certificate. To provide assurances as to the authenticity and integrity of the certificate, the CA attaches its own digital signature to the certificate.

Regulating Certification Authorities

In theory, any trusted person or entity can be a CA, including a private enterprise or a government authority.[179] Many practicing CAs are entities that have created public confidence through their history of providing services, such as banking or postal services.[180] Some jurisdictions, such as Japan and Hong Kong, have enacted

---

[179] *See* <http://www.pkiforum.org> for industry group and lists a number of private companies that will act as a certification authority.

[180] John Angel, *Why Use Digital Signatures for E-commerce?*, 2 The J. of Information, Law & Technology (1999) available at <http://www.law.warwick.ac.ulc/jilt/qq-2/angel.html>.

laws granting ministers the power to accredit CAs.[181]

The European Commission's Directive on Electronic Signatures provides that no EU member state can require public accreditation of CAs, on the basis that such a requirement would unduly restrict the development of the CA market. Voluntary accreditation schemes are permitted, however, as a way of promoting consumer confidence. The directive requires that such voluntary accreditation must be based on objective, transparent, proportionate, and non-discriminatory criteria. The directive also sets out a list of criteria that must be met if a certificate issued by a CA is to entitle a signature to preferential treatment.

Liability of Certification Authorities and Subscribers

A PKI regulatory regime can apportion liability for inaccuracies in the certificates issued and relied upon by contracting parties.

The following acts of participants in a PKI can contribute to a loss for which the CA or others should be responsible:

(1) fraud by the CA's employees, such as intentional issuance of false certificates;

(2) negligence on the part of the CA's employees, such as negligently issuing improper certificates or negligently disclosing confidential information;

(3) fraud by a subscriber, such as impersonating another user;

(4) negligence on the part of the subscriber, such as losing the private key; and

(5) fraud by other parties.

Liability for fraud, either by the CA or the subscriber, is relatively easy to address (unless such fraud is facilitated by another party's negligence), because the fraudulent party should bear the liability and loss. For example, legislation in Singapore and India makes it an offense, punishable by monetary penalties or imprisonment, to knowingly request or issue a fraudulent certificate.[182]

From a legal policy perspective, a more difficult issue is whether a CA should be subject to mandatory minimum standards or warranties; in other words, whether to impose minimum standards on the CA or to permit CAs to contract out of warranties or liability altogether. Minimum mandatory standards may increase confi-

---

[181] *See e.g.* Japan ESCS, *supra* n. 129, art. 34.

[182] Singapore ETA, *supra* n. 127; EU, E-Signature Directive, *supra* n. 170, at secs. 25-26; India, *Commerce Act* at secs. 26-27 (1998).

dence in the CA system. They may also increase the cost and complexity of such systems. Many jurisdictions have not yet proposed legislation to address these issues because of the speed of change in the technologies used in PKIs and by CAs and because of the lack of consensus on the proper approach to take. Some approaches are, however, emerging.

The UNCITRAL Electronic Signature Model Law requires CAs to take reasonable care to ensure the accuracy and completeness of information in the certificate.[183] Other jurisdictions require CAs to give a mandatory warranty that the certificate contains no information that the CA knows to be false.[184]

Many of the U.S. state digital signature regimes permit the CA or distributor of the relevant software to produce the digital signature, to disclaim liability for everything but the technical operation of the system.[185] This means that the CA can contract out of all liability with respect to the content or accuracy of the certificate, but not for the mechanical operations of issuing, verifying or revoking digital signature certificates.[186]

The European Electronic Signature Directive[187] creates a framework within which secure electronic authentication technologies may be used. The directive imposes liability on CAs with respect to the accuracy of the contents of the certificate (although in some cases the CA will not be liable if it can prove it has not acted negligently).[188]

A different legislative approach is to create a presumption that a person relying on a digital signature did rely on the certificate issued by the CA. If the certificate is flawed, this presumption will make it easier for the person relying on the signa-

---

[183] UNCITRAL (E-commerce), *supra* n. 142, art. 9.

[184] United States, Minnesota, *Minnesota Electronic Authentication Act* sec. 325.

[185] The *Utah Digital Signature Law* makes certification authorities liable only if they fail to comply with their own specified certificate practice statement and procedure, but does not require any minimum level of content or confirmation in the certificate practice statement and procedure. *Utah Code Ann.* Sec. 46-3-101 et seq. *See also* Illinois, *E-commerce Security Act* 1998, 5 Ill. Comp. Stat. 175.

[186] Another variation is to allow parties to contract out of accuracy or completeness in the certificate, but if they do not contract out then default minimum standards apply. *See India Commerce Act* 1998, part VII.

[187] EU, E-Signature Directive, *supra* n. 166.

[188] *Id.*, art. 6.

ture to establish the liability of the issuer. This approach is used in Singapore[189] and India.[190]

No regimes hold a CA strictly liable for all potential losses. The level of mandatory liability of a CA under the European approach provides Internet consumers and merchants with greater confidence in the authentication system, but it may also make CA services more expensive in the European Union than in the United States. Not only is the increased expense a problem for some small businesses, but a CA may find it economically undesirable to offer services for infrequent users or small-value transactions.

A related issue is what, if any, level or scope of responsibility the subscriber or holder of the digital signature is required to satisfy. The UNCITRAL Electronic Signatures Model Law requires holders of the digital signature to exercise reasonable care to avoid unauthorized use of signature creation data, to alert others of a risk that such data may have been compromised, and to ensure the accuracy and completeness of material representations made by the signatory in relation to the certificate.

Certification Authority Cross-Border Recognition

An emerging issue is how to deal with the acceptance of digital certificates across borders and across CAs. Because e-commerce often crosses jurisdictional boundaries, parties to a transaction may deal with a number of different CAs, each governed by a different set of rules. Harmonization of technical standards, business processes, and legal frameworks is critically important.

If there is no agreement on the recognition of certificates or digital signatures, e-commerce could be seriously impaired. Without the confidence that comes from that certainty and security, use will be dampened. As well as dealing with the legal issues of cross-border recognition, CAs must also deal with technical considerations, such as compatibility of software and workable procedures for accepting and evaluating certificates issued by other CAs. A number of organizations have been debating this question.[191]

---

[189] Singapore ETA, *supra* n. 127, sec. 23.

[190] *Id.*, sec. 24.

[191] *E.g.* ABA Section of Science and Technology Law, *PKI Assessment Guideline* <http://www.abanet.org/scitech/ec/isc>; European Forum For Electronic Business Pki Challenge project <http://www.eema.org/pki-challenge/>; CA-CA Interporeability, White Paper (Mar. 2001) <http://www.pkiforium.org/pdfs/ca-ca_interop.pdf>; European Electronic Signature Standards Initiative <http://www.ict.etsi.org/eessi-homepage.htm>;

The UNCITRAL Electronic Signature Model Law states that in determining the effectiveness of a certificate or digital signature, no regard shall be had to geographic location of the signatory or issuer, or the location where the signatory or certificate originated.[192] The central issue should be reliability, not place of origin.

A number of approaches have been taken to achieving interoperability between CAs, both within a jurisdiction and internationally. The following three approaches are examples.[193]

(1) *Cross-certification*: This approach involves one CA issuing a certificate to another CA, and bilateral agreements between individual CAs.

(2) *Bridge CA*: This model uses a central CA with which the other CAs enter into a cross-certification agreement. All CAs are then able to rely on each other's certificates, without having to enter into numerous individual agreements. The United States Federal Bridge CA is being developed for use by federal government departments and agencies and is expected to extend eventually to federal-state communications and beyond.

(3) *Cross-recognition*: This approach involves recognition without agreements between individual CAs. Instead, individual CAs would be licensed or accredited by some trusted authority, and this license or accreditation would be relied upon by others in deciding whether to trust that CA. A variant of this approach was suggested in the Australian Government Gatekeeper project. The Australian government would issue a CA with a Gatekeeper Accreditation Certificate which would assure third parties that the CA had met the criteria of the government body. Japan has also taken this approach. There, the government has the power to grant accreditation to both Japanese and foreign CAs.[194]

Australian Gatekeeper Project, <http://www.govonline.gov.au/projects/publickey/index.asp>; United Kingdom, The Communications-Electronic Security Group information <http://www.cesg.gov.uk/>; United States Federal Bridge Certification Authority being developed by the Federal Chief Information Officers' Council <http://www.cio.gov/fbca/>.

[192] UNCITRAL (Electronic Signature), *supra* n. 131, art. 12.

[193] For a general discussion of the possible business structure, *see* CA-CA Interoperability – White Paper (Mar. 2001) <http://www.pkiforum.org/pdfs/ca-ca_interop.pdf>.

[194] *Id.*

Without the ability to accept digital signatures across borders and CAs, global e-commerce over the Internet will be restricted because businesses and consumers will not have the confidence in the system to effect large or critical cross-jurisdiction transactions over the Internet.

5.6. Balancing Confidence against Cost and Complexity

Underlying each of these electronic contracting issues is the issue of confidence. Confidence in electronic communications will, to different degrees, require confidence in the identity of the other party, in the integrity of the communication and in the confidentiality of the communication.

These issues are difficult to address because the most effective approaches are expensive and complicated to implement. For example, use of digital certificates within a PKI system may be most effective to ensure the identities of the parties, integrity of the communications and confidentiality. However, because of the cost and complexity, this approach is generally impractical for smaller or ad hoc B2B transactions and for B2C transactions.

Legal frameworks should allow for flexibility, and the ability of the participants to find the proper balance in each situation between confidence on the one hand and cost and efficiency on the other. The following chart provides some examples of Internet uses and an assessment of the degree of importance of the issues of identity, integrity, and confidentiality. The issues can then be addressed, as appropriate to each situation, through a combination of a legal framework, business practices, and technology.

In order to avoid unnecessary cost and complexity, users of e-commerce ought to be able to obtain only the authentication product required to enable their transaction or activity. From a policy perspective, legal frameworks should be flexible, and CAs and other facilitators should be discouraged from offering only bundled solutions.

6. Consumer Protection

6.1. Overview

Facilitating e-commerce not only involves making it easier for merchants to sell online and across borders. It also involves fostering consumer trust and confidence about conducting commercial transactions online. Consumers are cautious about

Table 2.

	Confidence Issues			
Fact Pattern	*Repudiation of Identity*	*Repudiation of receipt*	*Integrity of Communication*	*Confidentiality of Communication*
Sale of books over the Internet to consumers, with payment by credit card.	Important to merchants, if there is fraudulent use of a credit card it is the merchant that generally bears the loss, under the terms of the credit card contract.	Not relevant.	Not relevant because if consumer orders the wrong book or the invoice is for the wrong amount, a return or refund business process usually exists to fix the problem.	Important, particularly for credit card information.
Numerous drafts of a highly confidential deal being sent between two lawyers.	Not relevant.	Not relevant.	Important.	Important.
Commercial contracts on a business-to-business exchange for large amounts of commodity raw materials to make steel.	This can be addressed by requiring participants to agree that any transactions occurring between the participants are their responsibility regardless of whether in fact they effected the transaction.	This can be addressed in the same manner as for repudiation of identity.	May be important.	Not relevant, if prices are available publicly on the B2B exchange. Important, if commercial terms are different between buyers.

making purchases over the Internet.[195] Therefore, protecting consumers who purchase products and services over the Internet is a significant policy objective for facilitating electronic commerce.[196]

To promote trust and confidence in electronic commerce, consumers' economic and legal interests need to be protected. Consumers are particularly concerned by the issues related to (a) accessibility and affordability of products and services; (b) transparency and clarity of information; (c) fair marketing practices, offers, and contract terms; (d) protection of children against unsuitable content; (e) security of payment systems; (f) the apportionment of responsibility and liability; (g) privacy and the protection of personal data; and (h) access to efficient systems of redress and dispute resolution.[197]

International consumer protection policies to promote electronic commerce generally take into account the principles of "equivalent protection," "harmonization," and "international consistency." The "equivalent protection" principle promotes the policy that consumers should not be afforded any less protection in e-commerce than in other forms of commerce. The consumer should be entitled to the same rights regardless of the medium of commerce used to make a purchase. The "harmonization principle" reflects the policy objective that consumer protection laws related to e-commerce be harmonized across jurisdictions without requiring any jurisdiction to lower its standards. The "international consistency" principle fosters the objective that consumer protection laws be consistent with

---

[195] The latest survey from Consumers International reports that online shoppers face significant challenges and risks with goods failing to arrive or refunds never credited. The global federation of more than 260 consumer organizations in 120 countries also found that only one in five sites provided clear information on the total cost of a transaction. Report available at <http://www.consumerinternational.org/C1_Should_I_buy.pdf>. *See also* Consumers International, *Consumer @ Shopping: An International Comparative Study of E-commerce* (Sept. 1999) <http://www.consumersinterantional.org> and the follow up *Consumer @ Shopping II* (to be released). *See also Why Aren't More People Online?*, *supra* n. 15. *See also* Communication from the European Commission, *Consumer Policy Action Plan* 1999-2001<http://www.europa.eu.int/comm/dgs/health_consumer/library/legislation/ap/ap01_en.pdf>.

[196] UNCTAD E-Commerce and Development Report, *supra* n. 2, at 38.

[197] European Union Resolution of 19 Jan. 1999 on the *Consumer Dimension of the Information Society*, 1999 O.J. (C 023) 1 <http://www.europa.eu.int/eur-lex/en/lif/dat/1999/en_399Y0128_01.html>.

principles of consumer protection established by international bodies such as the OECD.[198]

Consumer protection policies should promote the active participation of all stakeholders including governments, businesses, and consumers. Online businesses should be responsible for developing and following fair practices and ensuring proper online disclosures. Consumers need to act carefully and responsibly. Governments can provide a framework to facilitate the accomplishment of the above objectives. Governments can also provide a framework for fair and cost-effective dispute resolution processes.[199]

A significant amount of effort is being made around the world to enact or revise legislation and codes of practice and to establish new guidelines governing consumer protection for electronic commerce. For example, the WTO has established a work program on electronic commerce and published a study which identifies a range of issues including those related to consumer protection.[200] The OECD, after considerable study and commitment to the issue[201] adopted *Guidelines for Consumer Protection in the Context of Electronic Commerce* (OECD Consumer Protection Guidelines).[202] The OECD Consumer Protection Guidelines have been the basis for consumer protection legislation in a number of countries[203] including

---

198 *Guidelines for Consumer Protection in the Context of Electronic Commerce*, OECD <http://www.oecd.org>; Industry Canada, *Principles of Consumer Protection for Electronic Commerce: A Canadian Framework* <http:://www.strategis.ic.gc.ca/SSG/ca01182e.html>.

199 *Id.*, OECD Consumer Protection Guidelines.

200 WTO Declaration on Global E-commerce, *supra* n. 9.

201 *See Dismantling the Barriers to Global Electronic Commerce*, OECD (Turku, Finland, 19-21 Nov. 1997), DSTI/ICCP (98) 13/Final (OECD Dismantling the Barriers to Global E-Commerce); *Ministerial Declaration on Consumer Protection in the Context of Electronic Commerce* (Ottawa, 7-9 Oct. 1998) <http://www.oecd.org>; *ICCP Special Session on Codes of Conduct for Electronic Commerce*, OECD (13 Oct., 1999) <http://www.oecd.org>; *OECD Consumer Protection in the Electronic Market Place*, dtfti/(CP98)13/final (Dec. 22, 1998) <http://www.oecd.org>.

202 Available at <http://www.oecd.org>.

203 For a compilation of OECD member country consumer protection laws, *see* OECD, Directorate for Science, Technology and Industry Committee on Consumer Policy, *Inventory of Consumer Protection Laws, Policies and Practices Applied to E-commerce* (Mar. 1, 2001) <http://www.olis.oecd.org/olis/>.

Australia,[204] New Zealand,[205] and Canada.[206] The European Union has adopted a Council Directive on Legal Aspects of Electronic Commerce.[207] The European Union has also passed a Distance Selling Directive[208] and a privacy directive.[209] It has also proposed a directive concerning the distance marketing of consumer financial services[210] and a directive on electronic money,[211] each of which contain consumer protection provisions related to various forms of electronic transactions.

Other countries, such as the United States, have approached consumer protection over the Internet by relying on industry self-regulation combined with the enforcement of existing laws to consumer transactions over the Internet.[212] In the

---

[204] *A Policy Framework for Consumer Protection in Electronic Commerce.* <http://www.treasury.gov.au/publications/ConsumerProtectionInElectronicCommerce/index.asp>.

[205] New Zealand, Model Code for Consumer Protection in E-commerce (Oct. 2000) <http://www.consumer-ministry.gov.nz/Model-Code.html>. This Model Code has been drafted in a plain English style that should make it easier for merchants to understand and implement.

[206] *Principles of Consumer Protection for E-commerce: A Canadian Framework*, Working Group on E-commerce and Consumers. The OECD Guidelines were also influential in the development of model Canadian provincial legislation regulating Internet sales. *See Internet Sales Contract Harmonization Template* (May 29, 2001) <http://www.strategis.ic.gc.ca/SSG/ca01642e.html>.

[207] *European Parliament and Council Directive on Certain Legal Aspects of Electronic Commerce in the Internal Market*, COM (1998) 586 Final-98/03125 (COD), adopted Dec. 13, 1999. Member states had until July 19, 2001 to bring into force the laws, regulations and administrative provisions necessary to comply with it.

[208] EC European Parliament and Council, Directive 97/7 of May 20, 1997, *Protection of Consumers in Respect of Distance Contracts.*

[209] Directive 95/46/EC of the European Parliament and of the Council of Oct. 24, 1995, *Protection of Individuals with Regard to the Processing of Personal Data and On the Free Movement of Such Data.*

[210] *Directive of the European Parliament and of the Council Concerning the Distance Marketing of Consumer Financial Services*, COM (1999) 468 Final-98/0245 (COD), submitted by the Commission on Nov. 19, 1998.

[211] *Proposal for a European Parliament and Council Directive on the Taking Up, the Pursuit and the Potential Supervision of the Business of Electronic Money Institutions*, OJ C 317/1998.

[212] Clinton & Gore, *supra* n. 9, *A Coordinated Strategy.*

United States, for example, the Federal Trade Commission (FTC) has been active to assert that its laws, regulations, and guidelines are as applicable to electronic commerce transactions as to other transactions. Various publications of the FTC such as *Advertising and Marketing on the Internet*, *The Rules of the Road*, *Guide to Online Payments* and *Dot Com Disclosures* explain the FTC's position on the application of U.S. laws to protect consumers on the Internet.[213] The FTC also enforces U.S. laws by holding "Internet surf days" during which FTC enforcement staff surf the Internet reviewing, among other things, website privacy policies, advertising, and disclosure statements. Non-compliances are identified and website operators are contacted. Website operators that do not change their practices may be fined or subject to penalties.

6.2. Policy Considerations

Consumer protection policies for electronic commerce generally address the following concerns:

(1) transparency and the right of the consumer to receive sufficient and reliable information before, and where appropriate, after the transaction;

(2) nondiscrimination in the access to products and services, and consideration of the needs of vulnerable consumers;

(3) protection of consumers from unsolicited, misleading, and unfair marketing practices, including advertising;

(4) protection of a consumer's health, safety, and privacy, including protection against the misuse of personal information;

(5) information and education of consumers to enable them to develop the appropriate skills;

(6) consultation of consumers when developing new policies or regulatory mechanisms; and

(7) representation of consumers interests in relevant monitoring and supervisory bodies.[214]

The above principles are discussed below in further detail.

---

[213] These three papers are available at <http://www.ftc.gov>.

[214] OECD Consumer Protection Guidelines, *supra* n. 198.

Information Provision

Consumers should be provided with clear and sufficient information to make an informed choice about whether and how to make a purchase.[215] Merchants are encouraged to use plain and appropriate language, and avoid using jargon or "legalese." They are also encouraged to provide sufficient information and purchase terms so that the consumer can easily review them prior to purchase and keep them for future reference (either by saving them electronically or by printing them). Merchants are also advised to clearly distinguish between the marketing message and the purchase terms.

Merchants are also urged to make the following information available to the consumer, prior to the completion of a purchase:

(1) merchant identity, location of business operations, contact details including e-mail address and phone numbers, any registration numbers or licenses, any accreditation and any other information necessary for the consumer to verify the merchant's legitimacy;

(2) fair and accurate description of goods or services, together with any associated warranties and geographical restrictions;

(3) description of types of delivery mechanisms including any expected delay to delivery and any differences in associated costs;

(4) cancellation, return, and exchange rights and procedures (including any associated costs);

(5) types of payment that will be accepted;

(6) full price to the consumer including currency, shipping, any taxes or duties and any fees or discounts based on payment types;

(7) level of privacy, including merchant's privacy policy;

(8) security mechanisms to protect confidentiality and integrity of information being exchanged;

(9) rights of withdrawal, such as the seven working day "cooling-off" period provided for in the EU Distance Selling Directive; and[216]

(10) complaint procedures.

---

[215] *See* Sookman, *supra* n. 128, at 10-32.

[216] Directive 1997/7/EC of May 1997 on the protection of consumers in respect of distance selling contracts, 1997 O.J. (L144) 19, art. 6 (EU Distance Selling Directive).

Merchants are also encouraged to provide consumers with their own record of the transaction that can be printed and stored by the consumer.

Canada has taken an innovative approach to requiring information disclosures in the context of Internet sales transactions with consumers. In May 2001, Canadian federal, provincial, and territorial ministers adopted model legislation, the *Internet Sales Contract Harmonization Template* (Internet Template),[217] for consumer protection legislation in Canada governing Internet sales and service contracts. The Internet template covers contract formation, cancellation rights, credit card charge-backs, and information disclosures to consumers entering into Internet sales contracts.

Contract Formation

Merchants should take reasonable steps to ensure that the consumer in fact intended to purchase, and that the consumer agreed to purchase only after having received all the necessary information to make an informed purchase decision. This principle encourages online businesses to design their online purchase processes so that it is clear what constitutes an offer and what constitutes an acceptance and what terms are included in the purchase contract. It also encourages the development of processes whereby the purchaser is required to confirm the intention to purchase on the specified terms more than once in order to avoid an accidental purchase.[218] Purchasers should also receive a purchase acknowledgement summarizing the terms of the purchase. Where a multistep confirmation process is not used, the purchaser should be allowed a reasonable period of time to cancel the purchase order (in addition to, but overlapping with, any "cooling-off" period).

The OECD Guidelines require businesses engaged in electronic commerce to pay due regard to the interests of consumers and act in accordance with fair business, advertising, and marketing practices. The guidelines require that:

---

[217] *Supra* n. 206, <http://strategic.ic.gc.ca/sc_consu/consaffairs/engdoc/oca.html>.

[218] For example, there is a "three-click" purchase model that requires: 1. Consumer express interest to purchase by, for example, adding it to the "shopping cart." 2. Consumer has opportunity to review all details of the purchase and is required to "click" to confirm that they are correct. 3. Consumer is required to "click" again in order to place the order and this is accompanies by clear language stating that this is the final stage of placing the order. This three-click model is recommended by Consumers International, available at <http://www.consumersinternational.org>. This type of a "three-click" process is consistent with the OECD Consumer Protection Guidelines, *supra* n. 198.

(1) Businesses should not make any representation, or omission, or engage in any practice that is likely to be deceptive, misleading, fraudulent or unfair.

(2) Businesses selling, promoting or marketing goods or services to consumers should not engage in practices that are likely to cause unreasonable risk of harm to consumers.

(3) Whenever businesses make information available about themselves or the goods or services they provide, they should present such information in a clear, conspicuous, accurate, and easily accessible manner.

(4) Businesses should comply with any representations they make regarding policies or practices relating to their transactions with consumers.[219]

Complaint Mechanism, Dispute Resolution and Redress

Just as they do in the "bricks and mortar" world, consumers in the electronic marketplace will face situations where products arrive broken, defective or in some way simply do not meet expectations. They will need to have access to effective complaint and redress mechanisms to help resolve disputes. The global nature of the Internet may make efforts to resolve disputes between consumers and businesses located in different parts of the world time consuming and difficult. Addressing consumer problems necessitates developing mechanisms to resolve differences quickly, easily, and fairly.[220]

The issue of consumer redress has been the subject of much controversy. OECD Consumer Protection Guidelines acknowledge the difficulty of defining the scope of redress to which consumers should be entitled. The OECD recommends that the guiding principle be that consumers have meaningful access to fair and timely alternative dispute resolution and redress mechanisms without undue cost or burden. The International Chamber of Commerce (ICC) proposed a three-step process for resolving online disputes. The steps comprise a merchant internal complaint mechanism, an online ADR mechanism, and recourse to legal action.[221] These steps

---

[219] Guidelines for Consumer Protection *supra* n. 198, at 4.

[220] *Consumer Protection in the Electronic Market Place*, OECD, DSTI/cp(98) 13/Final, Dec. 22, 1998 www.oecd.org>.

[221] International Chamber of Commerce, E-commerce Project Ad hoc Task Force, *Jurisdiction and Applicable Law in E-commerce* (June 6, 2001) <http://www.iccwbo.org/home/statements_rules/statements/2001/jurisdiction_and_applicable_law.html>.

were advocated on the basis of low cost and the potential to overcome geographic and cultural barriers.

A difficult question in developing policies to promote consumer remedies for e-commerce relates to the right of online merchants to select the governing law and choice of venue for resolving disputes. The OECD Consumer Protection Guidelines acknowledge the problem of applicable law and jurisdiction related to Internet transactions and leave it up to individual governments to determine whether "the existing framework for applicable law and jurisdiction should be modified, or applied differently, to ensure effective and transparent consumer protection."[222] The European Union approach is to permit Internet consumers the right to bring actions for redress in their state of residence.[223] In the United States choice of law and forum selection clauses are often enforced, even in standard form contracts, often referred to as "contracts of adhesion."[224] Not all courts, however, enforce forum selection clauses in Internet-based agreements.[225]

---

[222] *Supra* n. 202, sec. VI.

[223] *See* Rome Convention *supra* n. 60, arts. 5, 7. *See also* recent amendments to the Brussels Convention, *supra* n. 60.

[224] *See e.g. State ex rel Meierhenry v. Spiegel*, 277 N.W. 2d 298 (S.D. 1979); *see also Williams v. America Online, Inc.*, (2001 W.L. 135825); *Specht & Gibson et al. v. Netscape Communications Corp. and America Online, Inc.* Civ. Action No. 00 Civ. 4871 (S.D.N.Y. July 3, 2001).

[225] In *America Online, Inc. v. The Superior Court of Alameda County*, Super. Ct. No. 827047-2 (Cal. C.A. June 21, 2001) for example, a California Appellant Court refused to give effect to a forum selection clause in a class action lawsuit against it. The court noted that California law "favors forum selection agreements only so long as they are procured freely and voluntarily, with the place chosen having some logical nexus to one of the parties or the dispute, and so long as California consumers will not find their substantial legal rights significantly impaired by their enforcement." Further, "to be enforceable, the selected jurisdiction must be 'suitable', 'available' and able to 'accomplish substantial justice.'" The court refused to permit AOL to rely on its Virginia choice of law and exclusive venue provision as the enforcement of the contractual forum selection and choice of law clauses would operate as a functional equivalent of a contractual wavier of a California consumer protection law. Further, Virginia law did not allow consumer lawsuits to be brought as class actions and the available remedies were more limited than those available by California law.

Security of Payment and Personal Information

Merchants should take all reasonable steps to ensure that a consumer's personal information is transmitted securely and maintained in a secure environment.[226] In the context of consumer transactions over the Internet, personal information includes payment information, such as credit card details and e-mail addresses. It can also include persistent identifiers such as cookies,[227] a computer service number, clickstream information,[228] and other data in electronic form which can be used directly or indirectly to identify an individual.[229] It is generally recognized that a consumer has a responsibility to take reasonable steps to conduct transactions safely and securely. In this regard, a consumer protection policy should encourage consumers not to give out personal information over a non-secure website.

Engaging with Minors

Merchants must take special care when targeting minors, or when it is reasonable that a minor may be attracted to the website. When interacting with minors, a merchant should take reasonable steps to ensure that the potential consumer is not a minor. Unless the merchant has a reasonable belief that the potential consumer is not a minor, the parent's consent should be obtained before personal information is collected from, or before a contract is entered into with, a minor.[230]

---

226 OECD Consumer Protection Guidelines, *supra* n. 198, sec. V and Canadian Framework and Internet Sales Template, *supra* n. 206.

227 Cookies are short pieces of data used by web servers to help identify web users who visit a particular server's site. They are stored on the user's machine and alert a server when a user visits a particular server's site to the fact the user has visited that site before.

228 Clickstream information is a virtual trail that a user leaves behind while navigating the web. It is a record of the user's activity on the internet, including every website and webpage that the user visits, how long the user was on a page or site, in what order the pages were visited, any newsgroups the user participates in, and email addresses of mail that the user sends and receives.

229 Sookman, *supra* n. at 8-26 to 8-35. *See also* the Regulations to the U.S. *Children's Online Privacy Protection Act* of 1998 (U.S. COPPA) definition of "Personal Information" <http:// www.F.TC.gov>.

230 Australia, Consumer Affairs Division, Department of Treasury, Building Consumer Sovereignty in E-commerce, *A Best Practice Model for Business* sec. 24 (May 2000) <http://www.ecommerce.treasury.gov.au/html/build.htm>; U.S. *Children's Online Privacy Probation Act* of 1998.

SPAM

An important policy issue is how best to address the problems associated with unsolicited commercial e-mail solicitations, also known as "SPAM." Jurisdictions which have developed policies to deal with this problem have taken either an "opt-in" or "opt-out" approach. The "opt-in" approach requires consent from consumers before commercially unsolicited e-mails can be sent. The "opt-out" approach permits merchants to send unsolicited e-mails unless a recipient requests otherwise.

The EU Committee for Consumer Policy that is responsible for considering the issues associated with SPAM has recommended against a policy requiring e-marketers to obtain a recipient's consent prior to sending unsolicited commercial e-mail.[231] This policy is reflected in the "opt-out" approach adopted in the EU E-Commerce Directive.[232] In each EU Member State there is an "opt-out" registry. Individuals who do not wish to receive unsolicited commercial communications can register with these registries. A merchant who wishes to send SPAM to a consumer must ensure that the targeted recipient is not listed in the opt-out registry in the consumer's country. European Union Member States can, however, provide for more restrictive provisions, including provisions which require "opt-in" consents.[233] Under the EU E-Commerce Directive, ISPs are not required to carry unsolicited e-mails.

In the United States, approximately 19 of the states have either enacted or are in the process of enacting legislation to limit or prohibit unsolicited commercial e-mails.[234]

Consumer and Merchant Awareness and Education

Government, business, and consumer groups should promote consumer awareness about the safe use of electronic commerce. Many countries are providing

---

[231] European Union's Citizen's Rights and Freedoms, Just and Home Affairs Committee. *See also* U.S. COPPA, and the regulations made pursuant thereto which set out how the United States has approached this issue, *infra* n. 267 and accompanying text.

[232] *Supra* n. 45, art. 7.

[233] For example, Austria, Denmark, Finland, Germany, and Italy.

[234] For example, California, Colorado, Connecticut, Delaware, Idaho, Illinois, Iowa, Louisiana, Missouri, Nevada, North Carolina, Oklahoma, Pennsylvania, Rhode Island, Tennessee, Virginia, Washington, and West Virginia. For a summary of the status of U.S. state SPAM laws, *see* <http://www.spamlaws.com/state/summary.html>.

education to consumers and merchants with respect to e-commerce. For example, the United Kingdom government has developed an extensive website presence to assist in educating merchants and consumers on the implications of the EU E-Commerce Directive.[235] The European Commission also has online resources for consumers and merchants focusing on education and awareness.[236] The Singapore government has developed a business guide to promote usage of e-commerce and development of e-commerce related technologies.[237]

International organizations can also promote awareness of consumer protection issues related to electronic commerce. For example, the International Telecommunication Union has created a website that lists links on consumer protection for a number of countries including Canada, Australia, and the United States.[238]

7. Privacy

7.1. Introduction

The Internet has the capacity to be the most effective data-collector in existence.[239] The Internet, and in particular the worldwide web, is a rich source of information about online consumers. Websites collect a great deal of personal information explicitly, through registration pages, survey forms, order forms, online contests and

---

[235] Available at <http://www.dti.gov.uk/cii/>; *see also* for education for businesses <http://www.ukonlineforbusiness.gov.uk>.

[236] *See* <http://www.europa.eu.int/comm/consumers/index_en.html>.

[237] Singapore Business Guide for Implementing E-commerce sets out a guide for the steps a company must go through when implementing e-commerce as follows: Step 1 : Understand how e-commerce is changing the business. Step 2 : Analyze business processes and plan for the change. Step 3 : Choose between in-house implementation or outsourcing. Step 4 : Design for audience – Simplicity is the key. Step 5 : Put operational processes in place. Step 6 : Update and improve constantly. Step 7 : Provide impeccable customer support. Step 8 : Make yourself known. Step 9 : Encourage usage. *See* <http://www.ec.gov.sg/forward/step.html>.

[238] *See* <http://www.itu.int/ITU-D/ecdc/UsefulLinks/consumerprotection.html>.

[239] Susan Gindin, *Lost and Found in Cyberspace: Informational Privacy in the Age of the Internet*, 34 San Diego L. Rev. 1153 (1997), available at <http://www.info-law.com/lost.html>.

other means, and by using systems in ways that are not obvious to online consumers. Through cookies, tracking software, and other persistent identifiers, website owners are able to follow consumers' online activities and gather information about their personal interests and preferences.[240] The online environment provides for unprecedented opportunities for the compilation, analysis, and dissemination of such information. While businesses have always collected some information from consumers in order to facilitate transactions, the Internet allows for very efficient and inexpensive collection of a vast array of personal information. The prevalence, ease, and relatively low cost of such information collection distinguishes the online environment from the more traditional means of commerce and information collection and thus raises consumer privacy concerns.[241]

The Internet has a broad spectrum of participants, an extraordinarily quick pace of change, a significant decentralization of information processing activity and no deference for jurisdictional boundaries. A session on the Internet may involve websites located in different territories. Even a visit to a single website can result in transmissions of data to many territories. Online directories, cookies, search engines, log analyses, intelligent agents, banner advertising, online shopping, to name just a few of the activities and infrastructure elements, underscore the increasing tendency, capability, and commercial pressure to gather and use personal information online. In the Internet environment, there is an enormous positive need for reliable personal information and its commercial value creates very strong pressures for massive collection of personal data.[242]

Studies demonstrate that consumers are concerned about privacy, particularly in relation to disclosing personal information over the Internet.[243] Numerous

---

[240] Federal Trade Commission, *Self-Regulation and Privacy Online: A Report to Congress* (July 1999) <http://www.ftc.gov/reports/privacy3/toc.htm>.

[241] *Id.*

[242] Joel R. Reidenberg *et al.*, *Data Protection Law and Online Services: Regulatory Responses, Study for the Commission of the European Community* (Dec. 1998) <http://www.europa.eu.int/comm/dg15/en/media/dataprot/studies/regul.htm>.

[243] United States Department of Commerce *The Emerging Digital Economy* <http://www.ecommerce.gov>; *Privacy Online: A Report to Congress* (Federal Trade Commission June 1998), available at <http://www.ftc.gov/reports/privacy3/toc.htm>; U.S. FTC Self-Regulation 1999, *supra* n. 240; *Privacy Online: Fair Information Practices in the Electronic Market Place: a Report to Congress* (Federal Trade Commission 2000), available at <http://www.FTC.gov>.

studies have also warned that consumers will distrust online merchants and will remain wary of engaging in electronic commerce until meaningful and effective consumer privacy protections are implemented.

Lack of privacy may result in the online marketplace failing to reach its full potential.[244] It is therefore critical to developing an overall legislative structure for electronic commerce to develop policies that promote trust and confidence that personal information about individuals will be dealt with in accordance with internationally recognized fair information practices.

Privacy protection laws are intended to provide a series of rights for individuals such as the right to receive information whenever data about them is collected, the right of access to data, the right to have data corrected, and the right to object to certain types of data processing.[245] These rights are reflected in privacy or data protection laws that have been enacted in many countries.[246]

---

[244] On this issue, *see e.g. The Canadian Electronic Commerce Strategy* (Industry Canada 1998), available at <http://e-com.ic.gc.ca>; OECD, *Dismantling the Barriers to Global E-Commerce, supra*, n. 201; United States Department of Commerce, *The Emerging Digital Economy* <http://www.ecommerce.gov>; U.S. Department of Commerce, *Privacy and the NII: Safeguarding Telecommunications – Related Personal Information* (Oct. 1995) <http://www.ntia.doc.gov./ntiahome/privwhitepaper.html>; *Privacy Online: A Report to Congress* (Federal Trade Commission June 1998), available at <http://www.ftc.gov/reports/privacy3/toc.htm>; U.S. FTC Self-Regulation Report 1999, *supra* n. 240; Ann Cavoukian, Ontario Information and Privacy Commissioner, *Privacy: The Key To Electronic Commerce* (Apr. 1998) <http://www.ipc.on.ca>.

[245] Privacy protection has also been recognized as a fundamental human right. For example, art. 17 of the International Covenant on Civil and Political Rights which establishes privacy as one of the internationally recognized human rights. The right recognized there states: "No one shall be subjected to arbitrary interference with his privacy, family, home or correspondence, nor to attack upon his honour and reputation. Everyone has the right to the protection of the law against such interference or attacks."

This right is also recognized in article 12 of the Universal Declaration of Human Rights, G.A. Res. 218 A (iii), U.N. Doc. A/810 at 71 (1948) and in art. 8 of the European Convention for the Protection of Human Rights and Fundamental Freedoms, 213 U.N.T.S. 221. Art. 8 of the Convention reads "Everyone has the right to respect for his private and family life, his home and his correspondence." This article's focus, however, is on information privacy.

[246] Argentina, *Personal Data Protection Act (2000)* <http://www.privacyinternational.org/countries/argentina/argentine-dpa.html>; Australia, *Privacy Act 1988* <http://www.austii.edu.au/au/legis/cth/consol_act/pa1998108/> as amended including *Privacy Amendment (Private Sector) Act* No. 155 (2000) <scaleplus.law.gov.au/comact/10/6115/top.htm>;

7.2. Core Information Privacy Principles

There have been several attempts to develop complete and comprehensive sets of internationally recognized fair information practices that incorporate information privacy rights. These principles, which are set out below, reflect a consensus among the international community concerning the core principles related to privacy.

Austria – *Datenschutzgesetz* (1978) <http://www.ad.or.at/office/recht/dsg.htm> (in German) as amended by the *Datenschutzgesetz (Data Protection Act)* (2000), BGBI Nr. 1999/165 (summary available at <http://www.privacyexchange.org/legal/nat/omni/austriasum.html>); Belgium – *Belgium Data Protection Act of 1992* (summary available at <http://www.privacyexchange.org/legal/nat/omni/belgiumsum.html>); Canada, *The Personal Information Protection and Electronic Documents Act* (2000) <http://www.parl.gc.ca/36/2/parlbus/chambus/house/bills/government/c-6/c-6_4/c-6_cover-e.html>; Czech Republic, *Act of 29 April 1992 on Protection of Personal Data in Information Systems* <http://www.psp.cz/> (in Czech) (summary available at <http://www.privacyexchange.org/legal/nat/omni/czechsum.html>); Denmark, *The Public Authorities' Registers Act (*1991) <http://www.registertilsynet.dk/lovgivning/maina.html> (in Danish); and *The Private Registers Act* (1987) <http://www.registertilsynet.dk/lovgivning/main1html> (in Danish); Finland, *Personal Data Act* (523) 1999 amending and replacing the *Personal Data File Act* (1999) <http://www.om.fi/1077.htm> (in Finnish) (summary available at <http://www.privacyexchange.org/legal/nat/omni/finlandsum.html>); France, *An Act on Data Processing, Data Files and Individual Liberties, Law No. 78-17* <http://www.cnil.fr/textes/ttext.htm> (in French); Germany, *Federal Data Protection Act* (1990) <http://www.datenschutz-berlin.de/gesetze/bdsg/bdsgeng.htm>; Greece, *Law on the Protection of Individuals with regard to the Processing of Personal Data*, Law No. 2472 <http://www.privacyexchange.org/legal/nat/omni/greece.html>; Hong Kong, *Personal Data (Privacy) Ordinance* <http://www.privacy.com>.hk/contents.html>; Hungary, *Act LXIII of 1992 on the Protection of Personal Data and disclosure of Data of Public Interest* <http://www.privacyinternational.org/countries/hungary/hungary_privacy_law_1992.html>; Iceland, *Act on Protection of Individuals with Regard to the Processing of Personal Data* <http://www.mannvernd.is/english/laws/act.dataprotection.html>; Ireland, *Data Protection Act* (1988) <http://www.dataprivacy.ie/6ai.htm>; Israel, *Protection of Privacy Law* (1981) <http://www.law.co.il/computer-law/privacy_law_english.htm>; Italy, *Protection of Individuals and Legal Persons Regarding the Processing of Personal Data Act* <http://www.privacyexchange.org/legal/nat/omni/italy.html>; Japan, *Law for the Protection of Computer Processed Personal Data Held by Administrative Organs* (1988); Latvia, *Personal Data Protection Law* (2000) <http://www.privacyexchange.org/legal/nat/omni/latvialaw.html>; Luxembourg, *Act Regulating the Use of Nominal Data in Computer Processing* (1979) (summary available at <http://www.privacyexchange.org/legal/nat/omni/luxemsum.html>); Netherlands,

7.2.1. OECD Guidelines

One of the first attempts to develop a complete and comprehensive set of internationally recognized fair information practices was the *Guidelines Governing the Protection of Privacy and Transborder Flows of Personal Data*, prepared by the Organization for Economic Cooperation and Development in 1980 (the OECD Guidelines).[247] The principles in that document have served as the model for privacy legislation in many countries.

At the core of the OECD Guidelines is a set of eight principles to be applied to both the public and private sectors: (a) the collection limitation principle, (b) the data quality principle, (c) the purpose specification principle, (d) the use limitation principle, (e) the security safeguards principle, (f) the openness principle, (g) the individual participation principle, and (h) the accountability principle.

The principles identified in the OECD Guidelines outline the rights and obligations of individuals in the context of automated processing of personal data, and the rights and obligations of those who engage in such processing. They apply to personal data, whether in the public or private sectors, which pose a danger to

---

Personal Data Protection Act (2000) <http:// home.planet.nl/%7eprivacy1/wbp_en_rev.htm>; New Zealand, *Privacy Act (*1993) <http://rangi.knowledge-basket.co.nz/gpacts/public/text/1993/an/028.html>; Norway, *Act No. 48 of 9 June 1978 Relating to Personal Data Filing System* <http://www.datatilsynet.no/arkiv/engelsk/LOV-ENG.html>; Poland, *Act of August 29, 1997 on the Protection of Personal Data* <http://www.privacyexchange.org/legal/nat/omni/poland.html>; Portugal, *Act on the Protection of Personal Data (*1998) <http://www.cnpd.pt>; Russia, *Federal Law on Information, Information and Information Protection* (1995) <http://www.datenschutz-berlin.de/gesetze/internat/fen.htm> (excerpts). In addition, a draft *Law on Personal Data* has been pending in the Russian Duma (the lower chamber of the Russian Parliament) since 1996; Slovenia, *Personal Data Protection Act,* RS no. 55/99 <http://www.privacyexchange.org/legal/nat/omni/slovenia.html>; Spain, *Law 15/1999 of 13 Dec. 1999 Relating to the Protection of Personal Data* <http://www.agenciaprotecciondatos/datd1.htm> (in Spanish); Sweden, *Personal Data Act* (1998) <http://www.datainspektionen.se/PDF-filer/ovrigt/pul-eng.pdf>; Switzerland, *Federal Law on Data Protection* (1992) <http://edsb.ch/framese.html>; Taiwan (China), *Computer-Processed Personal Data Protection Law of 11 Aug. 1995* <http://www.privacyexchange.org/legal/nat/omni/taiwan.html>; United Kingdom, *The Data Protection Act* (1988) <http://www.hmso.gov.uk/acts/acts1998/19980029.htm>.

[247] *See* OECD web site at <http://www1.oecd.ong/dsti/sti/it/secur/prod/PRIV-EN.HTM>.

privacy and individual liberties because of the manner in which it is processed, or because of its nature or the context in which it is used.

The core privacy principles contained in the OECD Guidelines are as follows:

(1) *Collection Limitation Principle*: There should be limits to the collection of personal data and any such data should be obtained by lawful and fair means and, where appropriate, with the knowledge or consent of the data subject.

(2) *Data Quality Principle*: Personal data should be relevant to the purposes for which they are to be used, and, to the extent necessary for those purposes, should be accurate, complete, and kept up-to-date.

(3) *Purpose Specification Principle*: The purposes for which personal data are collected should be specified not later than at the time of data collection and the subsequent use limited to the fulfillment of those purposes or such others as are not incompatible with those purposes and as are specified on each occasion of change of purpose.

(4) *Use Limitation Principle*: Personal data should not be disclosed, made available or otherwise used for purposes other than those specified in accordance with the Purpose Specification Principle except: (a) with the consent of the data subject; or (b) by the authority of law.

(5) *Security Safeguards Principle*: Personal data should be protected by reasonable security safeguards against such risks as loss or unauthorized access, destruction, use, modification or disclosure of data.

(6) *Openness Principle*: There should be a general policy of openness about developments, practices, and policies with respect to personal data. Means should be readily available of establishing the existence and nature of personal data, and the main purposes of their use, as well as the identity and usual residence of the data controller.

(7) *Individual Participation Principle*: An individual should have the right: (a) to obtain from a data controller, or otherwise, confirmation of whether or not the data controller has data relating to him; (b) to have communicated to him, data relating to him within a reasonable time; at a charge, if any, that is not excessive; in a reasonable manner; and in a form that is readily intelligible to him; (c) to be given reasons if a request made under subparagraphs (a) and (b) is denied, and to be able to challenge such denial; and (d) to challenge data relating to him and, if the challenge is successful to have the data erased, rectified, completed or amended.

(8) *Accountability Principle*: A data controller should be accountable for complying with measures which give effect to the principles stated above.[248]

The OECD Guidelines also contain the following principles of international application:

(1) Member countries should take into consideration the implications for other member countries of domestic processing and re-exporting of personal data.
(2) Member countries should take all reasonable and appropriate steps to ensure that transborder flows of personal data, including transit through a member country, are uninterrupted and secure.
(3) A member country should refrain from restricting transborder flows of personal data between itself and another member country except where the latter does not yet substantially observe these guidelines or where the re-export of such data would circumvent its domestic privacy legislation. A member country may also impose restrictions in respect of certain categories of personal data for which its domestic privacy legislation includes specific regulations in view of the nature of those data and for which the other member country provides no equivalent protection.
(4) Member countries should avoid developing laws, policies, and practices in the name of the protection of privacy and individual liberties, which would create obstacles to transborder flows of personal data that would exceed requirements for such protection.[249]

The above principles are to be implemented by member countries through the establishment of legal, administrative or other procedures or institutions for the protection of privacy and personal data. This may include the adoption of appropriate domestic legislation; encouraging and supporting self-regulation such as codes of conduct; providing reasonable means for individuals to exercise their rights in respect of personal information; providing for adequate sanctions and remedies for breaches of the means used to implement the principles; and ensuring that there is no unfair discrimination against individuals about whom personal information is held.

In 1997, the Information, Computer and Communications Policy Division submitted a document to the OECD Group of Experts on Information Security and

---

[248] *Id.*

[249] *Id.*

Privacy. That document was subsequently issued in 1998 as a paper entitled, *Implementing the OECD "Privacy Guidelines" in the Electronic Environment: Focus on the Internet.*[250] That report was a study of concerns relating to privacy and the burgeoning development of the Internet and the special challenges to the protection of privacy posed by the electronic age and e-commerce in particular. The report reaffirmed that the OECD Guidelines were generic guidelines for the protection of privacy and the handling of personal data and suggested the following actions:

(1) to reaffirm that the Privacy Guidelines are applicable with regard to any technology used for collecting and processing data;

(2) for those businesses who choose to expand their activities to information and communication networks, to encourage them to adopt policies and technical solutions which will guarantee the protection of the privacy of individuals on these networks, and particularly on the Internet;

(3) to foster public education on issues related to protection of privacy and the use of technology.

The report suggested that the OECD would be a good place to undertake the necessary study of these issues in light of its history in developing the Privacy Guidelines and its established competence in dealing with issues relating to the development of the global information society.[251]

7.2.2. Council of Europe Convention

The OECD Guidelines were followed by the adoption of the *Convention for the Protection of Individuals with Regard to Automatic Processing of Personal Data* by the Council of Europe (the "Convention"). The Convention, which took effect in 1985, also established standards for the quality of data and security of data which is held in automated files or subject to automatic processing in the public and private sector.

---

[250] *Implementing the OECD "Privacy Guidelines" in the Electronic Environment: Focus on the Internet* (OECD 1998) <http://www.oecd.org/dsti/sti/it/secur/prod/reg97-63.htm>.

[251] The reader may also be interested in consulting the 1992 OECD Guidelines for the Security of Information Systems <http://www.oecd.org/dsti/sti/it/secur/index.htm>, and a Review of the Guidelines published in 1998 which is available from the Head of Publication Services, OECD, 2 rue Andre-Pascal, 75775 Paris Cedex 16, France.

The basic principles for data protection set out in the convention consist of the following:

(1) *Quality of Data*: Personal data undergoing automatic processing shall be: (a) obtained and processed fairly and lawfully; (b) stored for specified and legitimate purposes and not used in a way incompatible with those purposes; (c) adequate, relevant and not excessive in relation to the purposes for which they are stored; (d) accurate and, where necessary, kept up to date; and (e) preserved in a form which permits identification of the data subjects for no longer than is required for the purpose for which those data are stored.

(2) *Special Categories of Data*: Personal data revealing racial origin, political opinions or religious or other beliefs, as well as personal data concerning health or sexual life, may not be processed automatically unless domestic law provides appropriate safeguards. The same shall apply to personal data related to criminal convictions.

(3) *Data Security*: Appropriate security measures shall be taken for the protection of personal data stored in automated data files against accidental or unauthorized destruction or accidental loss as well as against unauthorized access, alteration or dissemination.

(4) *Additional Safeguards for the Data Subject*: A person shall be enabled: (a) to establish the existence of an automated personal data file its main purposes, as well as the identity and habitual residence or principal place of business of the controller of the file; (b) to obtain at reasonable intervals and without excessive delay or expense confirmation of whether personal data relating to him are stored in the automated data file as well as communication to him of such data in an intelligible form; (c) to obtain, as the case may be, rectification or erasure of such data if these have been processed contrary to the provisions of domestic law giving effect to the basic principles set out in articles 5 and 6 of this convention; and (d) to have a remedy if a request for such confirmation or, as the case may be, communication, rectification or erasure as referred to in paragraphs (b) and (c) of this Article is not complied with.

(5) *Sanctions and Remedies*: Each party undertakes to establish appropriate sanctions and remedies for violations of provisions of domestic law giving effect to the basic principles for data protection set out in this section.

(6) *Extended Protection*: None of the provisions of this section shall be interpreted as limiting or otherwise affecting the possibility for a party to grant

data subjects a wider measure of protection than that stipulated in this convention.[252]

7.2.3. United Nations Guidelines Concerning Computerized Data Files

On December 14, 1990, the United Nations General Assembly adopted *Guidelines Concerning Computerized Personal Data Files* (the "U.N. Guidelines"). The U.N. Guidelines set out the following ten principles concerning the minimum guarantees that should be provided in national legislation:

(1) *Principle of lawfulness and fairness*: Information about persons should not be collected or processed in unfair or unlawful ways, nor should it be used for ends contrary to the purposes and principles of the Charter of the United Nations.

(2) *Principle of accuracy*: Persons responsible for the compilation of files or those responsible for keeping them have an obligation to conduct regular checks on the accuracy and relevance of the data recorded and to ensure that they are kept as complete as possible in order to avoid errors of omission and that they are kept up to date regularly or when the information contained in a file is used, as long as they are being processed.

(3) *Principle of the purpose-specification*: The purpose which a file is to serve and its utilization in terms of that purpose should be specified, legitimate and, when it is established, receive a certain amount of publicity or be brought to the attention of the person concerned, in order to make it possible subsequently to ensure that:

(a) All the personal data collected and recorded remain relevant and adequate to the purposes so specified;

(b) None of the said personal data is used or disclosed, except with the consent of the person concerned, for purposes incompatible with those specified; and

(c) The period for which the personal data are kept does not exceed that which would enable the achievement of the purpose so specified.

---

[252] *Convention for the Protection of Individuals with Regard to Automatic Processing of Personal Data* arts. 5, 6, 7, 8, 10, and 11 (Jan. 28, 1981) <http://conventions.coe.int/treaty/en/Treaties/Html/108.htm>.

(4) *Principle of interested-person access*: Everyone who offers proof of identity has the right to know whether information concerning him/her is being processed and to obtain it in an intelligible form, without undue delay or expense, and to have appropriate rectifications or erasures made in the case of unlawful, unnecessary or inaccurate entries and, when it is being communicated, to be informed of the addressees. Provision should be made for a remedy, if need be with the supervisory authority specified in principle 8 below. The cost of any rectification shall be borne by the person responsible for the file. It is desirable that the provisions of this principle should apply to everyone, irrespective of nationality or place of residence.

(5) *Principle of non-discrimination*: Subject to cases of exceptions restrictively envisaged under principle 6, data likely to give rise to unlawful or arbitrary discrimination, including information on racial or ethnic origin, colour, sex life, political opinions, religious, philosophical and other beliefs as well as membership of an association or trade union, should not be compiled.

(6) *Power to make exceptions*: Departures from principles 1 to 4 may be authorized only if they are necessary to protect national security, public order, public health or morality, as well as, *inter alia*, the rights and freedoms of others, especially persons being persecuted (humanitarian clause) provided that such departures are expressly specified in a law or equivalent regulation promulgated in accordance with the internal legal system which expressly states their limits and sets forth appropriate safeguards. Exceptions to principle 5 relating to the prohibition of discrimination, in addition to being subject to the same safeguards as those prescribed for exceptions to principles 1 and 4, may be authorized only within the limits prescribed by the International Bill of Human Rights and the other relevant instruments in the field of protection of human rights and the prevention of discrimination.

(7) *Principle of security*: Appropriate measures should be taken to protect the files against both natural dangers, such as accidental loss or destruction and human dangers, such as unauthorized access, fraudulent misuse of data or contamination by computer viruses.

(8) *Supervision and sanctions*: The law of every country shall designate the authority which, in accordance with its domestic legal system, is to be responsible for supervising observance of the principles set forth above. This authority shall offer guarantees of impartiality, independence *vis-à-vis* persons or agencies responsible for processing and establishing data, and technical competence. In the event of violation of the provisions of the national law implementing the aforementioned principles, criminal or other

penalties should be envisaged together with the appropriate individual remedies.

(9) *Transborder data flows*: When the legislation of two or more countries concerned by a transborder data flow offers comparable safeguards for the protection of privacy, information should be able to circulate as freely as inside each of the territories concerned. If there are no reciprocal safeguards, limitations on such circulation may not be imposed unduly and only in so far as the protection of privacy demands.

(10) *Field of application*: The present principles should be made applicable, in the first instance, to all public and private computerized files as well as, by means of optional extension and subject to appropriate adjustments, to manual files. Special provision, also optional, might be made to extend all or part of the principles to files on legal persons particularly when they contain some information on individuals.[253]

7.3. Approaches to Privacy Legislation

The history of data protection legislation around the world has reflected the effort to balance what countries perceive as the fundamental right to privacy and legitimate needs for government and business to obtain and use personal information. While there has been a general consensus concerning fundamental principles concerning privacy, different approaches have been taken to protect the privacy of individuals. The following is a summary of some of the approaches taken internationally.

7.3.1. European Union

The *European Union Data Protection Directive* was adopted in October 1995 and took effect on October 25, 1998. The two objectives of the directive are the protection of the fundamental rights and freedoms of natural persons, and in particular, the right to privacy with respect to the processing of personal data, and the requirement that member states do not restrict or prohibit the free flow of personal data between member states for reasons not permitted by the directive.

The directive applies to the "processing" of "personal data." Personal data is defined to mean, "any information relating to an identified or identifiable natural

---

[253] *Guidelines for the Regulation of Computerized Personal Data Files* <http://www.hri.ca/uninfo/treaties/72.shtml>.

person (a data subject)." An identifiable person is one who can be identified, directly or indirectly, in particular by reference to an identification number or to one or more factors specific to the person's physical, physiological, mental, economic, cultural or social identity.[254] The term "processing" is defined to mean, "any operation or set of operations which is performed upon personal data, whether or not by automatic means, such as collection, recording, organization, storage, adaptation or alteration, retrieval, consultation, use, disclosure by transmission, dissemination or otherwise making available, alignment or combination, blocking, erasure or destruction."[255]

The directive sets out the following principles which apply to the legislation that member states must adopt for the protection of personal information:

(1) personal data must be processed fairly and lawfully;

(2) personal data must be collected for specified, explicit and legitimate purposes and not further processed in a way incompatible with those purposes;

(3) further processing of data for historical, statistical or scientific purposes shall not be considered as incompatible provided that Member States provide appropriate safeguards;

(4) personal data must be adequate, relevant and not excessive in relation to the purposes for which they are collected and/or further processed;

(5) personal data must be accurate and, where necessary, kept up to date;

(6) every reasonable step must be taken to ensure that data which are inaccurate or incomplete, having regard to the purposes for which they were collected or for which they are further processed, are erased or rectified;

(7) personal data must be kept in a form which permits identification of data subjects for no longer than is necessary for the purposes for which the data were collected or for which they are further processed; and

(8) Member States shall lay down appropriate safeguards for personal data stored for longer periods for historical, statistical or scientific use.[256]

The directive establishes rules designed to ensure that data is only transferred to countries outside the European Union when its continued protection is guaranteed

---

[254] *European Union Data Protection Directive* art. 2(a) (Feb. 1995) <http://www.privacy.org/pi/intl_orgs/ec/final_EU_Data_Protection.html>.

[255] *Id.* at 2(b).

[256] *Id* at art. 6.

or when certain specific exemptions apply. Accordingly, articles 25 and 26 of the directive contain rules designed to ensure that the high standards of data protection established by the directive are not undermined given the ease with which data can be transmitted on international networks.[257]

The directive requires members to permit transfers of personal data only to countries outside the European Union where there is adequate protection of such data, unless one of a limited number of specific exemptions apply. The adequacy of the level of protection afforded by a third country is to be assessed "in the light of all the circumstances surrounding a data transfer operation or set of data transfer operations." Particular consideration is to be given to "the nature of the data, the purpose and duration of the proposed processing operation or operations, the country of origin and country of final destination, the rules of law, both general and sectoral, enforced in the third country in question and the professional rules and security measures which are complied with in that country."[258] The directive goes on to state that the commission may decide that a third country "ensures an adequate level of protection" "by reason of its domestic law or the international commitments it has entered into" for the protection of the private lives and basic freedoms and rights of individuals.[259]

Considerable debate has ensued concerning what constitutes an "adequate level of protection" so as to enable the transfer of personal data to a third country. To clarify its position, the Working Party of the European Commission published a working document setting out the criteria to be applied.[260]

To resolve the dilemma of the potential for the directive's adequacy provisions inhibiting commerce with the United States, considerable negotiation took place between the United States Department of Commerce and the European Community on the adequacy of International Safe Harbor Principles[261] that would help

---

[257] *Id.*, arts. 25, 26.

[258] *Id.*, arts. 25(1), 25(2).

[259] *Id.*, art. 25(6.).

[260] *Transfers of Personal Data to Third Countries: Applying Articles 25 and 26 of the EU Data Protection Directive*, adopted by the Working Party on July 24, 1998. *See also* Charles D. Raab *et al.*, *Application of a Methodology Designed to Access the Adequacy of the Level of Protection of Individuals with Regard to Processing Personal Data: Test of the Method on Several Categories of Transfer* (European Commission Final Report, Sept. 1998).

[261] For a list of the Safe Harbor Documents, *see* <http://www.ita.doc.gov/td/ecom/menu.html>.

U.S. organizations comply with the directive.[262] On July 26, 2000, after two years of negotiation, the European Commission approved the safe harbor privacy principles developed by the United States to ensure corporate compliance with the directive.[263] Under the terms of the U.S.-EC agreement, many U.S. companies that want to continue transferring personal data from Europe must commit to respecting detailed standards of notice, user choice, data access, and security. Making that commitment will put the companies into "safe harbor" against regulation under the directive.

7.3.2. Privacy Protection in the United States

For a combination of historical, cultural, and political reasons, the private sector in the United States has been virtually unregulated with respect to its collection, use, and disclosure of personal information. The United States has a highly developed system of privacy protection under tort law, however. Although right of privacy is not specifically guaranteed by the United States constitution it has been held that it protects a right of privacy in making certain intimate personal decisions free from governmental interference. In this regard, some information privacy protection can be found in the First and Fourth Amendments of the United States Constitution.[264] The United States Congress has also addressed specific needs for informational privacy and security by enacting specific statutes such as the *Electronic Communications Privacy Act* of 1986, the *Computer Fraud and Abuse Act*, the *Privacy Protection Act* of 1980, the *Privacy Act* of 1974, the *Computer Matching and Privacy Protection Act* of 1988, and the *Fair Credit Reporting Act*.[265]

There are recent indications that the U.S. approach of self-regulation may be changing. For example, a May 2000 report of the FTC entitled *Privacy Online: Fair Information Practices in the Electronic Marketplace*, concludes that legisla-

---

262 The International Trade Administration, *Electronic Task Force Documents*, showing the Commerce Department's work to Develop Safe Harbour Principles <http://www.ita.doc.gov/ecom/menu.htm>.

263 Keith Perine, *EC Will Stand By 'Safe Harbor' Deal*, The Standard (July 27, 2000), available at <http://www.thestandard.com/article/display/0,1151,17197,00.html>.

264 Susan Gindin, *supra* n. 239. *See also* sec. 8.14(b)(i).

265 These Acts are summarized in Gindin, *id.*

tion is necessary to implement and enforce fair information practices online.[266] The FTC noted that self-regulation by the online industry has not been sufficient to protect consumers and recommended that legislation be enacted to establish basic standards of practice for the collection of information online and to grant an agency the authority to enforce such standards.

While no comprehensive legislation has been enacted in the United States that applies to all private sector businesses, legislation has been passed to address particular privacy concerns. To address the protection of personal information of children, the United States enacted the *Children's Online Privacy Protection Act* of 1998 (COPPA). The act requires the operators of websites directed to children under thirteen or who knowingly collect information from children under 13 on the Internet to (a) provide parents notice of their information practices; (b) obtain prior, verifiable parental consent for the collection, use, and/or disclosure of personal information from children (with certain limited exceptions); (c) upon request, provide a parent with the ability to review the personal information collected from his/her child; (d) provide a parent with the opportunity to prevent the further use of personal information that has already been collected, or the future collection of personal information from that child; (e) limit collection of personal information for a child's online participation in a game, prize offer, or other activity to information that is reasonably necessary for the activity; and (f) establish and maintain reasonable procedures to protect the confidentiality, security, and integrity of the personal information collected. The act required the FTC to adopt regulations implementing its requirements. These regulations came into effect on April 21, 2000.[267]

The United States federal government also enacted sweeping new privacy legislation to protect consumer information collected by financial institutions. Under the *Gramm-Leach-Bliley Act*, financial institutions are required to have written privacy policies that must be disclosed to customers. The disclosure of a financial institution's privacy policy must take place at the time a customer relationship is established and not less than annually during the continuation of the relationship. In addition, consumers can opt out of allowing private financial information shared with most third parties without their permission. Federal and state regulators are directed to establish comprehensive standards for ensuring the security and

---

[266] *See* <http://www.ftc.gov/reports/privacy2000/privacy2000.pdf>.

[267] The Regulations are published at <http://www.ftc.gov>.

confidentiality of consumers' personal information. The new federal privacy protections will not supersede any stronger privacy protection provided under state law.[268]

7.3.3. Legislation Based upon Model Codes

A novel legislative approach to protecting personal information was adopted by Canada when it enacted the *Personal Information Protection and Electronic Documents Act (*PIPEDA*)*.[269] The fair information practice principles established by this law are based upon the Canadian Standards Association's Model Code for the Protection of Personal Information (the CSA Model Code). The CSA Model Code consists of ten privacy principles which are based on the OECD Guidelines, but revised to reflect the Canadian context and the new challenges of privacy protection in the information age. The CSA Model Code was developed for the Canadian Standards Association by a Technical Committee made up of representatives of the Canadian Federal Government, industry, privacy commissions, and advocacy groups. It was developed as a voluntary code, which private organizations could adopt if they chose, and which they could modify to suit their own particular requirements as needed. The Standards Council of Canada adopted the CSA Model Code as a National Standard in 1996. This made Canada the first country in the world to adopt such a standard.

The CSA Model Code has generated significant international interest. In May 1996, the consumer policy group of the International Organization for Standardization (ISO) passed a unanimous, twenty-five country resolution in favor of a proposal to develop an international standard on privacy based on the CSA Model Code. As such, this standard may form the basis for legislation in other countries.

The ten interrelated principles that form the basis of the CSA Model Code are the following:

(1) *Accountability*: An organization is responsible for personal information under its control and shall designate an individual or individuals who are accountable for the organization's compliance with the following principles.

---

[268] *See also Individual Reference Services Group, Inc. v. FTC*, Civ. Action, No. 00-1828 (Esh.) (D.C. 2001) (motion seeking judicial review of the regulations promulgated to implement title V, subtitle A of the Gramm-Leach-Bliley Act dismissed).

[269] Personal Information Protection and Electronic Documents Act, S.C. 2000 c.5 (Can.).

(2) *Identifying Purposes*: The purposes for which personal information is collected shall be identified by the organization at or before the time the information is collected.

(3) *Consent*: The knowledge and consent of the individual are required for the collection, use, or disclosure of personal information, except where inappropriate.

(4) *Limiting Collection*: The collection of personal information shall be limited to that which is necessary for the purposes identified by the organization. Information shall be collected by fair and lawful means.

(5) *Limiting Use, Disclosure, and Retention*: Personal information shall not be used or disclosed for purposes other than those for which it was collected, except with the consent of the individual or as required by law. Personal information shall be retained only as long as necessary for the fulfillment of those purposes.

(6) *Accuracy*: Personal information shall be as accurate, complete, and up-to-date as is necessary for the purposes for which it is to be used.

(7) *Safeguards*: Personal information shall be protected by security safeguards appropriate to the sensitivity of the information.

(8) *Openness*: An organization shall make readily available to individuals specific information about its policies and practices relating to the management of personal information.

(9) *Individual Access*: Upon request, an individual shall be informed of the existence, use, and disclosure of his or her personal information and shall be given access to that information. An individual shall be able to challenge the accuracy and completeness of the information and have it amended as appropriate.

(10) *Challenging Compliance*: An individual shall be able to address a challenge concerning compliance with the above principles to the designated individual or individuals accountable for the organization's compliance.[270]

PIPEDA imposes an important limitation on the collection, use, and disclosure of personal information. It states that an "organization may collect, use or disclose personal information only for purposes that a reasonable person would consider

---

[270] CSA Model Code for the Protection of Personal Information. *See* CSA website at <http://www.media-awareness.ca/eng/issues/priv/laws/csacode.htm>.

appropriate in the circumstances."[271] Unlike other principles in the CSA Model Code which premise their operation upon openness and consent of the data subject, this principle does not enable organizations to obtain the consent of data subjects for the collection, use or disclosure of personal information for any purpose. To this extent, PIPEDA goes beyond many of the voluntary codes of fair information practices previously established in Canada or recommended for use in other countries.

8. Taxation

8.1 Overview

The globalization of traditional commerce requires coordination of national taxing systems. The advent of e-commerce adds new urgency to this requirement. The ideal goal of effective taxing and administration of e-commerce is harmonization across jurisdictions and neutrality as between traditional commerce and e-commerce.[272]

It is only within the last decade that harmonization of national tax systems with respect to traditional commerce has moved to the top of the international policy agenda. Prior to this, tax harmonization had been a relatively arcane aspect of tax law, with international considerations rarely influencing the thrust of domestic tax reform. A leader in the development of international harmonization efforts has been the OECD.[273]

Analyzing the tax consequences of e-commerce transactions can be difficult due to the complexity and lack of coordination among national taxing systems. In theory, an online merchant of physical goods could be required to analyze the tax liability associated with the transaction in every jurisdiction connected to the transaction including where a customer is domiciled (country, state, municipal), where

---

[271] Model Code, *supra* n. 270, sec. 5(3).

[272] For a brief discussion, *see* UNCTAD E-commerce and Development Report, *supra* n. 2, at 39-40.

[273] See *OECD Model Tax Convention on Income and on Capital* (June 1988). The OECD Conventions were developed by the OECD on a consensus basis among the member countries. They are not legally binding on the member countries until and unless each member country implements it by enacting domestic legislation.

servers are located, where contracts are entered into, where inventory is stored or shipped to and where the merchant's place of business is located.

E-commerce transactions and order fulfillment can take two forms: (1) where the Internet is used to order (and pay for) physical goods or services that must be delivered by conventional means; or (2) where the Internet is used to order, pay for and deliver the goods and services, such as digitized software or digitized music (sometimes known as a "pure e-commerce transaction").

The pure e-commerce transaction causes difficulties in the audit and enforcement process because the delivery of the product or service does not occur through the usual physical channels. Although the physical delivery of the goods associated with traditional commerce provides one more audit trail than for a pure e-commerce transaction, tax audits generally follow the money rather than the goods. Pure e-commerce transactions are particularly difficult in the administration and enforcement of value added taxing systems.

Two major types of taxes that affect e-commerce transactions are income tax and value added tax. Income tax is generally imposed on the income (defined in a wide variety of ways) generated by a business. Value added tax is concerned with taxing individual transactions on the basis of factors such as consumption. Examples include the value added tax in the EU countries, known as VAT, and goods and services tax in Australia, Canada and Singapore,[274] known as GST.

To date, the general approach to taxing e-commerce has been to build on the taxing systems for traditional commerce. The existing tax rules for traditional commerce have been applied substantially as is, with adjustments recognizing the inherent differences between traditional commerce and e-commerce.[275] In this regard,

---

[274] For a summary and overview of income tax and "permanent establishment" as well as GST application in the Asia Pacific region as of March 2001, *see* Robert E. Meldman & Daniel P. Cooper, *Taxation of E-commerce and Its Effects on Asian Business*, originally published in LAWASIA (Mar. 2001) <http://www.rbvdnr.com/Articles/tax/ecommerce.htm>.

[275] *See e.g.* Australian Tax Office, *Tax and the Internet Discussion Report* (Aug. 1997), Australian Tax Office, *Tax and the Internet Second Report* (Dec. 1999) <http://www.ato.gov.au>; Netherlands Ministry of Finance, *Taxation in a World Without Distance* (May 1998) <http://www.minfin.nl/uk/taxation/tax_home.htm>; Revenue Canada, *E-commerce and Canada's Tax Administration*, April 1998 <http://www.rc.gc.ca/ecomm/>; Revenue Canada, *A Response by the Minister of National Revenue to his Advisory Committees Report on E-commerce* (Sept. 1998) <http://www.rc.gc.ca/ecomm/>; New Zealand Inland Revenue, *Taxation and the Electronic Medium* (April

the OECD has been actively identifying, consulting, and reporting on various aspects of e-commerce and taxing systems. A number of technical advisory groups, known as TAGs, have been established by the OECD to consider these issues.

8.2. OECD Principles of Taxing Systems

In late 1988, the OECD Taxation Framework Conditions ("OECD Taxation Framework")[276] were established. The fundamental proposition of the OECD Taxation Framework is that the principles that guide governments in relation to traditional commerce should also be applied to e-commerce. The five key principles for evaluating the operation of tax systems in the context of e-commerce are:[277]

(1) *Neutrality*: taxation should be neutral and equitable between e-commerce and conventional commerce. Effectively, this requires taxpayers in similar situations carrying out similar transactions to be subject to similar levels of taxation.

(2) *Efficiency*: compliance costs for taxpayers and administrative costs for tax authorities should be minimized as far as possible.

(3) *Certainty and Simplicity*: clear and simple tax rules should apply so that the taxpayers can predict the tax consequences of a transaction.

(4) *Effectiveness and Fairness*: tax rules should produce the right amount of tax at the right time. The potential for evasion and avoidance should be minimized.

(5) *Flexibility*: so as to keep pace with technological and commercial developments, tax systems should be flexible and dynamic.

These principles are appropriate for both income tax and value added tax regimes.

1998) <http://www.ird.govt.nz/resource/taxaint/index.htm>; United Kingdom Inland Revenue and HM Customs and Excise, *A GIIC Perspective, E-commerce: U.K. Taxation Policy* (Oct. 1998) <http://www.inlandrevenue.gov.uk>; E-commerce Committee for the Global Information Infrastructure Commission, *E-commerce Taxation Principles: GIIC Perspective* <http://www.giic.org/focus/ecommerce/ectax.html>; United Kingdom Inland Revenue, *E-commerce: The U.K.'s Taxation Agenda* (Nov. 1999) <http://www.inlandrevenue.gov.uk>; Ireland Revenue, *E-commerce and the Irish Tax System* (June 1999) <http://www.revenue.ie>.

[276] The OECD Taxation Framework is available at <http://www.oecd.org/daf/fa/e_com/framewke.pdf>.

[277] *Id.*, at 4.

The OECD Taxation Framework recommends that the present international taxing norms be clarified in their application to e-commerce, especially as they relate to the OECD Model Tax Convention[278] and the concept of permanent establishment.

8.3. Income Tax

8.3.1. Permanent Establishment

Generally, a country assesses income tax on persons who carry on business in the country by having a permanent establishment there. Most international treaties follow the OECD Model Tax Convention definition of "permanent establishment." That term is defined there to be a "fixed place of business through which the business of an enterprise is wholly or partially carried on."[279]

The "permanent establishment" concept is used to reconcile the different tax effects of "residence-based" and "source-based" income tax systems. Countries with residence-based tax systems typically tax individuals and businesses resident in that country on their worldwide income (i.e., regardless of where it is earned). Source-based tax systems typically tax individuals and businesses on income earned in that country (i.e., regardless of where the business is resident). As residence- and source-based systems can lead to double taxation in international transactions, the international tax treaties have the effect of providing "tax credits" to individuals resident in residence-based countries for income earned in source-based countries.[280]

The "permanent establishment" concept was developed at a time when the underlying assumption was that not much income could be generated without a substantial physical presence in another jurisdiction. E-commerce greatly reduces the need for a physical presence in a country in order to sell goods or services to persons in that country. Accordingly, for a country with a source-based tax system, e-commerce can result in significant income tax shortfalls for sales by foreign merchants to local businesses and consumers. Countries that are net exporters

---

[278] OECD Model Tax Convention on Income and on Capital, *supra* n. 273.

[279] *Id.*, art. 5.

[280] Canada has both residence- and source-based taxation (withholding tax and taxes levied on carrying on business are both source based). Dual residence can also lead to double taxation in Canada.

of goods and services generally support the continued use of the concept of "permanent establishment." Countries that are net importers of goods and services delivered over the Internet are more likely to question whether the concept of permanent establishment should continue to be the central concept related to the jurisdiction to tax.[281]

The following are two key fact scenarios that are generally thought to constitute a permanent establishment for traditional merchants, and that proponents of the concept of permanent establishment have attempted to reconcile with the e-commerce business model:

(1) The fixed place of business or physical presence in a country of a merchant. This generally does not include a fixed place of business that is not directly involved in the income-earning process, but is of a preparatory or ancillary nature (e.g., premises for storage or for mere information gathering purposes).

(2) A dependent agent who can conclude contracts for the business in that country. An employee is a dependent agent. An independent reseller or agent that is carrying on his or her own business does not generally constitute a dependent agent.

The OECD has extensively researched, consulted, and reported on the issue of permanent establishment.[282] The OECD approach has been to attempt to reconcile the realities of the Internet with the legacy concepts created for traditional commerce by focusing on practical issues, such as whether a website or server constitutes a physical presence or whether an ISP or a website constitutes a dependent

---

[281] *See Tax and the Internet*, discussion report of the ATO Electronic Commerce Project and Tax and the Internet – Second Report (Dec. 1999) <http://www.ato.gov.au>.

[282] The following are relevant OECD reports and discussion papers: Technical Advisory Group (TAG) on Treaty Characterization of E-commerce Payments, *Clarification on the Application of the Permanent Establishment Definition in E-Commerce: Changes to the Commentary on the Model Tax Convention on Article 5: The Final Report on Treaty Characterization Issues Arising from E-commerce;* Business Profits TAG, *A Discussion Draft on Attribution of Profit to a Permanent Establishment Involved in E-commerce Transactions* (for public comment). All these reports and discussion papers are available at <http://www.oecfd.org/daf/fa/e_com/public_release.htm>.

agent. Although this approach is not without its skeptics, an alternative workable approach has not yet been developed by the OECD.[283]

8.3.2. Location of Website or Server/Storage Facility

A website consists of a number of "pages" created in programming languages such as "html" (hypertext mark-up language). Computer code and related data that comprises a website must exist physically on a piece of computer equipment, such as a computer server. When a user accesses a website that is hosted on a server, the server is programmed to automatically determine the correct web page to "send" to the user over the Internet. The server is able to process information such as the name and address of the user, payment, collection, and shipping information and provide user-specific information or queries.

In December 2000, the OECD released a report in which it tried to clarify the relationship between an Internet presence and a permanent establishment (OECD Tax Clarification).[284] The clarification states that:

(1) a website cannot, in itself, constitute a permanent establishment;

(2) a website hosting arrangement typically does not result in a permanent establishment for the merchant that carries on business through that website; and

(3) a place where computer equipment, such as a server, is located may in certain circumstances constitute a permanent establishment. This requires that the functions performed at that place be significant as well as an essential or core part of the business activity of the enterprise. For example, a server could constitute a permanent establishment for a hosting business that is selling space on the server, but not for an e-commerce merchant.

Certain countries, including the United Kingdom, have taken a similar view that a website, by itself, is not a permanent establishment, and that a server, by itself, is

---

[283] OECD Deliberations, *E-commerce and Permanent Establishment Issues*, Twelfth Annual Institute on Current Issues in International Taxation, December 10, 1999, Washington D.C. <http://www.pwcglobal.com/extweb/manissue.nsf/DocID/897938C56EDFDB2585256882004E6DCF>; *Tax and Internet Discussion Report*, *supra* n. 275; *Tax and Internet Second Report*, *supra* n. 275.

[284] OECD, *Progresses towards achieving an International Consensus on the tax treatment of e-commerce*, News Release, (Feb. 12, 2001) <http://www.oecd.org/media/release/nw01-15a.htm>.

insufficient to constitute a permanent establishment of a merchant that is conducting e-commerce through a website hosted on the server.[285] The U.S. Treasury, in its White Paper,[286] took the position that the use or lease of a computer server generally does not create a permanent establishment, by analogizing the server to traditional commerce facilities used for storage and display. Where a business sells information instead of goods, the White Paper opines that "a computer server might be considered the equivalent of a warehouse, which is excepted from the definition of permanent establishment."[287] Nevertheless, where the server is integral to the business (*e.g.*, the business of an ISP), the White Paper recognizes that the exception may no longer apply.

If a server, of itself, creates a permanent establishment, online merchants could place servers in low- or no-tax jurisdictions to satisfy the permanent establishment requirement of that country, anticipating that obligations in tax treaties may preclude other countries from taxing. As a server is relatively small and inexpensive to locate anywhere in the world, merchants could move servers from country to country in order to manipulate tax treatment.

8.3.3. Dependent Agent

The OECD Tax Clarification states that a dependent agent of another business is not constituted by an ISP nor a website, even with "intelligent" software that accepts purchase orders automatically and without human involvement.[288] The U.S. Treasury White Paper,[289] consistent with the OECD conclusion, considered that a server could not constitute a dependent agent because the activities or services performed by the server do not include contractual authority that is normally associated with a dependent agent.

---

[285] U.K. Inland Revenue has taken the position that a mere website or server does not constitute a permanent establishment for U.K. income tax purposes, *see* <http://www.inlandrevenue.gov.uk/e-commerce/ecom15.htm>.

[286] Department of the Treasury, Office of Tax Policy, U.S. Treasury, *Selected Tax Policy Implications of Global E-commerce* (Nov. 1996) <http://www.caltax.org/!treas-ec.html>.

[287] *Id.*, at art. 5, para. 4(a) excludes from the definition of permanent establishment the use of facilities solely for the purpose of storage, display or delivery of goods or merchandise belonging to the enterprise.

[288] *Supra* n. 284.

[289] *Supra* n. 286.

Significant issues still remain to be resolved relating to the permanent establishment concept as it applies to e-commerce. Two key issues are:

(1) whether the concept of permanent establishment is appropriate, given that a business can conduct a substantial amount of e-commerce, unlike traditional commerce, without a physical presence in a country; and

(2) whether harmonization or significant consensus is possible with the permanent establishment concept given that for e-commerce it favors exporting nations over consuming nations.

8.4. Value Added Tax

Value added tax is a tax on the sale of goods and services that is normally applied at all stages of the production process. VAT is charged by the merchant and then credited by the users of the inputs in the course of doing business. An invoice is created for each transaction with a separate line item for VAT. The VAT system relies on invoices prepared by each merchant in the distribution chain that is a VAT-registered business. The final consumer is generally not a VAT-registered entity, and so ultimately pays the VAT.[290]

Many value added tax regimes provide for a "reverse" assessment that makes the consumer responsible to remit the VAT, when the merchant is not a registered taxpayer for that jurisdiction. In the consumer context, it is impracticable to expect consumers to self assess and remit value added tax for their online purchases. This is especially true in the case of pure e-commerce transactions, where the goods are delivered over the Internet and there is no physical delivery of the goods through customs into the consumer's country. The pure e-commerce transaction makes it nearly impossible for a country to effectively administer and enforce certain aspects of a VAT system.

In the OECD, all countries except for the United States, have or will soon have a VAT/GST system.[291] For countries in the EU, VAT contributes approximately

---

[290] The U.S. sales and goods tax system is different in that final users (usually retail consumers) pay the taxes, principally only on tangible property (with exceptions) and usually not on services. Business inputs generally are exempt from the tax.

[291] *See* Catherine L. Mann, *Transatlantic issues in E-commerce* (Institute for International Economics, Working Paper 00-7, Oct. 2000) <http://www.iie.com/catalog/wp/2000/00-7.htm>.

30% of total tax revenues.[292] In the U.S. states, sales and goods tax averages at approximately 12% of state total tax revenue.[293]

OECD Approach

A report from the Working Party on Consumption Taxes released for public comment (OECD Consumption Tax Report),[294] considers it critical to define the principle of taxing in the place of consumption more clearly, and to identify the collection mechanisms that can best support the practical operation of that principle, in the e-commerce context.

The OECD Consumption Tax Report proposes guidelines to define the place of taxation for cross-border services and intangible property by reference to the business establishment of the recipient business in the case of B2B (business-to-business) transactions, and by reference to the recipient's usual jurisdiction of residence for B2C (business-to-consumer) transactions.

On collection mechanisms, the report identifies a self-assessment mechanism for B2B transactions as the most viable option. For B2C transactions, the report points toward the potential in the medium term for technology-facilitated options, while accepting that, in the interim, simplified registration-based mechanisms may be required. The report recognizes that further work is necessary in several areas, and recommends that this continue to be pursued in partnership with business.[295]

WTO, U.S., and EU Approaches

The WTO Declaration on Global E-commerce[296] states that members of the WTO will continue the practice of not imposing customs duties or other new taxes on electronic transmissions. Broadly consistent with this approach, the United States has legislated to affirm that domestic Internet transactions were free of any "new"

---

[292] *Id.*

[293] *Id.*

[294] *Consumption Tax Aspects of E-commerce* (for public comment) (Committee's Working Party No. 9 on Consumption Taxes) <http://www.oecd.org/daf/fa/e_com/public_release.htm>.

[295] *OECD Progresses towards achieving an International Consensus on the tax treatment of e-commerce*, News Release, (Feb. 12, 2001) <http://www.oecd.org/media/release/nw01-15a.htm>.

[296] *Supra* n. 9.

taxes until October 2001. This moratorium was recently extended in the United States. The United States has also proposed that, in the interests of tax neutrality, the tangible counterparts to the digital products sold over the Internet also be exempt from tax.[297] This is referred to as a "harmonizing down" approach.

The European Union is adopting a different tack with its "harmonizing up" approach. The European Union has categorized all digital downloaded products as "soft goods," and classified them as services subject to VAT.[298] In July 1998, the EU endorsed a number of guidelines as a first step towards ensuring that the EU's VAT system would function in the world of e-commerce as follows:

(1) Existing forms of taxes, specifically VAT, should be adapted to e-commerce so that they are enforceable and so that the compliance burden for e-commerce operators is as light as possible.

(2) Electronic invoicing, declarations, and payments should be possible for VAT liable transactions within the European Union.

(3) Online supply of a digitized product is to be treated as the supply of a service, not a good. Consumption of services within the European Union should be taxed within the European Union, whatever the origin and whether supplied by e-commerce or otherwise. Services supplied by EU merchants for consumption outside the EU are not to be subject to EU VAT, but VAT on related inputs would be deductible.

(4) Merchants, whether residents of the European Union or not, transacting e-commerce with EU residents that are not VAT-registered entities (i.e., individual consumers) should apply, collect, and remit VAT on products downloaded from the Internet.

---

[297] This recommendation was not included in the legislation. An example follows of how tax structures can drive against business decisions and economic efficiencies. Barnes and Noble is a "brick and mortar" bookseller in the United States. After the success of Amazon.com, an online bookseller, Barnes and Noble entered the e-commerce arena. In order for BarnesandNoble.com to benefit from the U.S. Internet tax moratorium and avoid the "nexus" (or physical presence) – as Amazon.com did – a separate subsidiary of Barnes and Noble had to be created. *See* Mann, *supra* n. 291, at 8.

[298] *See* The European Parliament and the Economic and Social Committee on E-commerce and Indirect Taxation, *Communication from the Commission of 17 June 1998 to the Council* <http://www.europa.eu.int/scadplus/leg/en/lvb/l31041.htm>.

(5) Non-EU merchants should establish a tax identity or presence within the European Union in order to determine which rate of tax to charge when engaging in B2B.

9. Copyright and Related Rights

9.1. Overview

Digital technology, and particularly the Internet, has led to new opportunities for copyright creators and owners to exploit and disseminate works and for users to enjoy them. This technology also allows copyright works to be created entirely in, or converted from, almost any other format into digital form. It has facilitated new uses of copyright works and new opportunities for copyright owners unforeseen when most copyright laws were drafted. It has given rise to a variety of issues as to what is the proper balance between the rights of creators to exploit their works and the rights of users to use and freely disseminate works,[299] what constitutes infringement of copyright in cyberspace and how the rights of copyright owners can practically be enforced.

Many, if not all, of a copyright owner's exclusive rights are being affected by digital and communication technologies. The potential effects on the reproduction right are perhaps the most obvious. The right to reproduce a work is one of the most important rights conferred by copyright legislation. It is an especially important right given the ease with which works in traditional formats can be digitized, processed in machine readable form, and transmitted to unlimited numbers of recipients.[300] This ease of diffusion highlights the potential for abuse.

Digital networks are making it faster and easier to transmit copyright works to all users of the Internet anywhere in the world. Copying, public performances, and

---

[299] *See* Lawrence Lessig, *The Future of Ideas: The Fate of the Commons in the Connected World* (Random House 2001). In addition, the Internet has blurred the distinction in the papered world between author and publisher, which may raise issues of content regulation peculiar to the Internet. *See* Lawrence Lessig, *Code and other Laws of Cyberspace* (Basic Books 1999). *Cf.* discussion in § 10.5 *infra.*

[300] For an example of how fast a work can be distributed over the Internet *see Religious Technology Centre v. Netcom Online Communication Services Inc.*, 32 U.S.P.Q. (2d) 1545 (N.D. Cal. 1995).

distribution and other forms of infringement are easier, less expensive, and more difficult to detect and measure. Multiple users are able to download and redistribute works at the click of a mouse. Copies of a work can easily be made available to the public through the Internet. This makes the work available to millions of potential customers; it also exposes the work to millions of potential pirates. The Internet has created a new publishing medium in which anyone with a computer can, in effect, become an unauthorized publisher and marketer of other peoples products in their original or altered forms.

The key copyright issues that arise from digital technology are: the right to copy copyright works; the right to communicate copyright works to the public, including the transmission of works to audiences over the Internet such as by webcasting, the making available of works on the Internet and the retransmission of free-to-air broadcasts using digital technology; whether, and in what circumstances, ISPs and other Internet intermediaries should be liable for copyright infringement including the activities of their subscribers; the legal protection of technological protection measures and electronic rights management information; the legal protection of electronic databases; and whether any new exceptions or permitted uses are required to protect the interests of the users of copyright works and the wider public interest in the digital age.[301]

---

[301] For recent policy papers that describe the issues that arise from digital technology, *see* New Zealand, Ministry of Economic Development, Competition and Enterprise Branch, *Digital Technology and the Copyright Act 1994: A Discussion Paper* (July 2001);Canada Intellectual Property Policy Directorate, Industry Canada and Copyright Policy Branch, *Consultation Paper on Digital Copyright Issues* (June 22, 2001); Bruce A. Lehman, *Intellectual Property and the National Information Infrastructure: The Report of the Working Group on Intellectual Property Rights* (United States) <http://www.uspto.gov/web/offices/com/doc/ipnii/>; Ministère de la Culture de la Francophonie (France), *New Technologies, Author's Right and Neighbouring Rights: Copyright and Related Rights in the Information Society*; Commission of the European Communities, Com (95) July 19, 1995, *A Report on Discussions by The Working Group of the Subcommittee on Multi-Media Copyright Council: Study of Institutional Issues regarding Multi-Media* (February 1995); *Highways to Change: Copyright in the New Communications Environment*, Report of the Copyright Convergence Group (August 1994); *Copyright and the Information Highway*, Final Report of the Subcommittee on Copyright (March 1995) (Canada); Industry Canada, *The Cyberspace is Not a No Law Land: A Study of the Issues of Liability For Content Circulating on the Internet* (February 1997). *See* also Lessig, *supra* n. 299.

From a developmental standpoint, it is recognized on the one hand that where intellectual property rights, such as copyright, are not protected by national law, holders of copyrighted software (or hardware with imbedded software) will be reluctant to export to that jurisdiction. Accordingly, developing countries wishing to expand economic growth through e-commerce, but where the protection of intellectual property rights is unclear, will face challenges of encouraging vendors to invest in those countries. On the other hand, while beyond the scope of this article, it is also recognized that there is a contrary view held by some in the development community that continued protection of rights held by those in the developed world actually depresses growth and development in developing countries – developing countries merely effect transfer payments to rights holders in the developed world while providing disincentives at home for innovation and growth of local high-tech industries.[302]

9.2. International Standards

International standards play an important role in ensuring that comparable levels of protection are provided around the world and that domestic copyright owners receive protection in foreign countries. The harmonizing of international standards also facilitates the free movement of goods, services and financial capital. Through the TRIPS Agreement (Trade Related Aspects of Intellectual Property Rights), one of a number of trade-related agreements administered by the WTO, and the 1996 WIPO agreements on intellectual property rights, governments have made some progress in agreeing to common international standards of protection. However, to facilitate the development of electronic commerce, particularly as it relates to intangible property, it is important that countries move rapidly to implement these agreements in national legislation.[303]

The 1996 WIPO agreements on intellectual property rights set out international standards to address the use of digital technologies and the Internet for copyright and related rights. These agreements are contained in the two WIPO Internet

---

[302] The authors, while not taking sides in this debate, wish to point out the existence of the debate surrounding proprietary and "open" approaches, and related issues of protection of intellectual property rights, as it potentially affects growth and development of e-commerce in the developing world. For a recent apologetic from the developing world, *see e.g.* NACI, *Open Software & Open Standards in South Africa: A Critical Issue for Addressing the Digital Divide*, <http://www.naci.org.za/docs/opensource.htm>.

[303] OECD, *Dismantling the Barriers to Electronic Commerce*, *supra* n. 201.

Treaties (the WIPO Treaties): the WIPO Copyright Treaty (WCT) and the WIPO Performances and Phonograms Treaty (WPPT). In particular, the WIPO Internet Treaties establish international standards in relation to the right of communication to the public and the right of making available to the public; technological protection measures; rights management information; and limitations and exceptions to the rights of copyright holders. Some of the issues associated with these subjects are discussed below.

9.3. The Making Available Right

Copyright grants the owners of works the right to authorize the first publication of their works and later to control the making of copies. The Internet makes it easy for a single legitimate copy of a work to be lawfully acquired and stored on a computer connected to the Internet and thereby made "available" to the public.

The right to make a work "available to the public" provides protection beyond the mere right of reproduction by making it an infringement to offer the work to the public so that others might make illegal copies from it. A closely related concept is the "making available" of a work on the Internet for on-demand access, whereby copies of works are stored on computer networks that can be accessed by persons from a place and at a time of their choosing.[304]

The WCT provides for a new exclusive right to authorize the making available of works to the public as part of the "right of communication." The WPPT provides an equivalent right to producers of phonograms but calls it the "right of making available." Both treaties are intended to apply to the dissemination of works over the Internet. For example, the WPPT gives authors and producers of phonograms the exclusive right to make their works available to the public "in such a way that members of the public may access those works from a place and at a time individually chosen by them." What is key to the operation of these provisions is that there is no need to demonstrate that any member of the public has accessed or reproduced works made available over the Internet. It is sufficient that there is a possibility of the works being accessed.

The right to make works available to the public has been gaining approval internationally with the adoption of the WIPO Treaties. For example, the United States and Japan have embodied the protections of the WCT and WPPT into their copyright law. The European Union has also made it a requirement for its member

---

[304] *See* New Zealand, *supra* n. 301.

states under the European Union *Directive on the Harmonization of Certain Aspects of Copyright and Related Rights in the Information Society*.[305] Article 3 provides for the right to authorize or prohibit the communication of works to the public by wire or wireless means. The right includes the making available to the public of works in such a way that members of the public may access the works from a place or time individually chosen by them.

9.4. Protection and Anti-Circumvention

In the digital environment, perfect copies can instantaneously be transmitted and retransmitted around the globe at the speed of light, effectively taking reproduction control away from the copyright owner. To address these challenges, publishers of works are attempting to build technical protection measures into data, software, and hardware. These measures, however, are frequently met with tactics designed to circumvent these technological measures. Legislation designed to prevent the use and distribution of circumvention technologies is therefore important in aiding copyright owners to exploit new technical means of protecting copyright works.

Both the WCT and the WPPT acknowledge the need for adequate legal protection against circumvention.[306] The WCT and the WPPT include provisions that oblige member countries to provide "adequate legal protection and effective legal remedies" against the circumvention of effective technological measures that are used by copyright authors and owners, in connection with the exercise of their rights under those treaties or under the Berne Convention.

To implement the treaties, the United States enacted the *Digital Millennium Copyright Act* of 1998 (DMCA). The DMCA contains three prohibitions related to circumvention. First, it prohibits the act of circumventing a technological measure that effectively controls access to a work protected by the Copyright Act.[307] A second provision forbids trafficking in technology or products designed to

---

[305] Directive 2001/29/EU of the European Parliament and the Council of 22 May 2001 [hereinafter *EU Copyright Directive*].

[306] World Intellectual Property Organization (WIPO) *Copyright Treaty*, art. 11; WIPO, *Performers and Phonograms Treaty*, art. 18.

[307] 17 U.S.C. sec. 1201(a)(1)(A). *See* also, Lawrence Lessig, *Open Code and Open Societies* 10 <http://cyber.law.harvard.edu/works/lessig/opensocd1.pdf>, where he argues that the anti-circumvention provisions actually suppress innovation.

circumvent a technological measure that controls access to a copyrighted work.[308] The DMCA's third anti-circumvention provision prohibits trafficking in technology designed to circumvent measures that protect a copyright owner's rights under the *United States Copyright Act*.[309]

The DMCA applies to technology that blocks access to copyrighted works, such as devices that permit access to an article on an Internet website only by those who pay a fee or have a password. It also applies to technology that protects the work itself from being copied such as a device on the same website that prevents the viewer from copying the article once it is accessed.[310]

---

[308] Sec. 1201(a)(2) provides that:

> "No person shall manufacture, import, offer to the public, provide, or otherwise traffic in any technology, product, service, device, component, or part thereof, that
>
> (A) is primarily designed or produced for the purpose of circumventing a technological measure that effectively controls access to a work protected under [the Copyright Act];
>
> (B) has only limited commercially significant purpose or use other than to circumvent a technological measure that effectively controls access to a work protected under [the Copyright Act]; or
>
> (C) is marketed by that person or another acting in concert with that person with that person's knowledge for use in circumventing a technological measure that effectively controls access to a work protected under [the Copyright Act]."

[309] *See* 17 U.S.C. sec. 1201(b). Sec. 1201(b)(1) provides that:

> "No person shall manufacture, import, offer to the public, provide, or otherwise traffic in any technology, product, service, device, component, or part thereof, that:
>
> (A) is primarily designed or produced for the purpose of circumventing protection afforded by a technological measure that effectively protects a right of a copyright owner under this title in a work or portion thereof;
>
> (B) has only limited commercially significant purpose or use other than to circumvent protection afforded by a technological measure that effectively protects a right of a copyright owner under this title in a work or a portion thereof; or
>
> (C) is marketed by that person or another acting in concert with that person with that person's knowledge for use in circumventing protection afforded by a technological measure that effectively protects a right of a copyright owner under this title in a work or a portion thereof."

[310] S. Rep. No. 190, 105th Cong., 2d Sess. 11-12 (1998).

To balance the need for protection with the policy of promoting access to work, the DMCA provides several exceptions to these prohibitions. The statute permits an individual to circumvent an access control on a copyrighted work, or, in limited circumstances, to share circumvention technology: (a) in order for a school or library to determine whether to purchase a copyrighted product; (b) for law enforcement purposes; (c) to achieve interoperability of computer programs; (d) to engage in encryption research; (e) as necessary to limit the Internet access of minors; (f) as necessary to protect personally identifying information; or (g) to engage in security testing of a computer system.[311]

In addition, the DMCA provides that its prohibition on access circumvention itself,[312] would not apply to users of certain types of works if, upon the recommendation of the Register of Copyrights, the Librarian of Congress concludes that the ability of those users "to make non-infringing uses of that particular class of work" is "likely to be adversely affected" by the prohibition.[313] The statute makes clear, however, that any exceptions adopted by the Librarian of Congress are not defenses to violations of the anti-trafficking provisions.[314]

Several U.S. cases have used the provisions of the DMCA to grant injunctions restraining distribution of software over the Internet designed to defeat technological measures used by the owner or publisher of works. For example, in *Real Networks Inc. v. Streambox, Inc.*,[315] the plaintiff Real Networks obtained a preliminary injunction restraining the defendant Streambox from distributing and marketing products known as the Streambox BCR and Ripper. The Streambox BCR was enjoined because at least part of it was primarily, if not exclusively, designed to circumvent the access control and copy protection measures that Real Networks affords to copyright owners. An injunction was also obtained in *Universal City Studios, Inc. v. Reimerdes*[316] to restrain the dissemination over the Internet of a program designed to circumvent protection measures used by publishers of DVDs known as DeCSS.

---

[311] *See* 17 U.S.C. sec. 1201(d)-(j).

[312] *Id.*, sec. 1201(a)(1)(A).

[313] *Id.*, sec. 1201(a)(1)(B).

[314] *Id.*, sec. 1201(a)(1)(E).

[315] No. C99-2070P (W.D.Wash., Jan. 18, 2000).

[316] 111 F. Supp. 2d 294 (S.D.N.Y. 2000).

The WIPO Treaties allow for varying methods of addressing circumvention technologies. In Japan, circumvention has been addressed through the regulation of parts, programs, and devices designed with the purpose of thwarting protection technology. Copyright is bolstered by prohibiting making protected material susceptible to unauthorized reproduction. Australia has chosen to focus on outlawing not just the manufacture and trade in devices, but also services which lead to circumvention. The EU Copyright Directive requires members to provide "adequate protection against the manufacture, distribution, sale, rental, advertisement for sale or rental, or possession for commercial purposes of devices, products or components or the provision of services" which are intended to result in circumvention.[317] In effect, this provision gives rightholders control over the manufacture and distribution of anti-circumvention devices.

In many countries in the developing world, growth and development of a vibrant e-commerce and Internet-based economy depends on developing local content and, in many cases, using local language. In some cases proprietary software, some of which is protected (through anti-circumvention provisions for example) by the laws discussed in the foregoing paragraphs does not support local languages, and the cost of updating this software to accommodate local conditions may be prohibitive.[318] The challenge for policy makers in developing countries as they consider elaborating appropriate legal frameworks is, therefore, to find the right balance in protecting rights in order to ensure both a legally certain environment for investment and one that is at the same time supportive of innovation and responsive to local needs.

9.5. Rights Management

A separate but related issue is that of rights management. Rights management allows the owner of a work to imbed or "watermark" its works so that information about the work and the authorized use travel with it. Examples include the name of the author, title of the work, and to whom the copy was originally licensed. Rights management information is designed to ensure that the creator of the work is given proper credit and can track and monitor the use of the work once distributed. The music industry, for example, believes that rights management provides an effective way to track music downloads for a royalty-based exchange. The overlap

---

[317] *Supra* n. 305, art. 6.

[318] *See e.g* NACI Paper, *supra* n. 302.

issues with anti-circumvention are obvious, but rights management is generally treated as a separate category and is embodied in different articles of the WIPO Internet Treaties.[319]

The WIPO Treaties include provisions that require member countries to provide adequate and effective legal remedies against the unauthorized removal or alteration of rights management information; or, the unauthorized distribution, importation for distribution, broadcast or communication to the public of copyright works (or copies of such works), knowing that such information has been removed or altered without authority.[320] Under these provisions, the person performing the unlawful activity must have actual or constructive knowledge that the activity will induce, enable, facilitate or conceal the infringement of a copyright owner's rights.

Australia has recently implemented the rights management portion of the WIPO Treaty in its *Copyright Amendment (Digital Agenda) Bill*. The EU Copyright Directive also requires member states to implement these provisions.[321] Under the EU Copyright Directive, the removal, alteration or the making available of a work with reasonable grounds to know that rights management has been altered or removed is prohibited.

9.6. Retransmission

Historically, copyright law has permitted the retransmission of electromagnetic signals over the airwaves. With the advent of cable television, direct to home (DTH) satellites and multipoint wireless systems most countries created statutory compulsory licenses which permit the retransmission of signals other than by air waves. A rationale was that it would promote the creation of the necessary infrastructure and expand access to new communication networks.[322]

With the advent of the Internet, new forms of retransmission became possible. The significance of Internet retransmissions to rightholders became known in 1999 when a Canadian website, www.iCraveTV.com, attempted to stream nine Canadian and eight American over-the-air television signals on its site. The operators of

---

[319] *See* New Zealand, *supra* n. 301.

[320] WCT Art. 12; WPPT Art. 19.

[321] *Supra* n. 305, art. 7(1)(a)(b).

[322] *See* New Zealand, *supra* n. 301.

the site claimed not to be infringing copyright. They asserted they were protected like cable operators as retransmitters under the compulsory license provisions of the Canadian *Copyright Act*. The operators of the site were sued by various Canadian television broadcasters and Canadian and United States producers who alleged infringement of copyright.[323] The case was settled, however, and no decision was reached in Canada.[324] A preliminary injunction against the service was, however, obtained in the United States.[325]

The Agreement on Trade-Related Aspects of Intellectual Property Rights (TRIPS) requires WTO members to provide broadcasting organizations with the right to control retransmission of their broadcasts.[326] Exceptions can, however, be made to this right in certain circumstances.[327] The WCT and WPPT do not include provisions that expressly deal with Internet retransmission, although the issues concerning copyright and the rights of broadcasting organizations are currently on the work program of the WIPO Standing Committee on Copyright and Related Rights in anticipation of new international standards concerning copyright in relation to broadcasting and related transmission issues.[328]

---

[323] The Canadian Act provides it is not an infringement of copyright to communicate to the public by telecommunication any literary, dramatic, musical or artistic work if: the communication is a retransmission of a local or distant signal; the retransmission is lawful under the Broadcasting Act; the signal is retransmitted simultaneously and in its entirety, except as otherwise required or permitted by or under the laws of Canada; and in the case of the retransmission of a distant signal, the retransmitter has paid any royalties, and complied with any terms and conditions, fixed under the Act. Section 31(2). The legislative scheme allows cable operators, under certain conditions, to retransmit local signals, without charge. *See Re Statement of Royalties to be Collected for Performance in Canada of Dramatico Musical or Musical Works*, 52 C.P.R. (3d) 23 (Copyright Board) (1993), aff'd (1994), 58 C.P.R. (3d) 190 (Fed. C.A.).

[324] *See Alliance Atlantis Motion Picture Distribution Inc. et al v. TV Radio Now, Corp.*, 00-CL-3641 (Ontario Superior Ct. of Justice).

[325] *See National Football League v. TV Radio Now Corporation*, Civil Action no. 00-120; Civil Action no. 00-121.

[326] Trade-Related Aspects of Intellectual Property Rights, at art. 14 (3).

[327] TRIPS, art. 14(6).

[328] *See* New Zealand, *supra* n. 301.

9.7. Databases

The advent of computers and their widespread use has created new industries dedicated to the collection, arrangement, and dissemination of information. For a compiler, the computer offers tremendous advantages over traditional methods of storing huge amounts of information, including faster retrieval speed, greater storage capacity, increased accuracy of the information, and the ability to share the information over networks and through telecommunications.[329] Computer databases organized through powerful information processing technologies today are central to the operation of many businesses and have the potential of virtually replacing traditional forms of information handling and publication. It is therefore important that the labor, skill, and expense associated with collecting and storing computerized information be protected from piracy.

There has been significant debate in copyright law as to the level of originality required for copyright to subsist in a compilation of data. It is accepted that for a work to be "original," it must be independently created by the author; that is, it must not be copied from another work. But there is a further requirement; the disagreement concerns the nature of that requirement. On this issue there are two schools of thought. On the one hand, there are those who say that copyright will only protect intellectual effort, and unless there is at least some intellectual labor in the creation of the work, it cannot be "original." On the other hand, there is a school that argues that at least in respect of a compilation, the originality requirement would be satisfied if there has been some effort expended in producing the work, especially effort in gathering or collecting the factual data that is reproduced, though there be no ingenuity in the arrangement or presentation of that data.[330]

Under United States law, for example, "industrious collection" or "sweat of the brow" alone are insufficient to render a compilation original for copyright purposes, even if the means used to discover or collect the information for the compilation is creative.[331] In *Feist Publications Inc. v. Rural Telephone Services*

---

[329] Jack B. Hicks, *Copyright and Computer Databases: Is Traditional Compilation Law Adequate,* 65 Texas L. Rev. 993 (1987); U.S. Congress, Office of Technology Assessment, *Intellectual Property Rights in an Age of Electronics and Information* ch. 3 (1986).

[330] For a good discussion of these views *see Telstra Corporation Ltd. v. Desktop Marketing Systems Pty. Ltd.* [2001] F.C.A. 612 (Aust. F.C.).

[331] *Bellsouth Advertising & Publishing Corp. v. Donnelly Information Publishing, Inc.*, 999 F.2d 1436 (11th Cir. 1993).

Co.[332] the United States Supreme Court stressed, and later United States courts have required, that three distinct elements be present for a work to qualify as a copyrightable compilation: (1) the collection and assembly of preexisting material, facts, or data; (2) the selection, coordination, or arrangement of those materials; and (3) the creation, by virtue of the particular selection, coordination, or arrangement and minimal creativity, of an "original" work of authorship and not something so mechanical or routine, entirely typical, or obvious as to require no creativity whatsoever.[333]

Some jurisdictions have introduced new legislation to protect makers of databases against the unauthorized extraction and reutilization of the contents of databases for commercial purposes. In this regard, the Council of the European Communities has passed a directive which, among other things, confers upon owners of databases "a right to prevent unauthorized extraction" from a protected database.[334] The EU Database Directive became effective in the 15 European member states as of January 1, 1998, and has since been enacted into the national laws of all EU member states.

The EU Database Directive creates a two-tier system for the protection of databases comprising a copyright protection for original databases and a *sui generis* right rewarding the non-creative efforts of database makers.[335] Under a reciprocity requirement, the EU Database Directive will not provide protection for foreign companies unless their home states adopt comparable legislation.[336]

The United Kingdom has adopted regulations to grant database providers copyright protection in accordance with the EU Database Directive. By complying with

---

[332] *Feist Publications Inc. v. Rural Telephone Services Co.* 111 U.S. 1282 (1991).

[333] *See Key Publications Inc. v. Chinatown Today Publishing Enterprises Inc.*, 20 USPQ2d 1122 (2nd Cir. 1991); *Kregos v. The Associated Press*, 19 USPQ (2d) 1161 (2nd Cir. 1991); *U.S. Payphone, Inc. v. Executives Unlimited of Durham, Inc.*, 18 USP.Q. 2d 2049 (4th Cir. 1991).

[334] *See* EEC, *Amended Proposal for a Council Directive on the Legal Protection of Databases*, COM(93) 464 Final-SYN 393 Brussels, October 4, 1993, Chapter III [hereinafter *EU Database Directive*].

[335] J. Gaster, *The EC sui generis right revisited after two years: a review of the practice of database protection in the 15 EU Member States,* 5 Communications Law 87(2000).

[336] Art. 11 of the *EU Database Directive* limits protection to database providers who are nationals of a member state or who have their habitual residence in the territory of the European Community.

the EU Database Directive, the United Kingdom has ensured that its database providers will have statutory protection not only in the United Kingdom but in the European Union as well. The Copyright and Rights in Database Regulations[337] were passed in the United Kingdom on December 18, 1997. Like the EU Database Directive, the Regulations create a two-tiered protection for databases. First, the Regulations provide full copyright protection for databases which by reason of selection or arrangement of their contents constitute the author's own intellectual creation. Owners of copyright in databases have the same 70-year right as do other owners of copyright.[338] Second, the Regulations also create a *sui generis* "database right" for database compilers who can show substantial investment in either obtaining, verifying, or presenting of the contents of the database. The "database right" guarantees 15 years of protection against extraction and use. This *sui generis* protection is intended to provide protection for a compiler's skill, labor, and judgment.[339]

WIPO has also considered a *Draft Treaty on Intellectual Property in Respect of Databases*. The WIPO draft database treaty, which was considered by WIPO in December 1996 was relatively similar to the provisions of the EU Database Directive. This treaty was withdrawn because no agreement could be reached by member countries.

---

[337] United Kingdom, *The Copyright and Rights in Databases Regulations,* S.I. 1997 no. 3032 [hereinafter the *Regulations*].

[338] A. Charkiewicz, *Database Protection in the U.K. – Past, Present and Future*, Copyright World 14 (Dec. 2000).

[339] The *Regulations* were recently applied for the first time to protect a database in the case of *British Horse Racing Board Ltd. v. William Hill Organization Ltd.*, The Times (Feb. 23, 2001). In that case, the British Horse Racing Board succeeded in protecting its database of races and horses running in them from use by an Internet betting site run by a bookmaker, who had previously been freely permitted to access the database for purposes of setting odds. The case is currently under appeal to the European Court of Justice.

10. Regulation of Content and Criminal Activities

10.1. Overview

Regulation of content and of criminal activities on the Internet are controversial subjects. This chapter deals first with content-related laws, regulations and other restrictions, whether or not they are defined as "criminal." It also deals with the new Cybercrime Convention, and criminal activities generally, whether or not related to content, such as malicious hacking and distribution of viruses.

The issues related to regulation of e-commerce and Internet content are complex and dynamic. Debate on the issues often suffers from oversimplification and from the application of outdated paradigms. In the early days of the Internet, many users and some governments opposed almost any form of regulation. Today, almost no one would dispute the right of government and the courts to regulate and even prohibit the dissemination of some types of content, such as the distribution or sale of child pornography or the intentional transmission of computer viruses. At the other end of the spectrum, regulation of political content is controversial. The dynamic nature of the debate on Internet content regulation can be seen in the aftermath of the events of September 11, 2001. Even in countries such as the United States and the United Kingdom, where regulation of political content was anathema to many, there now seems to be greater public support for regulation of "terrorist" political content.

In the early days of the Internet, many users and commentators treated the Internet as a law-free zone. As late as five years ago, John Perry Barlow's celebrated "Declaration of Independence of Cyberspace" declared on behalf of Internet users that "[Governments] have no moral right to rule us nor do [they] possess any methods of enforcement we have true reason to fear."[340] Early attempts to regulate any content or activities on the web were often met with scorn and circumvented by users. One common tactic to bypass attempts to regulate content was to use intermediaries, such as those that stripped IP addresses to hide the identity of senders of e-mail or other Internet content.

The Internet continues to be regarded as a revolutionary communications medium due to its ability to circumvent and undermine traditional laws and regulatory structures. The decentralized nature and redundant transmission capabilities

---

[340] *See* <http://www.eff.org/~barlow/Declaration-Final.html>. *See also The Internet and the Law: Stop signs on the web*, The Economist (Jan. 13, 2001).

of IP packet networks make detection and censorship of content far more difficult than with traditional circuit-switched networks. As a result, early government efforts to restrict Internet use often proved futile.

Most citizens and governments in industrialized Western economies watched with tacit approval as the Internet was used to disseminate information that penetrated walls established by the world's few remaining totalitarian regimes. Similarly, IP telephony has helped to undermine the longstanding revenue settlement systems (based on negotiated "accounting rates") that had maintained international telephone tariffs at rates that were well above costs. IP telephony also added greater anonymity to telephone calling. The sheer volume of global Internet traffic and the wide diversity of its routing make eavesdropping on IP telephony calling very difficult.

"Freedom of the Internet" was promoted and defended with particular vigor in the United States, based on national traditions of individualism, liberalism, faith in laissez-faire free-market principles, and on the protection of free speech enshrined in the U.S. Constitution.[341] However, over the past decade, increasing concerns have been voiced about the "lawless" nature of the Internet.

Some societies, particularly those based on more communal traditions than those of the United States, have never accepted the proposition that content that was illegal in the press or other media should be tolerated on the Internet. Countries

---

[341] For an analysis of the differing philosophical and legal underpinnings of Internet content regulation in the United States and Singapore, *see* Joseph C. Rodriguez, *Comparative Study of Internet Content Regulations in the United States and Singapore: The Invincibility of Cyberporn,* 1 Asia-Pacific Law & Policy Journal (Feb. 2000) (available at <http://www.hawaii.edu/aplpj/pdfs/09-rodriguez.pdf>). In the United States there have been several attempts to regulate offensive content on the Internet. Many such attempts have been ruled unconstitutional under either the Commerce Clause or under the first amendment to the United States constitution. *See American Library Association v. Pataki,* 969 F. Supp. 160 (S.D.N.Y. 1997); *American Civil Liberties Union et al. v. Johnson*, 4 F. Supp. 2d 1029 (D.N. Mex. 1998); *Cyberspace Communications, Inc. et al. v. Engler*, 55 F. Supp. 2d 737 (E.D. F. Ch. 1999); *People v. Wheelock*, 990875-7 (Costa County Superior Court, January 3, 2000); *State of Washington v. Heckel* (Wash. Sup. Ct. King Co., March 10, 2000); *Reno v. American Civil Liberties Union (Reno)*, 521 U.S. 844, affirming *American Civil Liberties Union v. Reno*, 929 F. Supp. 824 (E.D. Pa. 1996); *ACLU v. Reno (Reno II)*, 31 F. Supp. 2d 473 (E.D. Pa. 1999); *American Civil Liberties Union of Georgia v. Miller*, 43 U.S.P.Q. 2d 1356 (N.D. Geor. 1997); *Mainstream Loudoun v. Board of Trustees of the Loudoun County Library*, Civil Action No. 97-204-A (E.D. Vir. 1998); *PsiNet Inc. v. Chapman* Civ., Act. no.3:99 Cv 00111 (W.D.Virg. 2000).

like Singapore and China, where the population generally accepted more communal traditions of Confucianism over U.S.-style individualism, were among the first to enact laws that broadly regulated Internet content. In Singapore, ISPs were licensed and required to use proxy servers as filters to block access to websites that the government deemed objectionable.[342] In China, a "Great Firewall" was erected, to filter much of the content available to most Internet users. But these countries were far from the only ones that had taken steps to regulate the Internet.

It has been said that the year 2000 will be remembered as the year when governments around the world started to regulate the Internet in earnest.[343] In the new millennium, the novelty of the Internet and initial public amusement about viruses, hacking, and objectionable content all seemed to wear off.[344] The Internet had become ubiquitous, and its misuse was increasingly recognized as capable of inflicting serious damage to both public and private interests.

Since the start of Y2K, governments and courts significantly accelerated legislative and judicial action to regulate certain types of Internet content and activities. The Council of Europe, a group of 41 countries that includes all EU members, worked in earnest, with the participation of the United States, Canada, and other countries to develop the first international treaty on cybercrime.[345] In November 2000, a French court issued its landmark decision against Yahoo, aimed at preventing access to the hundreds of neo-Nazi websites that are illegal in Germany, France, and other European countries, but that continued to operate in the United States under the protection of the First Amendment to the U.S. Constitution.[346] Subsequently, a U.S. Federal Court judge refused to enforce the order of the French Court on the basis that Yahoo (a California-based company) was entitled to the protections of the U.S. Constitution, specifically the First Amendment that protects free speech including in the commercial context.[347] Other countries around the world have begun to enact laws aimed at stemming the worst abuses of the

---

[342] *Id.*; *see* discussion *infra* "Who is Regulated and How" on the use of proxy servers and filters.

[343] *The Internet and the Law: Stop signs on the web*, The Economist (Jan. 13, 2001).

[344] *When the anarchy has to stop*, New Statesman (Oct. 15, 2001).

[345] *See infra* n. 382.

[346] For discussion of the Yahoo case, *see supra* n. 24.

[347] *Yahoo v. La Ligue Contre le Racisme et L'Antisémitsme et al.*, 145 F. Supp. 2d. 1168 (N.D. Cal. 2001).

Internet. More significantly, as illustrated by the Cybercrime Treaty, there seems to be an increasing willingness of countries, including the United States, to work together on regulation of harmful Internet content and activities.

10.2. What is Regulated?

A wide range of different policy concerns have motivated governments to regulate Internet-related content and activities. In some cases, specific types of content are targeted; in others, specific activities related to certain content, such as the sale of certain types of content to minors. In yet other cases, harmful activities, that do not involve "content" *per se*, such as spreading viruses or hacking into private computer systems, are the focus of regulation.

Table 3 illustrates the main policy concerns underlying current government or judicial action to regulate Internet content and harmful Internet-related activities.[348] The table provides examples of the types of content and activities that are the subject of these policy concerns, as well as the regulatory approaches that have been implemented or that are currently under discussion. Of necessity, the table is selective. New approaches, and the technology to implement them, continue to be developed. The table focuses on the main approaches used around the world today, but includes some alternative and rather unusual approaches, in order to illustrate the wide-ranging measures governments have considered. A good example of an unusual approach included in the table is Myanmar's law to ban all unauthorized use of a modem in the country.[349]

As the table illustrates, in some cases similar approaches are used to address different types of content. In some cases, the same regulatory approaches, such as filtering, are applied in different ways for different types of content, or in different countries. The following sections of this article discuss the most common regulatory approaches. The last three policy concerns listed in the table are dealt with in separate sections of the article, namely consumer protection, protection of individual privacy, and protection of intellectual property.

---

[348] The classification of content and activities in the table is based, in part, on a classification developed by the European Union in the Communication from the Commission to the Council, the European Parliament, Economic and Social Committee and the Committee of the Regions on Illegal and Harmful Content on the Internet of 16 October 1996, COM (96) 0487 <http://www.ispo.cec.be/legal/en/internet/communic.html>.

[349] For a summary of other approaches used to regulate Internet content in different countries, *see* Peng Hwa Ang, *How Countries are Regulating Internet Content* (1997) <http://www.isoc.org/inet97/proceedings>.

Table 3. Approaches to Regulation of Internet Content and Activities

Policy Concern	*Examples of Regulated Content and Activities*	*Regulatory Approaches*
Protection of Minors	• Pornography • Violence	• Application of existing criminal laws • International treaty (Cybercrime Treaty) • ISP self-regulation • Filters • Labeling • Government inspection of content (*e.g.* early "Minitel" approach in France) • ISP Licensing (*e.g.* Singapore)
Protection of Human Dignity	• Inciting racial or religious hatred or discrimination	• Application of existing or modified national criminal and human rights laws • Filters • Labeling • International treaty (*e.g.* proposed protocol on hate speech)
National Security	• Terrorist activities • Bomb-making instructions • Illegal drug trade	• Modification of existing criminal law (*e.g.* post Sept. 11 bills in U.S., U.K., Canada, etc.) • International coordination • Filters (*e.g.* Chinese proxy servers) • Banning unauthorized use of modems (Myanmar)
Security of Information and Communications	• Electronic harassment • Interference with databases or communication (hacking, altering data, etc.)	• New or modified national laws including privacy and data protection laws • International treaty (Cybercrime Treaty) • ISP self-regulation

Policy Concern	*Examples of Regulated Content and Activities*	*Regulatory Approaches*
Preventing or Detecting Other Criminal Activities	• Tax evasion • Money laundering • Illegal gambling • Conspiracy to rob a bank • Credit card fraud	• Application of existing criminal laws • Judicial authorization for interception of communications or access to databases • International co-ordination • Labeling
Protection of Reputation	• Defamation • Unauthorized use of personal names	• Application or modification of national defamation laws (and "jurisdiction shopping") • International coordination
Promotion of National Culture or Sovereignty	• Domestically produced content • Culturally-significant content (e.g. national culture, underrepresented types of content)	• Hands-off regulation, with subsidies to produce domestic or diverse content • Subsidies or policies to promote local portals that increase access to domestic content • Laws and policies to filter or redirect content (via proxy servers, etc.) • Regulation of portals and electronic gateway devices to promote those that provide priority access to certain types of content
Consumer Protection	• Fraud • Misleading advertising • Securities fraud	• New and modified consumer protection laws • Self-regulation including codes, trust seals and ADR • International harmonization
Protection of Individual Privacy	• Unauthorized distribution and use of personal data	• New national laws (*e.g.* Canada's PIPEDA) • International harmonization • Self-regulation, including codes & trust seals • Filtering

Policy Concern	*Examples of Regulated Content and Activities*	*Regulatory Approaches*
Protection of Intellectual Property	• Unauthorized distribution of copyrighted works: text, video, music, software, etc. • Unauthorized use of trade names and copyright works	• New national IP laws (*e.g.* U.S. Millennium Copyright Act), incl. "notice and take down process" • International Treaty (*e.g.* WIPO: WTC, WPPT), and harmonization of domestic IP laws • Anti-circumvention measures and rights management (watermarking) of protected works

10.3. Who Regulates Content?

The laws and policies of different jurisdictions may distribute responsibility for regulating Internet content and activities among a number of different types of parties. These include:

(1) *Legislatures*: national, state, provincial or other local legislatures, that enact laws that directly prescribe content rules to be followed by content providers or distributors;

(2) *Law enforcement agencies*: that investigate and prosecute breaches of such legislation;

(3) *Courts*: that interpret and apply the law in cases of criminal prosecution or civil litigation, and that determine breaches of content laws;

(4) *Self-regulation agencies*: industry organizations, or organizations that combine representation from industry, public interest, consumer, and government representatives;

(5) *National broadcasting regulators*: that are authorized to enact regulations, orders or other subordinate legislation that determine what types of content are restricted, and that sometimes have enforcement powers;

(6) *Other government regulatory agencies*: such as copyright boards, and national administrators of country code top-level domains (ccTLDs);[350]

[350] *See* discussion of the domain name system, in chapter 4 of this article.

(7) *Alternative dispute resolution agencies*: special or general-purpose arbitrators or mediators;

(8) *International agencies*: international organizations or tribunals.

To date, the most common approaches adopted to regulate Internet content are self-regulation and legislated approaches that combine elements (1), (2), and (3) from the above list. Under the latter type of approaches, laws are enacted to criminalize or to establish civil penalties for distribution of certain types of content. Law enforcement officials or interested parties are then authorized to commence criminal or civil legal action to enforce the laws. The courts apply the laws to the facts of different cases to determine whether there have been breaches of the law, and if so, what legal remedies should apply.

However, self-regulation and Internet content laws are neither the only options, nor necessarily the best ones, for governments seeking to regulate objectionable Internet content. A specialized regulatory agency, other than a court, may be authorized to develop and/or enforce Internet content regulations. Perhaps the best-known example is the Singapore Broadcasting Authority (SBA), which was authorized to develop an Internet Code of Practice, to determine which Internet content would be prohibited in Singapore.[351]

The Singapore Internet regulation model has been heavily criticized by commentators in the United States and some other liberal democracies. Critics argued that the SBA's approach was tantamount to "censorship." However, much of the prohibited material prescribed by the SBA was similar to the types of material prohibited under laws of Western democracies. Other content prohibited by SBA covered subject matter that many citizens of Western democracies would actually prefer to see eliminated from public areas of the Internet. These include explicit sexual behavior, incest, pedophilia, bestiality, necrophilia, acts of extreme violence or cruelty, and material that incites or endorses ethnic, racial or religious hatred, strife or intolerance.[352]

However, many observers criticized the broad and vague definitions of "prohibited material" developed by the SBA. For example, the 1997 amendment to the SBA's Internet Code of Practice defined prohibited material as "material that is objectionable on the grounds of public interest, public morality, public order,

---

[351] *See* <http://www.sba.gov.sg/Internet.htm>.

[352] *Id.*

public security, national harmony … [etc]."[353] Ultimately, the SBA failed to effectively restrict access to prohibited Internet material in Singapore, due to a combination of factors including lack of enforcement and the ease with which the enforcement mechanisms could be circumvented.[354]

The apparent failure of Singapore's SBA Internet regulation model is not so much an indictment of the use of specialized tribunals to determine which Internet content should be restricted as it is a case study in the problems faced by any one country in acting unilaterally to attempt to enforce such restrictions.

In other countries where specialized tribunals regulate the content of broadcasting programming, consideration has been given to extending such regulation to the Internet. In Canada, for example, the Canadian Radio, Television, and Telecommunications Commission (CRTC) considered whether to regulate certain types of Internet content described as "new media," as it was legally authorized to do under the Canadian *Broadcasting Act*. After an extensive review, the CRTC decided to exempt Internet "programming" from broadcasting regulation.[355] In making its decision not to regulate Internet content, the CRTC cited, among other things, the views of parties who filed comments arguing that Canadian laws of general application, coupled with self-regulatory initiatives, would be more appropriate for dealing with offensive and illegal content over the Internet, than would be the Canadian *Broadcasting Act* or *Telecommunications Act*.

The problems associated with unilateral enforcement of Internet content in any single country would undermine the role of many of the other types of possible regulatory agencies listed above, such as national copyright boards, national arbitration or mediation organizations, and self-regulation agencies. The real problem is that, with currently available technologies, neither the courts, nor any other tribunal in a single country, have been able to effectively enforce regulations on Internet content available to their nationals.

However, two trends discussed in the next section of this article may change the enforcement environment significantly. First, filtering and labeling technologies are evolving, and their penetration may be promoted by business and government

---

[353] *Id.*; *see also* Rodriguez, *supra* n. 341.

[354] *See* discussion of filters and proxy servers below; *see also* Rodriguez, *supra* n. 341.

[355] *Exemption Order for New Media Broadcasting Undertakings,* Public Notice CRTC 1999-197 (Dec. 17, 1999); The background and rationale for the CRTC's decision to exempt Internet-based broadcasting and "new media" services is set out in Broadcasting Public Notice CRTC 1999-84, *New Media* (May 17, 1999).

to such an extent that national regulators may be able to effectively regulate distribution of Internet content to most users in their countries most of the time. Second, the success of initiatives to promote international agreements to effectively regulate certain types of content, such as copyright works and the criminal content covered by the Cybercrime Treaty[356] and the proposed new hate speech protocol,[357] may lead to renewed enforcement efforts. This will be particularly true if countries that produce significant amounts of the Internet's content, and especially the United States, join in such international agreements. If this occurs, there may be a renewed interest in having quasi-judicial tribunals with expertise in Internet matters, instead of the courts, apply laws to determine specifically which type of Internet content and activities should be prohibited.

To date, international organizations, such as WIPO and the Council of Europe, have played a key role in developing international treaties to regulate certain types of Internet content. If the trend to adoption of international treaties to regulate the Internet continues, the question that will inevitably arise is whether existing or new international tribunals or other types of international organizations should also be given greater enforcement powers to implement such treaties.

10.4. Who is Regulated and How?

Once national legislation or international treaties determine what types of content are regulated, and who regulates it, the next questions are:

(1) Who to regulate in the chain of creation and distribution of Internet content?

(2) How to regulate such players?

In most cases, a number of players are involved in the creation and distribution of Internet content. Some are actively involved in content creation or in its sale or distribution to end users. Others play more passive roles. In many cases, players in the distribution chain have no direct control or knowledge of the information content of the digital bitstreams they transmit.

Table 4 illustrates some of the main functions performed by different players in the creation and distribution of Internet content. With the increasing convergence of players in the information and communications technology industries, many players perform two or more of the functions described in the table.

---

[356] *Infra* n. 382.

[357] *Id.*

Table 4. Key Functions in the Creation and Distribution of Internet Content

Function	*Comments*
Author	Individual, corporate or institutional creator of the content (e.g. photographer of pornographic image, writer of hate literature).
Internet Content Provider (ICP)	Entity responsible for the content of a website or other source of electronic information sold or otherwise made available to the public.
Internet Service Provider (ISP)	Depending on the context, the term "ISP" is used to describe entities that provide many different types of services related to the Internet. Most commonly, the term is used to describe Internet Access Providers (below). In addition to providing access to the World Wide Web, Usenet and other forums, many ISPs provide Internet-based services such as e-mail and act as portals.
Internet Access Provider (IAP)	Often called an ISP, this is the entity that provides end-users with access to the Internet. The physical means of access to IAPs by end users is generally provided by telecommunications service providers (below).
Internet Portal	Internet websites that provide links to other websites and to information provided by third parties, with or without playing a role in selection of the information or monitoring its contents.
Telecommunications Service Provider (TSP)	Called telecommunications common carriers in some countries, these entities provide simple telecommunications transmission services, via their own infrastructure or that of third parties. TSPs connect end-users with ISPs by means of dial-up access through the public switched telephone network, cable TV lines, wireless channels, and dedicated wireline telecommunications circuits. Traditionally, TSPs have no control or knowledge of the contents of telecommunications traffic they transmit. TSPs are also the major providers of Internet backbone links, which connect IAPs, other ISPs and ICPs to each other.

Who to regulate?

As the foregoing table illustrates, the degree of responsibility of the various players in the Internet content chain varies significantly. At one end of the spectrum are Internet content providers who author illegal works, for example individuals operating a website selling child pornography photographs they have taken. At the other end are telecommunications service providers, such as WorldCom or NTT, that act as major Internet backbone providers transmitting digital bitstreams without regard to their contents.

The question of which legal entity to regulate is complicated by the dynamic nature of the Internet industry. Some individuals or legal entities perform only one of the functions listed in the table. Others may perform several or even all of the functions. Accordingly, it is necessary to focus on the functions performed and the relationship of such functions to the regulated content. Regulatory liability may be imposed on a legal entity with respect to one of the functions it performs, such as acting as an Internet portal, and not others, such as acting as a telecommunications service provider.

It is often difficult to enforce laws against authors or Internet content providers. They may have no resources, may be outside of the jurisdiction, difficult to locate or anonymous. Consequently, while content-related laws may impose liability on these players, the laws may also impose it on others further down the chain toward the end-user, where those other players have knowledge and the ability to control distribution of the regulated content.

Other players down the chain, including portal operators and other ISPs, are often easier to regulate since they are identifiable and may have offices or other assets in the jurisdiction. Moreover, they may be perceived to be "accessories" in the distribution of illegal content in that they may profit from it. In supporting a policy of imposing liability on distributors of Internet content, comparisons are often drawn with distributors or "publishers" of information in other media. It has often been argued that Internet content providers and other intermediaries have been subject to far fewer legal responsibilities to date than have other forms of media.[358]

---

[358] *See* Michael Deturbide, *Liability of Internet Service Providers for Defamation in the U.S. and Britain: Same Competing Interests, Different Responses*, 3 The J. of Information, Law & Technology (2000) (available at <http://www.elj.warwick.ac.uk/jilt/00-3/deturbide.html>) (where he argues that, in the United States at least, there has been an enormous discrepancy between the liability standard imposed on electronic versus other forms of media).

Policy arguments developed in the context of illegal distribution of copyright material may also apply to other illegal content. A U.S. White Paper has argued that "intermediaries" that distribute copyright material ought to be liable on the basis that:

> Copyright would lose much of its value if third parties such as publishers and producers were insulated from liability because of their innocence as to the culpability of the persons who supplied them with the infringing material … Online service providers have a business relationship with their subscribers. They – and, perhaps, only they – are in the position to know the identity and activities of their subscribers and to stop unlawful activities. And, although indemnification from their subscribers may not reimburse them to the full extent of their liability and other measures may add to their cost of doing business, they are still in a better position to prevent or stop infringement than the copyright owner. Between these two relatively innocent parties, the best policy is to hold the service provider liable.[359]

It can also be argued that intermediaries in the content distribution chain are in a better position to allocate costs associated with control of the illegal distribution of content. Some intermediaries, including some portal operators and other ISPs are able to require content providers to sign contracts relating to access to the public through their websites. These contracts may require the content providers to compensate the intermediaries if the latter are held liable for the content. Some intermediaries may be able to obtain insurance for content liability. More important, the intermediaries may be in the best position to apply human resources and search technologies to identify and remove content that exposes them to potential liability. If monitoring or removing improper content increases their costs, some intermediaries may be able to pass increased costs on to their customers.

However, these arguments should not be overstated. Most intermediaries in the Internet content supply chain face the same challenges in enforcing content restrictions as do law enforcement officials, and they often have fewer resources. It is unusual, and probably impracticable, for content distributors to seek financial security from end-users or other third parties who provide content (e.g., on open forums). Consequently, intermediaries may be unable to recover costs from any

---

[359] U.S. Department of Commerce, *Intellectual Property and the National Information Infrastructure: The Report Of The Working Group On Intellectual Property Rights* 117 (Sept. 1995).

but the largest content providers. Content insurance may be prohibitively expensive or unavailable. A content intermediaries' market may not bear the additional costs involved in monitoring, filtering or removing content. Consequently, imposition of liability on intermediaries could make their business uneconomic, and excessive content regulation would significantly reduce the availability of information on the Internet and the efficiency of e-commerce.

Finally, even if a government chooses not to impose liability for transmitting inappropriate content, it may still develop legislation that relies on Internet intermediaries such as ISPs to enforce laws aimed at preventing dissemination of illegal content or conduct of illegal activities over the Internet. ISPs can be required to provide information in their possession or control with respect to the providers of illegal content or perpetrators of illegal activities.[360] Such measures require a balancing of interests, including the rights to privacy of Internet users. Governments may wish to ensure that the nature of the interest sought to be protected warrants the intrusion on the privacy of a content provider. That may require instituting rules to ensure due processes to consider privacy rights before making a decision to require ISPs to reveal the identities of their subscribers or users.

Knowledge and Control of Content

The most commonly used approach to determine who to regulate in the content supply chain is to focus on those that have knowledge and control of the content. Governments and courts have generally been reluctant to impose liability on Internet intermediaries for content in the absence of some degree of knowledge and control over the inappropriate content.[361] Most current legislative and policy debates about

---

[360] *See e.g.* the U.S. case of *United States v. Hambrick*, 55 F. Supp. 2d 504 (W.D. Wa. 1999), in which a subscriber moved to suppress evidence obtained when state police issued a subpoena to his ISP. The ISP disclosed his name, address, credit card number, e-mail address, home and work telephone numbers, fax number and the fact that he was connected to the Internet at a certain site. The subscriber claimed that he had a reasonable expectation of privacy in the information he provided to his ISP. The court held that the *Electronic Communications Privacy Act* did not create a privacy right in the information one discloses to an ISP, nor does a person generally have a privacy right in personal information. Of course, the result may be different in jurisdictions with different and/or more stringent privacy legislation.

[361] For example, the German *Information and Communication Services Act* of 1997 (known as the "German Multimedia Act") (Informations- und Kommunikationsdienste-Gesetz – IuKDG) (Aug. 1, 1997), English translation <http://www.iid.de/iukdg/iukdge.html>,

who should bear liability for distribution of restricted or prohibited content have similarly focused on the elements of knowledge and control.[362]

It has sometimes been proposed that only those players that have "actual knowledge and control" of content should be liable. However, this standard is subject to criticism. The main concern is that such a standard would permit some players in the Internet content chain to avoid liability for distributing illegal content by intentionally arranging their business in such a way that they will neither obtain actual knowledge of content, nor the legal ability to control it, even where they could technically do so.[363] Another concern is that a specific player in the supply chain is

---

only holds Internet intermediaries liable where they have knowledge of offensive content and are technically able to block such content. *See also* U. Wuermeling, *Multimedia Law – Germany* (1998), 14 Computer Law & Security Report 41-44, for a summary; *see also* Lee Bygrave, *Germany's Teleservices Data Protection Act*, 5 *Privacy Law & Policy Reporter* 53-55 (1998). However, some legislative approaches impose liability on Internet intermediaries even where actual knowledge of infringement is absent. The EU Copyright Directive, *supra* n. 305, which will come into force in December 2002, will impose liability on any party who "knows or who has reasonable grounds to know" that their activity may be "inducing, enabling, facilitating or concealing" an infringement of copyright. Similarly, in the United Kingdom, section 1 of the *Defamation Act* provides that a person will have a defense to a defamation action if that person "did not know, and had no reason to believe, that what he did caused or contributed to the publication of a 'defamatory statement'." The phrases "reasonable grounds to know" and "no reason to believe" impose a constructive knowledge standard on Internet intermediaries which would require them to take reasonable steps to make themselves aware of infringing or defamatory content. Numerous sections of the U.S. DMCA, *supra* n. 307, hold that ISPs will not be liable for content unless they have "actual knowledge that the material or activity is infringing".

[362] *See e.g.* Christian Koenig, Ernst Röder & Sascha Loetz, *The Liability of Access Providers: A Proposal for Regulation based on the Rules concerning Access Providers in Germany*, 3 Int. J. of Communications Law and Policy (Summer 1999) available at <http://www.digital-law.net/IJCLP/3_1999/ijclp_webdoc_7_3_1999.html>. The authors of this article point out that sec. 5(2) of the German *Multimedia Act* states that ISPs "shall not be responsible for any third-party content which they make available for use unless they have knowledge of such content and are technically able and can reasonably be expected to block the use of such content."

[363] *See e.g.* the IP and NII White Paper, *supra* n. 359, which raised the argument that allowing ISPs to shield themselves behind the twin requirements of actual knowledge and control over content would unfairly (and dangerously) allow "one class of distributors

best positioned to detect and control illegal content, at the lowest cost, even if it does not currently do so. Consequently, the debate is currently focused more on the issue of whether a player has a reasonable ability to know and control the Internet content it distributes, than whether it has actual knowledge and control.

In this regard, legislation and enforcement must strike a balance. In some cases, intermediaries in the content chain should clearly be exempt for liability due to their very limited ability to know about or control contents. The high costs that would be incurred to gain knowledge of Internet content or to control it must also be taken into account. It is widely accepted that entities that act solely as "common carriers," that is, pure telecommunications service providers (TSPs), should not be liable for distribution of content. Indeed the laws of some countries specifically prohibit pure TSPs from interfering with or controlling the content of telecommunications traffic they carry, at least in the absence of orders from law enforcement or regulatory authorities.[364]

In the case of Internet or IP traffic, the content transmitted by TSPs is broken down into many different "packets" of data. The packets that compose a single message or item of content may take various different routes to reach their destination and may not reach their destination in their original order. Information contained in the packet "headers" allows the destination computers to reassemble the packets into a coherent item of information. Thus even if a TSP were to review each packet it transmits, it might not be able to ascertain the content of the information without intercepting all other packets that comprise the specific content being transmitted. In some instances, particularly in the case of Internet backbone networks, all of the packets are not transmitted over a single TSP network. Further, even if a backbone TSP could identify harmful content, it may have no way of identifying the original content provider or of cutting off future transmissions from that content provider, since the backbone TSP is likely to have received the packet from another TSP further up the supply chain. Consequently, pure TSPs are generally exempted from liability from content regulation.

---

to self-determine their liability by refusing to take responsibility. This would encourage intentional and wilful ignorance."

[364] For example, sec. 36 of the Canadian *Telecommunications Act*, S.C. 1993, ch. 38, provides that: "Except where the Commission approves otherwise, a Canadian carrier shall not control the content or influence the meaning or purpose of telecommunications carried by it for the public."

Another exemption from liability often applies to Internet intermediaries that only handle or copy illegal material as part of the transmission process or temporary storage related to such transmission.[365]

The extent of knowledge and control required to warrant imposing liability on intermediaries is a more difficult question. The standards of knowledge most commonly cited in the commentaries and reflected in legislation are those of negligence and willful blindness. That is, an intermediary will be held liable for illegal content it makes available if it was willfully blind to or ought reasonably to have known of the illegal content. A standard of willful blindness is satisfied if an intermediary is aware of facts or circumstances from which an impugned activity is apparent.[366] The standard of negligence under common law asks whether a reasonable person in similar circumstances would have known of the presence of the illegal content. Actual knowledge is rarely relevant because it is difficult to prove.

Another approach is a "notice and take-down requirement,"[367] which relies on notification to an Internet intermediary to provide it with knowledge of illegal or infringing content, and then imposes liability if it fails to remove the offending content. However, this approach can have unanticipated side effects. For example, legislation might set a standard holding an ISP liable for defamatory statements

---

[365] For the U.S. DMCA, *supra* n. 307, in the United States <http://www.educause.edu/issues/dmca.html>, as well as the EU E-Commerce Directive, *supra* n. 45, include provisions designed to shield from liability Internet distribution intermediaries that are merely technically involved in the communication. The U.S. DMCA expressly exempts ISPs from liability where they are solely transmitting or routing content or merely providing connections between parties. Similarly, the E-Commerce Directive, provides exemptions for caching, hosting or acting as a mere conduit.

[366] In the U.S. DMCA *supra* n. 307, for example, the language frequently used is "in the absence of such actual knowledge, is not aware of facts or circumstances from which infringing activity is apparent."

[367] *See e.g.* U.S. DMCA sec. 512(c)(3), *supra* n. 307, which requires a notification to include a physical or electronic signature of an authorized representative of the owner of the allegedly infringed IP right, an identification of the copyrighted work, an identification of the allegedly infringing material, sufficient contact information, a statement that the authorized representative has a "good faith belief" that the content is infringing and a statement that the information in the notification is accurate (where misrepresentation carries a penalty of perjury). An ISP is entitled to disregard (and will not be deemed to have constructive knowledge of infringement) most notices which do not meet the above requirements.

only if it fails to remove the statement or any link to the statement after receiving notice from any person that the statement is defamatory. Such an approach could have a significant impact on free speech. The ISP would either have to remove the statement or risk being held liable. If individuals become aware that they can have anything they want removed by simply complaining about it, many may do so. Not only would this increase the cost of legal compliance for the ISP, but it could have a chilling effect on free speech, which may outweigh the beneficial effect of the legislation. Some legislation has addressed this concern by including requirements in the notice intended to provide some assurance that the complaint is *bona fide*.[368]

In determining the degree of knowledge and control required to impose liability, other factors are relevant, including: (a) the importance of the public concern underlying the laws being enforced; (b) the costs of the proposed measures; and (c) negative impacts on other public interests.

The ability of an Internet intermediary to control content is dependent on the type of function it performs and the technology it utilizes. As indicated by the discussion of filters and labeling, below, the technology related to control of content is in a state of evolution. Accordingly, legal and policy standards regarding imposition of liability for dissemination of illegal content are in a state of flux. These standards should take into account the efficacy of available technologies, as well as costs of implementing and maintaining measures to detect and control dissemination of inappropriate content. Legal and policy standards should be revisited periodically to take account of such technological developments.[369]

---

[368] *See e.g.* U.S. DMCA sec. 512(c)(3), *supra* n. 307, which requires a notification to include a physical or electronic signature of an authorized representative of the owner of the allegedly infringed IP right, an identification of the copyrighted work, an identification of the allegedly infringing material, sufficient contact information, a statement that the authorized representative has a "good faith belief" that the content is infringing and a statement that the information in the notification is accurate (where misrepresentation carries a penalty of perjury). An ISP is entitled to disregard (and will not be deemed to have constructive knowledge of infringement) notices which do not meet the above requirements.

[369] Perhaps the best example of changing legal and policy standards can be found in the French *LICRA v Yahoo* case, *supra* n. 24. Similar issues have arisen in Germany, where the *Multimedia Law* exempts ISPs from liability for content posted by third parties unless they have knowledge of such content and unless blocking its use is technically possible and can be reasonably expected. ISPs in the German state of Nordrhein-Westfalen

IP-Address Tracking

IP-address tracking techniques are currently the focus of much debate about the ability to control distribution of content. These techniques track the IP address of ISPs and potentially other players in the Internet chain, from users to Internet content providers. The ability to identify the players in the content distribution chain provides opportunities to detect and block the delivery of certain types of content to certain classes of users.

IP-address tracking techniques are already being used for a number of e-commerce applications. For example they are used on websites to call up different types of banner advertisements for different users, depending on the country from which they access the site.[370] In fact, work on the development of more advanced labeling techniques is being driven by the demands of e-commerce more than by the demands for government regulation of content and illegal activities. According to *The Economist*:

> These [IP-address tracking] technologies are likely to become more efficient. The demands of e-commerce rather than governments are driving improvements. ... Online companies will certainly also make use in future of a controversial feature called IPV6, designed by the Internet Engineering Task Force (IETF). At present, the anonymity of most Internet users is more or less protected because service providers generally assign a different IP address each time someone logs on. But IPV6 includes a new, expanded IP address, part of which is the unique serial number of each computer's network-connection hardware. Every data packet sent will carry a user's electronic fingerprints. ... The holy grail for e-commerce ... would be a system in which users had permanent digital certificates on their computers containing details of age, citizenship, sex, professional credentials, and so on. ... Lawrence Lessig, a law professor at Stanford University, warns that e-commerce firms will push for such certificates and that governments may one day require them.[371]

---

have recently been ordered to block access to certain neo-Nazi and other offensive sites, raising the question of exactly what "reasonable" and "technically possibly" actions must be taken in order to comply with the order. Thus, the standard of control will stand to be determined from a technological as well as a legal perspective.

[370] For a description of this technology and the privacy implications of its use, *see DoubleClick Inc. v. Privacy Litigation* C.V. 0641 (N.R.V.) (S.D.N.Y. Mar. 28, 2001), In re Intuit Privacy Litigation 2001 U.S. Dist. Lexis 5828 (CC.D. Cal. 2001).

[371] Economist *supra* n. 343, at 22.

Although IP-address tracking techniques are far from perfect today, they are already being used in the regulation of prohibited content. The most celebrated case to date is *UEJF and Licra v. Yahoo! Inc. and Yahoo France*.[372] In that case, a French court addressed the longstanding issue of prohibiting the sale via the Internet of artifacts related to the Holocaust in contravention of French law. The court found that since the artifacts were being made available to French users on Yahoo auction websites, Yahoo must block access to the forbidden material by French users. The judgment was seen as a precedent for imposing worldwide liability on a U.S.-based ISP for distribution of illegal content.

The court heard extensive arguments about the ability of Yahoo to implement the court's judgment. The court appointed a panel of technological experts to determine whether it was technically feasible for Yahoo to comply with the court's orders. The experts concluded that, using IP-address tracking techniques, it would be possible to block up to 90% of French users from accessing the prohibited parts of the U.S. site. Yahoo was ordered to apply these techniques. In the aftermath of this decision, there continues to be a considerable debate about the practical ability to use current IP-address techniques to enforce Internet content regulation.[373]

The desire and ability of some Internet content providers and users to retain their anonymity will undermine the effectiveness of IP-address tracking techniques. Many law abiding Internet users seek to remain anonymous in their online dealings for a variety of good reasons.[374] In response to these concerns, many ISPs permit their customers to use pseudonyms online. In addition, several products

---

[372] *Supra* n. 24.

[373] In *Nazis, Porn and Politics: Asserting Control Over Internet Content*, 2 The J. of Information, Law and Technology (2001) (available at <http://elj.warwick.ac.uk/jilt/01-2/penfold.html>), author Carolyn Penfold argues that technological means to implement the decision do not exist. Similarly, she notes that, in Australia, a bill which would have imposed an obligation on ISPs to block access by users to prohibited content was greatly watered down once the government came to recognize the enormous technological difficulties (and resultant liability burden on domestic ISPs) inherent in attempts to prevent end users from accessing content. She concludes that "the Australian legislation [...] was said to be the embodiment of symbolic politics, the government knew the legislation couldn't work but wanted anyhow to be seen to act."

[374] The ability of the Internet to collect and collate information about individuals from a number of different sources has recently been a source of concern to consumers groups around the world. Demands for Internet privacy have increased in many countries. Well-organized, high-profile pressure groups such as the Electronic Frontier Foundation (*see*

and services are available to enable individuals to retain their anonymity online.[375] The introduction of Internet-related privacy legislation in recent years has also added a counter.[376] These developments only serve to compound the difficulty of locating content providers.

Filtering

Filtering software can be installed at various points to block access to websites or to various areas of the Internet. It can be installed on a PC, on ISP or IAP servers, or at gateways that provide Internet access to a whole city, region or country. Filtering software has been used by parents on home computers to prevent their children from accessing adult sites. A number of ISPs provide filtering services that permit their subscribers to block access to certain sites from anyone, such as their children, that use the ISP's services to access the Internet.

More controversial is the use of proxy servers as filters of Internet content for whole regions or countries. Proxy servers act as intermediaries between the Internet and all users on a corporate or organizational network or intranet. In most cases, the functions of proxy servers include caching Internet content for ease of access and providing added security and administrative control over an intranet. However, proxy servers can also filter out or prevent access to specified websites or websites that use specified words, domains, or other parameters.

The best-known example of the use of proxy servers to filter Internet content available to a whole country is China. China's Great Firewall has proven to be a reasonably effective filter, since a large proportion of the country's Internet users

---

<http://www.eff.org/>), take an active role in supporting and advocating online anonymity. The adoption of Internet privacy measures is also a major issue today for more traditional organizations such as the American Civil Liberties Union. Participation of these advocacy groups makes it clear that the demand for anonymity does not come solely from those seeking to conduct illegal activities online. Many law abiding individuals and organizations support online anonymity for reasons related to their belief in freedom of speech, personal safety, and freedom from harassment and unwanted Internet solicitations.

[375] Such as Anonymizer.com and similar services.

[376] A few examples are the *Children's Online Privacy Protection Act* in the U.S., the *Data Protection Act* in the United Kingdom and the *Personal Information Protection and Electronic Documents Act* in Canada. Such legislation and related privacy issues are discussed in chapter 7 of this article.

access the Internet from work or a public place through computers which are connected to proxy servers that act as gateways between the country and the global Internet.[377] Similarly, proxy servers have been used as filters by all ISP's licensed by the Singapore Broadcasting Authority to provide Internet access services in Singapore.[378] It is possible, of course, in countries such as China and Singapore, for some users to bypass proxy servers by dialing up an international number to access the Internet. However, the cost to users reduces the incentive to bypass, as long as users do not consider it essential to access the blocked sites.

In countries with diverse and competitive Internet access providers, the use of proxy servers as filters has largely been limited to voluntary blocking programs, and to self-regulation by some ISPs. However, the mandatory use of filtering software by ISPs may be subject to renewed interest if the trend toward regulation of Internet content continues.

Self regulation

This chapter has focused on the legal and policy issues related to regulation of Internet content and certain illegal Internet activities by government agencies and the courts. However, self-regulation by the Internet industry remains a promising means of both screening out undesirable content and of avoiding heavy-handed content regulation by governments and the courts. Many government agencies and responsible businesses associated with the Internet have promoted self-regulation by the Internet industry as a means of restricting public exposure, or at least access by minors, to the most harmful types of content.

A number of codes of conduct have been adopted by ISPs around the world. Approaches used by ISPs may include filtering, IP-address tracking, blocking access to certain sites based on public complaints, and periodic reviews of website content accessed through portals run by an ISP.

Public education and public surveillance are also being promoted as a means of controlling the spread of harmful content on the Internet. For example, the European Commission recently allocated six million Euros to an Internet safety project as part of its Safer Internet Action Plan. The funding will be used for a public awareness campaign on the dangers of children using Internet chat rooms. Some

---

[377] *The Economist*, *supra* n. 343.

[378] Rodriguez, *supra* n. 341.

funding will also be used to establish hotlines to allow the public to report harmful content found on the Internet.[379]

At this stage, it is still early to determine to what extent self-regulation will be a viable option. The diversity of suppliers on the Internet access side make it difficult to establish industry-wide approaches to self regulation even within a single country, let alone at the international level. As a result, governments are likely to continue to feel the need to supplement self-regulation with mandatory laws and prohibitions to prevent abuses involving the most harmful types of Internet content.

Licensing

A number of countries require government licenses for Internet access providers and certain other types of ISPs. Licensing of Internet-related businesses has generally been regarded as unnecessarily intrusive in the dynamic Internet markets of Europe, North America, and many other countries. In fact, the currently proposed European Commission Directive on authorization of electronic communications networks and services severely limits the powers of European Union Member States to impose specific licenses or even general authorizations on Internet-related service providers, such as ISPs.[380] The policy of many other countries is to deregulate Internet-related services and to rely on market forces to develop Internet markets.

Where licensing of Internet access providers and other ISPs is required, governments can use license conditions and regulation of licensees as a means of controlling content. The best-known example is the case of the Singapore Broadcasting Authority. As previously discussed, the SBA required licensed ISPs to use proxy servers as filters to prohibit access to "prohibited material" prescribed in the SBA's Internet Code of Practice.[381]

---

[379] *Europe hopes to outlaw hate speech online*, Cnet New.Com (Nov. 12, 2001) <http://news.cnet.com/news/0-1005-200-7850494.html>.

[380] Proposal for a Directive of the European Parliament and the Council on authorization of electronic communications networks and services, CEC, COM (2000) 386 (12 July 2000).

[381] *Supra* n. 341.

10.5. The Cybercrime Treaty and Other Initiatives

Introduction

It is evident that efforts to criminalize distribution of certain types of content and illegal activities over the Internet will require international coordination. As the experience of Singapore and other countries illustrate, it is very difficult for any one country to effectively enforce prohibitions against illegal conduct in cyberspace. Since domestic laws are inadequate, international legal instruments must be adopted to address the borderless nature of the Internet.

The Convention on Cybercrime[382] (Convention or Treaty), drafted by the Council of Europe,[383] is the first international treaty on crimes committed through the Internet and other computer networks.[384] The main objective of the Convention is "to pursue a common criminal policy aimed at the protection of society against cybercrime, *inter alia* by adopting appropriate legislation and fostering international co-operation."[385]

After a lengthy gestation period, which included discussions with non-members of the Council, such as the United States and Canada, the Convention was formally adopted by the Committee of Ministers of the Council of Europe on November 8, 2001. The Convention is non-binding and must be ratified by individual countries, and its provisions incorporated into national law. Signature by member states of the Council of Europe took place on November 23, 2001 at the International Conference on Cybercrime.[386] The Convention will enter into force once it has been ratified by five states, three of which must be members of the Council of Europe.[387]

---

[382] Council of Europe, *Draft Convention on Cybercrime* <http://conventions.coe.int/Treaty/EN/projets/FinalCybercrime.htm>.

[383] The Council of Europe is an international organization based in Strasbourg, France. It has 43 member states, including all 15 members of the European Union. The Council deals with major issues facing Europe other than defence. *See* <http://www.coe.int>.

[384] Council of Europe, *First international treaty to combat crime in cyberspace approved by Ministers' Deputies* <http://press.coe.int/cp/2001/646a(2001).htm>.

[385] *See* Preamble, *supra* n. 382.

[386] *Supra* n. 382, para. I.

[387] *Supra* n. 384.

The Convention only covers limited types of "illegal content," namely those related to child pornography. However, it covers far more than content-related crimes. According to the Council of Europe, "cybercrime" is a term used to describe "any crime that in some way or other involves the use of information technology."[388]

The principal aims of the Convention, as outlined in the Explanatory Report to the Convention on Cybercrime, are as follows:[389]

(1) harmonizing the domestic criminal substantive law elements of offenses and connected provisions in the area of cybercrime;

(2) providing for domestic criminal procedural law powers necessary for the investigation and prosecution of cybercrime offenses and other offenses committed by means of a computer system or related evidence in electronic form; and

(3) setting up a fast and effective regime of international cooperation.

Essentially, the Convention criminalizes activities that would constitute cybercrime and also provides for powers to combat cybercrime at both the domestic and international levels.[390] The Convention deals with violations of network security, computer-related fraud and forgery, child pornography, and copyright infringement.[391] Search and seizure of computer networks and interception are among the powers and procedures prescribed by the Convention to facilitate the detection, investigation and prosecution of cybercrime.[392] At the same time, the Convention endeavors to protect the development of information technologies as well as fundamental human rights.[393]

---

[388] Commission of European Communities, *Communication from the Commission to the Council, the European Parliament, the Economic and Social Committee and the Committee of the Regions: Creating a Safer Information Society by Improving the Security of Information Infrastructures and Combating Computer-related Crime* 9 <http://europa.eu.int/SIPO/eif/InternetPoliciesSite/Crime/CrimeCommEN.html>.

[389] Council of Europe, *Convention on Cybercrime, Explanatory Report* (adopted Nov. 8, 2001) para. 16 <http://conventions.coe.int/Treaty/EN/projets/FinalCyberRapex.htm>.

[390] *See* preamble, ch. II, ch. III, *supra* n. 382.

[391] *Supra* n. 382, arts. 2-10.

[392] *Supra* n. 382, arts. 19-21.

[393] *Supra* n. 382, preamble.

Key Terms

The Explanatory Report to the Convention notes that Convention parties are not required to have verbatim definitions in their domestic laws if the concepts covered in their domestic laws are consistent with the Convention and there is an equivalent framework for its implementation.[394]

Article 1 contains the definitions of four key concepts: computer system; computer data; service provider; and traffic data. A computer system is defined in the Convention as a device consisting of hardware and software which performs automatic processing of data. Computer data means any representation of facts, information concepts in a form suitable for processing in a computer system. Service provider is broadly defined to extend to both public and private entities that provide users with the ability to communicate as well as entities that process or store computer data on behalf of those public and private entities. Traffic data is treated as a category of computer data that is subject to a specific legal regime, which allows national legislatures to provide different protection levels according to the sensitivity of the traffic data. The Convention defines traffic data as data generated by a computer system in a chain of communication in order to route the communication from its origin to its destination. The definition provides a list of categories of traffic data based on the origin of a communication, destination, route, time, date, size, duration, and type of underlying service.

Measures to be Taken at the National Level

Chapter II of the Convention covers both substantive and procedural criminal law.[395] Section I of Chapter II deals with substantive criminal law issues and covers criminalization provisions and related provisions regarding cybercrime.[396] A total of nine offenses are categorized under four titles:

(1) *Offenses Against the Confidentiality, Integrity, and Availability of Computer Data and Systems*: This category deals with illegal access, illegal interception, data interference, system interference, and the misuse of devices. Illegal access under article 2 is the intentional access, in whole or in part, of a computer system without a right. Illegal interception is a criminal offense under article 3 if there is an intentional interception without right,

[394] *Supra* n. 382, para. 22.

[395] *See* sec. 1 ch. II for substantive law. *See* sec. 2, ch. II for procedural law. *Supra* n. 382.

[396] *Id.*

by technical means, of non-public computer data transmissions involving a computer system. Under article 4, data interference is a criminal offense where there is intentional damaging, deletion, deterioration, alteration or suppression of computer data without right. System interference through intentional serious hindering of the functioning of a computer system by inputting, transmitting, damaging, deleting, deteriorating, altering or suppressing computer data, without a right, is a criminal offense under article 5. Article 6 criminalizes the misuse of a device where there is intentional commission of specific acts of misuse of certain devices or access to data for the purpose of committing offenses against the confidentiality, integrity, and availability of computer data systems under articles 2 through 5.

(2) *Computer-related Offenses*: The offense of computer-related forgery under article 7 is essentially a parallel offense to the forgery of tangible documents. Article 8 criminalizes manipulation during data processing where there is an intention to effect an illegal transfer of property such that it is computer-related fraud.

(3) *Content-related Offenses*: Article 9 makes it a criminal offense to produce, offer or make available, distribute or transmit, procure, or possess child pornography through a computer system.

(4) *Offenses Related to Infringement of Copyright and Related Rights*: Article 10 criminalizes willful infringement of copyright and neighboring rights arising from the international copyright agreements listed in the article,[397] where such acts were committed by means of a computer system and on a commercial scale.

The fifth title is "ancillary liability and sanctions." Article 11 criminalizes the intentional aiding or abetting of the commission of offenses under articles 2 to 10 of the Convention. Corporate liability is criminalized under article 12. Article 13, which deals with sanctions and measures, provides that Convention parties can invoke legislative or other measures as needed.

Procedural issues are dealt with in section II of chapter II. The scope of the procedures extends beyond the offenses enumerated in section I and applies to any

---

[397] Paris Act of July 24, 1971 of the Bern Convention for the Protection of Literary and Artistic Works, the Agreement on Trade-Related Aspects of Intellectual Property Rights and the WIPO Copyright Treaty, with the exception of any moral rights conferred by such Conventions, *supra* n. 382, art. 10.

offense committed by means of a computer system or involves evidence in electronic form. The conditions and safeguards applicable to the procedural powers are contained in Article 15. Procedural powers in the Convention include: expedited preservation of stored data, expedited preservation and partial disclosure of traffic data, production orders, search and seizure of computer data, real-time collection of traffic data, and interception of content data.

Jurisdictional provisions are provided in section III of chapter II.[398]

International Cooperation

Section I of chapter III outlines the general principles relating to international cooperation in article 23. The Convention provides that international cooperation between the parties should exist "to the widest extent possible."[399] The scope of cooperation extends not only to criminal offenses related to computer systems and data, but also to the collection of evidence of a cybercrime in electronic form.[400] As a third general principle, cooperation must accord with the provisions of chapter III and with international agreements on criminal matters. Accordingly, section I provides provisions regarding extradition and mutual assistance in situations with and without applicable international agreements on criminal matters.[401] Specific mechanisms to facilitate international cooperation are provided for in section II.[402]

Other Initiatives – Cybercrime and Hate Speech

Before adoption of the Cybercrime Convention, a number of countries enacted legislation aimed at hacking, viruses and other interference with electronic communications, computer networks or databases. A good example of an ambitious and fairly comprehensive law is Australia's Cybercrime Act 2001,[403] which was passed on September 27, 2001. The Australian Act includes seven offenses. The classification of serious computer offenses covers unauthorized access, modification or impairment with intent to commit a serious offense, unauthorized

---

[398] *Supra* n. 382, art. 22.

[399] *Supra* n. 382, art 23, para. 242.

[400] *Supra* n. 382, art. 23, para. 243.

[401] *Supra* n. 382, arts. 24-28.

[402] *Supra* n. 382, arts 29-35.

[403] No. 161 (2001); *see also* Christopher Ellison, Media Release, *New laws combat cyber terrorism* <http://law.gov.au/aghome/agnews/2001newsjust/e217_01.htm>.

modification of data to cause impairment, and unauthorized impairment of electronic communication.[404]

The remaining four offenses are categorized under other computer offenses which encompasses unauthorized access to or modification of restricted data, unauthorized impairment of data held on a computer disk, possession or control of data with intent to commit a computer offense, and producing, supplying or obtaining data with intent to commit a computer offense. The act also enhances the criminal investigation powers in the Australian Crimes Act 1914 and Customs Act 1901 with respect to the search, seizure, and copying of electronically stored data. The maximum penalty in the Cybercrime Act has been raised to ten years imprisonment.

Other countries that have not already done so can be expected to enact legislation to prevent the types of cybercrime covered by the Australian law.

More controversial are the new initiatives proposed to criminalize other types of content not covered by the Cybercrime Convention. First on the agenda for consideration is hate speech. Immediately after approving the Cybercrime Convention, the Standing Committee of the Council of Europe Parliamentary Assembly voted unanimously to add a protocol that defines and outlaws hate speech on computer networks.[405] It has been reported that drafters of the protocol are considering methods of preventing "illegal hosting," where servers are located in a country with more lenient laws, such as those of the United States, where there is greater legal tolerance for hate speech, as a result of the protections afforded by the First Amendment to the U.S. Constitution. The same report cites recent estimates that at present there are around 4,000 racist websites, including 2,500 in the United States.[406]

---

[404] *Supra* n. 382, secs. 477.1-477.3.

[405] *Europe hopes to outlaw hate speech online*, *supra* n. 379.

[406] *Id.*

Appendix

Selected Technical Terms, Organizations, Guidelines, and Legislation on E-Commerce

Technical Terms

Country-Code Top-Level Domain (ccTLD)

Digital Subscriber Line (DSL)

Domain Name System (DNS)

Electronic Data Interchange (EDI)

Generic Top-Level Domain (gTLD)

Internet Access Provider (IAP)

Internet Content Provider (ICP)

Internet Protocol (IP)

Internet Service Provider (ISP)

Megabits per second (Mbps)

Personal Identification Number (PIN)

Public Key Infrastructure (PKI)

Telecommunications Service Provider (TSP)

Very Small Aperture Terminal (VSAT)

Organizations

American Bar Association (ABA)

Asia Pacific Economic Cooperation (APEC)

European Economic Area (EEA)

European Commission (EC)

European Union (EU)

Internet Corporation for Assigned Names and Numbers (ICANN)

Organization for Economic Co-operation and Development (OECD)

International Telecommunications Union (ITU)

United Nations Conference on Trade and Development (UNCTAD)

United Nations Commission on International Trade Law (UNCITRAL)

United States National Conference of Commissioners on the Uniform State Laws (U.S. NCCUSL)

World Trade Organization (WTO)

World Intellectual Property Organization (WIPO)

Model Laws, Guidelines, and Conventions

ABA, Achieving Legal and Business Order in Cyberspace: Jurisdictional Issues created by the Internet (ABA Jurisdiction Report)

Convention of Jurisdiction and the Enforcement of Judgments in Civil and Commercial Matters (Brussels Convention)

Draft Convention on the Jurisdiction and the Enforcement of Foreign Judgments in Civil and Commercial Matters (Hague draft Convention on the Jurisdiction)

EC Convention on the Law Applicable to Contractual Obligations (Rome 1980) (Rome Convention)

General Agreement on Trade in Services (GATS)

Hague Conference on Private International Law (Hague Conference)

OECD Guidelines for Consumer Protection in the Context of Electronic Commerce (OECD Consumer Protection Guidelines)

OECD Taxation Framework Conditions (OECD Taxation Framework)

UNCITRAL Model Law of Electronic Commerce (1996) (Model Law)

UNCITRAL Guide to Enactment to the Model Law of 1996 (Guide to Model Law)

UNCITRAL Model Law on Electronic Signatures (2001) (E-Signatures Model Law)

EU Directives, Conventions and Reports

European Commission recommendation 94/820/EC relating to legal aspects of EDI

Directive 1995/46/EC of October 1995 Q.J. (L 281) on certain aspects of data protection (EU Data Protection Directive)

Directive 1997/7/ EC of May 1997 on the protection of consumers in respect of distance selling contracts, 1997 O.J. (L144) 19 (EU Distance Selling Directive)

Directive 1999/93/EC on a Community Framework for Electronic Signatures (EU E-Signature Directive)

Directive 2000/31/EC of June 8, 2000 on certain legal aspects of information society services, in particular e-commerce, in the Internal Market, 2000 O.J. (L178) (EU E-Commerce Directive)

Directive 2001/29/EU of 22 May 2001 on the harmonization of certain aspects of copyright and related rights in the information society (EU Copyright Directive)

Legislation

Australia

Electronic Transactions Act of 1999 (Commonwealth) (Australia ETA)

Canada

Uniform Electronic Commerce Act (Canada UECA)

France

Electronic Signature Bill (France – ESB)

Hong Kong

Electronic Transactions Ordinance (Hong Kong ETO)

Japan

Electronic Signature and Electronic Signature Certification Business Law (Japan – ESL)

Singapore

Electronic Transactions Act (Singapore ETAS)

United States

Anti-Cybersquatting Consumer Protection Act (U.S. ACPA)

Children's Online Privacy Protection Act (U.S. COPPA)

Digital Millennium Copyright Act (U.S. DMCA)

Uniform Computer Information Transactions Act (U.S. UCITA)

Uniform Electronic Transactions Act (U.S. UETA)

United States Federal Electronic Signature in Global and National Commerce Act (U.S. E-Sign)

INTELLECTUAL PROPERTY RIGHTS AND THE PROTECTION OF PUBLIC HEALTH IN DEVELOPING COUNTRIES

CARLOS M. CORREA*

This article focuses on the protection of intellectual property rights for pharmaceutical products from the perspective of developing countries. Mindful of the impact on both price and availability of medicines, the author subjects the international intellectual property rights regime, as well as common domestic practices, to critical scrutiny. Emphasizing that the WTO's Agreement on Trade-Related Aspects of Intellectual Property Rights does not impose international uniformity, Prof. Correa discusses all of the significant areas where developing countries have scope for fashioning their intellectual property law in ways that may best realize public health objectives while providing the necessary protections to rights holders within the internationally agreed upon framework.

---

* Carlos M. Correa is director of the Master's Program on Science and Technology Policy and Management of the University of Buenos Aires, Argentina, where he also directs the post-graduate course on intellectual property and the quarterly journal *Temas de Derecho Industrial y de la Competencia*. He is a member of the United Kingdom's Commission on Intellectual Property Rights (2001), and has been a consultant in the field of science and technology and intellectual property to numerous international organizations. He was director of the UNDP/UNIDO Regional Programme on Informatics and Microelectronics for Latin America and the Caribbean (1990-95). Among other positions in the Argentine national government, he was Undersecretary of State for Informatics and Development (1984-89), and a delegate in the negotiations of the Washington Treaty on Integrated Circuits and the TRIPS Agreement (1988-91). He is the author of numerous articles and books, among which are: *El regimen de patentes tras la adopción del Acuerdo sobre los Derechos de la Propriedad Intelectual Relacionados con el Comercio*, (6239 Jurisprudencia Argentina 2001), *Integrating Public Health Concerns into Patent Legislation in Developing Countries* (South Centre 2000); *Développements récents dans le domaine des brevets pharmaceutiques: mise en oeuvre de l'accord sur les ADPIC*, 1 Revue Internationale de Droit Economique (University of Louvain 2000); *Implementing national public health policies in the framework of the WTO Agree-*

The World Bank Legal Review: Law and Justice for Development: 161-205.

Contents

---

ments, 34 J. of World Trade 89 (No. 5, 2000); *Emerging trends: new patterns of technology transfer* in S. Patel, P. Roffe and A. Yusuf (eds.), *The International Transfer of Technology. The origins and aftermath of the United Nations negotiations on a Draft Code of Conduct* (Kluwer Law International 2000). Prof. Correa holds a Ph.D. degree (Law, Economics) from the University of Buenos Aires, Argentina.

Without further attribution, the author has drawn substantially on two of his previous publications: *Integrating Public Health Concerns into Patent Legislation in Developing Countries* (South Centre 2000) and *The TRIPS Agreement: how much room for maneuver?* which appeared in the *Journal of Human Development* (Vol. 2, Number 1, UNDP/Carfax Publishing, Taylor & Francis, Ltd. 2001) available at <http://www.tandf.co.uk>.

1. Introduction

The international framework on intellectual property rights (IPR) underwent dramatic changes during the 1990s. The adoption of the Agreement on the Trade Related Aspects of Intellectual Property Rights (TRIPS Agreement or Agreement)[1] as one of the outcomes of the GATT Uruguay Round, represented a "monumental change,"[2] due to its broad coverage and the availability of a system of dispute settlement that may lead to the imposition of trade sanctions. In addition, new treaties on copyright and related rights were developed under the auspices of the World Intellectual Property Organization (WIPO),[3] and many instruments dealing with IPR were adopted at the regional and bilateral levels.

The changes in IPR protection were driven by the concerted action of various industrial sectors (such as the pharmaceuticals, recording, semiconductors, and software industries), actively supported by the governments of developed countries, notably the United States. Such action aimed at both increasing and universalizing the standards of protection for IPR. Underlying this trend were growing private research and development (R&D) budgets, the vulnerability to copying of some R&D intensive products, and the perceived gaps and weaknesses of IPR protection in developing countries.

Developing countries reluctantly accepted the negotiation of IPR standards within the GATT framework. Though the developed countries largely prevailed in establishing standards of IPR protection comparable to those in force in their jurisdictions, developing countries strove to retain a certain flexibility so as to be able to adopt pro-competitive measures that mitigate the powers conferred to IPR holders. A number of World Trade Organization (WTO) members used such flexibility by establishing, for instance, exceptions to exclusive rights and compulsory licensing in their national laws. Despite the relatively large number of complaints submitted to WTO under the Dispute Settlement Understanding in relation to the

---

1 Agreement on the Trade Related Aspects of Intellectual Property Rights (Apr. 15, 1994) <http://www.docsonline.wto.org/GEN_viewerwindow.asp?D:/DDFDOCUMENTS/T/WT/MIN01/DEC1.DOC.HTM> [hereinafter *TRIPS Agreement*].

2 Sam Ricketson, *The Future of the Traditional Intellectual Property Conventions in the Brave New World of Trade-Related Intellectual Property Rights*, 26 Intl. Rev. of Industrial Property and Copyright Law 881-883 (no. 6, 1995).

3 *WIPO Copyright Treaty* (Dec. 20, 1996) and the *WIPO Performance and Phonograms Treaty* (Dec. 20, 1996) <http://www.wipo.int/treaties/ip/index.html>.

TRIPS Agreement, the legality of such pro-competitive measures was only formally tested in two cases. In a case initiated by the European Union against Canada,[4] the panel addressed the TRIPS-consistency of Section 55(2)(1) and (2) of the Canadian Patent Act (as revised in 1993) regarding the "early working" or "Bolar" exception. Upon a complaint by the European Union, a panel also examined section 110(5)(b) of U.S. copyright law – relating to the enjoyment of certain works by customers in business premises – in light of article 13 of the TRIPS Agreement.[5]

The emergence of HIV/AIDS epidemics and the actions and pressures exerted on some developing countries (as illustrated by the case of South Africa),[6] created considerable tension and a growing demand by developing countries to reaffirm and clarify the right of any WTO member to use the flexibility allowed by the TRIPS Agreement, particularly in order to implement public health policies. As a result, the Fourth WTO Ministerial Conference adopted a "Declaration on the TRIPS Agreement and Public Health,"[7] which clarifies certain aspects of the TRIPS Agreement of interest to developing countries.

This article describes first the main characteristics of the TRIPS Agreement.[8] Second, it examines the ways in which WTO member countries can use the flexibility of the agreement to promote competitive access to goods and technologies. Given the public health importance of access to pharmaceuticals and the concerns expressed by developing countries, the analysis focuses on the protection of IPRs in the pharmaceutical field.

---

4 *Canada-Patent Protection of Pharmaceutical Products*, WT/DS114/R (Mar. 17, 2000).

5 *United States-Section 110(5) of the Copyright U.S. Act*, WT/DS160/R (June 19, 2000), 17 U.S.C.A. §110 (5) (B) (Supp. 2001).

6 Patrick Bond, *Globalization, Pharmaceutical Pricing and South African Health Policy: Managing Confrontation with U.S. Firms and Politicians*, International Journal of Health Services (1999).

7 *Declaration on the TRIPS Agreement and Public Health*, WT/MIN(01)/DEC/W/2 (Nov. 14, 2001) [hereinafter *Doha Declaration*], available at <http://wto.org/english/the wto_e/minist_e/min01_e/mindecl_trips_e.htm>.

8 *See* Carlos Correa, *The TRIPS Agreement: how much room form maneuver?*, 2 J. of Human Development 79 (No. 1, Jan. 2001).

2. The TRIPS Agreement Standards of Protection

The agreement establishes minimum standards on copyright and related rights, trademarks, geographical indications, industrial designs, patents, integrated circuits, and undisclosed information (trade secrets). Hence, by its coverage, it is the most comprehensive international instrument on IPR. It deals with all types of IPR, with the sole exceptions of breeders' rights (only incidentally referred to) and utility models (or "petty patents").

The agreement is based on and supplements, with additional obligations,[9] the Paris, Berne, Rome, and Washington[10] conventions in their respective fields. In other words, the agreement is not to be viewed as a completely new and separate convention, but rather as an integrative instrument which provides "convention-plus" protection to IPR.[11]

The standards of protection set forth relate both to the availability of rights as well to their enforcement. The inclusion of detailed provisions on "enforcement" is one of the main innovations of the TRIPS Agreement with respect to pre-existing conventions on IPR. WTO member countries cannot, in the specific areas and issues covered by the agreement, confer a lower (or ineffective) protection. In exchange, members cannot be obliged to provide a "more extensive" protection (article 1.1.).

With the approval of the TRIPS Agreement, any controversy as to compliance with the minimum standards should be subject to a multilateral procedure of dispute settlement within the WTO, in accordance with the Dispute Settlement Understanding (DSU). Once the existence of a violation is determined, the affected country can apply trade retaliatory measures to the non-complying country, in any

---

[9] The provisions of the international conventions which are supplemented become binding even for countries that have not ratified them, except in the case of the Rome Convention (relating to producers of phonograms, performing artists, and broadcasting organizations) which only continues to be binding on states that have joined it.

[10] The provisions of the Washington Convention on the protection of layout designs of integrated circuits (1989), which has never entered into force, became however enforceable through the TRIPS Agreement.

[11] There are some cases, however, where "convention-minus" protection is granted, such as in the case of moral rights provided for by the Berne Convention. *See* Carlos Correa, *TRIPS Agreement: Copyright and Related Rights*, 25 Intl. Rev. of Industrial Property and Copyright Law (No. 4, 1994).

area covered by the WTO Agreement (for instance, it may increase tariffs on exports from the non-complying country). This mechanism provides an institutionalized, multilateral means to address disputes relating to IPR. It is aimed at preventing unilateral actions, such as those taken by the United States under Section 301 of its Trade and Tariffs Act.

The main stated goal of the agreement is "to reduce distortions and impediments to international trade, taking into account the need to promote effective and adequate protection of intellectual property rights, and to ensure that measures and procedures to enforce intellectual property rights do not themselves become a barrier to legitimate trade."[12]

The paradigm of protection adopted by the agreement aims at achieving a balance between the exclusive rights conferred to innovators and the interests of society in the diffusion of and further innovation on existing technology. Though it is recognized that intellectual property rights are "private rights," the underlying public policy objectives of national systems for the protection of intellectual property, including "developmental and technological objectives" are also recognized.[13] More specifically, articles 7 and 8 provide a framework for the interpretation and implementation of intellectual property rights.

Article 6 addresses the tension between free trade and the protection of IPR. It allows member countries to legislate on the international exhaustion of rights and, therefore, to admit parallel imports.

Unlike other components of the WTO system and despite the fact that the most appropriate level of IPRs varies by income level,[14] the TRIPS Agreement did not establish a special and differential treatment for developing countries. It only allowed such countries (as well as economies in transition) to delay the implementation of the Agreement (except national treatment and the most-favored nation obligations) until January 1, 2000. This period extends at least to January 1, 2016 in the case of least developed countries.[15] In the case of the countries that are

---

[12] The *TRIPS Agreement*, *supra* n. 1, at preamble.

[13] *Id.*

[14] World Bank, *Global Economic Prospects and the Developing Countries. Making Trade Work for the World's Poor* 129 (World Bank 2002).

[15] In paragraph 7 of the *Doha Declaration*, *supra* n. 7, the ministers agreed that: "… the least developed Members will not be obliged, with respect to pharmaceutical products, to implement or apply Sections 5 and 7 of Part II of the TRIPS Agreement or to enforce rights provided for under these Sections until 1 January 2016, without prejudice to the

bound to introduce patent protection for pharmaceuticals as a result of the TRIPS Agreement, patents will only be available for products for which a patent application was filed after January 1, 1995 (or for which priority was claimed after January 1, 1994).[16] This means that products for which a patent was applied for before those dates would remain in the public domain, unless the national law admits a retroactive ("pipeline") protection for such products. In addition, the granting of the patent may be postponed until January 1, 2005, provided that "exclusive marketing rights" are granted until the patent is granted or finally rejected, under the conditions established in article 70.9 of the agreement.

In sum, the adoption of the TRIPS Agreement allowed developed countries to universalize the core of their own IPRs systems. The agreement significantly expands and strengthens the standards of protection in most fields of IPRs. However, the agreement aims at balancing the rights of producers and users (article 7), and leaves some room for establishing pro-competitive measures that may facilitate access to protected technologies and goods.

3. Intellectual Property Rights and Public Health[17]

The protection of public health is one of the most pressing issues in developing countries. A large part of the world population still lacks access to essential drugs; in the poorest parts of Africa, for instance, over 50% of the population lack that access.[18] An estimated 1.5 billion people are not expected to survive to age 60, and more than 880 million people lack access to health care.[19] Of the more than 33

---

right of least-developed Members to seek other extensions of the transition periods as provided for in Article 66.1 of the TRIPS Agreement. We instruct the Council for TRIPS to take the necessary action to give effect to this pursuant to Article 66.1 of the TRIPS Agreement."

[16] *Paris Convention for the Protection of Industrial Property* art. 4 (July 14, 1967) <http://www.wipo.int/treaties/ip/index.html> [hereinafter *Paris Convention*].

[17] This section is substantially based on Carlos Correa, *Integrating Public Health Concerns into Patent Legislation in Developing Countries* (South Centre 2000).

[18] WHO, *Revised Drug Strategy. WHO's Work in Pharmaceuticals and Essential Drugs*, EB/RDS/RC/1 (WHO 1998).

[19] UNDP, *Human Development Report* (Oxford U. Press 1999).

million HIV-positive people in the world, 95% live in developing countries, and most of them cannot afford required drugs.[20]

There is broad recognition of the role that IPR can play in stimulating health-related research and development, particularly in the more advanced countries.[21] There is also recognition, however, that IPR have an impact on prices.[22] In the health sector, where denial of affordable access to treatment or pharmaceuticals can have life-or-death consequences, the conditions, including price, that determine access to medicines are critical matters, especially for the low-income segments of the population. It is quite clear that IPR are not the *only* factor determining access to medicines; but unaffordable prices may, in the absence of corrective measures, effectively discourage and block any attempt by governments in developing countries to increase access to medicines by the poor.

The TRIPS Agreement has important implications for the health sector;[23] it sets forth detailed obligations in respect of the protection of pharmaceutical inventions,[24] including the obligations:

- to recognize patents for inventions in all fields of technology, with limited exceptions;

---

[20] UNAIDS, *AIDS Epidemic Update* (Dec. 1998).

[21] On the little attention paid by pharmaceutical R&D to the specific needs of developing countries, *see* Robert and Bonita Beaglehole, *Public Health at the Crossroads. Achievements and Prospects* 220 (Cambridge U. Press 1997); Jeffrey Sachs, *Helping the World's Poorest*, The Economist (Aug. 14, 1999); Zafrullah Chowdhury, *The Politics of Essential Drugs. The Makings of a Successful Health Strategy: Lessons from Bangladesh* (Zed Books 1995); Médecins Sans Frontières, *Fatal Imbalance. The Crisis in Research and Development for Drugs for Neglected Diseases* (2001).

[22] *See Doha Declaration*, *supra* n. 7, para. 3.

[23] *See* H. Bale, *Uruguay Round Negotiations on Intellectual Property: A Step Forward?* (American University, Washington College of Law, Oct. 3, 1991) (3rd Annual Conference on International Trade); Velásquez, German & Boulet, *Globalization and Access to Drugs. Perspectives on the WTO/TRIPS Agreement* para. 4 (World Health Organization Action Program on Essential Drugs, Health Economics and Drugs DAP Series, No. 7, WHO/DAP/98.9, 1999).

[24] *See* Stefano Sandri, *La Nuova Disciplina Della Propietá Industriale Dopo I GATT-TRIPS* (CEDAM 1996); C. Correa & A. Yusuf, *Intellectual Property and International Trade. The TRIPS Agreement* (Kluwer Law International 1998).

- not to discriminate with respect to the availability or enjoyment of patent rights;
- to grant patent rights for at least twenty years from the date of application;
- to limit the scope of exceptions to patent rights and to grant compulsory licenses only under certain conditions;
- to effectively enforce patent rights.

The TRIPS Agreement also requires protection against "unfair commercial use" of data submitted for the marketing approval of medicines (article 39.3).

However, the agreement does not establish a *uniform* international law nor even uniform legal requirements. WTO member countries are obliged to comply with the *minimum* standards of the agreement, but they also have considerable room to develop their IPR laws in a manner that is responsive, among other things, to public health objectives and needs.[25] In implementing the TRIPS provisions, WTO member countries may legitimately adopt regulations that ensure a balance between the minimum standards of IPR protection and the public good. Moreover, they can adopt measures that are conducive to social and economic welfare (article 7), such as those necessary to protect public health, nutrition, and public interest in sectors of vital importance for their socioeconomic and technological development (article 8). Countries can also adopt measures to prevent the abuse of intellectual property rights (article 8.2).

---

[25] *Doha Declaration, supra* n. 7, para. 4 states:

> We agree that the TRIPS Agreement does not and should not prevent Members from taking measures to protect public health. Accordingly, while reiterating our commitment to the TRIPS Agreement, we affirm that the Agreement can and should be interpreted in a manner supportive of WTO Members' right to protect public health and, in particular, to promote access to medicines for all. In this connection, we reaffirm the right of WTO Members to use to the full the provisions in the TRIPS Agreement, which provide flexibility for this purpose.

3.1. Patentable Subject Matter

3.1.1. Exceptions

The TRIPS Agreement obliges all WTO members to recognize patents in all fields of technology (article 27.1).[26] This was a major victory for the pharmaceutical industry in the Uruguay Round, since more than 50 countries did not recognize patent protection for pharmaceuticals at the time the Round was launched. Article 27.1 does not permit the exclusion from patentability of medicines in general or, arguably, of specific groups thereof. Under this interpretation, WTO Members could not exclude from patentability even the "essential medicines" listed by the World Health Organization (WHO).[27]

There are two possible grounds for exceptions in the TRIPS Agreement under which pharmaceuticals might conceivably be excluded from patentability, but neither appears sufficient to justify such an exclusion, except in limited circumstances.

(1) *Public health* (article 8.1): This article explicitly recognizes the right of WTO members to adopt measures necessary to protect public health. Such measures would be subject to a test of "necessity" and of consistency with other obligations under the TRIPS Agreement. The consistency test as an element of the exception clause is a particular feature of this agreement and seems to rule out the flexibility that GATT 1947 (article XX (b))[28] and other WTO agreements, such as the agreement on technical barriers to trade and the agreement on the application of sanitary and phytosanitary measures, offer when it is necessary to derogate members' obligations in order to pursue public health objectives.

---

[26] According to art. 27(1), "patents shall be available for any inventions, whether products or processes, in all fields of technology." *TRIPS Agreement*, *supra* n. 1.

[27] Most of the drugs in the WHO list of Essential Medicines are off-patent, and the list does not include high-priced drugs. Given the methodology used for establishing that list, the non-patentability of such drugs may not be a significant issue for developing countries. *See* Médecins Sans Frontières, Health Action International & Consumer Project on Technology, *Open Letter to the WTO Member Countries on TRIPS and Access to Health Care Technology* (Nov. 12, 1999).

[28] This article recognizes the importance of sovereign nations being able to promote domestic health interests, even if contrary to their general obligations under the WTO agreements. However, to date, Article XX(b) has been interpreted and applied rather narrowly in GATT/WTO case law, and it is doubtful whether GATT Article XX(b) would apply in the TRIPS context. *See* the Panel Report in *USA v. India – Patent Protection for Agricultural and Chemical Products*, WT/DS50/R para. 7.19 (Jan. 16, 1998).

The implications of the "consistency" test are undefined, and were one of the key concerns that led developing countries to propose a clarification on the right to adopt public health measures at the fourth WTO Ministerial Conference. Though the final text does not fully reflect the position of developing countries[29] and does not modify the language in article 8.1, it does indicate that IPR protection should not be enforced at any cost, and that there might be situations in which public health measures may take precedence over such rights.

(2) *Ordre public* or *morality* (article 27.2): There is no universally accepted notion of *ordre public*[30] or *morality*, leaving WTO member countries some flexibility to define which situations are covered, depending upon their own social and cultural values. Article 27.2 itself indicates that the concept is not limited to "security" reasons; it also relates to the protection of "human, animal or plant life or health" and may be applied to inventions that may lead to "serious prejudice to the environment."

Non-patentability under article 27.2 would be permissible if necessary to prevent commercial exploitation. In other words, it may not be possible to declare the non-patentability of a certain subject matter while permitting at the same time its distribution or sale.[31]

---

[29] Developing countries proposed the following text: "Nothing in the TRIPS Agreement shall prevent Members from taking measures to protect public health. Accordingly, while reiterating our commitment to the TRIPS Agreement, we affirm that the Agreement shall be interpreted and implemented in a manner supportive of WTO Members' right to protect public health and, in particular, to ensure access to medicines for all. In this connection, we reaffirm the right of WTO Members to use, to the full, the provisions in the TRIPS Agreement which provide flexibility for this purpose." (JOB(O1)/155, Oct. 27, 2001).

[30] For instance, under the Guidelines for Examination of the European Patent Office "ordre public" is linked to security reasons, such as riot or public disorder, and inventions that may lead to criminal or other generally offensive behavior (Part C, chapter IV, 3.1). Traditionally, "ordre public" in United States law referred to an invention that was "frivolous or injurious to the well-being, good policy, or sound morals of a society." *See Lowell v. Lewis*, as quoted in Chisum & Jacobs, *Understanding Intellectual Property Law, Legal Text Series* 25 (Matthew Bender 1992). In the United States, "the trend is to restrict this subjective public policy approach to utility." *Id.*

[31] *See* Correa & Yusuf, *supra* n. 24, at 193. For a different opinion, *see* Dan Leskien & Micheal Flitner, *Intellectual Property Rights and Plant Genetic Resources: Options for a Sui Generis System* (IPGRI Issues in Genetic Resources No. 7, 1997).

3.1.2. Substances Existing in Nature

Some pharmaceutical products are based on, or consist of, biological materials. These include compounds extracted from plants and algae as well as human proteins obtained by extraction or through genetic engineering techniques (e.g., interferon, erythropoietin, growth hormone).[32] Plants, in particular, are an indispensable source of medicines.[33]

Whether biological materials are patentable depends in significant part on whether they are characterized as "inventions" (and therefore patentable) or "discoveries" (not patentable). Different patent law traditions treat this question differently.

The TRIPS Agreement requires the patentability of microorganisms and of nonbiological and microbiological processes for the production of plants and animals (article 27.3.b). However, national laws vary considerably in characterizing biological materials as inventions or discoveries. In some jurisdictions such as the United States, an isolated or purified form of a natural product, including genes, is patentable.[34] The European Directive on Biotechnological Inventions (No. 96/9/EC of March 11, 1996) adopts a similar approach.[35] The directive, essentially declaratory of long standing law throughout much of Europe, establishes that "biological material" and substances isolated from nature (such as new antibiotics) will be considered patentable.[36]

---

[32] For instance, a patent claim relating to a protein isolated from nature reads as follows: *Homogeneous erythropoietin characterized by a molecular weight of about 34,000 dalton on SDS PAGE, movement as a single peak on reverse phase high performance liquid chromatography and a specific activity of at least 160,000 IU per absorbance unit at 280 nanometers* (U.S. patent No. 4,677,195). This claim was deemed invalid by a U.S. court as overly broad and indefinite.

[33] John Lambert, Jitendra Srivastava & Noel Vietmeyer, *Medicinal Plants. Rescuing a Global Heritage* (World Bank Technical Paper No.355, 1997).

[34] S. Bent, R. Schwab, D. Conlin & D. Jeffrey, *Intellectual Property Rights in Biotechnology Worldwide* 123 (Stockton Press 1991); Philip Grubb, *Patents for Chemicals, Pharmaceuticals and Biotechnology: Fundamentals of Global Law, Practice and Strategy* 213 (Clarendon Press 1999). The extent of patentability of biological materials in the United States has not yet been addressed by the Supreme Court.

[35] Art. 3(2) reads as follows: "Biological material which is isolated from its natural environment or processed by means of a technical process may be the subject of an invention even if it already occurred in nature."

[36] *See* Grubb, *supra* n. 34; *see also* Giuseppe Sena, *Directive on Biotechnical Inventions:*

The TRIPS Agreement does not define what an "invention" is; it only specifies the requirements that an invention should meet in order to be patentable. This leaves member countries considerable freedom to determine what should be deemed an invention, and to exclude from patentability any substance which exists in nature.[37] In particular, DNA molecules may be regarded as building blocks of nature, which should be free for use by the scientific community and for any productive application.

3.1.3. New Uses of Known Products

Pharmaceutical patents rarely relate to new chemical entities, that is, active ingredients that represent a fresh contribution to the stock of products available for medicinal use. A great number of pharmaceutical patents protect processes of manufacture, formulations, systems of delivery, and new uses of a known product.[38]

A "use" claim may be either a *product* claim or a *process* claim, depending on the context. In Europe, *first medical indications* have been dealt with as product claims, whereas *second medical indications* have been considered as process claims.

A first indication issue arises when a new therapeutic use is found for a known product which had no previous pharmaceutical use. Because patents protect inventions but not discoveries, the discovery of a new purpose for a product cannot render a known product patentable under general principles of patent law.[39] Therefore, the patentability of the *product as such* would be rejected. Some countries, however, have adopted special rules for the protection of the *first indi-*

Patentability of Discoveries, 30 Intl. Rev. of Industrial Property and Copyright Law 736-738 (No. 7, 1999) who suggests the use of compulsory licenses to remedy the possible negative effects on subsequent research that may result from the extension of patentability to simply isolated materials.

37 The Agreement obliges Member States to protect "microorganisms" but nothing in the Agreement can be interpreted as requiring the patentability of microorganisms found in nature and not "invented," for instance, by alteration through genetic engineering.

38 *See* N. Zaveri, *Patents for Medicine: Balanced Patent Law –The Need of the Hour* 71 (Indian Drug Manufacturers' Assn. 1998).

39 Unless in connection with the new purpose the product is forced to be present in an amended new form. *See e.g.* Bernd Hansen & Fritjoff Hirsch, *Protecting Interventions in Chemistry: Commentary on Chemical Case Law under the European Patent Convention and the German Patent Law* 104 (Wiley-VCH 1997).

cation of a known product, expanding the scope of protection beyond its ordinary boundaries.[40]

Under the TRIPS Agreement, countries are free to expand patent protection beyond the general principles of patent law, but they are under no obligation to do so. WTO member countries are thus free to decide whether or not to allow the patentability of products for *first indication*.

In other cases, a new use is discovered for a product that already has pharmaceutical use.[41] Many national laws treat the new use as *process* patent claims of one of two kinds: "use" claims (such as "the use of X as an antihistaminic") or claims on one or more actual process steps (e.g. "a method of preventing …").[42] The patenting of use inventions depends on whether the purpose of the use is novel and non-obvious. Method inventions may be judged independently of the purpose. Even if intended for a novel purpose, the key consideration in determining the patentability of a method invention is whether it could be anticipated by other methods.[43]

Patent applications on the second medical indication of a known product are usually written as instructions to the physician on how to employ a certain composition to treat a particular disease. Such applications are accepted in some countries. The European Patent Office began granting such applications in 1984, when they were framed under the "Swiss formula."[44]

---

[40] In Europe, for example, a legal fiction allows the patentability of a known product for such an indication. Under article 54(5) of the European Patent Convention, the identification of the first medical indication of a known product may suffice to get a patent on the product. *See e.g.*, Werner Stieger, *Article 54(5) of the Munich Patent Convention: An Exception for Pharmaceuticals,* 13 Intl. Rev. of Industrial Property and Copyright Law (No. 2, 1982); Grubb, *supra* n. 34, at 218. The United States, by contrast, has adopted a more restrictive approach, confining patents on uses to a particular "method-of-use." Such method-of-use patents do not encompass protection of the product as such. *See e.g.* Robert P. Merges, *Patent Law and Policy: Cases and Materials* 489 (Contemporary Legal Educational Series 1992).

[41] This was the case, for instance, of nimodipine, a known cardiovascular agent for which an application to cerebral disorders was found.

[42] *See* Grubb, *supra* n. 34, at 208.

[43] *See* Hansen & Hirsch *supra* n. 39, at 120.

[44] "Use of X for the manufacture of a medicine to treat Y." *Id.* 339.

However, countries may deem an "invention" consisting of the second use of a substance non-patentable because it fails to satisfy various traditional patent requirements:

- it is a "discovery";
- it does not meet the requirement of industrial applicability;
- it is equivalent to a method of therapeutic treatment (when such methods are deemed non-patentable);[45] and
- the "Swiss formula" suffers from "the logical objection that it lacks novelty, since it claims the use of the compound for preparation of a medicament, and normally the medicament itself will be the same as that already used for the first pharmaceutical indication."[46]

As in the case of the first indication, nothing in the TRIPS Agreement obliges countries to introduce additional protection for the second indication. While the TRIPS Agreement obliges member states to protect *products* and *processes* (articles 27.1 and 28), it does not specifically refer to the protection of new uses, thus leaving member countries free to choose whether or not to protect them. In principle, a country that broadly excludes methods of medical treatment could also broadly exclude new therapeutic uses for old products.

3.1.4. Methods for Treatment and Diagnostics

Developing countries could consider the exclusion from patentability of diagnostic, therapeutic, and surgical methods for the treatment of humans or animals.[47] Most countries do not grant patents on such methods due to ethical reasons or to difficulties with actually enforcing those patents. In addition, a method that is applied to the human body is not considered industrially applicable and, hence, does not comply with one of the key patentability requirements of most patent laws. However, in the United States, patent practice increasingly favors the patenting of

---

45 *See* the following subsection.

46 *See* Grubb, *supra* n. 34, at 221.

47 For instance, U.S. patent No. 4,188,395 claimed "a method combating circulatory diseases in warm blooded animals in need of such treatment orally or parenterally which comprises administering to the animals an amount effective for combating circulatory diseases relating to heart action and blood pressure an active compound according to claim 1 either alone or in admixture with a diluent or in the form of a medicament."

medical methods if they satisfy the definition of process and the other conditions of eligibility.[48]

Article 27.3(a) of the TRIPS Agreement explicitly allows members not to grant patents for methods for therapeutic and surgical treatment and for diagnostics.[49] Even in the absence of specific provisions excluding the patentability of the referred methods, they may be deemed ineligible for protection due to the lack of industrial applicability, one of the essential requirements for patentability.

If the patentability of such methods are, however, admitted by national laws, its implications for the supply of health services should be assessed. Diagnostic, therapeutic, and surgical patents, even if rarely granted, may negatively affect low-income patients' access to required treatments, particularly in new areas such as gene therapy.[50]

In any case, the non-patentabilty of methods would not affect the patentability of equipments and substances necessary to execute them.[51]

3.1.5. Traditional Medicines

Traditional medicine – medicine based on the use of natural products and the knowledge held in indigenous and local communities – is of great importance in the health-care systems of many developing countries. It has been estimated that around 7,500 plant species are utilized in indigenous medicine, many of which (such as indigo) have multiple uses.[52] There are two major obstacles to affording patent protection to traditional medicine. First, the novelty requirement will generally impede the patentability of such products. Second, policy choices made to increase

---

[48] A bill enacted in 1996 (amending U.S. patent law, 35 U.S.C. 287.c) determined, however, that the use of patented surgical procedures is protected from infringement suits. *See* Grubb, *supra* n. 34, at 220.

[49] Including when they apply to animals.

[50] Though the gene therapy methods may not be patentable as such (if the suggested exclusion is provided for) the vectors and constructs that may be used could be patentable, as well as *ex vivo* process steps not involving the administration of the transformed cells to the patient (Grubb *supra* n. 34, at 244).

[51] In cases where the protection of such equipments and/or substances could lead to a *de facto* monopolization of the non-patented method, governments may have recourse to compulsory licenses.

[52] *See* Darshan Shankar, *Tribal and Rural Farmer-Conservers* 170 (Agrobiodiversity and Farmers' Rights No. 14, Swaminathan Research Foundation 1996).

access to medicines – including a limitative approach towards the patentability of naturally occurring products and uses of existing products, as well as strict patentability requirements – may lead to the exclusion of protection for most traditional medicinal products.

Moreover, national patent protection of traditional medicine will not address "biopiracy" concerns. Since the granting of patents is dependent on each *national* law, the non-patentability in one country does not mean that traditional knowledge could not be patented in another country without the authorization of the communities that developed or possessed that knowledge. In these cases it may be necessary to request the nullification of the patent, if wrongly granted, in the foreign country.[53]

Many proposals have been made to protect traditional knowledge (including of medicinal use) through a *sui generis* regime. This is the case, for instance, of proposals relating to "tribal," "communal" or "community intellectual rights,"[54] and "traditional resource rights," among others.[55] The establishment of such a regime would not conflict with the TRIPS Agreement to the extent that the scope of intellectual property protection would be enlarged rather than restricted. Moreover, if a special regime were established, it would be outside the scope of the TRIPS Agreement, which only applies to the categories of intellectual property rights specified in its article 2.

Other approaches, outside of the intellectual property sphere, may also serve to promote the use of traditional knowledge for preventive and curative health care, or to block unauthorized appropriation by foreign countries. Act No. 8423 (1997) of the Philippines, for example, aims "to accelerate the development of traditional and alternative health care" by improving the manufacture, quality control, and marketing of traditional health care materials (Section 3.d).[56]

---

[53] One example of this was the action initiated by the government of India in relation to a patent on turmeric granted in the United States, which was finally revoked.

[54] *See* Tewolde Egziabher Berhan, *A Case of Community Rights*, in *The Movement of Collective Intellectual Rights* 38 (S. Tilahun & E. Sue eds., The Inst. For Sustainable Development/The Gaia Foundation 1996).

[55] *See* Darrell Posey & Graham Dutfield, *Beyond Intellectual Property: Toward Traditional Resource Rights for Indigenous Peoples and Local Communities* (Intl. Development Research Centre 1996).

[56] There is no intention to discuss here the different suggestions for the protection of traditional knowledge, nor to propose the adoption of any of them. The purpose here is only to indicate the need to consider this issue at the national level.

3.2. Patentability Requirements

Under the TRIPS agreement, to qualify for a patent, an inventor must show that his or her invention is novel, manifests an "inventive step" (i.e., that the invention is non-obvious) and is industrially applicable (article 27.1).

The manner in which these criteria are defined and applied is a crucial determinant of the pool of knowledge that is subtracted from the public domain. This issue is acutely important for pharmaceuticals. The registration of a large number of patents on pharmaceutical compositions, therapeutic uses, polymorphs, processes, and/or forms of administration relating to an active ingredient often permits the owner company to create a high barrier against competition. If aggressively enforced through "strategic,"[57] or even "sham," litigation practices[58] as a tool to discourage competition by other companies, those (secondary) patents may unduly extend the market power conferred by the original patent.[59] Such abuses may be particularly severe in developing countries where there is a lack or limited tradition in controlling such practices under antitrust regulations.

It is hard to undo the granting of overly broad patents and secondary patents. Once a patent has been granted, it is presumed valid. Challenging parties bear the burden of proving that the patent was wrongly issued. Consumers, especially in developing countries, rarely have the resources to challenge overly broad patents, though they bear the cost in higher prices and decreased access to patented goods.

Strong inter-firm competition in the pharmaceutical industry has led to numerous challenges of pharmaceutical patents by affected competitors.[60] But smaller,

---

[57] *See* John Barton, *Adapting the Intellectual Property System to New Technologies*, 10 Intl. J. of Technology Management (No. 2/3, 1995).

[58] The doctrine on "sham" litigation applies when a lawsuit is baseless and there is an intent to use it as a tool for monopolization. Federal Trade Commission Staff, *Anticipating the 21st Century: Competition Policy in the New High-tech Global Marketplace* vol. 1 (1996).

[59] *See* the U.S. Supreme Court decision in *Walker Process Equipment Inc. v. Food Machinery & Chemical Corp.* 382 U.S. 172 (1965). and subsequent case law on antitrust liability when there is an attempt to enforce invalid patents. *See e.g.* Arun Chandra, *Antitrust liability for enforcing a fraudulent patent in the United States* in *Patent World* (Apr. 1999).

[60] For an analysis of the vast litigation involving pharmaceutical patents, *see e.g.* Trevor Cook, Catherine Doyle & David Jabbari, *Pharmaceuticals, Biotechnology & the Law* (1991); Harold Wegner, *Patent Law in Biotechnology, Chemicals & Pharmaceuticals* (Stockton, Chippenham 1994); Hansen & Hirsh *supra* n. 39; Grubb *supra* n. 34.

generic firms in developing countries often do not have the resources to undertake such costly litigation. Moreover, the wave of mergers and acquisitions that has taken place in the 1990s has dramatically reduced the number of major players and accentuated the oligopolistic structure of the industry. This trend increases the importance of administering the patent system to protect competitors and the public from restrictions derived from patents granted on the basis of insufficiently precise patentability criteria.

The flexibility or strictness in the application of the patentability criteria may vary across countries and over time. The correct interpretation and application of the patentability criteria are crucial for balancing public and private interests, and also to help avoid excesses that undermine the credibility of the patent system. As noted by the World Bank, "countries could set high standards for the inventive step, thereby preventing routine discoveries from being patented."[61]

3.2.1. Novelty

The patent system was conceived to reward the inventor for contributions to the pool of existing knowledge. The criteria used to define what is *new* are key determinants of the scope of possible limitations to the free access and use of technical knowledge and products in the public domain. The stricter the novelty and other requirements, the smaller the number of applications that will lead to a patent grant.

The test of novelty considers how much distance separates one claimed invention from prior art. It applies before the existence of inventive step is considered.

The novelty requirement in modern patent laws is generally based on an assessment of the prior art on a universal basis, that is, anywhere in the world. Generally, novelty is destroyed by previous written publication, prior use, or other form of public communication of the invention.

Within this framework, the legal definition and application of the novelty requirement significantly differ among countries. In some jurisdictions a flexible standard is applied, thus permitting the granting of a great number of patents. For instance, in the United States, disclosure that has taken place outside the United States is only destructive of novelty when made in a written form.[62]

---

[61] World Bank, *Global Economic Prospects and Developing Countries: Making Trade Work for the World's Poor* (World Bank 2002).

[62] This may permit the patenting in that country of knowledge, including of indigenous communities, used but not published in written form outside the United States. *See e.g.*

National legislation and practice differ on numerous other important questions:

- The United States, for instance, requires complete disclosure in a *single* publication to destroy novelty, despite the fact that a skilled person may have been able to derive the invention without effort from a combination of publications.
- In some cases, disclosure may not have been made *expressis verbis* in a prior writing, but may be implicit. If a "photographic" approach to novelty (i.e., only based on explicitly disclosed information) is applied, equivalence to an invention implicitly disclosed in the prior art may not be sufficient to deny patentability. The result, in these instances, can be the patenting of pieces of existing knowledge (prior art). This result can be avoided by following the European Patent Office's practice of considering implicit teachings to be disclosed and part of prior art.[63]
- Another aspect left to national legislation is to establish whether novelty would only be destroyed when the anticipation *enabled* the execution of the invention, or whether a mere disclosure of the prior art would be sufficient – for instance, where a compound was made and tested even if a clear description of its properties or a method of making it were not available.[64]

3.2.2. Inventive Step

Even if novel, an invention is not patentable if its technical teaching would or could have been discovered in due course by a person with average skills in the respective field. In United States practice, for example, courts applying the nonobviousness standard (the U.S. equivalent to inventive step) undertake a three-step factual inquiry, examining:

(1) the scope and content of the prior art to which the invention pertains;

(2) the differences between the prior art and the claims at issue;

(3) the level of ordinary skill in the pertinent art.

Carlos Correa, *Access to Plant Genetic Resources and Intellectual Property Rights* (Commission on Genetic Resources for Food and Agriculture, FAO Background Study Paper No. 8, 1999).

63 *See* Hansen & Hirsch *supra* n. 39, at 96.

64 This was the approach adopted by the U.K. Patent law of 1977. *See* Cook, Doyle & Jabbari *supra* n. 60, at 79.

Courts then make a final determination of non-obviousness by deciding whether a person of ordinary skill could bridge the differences between the prior art and the claims at issue given the relevant prior art.[65] Though sometimes difficult to apply, the inventive step or non-obviousness requirement is critical to prevent the granting of patents on trivial developments.

The inventive step is often evaluated by considering the "unexpected" or "surprising" effect of the claimed invention. U.S. courts, however, currently reject this approach and stress that patentable inventions may result from either painstaking research, slow trial and error, or serendipity.[66]

Many countries' case law holds that there is no inventive step whenever it would be obvious – for a person with average skills – to test new matter with a significant likelihood of success. In the United States, the existence of an inventive step in relation to chemical compounds has been judged by taking into account the structural similarity between the claimed and the prior art compounds, the prior art suggestion or motivation to make the new compound, and the obviousness of the method of making the claimed compound.[67]

As in the case of novelty, national laws may be more or less stringent in evaluating inventive step or "non-obviousness." Moreover, in any domestic legal system, courts may elevate or relax the inventive step standard at different intervals in response to either prevailing attitudes towards competition, the perception of a need to protect new technologies (such as computer programs and biotechnological inventions), or the availability (or lack thereof) of alternative forms of protection in unfair competition laws, utility model laws, or the like.

In establishing the existence of inventive step, it is generally necessary to consider not only the knowledge derived from a single prior document, but also the combined knowledge of existing literature, patent documents, and other prior art. However, current U.S. practice disfavors such an approach and holds that "the subject matter of a claim is not rendered obvious by prior art unless there is some specific suggestion or teaching in the prior art that points the way to it."[68]

---

[65] *See* Jay Dratler, *Intellectual Property Law, Commercial, Creative, and Industrial Property* sec. 2.03[3] (Law J. Press 1999).

[66] *Id.*

[67] However, in *In re Thomas F. Deuel et al, 51 F.3d 1552* (Fed. Cir. 1995), these criteria were relaxed. The patenting of gene sequences has been allowed despite the fact that the sequencing of genes has become a standard technique.

[68] *See* Dratler, *supra* n. 65.

In the chemical and pharmaceutical field, there is often a close structural relationship between a compound which is claimed as new and inventive, and known compounds, such as salts of acids, bases, isomers, and homologues. In these cases it may be often deemed *obvious to try* the new compound, thus leading to its non-patentability. The European Patent Office, for instance, has taken the view that the fact that certain advantages were predictable made it obvious to prepare a new compound.[69] By contrast, in the United States, the presence of a predictable advantage is not deemed sufficient to exclude patentability.[70]

The TRIPS Agreement is not specific with respect to the issue of inventive step. Article 27.1 establishes that patents shall be granted to protect inventions which "involve an inventive step" and in a footnote, it allows member countries to interpret "inventive step" as synonymous with "non-obvious."

There is no agreement to harmonize the standard of inventive step/non-obviousness in practice. This suggests that developing countries may be well advised to consult and coordinate on this issue, possibly through their regional organizations.

A possible option for developing countries is to define and apply strict criteria for inventive step, in order to avoid the granting of patents that may unduly block competition in health-related products and processes. Such strict criteria may prevent the protection of locally developed "minor" innovations. But these innovations may be covered by utility models (or other forms of *sui generis* protection for know-how to provide compensatory rewards without exclusive property rights), rather than by diluting the inventive step requirement.

3.2.3. Industrial Applicability

The third criterion for patentability relates to the industrial applicability of the invention. Patent law around the world aims to protect technical solutions to a given problem, not abstract knowledge. The application of this criterion to health-related inventions is particularly important *vis-a-vis* inventions consisting of *uses* of a product since uses of health-related inventions may be considered as methods of treatment of the human body, not industrially applicable, and therefore not patentable.

---

[69] Technical Board of Appeal, T 154/82, IPD 7031.

[70] *See* Grubb, *supra* n. 34, at 195-196.

Countries differ in their treatment of industrial applicability. Under U.S. law, certain developments that do not lead to an industrial product may be patented: an invention only needs to be operable and capable of satisfying some function of benefit to humanity ("useful").[71] This usefulness concept is broader than the "industrial applicability" concept required in Europe and other countries. The U.S. rule permits the patentability of purely experimental inventions that cannot be made or used in an industry, or that do not produce a technical effect,[72] as illustrated by the large number of patents granted in the United States on "methods of doing business."[73]

The application of the industrial applicability requirement is often complex in the chemical, pharmaceutical, and biotechnology industries, where there are particular problems relating to the acceptable degree of speculative information. Thus, in the United States mere speculation about chemical homologues would be insufficient, while *in vitro* testing in animal tumor models of products intended for human use may be deemed sufficient.[74]

The TRIPS Agreement does not define the concept of industrial applicability and, therefore, leaves countries with considerable flexibility on this matter.[75]

Developing countries, particularly those implementing for the first time the patenting of product pharmaceutical inventions, should carefully craft their policy in these areas to ensure that patents are granted to real contributions to the prior art and to avoid granting trivial patents that impede competition. Poor drafting or administration of patent laws may also permit abusive practices that illegitimately extend patent protection beyond the 20-year term.

There are various ways in which barriers are frequently raised around products in the public realm, or patents on the point of expiring, with the aim of preventing legitimate competition. One of them is the patenting of polymorphs, described above. Other means employed artificially to delay the marketing of competing products include patenting of:

---

71 *See* Chisum & Jacobs, *supra* n. 30, 2-50.

72 *See* David Bainbridge, *Intellectual Property* 270-72 (Pitman 1992).

73 *See The Growing Flood of 'Wall Street' Patents*, in Patnews (Internet Patent News Services) (Sep. 29, 1999).

74 *See* Dratler *supra* n. 65, sec. 2.03[2].

75 It allows a member country to consider that "capable of industrial application" is synonymous to "useful." *See TRIPS Agreement, supra* n. 1, art. 27.1.

a) *Pharmaceutical forms:* these are particular ways of administering an active ingredient, which may be unpatented, in combination with certain additives;[76]

b) *"Selective" inventions*: these occur when a single element or group of elements of an already known large group are selected in order to take out a patent based, for example, on a feature that was not specifically described in an earlier patent for the larger group;

c) *"Analogy" processes*: this relates to processes that are not in themselves innovative, but which allow a product with innovative features to be obtained;

d) *Combinations of known products*;

e) *Optical isomers*: this takes advantage of the property of many chemical compounds to present two mirror forms, frequently after the mixture of both forms has been patented ("racemic" mixture) an application is made for a patent for the most active isomer;

f) *Active metabolites*: this involves patenting the active metabolite of a particular compound that produces the desired effect in the body;[77]

g) *Parent substances*: these are compounds which, although themselves inactive, produce a therapeutically active ingredient "parent substance" when metabolized in the body;

h) *New salts of known substances*;

i) *Variants of known manufacturing processes*;

---

[76] The practical consequences of this type of patent may be significant. For example, in Thailand – where there are serious problems of HIV infection – there is no current patent for didanosine ("ddl") as such. Nevertheless, the firm Bristol Myers Squibb (which did not discover the product, but purchased it under license from a federal United States laboratory) patented a formulation of "ddl" thereby blocking the Thai Government's attempts to purchase the drug at a price that was more affordable to its population. The Thai Government is currently examining the possibility of granting a mandatory license or of applying for the patent to be declared void.

[77] For example, after terfenadine had been on sale for several years, a patent was obtained for the relevant active metabolite. The courts decided that it was an unacceptable attempt to extend the original patent. *See* Grubb, *supra* n. 34, at 212.

j) *New uses for known products.*[78]

In sum, the TRIPS Agreement permits WTO members to define their policies on the scope of patentability in pharmaceuticals, and they should do so with an aim to rewarding genuine inventiveness and preventing the use of patents as a mere commercial tool to exclude legitimate competition, which is vital to increase access to medicines.

3.3. Exceptions to Exclusive Rights

All national patent laws contain exceptions to the exclusive rights granted by a patent, with the content and scope of those exceptions varying widely. Some exceptions are particularly relevant for the health area.

All of the exceptions considered below are recognized in some fashion in many developed countries. Outright exceptions to the exclusive rights of a patent (which operate without the need of a specific authorization by a court or administrator, and in favor of any third party) may be extremely important in fostering innovation, promoting the diffusion of technologies, or facilitating access at the lowest possible prices to health-related goods.

Article 30 of the TRIPS Agreement treats the exceptions issue only in general terms and leaves WTO member states with considerable freedom to define the nature and extent of exceptions to the exclusive rights of patent owners.[79] Comparative law reveals different types of exceptions that may be provided for within the scope of article 30. However, national practice is not a blank check, and any particular exception may be challenged before WTO tribunals.

Conversely, the boundaries of article 30 may be affected by new state practice, which may result from the wholesale adoption of certain practices by many developing countries or their regional organizations. Such a strategy would not save any given practice that constituted a clear violation of the TRIPS Agreement, but it might produce a differential approach in any judicial review where the violation was not clear.

---

[78] An example of a patent for the *use* of a known drug is AZT (Retrovir), which was synthesized in 1964 by the Michigan Cancer Foundation as a possible anti-cancer drug. Another more recent example is sildenafil ("Viagra").

[79] Exceptions to exclusive patent rights must meet three conditions: they should be limited, not unreasonably conflict with the normal exploitation of the patent, and not unreasonably prejudice the legitimate interests of the patent owner. These conditions are to be applied taking into account the legitimate interests of third parties.

3.3.1. Experimental Use

A basic objective of the patent law is to promote innovation. Overly broad patent rights may harm innovation, however.[80] One mechanism to address this problem is through a patent exception relating to research and experimentation, permitting use of the invention without compensation to the owner for such purposes. An experimental use exception may foster technological progress based on "inventing around" or improving a protected invention, as well as permit evaluation of an invention in order to request a license, or for other legitimate purposes, such as to test whether the patent is valid.[81]

While the experimentation exception is rather narrow in the United States,[82] many countries (notably in Europe) explicitly authorize experimentation on an invention without the consent of the patent owner, for scientific as well as commercial purposes.[83]

An experimental use exception, including one for certain commercial purposes, seems to fall clearly within the category of admitted exceptions under article 30 of the TRIPS Agreement. However, actual application of such an exception that leads to rival products not significantly different from the patented product may be deemed an infringement under the "doctrine of equivalents" in some countries' national case law.

A provision on this matter may be drafted in more or less broad terms, depending on the general policy adopted and on the expected implications of such exception on foreign investment, transfers of advanced technology, and local research and development.

---

[80] *See* Roberto Mazzoleni & Richard Nelson, *The Benefits and Costs of Strong Patent Protection: A Contribution to the Current Debate*, 27 Research Policy (1998).

[81] *See* Rebecca Eisenberg, *Patents and the Progress of Science: Exclusive Rights and Experimental Use*, 56 U. of Chicago L. Rev.1017 (1989); David Gilat, *Experimental Use and Patents* (IIC Studies Vol. 16, VCH 1995).

[82] *See* Wegner, *supra* n. 60, at 267

[83] *See* W. Cornish, *Experimental Use of Patented Inventions in European Community States*, 29 IIC 736 (No. 7, 1998).

3.3.2. Early Working[84]

Another exception specifically applicable to pharmaceutical patents[85] relates to using an invention without the patentee's authorization for the purpose of obtaining approval of a generic product before the patent expiration date. This procedure may permit the marketing of a generic version promptly after the patent expires. Since generic competition generally lowers prices,[86] this exception – known in the United States as the "Bolar" exception[87] – promotes the affordability of off-patent medicines.

The availability of generics either under a brand name ("branded generics") or a generic name ("commodity generics") would lead to increased competition in the pharmaceutical market, and to correspondingly lower prices for consumers and improved affordability of drugs.[88]

The "Bolar" (early working) exception was first introduced in the United States by the U.S. Drug Price Competition and Patent Term Restoration Act (1984), and has been explicitly adopted by Canada, Australia, Israel, Argentina, and Thailand. In many European countries it has been recognized by case law based on the experimental use exception.

The Supreme Court of Japan has also ruled (on April 16, 1999) on the validity of experiments made before the date of expiration of the patent for the purpose of an authorization petition for selling after such date. The Court argued that "it is one of the basic principles of the patent system to allow anyone to exploit freely a new technology after the expiry of the patent term, thereby generating a benefit to society." Given the need to undertake clinical trials in order to obtain approval for commercialization of a generic product, the court found that manufacturing the

---

84 This concept should not be confused with "working requirement," that is, the obligation imposed on the patent owner to "work" the invention, within certain periods from filing or grant.

85 It may also apply to agrochemical products and other products the commercialization of which is subject to prior administrative approval.

86 *See* WHO, *The World Drug Situation* 31 (World Health Organization 1988).

87 It is named "Bolar" after a case judged by U.S. courts in *Roche Products Inc. v. Bolar Pharmaceutical Co.* (733 F. 2d. 858, Fed. Cir., cert. denied 469 US 856, 1984). *See also* B. Coggio & F. Cerrito, *Immunity for Drug Approval Process,* New York L. J. (Mar. 9, 1998).

88 *See* WHO, *supra* n. 86, at 31.

patented product for that purpose was not an infringement of the patent, since otherwise "third parties would not be in a position to exploit freely the patented invention for a certain period of time even after the patent had expired. This, in turn, would contradict the basic principles of the patent system."[89]

Some countries, such as the United States and Israel, have adopted the "early working" exception while simultaneously extending pharmaceutical patent terms, but other laws need not include this linkage.

Given that commercialization of the generic product does not take place until after the expiration of the patent, the early working exception can be regarded as fully compatible with article 30 of the TRIPS Agreement.

In the case of Canada, the law established a "Bolar"-type exception that not only allowed tests with the invention, but also production and stockpiling of the product for release immediately after the expiration of the patent (Section 55(2)(2) of the Patent Act 1993). The European Union requested a panel against Canada under the WTO dispute settlement mechanism in connection with this exception. The panel decision confirmed that an early working exception is *consistent* with the TRIPS Agreement, even in the absence of an extended period of protection for the patent. However, the panel considered that the right to manufacture and stockpile before the expiration of the patent was not consistent with said Agreement (*see* WT/DS114/R, March 17, 2000).

The World Health Organization and the Joint United Nations Programme on HIV/AIDs (UNAIDS) have supported the establishment of an "early working" exception in national laws "for the rapid production of generic products in order to promote competition and contain drug expenditure."[90]

The "early working" exception, as noted above, may in some cases be considered as part of the experimental use exception. However, given the importance of this issue, and the uncertainty surrounding judicial interpretation, it seems advisable to include a specific provision on the matter.

---

[89] *Ono Pharmaceuticals Co. Ltd. v. Kyoto Pharmaceutical Co. Ltd.,* Case No. Heisei 10 (Ju) 153, 1998.

[90] WHO, *Trade and Public Health: Statement of the World Health Organization (WHO) at the Third WTO Ministerial Conference* 2 (Seattle, Nov. 30 – Dec. 3,1999) (WHO 1999); UNAIDS, *Statements of UNAIDS at the Third WTO Ministerial Conference* 2 (Seattle, Nov. 30 – Dec. 3,1999) (UNAIDS 1999).

3.3.3. Parallel Imports

Parallel imports involve the import and resale in a country, without the consent of the patent holder, of a patented product which was put on the market of the exporting country by the title holder or in another legitimate manner. For example, a company may buy a patented machine sold in Germany and then resell it in Canada – where the same patent is in force – without the patent holder's permission.

The underlying concept for allowing parallel imports is that since the inventor has been rewarded through the first sale or distribution of the product, he or she has no right to control the use or resale of goods put on the market with his/her consent or in otherwise authorized form. In other words, the inventor's rights have been "exhausted."[91]

Parallel imports, where allowed, cover legitimate products, not counterfeited products.[92] In some instances, however, parallel imports have been admitted (on a regional scale) even when originating in a country where the product was not protected.[93]

In economic terms, the acceptance of parallel imports may prevent market segmentation and price discrimination by title-holders on a regional or international scale. In other words, parallel imports allow consumers effectively to shop on the world market for the lowest price for a patented good.[94] Parallel imports may be of

---

[91] The doctrine of "exhaustion of rights" may be applied at the national level (rights are deemed exhausted domestically and the commercialization in foreign countries is not deemed to have exhausted the patentee's rights), at the regional level, as in the case of the European Community (exhaustion is deemed to have occurred if commercialization took place in a country member of a regional agreement), or at the international level. The presentation made in the text refers to this latter case.

[92] Abundant literature and considerable case law (particularly in the European Community) exists on the doctrine of exhaustion and parallel imports. *See* Frederick Abbott, *First Report (Final) to the Committee on International Trade of the International Law Association on the Subject of Parallel Importation,* 1 J. of Intl. Economic Law 497 (No. 4, 1998).

[93] *See* the decisions of the European Court of Justice in *In re Merck v. Stephar*, *Merck v. Primecrown*, and *Beecham v. Europharm,* European Court of Justice, Dec. 5, 1996, joined cases C-267/95 and C-268/95.

[94] In some countries, laws have established regulations providing for exclusive licensing agreements for the importation and distribution of goods. These kinds of regulations restrict competition and may practically impede parallel importation.

particular importance in the health sector, since the pharmaceutical industry generally sets prices differently throughout the world for the same medicines. Importation of a patented medicine from a country where it is sold at a lower price will enable more patients in the importing country to gain access to the product, without preventing the patent owner from receiving the remuneration for the patented invention in the country where the product was first sold.

On the negative side, states must evaluate the argument that there is an economic risk that the doctrine of exhaustion may discourage price discrimination favoring the developing countries. It has been argued that were parallel imports to be admitted generally, companies would tend to charge a single price worldwide, leading to an increase in the (supposedly lower) price that may otherwise be charged in low-income countries.[95] The pharmaceutical industry is reportedly concerned with the possible leaks across markets that could reduce its profit margins and thereby its ability to recoup R&D investments. There are further questions concerning parallel importing from markets where pharmaceutical prices are regulated. For these and other reasons, states need carefully to monitor the actual implementation of their exhaustion policy.

Parallel imports have been admitted in many developed and developing countries, on a regional or international scale, for all or some areas of IPR. For instance, in the European Union (EU) the European Court of Justice has applied the doctrine of *regional* exhaustion of rights to the entire EU and to different types of IPR, in order to prevent market segmentation.[96] Once a patented product has been sold in an EU country, it can be resold in any other member country without infringing on the IPR holder's rights.

---

[95] However, prices levels are generally established in different countries according to the consumers' ability to pay. Hence, the setting of a single world price may not be economically viable.

[96] In the case of the United Kingdom, however, the principle of international exhaustion has been admitted in some cases. *See* Stephen Whybrow, *The Limits of Parallel Imports in Europe*, (Managing Intellectual Property, Sept. 1997); *see also* Anna Carboni, *Zino Davidoff S.A. v. A &G Imports Limited: A Way Around Silhouette?*, European Intellectual Property Review (No. 10, 1999) on the "Davidoff" case. The European Court of Justice has accepted parallel imports even in cases where the product was not protected by a patent in the exporting country. *See Joint Cases C-267/95 and C-268/95, Merck & Co. v. Primecrown Ltd. and others*, 1 CMLR (Dec. 5, 1996).

Some countries recognize the international exhaustion of patent rights (and thus permit parallel imports) in case law,[97] while others expressly establish exhaustion principles in national patent law. The Andean Group "Common Regime on Industrial Property," as contained in Decision 344 of 1993, states that the patent owner cannot exercise exclusive rights in the case of "importation of the patented product that has been marketed in any country with the consent of the owner, a licensee or any other authorized person" (article 34. d).[98]

In the case of South Africa, the Medicines' Act has authorized the minister to prescribe "conditions for the supply of more affordable medicines in certain circumstances so as to protect the health of the public." The minister, "in particular may ... determine that the rights with regard to any medicine under a patent granted in the Republic shall not extend to acts in respect of such medicine which has been put onto the market by the owner of the medicine, or with his or her consent."[99]

---

[97] In Japan, for instance, the High Court of Tokyo held in *Jap Auto Products Kabushiki Kaisha & Anor v. BBS Kraftfahrzeug Technik A.G* (1994) that the parallel imports of auto parts purchased in Germany did not violate patents granted to BBS in Japan. In the Aluminum Wheels case, the Japanese Supreme Court affirmed, in July 1997, that Art. 4bis of the Paris Convention ("Independence of patents for the same invention in different countries") did not apply and that the issue of parallel imports was a matter of national policy of each country. For a (continued) review on current state practices in this area, *see* Abbott, *supra* n. 92, National Economic Research Associates (NERA), *Policy Relating to Generic Medicines in the OECD. Final Report for the European Commission* (Dec. 1998).

[98] Similarly, the Argentine Patent Law No. 24.481 (1995) provides that the rights conferred by a patent shall have no effect against: "any person who ... imports or in any way deals in the product patented or obtained by the patented process once the said product has been lawfully placed on the market in any country; placing on the market shall be considered lawful if it conforms to Section 4 of Part III of the TRIPS Agreement (art. 36.c)."

[99] South Africa, Medicines and Related Substances Control Amendment (Act no. 90, 1997) [hereinafter the Medicines' Act], art. 15c.a. As indicated by this text, the parallel import exception in South Africa is not general as in other countries mentioned above, but limited to medicines, and it is subject to the prior decision of the Ministry of Health. Despite these limitations, the South African law was challenged on this point by 42 pharmaceutical firms (which have, however, recently suspended their judicial action against the law) and it was included in the Special 301 "Watch list." However, USTR announced, on December 1, 1999, the removal of South Africa from that list. For more details on this case, *see* Bond, *supra* n. 6.

The TRIPS Agreement permits parallel imports. Parallel importing is one of the measures that member countries may take to protect public health under article 8.1 of the TRIPS Agreement. More specifically, article 6 of the TRIPS Agreement establishes that each member country has the freedom to incorporate the principle of international exhaustion of rights – the underlying justification for parallel imports – in its national legislation.[100] If done, parallel importing must be permitted for patented goods in all fields of technology, and not only for health-related inventions.

Because article 6 gives complete freedom on the matter to member countries,[101] parallel importing rules cannot be challenged at the World Trade Organization as a violation of the TRIPS Agreement, although the authority of a dispute settlement panel to adjudicate the indirect impact of exhaustion on other rights and obligations remains uncertain.

Although article 6 appears to give member countries very broad leeway to implement parallel importation policies, the doctrine of international exhaustion as applied to patents remains controversial with respect to both legal and economic aspects. Some influential authorities contend that overuse of the exhaustion doctrine would conflict with the exclusive right of importation conferred by article 28.1 (a) and with the thrust of Article 27, which forbids discrimination "as to … whether products are imported or locally produced." It has also been argued that an international exhaustion of rights conflicts with the principle of territoriality and independence of patent rights established by the Paris Convention.[102]

Other authorities counter that article 28 is subject to article 6 and therefore cannot be subject to dispute settlement procedures at the WTO.[103] Footnote 6 to

---

[100] According to an UNCTAD study, "Member countries also have the option (under art. 6 of the TRIPS Agreement) to adopt a worldwide exhaustion doctrine that could build upon the experience of economic integration schemes of industrialized countries." *See* UNCTAD, *The TRIPS Agreement and Developing Countries* 34 (1996). Similarly, a document published by the World Health Organization, after review by the WTO, includes among the possible TRIPS-compatible exceptions "parallel importation of the protected product." *See* Velasquez and Boulet, *supra* n. 23, at 33.

[101] *See Doha Declaration*, *supra* n. 7, at 5 (d).

[102] Tsuda, Yoshiaki & Sakuma, *Research on Parallel Trade of Patented Products,* Patents and Licensing 10 (1996).

[103] Marco Bronckers, *The Exhaustion of Patent Rights Under WTO Law*, 32(5) Journal of World Trade (1998); Verma, *Exhaustion of Intellectual Property Rights and Free Trade.*

TRIPS article 28.1(a) states that "this right [of importing], like all other rights conferred under this Agreement in respect to the use, sale, importation or other distribution of goods, is subject to the provisions of Article 6." The footnote to article 51 ("...there shall be no obligation to apply such procedures to imports of goods put on the market in another country by or with the consent of the right holder...") also supports this position.

General GATT principles also seem to support the permissibility of parallel imports. Under the GATT 1947, member countries must treat imported products in a manner not less favorable than the like products of national origin (article III.4), while members cannot impose restrictions "other than duties, taxes or other charges" (article XI(1)).[104]

Further, widespread resort to the doctrine of international exhaustion by developing countries could acquire some weight as state practice, helping to resolve any legal uncertainty in this area.

The World Health Organization has explicitly supported the use of parallel imports to advance the principle "of preferential pricing in poor countries." WHO has stated that "in cases where drug prices are higher in poor countries than in richer ones, recourse to parallel imports in low-income countries in order to reduce prices might be appropriate, while preventing parallel exports to industrialized countries."[105]

Finally, it is important to emphasize that the issue of parallel imports is completely distinct from the issue of counterfeit pharmaceutical products. Parallel imports, by definition, relate to products which have been legitimately put on the

---

Article 6 of the TRIPS Agreement, 29 Intl. Rev. of Industrial Property and Copyright Law (No. 5, 1998).

[104] An interpretation of these provisions is not only that parallel imports are legitimate, but that the GATT *requires* WTO members not to forbid such imports. *See* Verma, *id.* The possible application of art. XX.d of GATT (which allows for exceptions when necessary to secure compliance, inter alia, with "the protection of patents, trademarks and copyrights") needs also to be considered in this context.

[105] WHO, *Trade and Public Health. Statement of the World Health Organization at the Third WTO Ministerial Conference* 2 (Seattle, Nov. 30 – Dec. 3, 1999) (copy on file with the World Health Organization). It should be noted that the prevention of parallel trade is an issue that needs to be addressed by the importing and not the exporting country. Thus, the acceptance of parallel importation in a given developing country would not prevent any other country, including industrialized countries, from treating parallel imports differently, to the extent that such treatment is consistent with GATT.

market, not to imitations of original products. Parallel imports would be subject, in principle, to the same import and other regulations applicable to any imported medicine.

3.3.4. Individual Prescriptions

Patent laws commonly exclude from the effects of the patent rights, medicines prepared for an individual case in a pharmacy or by a medical professional.[106] This exclusion, though not specifically provided for, may be deemed permitted under article 30 of the TRIPS Agreement.

3.4. Compulsory Licensing

Compulsory licensing enables a government to license the right to use a patent to a company, government agency or other party without the title holder's consent. A compulsory license must be granted by a competent authority to a designated person, who should generally compensate the title-holder through payment of a remuneration. Compulsory licenses do not deny patent holders the right to act against non-licensed parties.

3.4.1. Grounds for Granting Compulsory Licenses

The provision of compulsory licenses is a crucial element in a health-sensitive patent law. Such licenses may constitute an important tool to promote competition and increase the affordability of drugs, while ensuring that the patent owner obtains compensation for the use of the invention. The use of such licenses, however, has been generally opposed by the research-based pharmaceutical industry,[107] on the grounds that they discourage investment and R&D.[108]

---

[106] From a public health perspective, however, the proliferation of individual prescriptions may be risky to the extent that there are no quality assurance mechanisms to protect the consumers.

[107] *See* Bond, *supra* n. 6.

[108] On the impact of compulsory licenses on R&D in the United States, *see* Scherer, Speech, *The Patent System and Innovation in Pharmaceuticals* (Toulouse, Jan. 28-30, 1999) (presented to Colloque de Toulouse: Brevets Pharmaceutiques, Innovations et Santé Publique).

Most countries, including developed countries, make available some forms of compulsory licenses.[109] Such licenses are one of the mechanisms that states can use in order to promote competition and access to drugs. While it is advisable that national laws provide for a compulsory licensing system (as further elaborated below), it should be borne in mind that such a system is not intended to, and cannot fix problems arising from the defective granting of patents, for instance, when the novelty or inventive steps were not actually met. Hence, it is of critical importance to ensure that the patentability criteria are rigorously defined and applied in the pre-grant process.

Compulsory licenses are generally available for lack or insufficiency of working,[110] to remedy anti-competitive practices, for cases of emergency, governmental or "crown" use, and for other public interest grounds. Most developed countries provide for use of compulsory licenses. Many developing countries that have recently revised their patent laws have also defined a more or less comprehensive list of reasons for the granting of such licenses.

The World Health Organization has recommended the use of compulsory licenses where there is "abuse of patent rights or a national emergency" in order to ensure that drug prices are consistent with local purchasing power. UNAIDS has also recommended the use of such licenses, as provided under the TRIPS Agreement, "such as in countries where HIV/AIDS constitutes a national emergency."[111]

---

[109] *See* Correa & Bergel, *Patentes y Competencia* (Rubinzal-Culzoni ed., 1996); Correa, *Intellectual Property Rights and the Use of Compulsory Licenses. Options for Developing Countries* (Working Paper No. 5, South Center 1999).

[110] "Working" of a patent was originally understood as the execution of the invention in the country of registration. *See* Edith Penrose, *La Economía Del Sistema Internacional de Patentes* 131 (Siglo Veintiuno Editores 1974). The current trend in some countries is to admit that working may take place through importation. Art. 27.1 of the TRIPS Agreement has been interpreted by some (notably the research-based pharmaceutical industry) as excluding the possibility of requiring the local execution of the invention. *See also* the Brazilian patent law (1996) which established such obligation unless not economically viable (art. 68.1).

[111] UNAIDS, Speech, *Statement of UNAIDS at the Third WTO Ministerial Conference* 2 (Nov. 30-Dec. 3, 1999) (copy on file with UNAIDS).

Despite the provisions for compulsory licenses in many national laws, relatively few compulsory licenses have actually been granted.[112] But commentators generally agree that the mere authority to grant compulsory licenses promotes some degree of competition in its own right, and that the impact of the compulsory licensing mechanism therefore cannot be measured on the basis of the number of licenses granted. Ladas has noted that: "The practical value of the existence of compulsory license provisions in the Patent Law is that the threat of it usually induces the grant of contractual licenses on reasonable terms, and thus the objective of actually working the invention is accomplished."[113]

The TRIPS Agreement specifically allows member states to grant compulsory licenses on grounds to be determined by each member country (article 31). The TRIPS Agreement specifies some grounds for the granting of compulsory licenses but does not restrict the possible grounds to those cited.[114] In contrast, the agreement is quite specific with respect to the conditions to be met should a compulsory license be granted. These conditions include: the requirement – in certain cases – that a license be voluntarily requested before it is granted on compulsory terms, non-exclusivity, and an adequate remuneration to the patent holder.

A health-sensitive patent law may specifically provide for several grounds for compulsory licenses, notably:

- *refusal to deal:* when the patent holder refuses to grant a voluntary license which was requested on reasonable commercial terms[115] and, for instance, the availability of a product is negatively affected or the development of a commercial activity jeopardized;

---

[112] The largest number of compulsory licenses has probably been granted in Canada, under the 1969 law amendment that authorized automatic licenses on pharmaceuticals, and in the Unites States under antitrust laws.

[113] S. Ladas, *Patents, Trademarks and Related Rights - National and International Protection* 427 (Harvard U. Press 1975). Beier has recently presented a similar view in a comprehensive study on the matter. Compulsory licenses "through their mere existence as well as through the apprehension of compulsory license proceedings are liable to increase the willingness of a patent owner to grant a voluntary license." Friedrich-Karl Beier, *Exclusive Rights, Statutory Licenses and Compulsory Licenses in Patent and Utility Model Law*, 30 Intl. Rev. of Industrial Property and Copyright Law (No. 3, 1999).

[114] *See Doha Declaration*, *supra* n. 7, para. 5 (b).

[115] This ground is contemplated, for instance, in the U.K. patent law (art. 48.3d) and in China's patent law (art. 51).

- *emergency:* such as when urgent public health needs exist as a result of a natural catastrophe, war or epidemics;[116]
- *anticompetitive practices*: for instance, to correct excessive prices and other abusive practices;
- *governmental use*:[117] such as to provide health care to the poor;
- *lack or insufficiency of working of an invention needed for health care or nutrition;*
- *public interest:* broadly defined to cover other situations where public interest is involved.

The TRIPS Agreement provides special rules for compulsory licenses granted to government agencies or contractors. Countries' national legislation may eliminate a patent owner's right to seek an injunction to bar the government or a government contractor from using its patent, allowing the patent owner only the right to seek compensation (article 31(h)). This is, in fact, the practice in the United States, where the government may use patents without a license, and the patent owner's sole remedy is to seek compensation under 28 USC 1498.[118]

Some public health-concerned organizations have urged countries to grant compulsory licenses for the "essential drugs" listed by the World Health Organization (WHO). Such a policy may be of limited importance, however. Although new important therapeutic developments (*e.g.* for AIDS) may be patented and on the essential drugs list, most of the drugs on the list are off patent. Moreover, high-priced drugs (such as those useful to treat AIDS) are currently excluded from the list – and these are the medicines for which compulsory licensing may be most valuable.

---

[116] The situation of some African countries in relation to AIDS may be deemed, for instance, a public health emergency.

[117] This type of licenses is grounded, in some jurisdictions, on the concept of the eminent domain vested in the state.

[118] U.S. Executive Order 12889 regarding the implementation of NAFTA sec. 6 formally waives the requirement in NAFTA 1709.10.b to seek advance authorization from the patent owner on "reasonable commercial terms and conditions," if use of a patent is by or for the government. The government or its contractors are required to notify patent owners of the use, if there are reasonable grounds to know an invention is covered by a valid patent, but the government can proceed with use directly without seeking a license.

A national law provision subjecting "essential drugs" (either as listed by WHO or otherwise defined by a national government) to compulsory licenses would not contradict the obligation to consider each application for a compulsory license on its individual merits (article 31 (a)). Such a provision would specify one of the grounds for granting such licenses, but they could remain subject to case-by-case evaluation. Compulsory licenses for essential drugs would not relate to a full "field of technology" but to a limited number of inventions which are of utmost importance for public health, and thus may be deemed as not violating the article 27.1 prohibition on discrimination among fields of technology. Moreover, article 8.2 specifically authorizes measures necessary to protect public health. Measures necessary to protect public health are also accorded an exception to GATT rules. Article XX(b) of GATT 1947 specifically permits members to adopt measures necessary to protect public health which violate their general obligations under the GATT.

The process by which compulsory licenses are granted will influence the space enjoyed by a WTO member to grant compulsory licenses for health-related products. Countries will be in the strongest position to issue compulsory licenses if they establish the existence of health emergencies through public hearings and undertake serious negotiations with industry before issuing compulsory licenses. Action by many developing countries, or by their regional groups, dealing with common emergencies could also reinforce the legitimacy of compulsory licenses. Such measures are *not* necessary, however.

Countries should examine the potential negative impact of compulsory licensing, as with other measures limiting patentees' rights. The consequences include the possibility of discouraging foreign investment, transfer of technology, and research, including research into local diseases. Although it has been argued that there may be some risk that compulsory licensing will lead to the marketing of inferior products (since they will be manufactured without the patentee's cooperation), the production and commercialization of medicines are in all countries subject to prior approval and state controls.

The conditions for the application of compulsory licenses are of particular importance. Too burdensome procedures may effectively discourage the use of the system and deprive compulsory licensing of its potential value as a pro-competitive tool. Particularly important implementation issues are considered below.

3.4.2. Imports/Exports

The TRIPS Agreement does not restrict the possibility that a compulsory license be executed by means of the importation of the patented product.[119] This may, in fact, be the only viable means to execute a compulsory license in cases where the size of the local market does not justify local manufacturing, or where there is a need to promptly address an emergency situation. In a post-TRIPS scenario, however, in which most countries in the world will grant patent protection for pharmaceuticals, it will become increasingly difficult for a compulsory licensee to get independent sources of supply for a patented pharmaceutical. The patent holder may (for instance, through contractual prohibitions to export imposed on his licensees and distributors) effectively block the possibility of obtaining such products through imports. This will, in practice, significantly diminish the effectiveness of compulsory licenses as a tool to facilitate access to drugs. Nevertheless, the market needed for satisfactory economies of scale would vary by drug, so that for some drugs compulsory licenses would be effective even in medium-sized companies.

The compulsory licensee may import from a compulsory licensee in another country. In this case, the imported product would have been legitimately commercialized in the exporting country. Such importation may be deemed as legal parallel importation, since the patent owner would have obtained remuneration in the exporting country and exhausted his/her rights there.[120] If this interpretation were upheld, there would be in fact no need to get a compulsory license to import.

A further question would be, however, whether a compulsory licensee would be authorized to export. The TRIPS Agreement stipulates that a compulsory license must be "predominantly" for the supply of the domestic market (article 31.f). Hence,

---

[119] The importation of the product was a key element in the Canadian compulsory system mentioned above, as revised in 1969. *See* Donald McFertridge, *Intellectual Property, Technology Diffusion, and Growth in the Canadian Economy*, in *Competition Policy and Intellectual Property Rights in the Knowledge-Based Economy* 83 (Robert Anderson & Nancy Gallini eds., U. Of Calgary Press 1998). If the compulsory licensee imported legitimate products (sold in a foreign country by the patent holder or with his consent), its acts could be covered under an exception for parallel imports.

[120] The admissibility of this interpretation may, however, be challenged in the WTO on the basis that a compulsory license does not imply the "consent" of the patent owner, as required in some jurisdictions in order to determine that one's rights have been exhausted.

exports are possible, though they should probably not constitute the main activity of the licensee with regard to the licensed product. The article 31.f limitation, however, may not apply when a compulsory license has been granted to remedy anti-competitive conduct (article 31.k). This exception corresponds to the practice followed in the United States in cases of compulsory licenses granted under anti-trust legislation.[121]

Whatever the approach taken, it is clear that successful compulsory licensing requires that adequate alternative sources of supply be secured, either through local manufacturing (which may be unfeasible for small countries) or importation.

3.4.3. Registration

The value of the compulsory licensing system may be undermined if a licensee faces obstacles to registering (gaining approval to market) the protected product. Such obstacles may originate from an expansive interpretation of article 39.3 of the TRIPS Agreement, as reportedly promoted in developing countries by the U.S. government.

Article 39.3 of the TRIPS Agreement obliges countries to protect confidential data[122] submitted for the registration of new chemical entities, only if their generation involved a "considerable effort." Article 39.3, however, does not create exclusive rights on such data. The only protection arguably conferred under the agreement is against "dishonest" commercial practices in the framework of unfair competition law.[123]

Some countries provide exclusive data protection, but these are not mandated by the TRIPS Agreement. In Europe, the first applicant may obtain exclusivity for the use of test data for six or ten years from the date of authorization,[124] while

---

[121] *U.S. v. Western Elec.. Co. Inc.*, Civ. No. 17-49, 1956 Trade Cases (CCH) 168, 246, Sx (E) (3) (D.N.J. 1956); *U.S. v. International Bus. March. Corp.*, Civ. No. 72-344, 1956 Trade Cases (CCH) 68, 245, SxI (q) (4) (S.D.N.Y. 1956); *U.S. v. Imperial Chem. Indus. Ltd.*, 100 F. Supp. 504 (S.D.N.Y. 1952) (Final judgment).

[122] These data generally consist of the results of tests made with a new product in order to prove its efficacy and lack of negative effects. They do not involve any inventive step, and are protected under the TRIPS Agreement in recognition of the investment made for their production, rather than on their value as "intellectual" assets.

[123] *See* Dessemontet, in Correa and Yusuf, *supra* n. 24, at 258.

[124] European Union Directive 65/65, as amended by Directive 87/21.

under NAFTA, a minimum five-year period of exclusivity is recognized.[125]

It is important to note that article 39.3 of the TRIPS Agreement does not apply to pharmaceutical products which are not new, and that it only obliges to protect test data relating to "chemical entities," thus apparently excluding polymorphs, compositions, delivery systems or uses, even if new. In addition, once data on a new drug have been submitted, national health authorities may approve subsequent applications of generic products on the basis of similarity,[126] since such authorities will not have to examine or rely on confidential information.[127]

Some developing countries have been under pressure to adopt standards of protection on confidential data beyond those required by the TRIPS Agreement. The adoption of such standards may lead to a restriction of legitimate generic competition for products which are already in the public domain, particularly if exclusive rights were recognized. This issue, therefore, requires careful examination in the context of a policy aimed at increasing access to medicines.

Compulsory licenses may legitimately be granted for the importation, as well as the manufacture, of a protected product. Importation will be crucial for developing countries with limited technological or financial capabilities to undertake manufacturing of the protected product and to address emergency or anticompetitive situations, in which rapid action is necessary.

The duration of a compulsory license is an important issue. If the term is too short, there may be no incentive for a third party to request or accept a license. General practice is for compulsory licenses to be granted for the remaining term of the patent. This is the solution proposed above, with an exception when justified by reasons of public interest.

Determination of the remuneration to be paid to the patent holder is a key issue. The respective royalty rates may be established on the basis of the rates generally applicable in the respective sector.[128] Another possible method may be to define a

---

[125] *North American Free Trade Agreement* art. 1711.6 (Jan. 1, 1994) <http://www.nafta-sec-alena.org/english/index.htm>.

[126] On the concept of "similarity" under European law, *see* the decision by the Court of Justice of the European Communities, Case 386/96 (Dec. 3, 1998).

[127] This reasoning has been applied by the Supreme Court of Canada in *Bayer Inc., The Attorney General of Canada and the Minister of Health, Apotex Inc. and Novopharm Ltd.* (May 19, 1999), to admit the registration of a "similar" product even *before* the expiration of the five years exclusivity period in force in that country.

[128] Argentine Patent Law, art. 43 (1995).

"reasonable" royalty as that which a third party would pay for a voluntary license. This method, introduced by U.S. law in 1922, has been extensively applied in U.S. case law relating to the infringement of patent rights.[129] In the case of compulsory licenses for U.S. governmental use, however, the remuneration may be based on what the owner has lost, not on what the licensee has gained.[130]

The practice in Canada (while a system of compulsory licenses was in force), was to require royalty rates of 4% of the sales price of the medicines under the license.[131] In India, the applicable policy guidelines normally limit royalty payments to a maximum of 4% of net sales, while royalties of up to 8% have also been reported.[132]

In order to determine compensation, authorities may require the patent holder to disclose product-specific R&D investments, revenues, and other relevant economic data, while ensuring adequate protection of any confidential commercial data. They may also take into account the domestic market share in the total world market for the licensed product in order to determine what proportion of actual R&D costs the country should fairly bear. In commercial practice, royalty rates usually range from 0.5% to 10% of the net sales of the licensed product, depending on the market volume and turnover of the specific product,[133] and on the stage of the technology in the life cycle, among other factors.[134]

It should be noted, finally, that the review of a decision granting a compulsory license may be made by an administrative or judicial body, and that the patentee's rights to such review may be limited – in accordance with the TRIPS Agreement – to the legal validity of the license and to the accorded remuneration.

---

[129] *See* Chisum & Jacobs, *supra* n. 30, para. 20(02)(2). In the area of copyright, the U.S. Court of Appeals for the District of Columbia has recently held that "reasonable" royalty rates under § 801(b) of the Copyright Act does not mean "market rates," but a rate determined according to statutory criteria. *See Recording Industry of America v. Library of Congress*, D.C. Cir. no. 98-1263 (1999).

[130] *Leesona Corp. v. Unites States*, 599 F.2d 958, 969 (1969).

[131] *See* McFertridge, *supra* n. 119, at 83

[132] *See* David Graber, *Foreign Countries Licensing Practices Cited in USTR's Annual Trade Barriers Report*, World Licensing Law Report/BNA No.4, 3 (1999).

[133] Peter Niess, *Technology Evaluation and Pricing*, Tech Monitor 16 -17 (1999).

[134] Kumar, Vinay & Bhat, *Estimating Payments for Technology. A Framework for SMEs* 21 (Tech. Monitor 1999).

4. Protection of Data

A component of any public health policy that needs to be carefully considered relates to some of the conditions for the registration of pharmaceutical products. Certainly, such products need to comply with adequate standards of efficacy and toxicity in order to be safe for consumers. As a condition to register new products, national authorities normally require the submission of data relating to efficacy and toxicity. The legal protection of such data, particularly in respect of the use thereof to treat subsequent applications for similar medicines, has raised different approaches and considerable controversy.

The issue of data protection is addressed by article 39.3 of the TRIPS Agreement, which leaves considerable room for member countries to implement the obligation to protect said data against unfair competition practices. The Agreement provides that "undisclosed information" is regulated under the discipline of unfair competition, as contained in article 10 bis of the Paris Convention. With this approach, the agreement clearly avoids the treatment of undisclosed information as a "property" and does not require to grant "exclusive" rights to the data possessor.

The subject matter of the protection under article 39.3 is test data, that is, the results of trials carried out by the originator company in order to prove the efficacy and safety of the product. This information is obtained by applying standard protocols on a certain chemical substance, and does not constitute a creative contribution. This is acknowledged by the TRIPS Agreement, which makes this kind of protection conditional upon the fact that there should have been a considerable effort to develop this information: the underlying concept is not the protection of creation but the protection of *investment*. Furthermore, the TRIPS Agreement requires this protection only in respect of *new chemical entities*. There is no need to provide it for a new dosage form or for new use of a known product.

The protection to be granted is against "unfair commercial use" of the relevant protected information. This means that a third party could be prevented from using the results of the test undertaken by another company as background for an independent submission for marketing approval if the respective data were acquired through dishonest commercial practices. Such a party could, obviously, independently develop the relevant data and information, or obtain them from other sources. However, the duplication of tests to reach results that are already known will certainly be highly questionable from a social cost-benefit point of view. Article 39.3 would also permit a national competent authority to rely on data in its possession to assess a second and further applications relating to the same drug, since this would not imply an "unfair commercial use."

In some jurisdictions, such as the United States and the European Union, additional ("TRIPS-plus") protection for data submitted for registration is granted. In the Untied States, the originator of the information is given a five-year exclusivity period for the use of this information.[135] In the European Union, this period is for 10 years. During the data exclusivity period, a subsequent applicant cannot rely on the information from the first registration, so it will not be able to register the same product unless it develops its own clinical test data.

However, this is not the concept of the TRIPS Agreement, which does not require the granting of exclusive rights. Under the standard adopted under the agreement, in order to approve subsequent applications, national authorities may rely, for instance, on the registration made in third countries which apply high sanitary standards,[136] or on data which are already available to them,[137] provided that the equivalence (or "similarity") of the products is demonstrated.

In sum, under the TRIPS Agreement, countries have options to decide how they wish to regulate the protection of undisclosed information submitted for the registration of pharmaceutical products. They can opt for TRIPS-plus protection by granting data exclusivity, or for strictly following the TRIPS standards. In making this choice, policymakers will have to weigh the protection of the interests of originator companies against the importance of creating an environment that fosters competition and increases access to drugs.

5. Conclusions

The changes that took place in the intellectual property framework, particularly after the adoption of the TRIPS Agreement, are likely to have significant socioeconomic implications, particularly in the area of public health. The TRIPS Agreement extended the IPR protection for pharmaceutical products and reinforced the rights available to title-holders in all WTO members. In addition, the standards of

---

[135] If the product is not new, but data are submitted on new clinical investigations, a three-year exclusivity period is granted.

[136] This is the approach followed by Argentine Law No. 24.766.

[137] The Federal Court of Appeal of Canada held that the national authority is able, under Canadian law and NAFTA rules, to rely on confidential information available to it. *See Bayer Inc., the Attorney General and the Minister of Health and Apotex Inc. and Novopharm Ltd.* (May 19, 1999).

patentability and examination practices applied by patent offices in some industrialized countries permit, in many cases, the protection of marginal developments that allow titleholders to block or delay genuine competition. If such practices are transposed to developing countries, the problems of access to affordable pharmaceuticals may be seriously aggravated.

The demands exerted by some industrialized countries to obtain IPR protection, particularly in pharmaceuticals, even beyond the standards established by the TRIPS Agreement, prompted developing countries to seek clarification on the extent of some of the obligations imposed and on the flexibilities allowed by the Agreement. This objective materialized in the Declaration on the TRIPS Agreement and Public Health adopted by the Fourth WTO Ministerial Conference.

There are many aspects which have not been regulated by the TRIPS Agreement, or which may be dealt with under national laws within the room for maneuver left by the Agreement. WTO countries may implement a variety of solutions with an aim to integrate public health concerns in national laws, including in relation to the protectable subject matter as well as to the extent of rights conferred in the area of patents and data submitted for registration. Developing countries should utilize such room for maneuver to the fullest possible extent in order to ensure the realization of public health objectives, especially in relation to access to drugs.

ASSESSING A BILL IN TERMS OF THE PUBLIC INTEREST: THE LEGISLATOR'S ROLE IN THE LAW-MAKING PROCESS

ANN SEIDMAN and ROBERT SEIDMAN*

Elected representatives in developing countries and economies in transition strive to exercise their constitutionally-assigned role to ensure for their people a better present and a brighter future. However, too often existing institutions (defined here as society's repetitive patterns of behaviors) defeat the best intentions of deputies to effectuate transformation. Rejecting the claim that law cannot significantly modify institutions, the authors offer an institutionalist legislative theory and methodology to guide deputies in assessing whether a bill will effectively help to resolve the social problem it purports to address. The theory requires deputies to follow a decision-making model that employs reason informed by experience. At its operational core, the authors' approach centers around four basic questions: What social problems does the bill address? What explains those behaviors? What provisions in the bill will cost effectively change those causes of problematic behaviors? How to monitor and evaluate the new law's implementation? Building on an understanding of why people behave as they do in the face of a rule of law, the article assists deputies in deciding what questions to ask to learn the relevant facts and logic that underpin a bill's substance – i.e., that justify its detailed provisions. The article concludes with a checklist of questions deputies should ask about every bill, and a logical framework to structure a deputy's decision-making.

---

* Ann Wilcox Seidman has held numerous academic positions in the United States and abroad (including visiting distinguished professor, the School of Law, University of Witwatersrand, South Africa, 1998; Fulbright professor, Economics Department, University of Beijing, Peoples Republic of China, 1988-89; professor of economics and head of department (1980-82), University of Zimbabwe, 1980-83; professor of economics and head of department, University of Zambia, Lusaka, Zambia, 1972-74; senior lecturer, University of Dar es Salaam, Tanzania, 1968-72; and lecturer, University of Ghana, Accra, Ghana, 1962-66). She is the author, co-author, editor or co-editor of 24 books and reports on the development process and economics, and is the author or co-author of over 80 articles and published papers. She has served as a consultant on

The World Bank Legal Review: Law and Justice for Development: 207-256.

Printed in the Netherlands.

Contents

---

numerous assignments, particularly in Africa and East Asia. Dr. Ann Seidman holds a doctorate in development economics from the University of Wisconsin, Madison, Wisconsin (1968), an M.S. degree (economics) from Columbia University, New York, New York (1953), and a B.A. degree from Smith College, Northampton, Massachusetts (1947).

Robert B. Seidman is professor of law and political science, emeritus, Boston University School of Law. Other academic appointments include: visiting distinguished professor of law, University of Witwatersrand, South Africa, 1998; Fulbright professor of law, Peking University, 1988-89; professor of law and political science, Boston University, 1972-92; visiting professor of law, University of Zimbabwe, 1980-83; professor of law, University of Zambia, Lusaka, Zambia, 1972-74; visiting professor, University College of Dar es Salaam, Tanzania, 1968-70; professor of law, University of Wisconsin, 1966-72; special visiting research professor of law, University of Ghana, 1965-66; senior lecturer in law, University of Laos, 1964-65; and senior lecturer in law, University of Ghana, 1962-64. He has authored or co-authored 12 books and over 70 articles and published papers. He is a frequent consultant and adviser, particularly in Africa and East Asia. Robert Seidman holds an LL.B degree from Columbia University Law School (1948) and a B.A. degree from Harvard University (1941).

(1) Interest (incentives)
(2) Ideology (domain assumptions)
3.3.2. Objective factors
(1) Rule
(2) Opportunity
(3) Capacity
(4) Communication
(5) Process
3.4. Analyzing a bill's detailed provisions
3.4.1. General criteria of an adequate bill
3.4.2. Preliminary questions
(1) The bill's scope
(2) History and comparative law and experience
3.4.3. Alternative potential solutions
3.4.4. Conformity-inducing measures
(1) Direct measures
(a) Punishments
(b) Civil damages or penalties
(c) Rewards
(d) Changing ideologies
(2) Indirect measures
3.4.5. Will the proposed solution "work"?
(1) Do the bill's detailed provisions address causes?
(2) Do the rules create a complete legislative system?
(3) Are there adequate criteria and procedures to guide rule-making?
3.4.6. What probable costs and benefits will the new law entail?
(1) What to include?
(2) Making qualitative estimates
3.4.7. Monitoring and feedback systems
3.5. Summing up: A checklist of questions to ask about a bill
3.5.1. Introductory questions
3.5.2. The difficulty the bill aims to help resolve, and how it fits into the larger picture
3.5.3. Explanations of the interrelated causes of the behaviors that comprise the difficulty addressed by the bill
3.5.4. What possible alternative legislative schemes logically might help alter or eliminate the causes of existing problematic behaviors?

4. Conclusion

1. Introduction[1]

Almost half a century ago, when we first went to teach in newly independent Ghana's first university, President Kwame Nkrumah proclaimed, "Seek ye first the political kingdom, and all else shall follow." Most of the new constitutions, in

---

[1] In writing this article, we have used the opportunity to pull together ideas that we have developed elsewhere, mainly in writing and conducting workshops related to legislative drafting, and to think through their implications for legislators' exercise of their constitutionally-designated legislative power. Without further attribution, we have drawn substantially on other articles and books that we have written or edited, in many cases paraphrasing text and copying footnotes. Books include: Ann Seidman & Robert Seidman *State and Law in the Development Process: Problem Solving, Law and Institutional Change in the Third World* (Macmillan 1994); Ann Seidman & Robert Seidman, *Legislative Drafting for Market Reform: Some Lessons from China* (Janice Payne & Robert Seidman eds., Macmillan 1997); Ann Seidman & Robert Seidman, *Making Development Work: Legislative Reform for Institutional Transformation and Good Governance* (Thomas Walde, ed., Kluwer Law Intl 1999); Ann Seidman, Robert Seidman & Nalin Abeysekere, *Legislative Drafting for Democratic Social Change: A Manual for Drafters* (Kluwer Law Intl. 2000) [hereinafter the *Manual*]; Robert B. Seidman, *The State, Law and Development* (St. Martin's Press 1978); Ann Seidman & Robert Seidman, *State and Law in the Development Process* (St. Martin's Press 1994).

Also without further attribution, we have drawn on the following articles: Ann Seidman & Robert Seidman, *A General Theory of Law and Development*, 10 Praxis 45 (1993); Ann Seidman, Robert Seidman & Michael McCord, *A Theory and Methodology for Investigating the Function of Law in Relation to Government Institutions: The Case of the Development Bank of South Africa*, in *Administrative Law Reform* (Hugh Corder ed., Juta & Co., Ltd. 1994); Ann Seidman & Robert Seidman, *The Present State of Legislative Theory and a Proposal for Remedying its Sad Condition*, 8 J. Leg. Research [Korea] 319 (1995); Ann Seidman, Robert Seidman & Neva Makgatla, *Big Bangs and Decision-Making: What Went Wrong?* 13 B.U. Intl. L.J. 435 (1995); Ann Seidman & Robert Seidman, *Drafting Legislation for Development: Lessons from a Chinese Project*, 44 Am. J. Intl. L. 1 (1996); Ann Seidman & Robert Seidman, *Building Post-Apartheid Rural Institutions: Transforming Rural Reconstruction and Development Policies into Law*, in *Rural Development in Post-Apartheid South Africa* (D. Wiener ed., Africa World Press 1996); Ann Seidman & Robert Seidman, *Beyond Contested Elections: The Processes of Bill Creation and the Fulfillment of Democracy's Promises in the Third World*, 34 Harv. J. on Leg. 1 (1997); Ann Seidman, Robert Seidman & Theodosio Uate, *Assessing Legislation to Serve the Public Interest: Experiences from Mozambique*, 20 Statute Law Review 1 (1999); Ann Seidman & Robert Seidman, *International Transfer of Knowledge about Law – Lessons from China and the Lao People's Democratic Republic*,

developing and transitional countries alike, bestowed on the deputies "the legislative power." In the political kingdom, the deputies stood tall.[2]

Those deputies enacted many new laws. Only rarely did those laws succeed in significantly improving the majority of their constituents' lives. At the millennium, four-fifths of the world's people, living on only a fifth of the world's total product,

---

in *Yearbook of Law and Legal Practice in East Asia* (A.J. de Roo and R. W. Jagtenberg eds., 1998).

Also without further attribution, we have drawn on papers we have delivered at various conferences on relevant issues, including*:* Ann Seidman & Robert Seidman, *Using Reason and Experience to Draft Country-Specific Laws* (Ho Chi Minh City, Vietnam, Aug. 30-31, 1997) (paper read in absentia at the Conference on Vietnamese Law); Ann Seidman & Robert Seidman, *The Human Right to Development* (Colombo, Sri Lanka, 1999) (presented at the UNDP/Asia Conference); Ann Seidman & Robert Seidman, *Law and Development* (Hong Kong, Jan. 7, 2000) (part of the City University of Hong Kong, Distinguished Lecturer Series); Ann Seidman & Robert Seidman, *Law and Rural Land Tenures in China* (Haikou, China, 2000) (presented at the Conference on Chinese Rural Land Tenures); Ann Seidman & Robert Seidman, Keynote Address, *Is Law and Development Consistent with Social Reality?* (Copenhagen, Denmark, 2000) (given at the Conference of Danish Researchers in Development); Ann Seidman & Robert Seidman, *Drafting Defensively against Corruption*, (Washington, D.C., 2000) (presented at the World Bank Lawyers Forum).

Many of the assertions made here come from our own experiences in working with drafters, both on drafting and more general law-and-development issues, in Belize, Bhutan, Cambodia, China, Ghana, Indonesia, Kazakhstan, Lao P.D.R., Mozambique, Nepal, Nigeria, South Africa, Sri Lanka, Tanzania, Vietnam, Zambia, and Zimbabwe.

For many favors above and beyond the call of duty, our gratitude to Sue Morrison, and, for helpful comments, to Professors Wendy Gordon and Cynthia Barr, and to John Duke, Adam Shapiro, Justin Zeefe, and Matthew Miller.

2 The term "deputy" is used in reference to elected representatives in a country's legislative branch of power, i.e., the parliament or congress. A country's elected representatives are called "deputies" to highlight their function as standing for the interest of the public at large when legislating to promote the country's wealth. As explained in more detail later, this paper focuses on the duties of deputies to keep in mind the public interest, specifically the social impact of new legislation, when adopting the latter. In this vein, it points to the deputies as "trustees" of society's common good in the interest of the public at large as opposed to them serving the more narrow interests of a few constituencies such as their party and/or the individuals or groups that helped finance their electoral campaigns.

still struggled to survive.[3] Despite the new laws, people often lack adequate food and shelter, education and health, deprivations that keep them from leading the kind of life they value.[4] Everywhere people complain, "we have good laws, but poor implementation."

This article attempts to shed light on why the new laws did little to improve the situation. To help overcome the causes of new governments' too frequently ineffective law-making processes, it offers a solution to address the legislative problems following institutional legislative theory's problem-solving methodology.

We first locate the problem of law-making and its core skill, assessing a bill, in the larger context of development and transition. To exercise their constitutionally-assigned legislative power, deputies must undertake three main tasks: to debate and enact laws; to oversee government's implementation of the laws it enacts; and to maintain two-way communication channels with their constituents. For all three tasks, deputies must have the capacity to assess whether, in their countries' unique circumstances, the bills on which they vote will likely achieve their stated objectives.

We put forward two hypotheses to explain why deputies in so many countries voted in favor of so many seemingly transformatory bills that defied effective implementation. First, institutionalized legislative procedures fostered their role as agents for party or narrow constituencies, rather than as trustees for the public interest. Second, the deputies had no legislative theory to guide them in assessing a bill's likely social impact. Instead they frequently enacted bills that merely stated broad principles, that copied law from someplace else, that simply criminalized unwanted behavior, or that merely compromised competing interest groups' interests.

When a deputy votes to approve a bill, the "aye" vote signals that the deputy approved the bill's policy, priority, design, and form, and its particular resolution of the power struggle between groups concerned with the bill's subject matter. Of these, we discuss here only problems in connection with assessing the bill's design – i.e., whether the legislative program it prescribes will likely resolve the social problem at which it aims *in the public interest*. We assign the term "the public

---

3 United Nations Development Programme, *Human Development Report* (Oxford U. Press 1998).

4 World Bank, *World Development Report 2000/2001: Attacking Poverty* 1-5 (Oxford U. Press 2001).

interest" a populist meaning: When implemented, will the new law likely advantage the majority of the population, and especially its most vulnerable members?

The second part of the article offers an institutionalist legislative theory to assist a deputy in using facts and logic to determine a law's likely social consequences. It emphasizes as the key question a deputy must ask: *Why do people behave as they do in the face of a rule of law?* Building on the answer to that question, it shows how institutionalist legislative theory empowers a deputy to analyze the causes of problematic behaviors that a law seeks to resolve; and to assess whether, by inducing new behaviors that tend to overcome those causes, logically the proposed law's detailed provisions will likely help resolve social problems in the public interest. On that basis, we conclude by showing how a deputy may use that theory to decide what questions to ask to assess a bill.

2. The Larger Problem

This article addresses the seemingly narrow social problem of most deputies' inability to assess a bill's design. That inability inevitably hinders a legislature from enacting legislation required to meet the challenges of social, political, and economic institutional transformation that lie at the heart of development and transition. This chapter defines the nature and role of the institutions and behaviors that hinder lawmakers from using the legal order to effectuate transformation of existing institutions in the public interest.

2.1. Of law, institutions, and behaviors

The seizure of state power by new populist governments (conservative parties seldom lead anti-colonial revolutions) created a paradox. At the outset, the new leaders had small choice but to rule through inherited authoritarian governmental, social, and economic structures that perpetuated cruel disparities in power and privilege. To achieve their populist goals, they had to transform those institutions to serve the people.[5]

---

[5] One example illustrates the difficulties. In 1980, immediately after the ZANU government took power in Zimbabwe, the minister of transport instructed his civil servants to produce a new road construction plan, giving priority to roads in the long-neglected black rural sector. The civil servants came up with not a single new road to a black rural community. When asked why, they explained that, under existing regulations, before

Society consists of its inhabitants' repetitive patterns of behaviors.[6] We define "institution" as a repetitive pattern of behavior.[7] A country's institutions define its

---

recommending a new road, they had to follow rules which required analysis of the specified expected use, consequences for economic development, etc. They said they tried every black community in Zimbabwe but, within those colonially created rules, for not one could they recommend a new road. Imagine, throughout the former colonial world, the multiplication of those kinds of detailed rules which – unless consciously reformulated – continued to shape civil servants' behaviors!

6 *Cf.* Harry M. Johnson, *Sociology: A Systematic Introduction* 639 (Harcourt, Brace 1960); Harry V. Ball, George Eaton Simpson & Kiyoshi Ikeda, *Law and Social Change: Sumner Reconsidered*, 67 Am. J. Soc. 532 (1967); Edward Rubin, *The Legal Process, the Synthesis of Discourse and the Micro-analysis of Institutions*, 105 Harv. L. Rev. 1399, 1425-29 (2001). For example, the perceived difficulty of dealing with polluted underground water results from the repetitive behaviors of defined sets of people, such as farmers whose agricultural fertilizers run off into underground water courses or industrial managers whose factories do the same with equally poisonous wastes.

7 George Casper Homans, *The Nature of Social Science* 50-51 (Harcourt, Brace & World 1967); *cf.* Norman Uphoff, *Local Institutional Development* 9 (Kumanian Press 1986). This definition is contested. *Cf.* Sven-Erik Sjostrand, *On Institutional Thought in the Social and Economic Sciences*, in *Institutional Change* 9-12 (Sven-Erik Sjostrand ed., 1993) ("Institution" means "a human mental construct for a coherent system of shared (enforced) norms that regulate individual interactions in recurrent situations;" "institutionalization" means "the process by which individuals subjectively approve, internalize and externalize such a mental construct."); Douglass C. North, *Institutional Change: A Framework for Analysis*, in *Institutional Change* 36, 37 (Sjostrand ed., 1993) ("Institution" consists of "formal rules, informal constraints (norms of behavior, conventions and self-imposed codes of conduct) and the enforcement characteristics of both.") ("Organizations" consist of "groups of individuals engaged in purposive activity. The constraints imposed by the institutional framework (together with other constraints) define the opportunity set and therefore the kind of organizations that will come into existence.") ("The agent of change is the entrepreneur, the decision-maker(s) in organizations."); Johnson, *supra* n. 6, at 22 ("social institution" means a "complex normative pattern that is widely accepted as binding in a particular society or part of society").

For analyzing the law-making enterprise, the behavioral definition seems more useful: Law always addresses behaviors – law can only transform institutions by changing behaviors. Problem-solving holds that the key question becomes, *why* do those behavioral patterns exist? A drafter ought to count as important not merely the clarity and elegance of a bill's words, but also their likely effectiveness in bringing about the prescribed behaviors, and those behaviors' effectiveness in resolving the social problem at which

society.[8] Differing *institutions* distinguish Albania from Azerbaijan, England from Ethiopia, Zimbabwe from Zambia: their schools, banks, farms, courts, families, churches, hospitals, business enterprises, government bureaucracies – an endless list. To transform an institution deliberately, lawmakers must change that institution's constitutive repetitive patterns of behavior.

---

the law aims. To serve a drafter's needs, the definition of "institutions" ought to reflect the requirement that a bill should not merely change the *rules*, but change *behaviors*.

These utilitarian considerations suggest two reasons for the definition of "institution" used here: (a) Because solutions build on causes (or explanations), to build into the definition of "institution" only one possible explanation for repetitive patterns of behavior (for example, that the normative pattern is "widely accepted as binding,") Johnson, *supra* n. 6 tends to limit the investigation of explanations for those repetitive patterns, and thus contracts the range of possible legislative initiatives to change them. (b) To confine the definition of "institution" to the *rules* that prescribe the behavior (as does North, *supra*) can lead to focusing on the rules as distinguished from the behavior they will likely induce in the given circumstances; that is, it neglects the American legal realists' observation that the law-in-action systematically differs from the law-in-the-books. *See* Roscoe Pound, *Law in Books and Law in Action*, 44 Am. L. Rev. 12 (1910). *See also* Karl Llewellyn, *Some Realism About Realism – Responding to Dean Pound*, 44 Harv. L. Rev. 1222 (1931). That ignores the potential use of law to change institutions and thus to foster development. (North himself may avoid this trap by subsuming under the word "organization" what we subsume under "institution").

8 Seidman & Seidman, *State and Law in the Development Process* , *supra* n. 1, at 145-176. *Cf.* writings in the New Institutional Economics School; *see e.g.* Joel P. Trachtman, *The Applicability of Law and Economics to Law and Development: The Case of Financial Law, Emerging Financial Markets and the Role of International Financial Organizations* 26 (Joseph J. Norton & Mads Andenas eds., 1996); Mustapha K. Nabli and Jeffrey B. Nugent, *The New Institutional Economics and its Applicability to Development*, 17 World Development 1333, 1335 (1989); Oliver E. Williamson, *The Institutions and Governance of Economic Development and Reform*, Proceedings of the World Bank Annual Conference on Development Economics 171 (1995); and North, *supra*, n. 7, at 44 ("Third world countries are poor because the institutional constraints define a set of pay-offs to political/economic activity that do not encourage productive activity.") *See also* Antoni Z. Kaminski and Piotr Stralkowski, *Strategies of Institutional Change in Central and Eastern European Economies* in *Institutional Change* 139 (Sjostrand ed., 1993); and James G. March and Johan P. Olsen, *Rediscovering Institutions: The Organizational Basis of Politics* 143-148 (1989).

To channel behaviors into desired patterns, lawmakers have little choice but to use law.[9] As one of its primordial functions, law constitutes government's tool of choice for channeling behaviors. That proposition constitutes the very cornerstone of this article.

Law serves many functions – dispute settlement, declaration of society's "fundamental" principles, symbol of government's good intentions, and seal of legitimacy. As one of those law-jobs, the law orders social behaviors.

> The law-jobs are in their bare bones fundamental, they are eternal. Perhaps they can all be summed up in a single formulation: such arrangement and adjustment of people's behavior that the society (or the group) remain a society (or a group) and gets enough energy unleashed and coordinated to keep on with its job as a society (or a group).[10]

This article focuses on that fundamental law-job.

Invariably, at some point in developing a governmental program, government translates its seriously intended, publicly avowed policies – including development policies – into laws.[11] Only by prescribing desired behaviors can the tiny handful of elected lawmakers govern. The detailed substantive provisions of the law and its structure and form thus have significant consequences for the subsequent effectiveness of government's proposed program. But for the relevant law, the problematic behaviors at which it aims might change, but not necessarily along the paths that government desires.

---

[9] We define law broadly to include constitutional provisions, laws enacted by legislators at the national, regional, and local levels; judicial decisions; and regulations (sometimes termed "subsidiary legislation" or "implementing decrees") and other rules introduced or enforced by government officials – that is rules promulgated or enforced by the state.

[10] Karl Llewellyn, *The Normative, the Legal and the Law Jobs: The Problems of Juristic Method*, 49 Yale L. J. 1355, 1373 (1940).

[11] Franz von Benda-Beckmann, *Scapegoat and Magic Charm: Law in Development Theory and Practice*, 28 J. Legal Pluralism and Unofficial L. 129 (1989) ("In all contemporary societies salient elements of state policy have to be formulated in terms of law ... The involvement of law in development planning and practice is no coincidence; neither is it a matter of conscious choice. Development ... implies change. In as much as government agencies engage in development planning and implementation, they aim at changing behavior. In other words, they try to exercise power ... [S]tate law is the primary source of legitimation for the exercise of power by or in the name of state agencies").

To some, that law constitutes government's tool of choice for changing behaviors seems an odd proposition. Some nay-sayers deny that law can change social behaviors and therefore society. Society, they say, creates law; how can law change its own creator?[12] Law, some claim, arises out of political decisions; study politics, not law.[13] Others hold that, so complex are the causes of behavior in the face of a law, lawmakers can never use law purposefully.[14] Following deconstructionist theories of literary criticism, still others maintain that since a text always wallows in ambiguity, a law's readers necessarily interpret it at will.[15]

To defeat the nay-sayers, it suffices to cite but one or two instances where law has changed behavior. But for the income tax law, who would pay the tax? But for an election law, who could vote? The chain of decisions that end in effective institutional transformations stretches long and convoluted. Someplace in that chain there always appears a rule or set of rules. The details of that set of rules – its *design* and its *form* – make a difference in the program's effectiveness. In that sense, law is a "but for" cause of change.

2.2. The institutions of law-making

In many developing and transitional countries, there were two reasons why existing law-making institutions tended to discourage deputies from using reason and experience to argue for or against a bill. First, political institutions imposed strong incentives for deputies to hew the party line. Political parties controlled the process of nominating legislators to run for election. Party leaders tended not to renominate a deputy who – for whatever reasons – opposed a government bill. In a parliamentary (as opposed to a presidential) system, a vote against a government bill may bring down the government and require a new election. By voting against

---

12 James G. March and John P. Olsen, *Rediscovering Institutions: The Organizational Basis of Politics* (Macmillan 1989); David V. Williams, *The Authoritarianism of African Legal Orders: A Review and Critique of Robert B. Seidman's 'The State, Law and Development,'* 5 Contemporary Crises 255 (1980); *cf.* Yash Ghai, *The Role of Law in the Transition of Societies: The African Experience,* 35 J. African L. 8 (1991).

13 John Griffiths, *Is Law Important?*, 54 N.Y.U. L. Rev. 339 (1976).

14 Robert L. Kidder, *Connecting Law and Society: An Introduction to Research and Theory* (Prentice Hall 1983).

15 Joseph Singer, *The Player and the Card: Nihilism in Legal Theory*, 94 Yale L. J. 1 (1984).

a government bill, deputies risked their own seats. Some scholars have generalized these institutional tendencies as the basis of public choice theory.[16]

Second, the law-drafting institutions seldom produced for deputies' consideration bills competent to facilitate institutional transformation. Everywhere, deputies mostly voted on bills drafted in the executive branch – usually, by government officials, either in ministries or by a central drafting office, sometimes by foreign consultants. The deputies themselves rarely designed bills.

For reasons that we have reviewed elsewhere,[17] the bills presented that came before the legislature almost always took one of four forms: They (a) declared "grand principles" without detailed instructions about who must (or must not) do what to implement them; (b) slavishly copied foreign laws, frequently under the label of " international best practice," (c) criminalized unwanted behaviors; or (d) compromised between competing interests.

Save serendipitously, none of these four methodologies could produce effective laws, particularly in respect of the kinds of complicated bills required to transform complex institutions. To ensure that a law proves effective requires grounding it on an analysis of the place- and time-specific *causes* of the problematic behaviors that comprise the *social problems* which it aims to help resolve. None of the four methodologies could produce bills with *detailed* time- and place-relevant instructions. Without detailed instructions to both citizens and implementing officials, transformatory laws remain "good" laws – and never mind their implementation.

As to the first, to write a law in support of a "vision" simply requires describing the opposite – a mirror image – of the social problem's surface appearance. To write, for example, a law's "vision" calling for abolishing corruption says only that the law aims to address the social problem of corruption; it says nothing about the detailed legislative provisions the legislature would have to adopt to alter or eliminate the many very different causes of corrupt behaviors. By definition, drafting in terms of broad principles cannot produce the detailed instructions to social actors that transformation requires.

The second form of law-drafting, copying law, works no better. To adopt a law copied from elsewhere, legislators need only approve the proposed new law's

---

16 *Cf.* Daniel A. Farber & Philip P. Frickey, *The Jurisprudence of Public Choice*, 65 Tex. L. Rev. 5 (April 1987).

17 *See Manual, supra* n. 1 (absent a legislative theory to guide their decision-making, drafters fall back on methodologies that require no theory).

subject, usually in terms of its title – "check law" or "patent law."[18] That done, they need only accept the false notion that a bill containing provisions prescribed in other countries will likely work in their own country's conditions.[19] However, save by coincidence, a law or a presumed "international standard" will induce in its new home the same behaviors as in its original one *only* if the relevant factors in its addressees' social and physical surround, including the new country's implementing agency, closely resemble those in its place of origin.[20] A deputy cannot assume that congruence.

The third bill-designing procedure, criminalizing behavior, also does not require the drafter nor the deputy to determine whether a bill fits local circumstances. To vote for a bill that criminalizes unwanted behaviors, the legislators need only to assume the universal validity of Bentham's notion that a person acts only in response to a personal "calculus of pleasure and pain." By imposing criminal penalties and changing that calculus, criminal punishments alter a person's incentive for behaving problematically. In most developing and transitional countries, factors other than their private interests influence people's problematic behaviors. These include, for example, their lack of opportunity or capacity to behave otherwise or their countries' institutions' decision-making processes (especially, of the bureaucracies, courts, and other implementing agencies), frequently little changed from

---

18 Appalled by Lao's inefficient payments system, an international aid institution insisted that country's government enact a Check Law. Banks or bank branches existed in only two Lao cities. It seemed most unlikely that a law concerning only the legal consequences of making a check (and not creating appropriate new institutions) could magically develop a whole new set of payment institutions.

19 During the colonial era, Great Britain imposed on its African colonies a copied version of England's Black Acts. These acts aimed at poachers in England who put burnt cork on their faces to avoid gleaming in the moonlight. As copied into Africa, they made it a felony to wander about at night with intent to commit a felony – with a black face.

20 This proposition underpins the "Law of Non-Transferability of Law." *See* Seidman, *The State, Law, and Development*, *supra* n. 1, at 34. That "law" does not proclaim that a country ought never copy law; that depends upon the *relevant* circumstances. For example, if a polity presently without an effective check payment system enacts a proposed check law mainly to serve foreign businessmen, it makes sense to enact one more or less familiar to them. Even there, a drafter must attend to local circumstances. To require a checkholder to sign a protest before a notary public – as did an early draft of a Lao check law copied from elsewhere – will likely not work very well if, as in the Lao PDR at the time, neither a notary public law nor notaries public exist.

their non-democratic pasts. In the context of a socially accepted stable environment, criminal penalties may induce a few deviants to conform. Those penalties seem singularly impotent to induce the widespread behavioral transformations required to achieve development and transition.

Finally, as with the other three ways of preparing bills, interest contestation as a set of instructions to bill drafters and deputies also ignores local realities. A bill's proponents simply leap from the description of a social problem to their prescribed solution. That solution offers no guide as to the key questions concerning a bill's design: "Which requirements will best achieve the [proposed law's] basic goal? How specifically should these requirements be framed? Who should be responsible for implementing the legislation? What sort of enforcement strategy should be employed?"[21]

Without the tools to assess bills prepared in one of these four inadequate ways, many deputies justified voting the party line by the "busy legislator" argument: They had so many things to do that they had to leave the details of design and techniques to the central drafting office experts. Thus did the law-making institutions make it difficult for a deputy to assess a bill in terms of facts and rational argument – especially, in terms of the facts that define local conditions.

While dysfunctional law-making procedures can be a large part of the problem, in this article, we focus on how to overcome another key reason for deputies' apparent difficulties in enacting effective laws: Few deputies have the *capacity* to assess a bill's design in terms of the public interest.

2.3. Of legislative policy, priority, design, and technique

In this article, we focus on the assessment of a bill, not in terms of compromises between competing interest groups, but in terms of facts and logic. To specify the problematic legislators' behaviors discussed in this article requires unpacking legislative decisions into four symbiotic but distinct elements: a bill's *policy*, its *priority*, its *design*, and the *techniques* used in drafting it.

Legislative policy constitutes the decision to address legislation to an identified social problem. When the legislature of X-Land (a hypothetical developing country) enacts a new pensions law for the aged, it signifies approval to expend scarce legislative time and resources at this time to help resolve the problems of old-age poverty.

---

[21] Edward L. Rubin, *Legislative Methodology: Some Lessons from the Truth-in-Lending Act*, 80 Geo. L. Rev. 233, 240 (1991).

Legislative priority relates to the decision to devote resources to ameliorating this social problem at this time. By approving the X-Land pension bill, the deputies indicated their agreement with that bill's priority, i.e., its precedence over other bills then competing for legislative attention.

Legislative design comprises a bill's substantive details. Whether and how a law will affect behaviors (whether of its primary addressee or the implementing agency) depends on those detailed provisions. Legislative design has two aspects: (a) if obeyed, will the bill's prescribed behaviors mitigate the specified social problem? and (b) will the new law induce its prescribed behaviors? In short: Will it work?

The X-Land legislature's policy decision to introduce a pension plan did not settle that plan's details: Should the government fund the scheme through general taxation or through a payroll scheme? If a payroll scheme, how much should employers contribute? Employees? Should the money be paid into general revenues or into a separate fund? Who qualifies for the scheme? At what age? What benefits should go to deceased pensioners' spouses and dependents? How should officials resolve disputes concerning pensions? Etc., etc., etc.

Deciding to enact some sort of bill to address old age poverty through a pension plan, and to give that bill high priority only begins the deputy's task. The deputy must also ask: Will it work? Policy hides in the law's details. Those who design and draft a bill's details participate in defining its policy.

Legislative techniques comprise the ways by which legislative drafters chain a bill's words together. A thought and the words that express it intermingle so intimately that a change in the words alters the thought, just as a change in the thought requires changing the words.[22] The details define the policy – and drafters specify those details in words. By voting for X-Land's Old Age Pension Act, the deputies (by implication) approved the form in which the bill appeared. Because of the unity of form and content, approving the form implied approval of what the words say.

Before voting for a bill, a deputy must therefore assess it along all four of these dimensions: policy, priority, design, and techniques.[23] In this article, we focus only

---

[22] N. J. Jamieson, *Towards a Systematic Statute Law*, 3 Otaga L. Rev. [Dunedin] 342, 343 (1976) (observing that "the linguistic universe in which we live does not begin to manifest itself until we cease to mistake for a real distinction what we think to be a mere linguistic vehicle for the illusory substance of communication.")

[23] When a legislature approves a bill, it also approves the configuration of power that the bill embodies. In this paper, we do not discuss modalities for "getting to yes" – i.e., of

on the bill's *design*: Does the design translate policy into a bill which, when enacted, likely will actually resolve the specified social problem?

2.4. The want of capacity to make a deliberative argument

Typically, few deputies – often elected for reasons related to their popularity, especially their contribution to the cause of liberation – had much capacity to analyze available evidence in the ways required for deliberation. However, institutionalized procedural circumstances shaped the pressures that influenced deputies' decisions, and without a guide for assessing a complex, transformatory bill in the public interest, deputies could not carry out that essential task.

To assess a simple bill – say, a bill prohibiting spitting on the sidewalk in cities – does not require a complicated guide. The facts lie within everyone's ordinary experience. Most deputies, however, find it difficult or even impossible to make an independent assessment of a bill to reorganize the central bank, to set up an agricultural extension agency to assist subsistence farmers in entering the market, to provide finance to microenterprises, or to establish a new companies code – any bill which is aimed towards transforming a complex social, political or economic institution.

To make reasoned arguments about a bill's details – its design – deputies must have some kind of guide. They need a *legislative theory and methodology* to assist them, in the context of their countries' specific circumstances, in determining whether that bill's detailed provisions will likely facilitate the social change desired. Unless they can make that kind of assessment, elected legislators cannot effectively exercise their constitutionally-imposed legislative power in the public interest.

3. A Legislative Theory for Assessing Bills

Some laws work: We earlier mentioned income tax and election laws as examples. Other laws do not. Why do some laws induce something close to their prescribed behaviors, and others do not? That poses the central question for lawmakers: *Why*

---

achieving a workable compromise between competing interest groups. *See* Roger Fisher & William Ury, *Getting to Yes: Negotiating Agreement Without Giving in* (Bruce Patto ed., Houghton Mifflin 1981).

do people behave as they do in the face of a rule? Without a theory answering that question, and lacking personal expertise in a bill's subject matter, a deputy cannot assess a complex, transformatory bill – that is a bill that, when enacted, will help to transform the development institutions that still condemn peoples from developing and transitional countries to poverty and oppression.[24]

As the two foundation stones of an institutionalist legislative theory, this chapter's first section depicts a model to help answer the critical question of why people behave as they do in the face of a rule of law. The second section reviews the problem-solving methodology as an essential tool for assessing a bill. In that context, the third section reviews seven categories of possible reasons why, in the face of a rule of law, people may behave in problematic ways. The last section describes the factors a deputy should analyze in determining whether a bill's provisions will facilitate attainment of the social goals desired. By way of summing up, the chapter ends with a checklist of questions that a deputy should ask a bill's proponents in order to assess the likelihood that the bill's detailed provisions will help to resolve the social problem being addressed.

3.1. Why do people behave as they do in the face of a rule of law?

To understand why laws so often miss the mark of effective implementation, an adequate legislative theory must focus on why people behave as they do in the face of a rule of law. To answer that question, the institutionalist legislative theory incorporates the model in Figure 1. That model emphasizes that to ensure effective implementation, lawmakers must ensure that a law contains rules addressed to two sets of social actors.

The primary social actors, here called "role occupants" and pictured on the model's right, constitute the sets of persons whose behaviors the law's detailed rules aim to change. The implementing agencies, pictured on the model's left, include the sets of agency officials who under the new law must implement the rules addressed to role occupants. For the law to work – to ensure that the primary role occupants behave according to the rules directed to them – the law must also prescribe the implementing agencies' detailed behaviors. (The law that commands a citizen not to commit murder commands a police officer to arrest the murderer, and a judge to convict that murderer.) That explains why the familiar phrase that

[24] In this article, we do not attempt to discuss at length the function of perspective in the uses of a theory; we have done that in *State and Law in the Development Process, supra* n. 1.

Figure 1. A model of the legal system

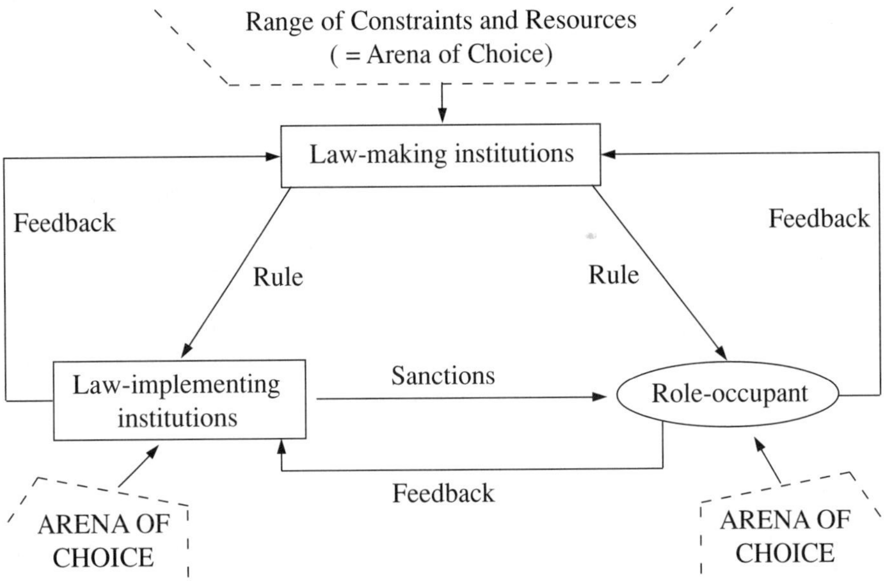

A model of the factors likely to influence a set of role occupants' behaviors in the face of a law.

"we have good laws, but they are poorly implemented" constitutes an oxymoron. A "good" law – a law that *works* – must induce appropriate behavior not only by the role occupant, but also by the implementing agency.

The model emphasizes that both the primary role occupants and the implementing agency officials behave as they do by making choices within the constraints and resources of their environments. That environment includes the legal rules and the expected behavior of the implementing agency. (In deciding the speed at which to drive, the motorist takes into account the law – the stipulated speed limit – and the expected behavior of the implementing agency – whether a police officer with a radar lurks behind the next bridge abutment.) The role occupant also takes into account other *non-legal* factors in the environment. (In determining speed, the motorist also takes into account the weather, the state of the pavement, the curves in the highway, and the amount of traffic.) Neither the behavior of implementing agencies nor the non-legal environment ever replicate themselves from one country to another. That explains why a law blindly copied from another time or place will not, save serendipitously, induce in its new environment the same behaviors it induced in its old environment.

An understanding of this model constitutes a basic premise of institutionalist legislative theory. It lays the essential foundation for the theory's problem-solving methodology. That methodology aims to facilitate the process of structuring the available evidence to answer the question, why, in the face of existing law, people behave as they do. The answer to that question holds the key to assessing whether a particular law's detailed provision will likely facilitate inducing the new patterns of behaviors essential to achieve desired institutional transformations.

3.2. Institutionalist legislative theory's problem-solving methodology

The roots of institutionalist legislative theory (including its problem-solving methodology) lie deeply embedded in John Dewey's philosophical pragmatism,[25] legal realism,[26] and law and society jurisprudence.[27] The theory requires that, in assessing a bill, the deputy adopt a decision-making model that employs reason informed by experience.[28] Its problem-solving methodology does not involve employing

---

[25] *See generally* John Dewey, *Theory of Valuation* 47-48 (U. of Chicago Press 1939); John Dewey, *Essays in Experimental Logic* (U. of Chicago Press 1916); John Dewey, *Logical Method and Law*, 10 Cornell L. Q. 17 (1925).

[26] *See* Llewellyn, *supra* n. 7; Llewellyn, *supra* n. 10.

[27] Law and society scholars tend to focus their research interests in explaining why people behave as they do in the face of a rule of law. *See* Philip C. Kissam, *The Decline of Law School Professionalism*, 134 U. Pa. L. Rev. 251, 299 (law and society research focuses on the effect of legal rules); Susan S. Silbey & Austin Sarat, *Critical Traditions in Law and Society Research*, 21 Law and Soc'y Rev. 165, 165 (1987) ("[Law and Society's] focus has been decentering, concerned not with what the law *is*, but what the law *does*.") *See* Nancy Levit, *Listening to Tribal Legends: An Essay on Law and the Scientific Method* 58 Fordham L. Rev. 263, 281 (1989). ("At the heart of law and society theory lies the conviction that an understanding of the law is possible only within the context of the surrounding social environment.") *See also* William J. Chambliss & Robert B. Seidman, *Law, Order and Power* (Addison-Wesley 1968).

[28] It seems doubtful that what we denote as "institutionalist legislative theory" qualifies as a "scientific" theory, if only because it probably defies falsification. *See* Levit, *supra* n. 27, at 268-272 (setting forth criteria for identifying a theory as "scientific.") It does

theory to construct an ideal-type model, applying the solution dictated by the model to the real world. Instead, it uses theory to guide an investigation of the real world, and reason to construct a solution based on the results of that investigation. In short, it uses theory, not as a metaphor, but as a heuristic.

As the institutionalist legislative theory's operational core, a four-step problem-solving methodology suggests an agenda of questions a deputy should ask to obtain the information needed to assess a bill.[29] Preliminarily however, the section below underscores three reasons why competent legislative theory must guide legislators in using facts and logic to judge bills' substance and form.

3.2.1. Reason informed by experience

Deliberation in the public interest lies at the heart of a democratic legislative process. That kind of deliberation requires that a deputy justify a bill by arguments that appeal from across the aisle. For three reasons, those arguments must rest on reason informed by experience. First, since, in any but the smallest society, people never agree on the same values, an appeal across the aisle cannot rely on assumptions of shared "values." Second, centuries-long social history teaches that reason informed by experience results in better normative propositions than the Oracle at Delphi, casting the bones, or reliance on the intuitions of a Great Leader, ethnic purity or muddling through.[30] Third, majority rule rests on the premise that

---

constitute a heuristic for best practice in developing legislation that actually solves perceived social problems in specific contexts. In that sense, it probably subsumes itself under the broad rubric of "practical reason," properly understood.

[29] A variety of authors propose a concept of problem-solving that differs from that put forward here. *See e.g.*, Ernest R. House, *Professional Evaluation: Social Impact and Political Consequences* (1993) (describes a methodology that the author denotes as "problem-solving;" that methodology tends to leave the determination of solutions to bargaining over conflicting claims and demands); Jack Stark, *The Art of the Statute* 15-16 (F. B. Rothman 1996) (problem solving described as a pragmatic process of incremental changes in existing laws: The drafter should think of a "spectrum" of solutions in order to choose between them, as well as "the purpose of the statutory provision causing the trouble, and on the relation of that purpose to the general law of which the vexing provision is a part ... After using these strategies to identify solutions, a drafter should begin to think like a lawyer [sic!], to commence the dialectical process of finding objections, countering them, finding other objections, etc.")

[30] *Cf.* Anthony Kronman, *Precedent and Tradition*, 99 Yale L. J. 1029 (1990).

the majority decision "can be viewed as the rationally motivated yet fallible result" of an ongoing decision-making process; "the outnumbered minority give their consent to the empowerment of the majority only with the proviso that they themselves retain the opportunity in the future of winning over the majority with better arguments and thus of revising the previous decision."[31] Only reason informed by experience – reliance on logically structured factual evidence – can serve to facilitate deliberation.

Thus, the legitimization of the process of majority empowerment lies in public expectations of rationality and reliance on factual evidence.[32] Long social experience and public expectations combine to underscore the necessity of justifying decision-making in terms of reason informed by experience.

3.2.2. The four steps

To guide deputies in asking logically necessary questions to obtain the facts they need to judge proposed legislation, institutionalist theory's problem-solving methodology incorporates the following four steps:

(1) What social problem does the bill address?

Problem-solving's first step calls for a description of the nature and scope of the social problem the bill seeks to address. That step involves two aspects. Because law necessarily addresses behaviors,[33] that description must do more than picture the existing problematic resource allocation patterns.[34] It must especially center

---

[31] Jurgen Habermas, *Between Facts and Norms: Contributions to a Discourse Theory of Law and Democracy* 167 (Willam Rehg, trans., MIT Press 1996).

[32] *Id.* at 304.

[33] Llewellyn, *supra* n. 10, at 1373 ("The law-jobs are in their bare bones fundamental, they are eternal. Perhaps they can all be summed up in a single formulation: such arrangement and adjustment of people's behavior that the society (or the group) remain a society (or a group) and gets enough energy unleashed and coordinated to keep on with its job as a society (or a group).") Some practical drafters understand that law aims only at behaviors. *See* Robert J. Martineau, *Drafting Legislation and Rules in Plain English* 65 (West Publishing 1991) (draft for "who does what.")

[34] Many social problems initially appear in the form of misused resources: polluted water, maldistributed incomes, inadequate social security payments, inflation. Laws cannot command those distorted resource patterns to mend themselves; they can only try to change the behaviors of those who contribute to their misdirection. A deputy must

attention on the relevant social actors' behaviors that contribute to those distorted resource use patterns. Beginning with problem-solving's first step, legislators should request the facts they need to assess *whose* and *what* behaviors the bill's design must change to overcome the problem described.[35] If (as usually occurs) existing law directs an agency to enforce the law, that agency's officials probably behave in ways that contribute to the problem.

(2) What explains those behaviors?

To change effectively the relevant problematic behaviors, a bill must prescribe new measures to alter the identified problematic behaviors. To avoid merely putting a salve on symptoms, those measures must change or eliminate those behaviors' causes. In problem-solving's second step, a deputy should ask for the evidence necessary to warrant the explanations advanced for the problematic behavior's causes.[36] Before its implementation, a deputy cannot expect a bill's proponents to supply evidence that demonstrates how that proposed solution will work. The deputy can, however, ask for facts that justify explanations as to the causes of relevant social actors' failure to comply with existing laws.

(3) What provisions in the bill will cost-effectively change those causes of the problematic behaviors?

In problem-solving's third step, the deputy must ask questions concerning the solution the bill proposes for the social problem identified in step one. The deputy

---

enquire what *behaviors* constitute the social problem at issue, and determine whether the proposed law will change those behaviors.

35 Eric J. Gouvin, *Truth in Savings and the Failure of Legislative Methodology*, 62 U. of Cincinnati L. Rev. 128, 131 (1994) (noting that a high proportion of drafting efforts that go awry stumble in the specification of the behaviors at issue.) The deputy should, of course, also enquire about the issues not examined in this paper: The legislative *policy* (i.e., whether the issue the bill addresses constitutes a true social problem, and its scope); its *priority* (i.e., whether it deserves legislative attention at this time); and the *legislative techniques* used. *See generally Manual, supra* n. 1.

36 Initially, those who draft bills can only draw on their existing knowledge to formulate educated guesses – hypotheses – as to the causes of the relevant social actors' problematic behaviors. The second part of a research report that explains and justifies a bill must first state those hypotheses, and second describe the facts to show that those hypotheses – revised in light of the facts as necessary – coincide with the available evidence. *See Manual, supra* n. 1, ch. 4-6.

should enquire whether the bill's details address the causes of those behaviors, and do so in the most cost-effective way. This key step in the problem-solving process underpins the claim that the bill's detailed solutions rest on reason informed by experience.

(4) How to monitor and evaluate the new law's implementation?

Finally, problem solving's fourth step calls for monitoring and evaluating the new law's effectiveness. (No law ever works exactly as anticipated. If it does not, the lawmakers must begin the whole process over again: Law-making, like life itself, requires dealing with one problem after another.)

As in every decision-making process, domain assumptions ("values and attitudes") inevitably influence every step in legislative theory's problem-solving methodology.

3.2.3. Domain assumptions

According to the popular view, in using an ends-means methodology to design a law the function of domain assumptions seems clear enough: They shape the law-makers' decisions as to the bill's objectives. In contrast, according to some, the problem-solving methodology here proposed naively assumes away the important role of domain assumptions in the law-making process.

As they do in every sort of decision-making, domain assumptions serve as criteria for relevance; without some form of criteria, no one can reach a decision – and that holds true for using the problem-solving methodology to assess a bill. That raises the central question: How do domain assumptions enter into the problem-solving process? In what sense can one claim that that methodology produces bills resting on reason and experience, when "values and attitudes" plainly have an important function – some say a decisive function – in determining the outcome?

The forms of domain assumptions appear as a continuum which fall into three main types. Some people permit unconsidered "intuitions" about the world to control their decisions. Others attempt to order their valuations into some kind of hierarchy of relative importance. Still others substitute for valuations of different imagined states of affairs, systematically coherent explanations of the real world (or Grand Theory).

Fully to ground decision on reason informed by experience, deputies must achieve some kind of intellectual control over their domain assumptions. Instead of the usual unexamined stew of domain assumptions, a deputy may invoke a Grand Theory, that is, a logically coherent set of propositions that purport to *explain* general social problems.[37] (The works of Adam Smith, Karl Marx, and Max Weber come immediately to mind; many alternatives exist.) Unlike the other forms of domain assumptions, one can use evidence to falsify a Grand Theory's explanatory propositions; that is, one can prove them inconsistent with the available facts. To guide decisions about the likelihood of a bill's provisions achieving their desired result, deputies can substitute for unexamined domain assumptions specific explanatory hypotheses suggested by Grand Theory as to particular problematic behaviors' causes. Then they may ask the bill's proponents whether available evidence falsifies those hypotheses.

In principle, in this way, decision-makers can verify specific explanatory hypotheses derived from Grand Theory by determining whether they prove logically consistent with the available country-specific "facts."[38] If a given explanatory hypothesis fails this test, deputies must reject it – and with it any legislative provisions that seemed logically designed to overcome the causes it specified. By substituting, where necessary, Grand Theory for unexamined domain assumptions, deputies can develop intellectual controls over the discretionary decisions they must make at each problem-solving step.

For example, in X-Land, using slash-and-burn cultivation, agricultural output seems desperately low. Local customary land tenures and inheritance rules have fragmented the land into tiny parcels, and make it impossible to buy or sell agricultural land. A bill proposes to resolve the problem of agricultural production by collectivizing the land into large parcels, and organizing large-scale producer cooperatives to farm it. A deputy with strong but unexamined libertarian "values" may reach a similar conclusion as to the bill's likely social impact as does another deputy who has studied and been persuaded by modern market-oriented economics. The deputy can generate specific hypotheses not inconsistent with the preferred Grand Theory, and put those to empirical test. Thus may a deputy put even domain assumptions under the discipline of reason informed by experience.

---

[37] Seidman & Seidman, *State and Law in the Development Process*, *supra* n. 1 at 86-90.

[38] Karl Popper, *The Logic of Scientific Discovery* (Hutchinson 1968). The proposition in the text expressly negates the central proposition of postmodernism, that one cannot determine the truth-value of a proposition about a matter of fact.

3.3. Possible causes of problematic behavior: The ROCCIPI categories

The second – and in some ways the key step – in problem-solving requires the deputy to enquire about the causes of the problematic behaviors at issue. Grounded on an understanding about how law influences behaviors, institutionalist legislative theory offers a set of categories to help a deputy generate explanatory hypotheses for those behaviors. Those hypotheses direct the deputy's search for the relevant country-specific facts required to demonstrate that a proposed bill's detailed provisions will likely work. Thus does legislative theory guide the research.

Legislative theory teaches that in the face of a rule of law people respond not only to the law-in-the-books, but also to the web of non-legal constraints and resources within which the law's addressees act. Institutionalist theory unpacks them into the following categories: Rule, Opportunity, Capacity, Communication, Interest, Process, and Ideology. (The mnemonic "ROCCIPI," composed of these categories' first letters, facilitates remembering them.)[39]

To ensure that a bill's detailed provisions address all the causes of problematic behaviors, deputies should review the ROCCIPI categories for possible explanations – preliminary hypotheses – for each set of role occupants' problematic behaviors. Those hypotheses, in turn, suggest questions a deputy may ask to discover whether a bill's detailed provisions rest upon the true causes of the problematic behaviors addressed. If the bill fails that test, the bill will likely not prove effective.

The ROCCIPI categories fall conveniently into two groups of causal factors, *subjective* and *objective.*

3.3.1. Subjective factors

Two sets of factors exist in the role occupants' own heads: their perceived interests or incentives; and their "ideologies" (that is, their domain assumptions). Intuitively, most people initially identify these subjective factors as the main causes of behavior.

(1) Interest (incentives)

This category suggests that role occupants behave in ways that, at relatively little cost, they perceive as likely to benefit themselves. It includes both material and

---

[39] The order of the categories in the "ROCCIPI" checklist have no significance; they ended up in this order merely to provide a mnemonic to facilitate remembering them.

non-material incentives, such as power and reference-group esteem. Interest-related explanations typically generate legislative measures that impose *direct conformity-inducing measures* – punishments or rewards – which purport to alter the role occupants' cost-benefit calculus. Social actors, however, seldom take into account only a law's paper penalty. Their behavior always depends in part on what they expect the implementing agency to do – not to speak of other, "non-legal" constraints and resources.[40]

A cautionary word – some writers expand the *Interest* category to include all possible explanations for behavior. The office of ROCCIPI's explanatory categories lies in pointing the deputy towards time- and place-specific explanatory hypotheses for the identified problematic behaviors. By expanding *Interest* (or incentives) to include everything, they deprive it of its explanatory power. To lay a foundation for assessing a bill's detailed provisions, the more detailed ROCCIPI categories can help legislators to identify all the probable, detailed, interrelated causes of problematic behaviors.

(2) Ideology (domain assumptions)[41]

Ideology constitutes the second subjective category of problematic behaviors' possible causes. Broadly construed, this category covers the subjective motivations not subsumed under *Interest*. These include everything from values, attitudes, and tastes, to myths and assumptions about the world, religious beliefs, and more or less well-defined political, social, and economic ideologies. Once again, some people tend to extend this category inclusively. That poses a seeming sociological paradox: Unless, even before its enactment, people's values and attitudes conform to a law, they will not likely obey it; if their values and attitudes already conform to a proposed law, enacting that law seems unnecessary. That paradox, some claim, proves that law cannot change people's behaviors. If that broad definition holds, the effort to use law to change behaviors chases after moonbeams.

---

[40] For example, some writers have explained altruistic behaviors by the wealth maximization principle, thus transforming philanthropy into its opposite, selfishness. Richard A. Posner, *The Economics of Justice* 67-68 (Cambridge, Massachusetts: Harvard U. Press, 1983). Does it really help understand philanthropic behavior to claim that it reflects only selfishness? *See Manual, supra* n. 1, ch. 5.

[41] *See generally* Alvin Gouldner, *The Coming Crisis of Western Sociology* (Basic Books, 1970).

Although ideologies do influence behaviors, effectively implemented laws can – and have served to – change both behavior and ideologies. For example, in the United States, the income tax law caused millions to change their behaviors: Whatever their sentiments for or against an income tax, they paid it. Implementation of the school desegregation decisions clearly altered the mind-set of many Southern white parents.[42]

Subjective factors – *Interest* and *Ideology* – offer partial explanations for problematic behaviors. They focus, however, on the causes of individuals' behaviors *within existing institutional structures*. As a result, legislative measures designed to alter these subjective factors rarely transform the dysfunctional institutions that perpetuate poverty and vulnerability.[43]

3.3.2. Objective factors

ROCCIPI'S objective categories – *Rule, Opportunity, Capacity, Communication and Process* – center attention on the institutional factors that help to explain problematic behaviors. Warranted by evidence, explanatory hypotheses suggested by these categories may lead to legislative proposals quite different from those directed to subjective causes.

(1) Rule

Most problems that lead to demands for legislative action do not suddenly pop up. Almost always, a considerable body of law exists concerning problematic behaviors.

---

[42] In 1954, only 15% of white parents in the south of the United States thought it proper that their children attend primary school with black children. Twenty-five years after the Supreme Court declared school segregation unconstitutional, 85% of white parents so believed. Surely the mere fact that non-segregation had become the law had some causative effect on those parents' ideologies. Most people believe behavior tracks one's values. Psychological findings about "cognitive dissonance" argue that the contrary also holds: If one must behave in a certain way, in time one's domain assumptions come to justify the behavior. L. Festinger, *A Theory of Cognitive Dissonance* (Row Peterson, 1957).

[43] For example, U.S. residential housing patterns – a non-subjective category – among other factors, apparently still contribute to the fact that today, 47 years after *Brown v. Board of Education of Topeka, Kansas,* 347 U. S. 483 (1954), a great many children still attend substantially segregated schools.

As emphasized above, that raises the central question legislators must ask: Why, in the face of existing rules of law, do people behave as they do?[44]

In reality, people behave as they do in the context, not of a *single* rule, but a *cage* of rules embedded in several laws.[45] A rule's detailed provisions may help to explain problematic behaviors for either of five reasons:

(1) Its wording seems vague or ambiguous, thus endowing its addressees with discretion to decide how to behave;

(2) Its provisions may not address the causes of the problematic behaviors at issue;

(3) Its provisions may permit implementing agency officials to behave in non-transparent, unaccountable, non-participatory ways;

(4) Its explicit wording may grant implementing officials unnecessary discretion in deciding whether and how to alter the problematic behaviors;

(5) Some sections of existing rules may permit or even command behaviors that contradict those prescribed by other laws (thus effectively requiring the law's addressees to choose which law to obey).

One case illustrates some of these possibilities: Despite a law that forbids dumping pollutants in rivers, *because* of the law's detailed provisions, people may still dump them there. Stated in ambiguous or confusing language, those provisions may leave their addressees unclear as to what they should (or should not) do. The law may leave existing implementing agency officials – for example, an agricultural extension agent – discretion to decide whether or not to stop farmers from using fertilizers although rains will likely wash these into nearby waterways. Other laws' provisions may permit or even command the people to behave in polluting ways; the agricultural extension law, for example, may authorize agents to encourage farmers to fertilize their crops. The law may not give the agricultural extension agency authority to help farmers learn how to increase productivity without using fertilizers. The law's implementing provisions may permit or even authorize extension agency officials to use non-transparent, unaccountable processes that hide

---

[44] The existing law always constitutes part of the explanation for problematic behaviors. The proof for this counter-intuitive statement lies in the methodology of problem-solving. The proposed new bill constitutes a *pro tanto* change in existing law. A proposed solution always addresses a cause of problematic behaviors. Therefore, existing law must count as a cause of perceived problematic behaviors.

[45] For our definition of "law," *see supra,* n. 9.

their (possibly corrupt) behavior in overlooking polluting activities. The law's wording may explicitly or implicitly grant the role occupants or implementing officials broad discretion to decide how to behave, leaving them scope to respond to inappropriate motivations.

(2) Opportunity

Do the circumstances of the rule's addressees enable them to behave as the law commands? Or, conversely, do those circumstances make it impossible for them to conform? For example, despite a law forbidding corrupt behavior, do government officials work in a non-transparent, non-accountable environment which gives them *opportunities* to benefit from behaving corruptly?[46]

(3) Capacity

This category should stimulate a deputy to ask whether the relevant actors have the knowledge, skills, and resources to behave as the law prescribes. For example, if subsistence farmers lack credit or technical expertise, they may lack the *capacity* to grow cash crops. Without adequate transport, agricultural extension agents may not have the *capacity* to help farmers increase productivity.

In practice, *Opportunity* and *Capacity* overlap. Nevertheless, whether considered singly or together, these categories achieve their purpose if they stimulate a deputy to ask for evidence about these kinds of possible explanations for the behaviors at issue.

(4) Communication

Where an existing law ineffectively prohibits the behaviors at issue, the role occupants' ignorance of the law may explain why they do not conform. Without knowing what a law commands, no one can *consciously* obey it. Legislators should enquire whether the responsible authorities have succeeded in *communicating* to – informing – the relevant actors about the rules, and how they should behave in conformity with them.

In many developing countries, institutionalized communications channels tend both to reflect and bolster existing skewed social structures. In most, governments publish new laws only in a gazette. The local media may publish reports on the more important laws. Ministries usually make sure their officials, in particular those assigned to enforce them, know about the laws' details. Urban elites,

[46] For examples, *see Manual*, *supra* n. 1, ch. 14.

especially formal-sector entrepreneurs, frequently learn about laws from their lawyers or business associations. Unless the responsible ministries make special efforts to inform them, however, the poor, especially the rural poor, seldom even hear about new laws – even those supposedly designed for their benefit. Semi-subsistence farmers may never learn that a new law aims to give them access to credit or to needed technology and skills.

(5) Process

This category may spur a legislator to ask questions about the criteria and procedures that control the processes by which role occupants decide whether and how to obey the law. Individuals usually make that decision by themselves; questions about the process by which they reach their decisions probably will do little to reveal the causes of their behaviors. However, in the case of a complex organization – a corporation, a non-government organization, a trade union, and especially a government implementing agency – *Process* often appears as ROCCIPI's most significant category.[47] Whose and what ideas, information, and feedback an implementing agency's officials take into account; whether they use transparent and accountable procedures in accord with clearly specified criteria: All these may influence their decision-making behaviors. As a basis for assessing whether a bill's provisions will effectively alter problematic decision-making behaviors, a deputy should ask detailed questions about the processes of decision under existing law.

Problem-solving's logic holds that sound "ought" propositions – a bill's detailed provisions – can rest on well-considered explanations for existing problematic behaviors. The seven ROCCIPI categories serve to guide a deputy in asking the questions necessary to determine whether a proposed bill's provisions logically rest on warranted explanations of why role occupants behave as they do in the face of existing law. After a conscientious search for falsifying evidence,[48] the deputy must assess whether the explanations on which a bill's detailed provisions logically rest in turn prove consistent with the available facts. That constitutes the necessary predicate for assessing the bill's detailed solutions – that is, its design.

---

[47] For more detailed analysis of *Process* as related to agencies assigned to implement legislation, consult *Manual, supra* n. 1, ch. 5.

[48] *See Manual, supra* n. 1, at 167-70.

3.4. Analyzing a bill's detailed provisions

In problem-solving's third step, institutionalist legislative theory guides the deputy in determining whether a proposed bill's detailed measures logically seem likely to alter or eliminate the causal factors identified in the second step.[49] This section discusses, in turn: (a) general criteria for an adequate legislative solution; (b) three preliminary questions a deputy should ask; (c) developing a menu of potential alternative solutions; (d) the bill's conformity-inducing measures; (e) determining whether the bill's provisions will likely work; (f) the bill's probable costs and benefits; and (g) the bill's monitoring and feedback mechanisms.

3.4.1. General criteria of an adequate bill

We suggest four general criteria which legislators should consider in determining whether a bill seems likely to prove adequate. First, logically, do the bill's provisions seem likely to alter or eliminate the warranted causes of the primary role occupants' and the implementing agency officials' problematic behaviors? Second, taken together with the relevant provisions of existing law, does the bill supply a complete legislative *system* for resolving the identified social problem? Third, since law and its implementation come in short supply, does the evidence demonstrate the bill's cost-effectiveness? Fourth, will the bill likely help to improve the majority's quality of life, especially for the poorest and most vulnerable? The succeeding sections discuss in more detail the questions a deputy should ask to assess whether a bill's solution will likely help solve the social problem it purports to address.

3.4.2. Preliminary questions

Preliminarily, a deputy should ask two sets of questions, one about the bill's scope, and the other about possible lessons from history and comparative law.

---

[49] A competent research report, grounded on the logically-organized relevant evidence, would contain the answers to these kinds of questions (*see Manual*, supra n. 1, chs. 4-5). Drafting and adopting parliamentary rules requiring that a bill's proponents supply such a research report seems an important element of reform designed to address the institutional explanations for the difficulties addressed in this article.

(1) The bill's scope

As a preliminary strategic choice, a deputy should ask if the bill's scope seems sufficiently narrowly defined. Since society constitutes a closely woven web of relationships, social problems inevitably appear closely interlocked. Frequently, governments propose great grab-bags of bills, containing subject-matters only tenuously held together by a common thread.

For example, as originally proposed, the Chinese bill for reforming the banking structure[50] not only provided for the creation of central, commercial, development, and agricultural banks, but also for the establishment and operation of stock exchanges and insurance companies. That broad scope multiplied the disputable issues on which lawmakers had to agree. One provision's supporters often jibbed at other provisions. Debates dragged on for years. To avoid "stuffing" the bill, the Chinese drafting team proposed an overall legislative *program* to address the original bill's many more or less related subjects. Within that larger program, they drafted, and the lawmakers enacted a separate central bank bill. Following further research and study, the lawmakers enacted additional bills relating to other kinds of banks, stock exchanges, and insurance companies.

In general, wise legislative policy seeks to narrow a bill's scope. In particular, if different agencies must implement measures relating to different aspects of a larger problem, legislators should ask whether two different bills would produce more readily understood – and more implementable – legislation.

(2) History and comparative law and experience

As a second preliminary question, with respect to the deputies' own country, deputies should ask about the social problem's history and about previous legislative efforts to resolve it. They should also enquire about other countries' laws and experiences. The answers to these questions may provide information that will help them to assess the proposed bill's likely social impact.

By the time someone in authority proposes drafting a bill to help resolve a problem, almost invariably, some law already exists touching the issue, and some agency probably has at least some more or less vague responsibility for implementing that law. Knowledge of the history that led to existing law helps in understanding the difficulty that the new bill proposes to address – for example, where the particular problem fits in the larger context, and whether the deputies should consider it as

---

[50] This comprised one of the 22 priority bills designated for preparation by the 1989 National Plan; *see* Payne & Seidman, *supra* n. 1.

part of a broader legislative program. That history may also offer insights into how people's perception of the specific difficulty has changed over the years; whether and how causes of the problematic behaviors may have changed over time; and why past legislative solutions at least partially failed. All these may help legislators assess whether the proposed bill's detailed provisions will likely prove successful.

That lawmakers cannot safely copy foreign law does not at all imply that they cannot also learn from foreign law and experience. Analysis of other countries' experience to solve a similar social problem through law may raise questions about (a) aspects of the difficulty which may not yet have appeared in the legislators' own country; (b) the causes of the problematic behaviors that contribute to the difficulty; and (c) ideas about alternative possible solutions and their probable consequences.

We reiterate: A law that induces a particular set of behaviors in one time and place will not, save serendipitously, induce the same behaviors at another time or place. A drafter should never blindly copy foreign law. It does not serve as a buffet, from which lawmakers can simply choose one that fits their taste. Before adopting even an idea from another country's law, legislators must know the facts, not only that foreign law's black letter text, but how it actually worked in its home country's unique circumstances. From foreign law there is nothing to copy, but much to learn.[51]

3.4.3. Alternative potential solutions

In considering a bill, a deputy should always ask for a menu of potential alternative provisions. As noted above, for that purpose, foreign law and experience frequently serves up a feast of alternative legal solutions for analogous problems. The scholarly literature often contains useful suggestions – not only in law reviews, but also journals in the relevant substantive discipline (for example, for a town planning act, the planning literature; for an agricultural extension agency law, agricultural journals.) Officials in the relevant ministries, and perhaps lawyers in the central drafting office, may have additional ideas. Deputies should also canvass their own constituents for proposals grounded in their own experience. Consideration of these alternatives might suggest provisions to improve the bill or even to substitute for it.

---

[51] *See* Rubin, in Payne & Seidman, *supra* n. 1; *see Manual*, *supra* n. 1, ch. 6.

3.4.4. Conformity-inducing measures

In assessing a bill, a deputy should focus attention on the kinds of implementing measures likely to prove effective in inducing role occupants to behave as desired. Seventy years ago Ernst Freund observed,

> "Enforcement clauses form a constant feature of regulative legislation, and it is therefore surprising how little thought has been given to them either as to general principle or as to detail ... Spasmodically, enforcement as a legislative problem arouses attention, and then there is talk about 'putting teeth into the law.' The result, as often as not, is the piling up of administrative powers and duties, without any realization of what their enforcement would mean, or that they are likely to remain unenforced."[52]

Conformity-inducing measures come in two modes, *direct* and *indirect* (or *roundabout).*

(1) Direct measures

In the older legal literature, and still in popular conception, law implies a sanction, and sanction means punishment. No sanction, no law, said Blackstone. When they did consider enforcement at all, lawmakers too often relied on criminal penalties. Experience has proven, however, that, more effectively than punishment, altering or eliminating the factors that cause problematic behaviors more likely ensures that a bill's measures will induce conforming behavior.

Of the seven categories of causes of problematic behaviors suggested by legislative theory's ROCCIPI checklist, punishment addresses only *Interest.* In principle, a reward for not behaving problematically serves as well as punishment. Both punishment and reward can also alter causes subsumed under *Ideology*. Logically, however, neither punishments nor rewards can alter the problematic behaviors that result from objective causes.

Criminal sanctions constitute only one of many kinds of direct measures; civil penalties and rewards can serve a similar deterrent purpose.

(a) Punishments

Lawmakers should consider three caveats with respect to punishment: First, they should resist the temptation to increase the amount of punishment instead of creat-

---

[52] Ernst Freund, *Legislative Regulation* 339 (The Commonwealth Fund, 1932).

ing more effective implementing agencies. Evidence shows that a law's general deterrent effect rarely depends solely on its prescriptions of specified amounts of punishment. Even though the penalty remains relatively small, a substantial threat of detection may deter crime. Absent the danger of detection, however, even severe punishments will not deter.[53] For many crimes – notably corruption – no clearly defined victim exists to report the crime.[54]

Second, in the criminal law, a powerful ethical injunction emphasizes that lawmakers should reserve the most serious punishment for the most serious offense. Corruption constitutes a serious offense. Murder and treason surely constitute more serious ones. If murder merits capital punishment, does corruption?

Third, as a leading sociologist suggested, "the usual punitive sanctions of fine or imprisonment are likely to be more effective where the prevailing behaviour of the majority of the population is already in accord with the goals sought by the statute."[55] Punishment seems particularly unlikely to ensure conformity in the case of transformatory law which, almost by definition, seeks to change widely prevalent behaviors.

(b) Civil damages or penalties

Punitive civil damages may impose a large additional penalty. At least at common law, criminal liability requires proof beyond a reasonable doubt. An action for a civil penalty or damages demands a somewhat lower burden. In the United States, a requirement in some laws that the defendant must pay attorney's fees to a

---

[53] Gary Becker hypothesizes that the deterrent effect of punishment equals the quantum of punishment threatened by a law discounted by the probability of detection, conviction and sentence. Gary S. Becker, *Crime and Punishment: An Economic Approach*, 76 J. Pol. Econ. 169 (1968). That proposition too easily leads a deputy to vote not for more funds to improve the criminal justice system, but (because it seems less costly) for higher and higher degrees of punishment. Becker's proposition is subject to considerable doubt, for most criminals do not commit a crime where a high degree of enforcement exists – and never mind whether the threatened sentence is five years or twenty-five years. Draconian punishments do not substitute for effective enforcement.

[54] Statutes may offer potential informers a share of fines or damages collected, shift the burden of proof to potential violators of the law, or establish special police units trained to search out the crime proactively. *See Manual, supra* n. 1, ch.14.

[55] Arnold Rose, *Sociological Factors in the Effectiveness of Proposed Legislative Remedies*, 11 J. Legal Education 470, 472 (1959).

successful plaintiff makes every lawyer a potential "private attorney general." Seizing the instrumentalities of crime – not only the narcotics or guns used, but also the automobile or boat – may add an additional dollop of deterrence. For professional misconduct, the suspension or revocation of a license serves as a direct conformity-inducing measure short of criminal action.

(c) Rewards

As a direct measure, a reward may serve a useful purpose in either of two situations. First, where the legislation permits different levels of conformity, it may prescribe different levels of rewards for different levels of achievement. That encourages creativity. Second, since many actors remain innately conservative, when introduced, transformatory laws frequently induce relatively few people to conform. To punish non-conformance, the authorities must proactively seek out the violators. Where a reward regime reigns, those who conform come forward to claim the reward. Rewarding those few who conform with transformatory prescriptions may well induce greater compliance at a lower cost than policing and punishing those who do not.

(d) Changing ideologies

Direct conformity-inducing measures may help to change "values and attitudes" (*Ideologies*). As illustrated by the U.S. desegregation experience, a law's very existence may help change ideologies; potentially, law has a distinct educative function.[56]

In general, over-criminalization poses serious problems. That does not mean that criminal punishments do not have their proper – though restricted – place. It does underscore the reality that a law which criminalizes unwanted behaviors will rarely foster significant social transformation.

(2) Indirect measures

Especially when proposing bills to implement institutional changes, indirect measures prove more effective in changing the "objective" causal factors – ROCCIPI's *Rule*, *Opportunity*, *Capacity*, *Communication*, and *Process*. These typically

[56] *Cf.* Alfred C. Ewing, *The Morality of Punishment* 104 (1929); Frederick Lawrence, *Punishing Hate: Bias Crimes under American Law* 49 (Harvard U. Press, 1999).

constitute the major hurdles blocking effective development. Here we suggest only a few examples of the seemingly limitless possibilities.[57]

By preventing preparatory steps toward unwanted behaviors, the bill may restrict a role occupant's *Capacity* to so behave – for example, to prevent a person from erecting an unsafe building, requiring a builder to obtain a building permit before breaking ground. The bill may also be designed to increase capacity to behave as the bill prescribes. For example, to invigorate small businesses it may assign a designated agency to provide business counseling to small, medium and micro enterprises. To overcome a failure to *Communicate* law, the bill may require an implementing agency to publicize its provisions – for example, by distributing fliers to stakeholders, or conducting workshops to enable stakeholders to discuss the law's implications. A Massachusetts law requires tobacco vendors to post a sign at the point of payment stating that the law forbids the sale of tobacco to minors. To improve an implementing *Process*, bills frequently prescribe an agency's structure and process of decision-making.[58]

Even to change subjective causes, like values and attitudes, indirect, roundabout conformity-inducing measures, instead of punishment or rewards, frequently prove more effective. To give two examples: After the introduction of democratic elections in 1994, the South African armed forces remained predominantly racist and white, Afrikaans-speaking, and Afrikaner-dominated. The new government required every soldier and sailor, starting first with the senior officers and ultimately reaching every recruit, to attend a seminar on the benefits of cultural diversity. To eliminate racial prejudice among student groups, the U.S. State of Pennsylvania enacted a statute requiring the Human Relations Commission to work with the Department of Education to prepare instructional materials.

Asking questions about the appropriate conformity-inducing measures constitutes only a part of the deputy's task in assessing a bill. What questions to ask to estimate its potential effectiveness?

---

[57] *See generally,* Robert Seidman, *The State, Law and Development Process, supra,* n. 1, ch. 9. The proposition in the text suggests that not all problematic behaviors result from perverse incentives, and that therefore "getting the prices right" does not serve as a universal blueprint for competent policy.

[58] *See Manual, supra* n. 1, ch. 5.

3.4.5. Will the proposed solution work?

(1) Do the bill's detailed provisions address causes?

A deputy should enquire of a bill's proponents how they expect the bill's provisions to work – that is, to demonstrate logically, with facts and in detail that those provisions will likely change or eliminate the causes of existing problematic behaviors. To do that, the deputy may ask what evidence suggests that, logically, the bill's provisions will likely alter or eliminate all the causes earlier identified by using the ROCCIPI categories.

(2) Do the rules create a complete legislative system?

Almost all of a law's provisions direct ordinary citizens and officials as to how to behave. In general, those provisions prescribe three kinds of behaviors: They command, they forbid, they permit.[59] Properly written, the bill's provisions should form a coherent, effective system. The deputy should ask questions to discover whether, in conjunction with other laws, the bill prescribes a system likely to prove effective. That requires seven sets of rules (most of which usually appear in other laws – but the deputy cannot assume that):

- Laws addressed to the primary role occupants;
- Laws addressed to implementing agencies, in general;
- Laws addressed to implementing agencies concerning sanctions and other conformity-inducing measures;
- Laws addressed to dispute settlement agencies;
- Laws addressed to funding agencies;
- Laws addressed to whoever must evaluate the law's implementation; and
- Laws addressed to judges and others who keep the corpus of the law in order (for example, coming-into-force provisions; scope-of-application provisions; consequential amendments; definitional clauses).

Consider, for example, a bill to take child hawkers out of the markets and into school. The deputy should enquire about:

- Laws addressed to child hawkers, their parents, and guardians;

[59] Stark, *supra* n. 29; *see* Martineau, *supra* n. 33. In English, to command, a bill uses "shall" or, in some jurisdictions, "must;" to forbid, "may not;" to permit "may." Practically every sentence in a bill should contain one of these words.

- Laws addressed to school officials, truant officers, and welfare workers in general;
- Laws addressed to Ministry of Welfare officials and to courts, with respect to sanctions;
- Laws addressed to Ministry of Welfare officials and to courts, with respect to dispute settlement;
- Laws addressed to the Ministry of Finance, with respect to funding;
- Laws addressed to whomever the law appoints to ensure evaluation of the new law's effectiveness; and
- Laws addressed to judges and other officials who keep the corpus of the law in order.

Frequently most of these laws already exist. For example, if in our hypothetical street hawkers' bill, courts will serve as the dispute settlement agency, no doubt the deputy will discover that existing laws concerning appointment of judges, court procedure, and the like require no change in light of the new law. The schools may have in place regulations that induce appropriate behavior by sufficient numbers of truant officers. Nevertheless, the deputy must enquire about all seven of these subsystems to ensure that, when enacted and in conjunction with relevant existing legislation, the new law becomes part of a system that works.

(3) Are there adequate criteria and procedures to guide rule-making?

Almost every bill requires some administrative rule-making. Sometimes, problems arise in conditions of rapid change. Sometimes the relevant problematic behaviors prove too many and too complex to permit the kind of detailed research required for formulating the kinds of detailed legislative provisions required for effective implementation. In these instances, legislators frequently grant to an administrative agency the power to draft and implement detailed regulations to deal with quite broad aspects of the larger social problem.

This kind of law has advantages and disadvantages. On the one hand, it may direct an agency to employ experts to conduct research and draft regulations to deal with each of the characteristic complex and changing conditions, and to revise those regulations when necessary. On the other hand, this raises a new form of the agency-trustee issue: In effect, the legislature will have granted a degree – sometimes a considerable degree – of their "legislative power" to unelected experts. As a minimum, the bill must impose limits on the agency's rule-making discretion by specifying in the law itself: (a) transparent, accountable, and – so far as possible – participatory procedures for making and enacting the regulations (*e.g.* provisions for public notice and comment, or for public hearings); and (b) clearly formulated criteria as to factors the agency may take into account in decision-making. Does a bill provide for legislative review of administrative rules? Does it facilitate public and legislative oversight of administrative proceedings?[60]

3.4.6. What probable costs and benefits will the new law entail?

(1) What to include?

Among the various potential solutions, the bill should prescribe the most cost-effective. Legislators should ask for facts to enable them to weigh those alternatives' relative costs and benefits. In particular, they should enquire about the bill's likely differential impact on various social strata and inchoate valued interests.

A law almost never affects society's diverse social groups equally. A regulation requiring a police commissioner to appoint as policemen only people six feet tall or taller discriminates against women – needlessly, because only a rare policing job requires brawn. In the United States, where an income tax law currently requires the rich to pay a somewhat higher percentage of their income as tax than the poor, a purportedly "neutral" ten percent across-the-board tax cut (proposed in 1999) would have given 62% of its proposed savings to the wealthiest 10% of taxpayers. Those with power and privilege always have channels of communication to political movers and shakers – including legislators. In contrast, the relatively powerless groups' interests frequently remain under-represented in the councils of power. Deputies should ask for evidence to enable them to assess a proposed bill's impact on these groups, particularly the poor, women, children and where they exist, ethnic minorities.

Laws may also differentially impact at least three sets of not always clearly formulated interests: the environment, human rights, and good governance. In some countries, people may value other inchoate interests.

Although many bills affect some aspect of the environment, in government the environment too seldom finds a strong advocate. As a minimum, the legislators should ask questions about every legislative proposal's likely environmental impact.

Whenever a legislative proposal has implications for human rights, a deputy should request more information. In some cases, those implications may appear

---

[60] Many devices exist to prevent an agency's arbitrary (and sometimes corrupt) decision-making behaviors; *see Manual, supra* n. 1, ch. 6.

obvious, as when a proposed bill gives officials the power to detain persons without trial, or imposes political controls over the press. Sometimes, however, a bill may affect human rights in less obvious ways. A legislative proposal for new roads may raise human rights issues concerning the taking of private lands. A proposal to build a hospital to serve a powerful, wealthy group – which already enjoys access to a developed health delivery system – may raise issues of discrimination against neglected poorer communities.

Increasingly, people have come to value good governance; without it, too often they lose out. To defend against corruption, a country requires more than criminal penalties (which rarely prove effective against corruption). It requires good governance – that is, transparency, accountability, stakeholder participation, and decision-making by rule. Legislators should always ask for facts as to whether and how proposed legislation provides for decision-making that meets those four criteria of good governance.[61]

(2) Making quantitative estimates

Deputies should always insist on an estimate of a new law's likely economic and social costs and benefits for these various groups and interests. They should, where possible, ask for those estimates in quantitative form.

In many cases it proves difficult to provide quantitative estimates. Then deputies should request information to enable them to weigh the relative impacts of non-quantifiable costs and benefits by specifying the factors involved in estimating each of them. Economic costs typically include government's out-of-pocket direct expenditures for personnel, buildings, and equipment. Governments usually pay for these out of current revenues or, over time, in the form of the principal and interest on loans. Especially in the short run, deputies may obtain reasonably accurate estimates of a particular law's direct budget costs for personnel, equipment, and services. For longer periods, unanticipated factors like inflation or goods shortages may make even these direct economic costs harder to estimate.

Deputies should also ask for government's indirect out-of-pocket costs. If, as its principal implementation measure, a proposed product liability law relies on individual lawsuits, government revenues must cover additional costs to the courts. These too may prove difficult to estimate. Who anticipated that, by the century's end, the United States' 1960s-70s expansion of prisoners' rights would increase prisoners' rights claims to half of the federal courts' case load?

---

[61] *Id.*

The private sector may also bear economic costs arising from a new law's impact on existing enterprises, present or future profits, employment or wage losses. These may include not only direct costs (for example, some form of tax increase), but also indirect costs. Building a new highway, for example, may leave a flourishing fast food restaurant some distance from the flow of traffic. That some of these economic costs may only appear over time makes it harder to estimate them; but better a guesstimate than no estimate at all.

The economic benefits generated by government's initial expenditures under a new law frequently appear only over time, making them harder than economic costs to estimate. Suppose that, to stimulate economic activity in a remote area, government builds a new highway. That may increase private sector employment and profits – but how many new jobs? Government may derive new tax revenue from the increased economic activity – but who can accurately predict how much? Depending on how they are managed, government capital investments may also produce more government income in the form of profits, increased fees for services, or interest on government loans. These future income flows, however, always remain difficult to predict in quantitative terms.

New legislation may also differentially bestow economic gains on private sector groups. A new road or a new school may benefit some, and disadvantage others. So may a new insurance law, or a new law on a father's obligation to support a child. A law's detailed provisions determine its impact on specific social groups. Uncertainty concerning many interrelated factors render these potential gains also difficult to estimate. Some politicians claim reduced taxes constitute a private sector gain. Which social group will benefit, however, depends not only on the particular kinds and amounts of taxes reduced, but also who will lose when government perforce eliminates some services. Reducing the education or health budget will likely most seriously impact the poor, who usually have no alternative fallback position. A shift from income or profit taxes to higher taxes on value added or consumer goods sales generally has a greater impact on the real incomes of the poor who pay a greater share of their income on consumer items than do the rich.[62]

---

62 A deputy should ask detailed questions about subsidies, especially tax subsidies. (A tax subsidy consists of a special tax concession to particular taxpayers. No difference exists between that and paying a cash subsidy equal to the amount the taxpayer would have paid in tax without that concession; hence "tax subsidy.") In particular, the deputy should ensure that no taxpayer gets a subsidy unless the subsidy induces the desired new behavior. Governments experience difficulty in accounting for tax subsidies, and in ensuring that it actually induces the behavior at which it is aimed. Preferably, a law should tax equal

Social costs and benefits usually involve intangible items like the quality of life (jobs and incomes, housing, recreational facilities), human rights, and environmental conditions. They generally prove even more difficult than economic costs and benefits to compare and assess. Typically, they too differentially affect the quality of life of society's historically disadvantaged. How, for example, to measure the impact on a family's life of a government decision to demolish their house in order to build a road through their property? Or the social impact of building a school or a hospital in a high-income area rather than a low-income area? Or the social costs of permitting timber companies to chop down swaths of natural forest, which over time will likely cause increased water runoff and flooding? Or the social benefits of increased spending on education to equip the community's poorest citizens so that many years later they may enjoy new employment and income opportunities? How to assess a law's effect in empowering the poor to play a more active role in governmental decision-making?

Despite the difficulties in measuring these non-tangible items, a deputy has the unenviable responsibility of pulling together, if only in descriptive or anecdotal form, whatever evidence exists as to a bill's potential social, as well as its economic, costs and benefits. Frequently, intangibles constitute a law's most important potential development impact. Lawmakers need whatever information they can get about them – and which social groups will most likely win or lose. They must request all the relevant information available as a basis for estimating at least a range of likely social costs and benefits, and do the best they can to decide whether the game seems worth the candle.

3.4.7. Monitoring and feedback systems

Inevitably, in part because the available evidence remains insufficient and in part because circumstances always change, laws produce unanticipated consequences. In accord with problem-solving's fourth step, deputies should ask what monitoring and feedback mechanisms the bill includes to enable them to find out whether, once enacted, the law actually induces the behaviors it prescribes, and whether it produces the desired social impact. If ongoing evaluation demonstrates the law does not produce its anticipated outcomes, the deputies may wish to revise some or all of its provisions.

---

taxpayers equally, and pay a direct subsidy to specific actors to induce conforming behavior. *See generally* Stanley Surrey, *Pathways to Tax Reform: The Concept of Tax Expenditures* (Harvard U. Press 1973).

In the largest sense, democracy itself constitutes a gigantic, if somewhat unsystematic, monitoring and evaluation system. Constituents whose toes a law's implementation may pinch can and frequently do complain to their legislative representatives. The legislature as a whole has a constitutionally assigned oversight duty. As an important function, many legislative committees oversee the work of particular ministries. That general system, however, too often does not lead to systematic or reliable monitoring. At least important transformatory laws should include built-in devices to ensure some kind of ongoing system for evaluating the new law, and reporting back on its results.

Many possible devices exist: A sunset clause (i.e., a clause by which the new law stipulates its own limited life, so that it will only continue if the legislature votes for it again; requiring a responsible officer (frequently the minister) to report periodically on the new law's operation; requiring an official, after a stated period, to appoint an evaluation commission; requiring a referendum at a fixed future time so voters can decide whether the law should continue.

A discussion of the advantages and disadvantages of possible monitoring mechanisms would exceed this article's scope. To reduce the dangers of corruption, governments have used a range of bottom-up and top-down monitoring techniques. More generally, a profession of evaluators and a library of books have appeared to facilitate the process of assessing legislative programs' social impact.[63] Deputies should familiarize themselves with that literature and decide which kinds of feedback mechanisms seem most likely to prove effective in particular circumstances. Also, as an aspect of their review of relevant laws and experience, a deputy should critically consider mechanisms that, elsewhere, apparently have provided useful feedback.

3.5. Summing up: a checklist of questions to ask about a bill[64]

To assess a bill, a deputy must ascertain its factual and logical foundation. In most countries, parliament usually receives a bill from its proponents accompanied by little more than a flimsy restatement of the bill in lay terms. Concretely, the task of assessing a bill reduces itself to learning what questions to ask to uncover that

---

63 *See generally Manual, supra* n. 1, ch. 6.

64 In almost every case, one or another of these categories may appear "empty;" that is, no causal factor of the kind the category suggests seems to exist. Legislators should not feel obliged to ask anything about a category if, after thinking about it, for the behavior at issue they can construct no plausible explanation subsumed by the category involved.

factual and logical foundation. A legislator seeking to assess a bill in terms of reason informed by experience requires a checklist of questions to ask.[65] The same checklist suggests questions to ask a minister or department official about a bill's provisions and suggests questions to ask officials, after its enactment, about that law's implementation and impact.

A deputy should treat this checklist as a flexible guide, not a straitjacket. Every bill constitutes a special case. Under each heading, a legislator must decide what specific questions to ask depending on the particular bill under consideration. For that, this checklist serves as a guide to relevance. It can guide the deputy to discover the information required to assess the proposed bill's design – and since policy lurks in the details, the bill's underlying legislative policy.

3.5.1. Introductory questions

(1) How would you summarize the bill's proposals to overcome the social problem addressed?

(2) Where and how does the bill fit into the government's larger legislative program?

(3) Does the history of efforts to deal with the problem in the country or in other countries offer lessons that might help to understand the reasons for introducing this bill at this time and in this form?

3.5.2. The difficulty the bill aims to help resolve, and how it fits into the larger picture

[This item, as well as the two following items, suggest questions to ask about the present situation].

(1) What evidence exists as to the surface appearance of the particular difficulty addressed by the bill in terms of its effect on human, physical, or financial resources?

---

[65] We derive this outline from the one we have recommended for drafters' use in formulating a research report to accompany and justify a bill's detailed provisions (*see Manual, supra* n. 1). Structured by legislative theory's problem-solving methodology, the outline specifies how to organize the available evidence logically to demonstrate that a bill's detailed provisions will likely alter problematic behaviors in ways appropriate to resolve the social problem at which it aims.

(2) What evidence exists as to whose and what behaviors contribute to the difficulty addressed by the bill?

(3) Does the history of either the difficulty or comparative law and experience provide, with respect to your country, insights into the nature and scope of the difficulty, or whose and what behaviors comprise it?

(4) What facts exist as to who benefits and who suffers from the present situation?

3.5.3. Explanations of the interrelated causes of the behaviors that comprise the difficulty addressed by the bill

[Using the ROCCIPI categories a deputy should ask questions about the evidence as to the (implicitly or explicitly hypothesized) interrelated causes of the role occupants' existing problematic behaviors. The deputy should ask those questions in turn about each set of primary role occupants and each implementing agency and each set of officials in those agencies. Where relevant, the deputy should ask questions about history and comparative law and experience as possible sources of additional hypotheses for explaining existing problematic behaviors. Here are the questions to ask of each set of these role occupants, agencies, and officials.]

(1) How does the existing "cage of rules" help to explain problematic behaviors?

(a) Exactly how does existing law address the problematic behavior at issue?

(b) Does existing law specify *in detail* what relevant role occupants and agencies shall, may, or may not do?

(c) Does existing law address non-legal causes of problematic behaviors?

(d) Does existing law in practice give to relevant actors non-transparent, unaccountable, non-participatory discretionary power? Does it prescribe adequate procedures for the exercise of that power?

(e) Does existing law explicitly or implicitly authorize all or part of the problematic behaviors at issue?

(2) What evidence exists as to what and how non-legal factors influence this set of role occupants' problematic behaviors?

(a) Objective factors

(i) Does this set of role occupants have the *Opportunity* and *Capacity* to behave in ways appropriate for helping to resolve the difficulty?

(ii) Have the relevant authorities *Communicated* the law's relevant details to this set of role occupants?

(iii) What criteria and procedures determine the *Process* by which this set of role occupants (especially if they constitute implementing agency officials) make decisions as to how to behave? If this set of role occupants constitutes implementing officials, how transparent are their decision-making *Processes*? How accountable? How participatory? Do they decide by rule?

(b) Subjective factors

(i) How and to what extent does this set of role-occupants' *Interests*, including the effect of potential sanctions, influence their behaviors?

(ii) How and to what extent does this set of role occupants' *Ideology* seem to affect their behaviors?

After obtaining the answers to these questions relating to the first set of role occupants, ask the same questions about the second set, then about the third set, and so on, to obtain the available evidence as to the possible interrelated causes of different sets of role occupants' problematic behavior.

3.5.4. What possible alternative legislative schemes logically might help alter or eliminate the causes of existing problematic behaviors?

(1) Does a review of the country's history of efforts to use law, or other countries' laws and experience, provide insights into possible solutions, other than the one proposed in the bill?

(2) Given the country's unique circumstances, does the proposed bill's legislative scheme seem preferable – and if it does, in what ways – to the available alternatives?

(3) Request a detailed description and explanation of the bill's major provisions – in lay language.

(4) Do the bill's prescriptions, taken in conjunction with existing law, create a viable *system* for dealing with the problem?

(a) Do almost all the sentences in the bill *command, allow or forbid* behavior (i.e., do they almost all contain the words "shall," "may," or "may not")?

(b) To determine whether these prescriptions amount to a complete *system*, consider the following sets of rules: Rules addressed to –

(i) primary role occupants;

(ii) implementing agencies and their officials generally;

(iii) implementing agencies, concerning sanctions;

(iv) dispute settlement agencies

(v) funding agencies;

(vi) officials concerned with monitoring and evaluating the law; and

(vii) officials who keep the corpus of the law in order (definitional clauses, coming-into-force and scope-of-application provisions, consequential amendments, etc.)

The following questions serve to amplify the answers to the previous questions, particularly as they relate to the likely effectiveness of the proposed implementing agencies:

(5) Do the bill's measures with respect to the primary role occupants seem likely to:

(a) Alter or eliminate the objective and subjective causes of their existing problematic behaviors?

(b) Induce them to behave in more appropriate ways?

(6) Will the bill's provisions with respect to the implementing agency officials' existing problematic behaviors likely:

(a) Change the objective and subjective causes of their existing problematic behaviors?

(b) Induce officials to behave in ways necessary to assist the primary role occupants to change their subjective perceptions and overcome the objective factors that might hinder them from behaving as the law prescribes?

(c) Ensure they employ transparent, accountable, and participatory decision-making processes?

(7) Do the bill's provisions prescribe adequate decision-making processes with respect to rule-making?

(a) In general, does the bill seem likely to ensure that the agency will make the kinds of decisions required to resolve the social problem at which it aims?

(b) Does the bill require the agency – and ensure its officials have the capacity – to do the necessary research to make sound rules?

(c) By specifying criteria that the agency may take into account, does the bill limit its officials' range of discretion as narrowly as possible while still enabling them to play the role required to help resolve the particular social problem?

(d) Does the bill require the agency decision-makers to employ specific, transparent, accountable, participatory rule-making procedures? Does it require decision by rule?

(8) Do the bill's estimated long-term social and economic benefits seem likely to outweigh its estimated long-term social and economic costs?

(a) On what facts do those estimates rest, especially for those more difficult to estimate –

(i) long-term economic costs; and

(ii) non-quantifiable social costs and benefits.

(b) What social impact will the bill likely have for –

(i) different social groups, especially the poor, women, children and minorities;

(ii) valued, but typically poorly represented interests, *e.g.*, the environment, human rights, and the rule of law (including the prevention of corruption).

(9) Do the bill's dispute-settlement provisions seem appropriate and sufficient to take care of anticipated disputes?

(10) Does the bill or other law provide adequate funding for implementation of its entire program?

(11) Does the bill contain appropriate instructions to judges and others who ensure it fits into the existing corpus of the law?

(a) Does the bill contain a General Principles (or "Objectives") clause sufficiently narrowly drawn to guide the relevant official in drafting regulations under the new law?

(b) Does it contain sufficient definitional clauses?

(c) Does it contain the necessary consequential amendments to existing laws to avoid conflicts?

(d) Does it provide for coming-into-force at an appropriate time?

(12) With respect to the bill's provisions for monitoring and evaluating the law's results after its enactment to determine whether that law proves effectively implemented and produces the desired social impact (problem-solving's indispensable fourth step):

(a) Why did the bill's proponents select the monitoring and evaluation system it proposes? Do the reasons seem sufficient?

(b) What alternative possible monitoring and evaluation devices might the bill contain, either in addition to or in place of those it proposes?

(c) What does foreign experience demonstrate as to the relative effectiveness of all these "feedback" devices?

4. Conclusion

The twentieth century's end saw increased poverty and a deepening gap between the "haves" and "have nots," not only within developing and transitional countries, but between their peoples and those of industrialized countries. In this article, we have used a problem-solving approach to try to explain why newly-elected legislators have so seldom deliberated and enacted laws in the public interest. In part, the causes seem embedded in existing legislative procedures which deny elected legislators the opportunity to exercise their constitutionally-designated legislative powers. (As a basis for changing those procedures, lawmakers may want to explore that hypothesis in their country's unique circumstances.) In part, the causes reflect the reality that few legislators have a legislative theory, methodology or techniques to guide them in assessing – and when necessary initiating – legislative proposals.

Addressing only the second of these explanations, this article has proposed an institutionalist legislative theory to guide elected deputies in assessing a bill. That assessment requires more than expertise in scanning the face of a bill. It requires the deputies to obtain information about the facts and logic on which a bill purports to rest. Only with that information can they enact laws with a high probability of effective implementation. Only by using reason informed by experience – facts and logic – can legislators exercise their constitutionally-designated legislative power as trustees for the public interest. Only as trustees can they build a better future for themselves and their constituents.

PROPERTY RIGHTS ISSUES IN COMMON PROPERTY REGIMES FOR FORESTRY

JOHN BRUCE*

In many developing countries, common property rights regimes for forests are difficult to discern: they are typically the result of original common property elements in customary legal systems on which several layers of subsequent law have been superimposed – colonial rule, post-independence law asserting new rights in the state, laws recognizing indigenous forms of land tenure alongside "modern" land law, and attempts at harmonizing and unifying national law with respect to

---

* John W. Bruce is senior counsel with the Environmental and Socially Sustainable Development and International Law Practice Group, Legal Vice Presidency, the World Bank. Previously he was director of the Land Tenure Center and adjunct assistant professor, Department of Forest Ecology and Management, University of Wisconsin-Madison; country representative/project specialist in customary law, Sudan Field Office, the Ford Foundation; and legal institutions advisor, Ministry of Land Reform and Administration, Ethiopia while serving with the U.S. Agency for International Development. He taught at the faculty of law, University of Khartoum, Sudan and has consulted for numerous international organizations and national governments. He has published over 30 articles and monographs (alone or with others) and has co-edited *Searching for Security of Land Tenure in Africa* (with Migot-Adholla, Kendall/Hunt 1994), and *Whose Trees?* (with Louise Fortmann, Westview Press 1988). John Bruce holds an S.J.D. degree from the School of Law, University of Wisconsin-Madison, a J.D. degree from Columbia University, and a B.A. degree from Lafayette College, Pennsylvania.

The author thanks the Land Tenure Center of the University of Wisconsin-Madison and the Community Forestry Programme of the United Nations Food and Agriculture Organization (FAO) as well as the World Bank's Environmental and Socially Sustainable Development and International Law Practice Group for their support with the research of this article. The author gratefully acknowledges permission granted by the Food and Agriculture Organization of the United Nations (FAO) for permission to reproduce from John Bruce, *Legal Bases for the Management of Forest Resources as Common Property* in FAO Community Forestry Note No. 14 (©FAO 1999).

The World Bank Legal Review: Law and Justice for Development: 257-305.

Printed in the Netherlands.

land. In this article, John Bruce cuts through this legal layer-cake, drawing heavily on the experience of the World Bank and the Food and Agriculture Organization of the United Nations and using examples from countries in Africa, Asia, the Middle East, and Latin America and the Caribbean. He concludes that common property regimes for forest management that offer greater autonomy and security of tenure deserve to be pursued, but that their effective realization will require clearly articulated and strong legal frameworks.

Contents

1. Introduction: Forestry and Community

Recognizing the need of local communities to utilize forests to generate an income, there has been a shift in government policies and development aid from mere conservation to sustainable use and management.[1] As the general forestry policy shifted, so too the World Bank has increasingly focused on poverty eradication and environmental stewardship, and natural resource management has taken its place alongside agriculture as a major concern in rural development. The growing focus on poverty eradication has directed attention towards natural resources management policies and project designs that meet the needs of those in poverty, as well as demands of the larger national and global communities. Nowhere is this shift in emphasis clearer than in the World Bank's work on forestry.[2] An earlier generation of World Bank-funded projects focused on commercial production, often for export and with foreign exchange needs very much in mind. Later, conservation concerns predominated. While concerns for the benefit of larger groups or legitimate national interests are still very much in play, the World Bank is now anxious to ensure that forestry projects also make significant contributions to local needs and livelihoods.

Today, designers and managers of development and conservation projects are seeking to establish or support community resource management as part of their projects. Disillusioned with the performance of the state as a resource manager, they now commonly resort to greater control of resource use by local communities. Donors and governments are increasingly opting for smaller, more participatory projects. They often find communities using land as commons, and there is a particular interest in exploring more thoroughly the role which community-managed

---

1 A good example of this policy shift is the World Wildlife Fund's (WWF) Forests for Life Campaign and the Alliance between the WWF and the World Bank, which was formed in 1999. *See* <http://www.panda.org/forests4life>, and <http://www-eds.worldbank.org/wwf>.

2 Various projects illustrate this change, *see* The World Bank, Operations Evaluation Department, *Impact Evaluation Report: Financing the Global Benefits of Forests – The Bank's GEF Portfolio and the 1991 Forest Strategy* (10/01/2000); *Country Case Study: China* (07/01/2000); *Country Case Study: Costa Rica* (07/01/2000); *Country Case Study: India* (07/01/2000); *Country Case Study: Brazil* (07/01/2000); and *Country Case Study: Cameroon* (07/01/2000), <http://www.wbln0018.worldbank.org./oed/oeddoclib.nsf/htmlmedia/pubcagr.html>.

commons can play in community forestry.[3] Numerous countries have substantial experience in community forestry and associated property arrangements, and these initiatives have been reviewed.[4] The World Bank has supported projects of this nature and judged them successful.[5]

2. Community Forest Projects and Programs

Community forest projects and programs can vary from one country to the next and achieve differing degrees of success in strengthening community access to and use of forests. Two examples are described below.

2.1. Two Examples

The Laos Forest Management and Conservation Program (FOMACOP) is supported by the World Bank, the Government of Finland, the Global Environmental Facility Trust Fund, and the Laotian Ministry of Agriculture and Forestry and Department of Forestry.[6] It has launched a pilot program for participatory management of production forests in Savannekhet and Khammaoune Provinces, encompassing 60 villages, 19,000 people, and 100,000 hectares of natural forest.

Historically, the law respected traditional rights of local communities. But protections were lost during the communist period, and today Laotian law does not recognize the extensive customary rights of local communities in forests. The new Forestry Law does however allow the state to devolve state-owned forests to local communities for management according to state-approved management plans, and to compensate them for their management activities.[7] Though there is some re-

---

3 M. McKean & E. Ostrom, *Common Property Regimes in the Forest: Just a Relict From the Past?*, 180 Unasylva 3-15 (1995).

4 J.E.M. Arnold, *Managing Forests as Common Property* (FAO Forestry Paper No. 136, 1999); John Bruce, *Legal Bases for the Management of Forest Resources* (FAO Community Forestry Note No. 14, 1999).

5 Some of these projects will be discussed in detail later in this article.

6 World Bank, *World Bank Project Data, Forest Management and Conservation Project, Lao People's Democratic Republic* <http://4.worldbank.org/sprojects/Project.asp?pid=P004196>.

7 Lao Peoples Democratic Republic, Forestry Law art. 7 (1996).

spect for customary forest rights in practice, there have been instances of officials granting cutting permits to outsiders against the wishes of local communities.

FOMACOP's Forest Management Sub-Program has used the opening provided by the 1996 law to work with the villagers in several ways. It helped them organize themselves into 33 Village Forestry Associations (VFA) with approved articles of association, involving 5,000 members from 41 villages, and supported VFA interaction with the Department of Forestry in the preparation of acceptable forest management plans. It also assisted the VFAs in concluding 50-year management contracts with the Department of Forestry, which include management plans. The villages and ministry staff have undertaken boundary demarcation and prepared land use maps and 10-year land use plans. They have completed pre-harvest inventories, prepared ten-year forestry-management plans and operational plans, tree marking, supervision of log felling and grading, and post-harvest assessments. The management plans are based on low-intensity harvesting, and on felling cycles of 5 to 10 years, with only one or two trees cut per hectare.

Sixty-nine percent of timber revenues for 1998-1999 went to the government in the form of royalties and other taxes; 19 percent went to logging contractors for the felling of trees and transporting of logs, and the remaining 12 percent went to the villages. The villages spent half of their revenues on sustainable forest management, including wages to villagers for labor and VFA administration costs. The remaining half was left available for development, welfare support, investments, and reserves, and averaged approximately U.S.$ 1,700 per village. The pilot experience has been promising, and evaluations have given it good grades for efficiency and sustainable resource use. However, the division of income from timber sales remains heavily skewed in favor of government, reflecting government's ownership of the forest and lack of recognition of customary rights. Most critically, the program is based on delegation of state authority by contract rather than secure vesting of rights of management in the associations. This has not prevented the creation of an attractive incentive structure for local participation. It remains to be seen whether the contracts will be consistently honored, and cutting by outsiders not allowed, especially when the project ends. Beyond the ten-year time frame of the current management plans, the sustainability of the program is subject to decisions made by the officials of the day.

2.2. Property Rights Strategies in Community Forest Projects and Programs

Property rights strategies are critical for these projects. Forests are among the land-based natural resources that development literature often denominates as "common property resources" or "common pool resources" because, in the developing world, the use of forests is frequently shared by one or more groups for hunting, gathering, firewood and timber extraction, and sacred purposes. Forests may be managed by community institutions. Owing to their physical extent and how frequently various groups make use of them, common-pool resources can be quite difficult to control and manage. Some are managed in a sustainable manner by effective community institutions and conventions, while others fall into the category of "open access," the free-for-all that Hardin has in mind when he argues that individual users of a common will in the absence of control inevitably over-utilize and degrade the resource.[8]

Governments are often confronted with choices as to whether to use common property management regimes, building or strengthening community institutions and empowering them to manage the resource, or to partition and individualize rights to the resource. Where a resource is managed well either as common property or individual property, the maxim, "if it isn't broken, don't fix it," will in practice apply. However, there are at least three circumstances in which choices need to be made:

- Where a resource has been subject to open access, but there is now a desire to create user incentives for sustainable use and management and a choice must be made to proceed on an individual or community basis;
- Where a resource has been under common property management but the system is being undermined by outside pressures, and the choice is whether to reinforce or reengineer the existing system or to partition the resource to household or individual users; and
- Where a resource has been under failed direct state management and its use, management and possibly ownership are to be devolved to smaller social units, households or communities.

These choices about property rights and their assignees have critical implications for the distribution of project benefits. Individualization, while simpler in design, may limit those who benefit from forestry. Forests in the developed world tend to be managed on a large scale by private forest owners, but in the developing world it is often unacceptable to create large forest ownerships for some individuals, and

---

[8] G. Hardin, *The Tragedy of the Unmanaged Commons*, 9 Trends in Ecological Evolution 199 (1994).

exclude most existing users. The existing users consider the forest theirs, and excluding them would be politically untenable, partly because this group includes the poorest and most vulnerable. The poor commonly earn a larger part of their livelihoods than others from common property resources, seeking to compensate for their lack of individually-owned resources. Women and other vulnerable groups rely on them disproportionately. However, partitioning forests into thousands of small forest holdings for household management is not a viable option. This makes the proper institutionalization, maintenance, and even expansion of community forestry management important in poverty reduction strategies, with partition a last resort.

3. The Common Property Solution

Realization of the potential of common property in supporting sustainable community resource management has in part grown out of the observations of development practitioners that local communities sometimes manage their resources effectively, even under substantial pressure. It is also due to the work of institutional economists who have reflected to good advantage on what precisely we mean by common property, why sustainable common property management is theoretically workable, and what might be the necessary conditions for effective common property management.[9]

Literature developed over the past decade examines "open access" situations, in which there are no social controls over use of the resource and where a "tragedy" of overuse may indeed be likely, as well as situations where the conditions for such control exist: a group with limited membership and a right to exclusive use of the resource, which then has the opportunity to regulate resource use by its members and also the incentive to do so, because the costs and benefits of disciplined, sustainable use are internalized to the group.[10]

---

[9] *Making the Commons Work: Theory, Practice and Reality* (D. Bromley ed., Inst. for Contemporary Studies Press 1992); D. Bromley, *Rules, Games and Common Property Resource Management* (E. Ostrom, E. Gardner & J. Walker eds., U. of Michigan Press 1994).

[10] John W. Bruce & Louise Fortman, *Property and Forestry*, in *Emerging Issues in Forestry Policy* (Peter Nemetz ed., U. of British Colombia Press 1992).

Common property is, as Bromley points out, simply property of a group.[11] It may be held in full private ownership or some other tenure. From an economic standpoint, its objective is much the same as individual property: to increase security of expectations, while reducing externalities and internalizing the costs and benefits of use decisions, thereby increasing incentives for efficient and sustainable use. Common property is one important way to ensure that communities have the confident expectation of long-term use of the land. It is a strategy to increase incentives for sustainable use by giving users a longer planning horizon. Communities can respond positively to the incentives for investment created by secure expectations, as do individuals on their own holdings.

Common property must be managed by a "community," which, as that word implies, has an affinity and shared sense of identity. This can be an extended family, a village, a lineage, a user group, a village, a tribe, or even a local administrative subdivision. It must not, by the economists' criteria, be too large, but it need not be private. In African countries, a village may in one decade be recognized as part of the state machinery, but in the next, revert to a quasi-private status. Local administrative units may be small enough so that they are communities in the normal sense of the word, and in these cases it would be too formal to exclude their arrangements for forest management from the common property category, though the arrangements of larger, more remote administrative entities do not qualify as common property.

Because management by a group is involved, common property resource management involves all the problems associated with collective action. Economists have puzzled over institutional frameworks that would solve these problems, and have developed a model for workable community resource management of "common property."[12] While derived from experiences with community management, it is, like other economic models, a simplification. In reality, common property regimes can be complex. Their success requires not only the legal and real empowerment over resources that property rights provide, but also adequate institutional arrangements for decision-making and enforcement, the requisite social capital, and a supportive political and legal environment. These are conditions that are often met only imperfectly, and cannot be perfected quickly or easily.

---

[11] D. Bromley, *supra* n. 9.

[12] *Id.*

In establishing or reinforcing a common property regime for community forestry, there are at least four questions that the theoreticians of common property tell us must be answered:[13]

- *Scale*: On what scale can the forest be managed? The answer is affected by the scale at which effective community institutions exist or can be created, but also by minimum scale requirements for forestry.
- *Management Organization*: What is the community that is to manage the resource? Is it to be an inclusive local community or a user group constituted specifically for the purpose? Is it adequately organized for the purpose and does it have the requisite social capital? Does it have the legal recognition that allows it to hold property rights?
- *Control over the Resource*: The community must be empowered to manage the resource, and that implies both the power to control use by members and the power to exclude or limit access by non-members.
- *Supportive Environment*: Is there a supportive legal and political environment? Will government respect community rights and refrain from allocating the land to others? Will outsiders respect properly constituted common property? If they trespass, can they be sanctioned effectively?[14]

Common property forestry is urged as an efficient approach, but there are other important values reflected in the literature on common property.[15] One is the need to maintain access to critical resources for the many rather than the few, and especially to preserve the access of the rural poor. In some cases, the survival of minority peoples depends upon the safeguarding of the rights of those communities in

---

[13] *Id.*; S.V. Ciriacy & R.C. Bishop, *Common Property as a Concept in Natural Property*, 15 Natural Resources Journal 713 (1975); E. Ostrom, *Neither Market nor State: Governance of Common-pool Resources in the Twenty-first Century* (Intl. Food Policy Research Inst. 1994).

[14] *See generally* Brent Swallow, Ruth Meinzen-Dick, Lee Ann Jackson, Timothy Williams, T. Anderson White, Panel, *Multiple Functions of Common Property Regimes* (Berkeley, California, Intl. Assn. for the Study of Common Property, 6th Annual Conference, June 7, 1997) (copy on file with the Environment and Production Technology Division, Intl. Food Policy Research Inst./CGIAR System-Wide Program on Property and Collective Action, EPTD Workshop Summary Paper No. 5, 1997).

[15] *See e.g. Whose Trees?: Proprietary Dimensions of Forestry* (Louise Fortmann & John W. Bruce eds., Rural Studies Series, Westview Press 1988) [hereinafter *Whose Trees?*].

their lands and forests.[16] Finally, strengthening community tenure in resources may be the only way to protect natural resources when they are beyond the effective control of weak states. The World Bank's experience with natural resource management in remote areas of Colombia in the mid 1990s led it to support extensive titling of natural resources to indigenous and Afro-Colombian communities.

3.1. Titling Community Territories for Natural Resource Management in Colombia

The World Bank-supported Colombia Natural Resources Management Program[17] began in 1994, and during loan preparation the concept of titling of indigenous territories was introduced under an Operational Directive.[18] There was such uncertainty over the authority to use and control land and natural resources in the heavily forested (77%) Choco Region that the project could not go forward without addressing the problem.

Land sales by government in the region had displaced some inhabitants and threatened others, resulting in declining security of tenure. The new constitution in 1991 and subsequent laws in 1993 and 1995 provided local communities in historic occupation of the extensive and largely unmanaged public forest lands with the capacity to register rights in their territories. After consultation with local communities, a project was designed that included titling and demarcation of indigenous reserves, titling of Afro-Colombian territories, and local participation through regional committees. About a tenth of the budget of the U.S.$ 39 million project has gone for this component, and the project ended in 2000.

The project worked closely with local communities and with the Integral Peasant Association of the Middle Atrato (ACIA). The first few years of the project concentrated on community capacity-building, and awareness-raising through workshops and publications. Regional committees were established, and developed the principles and criteria to guide titling. Community councils were also

---

[16] Roger Plant, *Land Rights and Minorities* (Minority Rights Group 1994); *Culture, Resources, and Conflict*, 19 Cultural Survival Quarterly (1995); *Land and* Resources, 14 Cultural Survival Quarterly (1990).

[17] World Bank, *World Bank Project Data, Colombia Natural Resources Management Program* <htttp://www.4.worldbank.org/sprojects/Project.asp?pid=P006868>.

[18] World Bank, *Operational Manual, Operational Directive OD 4.20, Indigenous Peoples* (Sept. 1991), <http://wbln0011.worldbank.org/Institutional/Manuals/OpManual.nsf>.

created. Boundaries between ethnic territories were established through inter-ethnic consultation and agreements, and then demarcated and titled to the communities. When ethnic conflict over a territory developed, inter-ethnic regional committees proved highly effective sites for conflict resolution. The World Bank was perhaps not as aware of the potential for conflict around these issues at the outset, but the avoidance of future conflict should be one of the lasting contributions of the project.

In total, 83 titles were granted to 404 communities, affecting nearly twenty thousand families and nearly two million hectares. The land has been protected against government land sales, and a basis established for sound natural resource management. In spite of the project's success and the positive local reception of the titling of ethnic territories, the project points up the vulnerability of activities in forested areas to insurrections. It is not possible at the current time for activities under the project to proceed.[19]

4. Common Property as Law and Custom

There is a duality in the normative life of many developing countries that represents both an opportunity and a complication for those who deal in common property solutions. The duality is between customary law and national legislation. These often exist in parallel and sometimes in conflict. The opportunity lies in the rich common property elements in customary legal systems, while the complication lies in the poor articulation between these systems in national law and the uncertainties that this creates.

First, the opportunity: customary property rights systems in developing countries often (though not invariably) emphasize communal natural resource management. There has been a growing understanding among development planners that indigenous tenure systems possess important normative and institutional resources for managing natural resources, for targeting benefits of project activities on the rural poor and for preserving the access of poorer members of these communities to those resources. Is it not then possible to rely upon them rather than legislating new rights and institutions?

---

[19] Bettina Ng'weno, Address, *Titling Collective Property, Participation, and Natural Resource Management: Implementing Indigenous and Afro- Colombian Demands, A Review of Bank Experiences in Colombia* (World Bank Oct. 15, 2000).

Reliance on customary common property institutions will be the solution in some cases, but caution is necessary. A village or lineage's "communal lands" are lands over which the community exercises administrative control, and even residual rights, but the lands often include parts which are subject to perpetual, inheritable individual rights as well as areas of land which are indeed community owned and managed. Moreover, land use in customary commons tends not to fall neatly into the boundaries expected in common property solutions. Instead, one often finds overlapping use rights and fuzzy boundaries. For instance, an area enjoyed as a commons for woodcutting, hunting, and bee-keeping by a village is also part of the customarily recognized commons of another group, such as pastoralists visiting the area on a seasonal basis. Such complexities can be managed, but must be recognized. Failure to address them creates exclusions that engender conflicts.

However, the duality between customary law and national legislation also leads to complications in developing countries. The root of the problem lies in colonial history. Colonial powers introduced western tenure forms alongside indigenous systems, but this was usually limited to modest land areas where holdings had been demarcated and surveyed. There was sometimes explicit recognition by colonial law of certain customary land rights, but in other cases customary rights were unrecognized and unenforceable in colonial courts. Recognition often involved considerable distortions of those systems to serve colonial policies.[20]

Such recognition however tended to be limited to farmland, with the state claiming pastures and forests for itself and seeking to extinguish traditional use rights. For the latter categories of land, there was a much greater uniformity than with regard to farmland and residential land. Across continents and across different colonial traditions, the clear and consistent theme of colonial natural resource management was concentration of control over those resources in the hands of the state.

The typical outcome is a legal layer-cake. At the bottom are a variety of local, community-based systems whose formal validity may or may not be recognized by statutory law. They may have been distorted or impaired by attempts to replace them, but they usually determine who actually gets to use land. Above them is a layer of national legislation originating in the colonial era or later, in socialist times, that contains extensive claims to state ownership of natural resources traditionally managed communally. Over these is often a third or even fourth layer of

---

[20] M. Chanock, *Law, Custom and Social Order: the Colonial Experience in Malawi and Zambia* (Cambridge U. Press 1985).

national legislation which attempts to replace the legal dualism with a unified national land law but which has never been effectively implemented. Normative confusion and conflict abound. In dealing with this situation it is useful to adopt the Austinian habit of accepting the legal preeminence of the state.[21] It is better to think of these conflicting bodies of rules as the normative expression of the "semi-autonomous social spheres" of local, regional, and national authorities.[22] There is a major tension between these systems concerning land and natural resources, and forests in particular.

How can these and other problems best be handled in national legislation to facilitate the creation and support the functioning of common property institutions for the forestry sector? The next section of this paper reviews some experiences. But a caution at the outset: one cannot derive through such a review legal forms that are universally "right" for common property forestry management. There are of course lessons to be learned, but there is no axiom more basic to the study of law and society than that a legal rule (a command to act or refrain from acting in a certain way) will produce different behavior on the part of individuals differently situated. "Differently situated" can refer to economic classes or social groups, or cultural and political milieus. The clear implication is that different legal solutions will be required for different contexts, and in the next section of this article, the material on national experiences is organized according to regions of the world.

5. Common Property in National Law

5.1. Overview

The index of laws for Country X will not direct the reader to laws on common property. Common property is a reality on the ground, and the topic of much modeling by economists. The reality is however treated by statutory law in almost all countries in an unfocused and fragmented fashion. There is no single statute or even field of law that covers all of common property. Rules that structure common property are embodied in legislation dealing with several substantive areas, including property, the law of associations, administrative law, and natural resources law.

---

[21] *The Austinian Theory of Law* (J. Brown ed., 1906).

[22] S. F. Moore, *Law As Process* (Routledge & Kegan Paul 1978).

Common property theory directs us to the relevant areas of law. Oakerson's model notes three fundamental normative requirements: (a) rules establishing collective choice (institutional form); (b) rules regulating the use of the commons (including exclusion of non-members); and (c) rules defining external arrangements.[23]

These requirements correspond roughly to particular areas of law within national legal systems, and those bodies will differ depending on whether the organization managing the common property is private or public:

- Rules establishing collective choice provide for the constitution and legal personality of the community, and the delimitation of its membership, its authority to control their activities and the processes by which the community makes decisions concerning the commons. The general body of law in which such issues are handled is the law of associations, including the law of corporations, cooperatives, and other private organizations. It details the ways in which people must organize themselves in order to be recognized by the state and hold property rights. Public administrative law may be applicable rather than the law of associations if the community is organized as a creature of public law, such as a unit of local government.
- Rules conferring management authority and regulating use of the commons govern the activities of the members and non-members with respect to the commons, usually limiting use by the former and excluding use by the latter. Property law is generally the main source of such authority, though conservation law and other bodies of law can also be important.
- Rules defining external arrangements include those which define the relationship between the community proprietor of the commons and external actors, which may include neighboring communities or their individual members; it may also include more remote external actors, as well as government at the local, regional, and national levels. Relations with neighboring communities and even more remote actors will be governed primarily by property law, especially as regards the right of exclusion, but the law of dispute resolution will also play a key role. Dispute settlement is one of the key areas in which a common property system needs support from govern-

[23] R. J. Oakerson, *Analyzing the Commons: a Framework*, in *Making the Commons Work: Theory, Practice, Reality, supra* n. 9; R. J. Oakerson, *A Model for the Analysis of Common Property Resources Management* (Natl. Academy Press 1986).

ment, and the need may extend to disputes within the community as well as with outsiders. Relations between the government and a common property management institution will be affected by the legislation establishing and empowering the ministries or agencies which provide relevant services to the local community, and in the legislation which establishes the hierarchy of government down to the local level. The community may be a part of that hierarchy, if it is a unit of local government.

- Relevant across all three of the above categories are specialized statutes regulating the use of natural resources generally, or more commonly a particular resource, such as forests or pasture. This resource-specific legislation is often the law with which public officials such as forestry officers are most familiar, because it is specific to the resource with which they deal. It often provides some special option, such as a simplified form of organization and authority for community management of the resource, but it almost never is itself sufficient to the legal needs of common property management, nor does it exclude the possibility of the more general and complex forms of organization and authority available in the national legal system.

The conclusion is that there is no all-purpose "common property statute" in any national law. In the concluding chapter, we can consider whether such a statute would be a good thing, but for now we must, like local people engaged in community forestry, take the statute law as we find it. Figure 1 seeks to summarize the relevant areas of formal law. It recognizes that some local common property institutions are public rather than private, and others are hybrids, with different bodies of law relevant in the different cases. Property rights are a legal source of management authority.

The remainder of this section first examines the patterns established by colonial laws, which often undermined local traditions of commons. It then examines numerous national experiences, and seeks to identify trends that are developing in this area of law. The countries reviewed were selected to provide a considerable variety of legal forms, and in light of the availability of information.

5.2. The Colonial Inheritance

The development of a dichotomy between indigenous and national statutory law originated in most developing countries through imposition of colonial law at the national level. In all cases colonial law has been an important influence, and so it is appropriate to begin here.

The colonialists had their own traditions of commons. The English term "the commons" comes out of the law of feudal England, and was land to which rights

Figure 1. Legal Bases: Common Property

	Public Common Property Institutions	*Private Common Property Institutions*
INSTITUTIONAL FORM (RULES ESTABLISHING COLLECTIVE CHOICE)	Local government law Cooperative law Forestry law	Law of associations Cooperative law Corporation law Foundation law Registration law Forestry law
MANAGEMENT AUTHORITY (INCLUDING TENURE)	Constitution Local government law Property law Cooperative law Forestry law Contract law	Constitution Property law Forestry law Contract law
RELATION TO EXTERNAL ACTORS	Local government law Administration of justice law Forestry law Property law Contract law	Local government law Administration of justice law Forestry law Property law Contract law

of commonage applied. The land was that of the feudal lords, and their subjects were granted rights over the land in exchange for farming the land or carrying out other functions for the lords. This concept was not carried over into the colonies, and judges tried instead, with poor results, to apply concepts such as tenancy in common to customary communal ownership.[24] The situation was more satisfactory in those English colonies where indirect rule was applied, and where there

[24] R. W. James, *Land Tenure Reform in Developing Countries: From Westernization to Indigenization*, 9 East Africa Law Rev. 1-46 (1976).

was recognition of customary law in colonial statute. This law was developed through the decisions of colonial courts, in the English common law tradition. The colonial power pursued its land policies through the courts.[25] In the later colonial period, large areas of forest land were declared reserves, for direct management by the colonial state.

In francophone colonies, a somewhat different pattern emerged based on a strong French tradition of centralized forest management by the national state. The colonial forest code for French West Africa[26] declared that lands which were vacant and without owners belonged to the state. The criterion for recognition of such occupation excluded most uses other than agriculture, and this led to vast areas of forest and range vesting in the state. Under this law, the mission of the Forest Service evolved over the years into a repressive policing role. Local rights to forest use were denied, reflecting a centuries-old French state policy of restricting traditional peasant access to French forests in order, in part, to preserve the state's monopoly over the commercial use of increasingly valuable forests.[27]

It is necessary to turn to Latin America, and the heritage of Spanish law, to find a very direct transfer of common property traditions of the metropole to the colony. The region's history has provided opportunities for community forestry to rural people in some countries through a common property institution of Castilian origin: the *ejido*. In Latin America, public land is either *ejido* or *baldia*. Ejido refers to land that belonged to the municipalities at the time of colonization, and municipal lands subsequently acquired. This land cannot be sold or mortgaged. Baldia refers to government-owned land, which is not ejido land and has no other legal owner. The government may sell or assign this land. If government assigns the land to a municipality, it becomes ejido land.[28] These forms have been key legal vehicles for common property forestry in some countries of the region, such as Mexico and Guatemala. Elsewhere, new forms have arisen.

---

[25] Z. Mustafa, *The Common Law in the Sudan: an Account of the "Justice, Equity, and Good Conscience" Provision* (Clarendon Press 1971); *Whose Trees?*, *supra* n. 15; Robert B. Seidman, *The State, Law and Development* (Methuen 1976).

[26] French West Africa, Forest Code (July 4,1935).

[27] S. Pinctl, *Some Origins of French Environmentalism: An Exploration*, 37 Forest and Conservation History 80 (1993).

[28] S. E. Hendrix, *Property Law Innovations in Latin America with Recommendations*, 18 Boston College Intl. Law Rev. 1-58 (1995).

The post-colonial period has seen extensive and diverse experimentation with the legal frameworks for community forestry, and this experience is reviewed below.

5.3. Latin America: Diversification and Indigenization

In recent decades, there has been a virtual explosion of legal arrangements purporting to confer authority to manage forests on local communities. Historically, the ejido has played a major role, and its role has continued to develop and change, as will be seen in the brief review below of the experience with ejidos in Guatemala and Mexico.

In Guatemala, a unique system of community forest management exists among the Quiche Maya living in the highlands of southwestern Guatemala. As much as 25% of this region is held communally. The system has survived through integration into an imported Spanish commons institution. When the Spanish sought to repress Mayan institutions beginning early in the 18th century, they imported the Castilian notion of the ejido, village common property used for threshing, garbage disposal, and other general necessities. Land which had been communally managed in pre-Columbian times was awarded as ejidos to the *pueblo* (town), usually the main settlement in the *municipio* (township), and the *aldeas* and *caserios* (villages) around the pueblo.[29]

As ejidos, these remain in practice closed corporate communities, with membership based on birth in the community. Each is governed by a village council elected annually by the village assembly. The council assesses requests to extract trees, create and enforce rules, oversee the activities of the forest guards, and in some cases, manage nurseries. The ejidos have been threatened by both pressures to individualize land tenure and by governmental regulation of forest use, but there is evidence that they have effectively husbanded forest resources.[30]

While ejidos in Guatemala have struggled in an unfriendly policy context, in Mexico they were the organizational cornerstone of the land reforms after the Mexican Revolution, and enshrined in the Mexican Constitution of 1917. Ejidos

---

[29] R. Hill & J. Monaghan, *Continuities in Highland Maya Social Organization: Ethnohistory in Sacapula, Guatemala* (U. of Pennsylvania Press 1987).

[30] M. Castellon, *Communal Forest Preservation in Totonicapan* (Thesis, U. of Wisconsin-Madison 1992); I. Lebot, *Tenencia y Renta de la Tierra en el Altiplano Occidental de Guatemala*, 13 Estudios Sociales Centeroamericanos 69-95 (Feb.-Apr. 1976).

had existed earlier in Mexico, but now they became the form for organizing land reform beneficiaries, and the entity which actually received title to the land. Presently there are 29,000 ejidos in Mexico, covering about 50% of the country.

Ejido forests are common property, but a 1947 law allowed the government to grant concessions to forests on ejido lands. This was the primary means of forest exploitation until the early 1980s, when ejidos began to organize into regional associations and assert their right to directly manage their forest resources.[31] The new control over marketing of timber products produced considerable surpluses for local communities, and they began to move into processing. The ejido has also been utilized in non-indigenous communities, as where resin-tappers in Michoacan State agreed to communal exploitation of forest resources on their individual territories subject to their right to tap resin and a stumpage payment.[32]

Under a 1991 reform, the ejido now has full ownership of its land rather than just use rights. The commons areas may not be alienated permanently, but the ejido board can lease out the use of the land for as long as 30 years, and may authorize a pledge of the use of the land as security for a loan. A creditor may foreclose, but at the end of the term of the use right, the land reverts to the ejido. The new legislation of 1991 has spurred reorganization of community forestry enterprises.

While in Mexico and Guatemala the ejido has played the key role in common property forestry, alternative institutional developments are now proliferating. In Brazil, the traditional rubber estate is used as a model for extractive reserves. Individual holdings within the traditional estate had no visible boundaries, but rights to trails were assigned and recognized. The Chico Mendes extractive reserve contains 19 former rubber estates. The extractive reserves belong to the government, which grants usufruct rights for 30 years (with renewal options) to

---

[31] R. L. Arzola & P. Gerez Fernandez, *The Permanent Tension*, Cultural Survival Quarterly 42-44 (Spring 1993); N. Forster & D. Stanfield, *Tenure Regimes and Forest Management: Case Studies in Latin America* (Land Tenure Center, U. of Wisconsin-Madison Paper No. 147, 1993).

[32] Maria Angelica Sanchez Pego, *The Forestry Enterprise of the Indigenous Community of Nuevo San Juan Parangaricutiro*, in *Case Studies of Community-Based Forestry Enterprises in the Americas*, in *Papers Presented at the Symposium Forestry in the Americas: Community-Based Management and Sustainability* (U. of Wisconsin-Madison, Feb. 3-4, 1995) 139-140 (Land Tenure Center, U. of Wisconsin-Madison 1995).

traditional forest product extractor communities. There are now over three million hectares assigned under two reserve categories.[33]

In numerous countries of Latin America with land reform experiences in the 1960s and 1970s, models of communal land ownership were introduced for reform beneficiaries.[34] These were intended more to protect the holdings of reform beneficiaries from reconsolidation in large estates, rather than to provide a basis for communal management of the resource. Often these laws provided for titling based on established use, and Indian communities have utilized these provisions as a second-best approach to protecting their lands, seeking individual titles in the absence of a possibility of obtaining a community title. In the past decade there has been an increasing trend toward the liberalization of the property regime for these lands, allowing them to move into the market.[35] This further reduces their potential as a vehicle for common property forestry management.

In Brazil, the Indian Reserve is offered as a model. Davis and Wali[36] characterize this option as protectionist. It involves the identification and regularization of indigenous territories, but that process has moved slowly. In 1990, a study found 526 indigenous areas of which 90 were not identified, 80 identified but not interdicted, 67 interdicted, 93 delimited, 136 demarcated and confirmed by presidential decree, and only 60 fully regularized. That last category accounted for only 13% of the total area of indigenous lands. Steps are being taken to streamline the process, but Davis and Wali conclude that the National Indian Foundation as a bureaucratic institution lacks the technical competence, financial resources, and authority to defend these lands.[37] Encroachment is continuing. Moreover, they point out, the system does not recognize indigenous models of land tenure, social organization, and resource management. They note that the relevant articles in the Brazilian constitution of 1988 are broad enough to permit an alternative indigenous model, but so far this has not been implemented.

In addition, there are protected areas in Brazil, Venezuela, Peru, Bolivia, and other Latin American countries, established under conservation legislation. Davis

---

[33] Forster & Stanfield, *supra* n. 31.

[34] R. V. Casanova, *Derecho Agrario* (U. de los Andes 1990).

[35] Hendrix, *supra* n. 28.

[36] Shelton H. Davis & A. Wali, *Indigenous Land Tenure and Tropical Forestry Management in Latin America*, 23 Ambio 485-490 (1994).

[37] *Id.*

and Wali cite the Xingu Indian Park in Brazil as the classic model,[38] and many others have been created under pressure from the international conservation community. They protect territory, but do not provide a basis for sustainable resource management. The indigenous peoples do not have title to their land, all rights remaining vested in the government.

There are indigenous community models (sometimes called "native community" models) in Bolivia, Ecuador and Peru. These seem more promising as a basis for common property management. Land is given to the communities but under a standard western model of organization. For example, in the era of agrarian reform, Indian communities in Ecuador and Bolivia had to organize themselves into cooperatives to be allocated land. In 1974, the Peruvian government enacted a Jungle Law which enables native communities to register as legal entities and to hold land in that capacity.[39] But it limited the size of traditionally occupied or used land that could be titled, and it has been suggested that this will prove inadequate in the long term.[40] The Yanesha Forestry Cooperative (COFYAL) is located in the Palcazu Valley in the Peruvian Amazon. A 1974 Law of Native Communities had permitted these communities to hold land communally in a manner recognized by the state for the first time. Logging areas are established by the communities. There is communal extraction with income generated used for communal activities, and also individual extraction with approval of communal authorities. The communities are authorized to manage and develop the forest through extraction contracts. These are granted on behalf of the community by the Ministry of Agriculture, since the communities are not allowed to own the forest. If the community does not obtain an extraction permit, it cannot carry out the process and market forest products because they will be confiscated and fines levied.

COFYAL was formed in 1986, in reaction to aggressive settlement by *ladinos* (Spanish-speaking Europeanized local inhabitants or descendants of Spanish-Indian unions) in the region. The organizing committee proposed a cooperative as the most appropriate structure "because this structure resembles the Yanesha's traditional way to decide communal issues."[41] Proyecto Especial Pichis-Palacazu

---

[38] *Id.*

[39] *Id.*

[40] *Id.*

[41] M. Lazaro, M. Pariona & R. Simeone, *A Natural Harvest*, Cultural Survival Quarterly 48, 49 (Spring 1993).

(PEPP), the project administration for colonization in the area, had under local and international political pressure shifted its emphasis to natural resource management. It now assisted in the formation of the cooperative. Several communities were involved, covering a large territory.

As a funding condition, the U.S. Agency for International Development had required that ten Ayanesha communities in the Palcazu Valley receive land titles. The five indigenous communities in COFYAL managed some 2,000 hectares of production forest reserves and wood processing facilities. It was anticipated that another five native communities might eventually add 6,500 hectares of production forest.[42]

However, the situation of the cooperative deteriorated. There was suspicion among the members, based on management style, and there were difficulties in developing a full-time labor force for forest management consistent with other production responsibilities in traditional households. Significant problems of scale also emerged; the area may be too large to be manageable. Today, the cooperative has ceased to manage extraction, and local woodcutters are doing as they wish. Those reviewing the project cite complexity and unprofitability as undermining it, and also list an inadequate legal framework, though they do not specify in what sense this was the case.[43]

Another troubled experience with this model is the Chaquitano Indigenous Community in eastern Bolivia. A regional cultural organization, the Centro Intercomunal del Oriente Lomerio (CICOL) provided the impetus for this effort, and decided that only a government-granted timber concession could provide a legal basis for protecting Indian territory. Bolivian law did not recognize communal titles. CICOL initiated a forest management project in 1984 called the Lomerio Project, and obtained support from Oxfam America and HIVOS, a Dutch organization. At the outset of the project there was apparent agreement of 21 communities to cede their land to the regional organization for management. The project prepared a forest management plan and applied for a concession.

---

[42] Forster & Stanfield, *supra* n. 31.

[43] M. Benavides & M. Paruiona, *The Forestry Enterprise of the Indigenous Community-based Forestry of Nuevo San Parangaricutiro* in *Case Studies of Community-based Forestry Enterprises in the Americas: Papers Presented at the Symposium on Forestry in the Americas: Community-based Management and Sustainability* (U. of Wisconsin-Madison, 3-4 February 1995) (Land Tenure Center, U. of Wisconsin-Madison 1995); Lazaro *et al.*, *supra* n. 41.

As the project attempted to get underway, it was discovered that there was not a full consensus among communities. The communities were putting forward property rights claims to their traditional areas. The Catholic Church supported the notion that each Chiquitano has property rights in resources. Three communities withdrew from the project and demanded that their areas be respected, and even those remaining asserted property rights. A major renegotiation was necessary, which clearly demarcated the area that the regional organization would manage and log, but which was perhaps only 30% of the original area.[44]

In Ecuador, the Quichua Indians of Napo Province in the Amazon have established areas of resource use. An oil boom in the 1970s precipitated a land rush, and Indians began to apply for individual titles under the agrarian reform laws. They converted forest to pasture to demonstrate use. The *Programa de Uso y Manejo de Recuros Naturales* (PUMAREN) is a regional natural resource-management program established in 1988 by the Indian Federation (Federation of Indian Organizations of Napo), representing 60 communities. In its first phase, the project emphasized consolidation of land rights. PUMAREN urged Indians to seek community titles for their full territories, rather than individual titles under the agrarian reform acts. At the outset, less than half the communities had any legal rights, and only one-third had global title. Five years later, only 25% of the communities lack legal standing, and 60% have communal titles. PUMAREN was seeking to increase legalized indigenous territory through co-management agreements for protected areas.[45]

A final model discussed by Davis and Wali is termed the "indigenous territory" model.[46] They present the model as expressing the current demands of indigenous people's regional organizations, and urge that its critical elements must be to provide land access and security in terms consistent with Indian social and political organization and cultural notions of space. Such projects, they suggest, will tend to be larger than earlier projects, to allow integrated management of an ecosystem. They suggest as a model the Awa Ethnic Forest Reserve in Ecuador, noting that the Ecuadorian Awa avoided using the agrarian reform law, and managed to get the government to establish an ethnic reserve. They stress also the role to be played by

---

44 R. C. Smith, *Indians, Forest Rights and Lumber Mills*, Cultural Survival Quarterly 52-55 (Spring 1993).

45 Forster & Stanfield, *supra* n. 31.

46 Davis & Wali, *supra* n. 36.

indigenous communities in defining these reserves, and cite promising experiences with use of indigenous topographic teams to identify territories in Ecuador and in Peru.

While these new forms have produced a much wider range of options for common property management, there are few comprehensive reviews of all the options even at the national level. One survey of legal options for common property management in Costa Rica gives some idea of the variety of forms that now exists.[47] The study notes the fundamental orientation of the tenure system toward private ownership of land, and provides a list of organizational options that could apply to most Latin American countries. A considerable variety of organizational forms is available. Foundations are non-profit entities that have legal personality. They can own land, and could be used to manage common property. A solidarity association is an entity in which persons with similar aspirations and needs join together to promote those goals. They have legal personality and so can own land. They must have at least twelve members, and a formal constitution and by-laws are needed as well. Cooperative associations also have legal personality, and the organization enjoys limited liability. Cooperatives enjoy tax-free status, and this is true in quite a number of other Latin American countries as well. Unions could conceivably own common property as well, but at least twenty members are required, and a constitution, by-laws, and many other legal formalities are required.

Finally, community development organizations are an option. These must have a minimum of 100 and a maximum of 1,500 members. A constitution and by-laws are required. Such associations are required to coordinate activity with the municipality, and are constrained by the National Economic Development Action Plan.

More recently, Costa Rica has granted legal recognition to indigenous communities. Article 2 of the Costa Rican *Ley Indígena* contemplates (a) separate legal personality for the communities, apart from the state, (b) reserves to belong to the community, (c) recording of their title at the Deeds Registry, and (d) exemption from fees associated with recording of titles. The reserves are non-transferable, and community property cannot be sold, rented, given away, or mortgaged. The legal organization of the community is a "development association," in which only

[47] L. Espinoza & I. Murillo, *Estructuras Legales para el Manejo de los Recursos Naturales de Propriedad Comun Basada en la Tiera*, Centro de Derecho Ambiental y de los Recursos Naturales (1994) in S. E. Hendrix, *Legal Structures for the Management of Land-based Common Property Natural Ressources in Latin America* (LACTECH Bulletin No. 17, U.S. Agency for International Development 1996).

indigenous people can participate. The development association is required to maintain current land use of present forest land and use sustainable forestry practices under the state forestry program.[48]

5.4. Africa: Common Property in an Era of Law Reform

With very few exceptions, most countries in Africa underwent major reforms of their land tenure systems in the years following independence. A few were privatization reforms, such as that of Kenya, but most vested land in the state and envisaged either communal production (Tanzania); a system of state concessions for commercial agriculture (Guinea Bissau); a smallholder agriculture in which farmers held their land titles as leases or permits from the state, not from local communities, or some combination of these approaches. These were all reforms that sought to replace community-based tenure systems, and for the most part they proved impossible to implement.[49] The policy debate has in recent years swung back toward recognition and adaptation of community-based tenure systems rather than their replacement.[50]

In many countries, vast areas of forest land fell under concessions to members of governmental and commercial elites, depriving local communities of access to those forest resources. Villages were themselves included in these concessions. In Guinea Bissau, an explosion of concessions in the 1990s destroyed the ability of many communities to manage the resources upon which they have historically depended. There was a critical failure to provide legal recognition for community rights to land used for hunting and gathering.[51] A similar pattern occurred on a

---

[48] *See* Vincente Watson *et al.*, *Making Space for Better Forestry: Costa Rica Country Study* (James Mayers ed., Centro Cientifico Tropical & Intl. Inst. for Environment and Development, Policy that Works for Forests and People Series No. 6, 1998).

[49] John W. Bruce, *The Variety of Reform: a Review of Recent Experiences with Land Reform and the Reform of Land Tenure with Particular Reference to the African Experience*, in *Institutional Issues in Natural Resources Management* 13-58 (H. S. Marcussen ed., Roskilde U. Intl. Development Studies Occasional Paper No. 9, 1993).

[50] *Searching for Land Tenure Security in Africa* (John W. Bruce & S. E. Migot-Adholla eds., Kendall/Hunt 1994).

[51] John W. Bruce & Christopher Tanner, *Structural Adjustment, Land Concentration and Common Property: the Case of Guinea-Bissau*, in *Institutional Issues in Natural Resources Management* 101-112 (Hendrik Secher Marcussen ed., Roskilde U. Intl. Development Studies Occasional Paper No. 9, 1993).

much larger scale in Mozambique[52] and in other countries where the state claimed ownership of forest resources. Unfortunately, donor pressures for land law reform have until very recently emphasized the need for strong rights for farm and residential land, to the neglect of common property resources.

5.4.1. Tanzania

Tanzania provides a vivid case of the struggle over communal resources in the rush to property rights reforms. In the years immediately after independence, Tanzania moved rapidly to villagize peasants and encourage them to engage in communal productions or *ujamaa*. Working on a basis of broad government land ownership inherited from the colonial period, the government ran roughshod over community-based tenure rights, which had received greater recognition by the colonial government and law. The village landholdings created were often inadequately demarcated and simply administratively assigned to villages. A legal framework for village management, the Villages and Ujamaa Villages (Registration, Designation and Administration) Act of 1975, came only as an afterthought, and was repealed in 1982.

Under the Local Government (District Authorities) Act of 1982, villages can enact bylaws for land administration, but the system for national approval of such bylaws rendered the system ineffective.[53] At the same time, a new land policy called for demarcation of village lands, and formalization of a leasehold title for the villages. The potential of such leaseholds as a legal basis for community forestry in miombo woodlands[54] and other forest resources was subsequently noted and discussed in World Bank forestry sector documents.[55] However, there has been an ongoing conflict over how expansively the boundary lines of villages should be drawn. One school of thought favors giving them "enough" land, keeping some

---

[52] Gregory W. Myers, Julieta Eliseu & Erasmo Nhachungue, *Security, Conflict, and Reintegration in Mozambique: Case Studies of Land Access in the Postwar Period* (Land Tenure Center, U. of Wisconsin-Madison Research Paper No. 119, 1994).

[53] A. Hoben, John W. Bruce & L. Johannson, *Rural Land Policy in Tanzania* (Issues Paper, World Bank 1992) (copy on file with the author).

[54] Miombo describes the sparse open deciduous woodlands characteristic of dry parts of Eastern Africa.

[55] Hoben, Bruce & Johannson, *supra* n. 53.

land in government's hands for development on the concession model.[56] Others have argued that historic notions of village territories should be honored, and communities encouraged to develop those resources.[57]

Tanzania's National Land Policy called for titling of "specific common property resources" to villages.[58] The resource would be titled as the common property of the village. The World Bank provided technical assistance in the preparation of a new land law, and in addition funded grassroots initiatives for local management of forest resources.

In 1992 the World Bank supported the Forest Resources Management Program in Tanzania, and soon found itself involved in land policy and law reform. The intention of the project was to support community-based initiatives in forestry, but the underlying land tenure regime made it difficult to assure communities that their boundaries or rights over land and trees would be respected. Land policy was reviewed, and the World Bank supported the translation of the report recommendations into a white paper and then a new land law. The 1999 Land Act[59] and the 1999 Village Land Act[60] now provide a legal regime whereby a village council can register village lands, including village forests or other commons areas, in the name of the village, or register them in the name of a user group or association. This ended a long period of uncertainty about the legal ability of villages to protect and manage their own forest resources and provided the legal imprimatur for demarcating the territories of 3,560 villages in eight regions.

These clarifications provided villagers with greater security, enabling them to undertake grassroots initiatives such as those described by community forestry specialist Dr. Liz Wiley:

> Perhaps the most significant was the development undertaken by a World Bank-funded programme operating in Mwanza Region. Following a visit to Duru-Haitemba, the programme assisted district foresters to help villagers bring residual forest patches under protection and management. The approach

---

[56] *National Land Policy* (Tanzania, Ministry of Lands, Housing and Urban Development 1995).

[57] *Report of the Presidential Commission of Inquiry on Land Matters* (Government of Tanzania 1992).

[58] *National Land Policy, supra* n. 56.

[59] Tanzania, Act No. 5 (1999).

[60] Tanzania, Act No. 4 (1999).

> linked the Duru-Haitemba process, already described,[61] and the experiences of neighbouring Shinyanga Region, where grazing lands, not forests, were being protected through a revitalized traditional mechanism for setting aside *ngitiri* or grassland.

What are locally referred to as forest ngitiri resulted. Today, more than 1,300 ngitiri exist in the seven districts of the Mwanza Region with another 120 in the Tabora Region.[62] Several hundred are in effect village forest reserves, similar to those of Duru-Haitemba and Mgori. Most ngitiri are much smaller and under the jurisdiction of parts of the village community – sub-villages, women's groups or traditional societies. At least 500 ngitiri are individually owned. Few are larger than 10 hectares and some are less than one hectare.

The ngitiri initiative represents a very important branch of community-based forest management in Tanzania because it extends the approach and the opportunity to conserve resources into areas, not hitherto seriously considered, where the resource is much diminished. Moreover, the principles are brought into play at the household level of decision-making, encouraging individual farmers to reassess their farm resources with a view to protecting rather than clearing their residual woodland patches. This has proved particularly advantageous, in that it is in such small areas that silvicultural management techniques may be profitably applied. A growing number of farmers with very small ngitiri, acknowledged and protected by the wider community, now routinely thin and prune to produce only those trees for which they have most use."[63]

5.4.2. Francophone Africa

In Francophone Africa, work on legal reforms to facilitate community resource management and shift away from broad state management of natural resources has been limited to a few exceptional cases, such as Senegal, Guinea, and Niger. This

---

[61] Liz Alden Wily, *The Evolution of Community Based Forestry Management in Tanzania*, in *Proceedings of the International Workshop of Community Forestry in Africa, Participatory Forest Management: a Strategy for Sustainable Forest Management in Africa* 127-143 (Banjul/Gambia, April 26-30, 1999) (Food and Agricultural Organization 1999).

[62] Liz Wily & G. Morena, *Communities and Forests: What has been learnt and what is the way forward?* (unpublished study, Forest Resource Management Project, Dar-es-Salaam, Tanzania) (on file with the author).

[63] Wily, *supra* n. 61.

is in spite of a strong recent emphasis on the *terroirs villageois*[64] approach to natural resource management in the region. No clear debate on a legal framework comparable to the discussions in Tanzania has emerged in most countries, though extensive discussions on policy reforms have taken place, in particular the Praia Regional Conference on Land Tenure and Decentralization in the Sahel in 1994.[65]

In these countries, however, pressures have been building for a reform of the forest codes in the French tradition. The codes have been reviewed and faulted both for their failure to provide an adequate legal basis for community forestry and for undermining incentives for tree-planting on privately held land.[66] Studies in individual Sahelian countries have developed this critique,[67] and in 1993 a Sahelian Forestry Code Workshop listed the shortcomings of current forestry and related legislation: (a) excessive centralization and the existence of a state monopoly over forest resource management; (b) failure to recognize indigenous systems of forest

---

[64] *Terroirs Villageois* is a term used for West African land management programs that entrust management of the historic territories of villages to village administrators beginning in the 1980s, thereby reversing the prior trend of nationalization and direct administration of such land by the central government. Thomas M. Painter, *Approaches to Improving Natural Resources Use for Agriculture in Sahelian West Africa: a Sociological Analysis of the "Aménagement/Gestion des Terroirs Villageois" Approach and Its Implications for Non-Government Organizations* (CARE Agriculture and Natural Resources Technical Report Series No. 3, 1991).

[65] *See generally* Gerti Hesseling & Boubakar Moussa Ba *et al.*, *Le Foncier et la Gestion des Ressources Naturelles au Sahel, Conférence Régionale sur la Problématique Foncière et la Décentralisation au Sahel, Praia, Cap Vert, Expériences, Constraintes et Perspectives, Synthèse Régionale* (Permanent Inter-State Committe for Drought Control in the Sahel / CILSS, Organisation for Economic Co-operation and Development & Club Du Sahel 1994).

[66] Kent Elbow & A. Rochegude, *A Layperson's Guide to the Forest Codes of Niger, Mali and Senegal* (Land Tenure Center, U. of Wisconsin-Madison Paper No. 139, 1990).

[67] Kent Elbow & S. Lawry, *End of Tour Report: Forest Policy in Dakar* (SECID/ Louis Berger 1989); Rebecca J. McLain, *Recommendations for a New Malian Forest Code: Observations from the Land Tenure Center's Study of Land and Tree Tenure in Mali's Fifth Region* (Land Tenure Center, U. of Wisconsin-Madison Paper No. 109, 1992).

management and indigenous rights to forest resources; and (c) excessive reliance on punitive law, based on a system of permits and fines.[68]

A series of studies have sought to think through the conditions for a more decentralized system of forest management by local communities.[69] A generation of village woodlot projects failed because the villages concerned never felt a sense of ownership of those projects, and in retrospect the project planners exhibited a remarkable naiveté about incentives and motivation.[70] But there have since been successful co-management schemes on classified forest land, such as Guesselbodi in Niger.[71] Across the region there are a growing number of interesting experiments with organization of local communities to manage natural resources, such as the Near East Foundation's project at Bora in Mali.[72] More recently, there is a new generation of projects, still not adequately evaluated, which stresses the terroirs villageois approach, which seeks to provide for integrated management of village territories defined to include forest resources.[73]

Guinea has arguably led West Africa in both forestry code and property law reforms, but has had difficulty reconciling the visions of the drafters of the two new laws. The *Code Forestier*,[74] prepared with the assistance of FAO, provides for

---

68 Rebecca J. McLain, *Report on the LTC/CILSS Sahelian Forest Code Workshop* (Bobo-Dioulasso, Burkina Faso, 18-20 Jan. 1993) (Land Tenure Center, U. of Wisconsin-Madison 1993).

69 J. T. Thomson, *Participation, Local Organization, Land and Tree Tenure: Future Directions in Sahelian Forestry* (Club du Sahel, OEDC, CILIS 1983); A. Bocoum, Address, *Etude de cas de Bore: décentralisation de la gestion forestière* (Bobo-Dioulasso, Burkina Faso, Atelier Régional sur les Codes Forestiers au Sahel 1992); McLain, *supra* n. 67; J. Heermans & J. Fries, *Natural Forest Management in Semi-arid Africa: Status and Research Needs*, 168 Unasylva 9-15 (1992).

70 *Whose Trees?*, *supra* n. 15.

71 J. Heermans, *The Guesselbodi Experiment: Bushland Management in Niger*, 23/24 Rural Africana 67-77 (1985).

72 Rebecca J. McLain, *La Gestion Décentralisée des Fôrets de Bore et de Tarabe* (Mali: Programme Forestier de Douentza 1992).

73 See Painter, *supra* n. 64.

74 Guinea, Code Forestier, Ordinance 081/PRG/SGG/89 (Dec. 20, 1989).

classification of local community forests and management of those forests by local communities.[75]

Shortly thereafter, in 1992, a new land code[76] was drafted with financial assistance from the World Bank. The code reflects primarily urban concerns, and was in fact initially drafted just for urban areas, but later applied with some adjustments to the entire country. The code provides for the automatic conversion of land under customary rights to the private ownership of whoever is using it like an owner. It is an approach that can promote expansive and conflicting claims, especially where there are overlapping claims to the land.[77]

In the Fouta Jallon, where it has not yet been applied, it has increased tensions and competition over land to which both former master and former slave populations make claims. This has undermined prospects for a terroirs villageois approach to resource management. A program put in place by the University of Wisconsin's Land Tenure Center has attempted instead to use contracts to create smaller, discrete areas for community management. Such contracts may have considerable utility when project managers are confronted with uncertainties about the impacts of general laws.[78]

The experience in Guinea highlights the importance of coordinating provisions on community forestry management with general property law.

5.5. South and Southeast Asia: Contractual and Property Solutions

In South and Southeast Asia, there have been strong traditions of state control of forests. In India, large areas of forest were reserved for management by the state,

---

[75] *See* Rebecca J. McLain, *Nialama Classified Forest Management Study: Preliminary Findings, Koundou Watershed, Guinea* (unpublished report prepared for USAID/Guinea 1993) (copy on file with the author).

[76] *See* J.E. Fischer, *Tenure Opportunities and Constraints in Guinea: Resource Management Projects and Policy Dialogue*, 72 Land Tenure Center Newsletter 1-7 (1994/95).

[77] D. Tabachnick, *A Review of Natural Resources Law and Implementation of the Land Code in Guinea: Report prepared for USAID/Guinea* (Land Tenure Center, U. of Wisconsin-Madison 1994).

[78] J. E. Fischer, *Tenure Opportunities and Constraints in Guinea: Resource Management Projects and Policy Dialogue*, 72 Land Tenure Center Newsletter 1-7 (1994/95); J. E. Fischer, *Report on Natural Resource Management Practices and Tenure Constraints in the Diafore Watershed, Founta Jalon, Guinea* (Land Tenure Center Research Paper No. 122, U. of Wisconsin-Madison 1995).

while in the Philippines, the state claimed all untitled land, including most land in the country.

5.5.1. India

India's Joint Forestry Management (JFM) Program has attracted considerable attention. In 1988 a new forestry policy reversed a century of tight control of forests by the state, calling for popular participation in the reforestation of wastelands. The shift in policy was in part the product of numerous social movements in the 1970s. The largest was the Chipko movement, which drew attention to the plight of forest dwellers and forest dependent populations. The new policy drew upon several models, including the forest councils or *panchayats* in Uttar Pradesh, an earlier Social Forestry Program, and most proximately, the model developed in successful experiments in the Arabari Region of West Bengal. The JFM Program initiated by a 1990 circular order by the national government, is based on a shift of state control to a joint competence of state and federal government. States are encouraged but not required to participate in the program.

Under the JFM program, the Forest Service negotiates use agreements with local communities, which may be organized as a local government (panchayat), a cooperative, or a village forest committee. The community is allowed to collect non-timber forest products and receive a share in the proceeds of the sale of timber. No more grazing or farming is permitted on the lands under the agreement. The scheme is operational for a period of ten years, after which it must be renewed.[79]

JFM is best characterized as a co-management regime, and exhibits a relatively low degree of institutionalization of forestry management and low security of tenure on the part of the communities. In most states the forest protection committees remain informal, with no legal personality or status beyond their relationship to the state. In West Bengal, they are under direct supervision of local government. Exceptionally, in Haryana and Rajasthan they are registered under the Indian Societies Act, which governs corporations.[80] JFM also exhibits a low degree of security

[79] There is considerable variation among India's states, and the requirements of different provinces are reviewed in M. Poffenberger & C. Singh, *Emerging Directions in Indian Forestry Policy: Legal Framework for Joint Management*, Wasteland News 4-11 (Feb.-Apr. 1992).

[80] *Id.*

for the communities involved, the parties committing themselves to the arrangements for ten years.

Today, the village committees involved in the JFM Program remain very much the creatures of the program. They have often not acquired an autonomous existence. They lack leverage to negotiate improvement of the terms of access to land with the Forestry Department. There is skepticism in some communities that the program is just another method by which the Forestry Department is mobilizing peoples' labor to improve public lands, from which people will not in the end receive much benefit. There are also fears that to the extent these projects are successful, their benefits will be hijacked by local elites. Full reviews of the program are available in Lindsay[81] and Hobley.[82]

The variety of forums in which the JFM Program has been executed makes a conclusive evaluation difficult. In some states, the program has sought to build upon local experience with forest use, while in others it has not. Lindsay concludes that when applied by thoughtful foresters, JFM can be a mechanism for building upon and supporting existing local traditions and practices; applied thoughtlessly, it can be used to undermine these traditions and practices by imposing new structures and methods.[83]

A draft forestry law submitted by the government in 1994, but not yet enacted, reinforces the JFM program along its current lines. After an evaluation of the JFM Program in 2000, the program was extended on the basis of the existing administrative regulations and without sanction in the forestry law, which was not necessary because the land was state land given to local communities on contract.

5.5.2. The Philippines

In the Philippines, land classified as forest reserves owned by the government makes up over 50 percent of the nation's land mass. Human communities live on and earn their livelihoods from these same lands, in some areas their historical territories. Individual permits to cultivate and so-called *taungya* programs were

---

[81] Johnathan M. Lindsay, *Law and Community in the Management in India's State Forests* (Lincoln Inst. for Land Policy Working Paper 1994).

[82] M. Hobley, *Institutional Change Within the Forest Sector: Centralized Decentralization* (Rural Development Forestry Network, Overseas Development Institute 1995).

[83] Interview with Jonathan Lindsay, Legal Officer, Development Law Service, U.N. Food and Agriculture Organization (Mar. 17, 1997).

utilized after 1975 to try to regularize these situations. In 1982 a new Integrated Social Forestry Program (ISFP) was initiated[84] which provided not only for contracts for individual farmers, but also for Communal Forestry Stewardship Certificates (CFSCs), creating a legal basis for community management of forest reserve land. Individual stewardship certificates can be held within a CFSC area.

The CFSC provides a lease for 25 years, renewable for another 25 years, during which the community has exclusive rights to possess, cultivate, and enjoy all the produce of the land, and to restrict outsiders from using the land. The leases are signed with either a cultural community or a forestry association, commonly organized by an indigenous NGO under a contract with the Forestry Bureau, and finally incorporated as a non-stock, non-profit corporation. The appropriateness of this form has been questioned because of its complexity.[85]

The contract gives the community full rights to non-commercial use of the forest and non-forest resources, and the community is required to aid and cooperate with the Forestry Bureau in protecting the forests immediately adjacent to their communal forests. Stewardship conditions are attached, but these are for the most part stated in relatively general terms. By mid-1992 there were twenty-one agreements covering almost 68,000 hectares. They range in area from 50 to 15,000 hectares, though most fall within the range of 1,000 to 4,000 hectares.[86]

While the Forestry Bureau touts the success of the CFSCs, it has been reluctant to consider releasing this land from state ownership and the reserve system. From the point of view of local communities, in particular the ethnic minority communities, the CFSC leases are a stop-gap, a way station along the road to satisfaction of their demands for legal recognition of their ancestral rights.[87]

The legal bases for community forestry in the Philippines have continued to expand in recent years, and are now probably the most varied of any nation. Of special importance are new provisions for Certificates of Ancestral Domain Claims,

---

[84] Philippines, Law No. 1260 (1982).

[85] Owen Lynch & Kirk Talbott, *Balancing Acts: Community Based Forest Management and National Law in Asia and in the Pacific* (World Resources Institute 1995); Owen Lynch & Kirk Talbott, *Legal Responses to the Philippine Deforestation Crisis*, 20 New York U. Journal of Intl. Law and Politics 679-713 (1988).

[86] Owen Lynch, *Securing Community Based Tenurial Rights in the Tropical Forests of Asia* (Issues in Development Report, World Resources Institute 1992).

[87] A.B. Gatmaytan, *A Critical Appraisal of the Social Forestry Program*, 2 Philippine Natural Resources Law Journal 9-12 (1989).

provided in response to pressure from grassroots activists and donors. Under Administrative Order No. 2 of 1993 of the Department of Environment and Natural Resources, a process is laid out for delineating ancestral domains, the continuing validity of which was established under a long-ignored 1909 court decision stating that land occupied from time immemorial never became public land. The ancestral domains are perpetual, cannot be canceled for failure to meet standards of the department, and so constitute a much stronger community entitlement than grants under the other programs. A 1991 National Integrated Protected Areas Act provides clear legal safeguards for ancestral domains in biologically critical areas. The department has however lacked resources to make a significant impact in the demarcation of the ancestral domains.[88]

5.6. After Communism: Finding a Niche for Common Property

5.6.1. China

A considerable part of the world is still working within legal frameworks created under communism, although many are in the process of revising them to varying degrees. While communist governments treated forests as state property managed on an industrial scale by state enterprises, in some communist countries smaller areas were managed as collective forests, and the institutional arrangements for those collective forests are still of interest. In addition, it is instructive to examine how post-communist societies in the throes of privatization are grappling with the reform of the ownership and management of state forest resources.

In China, reforms have been incremental and under the control of the Communist Party. The 1982 Constitution[89] and the 1998 National Land Administration Law[90] made it clear that the land held by village collectives belong to the collectives themselves, not the state. The villages, encouraged by policy declarations, largely returned to family farming in the years after 1985, leaving as common property such resources as fish ponds and hillside land, which had often been deforested during the collective period. The 1984 Forestry Law[91] provided for the contracting out of afforestation of such hillside land, and asserted that while

---

[88] Lynch & Talbott, *Balancing Acts*, *supra* n. 85.

[89] Constitution of China arts. 9, 10.

[90] China, Land Administration Law ch. 2, arts. 8,10 (Aug. 29, 1998).

[91] China, Forestry Law art. 23 (Sept. 20, 1984).

the land remained owned by the village, the planter became the owner of the trees. Leases are now available for periods of fifty years and even more in some locales.[92]

A variety of organizational forms have been available because current law[93] does not set out rigorous requirements for different forms of organization, but only requires their registration for recognition. Similarly, provisions on terms of land allocations and leases have been permissive. The result has been to stimulate a good deal of experimentation. In both cases, one sees a distinctive attitude toward law and social change, one that sees law not as a tool for working social change but as a capstone for changes which have already been accomplished by administrative processes.

5.6.2. Albania

Albania presents a stark contrast to the Chinese case in several respects. Here a reform government has implemented the "big bang" version of decollectivization, with great energies going into law reform as the basis for a new system of private property. Decollectivization has been fueled by popular anger with the old structures, and accompanied by the destruction of the physical plant of many public enterprises. Working on projects in Albania, the author sensed a deep mistrust of collective projects.

Forests in 1991 were said to constitute 37% of the land in Albania, and all remain controlled by the State Forest Administration, consisting largely of production forests organized as localized "forest enterprises," directly managed by the state. In areas of coppice and shrub, local villagers could purchase licenses to graze their sheep and goats. A new Law of Forests and Forest Service Police[94] makes provision for *komuna* forestry, that is, forestry managed by the komuna, the lowest level of local government, just above the villages. Control may also be delegated by the komuna to a village. Komuna have areas of state forest within their boundaries but, unlike the Chinese case, these lie outside the boundaries of

---

[92] Shouying Liu, *Changes in the Property Rights System in Mountainous Regions and Farm Households' Responses*, in *Transition of China's Rural Land System: Papers from the Intl. Symposium on Rural Land Issues in China* (Beijing, China, 8-10 Oct. 1992) (Land Tenure Center, U. of Wisconsin-Madison Paper No. 151, 1995).

[93] China, Land Administration Law art. 11 (Aug. 29, 1998).

[94] Albania, Law No. 7223 (1992).

the villages. As a result, the breakup of the collectives into family holdings has left the villages without much land suitable for forestry.

The komuna, a new and relatively weak level of government, has not thus far been able to realize the potential of komuna forestry. State control is failing and enforcement mechanisms are breaking down. Some villages are staking out claims to areas of state forest which they have traditionally used, even building fences to keep out animals from other communities in a few cases.

There is an ongoing discussion of whether the komuna is the appropriate level of government for community forestry. One could imagine it as local government forestry, somewhat like county forestry in the mid-western United States. Alternatively, the komuna might delegate control to villages or even individuals. In mid-1994, three komunas in the Elbasan District south of Tirana were selected as pilot districts under an FAO community forestry program. In 1996, funding from the World Bank made it possible to expand the program to 30 komunas.[95] The community forestry effort focused on fuel wood and fodder production in a silvo-pastoral system, as well as on creating production of non-timber fuel products. A komuna and its user groups create a silvo-pastoral commission to establish a 10-year management plan, as the basis of a 10-year contract between the komuna and one or more user groups. User groups may include the entire village or a more limited group of residents, or an extended family. There is a joint commitment to an initial 3-year investment plan, including fencing and replanting, to re-establish production and use control. Regulation No. 308 of January 1996 provides a legal framework for this contracting out of use and administration of the komuna forests. Plans call for forty percent of the forests, largely excluding major timber production areas, to be transferred to komuna control by 2004. Due to the weakness of the komuna level of government, there has been some contracting to user groups directly by the Forestry Agency.

The state forestry bureaucracy in Albania is still legally in executive control of the forests, and its members are divided as to the wisdom and viability of delegating control of forest resources to local communities. High timber, it is generally agreed, can only be managed by the state or large commercial firms. For some, with former colleagues already ensconced in new private timber-harvesting firms, the future of large-scale commercial timbering appears to lie in a partnership between government and those firms.

---

[95] World Bank, *World Bank Project Data, Albania Forestry Project* <http://www4.worldbank.org/sprojects/Project.asp?pid=P00008271>.

5.7. The Near East: Islamic and Secular Solutions

Islamic law is the primary legal authority in Islamic states, and a source of law in many developing, secular states, which have significant numbers of Muslim citizens. In the latter case, Islamic law is sometimes treated as a discrete body of personal law for Muslims, and in others is simply viewed as the custom of particular Islamicized groups. In practice, rural Muslims commonly make no very clear distinction between their custom and Islamic norms, which have been melded together for centuries. Even in non-Islamic states, Islamic law often governs the family affairs of Muslims, including inheritance, and thus touches on land rights.[96]

In Muslim communities, one is often dealing with a three-layered legal system. There are pre-Islamic, customary practices, which may have been endorsed by Islam. There are specifically Islamic norms, originating in the Koran and the hadith[97] of the Prophet. Finally, there is the national (and in some federal systems, state) statutory law, which may have Islamic origins or may be based on Western models, either of colonial or more recent origin. Even countries such as Pakistan, which strongly asserts an Islamic identity, works with a body of statutory law concerning the environment and natural resource management which is largely inherited from the British.

There are distinctly Islamic legal institutions for natural resource management, and those working in Islamic contexts need to be aware of their potential. Bagader *et al.* have sought to deal comprehensively with the bases in Islamic thought for natural resource conservation.[98] They identify sources of conservationist values in Islam: the concepts that God has created nothing without a purpose for it, and that God has created a balance in nature which we should be reluctant to disturb. They note the existence of several distinctively Islamic institutions with conservation objectives.

The first is *hema*, which are reserves for pasture and forests. The Prophet, they note, abolished private reserves for the benefit of powerful individuals, but

---

[96] Charles K. Meek, *Law, Land and Custom in the Colonies* (2d ed., Frank Cass & Co. 1968).

[97] Hadith are the sayings of the Prophet Mohammed.

[98] Abubakr Ahmen Bagader *et al.*, *Basic Paper on the Islamic Principles for the Conservation of the Natural Environment* (2d ed., Intl. Union for the Conservation of Natural Resources, Meteorology and Environmental Administration of the Kingdom of Saudi Arabia 1990).

established public reserves for the common good. They note the broad potential of this institution for conservation purposes. They also note the special protection accorded plants and animals in the two sanctuary regions, or *haramayn*, of Mecca and Medina.

A second such institution is *wakf*, the Islamic charitable endowment. Islam encourages private contributions to the public good. A wakf involves the donation of property, including land, for religious purposes and for the benefit of the poorer sections of society. The ownership of such property vests in God, and its profits may be applied for the stated purpose. Once this dedication is made, the property may not be sold, given away or inherited. It remains the property of the Islamic community. Bagader notes that a wakf may take the form of a land trust dedicated in perpetuity to charitable purposes such as agricultural and range research, wildlife propagation and habitat development, a village woodlot, or a public cistern, well or garden; or it may take the form of a fund or endowment for the financing of such projects.[99] The governing authorities may set provisions and standards for such wakf lands and funds, and for the qualifications of their managers, so that the benevolent objectives of such projects may be efficiently fulfilled.

While individual wakfs have certainly been made with conservationist purposes, it has not proved possible to find any purposeful attempt to use this model broadly in conservation programming. Nonetheless, it may have a great deal of potential. Legitimizing the wakf model of setting aside resources for poorer elements in the community is especially interesting.

The institution of hema, by contrast, has been actively promoted in some countries in recent years, or at least suggested as a model for consideration in range planning.[100] A hema is a reserve, usually a seasonal pasture set aside to allow its regeneration. In these and other arid environments such forests are often scattered trees on those pastures, or scrub used primarily for grazing. There is no clear dividing line between the grazing land and forest land, and herders still graze their animals in the "forests" without much effective control. Violation of the hema is traditionally punished by the slaughtering of one or more of the trespassing

---

[99] *Id.*

[100] Omar Draz, Proceedings, *Revival of the Hema System of Range Reserves as a Basis for the Syrian Range Development Program* (First Intl. Range Congress, Denver, Colorado 1978); A. Masri, *The Tradition of Hema as a Land Tenure Institution in Arid Land Management* (FAO 1991).

animals, but in more recent times sanctions have generally been fines and, in the case of repeated offenses, imprisonment.

Hema is likely a pre-Islamic custom in the Near East, and indeed throughout the Mediterranean world.[101] The Prophet is credited with having made a number of supportive statements with respect to the custom. It has different names in different parts of the Near East. In Morocco, the Berber *agdal* of Oukaimedene in the High Atlas Mountains has been studied by Gilles, Hammoudi, and Mahdi.[102] It includes irrigated meadows, and is used for oxen, mules, and horses, rather than smallstock. Access is tightly controlled and use closely regulated. Artz, Norton, and O'Rourke attribute the stability of the agdal to its sacred nature, and they note that many agdals have similar religious connections but that others are secular.[103]

Draz[104] has actively promoted the idea of hema as an Islamic conservation model, and, with Eighmy and Ghanem[105] documented its history throughout the region. Draz[106] specifically notes its use in the Arabian peninsula for protection of forests as well as grazing resources.

5.7.1. Syria

Syria poses a particularly interesting case in which public policy and law have struggled with the revival of hema. At independence, Syria aspired to replace nomadic land use with irrigated farming, settling the pastoralists. Government abolished the Native Administration and with it tribal grazing territories. When

---

[101] A. Bourbouze & R. Rubino, *Terres Collectives en Méditerranée; Histoire, Legislation, Usages et Modes d'Utilization par les Animaux* (Réseau FAO Ovins et Caprins & Reseau Parcours Euroafricain 1992).

[102] J. L. Gilles, A. Hammoudi & M. Mahdi, *Oukaimedene, Morocco: a High Mountain Agdal*, in *Proceedings of the Conference on Common Property Resource Management* (Washington, DC, 21-26 April 1985) (National Academy Press 1986).

[103] N. Artz, B. Norton & J.T. O'Rourke, *Management of Common Gazing Lands: Timahdite, Morocco*, in *Proceedings of the Conference on Common Property Management* (Washington, DC, 21-26 April 1985) (National Academy Press 1986).

[104] Draz, *supra* n. 100.

[105] J. L. Eighmy & Y. S. Ghanem, *The Hema System: Prospects for Traditional Subsistence Systems in the Arabian Peninsula* (FAO/ESH Working Paper on Pastoral and Agropastoral Societies 1982).

[106] Draz, *supra* n. 100.

new water sources were provided in the absence of effective social control, widespread overgrazing and land degradation occurred. The authorities then attempted to re-establish hema for grazing cooperatives, but they could not regulate the initiative, and the condition of the range has deteriorated. There was a reluctance to enforce hema exclusion for fear of arousing old tribal rivalries.[107]

There are provisions in the Forestry Law of 1953[108] for "village forests," but it is not clear how the forests are to be established, or what property regime would exist for them. The provisions appear to envisage harvesting of forest products just for village use, rather than for commercial purposes. No land has been allocated to the villages for reforestation, and no economic village forests have been created so far.[109]

5.7.2. Other Islamic Countries

In other countries in the region, Islamic law plays only a limited role in natural resource management. Pakistan case studies of competition over forest resources at Hazara in the Punjab,[110] Chalt-Chaprote in the Gilgilit District,[111] and Azad Kashmir[112] are framed in terms which are not specifically Islamic, and involve conflicts between national law based on English legal models and customary tenure. The same would apply to the many countries of the Near East, which emerged from the colonial period with legal norms of French origin.

---

[107] Masri, *supra* n. 100.

[108] Syria, Forestry Law, Decree No. 66 (Sept. 21, 1953).

[109] M. A. Mekouar, *Mission Report on Forestry Legislation in Syria* (GCP/INT/539/ITA, FAO 1993).

[110] R. A. Azhar, *Communal Property Rights and Depletion of Forests in Northern Pakistan*, 18 Pakistan Development Review 643-651 (1989).

[111] S. Mumtaz & D. Nayab, *Management Arrangements of the Chaprote Forest and Their Implications for Sustainable Development*, 30 Pakistan Development Review 1075-1086 (1991).

[112] M. M. Cernea, *Land Tenure Systems and Social Implications of Forestry Development Programs*, in *Whose Trees?*, *supra* n. 15.

6. The Variety of Approaches: Some Explanatory Factors

What patterns exist in the diversity of legal forms reflected in the experiences reviewed above? Of course one cannot identify approaches to common property which are universally "right" for all community forestry contexts. Different legal arrangements are required for different contexts, and this is why the experiences with resource tenure examined in this paper have been presented in their historic, country context in the first instance, rather than described in more abstract terms.

But we can now usefully categorize the cases we have been dealing with, in a manner which illuminates the rationales behind the different legal approaches to common property. Some after all are legislative, others administrative, yet others contractual. Some provide robust rights to communities, while others do not.

One fundamental distinction, it is suggested, seems to be whether we are dealing with forests or forest lands which have been under direct control and management of the state or have either in law or fact been under the control of local communities.

Where the state has controlled the resource, as in the case of taungya in Burma or Indonesia, the Guesselbodi project in Niger, most JFM sites in India, or the areas to become komuna forests in Albania, the shift of such land to community forestry appears to be hesitant and conditional. The community groups do not receive strong property rights, and their freedom of action is constrained by negotiated management plans. These are co-management approaches which rely more on continued state supervision and negative sanctions rather than on the incentives provided by property rights. In those instances where the communities do have common property rights, they tend to be tenuous, and rights to trees and non-timber forest products rather than to the forest land itself. Because the roles to be played in management are weak, one tends not to find the creation of strong organizations to manage the use of the forest.

These efforts are viewed as experiments in reforestation and approached cautiously. Often this is degraded land, which is being entrusted to communities for reforestation. Often too the land is being turned over to groups from farming communities, whose initial preference might be to farm the land, and this again limits the willingness of the state to move to empowering grants of property rights. Of course the reluctance of forest administration bureaucracies to "let go," out of inertia or self-interest, is also a factor.

The limited role played by common property strategies in the situations discussed above need not remain quite so limited. If the initial projects are successful, and confidence in the ability of communities to manage these resources grows, then the time may come for a second stage of reform, in which those communities obtain longer, more secure and less conditional tenure in the resource. The term "tenure ladder" has been used in the literature on individual land rights to describe how squatters may become tenants and later become owners,[113] and the idea appears transferable to communities in the common property and community forestry context.

It is in Africa, where significant areas of forests are used regularly by inhabitants, that opportunities for stronger tenuring may exist. This could occur through recognition of customary rights to forests, or in the case of reserves, decentralization of real management authority to local communities. In some cases, where the forest is a modest and delimited area under the control of an indigenous institution, there is the potential for simply recognizing the indigenous property rights of the community. The Guinea Forest Code in effect does this, though it also then creates possibilities for the state to intervene if the forest is not adequately managed,[114] and this is the intent of the ineffective by-law provisions in Tanzania.[115] The half-hearted Syrian attempt to recognize hema after undermining them would fall in this category.

As an alternative to recognizing the indigenous title, a new title under statutory law can be conferred on the community. The CSFC in the Philippines does this when it provides a leasehold right in recognition of traditional occupation and claims to an area, and the Mexican ejido is a statutory recognition of a customary institution. Of course the local community's occupation will not always be customary. While village forestry lands in China may have long historical associations with the villages concerned, the land vested in the village by statute at the breakup of the commune system.

However, the case is somewhat different for community occupation of the forest land, one which does not create such ready opportunities for common property strategies. The cases mentioned above involve primarily occupation by farming people of a forest of modest dimensions within mixed farm and forest landscapes. But there are also cases of very extensive occupations of forests by forest-dwelling people, often seasonally mobile and more interested in secure

---

[113] William C. Thiesenhusen, *Broken Promises: Agrarian Reform and the Latin American Campesinos* (Westview Press 1995); Peter Donner, *Latin American Land Reforms in Theory and Practice: a Retrospective Analysis* (U. of Wisonsin Press 1992).

[114] *See supra* n. 74.

[115] *See supra* n. 53.

access to particular spot resources than in property rights to specific areas of land. When forest-dwellers get protection for their forest through declaration of protected areas, the protection is as much for flora and fauna as for human inhabitants.

One needs to look to the governance structures for each such protected area to determine whether the local people can be said to have attained any rights to resources or management authority. They for the most part do not, and where an attempt has been made for the communities to undertake management, as in the Yanesha Forestry Cooperative in Peru, this has been problematic. Here the potential of common property approaches is directly connected to fundamental decisions taken by the state about the nature and pace of the social and economic "development" for forest-dwelling peoples.

7. Conclusion: Securing Common Property under National Law

It is clear that the circumstances in which common property develops are so diverse that there can be no single optimum legal arrangement within which common property management can be constructed. Nothing can be more misguided than the suggestion overheard some years ago in a donor office that, since Guesselbodi "worked," all that was needed was for every country to have a "Guesselbodi law." If Guesselbodi worked, it was because it was designed with a clear vision of the potentials of the local situation.

What is needed then, in national legislation, is a full "menu" of legal options. That is, there is a need for the full range of property options and organizational forms discussed in this paper. It is important that this variety of options exist in general law, and specific provisions for community forestry should embrace, not limit those choices. For instance, workable common property does not grow in a simple way out of any one property formula, such as simple ownership. It grows out of security of expectations, conferring genuine autonomy in management, and this can be achieved under a range of legal arrangements. The diversity that requires different legal responses exists not simply among nations, but within nations. National law must seek to cater to that diversity of situations.

Are there certain fundamental needs to be met by the national legal system, beyond these menus of property rights and organizational forms? I suggest that national law must include:

a) Property protection in national constitutions should clearly protect not only individual property rights, but also community rights in property. There should be explicit recognition of the existence of such rights.

b) Laws on natural resource management, including the forestry law, should recognize existing indigenous forms of common property, and should recognize and provide juridical personality for the institutions that manage that common property.

c) The forestry law should include a regime for common property management of forests devolved from forest reserve land to local communities for management, and permit the eventual transformation of these to community reserves.

d) It should be clear that the options provided are not exclusive, and that communities can at their option organize themselves and acquire land in any way permitted by general law to do community forestry.

What is suggested here is provision of an openness to normative experimentation not unlike that achieved in the 1980s. But instead of China's semi-vacuum in law, which allowed experimentation, what is suggested is provision of a broad range of organizational and tenure forms, as legal options. The extent to which each of those options is promoted from time to time by ministries, NGOs, and donors should be a matter of policy, based on experimentation.

What can we conclude about the central question for this article, that of the need for robust property rights for communities engaging in community forestry? If land in forestry had no uses other than forestry, the answer would be easier. One could feel fairly confident in asserting that communities with robust common property regimes would do better in community forestry. But the concern is that forestry is not the only use for the land; that cultivation of other crops may be more profitable in the short run, or even in the long run; and that communities cannot be allowed to make that decision solely in light of their own interests. The communities in essence are being asked to bear the cost of a public policy that the land must be kept in forests. There is some substance to the concerns of the forest service that empowerment conferred too suddenly can lead to overexploitation under pressure of immediate necessities. Communities may need to develop social capital, and grow into the discipline required for sound resource use. And they may need the assistance of the state in bridging difficult times.

Under this rough calculus of control and incentives, it seems best to give forest-managing communities as much security as one can afford to give them: to impose the minimum necessary control to ensure the land remains in forests. They should have the latitude to innovate to increase the profitability of community forestry, for instance through greater emphasis on non-timber forest products. As community forestry operations are made more profitable, conditions can be loosened. Stronger tenure need not be a gift at the outset, but can be used to reward effective management. It should however always be the long-term objective, and be maximized to the extent feasible in each situation. The term *dépérissement*[116] may be appropriate, to indicate the potential for the state to increasingly shrink controls over community forestry.

This is a calculus that is directed primarily at those situations in which government has been in control of the forest, but is turning all or a portion of it over to a local community for management. Where a community or communities have been in control of the forest, the scale tips towards the incentive side, and a much stronger and immediate emphasis on property rights is possible and appropriate.

What then might the community forestry provisions for forestry law discussed above include? It would be futile to try to suggest a model provision on community forestry. Conditions differ, and require different approaches. For example, forestry departments are unlikely to play well the roles suggested below if they are dependent on funds from logging revenue. But it is possible to suggest some potentially valuable elements for most legal regimes for community forestry:

(a) The forestry department should be placed under an affirmative duty to develop community forestry initiatives, the objective being clearly stated as that of assisting local communities and their members to practice sustainable forestry to their economic and social advantage. It should be clear that community forestry may involve both timber and non-timber forest products, and well as such other traditional uses, including cultural and religious practices.

(b) Community access to land and tree resources should be dealt with, as with a provision that the forest service should recognize communities' customary rights in forest, or make state-owned forest land available to the communities. It should require the strongest feasible security of tenure for the community to provide adequate incentives for good husbandry, normally under a recognition of customary rights, or in the case of state-owned land, through long-term leaseholds or transfer of ownership to the community.

(c) The forestry department should be made responsible for helping communities constitute themselves as legally-recognized entities with legal person-

---

[116] The term *dépérissement* is the French translation used for Marx's "withering away of the state." It has been used to describe a decreasing state role in development programs, specifically irrigation projects. *See* Peter Bloch, Lucie Colvin *et al.*, *Land Tenure Issues in River Basin Development in Sub-Saharan Africa* (Land Tenure Center, U. of Wisconsin-Madison Research Paper 90, 1986).

ality and the ability to own property and to contract. The law may be written to confer such legal personality upon the communities, and the forestry department should have the responsibility of developing with those communities a statement of the existing organization of the community for management of the forest resource or in the case of new organizations, the articles of association or similar documents.

(d) The forestry department must be responsible for providing technical and financial assistance as appropriate. Where this assistance is substantial, it should be possible for the department to require in return that the community enter into a management agreement with the department governing management of the forest by the community, setting out a management plan for the forest resource and conditioning access to services, assistance, and in the case of state-owned forest, the forest itself, on compliance with the plan. Management contracts should make clear reference to the policy of gradual reduction of controls, and make this conditional on adequate performance.

(e) The management contract should be outlined, perhaps in a schedule to the legislation or regulations. It should clearly identify the forest and the community, and spell out the rights and obligations of both the community and the forestry department. It should set out a plan for use of the forest for a period of not less than fifty years, and should incorporate provisions on sales of forest products, distribution of proceeds from sales, and payment to the forestry department for services rendered or credit extended. It should provide for automatic renewal of the contract except for cases of breach, and should in cases of termination provide for adequate compensation to the community for any standing trees or improvements on the land.

(f) In initiating a community forestry project, the department and community should be required to involve all stakeholders in consultation in the project design stage. They should plan the project to accommodate the use of the forest by any third parties who have used it, or should compensate them for loss of that use. Overlapping rights can be handled through rights of way or other similar arrangements which provide continued recognition to overlapping uses that do not threaten sustainable management of the resource by the principal users.

(g) For situations where a resource has been utilized by multiple communities, and it is not feasible for any one community to assume exclusive management, the forestry law should allow shared management of such forest between a state agency and one or several local communities.

(h) The forestry department should be allowed to delegate any of its activities but not its responsibilities in support of community forestry to non-governmental or civil society organizations, subject to monitoring by the department to ensure compliance with the rules governing community forestry.

(i) There should be provision for community and administrative adjudication of disputes arising under community forestry projects, and for appeal of administrative decisions on those disputes to the judicial system.

(j) Provision should be made for participation by women in the management entity for the community forest.

If adequate legislative provisions are critical in structuring common property forestry, it became clear to the author that contractual relationships will also play a major role that is not often recognized in the literature. The management contract is already a key element in community forestry, but the Guinea case cited earlier suggests that contract also has an important role to play in sorting out the contested claims to land that often bedevil community forestry efforts. A contract among communities or users of forest resources binds them with regard to their use of the resource. Contracts and the negotiations which lead to them can be used to sort out competing claims and conflicts among stakeholders. The challenge is to get all the stakeholders to the table, and to reach agreement.

The state, while it may not recognize local common property, should nonetheless enforce such agreements among the parties to them. It is not bound by them, however. The fact that local users of state land agree how to manage it does not compel the state to recognize their right to use it. To attain that, it is necessary to bring the state into the negotiations through its local agents. Involving the forestry department or local government in the negotiations and as a signatory to the agreement confers state recognition on the arrangement, and makes it much more difficult for the state to ignore.

In conclusion, then, there seems reason to hope that introducing increasingly robust common property – greater autonomy, greater security of tenure – will enhance community forestry management. But we will reach that point in many parts of the world only through an extended "balancing act," to use the language of Lynch and Talbot.[117] Local communities and those working with them in community forestry need to persevere in their attempts to expand their rights in forest

[117] Lynch & Talbott, *Balancing Acts*, *supra* n. 85.

land, and communities will need to be prepared to defend those rights every day. The central message of this article is that those attempts may be short-lived unless adequate legal frameworks are provided for them.

THE QUALITY OF JUDGES

HON. SANDRA E. OXNER*

Many countries around the world are engaged in judicial reform as part of a wider effort to make state institutions more responsive to the needs of citizens, market requirements, and protection of the social fabric. Recognizing that the quality of judges is crucial for a well-functioning judiciary, this article discusses a number of key determinants of judicial quality, ranging from how judges are selected to how they are trained, compensated, evaluated, and disciplined. Judge Oxner draws on her 25 years of experience as a judge and her international expertise in teaching and advising on judicial reform initiatives to present these elements in light of prevailing international standards and the experience of a variety of countries.

---

* The Honorable Judge Sandra E. Oxner is a retired judge of the Nova Scotia Provincial Court, Canada, where she served for 25 years. She is a past president of the Canadian Institute for the Administration of Justice, chaired the education committee of the Commonwealth Magistrates' and Judges' Association, and is the founding and current president of the Commonwealth Judicial Education Institute. She has organized or taught in judicial education programs in Canada; the United States; England; Australia; East, South and West Africa; the Caribbean; Asia; Yemen; China; and Russia. Judge Oxner has been active in judicial reform as president of the Canadian Association of Provincial Court Judges, the Canadian Institute for the Administration of Justice, and the Commonwealth Magistrates' and Judges' Association, and as adviser to the World Bank, the Asian Development Bank, the Inter-American Development Bank, UNDP, CIDA, USAID, and the Ford Foundation. She is an officer of the Order of Canada. Her publications include *Evaluation of Judicial Education*, Educatus (June 1999); *Judicial Education and Judicial Reform* in *The Judiciary in Africa* (Juta & Co. Ltd. 1997); and *Judicial Education in the Commonwealth* (Report of the Tenth Triennial Meeting of the Commonwealth Magistrates' and Judges' Association 1994). Without further attribution, the author draws substantially on the second publication listed.

This article is based on a paper delivered by the author at a conference on Empowerment, Security, and Opportunity through Law and Justice held in St. Petersburg, Russia, sponsored by the World Bank and the Russian Federation (July 2001).

The World Bank Legal Review: Law and Justice for Development: 307-376.

Printed in the Netherlands.

Suggestions for improvement of current practices are made throughout the text. Because of the pernicious influence of corruption, the article also considers the types and causes of judicial corruption and offers a prescription for its reduction.

Contents

1. Introduction: The Role of the Judiciary and the Quality of Judges

> The judiciary shall decide matters before them impartially, on the basis of facts and in accordance with the law, without any restrictions, improper influences, inducements, pressures, threats or interferences, direct or indirect, from any quarter or for any reason.[1]

Judges decide. The settings in which they must render decisions are varied and frequently complex. In constitutional democracies in which a charter of rights defines the rule of law, the courts must measure legislative and executive actions against the state's constitutional authority. In jurisdictions which are not constitutional democracies, courts have the role of protecting the citizen from improper executive encroachment on their civil and human rights and implementing domestically international human rights treaties to which their country is a party. Judiciaries are also important state actors – a branch of government that serves generally to support the authority of the state when it acts within its constitutional powers.[2]

The judiciary has become a more powerful and visible branch of government. Reasons for this increased presence include: more state intervention in life; increased technology – from motor cars to e-commerce – giving rise to more

---

1 Seventh United Nations Congress on the Prevention of Crime and the Treatment of Offenders, *Basic Principles on the Independence of the Judiciary*, Principle 2, A/CONF.121/22 (Aug. 26-Sept. 6, 1985) <http://www.unhchr.ch/html/menu3/b/b/h_comp50.htm> [hereinafter referred to as *United Nations Basic Principles*].

2 C. Baar, *The Emergence of the Judiciary as an Institution*, 8 Journal of Judicial Administration 4, 217 (1999).

disputes to be resolved; the global community, which has given us global crime and crime detection, money laundering, and international drug traffic; the rise of human and civil rights advocacy; class and public interest actions; a more iconoclastic public demanding accountability of all public office holders; and a changed judicial role in many jurisdictions: from interpreting the law under the principle of parliamentary sovereignty to judicial policy making in constitutional democracies with charters of rights.[3] In countries of the civil law tradition, the trend from judge as passive referee to a more powerful force is seen in the "orality movement."[4] Thus the quality of judges is a vitally important aspect of the modern judicial system.

If the judiciary is perceived as inferior or even irrelevant because of a reputation of incompetence, corruption, inefficiency or an inability to bridge the gap between laws and justice; because the transaction costs are too great; because of other access issues such as language or distance; because it is illegitimate[5] as unrepresentative of the community, then the citizens will find alternate means of resolving civil disputes and protecting values, persons, and property. In such instances, differences among citizens – and sometimes between citizens and the state – will be settled outside of the formal justice system. Some will be illegal and socially destructive. Others, like traditional community-based extra judicial dispute settlement methods, may provide a useful social service. All may pose a threat to the status of the formal judiciary and lessen its ability to perform its important functions. The social contract will be weakened, and the courts will have a lesser opportunity to strengthen the state. The faith of the community in the courts will diminish, further weakening the judicial branch and lessening its ability to attract necessary state funding. In sum, a high-quality judiciary is indispensable to a well-functioning social order.

This article reviews the following as determinants of quality that would need to be taken into account in any meaningful judicial reform effort: judicial selection, training, remuneration, evaluation, and discipline. Because in too many countries high levels of corruption have perverted the system, this article reviews the nature and causes of corruption and offers a remedial set of measures.

---

3 *E.g.* Canada, Commonwealth Africa, India, and some Latin American countries.

4 *E.g.* France, Argentina, Mexico, Colombia, and Uruguay.

5 *E.g.* South Africa at the beginning of the post-apartheid regime.

2. Judicial Independence and International Judicial Independence Standards

Some progress has been made in determining the appropriate parameters of judicial independence in a democracy and determining minimum standards of judicial independence against which to measure legislative, executive, and judicial performance.[6] Since the early 1980s there has been a movement to develop the concept of judicial independence (and the integrity it protects) at the international level by the enumeration of its key features.[7] This began with the United Nations Draft Principles on the Independence of the Judiciary (1981) ("Siracusa Principles"), the International Bar Association's Minimum Standards of Judicial Independence (1982) ("New Delhi Standards"), the Montreal Universal Declaration on the Independence of Justice (1983) ("Universal Declaration"), U.N. Basic Principles on the Independence of the Judiciary (1985), Procedures for the Effective Implementation of the Basic Principles on the Independence of the Judiciary and the Draft Universal Declaration of Justice (1989) ("Singhvi Declaration").[8]

Following on these came the Beijing Statement of Principles of the Independence of the Judiciary in the Law Asia Region 1995,[9] the Universal Charter of the

---

[6] Article 10 of the earlier *Universal Declaration of Human Rights*, GA Res. 217 (III), UN GAOR, 3d Sess., Supp. No. 13, UN Doc. A/810 (1948) provides: "Everyone is entitled in full equality to a fair and public hearing by an independent and impartial tribunal in the determination of his rights and obligations and of any criminal charge against him." The list of international standards here is not exhaustive and omits regional charters and conventions that require independent and impartial tribunals, *e.g.*, the American Convention on Human Rights, the European Convention for the Protection of Human Rights and Fundamental Freedoms, and the African Charter on Human and Peoples Rights.

[7] David Malcolm, *Independence and Accountability: An Asian Pacific Perspective*, in *Comprehensive Legal and Judicial Development: Toward an Agenda for a Just and Equitable Society in the 21st Century* 219, 222 (Rudolf V. Van Puymbroeck ed., World Bank 2001).

[8] *Id*; *see* Singhvi Declaration, 25 *CJIL Bulletin* (Special Issue on Judicial Independence) (Geneva: Center for Independence of Judges and Lawyers, 1989). All the above noted documents may be found in this *CJIL Bulletin*, and are analyzed in chart A of the appendix.

[9] *Guide for Promoting Judicial Independence and Impartiality* appendix A (Technical Publication Series, USAID 2002).

Judge by the International Association of Judges 1999,[10] the European Association of Judges Charter 1999[11] and the Commonwealth Latimer House Guidelines on Judicial Independence 1999.[12]

An analysis of seven of these international standards on judicial independence may be found in chart A in the appendix. They identify, among other issues, the following key factors: security of tenure; an impartial appointment process based on objective facts and factors, including integrity, ability, and experience; an adequate and protected salary; freedom from transfer; freedom from interference from superior judicial officers in decision-making outside the appellate process; objective and transparent assignment of cases; protection from civil liability; physical security; executive support for judgment enforcement; absence of retroactive legislation; protection from abolition of courts; and sufficient budget to provide reasonable resources for the judges to do their work.[13]

A comparison of the standards reveals that the more recent Beijing Principles take more account of judicial accountability – responding to a more pressing need in 1995 than in the 1980s. It also shows how "watered down" the *Basic Principles* adopted by the United Nations are in comparison to other international standards. The present U.N. Special Rapporteur on the Independence of Judges and Lawyers offers the explanation that the weaker standards were necessary to obtain the support of the Eastern European bloc at the time of the General

---

[10] *Id.*

[11] *Id.*

[12] *Id.*

[13] Contemporary threats to judicial independence range from powers of chief judges and court administrators responsive or responsible to the Executive, to illegal removals from office, kidnappings and killings. The web page of the Centre for Independence of Judges and Lawyers (CIJL), available at <http://www.icj.org/press/press00/english/attacks.htm>, indicates that from January 1999 to February 2000, at least 412 jurists suffered reprisals in 49 countries for carrying out their professional duties. Of these, 16 were killed, 12 disappeared, 79 were prosecuted, arrested, detained or even tortured, 8 physically attacked, 35 verbally threatened and 262 professionally obstructed and/or sanctioned. The recent forced retirement of the Chief Justice of Zimbabwe because of court judgments striking down government strategies to curry election votes has generated concern in the international legal community. An IBA committee visited Zimbabwe to indicate this concern. (This information was obtained by the writer from Chief Justice Gubbay of Zimbabwe and Chief Justice Byron of OECS, a member of the IBA mission.)

Assembly endorsement.[14] It is also interesting to note that recent international judicial independence standards adopted by the European Association of Judges (regional group of the International Association of Judges) makes no mention of judicial accountability issues and rules out non-judicial participation in appointment and selection processes. These views reflect the current strong judicial control and lack of public accountability of some European judiciaries.[15] On the other hand, the most recent document, the Commonwealth Latimer House Guidelines, includes references to accountability and joins the Montreal Declaration and the Singhvi Declaration in requiring the goal of diversity in the appointment process.

How do you measure judicial independence? Many attempts to assess how "independent" a judiciary is have not been successful.[16] Part of this failure is caused by the difficulty of gathering comparative data, but the real problem is the difficulty of measuring the concept. Judicial independence is a "more or less," rather than a "yes or no" variable. Many core elements of judicial independence, or threats against it, are neither visible nor objectively measurable.

One attempt to assess the confidence of the community in its judiciary is shown by the World Economic Forum's survey results on "the perception of the judiciary as fair."[17] This survey ranks countries in order of the degree of confidence the business community has in the fairness of its national judiciary. A *World Development Report* survey[18] rated corporate confidence in the corporate area of legal systems of surveyed countries. Both surveys solicited comments from the business community. The latter is often an agent for judicial reform out of its interest in the

---

[14] P. Cumaraswamy, *International and Regional Standards for the Protection of Judicial Independence and the Role of the UN Special Rapporteur on the Independence of Judges and Lawyers* in *Larnaca Conference Papers* 11 (Commonwealth Magistrates' and Judges' Association 1998).

[15] *See generally* G. Di Federico, *Judicial Independence in Italy: A Critical Overview in a (Non-Systemic) Comparative Prospective Guide to Judicial Independence – Draft Report* pt. G (IFES/USAID, 2000).

[16] L. Hammergren, *Diagnosing Judicial Performance: Toward A Tool to Help Guide Judicial Reform Programs* (World Bank 1998), <http://www1. worldbank.org/publicsector/legal/judicialindependence.htm>; C. Larkins, *Judicial Independence and Democratization: A Theoretical and Conceptual Analysis* 44 Am. J.Comp. Law 605 (1996).

[17] *Ranking of Judicial Systems* in *World Competitiveness Yearbook* (IMD 1999).

[18] World Bank, *World Development Report 1998-9* at 181 (Oxford U. Press 1999).

predictability of court decisions to assist them in business decisions.[19] They also strongly support improvements in judgment enforcement, generally one of the weakest areas of the justice system in developing countries.

Of course, surveys representative of only one segment of the community may represent vested interests and should be used only in combination with surveys of other aspects of the community – judges, lawyers, court users, organized labor, professional associations, the community at large. In this way, a better-rounded picture could be produced. The question would still remain if the insidious non-visible threats to judicial independence would be revealed. Table one in this article sets forth a checklist of internationally accepted mechanisms to protect judicial independence. Using such a document,[20] in combination with comprehensive surveys[21] seeking both objective facts and subjective opinions, should produce a more accurate picture.

Larkins criticizes prior positivist efforts to measure judicial independence, listing the following weaknesses: (a) the reliance on formal indicators of judicial independence which do not match reality (he uses the example of the Argentinean judicial tenure guarantees that existed during the five judicial purges since the 1940s); (b) the dearth of information on the courts for comparative study; (c) the difficulties in determining the significance of judicial outcomes; and (d) the arbitrary nature of assigning a numerical score to some attributes of judicial independence. He also points out that judicial surveys are unreliable as judges are not likely to admit their decision was motivated by improper pressures. Larkins also criticizes reliance on subjective criteria, finding this equally problematic. In agree-

---

19 *See generally* Harvey Blair and Gary Hansen, *Weighing in on the Scales of Justice* (USAID Program and Operations Assessment Report No.7) (USAID Development Information Services Clearinghouse 1994).

20 Another such document is the ABA CEELI Chart for Measuring Independence available from the American Bar Association.

21 *See* H. Kritzer, *Using Public Opinion to Evaluate Institutional Performance: The Experience with American Courts* (unpublished paper delivered at the World Bank, Washington, D.C.) (July 14, 1999). This paper demonstrates that there is a difference between public perceptions of performance and actual performance and warns that reformers, who would base their prescription for institutional reform on perceptions rather than operational data, risk attacking the wrong problem with the wrong remedy (copy on file with the author).

ment with Rosenn,[22] he finds unreliable the methodology used in a Latin American study[23] which surveyed 84 social scientists and considers its conclusions as little more than "collective hearsay."[24]

While inadequate to paint a full picture, the use of a comprehensively drawn checklist, as in table 1 below, allows identification of internationally accepted components of, or mechanisms to support judicial impartiality and provides a goal to work toward.

Table 1. Checklist of Judicial Independence

- Impartial appointment process
- Impartial discipline process
- Adequate salary
- Constitutionally protected salary
- Security of tenure
- Physical security
- Civil immunity for judicial functions
- Freedom from interference in decision-making from superior judicial officers outside of the appellate process
- Integration of subordinate court as full members of the judiciary
- Emancipation of the subordinate court from the executive
- Articulated judicial ethical standards
- Judicial control of its own budget
- Judicial control of its own administration
- Constitutionally entrenched courts
- Freedom from geographic transfer without consent (unless it is term of employment)
- Judicial control of the curriculum and faculty of judicial education
- Lack of retrospective legislation
- Executive support to enforce judgments even against itself
- Executive support to prosecute and punish attempted or actual judicial corruption
- Executive restraint from interference in judicial decision-making processes
- Independent bar
- Government sensitive to public opinion
- Educated public demanding of an impartial judiciary
- Free and informed press

---

[22] K. Rosenn, *The Protection of Judicial Independence in Latin America* 19 U Miami Inter-Am. L. Rev. 11 (1987).

[23] K. Johnson, *Scholarly Images of Latin American Political Democracy in 1975*, 11 Latin American Research Review 129 (1976).

[24] Larkins, *supra* n. 16.

The use of checklists also assists in the development of baseline data that can be used nationally and comparatively to measure the independence of judiciaries. Such data are an essential tool for judicial reform projects that seek to strengthen judicial independence. However, it must be recognized by those using the charts and surveys that the information provided tells only part of the story and that such other measurements as those mentioned by Helmke[25] must be included. Only interpersonal research and an understanding of the social, political, and economic background of the jurisdiction involved and its legal culture will reveal facts necessary to complete the picture.[26]

Furthermore, regional comparison is important to gauge the ranking on the judicial independence continuum of different countries in a region. This often will provide more information useful to judicial reformers than comparisons with developed countries with different histories, cultures, traditions, and resources. Moreover, the amount of institutional protection required to produce an environment that nurtures an impartial judicial mind will vary between developed and developing countries, as well as between developing countries at different developmental stages. For example, control of the judicial budget is not an important issue in Canada and the United Kingdom. Their judiciaries have input into the preparation of their budgets, which are charged on the consolidated fund. The funds are received in accordance with the approved budget. This is to be contrasted with some transitional and developing jurisdictions where judiciaries have minimal input into their budget allocation, often wait months to receive paychecks and longer, if at

---

[25] G. Helmke, *Methods for Measuring Judicial Independence: Preliminary Findings for the Case of Argentina (1975-1995)* (unpublished paper referred to in Todd Foglesong, *The Dynamics of Judicial (In)dependence in Russia*, in *Judicial Independence in the Age of Democracy: Critical Perspectives from Around the World* 62, 68 (P. Russell and D. O'Brien, eds., University Press of Virginia 2001)).

[26] Shortly after the creation of the new nation of Eritrea, the author visited the judiciary of Eritrea. The judges appointed were heroes of the liberation war just concluded. They identified strongly with the executive branch of government they had fought to place in power and were disinterested in establishing mechanisms to protect judicial independence that would distance them from their former comrades in arms. In the words of Russell: "How judicial independence is understood and institutionally provided for depends very much on the status of law in society's political culture and on its general political circumstances." Peter Russell, *Conclusion* in *Judicial Independence in the Age of Democracy: Critical Perspectives from Around the World* 301, 307 (P. Russell and D. O'Brien, eds., University Press of Virginia 2001).

all, to receive their full budget allocation.[27] In countries with an independent and informed media, improper pressures placed on the judiciary have more opportunity to be exposed and remedied non-judicially.[28] Adequate judicial salaries and benefits, prestige of office, and peer pressure which exist in industrialized countries may be absent in developing countries. For these reasons more institutional protections are required in the latter.

3. Appointment

3.1. General

> Persons selected for judicial office shall be individuals of integrity and ability with appropriate training or qualifications in law. Any method of judicial selection shall safeguard against judicial appointments for improper motives. In the selection of judges there shall be no discrimination on the grounds of race, color, sex, religion, political or other opinion, national or social origin, property, birth or status except that a requirement that a candidate for judicial office must be a national of the country concerned, shall not be considered discriminatory.[29]

As indicated by the *United Nations Basic Principles*, the quality of people appointed to the judiciary is linked to the appointment process. This article discusses the appointment process by analyzing both the criteria of appointment and the process through which the appointment is made. The existing tension is between the wish of the executive to control the power of judicial appointment and the principle of judicial independence. Control over the appointment power is

---

27 Foglesong, *supra* n. 25 at 70. This is also a problem in Ukraine as the author was informed during a court diagnostic visit there in 1998. Notes in author's files.

28 Baar, *supra* n. 2 at 222 where Baar describes an incident where Canadian Cabinet ministers' attempts to influence judges were revealed to the Canadian public via the media, approximately 20 years ago. Two federal Cabinet ministers were forced to resign after it became clear that they had contacted judges to discuss a certain case. A set of guidelines was subsequently drafted and approved by the government prohibiting such contacts. A decade later another Cabinet minister was forced to resign for another attempt at "telephone justice."

29 *United Nations Basic Principles*, *supra* n. 1, Principle 10.

valuable to the executive to enable appointments of those who support government policies as well as for patronage purposes.[30]

What kind of person do we want as this more visible and powerful judge? What are the contemporary requirements for the judicial office? What are the ideal judicial qualities? What should be the criteria for judicial appointment?[31] The appropriate criteria will be examined in several ways: (a) analyzing day-to-day judicial duties and responsibilities;[32] (b) reviewing the results of New Zealand and Canadian judicial surveys on important judicial qualities; and (c) appointment criteria from jurisdictions studied that have articulated criteria. "The real substance of independence lies in the hearts and minds of the judges and the way in which from day to day they administer justice."[33]

The function of the judge is to serve the community by hearing and resolving disputes among citizens and between citizens and the state. To achieve public acceptance of judicial decisions, the judge's functions must both actually be and be perceived to be carried out impartially vis-à-vis the parties and the executive and legislative branches of the state. The judiciary is one of the last listening professions. A primary judicial function is to listen to the evidence given and the

---

[30] The 1867 confederation of Canada led to highly politicized appointments in at least a number of provinces and a corresponding diminution of respect for the judiciary. D. Bell, *Judicial Crisis in Post–Confederation New Brunswick*, 20 Manitoba L. J. 181 (1991).

[31] This article does not discuss the criteria for or the appointment processes of the judges of the apex court or of national chief justices. It uses the comparative of a high court judge and a mid career subordinate court judge. Where national judicial discipline processes vary for apex level judges, they are not included.

[32] *The Universal Declaration on the Independence of Justice* unanimously adopted at the final plenary session of the First World Conference on the Independence of Justice held at Montreal on June 10, 1983, held the objectives and functions of the judiciary to include: (a) administration of the law impartially between citizen and citizen and citizen and state; (b) the promotion, within proper limits of the judicial function, of the observance and attainment of human rights; and (c) to ensure that all people are able to live securely under the rule of law.

[33] D. Hope, Address, *Human Rights and Judicial Independence* (Cape Town, South Africa, 1997) (copy on file with the Commonwealth Magistrates' and Judges' Association); S.W.W. Wambuzi, Address, *Judicial Independence*, (Eritrea, 1996) (copy on file with the Commonwealth Judicial Education Institute); R. Devlin, *Judging and Diversity: Justice or Just us?*, 20 Provincial Judges Journal 4-22 (1996); *Valente v. The Queen* (1985) S.C.R. 673 (Can.).

arguments made. The judge must not only listen attentively, but must also be observed to do so.

The tasks of the judge are complex and diverse. They include the following: (a) chairing proceedings; (b) ensuring that witnesses are not harassed while not protecting them to the extent that cross-examination is hampered in exposing the truth; (c) ensuring that defendants, litigants, and witnesses are fully aware of their rights and have all the benefits with which the law and the constitution clothe them; (d) ruling on the law on evidentiary motions and instructing the jury on the law applicable to the case in hand; (e) delivering oral and written judgments; (f) exercising discretion in imposing criminal sentences; and (g) in some countries, making judicial policy in finding that legislation offends the constitution.[34]

In accordance with this analysis of the judicial tasks, a potential judge needs the following characteristics to perform his or her duties in an appropriate manner: integrity; legal skills; written and oral communication skills; patience; courtesy; common sense; introspective analytical skills; leadership; decisiveness; dignity; empathy; efficiency; and a thirst for learning. The complex and difficult tasks the judge has to perform should be clearly weighed against the criteria and procedures for appointment. These criteria and procedures are perceived differently by the judges themselves, the executive branch, the public at large, and the experts in judicial matters. The following section reviews the results of New Zealand and Canadian judicial surveys on important judicial qualities, and the criteria of appointment used in various jurisdictions.

3.2. Judicial Perceptions of Appointment Criteria

One method of determining criteria for judicial appointment is to ask judges.[35] The late Chief Justice Laskin of Canada listed a number of qualities that he felt were

---

[34] The function referred to in (g) may well be new to the judge. It was so for Canadian judges after 1981 on the inclusion in their repatriated constitution of a Charter of Rights and Freedoms. This function of becoming a judicial policy maker will become a function of the judges of England, Wales, and Northern Ireland as the citizens of these countries come this year under the protection of the European Charter of Rights. This will require English judges to determine if their legislation conforms to the European Charter.

[35] At a recent meeting of Canadian judicial educators attended by the author, it was suggested that computer literacy be added to the criteria for judicial appointment because of the tendency for judicial communication and aspects of education to be computer based.

essential to being a good judge: character; integrity; honesty; industry; life experience (which can include politics); flexibility of mind; knowledge of the law; and a willingness to listen – but indicated that not all were easily ascertainable in advance and some "must be taken on expectancy."[36] The former U.N. Special Rapporteur on the Independence of Judges and Lawyers, Dr. L.M. Singhvi, in his final report to the United Nations, put forward the following judicial qualities as prerequisites of a fair trial and credible and reliable adjudication: conscientiousness, equipoise, courage, objectivity, understanding, humanity, and learning.[37]

New Zealand judges have recently been asked to specify the different kinds of attributes an effective judge needs.[38] Knowledge of the law and wide legal experience were rated highly, followed by experience in the application of the law in specialist areas, an attribute rated more highly by men than women. Both men and women mentioned "people skills as an important aspect of professional experience." But women ranked management skills second, denoting the ability to juggle many different tasks or cope with pressure after legal experience and ahead of knowledge of the law and people skills.

When asked to list the most important personal qualities an effective judge required, male judges most favored fairness, impartiality, intellect, analytical skills, empathy, compassion, courtesy, sensitivity, and integrity. Women's favored options in order were empathy, compassion, an ability to listen, fairness, impartiality, common sense, a sense of humor, and an even temper. Both men and women judges agreed that an effective judge requires wide community experience particularly with other ethnic or socioeconomic groups, and active participation in a service capacity in the community.[39] Justice Cartwright went on to include in the list flexibility of mind, courage, and ingrained appreciation of ethical responsibilities. She

---

[36] B. Laskin, Address, *On Being a Judge* 6 (Goodman Memorial Lecture, Feb. 8-10, 1973) (copy on file with the University of Toronto Faculty of Law).

[37] L.M. Singhvi, Final Draft of Report Commissioned on Judicial Independence and Impartiality, E/CN.4/Sub.2/1985/18/Add.1 (United Nations Commission on Human Rights 1985).

[38] S. Cartwright, *The Judiciary: Qualifications, Training and Gender Balance*, in *Parliamentary Supremacy and Judicial Independence: A Commonwealth Approach* (J. Hatchard & P. Slinn eds., Cavendish Publications 1998).

[39] Judicial Working Group on Gender Equity, *Gender Equality in the New Zealand System: Judge's Perception of Gender Issues* (Judicial Working Group on Gender Equity, Nov. 1996).

also advanced the concept that a broad age range of the judiciary provides for the cross section of views which will emerge from different generations and ensures a sound line of succession towards seniority.

Judges in the Province of Alberta, Canada ranked desirable judicial qualities a little differently.[40] Their choices ranked in order of frequency were: industry and diligence; courtesy; empathy; patience; knowledge of the law; intelligence; and sense of fair play. As Professor MacKay points out, these judges esteemed humanity, patience, and courtesy at roughly the same level as knowledge of the law or intelligence.[41] He drew attention to the rather unusually low ranking of the qualities of "independence" and "objectivity."

3.3. Appointment criteria

Relatively few countries have adopted articulated criteria for judicial appointment. The agreement establishing the new Caribbean Court of Justice requires regard to the following criteria in making appointments to the office of judge: high moral character; intellectual and analytical ability; sound judgment; integrity; and understanding of people and society.[42]

Common law countries studied that have articulated appointment criteria include Canada, Trinidad and Tobago, South Africa, and the United Kingdom.[43]

---

[40] P. McCormick & I. Greene, *Judges and Judging: Inside the Judicial System* 103 (Lorimer 1990).

[41] A.W. MacKay, *Judicial Ethics: Exploring Misconduct and Accountability for Judges* (unpublished manuscript 1995) (copy on file with the Commonwealth Judicial Education Institute).

[42] Agreement Establishing the Caribbean Court of Justice para. 10 <www.sice.oas.org/trade/ccme/ccj1.asp>.

[43] See charts C and D in the appendix for a cross-country comparison of judicial appointment systems. The criteria for South Africa and the United Kingdom apply only to subordinate court judges. The criteria for Canadian judges are found in policy documents that come federally from the Office of Federal Judicial Affairs and provincially from the Minister of Justice. The criteria for Trinidad and Tobago are determined by the Judicial Service Commission. The criteria in the United Kingdom are determined by the Lord Chancellor in a policy document. The Canadian and United Kingdom criteria are widely disseminated in print form and are also available online. The South African criteria for magistrates are determined by the Magistrates' Commission and published by them in a policy document. Constitution of South Africa ch. 8, sec. 174(1) establishes the criteria for judges of "fit and proper persons."

Common to their listed criteria are integrity, commitment to public service, communication skills, social awareness, maturity and sound temperament/judgment, decisiveness, fairness, and courtesy. Canada and Trinidad and Tobago include humility and interest in developing the law, and an ability to listen. Canada includes patience and tolerance.[44] These are, of course, in addition to a statutory qualification of minimum professional experience and a reputation of professional competence. Several countries make reference to the need for the bench to include women and/or members of minorities to make it more reflective of the community it serves.[45] Canada is the only jurisdiction studied to pinpoint potential impediments to appointment: drug or alcohol dependency; civil or criminal actions; health; sexual harassment complaints; professional complaints and/or disciplinary actions; financial difficulties; and default of family support obligations.

It would seem then that in common law developed countries, there is a trend to articulate criteria far beyond professional experience, and in some cases, political affiliation or social standing – the unarticulated criteria of earlier times. Setting forth the broad-based criteria described above, in addition to requiring a written application, greatly expands the pool of judicial candidates. Such a recruitment process should improve the quality of judges and the legitimacy of the judiciary.

Is there any reason this reform would not work in developing and transitional countries? One response is that the field of candidates, particularly in the subordinate courts, is often insufficient to fill the vacancies (vacancy rates can be from 30 to 70 percent). Raising standards would make a bad situation worse.[46] However, the reasons judicial appointments are unattractive are inadequate salaries, poor working conditions, and lack of respect. A judicial reform project should address all of these issues and could therefore incorporate as part of the judicial reform "package" the broader articulated criteria.

---

44 We may not have come such a distance from the age of the famous adage that in appointing a judge a Lord Chancellor of England choose a gentleman and if he knows a little law so much the better.

45 *E.g.* Canada and the United Kingdom.

46 The author was advised by the head of a provincial Pakistan Public Service Commission, the examining authority for entrance level judges that, at the time, the need for judges was so great that when an insufficient number failed to pass the entrance examinations failing candidates were also accepted into the judiciary.

The European civil law countries studied did not specify appointment criteria, which is not to be wondered at in light of their tradition of controlling the training and regular evaluation of their judges from the beginning of their legal careers. An Italian case study shows that when judicial independence is equated with total judicial control of judicial processes, it is at the expense of other important values (such as accountability and guarantees of professional competency) and a series of negative consequences ensue.[47] Italy's experience shows that the very provisions intended to protect judicial independence when carried too far may be detrimental to judicial independence.

Latin American countries adopted the authoritarian nature of European judiciaries controlled by the executive and did not keep pace with European reform that transferred control to the judiciaries. Recent Latin American reforms scattered throughout the continent have changed this.[48] In many civil law countries the judiciary is in control of the appointment and promotion processes.[49] The adoption of publicly disseminated articulated appointment and promotional criteria and the inclusion of some non-judges and lay persons in the promotion process, where this is not presently the case, would improve the transparency and objectivity of the civil law promotion processes.

---

[47] G. Di Federico, *Judicial Independence in Italy: A Critical Overview in a (non-systematic) Comparative Perspective*, in IFES/USAID, *Guide to Judicial Independence – Draft Report* 1 (IFES/USAID 2000).

[48] *See e.g. Bolivia Constitution* art. 117 (1994) (removed from the National Congress the function of electing members of the Supreme Court and placed that power with a newly created Council of Judicature), and Dominican Republic Constitution art.23 (1994) (removed from the Senate the exclusive power to elect judges of the Supreme Court). The implementation of these provisions has been more difficult in some countries than in others and has brought mixed results, ranging from achieving a fully independent judicial system, such as in the Dominican Republic, to lesser degrees of independence.

[49] Foglesong, *supra* n. 25. *See* essays in *Transition to Democracy in Latin America: The Role of the Judiciary* (I. Stotzky ed., West View 1993). However, a new reform in Belgium creates an appointing body composed of 50 percent judicial and 50 percent non-judicial officials. Reforms in France proposed to achieve the same: F. Aucoin, *Judicial Independence in France* in IFES/USAID *Guide to Judicial Independence – Draft Report* pt.2-E (5) (USAID 2000). This is in accordance with the requirement of the European Charter of Rights that judicial appointment bodies have only 50 percent judicial membership.

3.4. Methodology

There are three traditional patterns for judicial appointment. One is a career judicial path shared by civil law and transitional countries and many developing common law countries. In this pattern the judges enter the judiciary at the bottom tier of the professional magistracy and hope to work their way upward to the high and supreme court and perhaps the chief justiceship. A second pattern is the appointment of judges of both subordinate and high courts from experienced members of the practicing bar (United States, United Kingdom, Canada, Australia, and New Zealand). This is predominantly the pattern in industrialized common law countries. A third pattern has emerged as developed common law jurisdictions are increasingly elevating members of subordinate court judges to the high court[50] and developing countries are appointing more practicing members of the bar directly to the high court in countries which previously had dominantly a career judicial path. This mixed path to the high court also exists through lateral entry at a senior level of the subordinate judiciary as is the case in Pakistan and France.

The high courts of developing common law countries are now therefore usually a mix of career path magistrates and appointments direct from the practicing bar. In some countries the high court will be dominantly career path magistrates and in others dominantly appointments direct from the practicing bar. This relates to the number of practicing lawyers in the country as well as the attractiveness in the national environment of a high court judicial appointment.

Recruitment difficulties to the subordinate courts have many aspects. In Pakistan, the position of subordinate court judge is seen to be without "clout" and, for most, it is a last career choice for university graduates. The judiciary therefore does not attract sufficient capable jurists of integrity but must, to run the courts, accept even those who have not passed the entry competitive examinations. In the Philippines, the author was advised that while there is a vacancy rate in the subordinate courts, capable candidates of integrity were not appointed because the positions were being saved for those more politically worthy.

---

50 In Canada, the appointments of three subordinate court chief judges to high court chief justiceships over the last 20 years indicates a change (Chief Justices Gold of Quebec and Ferguson and Kennedy of Nova Scotia). The elevation of women from subordinate to high courts is increasingly common in Australia, New Zealand, and Canada. The elevation of the family court to the supreme court level in Canada also elevated many subordinate court judges.

In all countries, the lure of the lucrative awards to be found at the bar by enterprising and capable lawyers keep many well qualified lawyers from benches of all levels. This is particularly true of developing countries and countries in transition to a market economy with a shortage of trained lawyers and outstanding opportunities for those who are at the commercial bar. A more prestigious subordinate court might well attract the more civic-minded young at a stage where judicial salaries would not be such an economic sacrifice. To make the subordinate court attractive to capable candidates of integrity requires increased salaries, increased jurisdiction, a workplace of equal quality of that of the high court, and demonstrated respect from the high court, legislature, and executive.

3.5. Recent Trends

In the common law countries that appoint judges from the bar there has been a sea change in the judicial appointment process although the change has been greater in some countries than others. Perhaps because of the recognition of the increased power of the judiciary, demands are being made that the appointment process be more transparent and that the bench be more reflective of the community.

The United States process of nomination with a public confirmation hearing by the Senate or of elections has always been a transparent operation. While none of the Commonwealth countries have opened the process to the extent of the U.S. practice, the following changes may be noted. Many countries now advertise judicial vacancies and require a written application from potential candidates. They ask for feedback not only from the senior members of the legal profession but also from selected members of the community at large. Advisory committees with lay representatives are asked to determine the merit of candidates against articulated criteria that can go far beyond legal experience and integrity.

The integrity of the selection process and personnel involved are issues recently addressed in many jurisdictions, but new formal structures have not necessarily solved the problems. In the Philippines, for example, some members of the judicial and bar commission, the appointing authority that was set up in the new constitution to buffer political influence, are considered politically biased. It is commonly heard that first instance judgeships go vacant because of a lack of applicants with the correct political affiliation. In an East African country, the judicial nominating authority nominated its chairman to be chief justice, and in one instance nominated a judge who had submitted an application for promotion so late as to preclude consultation. Both were appointed. While the former merely raised eyebrows, the latter process was considered improper and caused a meeting of the entire judiciary to be called to consider its position. Publicly disseminated rules of procedure which would cover these and other process issues would improve confidence in judicial service commissions.

Generally there are three methods of appointing judges – politically, judicially, or otherwise, perhaps through a body created by the constitution or a statute to which is given functions relating to the judiciary such as a judicial service commission. The structure and function of such commissions will vary from nation to nation in accordance with its historical and social practices. Its powers can include appointment, discipline, education, and other functions or one or more of these. Countries such as the United States,[51] Canada, the United Kingdom, Australia, and several Latin American countries come under the political appointment category. The methodology ranges however from the very transparent and accountable U.S. process to the closed Australian process, with the methodologies of Canada and the United Kingdom ranging in between. The U.S. federal appointment process is initiated by a review of the applicant by a broad-based community consultative committee[52] and proceeds on to recommendation by the president through a public Senate confirmation hearing. This achieves the necessary accountability, generally produces judges of merit of the same political persuasion as the president, but has the drawbacks of eliminating from play excellent candidates who do not wish their life to be the object of partisan political dismemberment at a public Senate hearing. This is not the general rule for most nominees below the Supreme Court. It can also have the drawback of appointing relatively nondescript judges who have accomplished little to antagonize anyone, or, when the Senate is equally divided, philosophically middle of the road men and women of no strong convictions on important but controversial issues – or convictions they have successfully managed to suppress, perhaps not the intellectual valor one would like to see in a judge.

---

[51] The United States federal judiciary was made accountable to the Senate by the writers of the Constitution. During the Kennedy years the present process of consultative groups was established. These are made up of lawyers and members of the public who screen candidates who have indicated their interest for judicial appointment in writing. They are measured against publicly available articulated criteria. Nominations are made to the President (often through the senior Senator of the president's party) and the chosen one is then subjected to a public federal senatorial confirmation. (This information was obtained from the Honorable Judge Rya Zobel, District Judge, Massachusetts.)

[52] This is also true of many states in the United States, such as Massachusetts.

The Canadian process requires written application by candidates who are then screened by broad-based community committees. These committees either categorize candidates as very acceptable, acceptable, or unacceptable or rank them in order of committee preference. While not bound by law, the cabinet generally is guided by the committee recommendations. Following the McKelvie Canadian Bar Report on judicial appointment, which identified the Canadian process as highly politicized, a reform process for federal judicial appointments was established in Canada in 1988.[53] The process starts off with a written application by the interested candidate that is sent to a consultative committee appointed by the minister of justice. The committee includes representatives of the bench, the bar society, and other persons, including lay persons, appointed by the minister. The committee reviews references, interviews the candidates and categorizes candidates as not qualified, qualified, and very qualified. Appointments are then made by the federal cabinet in the name of the head of state. There has been some criticism that the committee has been in some instances controlled by the political party in power. Similar reforms have been made in the Canadian provinces.

In England, until 1923, judicial appointments were made on a partisan political basis. From that time until recently, appointments were recommended to the head of state by the Lord Chancellor in a non-transparent process that resulted in a professionally well qualified, but homogeneous bench made up of male members of the elite of the English bar. Under the present Lord Chancellor the appointment process is as follows: (a) judicial vacancies from the high court down are advertised and applications invited (a high court appointment may be offered by the Lord Chancellor to someone who does not apply); (b) written criteria against which candidates will be measured are widely available (the field from which judges may be chosen has been widened to include solicitors as well as barristers); (c) an interview committee of one judge, one official of the Lord Chancellor's office and one lay person interview, consider and make recommendations to the Lord Chancellor on the applications for subordinate court positions; (d) the Lord Chancellor consults with senior members of the bar and bench on appointments to the higher courts; and (e) applications from women and members of minorities are encouraged. Recent changes in the judicial appointment process in England include electronic and print dissemination of the appointment process as well as widening of

---

[53] The Canadian federal appointment process is described in the judicial appointment policy manual. Canada, Department of Justice, *A New Judicial Appointment Process* (Ottawa: Communications and Public Affairs, Department of Justice, 1998).

the pool outside senior members of the bar. The consultation process, however, for senior judicial posts is still limited to senior judges, lawyers, and Lord Chancellor's office officials.

In the Australian federal appointment process, the executive consults only with senior members of the bench and bar. This is despite pressures from the bar and academics to widen the consultative process and include articulated criteria for greater transparency and representation.[54]

However, all three countries have demonstrated to varying degrees a commitment to appoint more women judges and, in the case of Canada, to appoint not only women but also minorities.[55] Italy, Japan, Spain, and several Latin American jurisdictions place the power of appointment in the judiciary. This total lack of accountability gives rise to a replication of the philosophy and social status of the existing bench and is inconsistent with the principle of judicial accountability.[56]

Other processes for judicial appointment include a combination of the executive, legislature, the judiciary, and the public. A good example of this is the process described in the new Constitution of South Africa for judicial appointments by which the president confirms an appointment via a consultative process between the judicial service commission, which is composed of members of the judiciary, leaders of parties represented in the national assembly, and provincial politicians. Judicial service commissions are in use in both the common law and civil law systems. Their composition and functions vary from appointment functions only (Philippines) to appointment and discipline functions (Trinidad and Tobago) to appointment, discipline, judicial education, and other functions (Uganda). Chart B in the appendix analyzes the composition, functions, and powers of a variety of judicial service commissions.

Different jurisdictions have different fears in designing an appointment and promotion process for the universally more powerful judge to best accommodate principles of judicial independence and judicial accountability. Many common law

---

[54] Law Council of Australia, *President's Message* (April 1977) <http://www.lawcouncil.asn.au>; Attorney General's Department, *Discussion Paper on Judicial Appointments, Procedure and Criteria* (unpublished manuscript Sept. 1993) (copy on file with the author).

[55] Office of Federal Judicial Affairs, *Lord Chancellor's Office Guidelines; Canadian Judicial Appointment Process* <http://www/cd.gov.uk>.

[56] *See supra* n. 49 for the European Council's recommendation that the recommending body for judges should have only 50 percent judicial membership.

countries fear executive interference through partisan politics in the appointment and promotion process and seek ways to eliminate this. The critics of European systems and those jurisdictions influenced by them, where judges control the appointment process, fear the weaknesses that nepotism and the "old boys network" bring to judicial quality. Contemporary analyses lament the lack of transparency in both the criteria and procedure of the appointment processes in most jurisdictions. They also regret that neither the selection process nor the judges selected properly reflect the community they serve. While the number of women on judiciaries is gradually increasing at least in common law countries, only those countries that have taken pains to specifically recruit women are seeing women in any number in the senior judiciaries. This is not so, of course, in transitional and some Latin American countries where the great number of female appointments to the bench reflects the low status of the judicial position.[57]

The vital importance of judicial selection requires careful crafting of the selection and appointment process. The methodology must prevent political or other improper influence from detracting from appointments. To preserve the integrity of the process the appointing authority would need to either justify its failure to accept the nominating body's recommendations or be limited to making appointments from the nominating body's recommendations. Appointment criteria based on merit, but going beyond legal skills and integrity to include interpersonal and communication skills, interest in public service, intellectual curiosity, and judicial skills such as patience, courtesy, and leadership, will bring diversity to the bench. This latter is unlikely to happen, however, unless diversity is incorporated into the selection process. A nominating or selecting body, not under the control of the executive, not totally composed of the judiciary, will bring differing community values to the definition of "merit." The composition of this committee will vary from jurisdiction to jurisdiction in accordance with national needs and culture.

The publication of judicial vacancies at all levels will promote transparency and prevent an "old boys network" appointment process. In addition, the publication of the criteria, process, and rules of procedure of the nominating or selecting body will promote transparency and confidence. Written application will widen the pool of candidates to include meritorious women, minority group members, and those without political or social clout.

---

[57] E. Buscaglia & M. Dakolias, *Judicial Reform in Latin America: Economic Efficiency vs. Institutional Inertia* (Georgetown University Working Paper Series No. 2367).

4. Training

4.1. General

The quality of judges depends also on strong training curricula and permanent skill enhancement and development for (a) aspirant judges, (b) newly appointed judges, (c) sitting judges, (d) judicial support staff, and (e) other stakeholders who may be interacting with judges in judicial processes. To ensure that adequate training is provided to judges, many countries have established judicial training institutions with different targets, but all with the same objective of improving the quality of judges. Judicial training improves the quality of judges by strengthening the fact and perception of the impartiality, competence, efficiency, and effectiveness of the judiciary and creates an environment for reform through knowledge.

The targets of judicial training institutes vary from one jurisdiction to another. Some offer training to subordinate court judges only (Sri Lanka[58]), some offer training to appeal court judges, high court judges, subordinate court judges (Canada[59]) and some offer orientation and continuing judicial education training to appeal court judges, high court judges, subordinate court judges, and judicial support staff (United States,[60] Malawi[61]).

Pre-appointment training is relatively rare in common law countries. There are exceptions. England and Wales gives training to the part-time judges whose part-time work, forms part of the criteria for appointment to judicial office. Some African common law jurisdictions, such as Zimbabwe and Uganda, have formalized training for lay magistrates. The Uganda program is under a statutory body called the Law Development Centre. It is chaired by a supreme court justice and gives a nine-month diploma course on the basics of substantive, procedural, and evidentiary law as well as ethics. The cost for tuition and accommodation is 2 million Uganda shillings (U.S.$ 1,112). Successful completion of the course qualifies one

---

58 Author's meeting with the Sri Lankan Judiciary (1999).

59 National Judicial Institute, *Annual Report 1995-1996,* at 4 (National Judicial Institute 1996).

60 Federal Judicial Center, *Annual Report 1999* (Federal Judicial Center 1999).

61 Discussions with the Honorable Chief Justice R.A. Banda, the Honorable Justice R.R. Mzikamanda and the Honorable Justice D. Tambala, Judicial Education Chairs, during visits to Malawi (1995-2000).

for a lay magistrate position. The course has been such a success, however, that there are more graduates than lay magistrate positions. Many graduates find employment in legal firms.[62] On the other hand, pre-appointment training is part of the judicial culture in the European countries of Italy, France, Germany, Portugal, and Spain.

Judicial education in Germany is under the supervision of the state justice ministry. The education process is composed of two examinations and an apprenticeship period. The first examination, with written and oral components, is prepared by state justice ministries assisted by university law faculties and follows three and a half years of university studies. This is followed by two years of apprenticeship training. The first year is devoted to three-month periods in civil courts, criminal courts, the prosecutor's office, administrative agencies, and private law offices. The second year of apprenticeship training is spent in courts or agencies of their choosing. The second examination, in which candidates for the judiciary must achieve a grade of high honors, is prepared, conducted, and graded by committees made up of judges, senior civil servants, and law professors. Only 50 percent of candidates achieve appointment to the judiciary.

In France, fifty years ago, *L'Ecole Nationale de la Magistrature* (ENM) was established at Bordeaux to train law graduates for the judiciary. ENM is under the administrative control of the ministry of justice.[63] Training lasts 31 months. The period of studies includes practical training in government administration or with a business corporation, 14 months at ENM, and 14 months in the courts. Candidates are paid a salary during their training, and on successful completion they are nominated, with the approval of the Superior Judicial Council, to judicial posts. Eighty percent of the judiciary is recruited directly from ENM. It is possible to enter the judiciary by a special examination (three percent) or by lateral recruitment[64] (12 percent). The cost of judicial training in France is 140,000,000 francs

---

[62] Information received from the Honorable Justice John Tsekooko, Chairman of the Law Development Center, Uganda (December 2000). In Zimbabwe the Justice College, chaired by the Chief Justice, trains lay magistrates. Both programs were inspired by the need for magistrates created by a lack of legally trained candidates for the positions.

[63] This describes the main category of candidates. There are two other minor streams.

[64] The lateral recruits are regarded suspiciously by the ENM as an executive intrusion upon the judiciary. *See* B. McKillop, *The Judiciary in France – Reconstructing Lost Independence*, in *Fragile Bastion: Judicial Independence in the 90s and Beyond* 126 (Helen Cunningham ed., Judicial Commission of New South Wales 1997).

(U.S.$ 23,430,000) per year, in the Netherlands is U.S.$ 20,008,500 per year, and the United States (1000 federal judges and support staff) is U.S.$ 17,495,000 per year.[65] This makes duplication of such training impossible for post-Soviet states and developing countries that follow the civil law pattern, who have difficulty in attracting suitable candidates to the judiciary and would like to adopt the European judiciaries' approach of training their own.

4.2. Levels of Judicial Education

There are four levels of judicial education. The first level of judicial education is the provision of information and "tools" necessary for judges to effectively do their jobs. This required information usually includes legislation, practice directions of higher courts, case reports, scholarly articles, bench books or manuals, and judicial journals and bulletins. Such information can be given by printed material, audio tapes, audiovisual tapes, electronic means (diskette or e-mail), local area networks, and by cable and satellite television as well as through collegial meetings. Discussions of issues in substantive and procedural law are the traditional first step in collegial judicial education programs. Ensuring judges understand new laws that define a shift of philosophy (as in the modernization of the legal framework to support a vibrant market economy or to promote an efficient court process) is a second level. The third level is teaching a judge new intellectual approaches, as in the judicial exercise of discretion. The exercise of discretion is common in areas such as sentencing and assessment of damages. In a country undergoing judicial reform the exercise of judicial discretion takes on new dimensions.

Inspiring the attitudinal change required to provide an impartial and accountable bench rising to social expectations is the fourth and most sophisticated level of judicial education. In some countries, the dominant attitudinal change required may relate to eliminating gender or racial bias. In others, the dominant attitudinal change required is to encourage the judicial culture of service to the community and the fact and perception of judicial integrity, independence, competence, efficiency, and effectiveness. Attitudinal and thinking process change is the most difficult area of education in any field. It requires motivated and inspired teachers who are respected and trusted by the judges – most often other judges skilled in this area.

---

[65] The author was advised of the budget of the Federal Judicial Center by the Honorable Judge Rya Zobel, Director; of the Dutch budget by Judge Rosa Jansen, Director of the Judicial Training Center, and of the budget of the French judicial training body by the Director of the French l'Ecole de la Magistrature (author's notes on file).

4.3. Impartiality, Efficiency, Competency, Effectiveness

How does judicial education support an impartial, efficient, competent, and effective judiciary? It does so by analyzing the weaknesses of the judiciary, designing programs to compensate for these weaknesses and presenting them to judges in a manner that is both effective in imparting knowledge and cost effective.

"Impartial" stands for both the reality and the perception of impartiality. This includes the concepts of: (i) an impartially minded and independent judiciary respected for its integrity; (ii) transparency – from the appointment process through to the rendering of judgments comprehensible to the public; (iii) a transparent and accessible judicial complaint process; and (iv) an articulated and publicized code of judicial ethics and conduct so that the community is aware of the standards it has the right to require of a judiciary. However, we should add that "impartiality" and "independence" are often used interchangeably. "Judicial impartiality" is used here to describe the desired judicial character and state of mind. "Judicial independence" refers to freedom from improper pressure in the decision-making process from any quarter. This concept of judicial independence identifies roles and responsibilities for the judiciary, the executive, the media, the legal profession, and the public (*see* Table 1 above).

The creation and support of an impartial mind has different focuses. For example, in the new states of Eastern Europe, the focus is on changing the judiciary from a bureaucracy mechanically applying the law and acting as a conduit for the delivery of political decisions, to an impartial, independent dispute resolution mechanism as well as a protector of the rule of law and civil and human rights. In other countries, judicial education places emphasis on attitudinal changes to improve judicial integrity and independence and to eliminate open and hidden bias from the judicial mind in fact finding, particularly in relation to gender and ethnic issues.

"Efficiency" includes efficient judicial court room management (placing the judge and not the bar in charge of case management), caseflow and process efficiency, reform of rules and procedures to narrow the issues down, encouraging timely settlements, court annexed and free standing mediation, and other alternative dispute resolution practices. Efficiency also relates to appropriate physical structures and adequate equipment and access to such judicial tools as statute books, precedent cases, legal texts, and other scholarly writing.

"Competency" relates to knowledge of substantive and procedural laws – no easy task for a generalist judge in the complex modern legal world, and almost impossible in developing countries where statutes, case reports, and textbooks are in short supply. Some courts have none. It also includes "judicial skills" such as chairpersonship skills and oral and written communication skills.

It is not enough for judges to be impartial, efficient, and competent. They must also be effective in interpreting and shaping the law to achieve a just solution. This may be achieved by the use of judicially developed techniques such as domestic application of international human rights norms, interpretation of constitutions, or through the judicial exercise of discretion. Integrity, legal competence, and valor are required to bridge the gap between the law and a just solution or to prevent decisions on technicalities that unnecessarily avoid the merits of the case. Knowledge and understanding of the community in which one lives is a prerequisite for an effective judge. Knowledge and understanding of the philosophy behind economic reform is also a prerequisite.

Judicial predictability is a second aspect of judicial effectiveness. A third aspect of judicial effectiveness is the collective judicial responsibility of listening to the community's complaints about the justice system and using its influence to shape the justice system to respond to responsible complaints. For example, judges do not generally consider a low rate of judgment recovery their responsibility. In many countries, difficulties in enforcing judgments can make successful litigation a hollow victory and bring the judiciary into disrepute. There are judicial, legislative, and administrative ways of improving judgment recovery. The judiciary has an interest and responsibility in supporting this and other necessary reforms in non-political ways.

To be effective a judiciary must be legitimate – trusted, respected, and relevant. A judiciary must not only be impartial, competent, efficient, and effective, but must be perceived to have those qualities. Transparency in procedure and process is required to achieve public faith as is an understanding by the judiciary that they perform a public service and need to respond to community expectations. Judges, like other players in the justice system, often need intellectual leadership to help them to understand fully the importance of this and to encourage them to lend their support to the application of means to achieve it.

4.4. Curriculum Development

How does a jurisdiction determine judicial education curriculum? In many common law countries, judicial education began with judges electing to spend their study time considering the law of evidence and procedure. However, community criticism of the justice system rarely seems to find fault with judicial application of the law of evidence and procedure.

The content of judicial education programming must respond to community perceptions of judicial weaknesses. The community (in this context) includes the judiciary, the bar, and court-users, as well as the business sector and society at large. Judicial education is expensive – one must take into the account the judge's days off the bench, the cost of maintaining courthouses and court staff during judicial absences, as well as travel and accommodation expenses for participants, and program delivery costs. To justify these expenditures, programming must go beyond the old standbys of evidence and procedure and visibly respond to areas of perceived weakness. A curriculum committee may employ several tools to identify areas requiring improvement: (a) a broad-based needs assessment survey of the community; (b) a review of complaints against judges; (c) a review of media complaints on justice issues; (d) an assessment of areas of the law that call for frequent appellate review; (e) an analysis of the role and function of a judge; or (f) a combination of all of the above, plus others.

The broad-based survey of court users and the public is the most important curricula development tool. It should be undertaken to identify areas of community perception of judicial weaknesses that judicial studies could strengthen. It is interesting to note that an additional benefit of such a needs assessment is that it often produces a prioritized list of needed judicial reforms. It also tends to enhance public confidence in the judiciary as soliciting court users' opinions assures the public of judicial sensitivity to the community it serves.

4.5. Detection of Factual and Legal Bias in Fact-Finding

The greatest power of a fact-finding judge lies in the function of accepting or rejecting evidence, as for all practical purposes a judge cannot be reversed on appeal in this area. Any finding of guilt or innocence or rights between parties determined by the facts is based on subjective beliefs of the trier of fact. In many jurisdictions a single judge sitting alone without a jury is the finder of fact.

A judge should also be aware, as most of any experience are, of the fallibility of the human powers of observation and memory. The experiments of psychologist Elizabeth Loftus have shown us how sympathy can make honest people see things inaccurately.[66] Many judges are of the view that their function in making findings of credibility is not in danger of being usurped by a lie detecting machine because

---

[66] Elizabeth Loftus, *Eyewitness Testimony* (Harvard University Press 1979); Elizabeth Loftus, *Memory, Surprising New Insights into How We Remember and Why We Forget* (Addison - Wesley Publishing Co. 1980).

in their experience most people have convinced themselves that their evidence is true by the time they get to the courtroom.

The science of fact-finding in judicial decision-making is an important but neglected issue. While legal writers have given some attention to this issue[67] their analysis is different from the process of belief and proof that is considered by Seniuk.[68] His work points out that because of the power of the finder of fact, the outcome of a case is often determined by which judge is drawn. This, in essence, leaves the outcome as much to chance as would the flip of a coin.[69] His conclusion is supported by mock findings of guilt or innocence made by judges in judicial education programs. Having viewed a video that depicts a trial in which a young female from a troubled past alleges a retired war-disabled veteran sexually assaulted her, the judges are polled for their verdicts. When used throughout the Commonwealth, the result has almost always been an approximate 40/60 split on the part of the experienced judicial decision makers.[70] Programmes assisting judges to analyze, detect, and improve biases in their fact-finding process are important to the success of the judicial reform process.

---

[67] R.S. Abella, *The Dynamic Nature of Equality*, in *Equality and Judicial Neutrality* 8 (Sheila Martin & Kathleen Mahoney eds., Hardwell 1987); B.L. Shientag, *The Virtue of Impartiality* in *Handbook for Judges* (Glenn R. Winters ed., The American Judicature Society 1975); Bertha Wilson, *Will Women Judges Really Make a Difference?* 28 Osgoode Hall Law Journal 507 (1990); W.L. Twining, *Theories of Evidence: Bentham & Wigmore* (Stanford U. Press 1985); N. Gold, C. Mackie & W.L. Twining, *Learning Lawyers' Skills* (Butterworths 1989); W.L. Twining, *Rethinking Evidence: Exploratory Essays* (Oxford 1990). For a number of articles considering an academic movement called the "new evidence scholarship," which considers the implications of decision theory, probability and statistics for the study of evidence, *see Decision and Inference in Litigation* 13 Cardozo L. Rev. No. 2 and 3 (1991) (symposium issue).

[68] G.T.G. Seniuk, Seminar, *Judicial Fact - Finding and a Theory of Credit* (Halifax, Canada, Feb. 16, 1994) (copy on file with the Nova Scotia Judicial Education Seminar).

[69] Rabelais' Judge Bridlegoose did decide cases by tossing a coin. Francois Rabelais, *Gargantua and Pantagruel* vol. 3, ch. 39-43 (J.M. Cohen trans., Penguin 1955). Another unusual story of a coin tossing judge is that of the Manhattan judge who used this method to decide the length of a jail sentence. He also asked courtroom spectators to vote on which of two conflicting witnesses to believe. He was removed from office in 1983 by the New York State Commission on Judicial Conduct, *The Times* (Feb. 3 1982).

[70] Experience gleaned from the use of the video at Commonwealth Judicial Education Institute programs.

Judges also need to be aware of analysis of schools of jurisprudence. It is important that they be assisted to be sufficiently introspective to identify the school into which they fall and to determine if there is a need to consider a changed jurisprudential approach to achieve justice in their decisions. This will involve the study of academic articles analyzing judicial approaches to decision-making, an analytical self study of the judge's decision-making process, and a philosophical consideration of the objectives of the justice system fuelled by taking time for academic reading.

5. Performance Evaluation

5.1. General

Judges have the least feedback and evaluation of any profession – at least in the superior courts and the subordinate courts of common law developed countries. In jurisdictions where the judicial office has been perceived as powerful and attracts respect, it is difficult for the legal profession to deviate from the traditional deferential stance to the judge or risk judicial wrath wreaked on the interest of future clients by being known as critical of a judge's conduct. In jurisdictions where the judicial office is held in low esteem and is at the bottom rung of the legal profession,[71] there is as little motivation to devise methodology for feedback as there is motivation for judicial behavioral change to correct judicial weaknesses exposed by the measurement. However, the democratic clamoring for judicial accountability in the industrialized democracies and the accepted need for a well-functioning judiciary in transitional and developing countries have raised interest in the development of methodology that will allow qualitative and quantitative measurement of judicial performance as a foundation step to improvement. Methodology for measuring judicial performance is in place in the United States.[72] Attempts to create such methodology are underway in Canada[73] and

---

[71] *E.g.* Some South American and transitional country jurisdictions.

[72] *E.g.* Massachusetts, New Jersey, Connecticut. *See* the National Center for State Courts, *Trial Court Performance Standards and Measurement System* (National Center for State Courts 2001).

[73] Nova Scotia Judicial Development Project, Institute of Public Administration, Dalhousie University.

Australia.[74] Multilateral and bilateral donor agencies are also interested in such evaluation methodology to provide measurements by which to evaluate judicial reform projects. A difficulty in drawing up judicial performance evaluation standards is to do so in such a way that judicial independence is not compromised.

Measurement of judicial performance may be quantitative[75] – relating to the efficiency of the judicial process and the individual judge, or it may be qualitative attempting to measure the competency, impartiality, and effectiveness of the judicial process or the performance of the individual judge. The quantitative evaluation is less difficult as it collates objective data such as number of cases filed per year, number of cases disposed of per year, number of cases pending at year end, clearance rate (ratio of cases disposed of to cases filed), congestion rate (pending and filed over resolved), average duration of case, number of judges per 100,000 habitants, workload per judge, work time per judge, length of time judgment rendered after close of case, etc. Further data may also be collected from those jurisdictions[76] that have time limits for the rendering of judgments counting from the close of the case.

In quantitative evaluation, two thoughts must be kept in mind. The first is that the desired end product of the justice system is not speed but justice, even accepting that "justice delayed is justice denied." The second is that there needs to be good judicial statistical data gathered by the courts before such measurements can be made. In many developing jurisdictions, the gathering of statistical data is considered by the judiciary and staff as secondary to the staff's role as judicial assistant. The Uganda experience has shown that until this attitude is changed the data gathered will not be sufficient or reliable enough to identify bottlenecks in the system or provide measurement of judicial performance.[77] Basic to quantitative

---

74 *E.g.* Family Court (Justice Neil Buckley), Brisbane, Australia.

75 Maria Dakolias, *Court Performance Around the World: A Comparative Perspective* (World Bank Technical Paper No. 430, 1999).

76 Nova Scotia, Canada, and the Philippines have time limits for the rendering of judgments counting from the close of the case. The Philippines has other time limits and sanctions if a judge does not achieve the deadline. Pakistan also expects subordinate court judges to complete a certain number of cases in a given time. The Philippine and Pakistan time limits are often honored in the breach or honored in a way that is counterproductive to the justice system.

77 *See* the United Nations Office for Drug Control and Crime Prevention's (UNODCCP) project against corruption in Uganda (1998-2000), funded by international donor

measurement of the judiciary is the entering of court data either manually or electronically in such a way that it is available for analysis.

The qualitative measurement of judicial performance has in most countries been left to the appeal courts. However, in the Philippines and South Africa in the common law world, errors in law or ignorance of the law amounting to gross incompetence is considered misbehavior triggering discipline or dismissal.[78] The qualitative assessment presents difficulties of subjectivity, attempting to measure immeasurables, lack of data, and reluctance of court users to evaluate individual judges. The qualitative assessment is particularly difficult in hierarchical developing countries where the culture depresses criticism of authority figures.

It is doubtful that performance appraisals will be accepted by developing country common law high courts or by judiciaries such as Italy the institutions of which favor independence over accountability. The social and legal cultures of the common law developing countries would be more amenable to judicial performance evaluations of the subordinate court judges. Applying different standards to the subordinate court could well, however, mitigate against reform efforts to support and improve its status.

It would be useful to attempt one pilot project in Africa, one in Latin America and one in Asia under the following conditions: leadership by a senior local judge interested in pursuing the concept, a design that totally separates the evaluation from the disciplinary process, destruction of all evaluations post project, and judicial participation on a voluntary basis. In the author's view, it would be counterproductive for the bar to initiate such a project without the support of the judiciary as it would exacerbate tensions between the bench and bar often caused by judicial reform initiatives.

5.2. Common Law Jurisdictions

Led by U.S. practice, in the last decade performance evaluations of judges of all levels have come into being. These contemporary feedback mechanisms are far from universal and indeed would be considered in many jurisdictions as an encroachment on judicial independence. To date they are used or are being considered in the United States, Canada, and Australia in the common law world.

---

agencies such as DANIDA, NORAD, UNDP, USAID, and the World Bank <www.undcp.org/corruption_judiciary.html>.

78 *E.g.* the Philippines. The Constitution of South Africa ch. 8, sec. 177(1)(a) includes "gross incompetence" as a criterion for judicial removal.

These vary from judiciary-initiated evaluation processes to bar-initiated evaluations. Some were initiated by the legislature by statute, others were conducted by the bar, others were initiated by the judiciary as a volunteer mechanism for self-improvement, and others were initiated as a judicially ordered feedback mechanism for self improvement.

In some U.S. states with elected judges, evaluations are published for the benefit of the voters. In non-elected jurisdictions, they are generally disclosed only to the judge or to the chief justice and judge. The volunteer Canadian pilot project took great care to separate the anonymous feedback from the disciplinary process and the information was made known only to the judge through a mentor chosen by him or her.[79] All material relating to the project was destroyed. In addition to providing the judge with information for improving personal performance, summaries of the evaluation results are also valuable to judicial education bodies to indicate areas of general weakness in judicial performance that may be improved through judicial education programs. The final recommendation of this project was that both the bar and bench involved found it useful and felt it should be continued.

Competitive examinations are written in some Asian jurisdictions by subordinate court judges at certain career level entry points. Annual performance appraisals by the chief judge of the judges of the subordinate court are common in Africa and Asia. This is a holdover from colonial days when magistrates formed part of the executive branch and came under civil service regulations.[80] These appraisals are a monitoring mechanism considered by some countries, such as Pakistan, to be essential information for promotion. Other countries, such as Uganda, are considering eliminating them. These annual performance reports can be an internal judicial independence issue and be threatening to the independence and integrity of the subordinate judge. There are no comparable annual performance appraisals for Commonwealth high court judges.

5.3. Civil Law Jurisdictions

In civil law jurisdictions, candidates enter by competitive examination and are promoted by judicially controlled promotion criteria. These processes have

---

[79] *Supra* n. 73.

[80] In some Asian jurisdictions such as Pakistan, civil service regulations still apply to the subordinate judiciary.

recently come under criticism for lack of accountability and transparency.[81] A European conference was held in 2000 at Maastricht in the Netherlands on the issue of performance evaluations. As a result of this, it is likely performance evaluation projects will be undertaken in civil law jurisdictions as well.

One project already in place is the new Belgian professional evaluation system.[82] In this, the president of the court of first degree and two peer judges evaluate each judge once a year. There are articulated criteria for both quantitative and qualitative performance evaluation that differ from court to court. If the judge receives an insufficient score, then the judge may be penalized financially for six months and the judge's file is sent to the minister of justice and the High Judicial Council. While this process is held to be distinct from the disciplinary system carried out through the Cassation Court, in light of the sanctions available and the communication of the file to the promotional authorities, the distinction appears to be blurred.

Appropriate judicial performance evaluations bring to the judiciary a much needed opportunity for professional self-improvement. They provide a very necessary and acceptable method of communication between the court users and the judge. Most judges want to do a good job and will strive to modify their behavior to respond to negative comments in the evaluations. Judges, who in their isolation rarely receive praise, will feel appreciated and be inspired by the positive aspects of the evaluations. For most effective results, care should be taken to design performance evaluation processes so that fire walls are built between the evaluation and the disciplinary process. This will go a long way to attracting judicial support. A further suggestion for easing into such a program would be to initiate it on a voluntary basis.

---

[81] Di Federico, *supra* n. 47.

[82] Interview with Judge Joelle Colaes, Antwerp (March 13, 2001).

6. Salaries

6.1. General

> The term of office of judges, their independence, security, adequate remuneration, conditions of service, pensions, and the age of retirement shall be adequately secured by law.[83]

Because of the importance of a proper level and system of compensation to attract high quality individuals to the bench, and to keep them, a word needs to be said about compensation. Inadequate judicial salaries are common in developing countries and are frequently cited as a major cause of corruption. There are five issues relating to judicial salaries: their adequacy, their constitutional or statutory protection, the methodology of determining them, their source, and the issue of bonus pay.

6.2. Adequacy

It is commonly accepted that an important mechanism to support individual judicial integrity is a salary commensurate with the responsibility and societal importance of the judicial position. Without adequate salaries, the judiciaries are unable to attract candidates of a caliber necessary to constitute courts in which the community has trust. There are vast discrepancies in judicial salaries. Supreme Court judges in Singapore earn U.S.$ 500,000 a year. In the Cayman Islands the salary is U.S.$ 250,000 a year tax free. It is difficult to compare judicial salaries because some jurisdictions include benefits that are economically greater than the salary attached to the office. There is also the difficulty of determining the buying power of the salary. Maria Dakolias in *Court Performance Around the World* uses a multiple of a national average salary to determine the national financial ranking of the judge.[84] Her study indicates that judicial salaries of commercial courts in Brazil are 33 times the average net salary, in Ecuador 18 times that of the average net salary, in France twice that of the average net salary, in Hungary two times that of the national average, in Panama 10 times that of the average net salary, in Peru 14

---

[83] *United Nations Basic Principles, supra* n. 1, Principle 11.

[84] Maria Dakolias, *Court Performance Around the World. A Comparative Perspective* (World Bank Technical Paper No. 430, 1999).

times that of the average next salary.[85] In Ukraine, salaries, while comparable to teachers, have also been compared to those of janitors, and payment is often delayed several months and is far below private sector salaries. In Pakistan, a starting judicial salary is equivalent to that of a taxi driver, and judicial salaries are linked to civil service grades.

Low pensions are another hazard to judicial independence, particularly in Asian common law countries as judges approaching retirement hope to find post-retirement government positions, such as a chair of a law reform commission, or of a judicial studies board. This provides the perception and perhaps reality of a judge seeking government favor by court decision. In all jurisdictions it is accepted that the more financially successful members of the bar earn incomes both from their law practice and related activities of such a size that appointment to an even well-paid bench causes a severe diminution of income. Income tax regulations in many countries make this transition even more economically damaging. It is also generally accepted that inadequate salaries give rise to corruption, especially at the lower levels of the judiciary. It is common to most judicial reform prescriptions that any reform package aimed at reducing corruption should include salary increases. It is understandable that it is difficult to reduce corruption among low-paid judges in developing or transitional countries with no social networks when they are forced to choose between the basic needs of their families or adhering to ethical principles. The need for money to buy a life saving medication for a dying child puts great pressure on principles of integrity.

However, there is no evidence that increasing salaries alone without taking other measures leads to significant reductions in corruption. While it is one element, the reduction of corruption is linked to increasing transparency and meritocracy in judicial appointment and discipline processes. As stated in a recent World Bank report "the contrasting results between the low impact of higher salaries, on the one hand, and the significant effect of meritocracy, on the other, exemplifies the need to conduct in-depth, empirical diagnostics within countries intent on formulating serious anti-corruption programmes."[86]

To this must be added, however, the fact that the challenges of judicial reform for judges are generally neither pleasurable nor profitable, but burdensome. Increases in judicial salary included in programs to improve transparency and

[85] *Id.*, at 26.

[86] Thomas Vinod *et al.*, *The Quality of Growth* ch. 6, 152 (Oxford U. Press 2000).

meritocracy in appointment and promotion, to implement an accessible, transparent judicial complaint system linked to a transparent, effective, fair, and efficient discipline system will assist in rallying judges to the reform cause.[87]

6.3. Constitutional or statutory protection of salaries

Influenced perhaps by the U.S. federal judges' salary being constitutionally protected from diminution during their tenure of office[88] many countries have placed a similar provision in their constitution. Other countries have sought to protect judicial salaries against diminution by statute.[89] Others have no protection at all.

6.4. Methodology for salary determination

In many common law jurisdictions, the determination of judicial salaries has historically been left for the executive branch to recommend in its budget to the legislature. This was an obvious control by the executive over the judiciary. The demonstrated importance given to buffering this control and maintaining adequate judicial salaries has led in the past few decades to a variety of mechanisms to have judicial salaries established by independent tribunals.[90] An interesting comment by Chief Justice Lamer of Canada was that judges had distinct functions from bureaucrats, and it was inappropriate to determine judicial salaries only by comparison with senior bureaucrats.

Judicial salaries are generally paid out of the judicial budget from the consolidated fund. This is an important protection so that judicial salaries are not

---

[87] The Chief Justice of Singapore in conversation with the author attributed his ability to achieve success in delay reduction reform to the high salaries (U.S.$ 500,000) he was able to arrange for the Supreme Court.

[88] Which is natural life. This has been interpreted to include inflationary rises. R. Wheeler and M. Fur-Arie, *Judicial Independence in the United States: Current Issues – Relevant Background Information* in *IFES/USAID Guide to Judicial Independence – Draft Report* pt. C, 2 (USAID 2000).

[89] *E.g.* Canada.

[90] *See* G. Winterton, *Judicial Remuneration in Australia* (Australian Institute of Judicial Administration Incorporated 1995). Examples include Australia and England. In Canada the subordinate court judges sued their provincial governments on this issue and were supported by the Supreme Court of Canada in *Reference re Remuneration of Judges of the Provincial Court of Prince Edward Island* [1997] 3 S.C.R. 3 (Can.).

jeopardized by lessening of national income at certain times of the year. Russia and other post-Soviet countries suffer from the difficulty of their salaries often being paid months in arrears.

6.5. Sources

In many countries, local or municipal governments augment the salaries paid to judges from the state treasury. Local or municipal governments often provide facilities for courtrooms. In many transitional countries and in the Philippines, local governments supply judicial accommodation, electricity, transportation, additional allowances, etc. These local authorities are litigants in the courts and the reality of increased corruption due to pressures placed on judges by their supporting local authorities is well documented.[91] An additional problem, illustrated in the Philippines, is that local authorities are of differing levels of wealth, and the courts and judges in the wealthier localities have working conditions and allowances far superior to their colleagues in the poorer localities.

6.6. Bonus Pay

Suggestions have been put forward of increasing court productivity by awarding bonus pay to productive judges. This raises the specter of judicial glossing over work for financial gain, particularly in judiciaries with low salaries. Any such scheme would need to balance the possible benefit in productivity against the possibility of a lower standard of justice delivered and judicial independence issues. Perhaps we could consider the possibility of bonus pay for an entire court on achieving a productivity level although valid arguments against this, including loss of collegiality, could be raised as well.

---

[91] M. Feliciano, unpublished paper, *Analysis of Administrative Cases Against Judges in the Philippines* (1999) (copy on file with the author); J.W. Baker, *The Philippine Justice System* 48 (Geneva: Centre for the Independence of Lawyers and Judges, 1997); Court Management Report 120 (Philippine Supreme Court).

7. Discipline and Dismissal of Judges

7.1. Code of Conduct

Many countries have adopted a code of judicial ethics and conduct.[92] Some countries have adopted codes of ethics and conduct for support staff.[93] These codes generally consist of canons or rules of judicial ethics and conduct. Some codes such as the American Bar Association Code provide illustrative examples of the application of each canon or rule. These illustrative annotations are at first hypothetical fact situations illustrating the application of the rule in different situations as perceived by the code drafters. As judgments on complaints are rendered by the disciplinary tribunal, summaries of these are also included in the annotations. The result of a well-annotated code is to more closely define acceptable and prohibited conduct and provide a service both to judges on how to conduct themselves and their affairs and to the public who know what to expect of their judges.

The application of the rules and canons is not an easy matter. Seminars on judicial ethics throughout the world have shown that highly respected judges have different views on different applications of the ethical rules. Some differ on when a "gift" becomes a "bribe." Some differ on the dangers of *ex parte* visits by litigants to judicial chambers. Conflict of interest rules are complex. A Law Lord recently misunderstood the conflict rules.[94] How much more difficult must it be for a young magistrate in a developing country to be clear on the appropriate conduct in a difficult situation and have the courage to stand on principle despite the inconvenience or worse caused by this stance?

Codes of judicial ethics and conduct should be developed in a participatory way by the judges and not be imposed from above. Provision should be made for the annotated code to be regularly updated and disseminated to the judges and to the public.

A code alone is unlikely to produce a change in behavior. An accessible transparent judicial complaint process and remedial and punitive sanctions for transgressions of the code are also required. Neither of these is effective, however,

---

[92] *E.g.* United States, Philippines, Kenya, Tanzania, Uganda, Malawi, and South Africa.

[93] *E.g.* United States and Malawi.

[94] *Judgement – In Re Pinochet*, 38 I.L.M. 430, 437 (1999) (U.K. House of Lords, Oral Judgement Dec. 17, 1998) (available at <www.parliament.the-stationary-office.co.uk/pa/ld199899/ldjudgmt/jd99…/pino1.htm>).

without a transparent, efficient, and effective discipline process that screens out frivolous or malicious complaints or matters properly dealt with as appellate issues and deals fairly, efficiently, and transparently with the remaining complaints. Charts E and F in the appendix show a cross-country comparison of elements of existing disciplinary processes.

7.2. Accessible Complaint Process

The accessibility of a complaint process must be determined in light of the society and culture of the jurisdiction. In countries with high illiteracy rates, for example, a requirement for a written complaint would deny access to many. Countries such as Bangladesh and Pakistan that require that complaints be funneled through their presidents obviously inhibit complaints. The accessibility to court users to initiate a complaint is all important.

It is also important that complaint processes be transparent at least to the extent that the complainant is advised of the consequences of his or her complaint. An appropriate complaint process involves an initial screening of complaints to remove the frivolous and malicious ones or those more properly an appellate matter and a mechanism for informal resolution of complaints that could be satisfied by an apology.

7.3. Disciplinary Process

A transparent, accountable, and fair judicial discipline process accommodates the opposing pulls of judicial independence and judicial accountability.

Charges or complaints made against judges in their judicial and professional capacities must be processed expeditiously and fairly under an appropriate procedure. The judge must have the right to a fair hearing. The examination of the matter at its initial stage must be kept confidential, unless otherwise requested by the judge. Judges should be subject to suspension or removal, only for reasons of incapacity or behavior that renders them unfit to discharge their duties. All disciplinary, suspension, or removal proceedings should be determined in accordance with established standards of judicial conduct. Decisions in disciplinary, suspension, or removal proceedings should be subject to an independent review. This principle may not apply to the decisions of the highest court and those of the legislature in impeachment or similar proceedings.[95]

---

[95] *Supra* n. 1, Principles 17-20.

In respect of every decision affecting the selection, recruitment, appointment, career progress, or termination of office of a judge, the European Charter envisages the intervention of an authority independent of the executive and legislative powers within which at least one half of those who sit are judges elected by their peers following methods guaranteeing the widest representation of the judiciary.[96]

In most civil law jurisdictions, removal and discipline processes are either under the control of judicial councils,[97] controlled by judges, or directed by a court.[98] The industrialized common law countries have retained for courts above the subordinate level the traditional removal process through the parliament and, except for the United States, have no disciplinary processes for misconduct that falls below the "good behavior" criteria for removal. The Canadian Judicial Council, composed solely of the national and provincial chief justices, has the statutory power to investigate allegations of judicial misconduct but is restricted to making recommendations to the minister of justice if it considers the misconduct sufficient for parliamentary consideration of removal. It has no sanctioning power, not even that of a reprimand, although the publication of decisions of investigative tribunals that do not recommend removal are often a *de facto* reprimand to the judge concerned. After achieving independence, developing common law countries, particularly in Africa, often replaced the parliamentary removal process for high courts and above with a removal and discipline process through a judicial service commission. Few, if any, have sanctions for lesser conduct than that which would constitute grounds for removal. In other countries, such as Pakistan, the removal power was placed in the hands of senior judges and the president. Subordinate court judges in Pakistan and Bangladesh are subject to the civil service rules of conduct.

Judicial councils have been established by statute in some industrialized common law countries[99] to handle allegations of misconduct against subordinate court judges. They have the power either to recommend removal or to impose lesser sanctions, remedial as well as punitive. Appeals are provided for through the regular court appellate process.

The problems of existing processes are these:

---

96 European Charter, Principle 1.3 <http://conventions.coe.int/Treaty/EN/Treaties/Html/122.htm>.

97 *E.g.* Italy, France, Spain and Latin American countries.

98 *E.g.* Belgium.

99 *E.g.* Canada.

(a) Closed judicial control does not meet contemporary requirements of judicial accountability. As was noted above, the European Charter suggests judicial discipline or removal be exercised through an independent authority with one half of the members being judges.[100] While this will no doubt be unacceptable to many common law and other jurisdictions, there should be some independent professional and lay participation in judicial discipline tribunals.

(b) The common law process of removal by parliament meets process accountability standards but the difficulty of legislative removal is such that it does not provide a responsive mechanism to complaints about judges. Only seven federal judges have been removed in the history of the United States, none in Canada in recent times, and none in England and the Caribbean.

(c) There is no process for disciplining Commonwealth high court judges for misconduct that does not constitute grounds for removal.

(d) The discipline of subordinate court judges by the executive offends the principle of judicial independence.

(e) Most existing judicial councils that have discipline authority are not sufficiently accountable, nor do their processes generally provide sufficient transparency.

(f) Some jurisdictions place judicial discipline in the hands of the supreme court. This court is overwhelmed with complaints, creating a heavy administrative burden on it and resulting in complaints that take years to resolve.

In conclusion, then, the following are offered as elements of a disciplinary process that would best serve the principles of judicial independence and public accountability for both high and subordinate courts:

(a) A judicial discipline body composed of a majority of judges, but with lay and professional representation;

(b) A transparent process for complaints that are passed to the hearing process;

(c) A screening process that eliminates frivolous, malicious, or properly appellate issues;

(d) Separate investigative and adjudicative bodies;

---

[100] *Supra* n. 96.

(e) Remedial and punitive sanctions less than removal for conduct insufficient to meet the removal criteria with the possibility of a judicial appeal from any finding of misconduct or sanction;

(f) Either a public hearing or publication of the hearing results;

(g) An efficient process which resolves complaints within a reasonable period; and

(h) A process that is fair to both the judge and the complainant, which allows the judge to be represented by counsel and offers the possibility of the state bearing at least a vindicated judge's legal fees.

8. The Judiciary and the Corruption Issue

8.1. General

> Judges shall uphold the integrity and independence of the judiciary by avoiding impropriety and the appearance of impropriety in all their activities.[101]

Because of heightened attention to the judiciary the ethics and conduct of judges have come under increased scrutiny in recent years. The iconoclastic attitude of people of contemporary western democracies has added judicial criticism to criticisms of other state actors. The traditional respect in common law democracies for the judge that used to prevent much criticism is eroding, perhaps caused by the higher visibility of the judiciary and their enhanced policy-making powers. Anti-corruption components, often including articulated codes of ethics and creation of accessible, transparent judicial complaint and discipline processes, are a common element in judicial reform programs.[102] Many jurisdictions have adopted or are considering a code of judicial ethics and conduct both for judges and judicial support staff.[103] Considerable judicial education time is given to this topic.

---

[101] *Beijing Statement of Principles of the Independence of the Judiciary in the LAWASIA Region*, Principle 7 (Aug. 19, 1995) <http://www.taunet.net.au/lawasia/beijing_statement.htm> [hereinafter the Beijing Principles].

[102] Commonwealth Judicial Education Institute, *Judicial Reform Grid* (Commonwealth Judicial Education Institute 2000)

[103] *E.g*. South Africa, Kenya, Tanzania, Ukraine, Guatemala, the Philippines, United States, one Canadian province. Canada has a 200-page judicial ethics guideline.

The dictionary indicates a difference between ethics and conduct. However, they are intertwined. "Ethics" is used in this paper to describe the personal integrity of the judge or judicial support staff member. It has been defined as "of or relating to moral action, conduct, motive or character, as ethical emotions; also treating of moral feeling, duty or conduct; containing precepts of morality; morals. Professionally right or befitting; conforming to professional standards of conduct."[104] "Conduct," as used in this paper, describes the actions of a judge on and off the bench. Some of these, such as seeing one party to a case privately, give rise to the perception or misperception of unethical behavior on the part of the judge even when it is not present. "Conduct" is used to describe manners and behavior. In jurisdictions where the judicial office is prestigious some manners and behavior do not meet the high standard which, in the mind of the community, is becoming to the judicial role.[105]

8.2. Judicial Corruption

> You shall appoint judges and officers in all your towns which the Lord your God gives you, according to your tribes. You shall not pervert justice; you shall not show partiality, you shall not take a bribe; for a bribe blinds the eyes of the wise and subverts the cause of the righteous.[106]
>
> Do not devour each other's wealth among yourselves through deceit and falsehood, nor offer your wealth as a bribe to the authorities that you may deliberately devour a part of other people's wealth through injustice.[107]

The recent focus on judiciaries has brought judicial corruption into the open and has revealed that it is a major problem[108] common to the judiciaries in the developing countries of Africa and Asia,[109] as well as in post-Soviet countries.

---

[104] *Black's Law Dictionary* 553 (Bryan A. Garner *et al.* eds., 6th ed., West 1990).

[105] The status of a judge is not considered prestigious in many Latin American countries nor in the lower courts of Russia and other post-Soviet countries.

[106] Deuteronomy 16:18-20.

[107] Koran 2:188 (Muhammad Zaffrullah Khan trans., 3d ed., Qurzon Press 1978).

[108] A cabinet minister of Bangladesh advised the author that up to 17 bribes must be paid by a civil litigant in Bangladesh prior to the trial.

[109] For example, corruption was so endemic in Georgia and Ethiopia that a "judicial cleansing" took place on the establishment of new democracies in these countries; J.W. Bakker

Corruption is not a major problem in the Anglophone Caribbean, although it is in many Latin American countries. It exists to a small extent in the state courts in the United States. Corruption has not been found to be an issue in the courts of Scandinavia, Canada, the United Kingdom, Australia, and New Zealand.

Transparency International (TI), an international NGO working alone or in partnership with other organizations such as the World Bank, has undertaken surveys in several countries to determine the ethical perception of the judiciary held by the community.[110] Other NGOs, such as the Social Weather Station in the Philippines, have also undertaken surveys to measure the community's perception of corruption.[111] These were widely published in that country. The results in each country showed the communities' perception of judicial corruption to be considerable. The Philippine survey showed the image of corruption was greater in the community at large than in the perception of court users.[112] This shows the importance of survey checks and balances.

This accumulation of baseline data to prove a perception of judicial corruption is the first step in a process to improve both the reality and perception of judicial integrity. Such data are necessary for the confrontation with the judiciary that sparks personal and institutional reform. This must begin with the awareness raising of what constitutes acceptable behavior and the creation of a more informed understanding of the costs of corruption.

The *TI Source Book* indicates that a major research project in New South Wales, Australia in 1994 by the state's Independent Commission Against Corruption found a willingness to take action against corruption dependent upon a number of factors, including the relationship between taking action and how harmful, undesirable or unjustified each scenario was considered to be. Factors which reduced the willingness to take action included: (a) a belief that the behavior was justified in the circumstance; (b) the attitude that there is no point in reporting corruption as nothing useful will be done about it; (c) a belief that the behavior was not corrupt;

& Jan Willem, *The Philippine Justice System* (Centre for the Independence of Lawyers and Judges 1997); *The TI Source Book: National Integrity Systems* 9 (Jeremy Pope ed., Transparency International 1997)(available at <www.transparency.org/documents/source-book/index.html>).

[110] *E.g.* Uganda and Tanzania.

[111] *See* J.W. Bakker & Jan Willem, *supra* n. 109.

[112] *Id.*

(d) a fear of both personal and professional retaliation; (e) a relatively low position within the organization; and (f) the employees' perception of the relationship with the perpetrator and the supervisor and the concern about insufficient evidence.[113]

8.3. Types and Causes of Corruption

A policy framework for preventing and eliminating corruption and enforcing the impartiality of the justice system came from a meeting of 16 experts convened by the Centre for the Independence of Judges and Lawyers (CIJL).[114] Based on the findings of CILJ, major acts constituting corruption of the judicial system are as follows: (a) bribery; (b) fraud; (c) utilization of public resources for private gain; (d) deliberate loss of court records;[115] and (e) deliberate alteration of court records. Corruption also occurs when instead of procedures being determined on the basis of evidence and the law, they are decided on the basis of improper influences, inducements, pressures, threats, or interferences, directly or indirectly, from any quarter or for any reason including those arising from: (a) a conflict of interest; (b) nepotism; (c) favoritism to friends; (d) consideration of promotional prospect; (e) consideration of post retirement placements; (f) improper socialization with members of the legal profession, the executive or the legislative branches; (g) socialization with litigants or prospective litigants; (h) predetermination of an issue involved in litigation; (i) prejudice; and (j) having regard to the power of government or political parties. In this list, the author would emphasize corruption in judicial appointment, promotion, and discipline processes. For example, the textbook perfect appointment process of the Philippines using a constitutionally enshrined Judicial and Bar Council has reputedly been perverted by political pressures on its members.[116] In Asian countries such as Nepal[117] and Pakistan[118] as well

---

[113] *The TI Source Book: National Integrity Systems, supra* n. 109.

[114] The meeting was held on March 15, 1999 in Geneva, Switzerland.

[115] In Uganda the High Court judges keep all active files assigned to them under lock and key in their personal offices out of fear they may disappear or be tampered with in the Registry files; author's mission to the Ugandan Judiciary (Feb. 2000).

[116] Author's meeting with the Philippine Judiciary and court users (2000).

[117] Author's meeting with the Nepal Judiciary and court users (2000).

[118] Author's meeting with the Pakistan Judiciary and court users (1998).

as European[119] and South American[120] countries, the non-transparent judicially controlled discipline processes do not function well because of the protectiveness of the "old boys network" who prefer not to sanction their own.[121] A further important cause of judicial corruption is support staff. This includes both clerks who profit by interfering for a bribe in the court process and court officers or private enterprises charged with the enforcement of court orders. This latter area is a major source of corruption in nearly all developing and transitional countries.

The causes of judicial corruption are many but center around human greed and opportunity to accumulate wealth dishonestly or human need so great that it defeats even strongly held ethical principles. Countries with enormous wealth such as the Philippines, Nigeria, and Angola but with poor wealth distribution suffer corruption to the same extent as poorer countries such as Malawi, where again what wealth there is, is not well distributed. Literature on corruption ties it to social, traditional, and economic causes. [122] Anti-corruption programs try to create a sense of values and standards of integrity on which peer pressure to combat corruption might be built. They also deal with mechanisms and institutions to police these standards.

A further cause of judicial corruption is pure lack of knowledge that the act performed is corrupt - for example, a judge will know he may not take a bribe but in what circumstances is a gift not a bribe? Or, when is a conflict of interest sufficient to require a judge to step aside from the case? Education programs and codes of ethics and conduct with illustrative examples will help here. However, attacking judicial corruption cannot be successfully done by the judiciary alone. Support from the bar is also essential. There is little hope of reducing corruption without executive support to prosecute those who pervert the justice system.

"Justice delayed is justice denied" is a well accepted adage. However, a major problem throughout all jurisdictions is delay. In many developing countries, it is far from uncommon for parties in civil cases to die or go bankrupt before judgment is rendered up to 20 years from initiation of the legal action. Delay creates many opportunities for corruption. Delay reduction reform is one of the most common

---

[119] Di Federico, *supra* n. 47.

[120] *Judicial Independence in the Age of Democracy, Critical Perspectives from Around the World* (P. Russell and D. O'Brien eds., University of Virginia Press 2001).

[121] Discussion with senior judges in Pakistan (1998) and Nepal (2000).

[122] *See* e.g. Edgardo Buscaglia & Maria Dakolias, *An Analysis of the Causes of Corruption in the Judiciary* (World Bank 1999).

prescriptions of judicial reform, and one that meets many obstacles. Failure comes in many ways but as recently pointed out by Zuckerman,[123] a politically powerful bar protecting its vested interests is a major obstacle to delay reduction in the countries he studied.

8.4. Anti-Corruption Prescription

The problem of corruption is multi-faceted, and any anti-corruption reform would have to be equally multi-dimensional. The following are offered as essential elements of any of such program:

(a) articulated objective criteria of appointment;

(b) transparent, impartial appointment and promotion processes with community representation and choice from a wide pool of candidates to create a judiciary reflective of the community;

(c) codes of judicial ethics and conduct for judges and support staff, developed in a participatory manner and containing illustrative detailed examples of violations of the code rules;

(d) wide dissemination of codes of ethics and conduct so that the community will understand the standards it has a right to require of the judiciary;

(e) an accessible, transparent, fair, and efficient complaint process and an education program for the community at large;

(f) a transparent, efficient, and fair discipline process with remedial and punitive sanctions;

(g) legal and judicial education on judicial ethics and accountability;

(h) education for support staff on ethics and accountability;

(i) delay reduction reform to eliminate opportunities for corruption, including elimination of procedural opportunities for corruption (*e.g.* storage of court records and assignment of cases);

(j) legislative and executive support for the elimination of judicial corruption and prosecution of those who pervert the justice system;

(k) public disclosure of judicial assets;

(l) judicial performance evaluation feedback;

[123] *Civil Justice in Crisis* (A. Zuckerman ed., Oxford U. Press 1999).

(m) collection of baseline data on community perception of judicial integrity for each court level;
(n) adequate and protected salaries for judges; and
(o) control by an effective national auditor general.

9. Conclusion

This article has examined international efforts to achieve "well functioning"[124] judges, the essence of a valued justice system. It reviewed judicial appointment criteria and methodology, judicial salaries and benefits, judicial performance evaluation, judicial integrity, judicial impartiality, judicial complaint and discipline processes, codes of judicial ethics and conduct and judicial education.

It also reviewed and analyzed international instruments and declarations relating to minimum standards of judicial independence, and considered these and other efforts to establish a standard against which to measure the independence of a judiciary. The article also discussed the issue of corruption of judges and support staff and explored the correlation between corruption and appointment and disciplinary and removal practices.

The purpose of the article was to provide a basis for discussion of the methodology of improving the quality of judges. To further this discussion, it set forth remedial recommendations, including articulated criteria of appointment; an impartial appointment process; an articulated, widely disseminated code of judicial ethics and conduct; an accessible, transparent, efficient and fair judicial complaint process; more efficient and transparent record keeping and case management procedures; an independent salary and benefits tribunal; and judicial education to support judicial reform.

Inclusion of these remedial recommendations in a judicial reform program offers a prescription for more effective implementation of judicial reform investments. The recommendations should be supported by historical analysis of contemporary problems and an understanding of human, social, cultural and political pressures that will work for and against reform. This will provide an essential

---

[124] "Well functioning" is the phrase used in international judicial reform discourse to describe a judge or judiciary performing at a level that attracts the confidence of the community.

background for the understanding of contemporary problems and identify historical, social, political, economic, and cultural obstacles to reform.

Like all areas of judicial reform, improving the quality of judges requires parallel concurrent reforms and behavioral change both within and without the judiciary.

Appendix

Chart A. International Instruments Relating to Judicial Independence

A = International Bar Association Minimum Standards of Judicial Independence, 1982[125]

B = Universal Declaration of the Independence of Justice (Montreal), 1983[126]

C = Singhvi Declaration, 1985[127]

D = U.N. Basic Principles on the Independence of the Judiciary, 1985[128]

E = Beijing Statement of Principles of the Independence of the Judiciary in the LAWASIA Region, 1995[129]

F = The Draft Commonwealth Latimer House Guidelines on Judicial Independence, 1999[130]

G = The Universal Charter of the Judge by the International Association of Judges, 1999[131]

Criteria	A	B	C	D	E	F	G
Principle of separation of powers			+			+	+
Constitutionally entrenched courts		+[132]					
Constitutional enshrined or guaranteed judicial independence	+[133]	+[134]		+			+[135]
Judges accountable only to the law (personal independence)			+	+			+

[125] *Supra* n. 8.

[126] *Id.*

[127] *Id.*

[128] *Supra* n. 1.

[129] *Supra* n. 9.

[130] *Id.*

[131] *Id.*

[132] Partially.

[133] Inferred.

[134] Inferred.

[135] Judicial independence must be insured by law.

Criteria	A	B	C	D	E	F	G
Judicial exclusive authority to define its competence as defined by law		+	+	+		+[136]	
Parallel tribunals not be created to duplicate the jurisdiction of the ordinary courts		+	+	+			
Judiciary conducts proceedings fairly and respects the rights of the parties		+	+[137]	+			+
Judges entitled to freedom of expression, belief, association, and assembly, and must conduct themselves in such a manner as to preserve the dignity of their office and the impartiality and independence of the judiciary		+[138]	+	+	+		
Judge from an abolished court should be transferred to another court of the same status	+	+			+[139]		
Executive not have the power to close down or suspend the operation of the courts		+	+				
Judicial appointments should be merit-based	+	+	+	+	+	-[140]	+
Anti-discrimination provisions (race, gender, religion etc.)		+	+	+	+		

136 Inferred.

137 Any allegations of a violation of rights of a party or witness warrant a full inquiry.

138 Subject to its being consistent with the dignity of their office and their impartiality and independence of the judiciary

139 If a court is abolished existing members of the court must be reappointed to its replacement or appointed to another judicial office of status and tenure. Members of the court for whom no alternative position can be found must be fully compensated.

140 Appointment criteria should be reflective of community.

Criteria	A	B	C	D	E	F	G
Judiciary participation in judicial appointment and promotion process unless the system has proven to work satisfactorily otherwise over a long period of time	+						+
Safeguards against improper influences over judicial appointments in place		+			+		
Judicial appointments and promotions by the executive not inconsistent with judicial independence	+						
Judicial promotions merit-based	+	+		+	+		+
Safeguards against improper influences over judicial promotion must be in place		+					
Disqualifications (incompatibility rules) protect judicial independence and impartiality	+[141]	+	+				
Guaranteed tenure during good behavior until a mandatory retirement age or expiration of the office term	+	+	+	+	+	+	+
Recommendation (1) against temporary & probationary judges (2) safeguards for part-time judges	+	+					
Remuneration of judges should be adequate	+	+	+		+	+	+

141 Judges may not serve in executive functions; serve as members of the legislature or of municipal councils (unless by long historical traditions these functions are combined); hold positions in political parties; practice law unless a temporary judge; engage in business activities.

Criteria	A	B	C	D	E	F	G
Adequate judicial budget/ resources to be provided		+			+[142]	+	
Freedom from interference in decision making from superior judicial officers outside of the appellate process	+	+	+		+		+
Only judicial appellate court can reverse judicial decisions	+[143]	+				+[144]	+
Description of manner in which cases are assigned	+						
Case assignment is internal matter of judiciary	+	+		+	+		
Integration of subordinate courts as judiciary's full members emancipated from the executive		+[145]					+[146]
Judicial decisions made without political pressure	+	+	+	+	+	+[147]	+
Judicial decisions made without improper influences by litigants or other interested parties	+	+	+	+	+		+
Judiciary in control of its administration	+[148]	+			+		

[142] The amount allocated should be sufficient to avoid excessive work loads.

[143] Inferred.

[144] Inferred.

[145] Inferred.

[146] Inferred.

[147] Inferred.

[148] Judicial matters should be exclusively within the responsibility of the judiciary, both in central judicial administration and the court level judicial administration. The central responsibility for judicial administration should preferably be vested in the judiciary, or jointly in the judiciary and the executive.

Criteria	A	B	C	D	E	F	G
Budget prepared by competent authority in collaboration with the judiciary, after judiciary submits estimate of budget requirements		+	+				
Budget prepared by the courts or in collaboration with the judiciary					+		
Judiciary administers own budget					+	+	
Civil immunity for judicial functions warranted	+	+	+	+[149]	+		+
A judge should behave so as to preserve the dignity of his office and the impartiality of the judiciary	+						+
Judge must diligently and efficiently perform their duties without any undue delays							+
Conflict of interest provisions, explicit or inferred	+[150]					+	
Need for safeguards to protect judges' independence with respect to their transfer to a different jurisdiction	+[151]	+[152]	+[153]		+[154]		+

149 Personal immunity from civil suits for monetary damages for improper acts or omissions in the exercise of their judicial functions. Judiciary is bound by professional secrecy with regard to their deliberations and to confidential information acquired in the course of their duties other than in public proceedings and shall not be compelled to testify on such matters.

150 A judge shall not sit in a case where there is a reasonable suspicion of bias or potential bias. A judge shall avoid any course of conduct, which might give rise to an appearance of partiality.

151 Power to transfer a judge from one court to another shall be vested in a judicial authority and preferably subject to the judge's consent, such consent not to be reasonably withheld.

152 Judge's transfer to another court without consent is prohibited unless the court is abolished, and the transfer is to another court of the same status.

153 Judge's transfer to another court without consent is prohibited within strict limitations.

154 Judge's transfer to another court without consent cannot be done by the executive unless in pursuance of a uniform policy after consultation with the judiciary.

Criteria	A	B	C	D	E	F	G
Judiciary should control judicial education curricula						+	
Provisions for judicial education		+[155]	+[156]			+	
Provisions for physical security of judges and families		+	+		+		
In some cases judges can serve on committees of inquiry	+[157]						+[158]
Judges may practice another legal profession after leaving office							+
Judges free to join professional judicial association	+	+		+	+		+
Jurisdiction of military tribunals must be confined to military offenses with right to appeal to a legally qualified appellate court		+			+		
Military takeover is recognized as a threat to judicial independence						+	
Judicial decisions are not subject to revision by executive branch	+	+	+			+[159]	+
Need for executive support to prosecute and punish attempted or actual judicial corruption							+[160]

[155] Continuing education should be available to judges.

[156] Judicial education should be organized, systemic, and ongoing under the control of an adequately funded judicial body. Judicial curricula should include the teaching of law, judicial skills, and social context issues.

[157] Judges may serve as chairs in cases where the process requires fact finding and evidence taking skills.

[158] Only if compatible with the duties and status of a judge and with judge's consent.

[159] Inferred.

[160] Inferred.

Criteria	A	B	C	D	E	F	G
Need for executive restraint from interference in judicial decision-making process	+[161]	+	+		+	+	+
Executive shall support enforcing judgments even against itself	+[162]	+	+			+[163]	+[164]
The power of pardon exercised cautiously so as to avoid misuse as an interference with a judicial decision	+						
Legislature shall not pass legislation, which retroactively reverses specific court decisions	+	+	+				+[165]
Legislature shall not change composition of the court to affect its decision-making		+					
Need for sufficient budget to provide reasonable resources for judges to do their work without an excessive workload	+	+	+		+	+	+
The number of the members of the highest court should be rigid and should not be subject to change, except by legislation	+						

[161] The executive shall refrain from any act or omission which preempts the judicial resolution of a dispute, or frustrates the proper execution of a judgment. The executive shall not have the power to close down or suspend the operations of the court system at any level. Government ministers shall not exercise any form of pressure on judges, whether overt or covert, and shall not make a statement, which adversely affects the independence of individual judges, or of the judiciary as a whole.

[162] The executive shall not frustrate the proper execution of a court judgment.

[163] Inferred.

[164] Inferred.

[165] Inferred.

Criteria	A	B	C	D	E	F	G
The legislature may be vested with the powers of removal of judges preferably upon recommendation of a judicial commission	+						
Terms and conditions of judges currently holding office should not be worsened by legislation	+					+	
Judges serving in abolished court shall not be affected except for their transfer to another court of the same status	+		+				
Court room proceedings should be open to the public and the media unless otherwise ordered by the judge on the basis of legal criteria		+					
Judicial decisions should be published and open to academic and public scrutiny	+[166]	+					
A reliable record of court room proceedings is maintained and available to the public		+					
Court houses provide a respectable environment for the dispensation of justice and are accessible to the citizens they serve	+[167]	+					
Criteria for discipline and removal should be fixed by law and clearly defined	+						
Judge can be removed for incapacity	+	+	+	+	+	+	

[166] The press and other institutions should be aware of the potential conflict between judicial independence and excessive pressure on judges.

[167] Inferred.

Criteria	A	B	C	D	E	F	G
Judge can be removed for being unfit to discharge duties/gross misconduct/misbehavior/criminal act	+	+	+	+	+	+	+[168]
Disciplinary process should ensure fairness to the judge	+	+					
Disciplinary proceeding should be held before a court or board predominantly composed of members of the judiciary and selected by the judiciary		+					+
Disciplinary process must not compromise judges' genuine independence							+

[168] Attention should be paid only to objective and relevant considerations.

Chart B. Judicial Service Commissions (JSC)

Composition, Functions, and Powers

A = The Judicial and Bar Council, Philippines

B = The Judicial Service Commission, South Africa

C = The Judicial and Legal Service Commission, Trinidad & Tobago

D = The Judicial Service Commission, Uganda

E = The High Council of Justice, Ukraine

F = The Judicial Service Commission, Zimbabwe

G = The Canadian Judicial Council, Canada

H = The Federal Circuit Judicial Council, United States

Comparison Criteria	A	B	C	D	E	F	G	H
Constitution sets rules on JSC staffing	+	+	+	+	+	+		
Law other than constitution sets rules on JSC staffing							+	+
President/executive can chose *non ex officio* members	+	+	+	+	+	+		+
Groups outside judiciary are represented on JSC	+	+	+	+	+	+		
Civil Society is represented on JSC	+	+	+	+				
Chief Justice is *ex officio* JSC Chairman	+		+				+	
JSC has authority to appoint judges	+	+	+			+		
JSC role is limited to advisory in appointing judges				+	+			
JSC has authority to discipline judges		+	+	+	+		+[169]	+

169 Authorized to review complaints and recommend removal to the Minister of Justice.

Comparison Criteria	A	B	C	D	E	F	G	H
JSC has authority to dismiss judges			+	+[170]				
JSC has powers in judges education				+			+	
JSC renders policy advice		+		+		+	+	
JSC has adjudicative powers	+							
JSC has administrative oversight powers								+

[170] Can make recommendations on judges' dismissal.

Chart C. Cross-country Comparison of Judicial Appointment Systems

High Courts in Canada, Pakistan, Philippines, South Africa, Trinidad & Tobago, Uganda, and Ukraine

A = Canada – Federal

B = Pakistan

C = The Philippines

D = South Africa

E = Trinidad & Tobago

F = Uganda

G = Ukraine

Comparison Criteria	**A**	**B**	**C**	**D**	**E**	**F**	**G**
Requirement of written application from applicants	+		+	+	+	+	+
Age requirements			+		+		+
Language requirements	+						+
Residency requirements							+
Competitive examination of all candidates							
Educational requirements					+		+
Minimal length of specified experience	+	+			+	+	
Character requirements	+		+	+	+		
Professional abilities requirements	+		+	+	+		
Criminal record disclosure	+						
Personal finances should be in order	+						
Absence of pending proceedings and complaints							
Good health	+		+				
Affirmative action							
Judiciary has control over appointment process							

Comparison Criteria	A	B	C	D	E	F	G
Parliament decides on permanent appointment							
Publishing & inviting comments on applicant lists			+		+		
Probation period		+					+
Tenure to retirement age during good behavior	+	+	+		+	+	+
Nominating body is different from appointing one	+[171]	-[172]	+[173]	+[174]	+[175]	+[176]	+[177]
Appointing body is outside judiciary	+	+	+	+	+	+	+

[171] In Canada judges are nominated by the minister of justice and the appointed by governor general in council.

[172] In Pakistan judges are nominated and appointed by the president.

[173] In the Philippines judges are nominated by the Judicial and Bar Commission and appointed by the president.

[174] In South Africa judges are nominated by the Judicial Service Commission and appointed by the president.

[175] In Trinidad and Tobago judges are nominated by Judicial and Legal Service Commission and appointed by the president.

[176] In Uganda judges are nominated by Judicial Service Commission and appointed by the president with approval of parliamentary appointments committee.

[177] In Ukraine judges are nominated by the Qualification Commission of Judges and appointed by the president for the first five-year term and then by the parliament permanently.

Chart D. Cross-country Comparison of Judicial Appointment Systems

Subordinate Courts in Nova Scotia (Canada), Pakistan, Philippines, South Africa, Trinidad & Tobago, Uganda, and Ukraine

A = Canada – Nova Scotia

B = Pakistan

C = The Philippines

D = South Africa

E = Trinidad & Tobago

F = Uganda

G = Ukraine

Comparison Criteria	**A**	**B**	**C**	**D**	**E**	**F**	**G**
Requirement of written application from applicants	+		+	+	+	+	+
Age requirements							+
Language requirements	+						+
Residency requirements							+
Competitive examination of all candidates		+					
Educational requirements	+			+	+	+	+
Minimal length of specified experience	+	+	+		+		
Character requirements	+			+			
Professional abilities requirements	+			+			
Criminal record disclosure				+			
Personal finances should be in order	+			+			
Absence of pending proceedings and complaints	+			+			
Good health	+						
Affirmative action	+			+			
Judiciary has control over appointment process							

Comparison Criteria	A	B	C	D	E	F	G
Parliament decides on permanent appointment							+
Publishing & inviting comments on applicant lists			+				
Probation period		+					+
Tenure to retirement age during good behavior	+		+	+	+	+	+
Nominating body is different from appointing one	+[178]	+[179]	+[180]	+[181]	[182]	[183]	+[184]
Appointing body is outside judiciary	+	-	+	+	+	+	+

178 In Nova Scotia, Canada judges are nominated by the minister of justice based on advice from the Advisory Committee and appointed by Nova Scotia Governor in Council (cabinet).

179 In Pakistan judges are nominated by the Public Service Commission and appointed by the Supreme Court.

180 In Philippines judges are nominated by the Judicial Service Commission and appointed by the president.

181 In South Africa judges are nominated by the Magistrate's Commission and appointed by the minister of justice and constitutional affairs.

182 In Trinidad and Tobago judges are nominated and appointed by the Judicial Service Commission.

183 In Uganda judges are nominated and appointed by the Judicial Service Commission.

184 In Ukraine judges are nominated by the Qualifications Committee for Judges and appointed by the president for the five-year probation period, and then by the parliament permanently.

Chart E. Cross-country Comparison of Disciplinary and Dismissal Proceedings

High Courts in Nova Scotia (Canada), Pakistan, Philippines, South Africa, Trinidad & Tobago, Uganda, and Ukraine

A = Canada

B = Pakistan

C = The Philippines

D = South Africa

E = Trinidad & Tobago

F = Uganda

G = Ukraine

Comparison Criteria	**A**	**B**	**C**	**D**	**E**	**F**	**G**
Complaint mechanism is accessible	+[185]		+[186]	+	+		
Screening body is appointed by judiciary	+		+				
Screening body has suspension authority			+	+	+	+	
Suspension pending inquiry must be with pay				+	+		
Screening body has investigation authority			+		+		
Judicial control over investigating tribunal	+	+	+				-
Judicial control over hearing tribunal	+	+	+		+		+
Hearings are public					+		

[185] Prior to military dictatorship: through President to Supreme Judicial Council of Pakistan.

[186] Must be supported by affidavit.

Comparison Criteria	A	B	C	D	E	F	G
Mandatory publication of judgment	+	+[187]	+	+	+	+[188]	
Judge's right to be present	+	+	+	+	+	+	
Judge's right to be represented by counsel	+	+	+	+	+	+	
Government must bear legal costs							
Remedial sanctions							
Punitive sanctions	-[189]	+[190]	+	+[191]	+	+	
Completion of proceedings within reasonable time	+						
Judiciary decides on judge's dismissal			+				
Criteria for dismissal are specified	+	+	+	+	+	+	+

187 If a decision to remove is taken.

188 If a decision to remove is taken.

189 Disapproval of conduct may be expressed.

190 Removal.

191 Removal.

Chart F. Cross-country Comparison of Disciplinary and Dismissal Proceedings

Subordinate Courts in Nova Scotia (Canada), Pakistan, Philippines, South Africa, Trinidad & Tobago, Uganda and Ukraine

A = Canada

B = Pakistan

C = The Philippines

D = South Africa

E = Trinidad & Tobago

F = Uganda

G = Ukraine

Comparison Criteria	**A**	**B**	**C**	**D**	**E**	**F**	**G**
Complaint mechanism is accessible	+	+	+[192]	+	+	+	+
Screening body is appointed by judiciary	+	+	+[193]		+	+	
Screening body has suspension authority	+		+			+	
Suspension pending inquiry must be with pay	+						
Screening body has investigation authority		+	+			+	
Judicial control over investigating tribunal	+	+	+[194]		+	+	
Judicial control over hearing tribunal		+	+				
Hearings are public							
Mandatory publication of judgment				+	+		

[192] Complaint must be supported by an affidavit.

[193] Appointment by statute.

[194] As designated by commission.

Comparison Criteria	**A**	**B**	**C**	**D**	**E**	**F**	**G**
Judge's right to be present	+	+	+	+	+	+	+
Judge's right to be represented by counsel	+	+					
Government must bear legal costs							
Remedial sanctions	+			+			
Punitive sanctions	+	+	+	+	+	+	+
Completion of proceedings within reasonable time	+						
Judiciary decides on judge's dismissal	-	+	+				
Criteria for dismissal are specified	+	+	+	+	+[195]	+[196]	+

[195] Conduct that violates "good behavior."

[196] Conduct that violates "good behavior."

RECENT LEGAL DEVELOPMENTS

THE FEDERAL REPUBLIC OF YUGOSLAVIA AND THE WORLD BANK

- *Membership and Other Matters (with annex on Bank assistance to Kosovo); and*
- *Proposed Trust Fund for the Federal Republic of Yugoslavia*

Note*

Other than with respect to the original members, membership in the International Bank for Reconstruction and Development (Bank) is open to International Monetary Fund member countries "at such times and in accordance with such terms as may be prescribed by the Bank."[1] While the admission of new members is a matter reserved to the Bank's Board of Governors, membership of one or more states succeeding to the rights and obligations of a previously admitted member country is a matter that is decided, within certain constraints, by the Bank's executive directors.

Among the constraints limiting the discretion of the executive directors in succession decisions is the requirement that the same conditions for succession must be applied equally to all states succeeding to the membership of a particular preexisting member. In addition, all conditions for succession – like all conditions for admission of a new member – must be relevant to the Bank and its work. Thus, for example, a succession decision may not rest on political considerations that the Bank is prohibited by its Articles from taking into account in its work.[2]

On February 25, 1993, the executive directors determined that the Socialist Federal Republic of Yugoslavia (SFRY) had ceased to be a member of the Bank and set forth the conditions under which each of the five successor republics to the

* Note contributed by Elizabeth B. Lin, Assistant to the Vice President and General Counsel, Legal Vice Presidency, The World Bank.

1 IBRD Articles of Agreement, art. II, sec. 1(b).

2 *Id.*, art. IV, sec. 10.

The World Bank Legal Review: Law and Justice for Development: 379-391.

SFRY (namely, Republic of Croatia, Republic of Slovenia, Former Yugoslav Republic of Macedonia, Bosnia and Herzegovina, and Federal Republic of Yugoslavia) could succeed to the SFRY's membership in the Bank.

The following two legal notes issued in October 2000 and March 2001 by the Vice President and General Counsel of the Bank address membership and succession issues with respect to the Federal Republic of Yugoslavia (FRY), the only successor country that had not yet succeeded to SFRY membership by that time. The first note explains the conditions for succession to membership as applied to FRY and addresses the question whether trust funds could be used to provide pre-membership assistance. On the latter issue, a 1999 legal memorandum was annexed that analyzed the legal basis for the Bank's assistance to Kosovo. The second note provides a detailed discussion of the legal basis for Bank assistance to FRY as a non-member in the context of a U.S. $30 million trust fund approved by the executive directors of the Bank and the International Development Association to assist in the financing of an emergency recovery and transition program for FRY.[3]

[3] Subsequent to these two notes, FRY met all conditions for membership and, by virtue of an express provision of the February 25, 1993 resolution of the executive directors, the country assumed membership in the Bank as of the date of that resolution.

MEMBERSHIP AND OTHER MATTERS

Legal Note by KO-YUNG TUNG
Vice President and General Counsel

October 12, 2000

Introduction

1. During the Management briefing of the Executive Directors of October 10, 2000 on the recent events in the Federal Republic of Yugoslavia (FRY), the General Counsel indicated that a note would be circulated to the Board on the legal matters relating to the membership of the FRY in the Bank. This note presents a short summary of the arrangements for membership of the FRY in the Bank.[4] The note also briefly discusses the possible use of trust funds to provide assistance to the FRY before membership, in response to a question raised at the Board meeting.

The Arrangements for Succession to Membership

2. In February 1993, following a similar decision of the International Monetary Fund (the Fund) of December 1992, the Executive Directors of the Bank decided that the Socialist Federal Republic of Yugoslavia (SFRY) had ceased to be a member of the Bank, and established a mechanism under which each of the successor Republics of the SFRY would succeed to its membership in the Bank when it had met certain requirements[5]. The requirements were that the successor Republic had:

(a) become a member of the Fund;

(b) notified the Bank, that (a) it has accepted, as successor to the SFRY, the Articles of Agreement of the Bank and the terms and conditions related to the shares of the Bank's capital to which it succeeded; and (b) it had taken all steps necessary to carry out these obligations (a legal opinion from the Federal Attorney General or another official acceptable to the Bank, confirming that all necessary steps have been taken, is also required);

---

[4] This note deals only with succession to membership in the Bank. Similar succession arrangements were put in place in IFC, IDA and MIGA.

[5] The Executive Directors of IFC, IDA, and MIGA took similar decisions.

(c) made such payments as are necessary with respect to the shares of capital stock to be allocated to it;

(d) entered into a final agreement with the Bank with respect to the loans made by the Bank to or with the guarantee of SFRY which the Republic would assume; and

(e) eliminated, or agreed with the Bank on a plan to eliminate, arrears, if any, in the servicing of Bank loans made to or with the guarantee of the SFRY to be assumed by the successor Republic.

Four of the five successor Republics, namely the Republic of Croatia, the Republic of Slovenia, the Former Yugoslav Republic of Macedonia, and Bosnia and Herzegovina, have become members of the Bank by fulfilling these requirements. The FRY has not met these requirements. There follows short comments on these requirements as they relate to the FRY.

Membership in the Fund[6]

3. In December 1992, the Executive Board of the Fund determined that the SFRY had ceased to exist and had therefore ceased to be a member of the Fund. The Fund also established a mechanism under which, when certain conditions were met, each successor Republic could succeed to the membership of the SFRY in the Fund.[7] Overdue payments to the Fund amount to around SDR 99 million (around $135 million). One of the conditions of succession is the actual clearance of the arrears.

---

6 The Articles of Agreement of the Bank (Article II, Section 1) make membership in the Fund a prerequisite to membership in the Bank. Neither the Fund Articles nor the Bank Articles make membership in the United Nations a prerequisite of membership in the Fund or the Bank, respectively.

7 Decision of the Fund Executive Board of December 14, 1992. The conditions are: (i) the successor Republic has notified the Fund within one month of the decision that it agrees to its share of assets and liabilities of the SFRY to the Fund as determined by the Fund (all successor Republics have fulfilled this requirement); (ii) the successor Republic notifies the Fund that it agrees, in accordance with its laws, to succeed to the membership of the SFRY in accordance with the decision of the Fund; and (iii) the successor Republic "has been found by the Fund to be able to meet its obligations under the Fund's Articles of Agreement;" and (iv) it has no overdue financial obligations towards the Fund or in the SDR Department.

This is to be contrasted with the situation in the Bank, where the condition is either that the successor Republic eliminates its arrears, or that it agrees with the Bank on a plan to eliminate them.

Formal Notification of Succession

4. In order to succeed to the membership of the SFRY, a successor Republic needs to notify the Bank, that (a) it has accepted, as successor to the SFRY, the Articles of Agreement of the Bank and the terms and conditions related to the shares of the Bank's capital to which it succeeded; and (b) it had taken all steps necessary to carry out these obligations (a legal opinion from the Federal Attorney General or another official acceptable to the Bank, confirming that all necessary steps have been taken, is also required). In addition to the formal notification of succession and legal opinion, the Bank would need to be provided with the legislation authorizing succession.

Capital Payments

5. Payments made by the SFRY on account of its shares of the Bank's capital were apportioned to the successor Republics on the same basis as the shares themselves.[8] As a result, no new USD payment is required of the FRY. As the FRY has adopted a new currency since 1993, it would need to make payments in this currency to replace the payments made in the old currency.

Agreement on the Bank Loans Assumed by the FRY

6. In January 1992, the Bank concluded agreements on an interim basis with the SFRY (consisting at the time of Serbia, Montenegro, Macedonia, and Bosnia and Herzegovina), with Slovenia and Croatia, and later with Macedonia after it had become independent, for the service of debt due for projects benefiting these Republics, subject to the overall guarantee of the SFRY. Under these interim agreements, each Republic agreed to ensure the service of loans allocated to it, and the SFRY agreed to continue to guarantee the loans until final agreements were reached with each Republic. Subsequently, the Bank reached final agreements with the Republic of Slovenia, the Republic of Croatia and the Former Yugoslav Republic

---

[8] The shares of the Bank's capital were apportioned on the basis of the apportionment of the SFRY's quota in the Fund.

of Macedonia, and the SFRY was relieved of any further responsibility with respect to loans assumed by these Republics.[9]

7. The Bank also reached agreement with the FRY on the Bank loans allocated to it. By exchange of letters dated February 24, 1993 and sent by fax, the FRY confirmed its responsibility for ensuring the service of loans to borrowers or for projects located in the Republics of Serbia and Montenegro, a list of which was attached to the letters. This agreement would need to be supplemented to update the tables setting out the amounts owed under loans assumed by the FRY and to remove the list of loans assumed by Bosnia and Herzegovina, since these loans have been terminated and replaced by the Consolidation Loans made by the Bank to Bosnia and Herzegovina in 1996.

Elimination of the Arrears, or Agreement with the Bank on a Plan to Eliminate the Arrears

8. IBRD loans to the FRY were placed in non-accrual status in September 1992. As of September 30, 2000, overdue principal, interest and charges to IBRD amounted to $1.7 billion. The Board decision of 1993 does not require that these arrears be paid before succession to membership can occur; it would be sufficient that the FRY agree with the Bank on a plan to clear these arrears.

The Use of Trust Funds to Provide Pre-membership Assistance to the FRY

9. In response to a question raised at the meeting on the possible use of trust funds to provide assistance to the FRY, there is set out in the Annex to this note a legal memorandum of July 8, 1999 from the Acting Vice President and General Counsel on "Bank Assistance to Kosovo—A Legal Analysis."[10] The legal framework for any such assistance to a non-member is provided by the Articles of Agreement, and in particular Article I (i) and Article III, Section 1 (a). Under these provisions, assistance to a non-member can be provided only in cases where the Executive Directors determine that such assistance would have clear benefits for the members of the Bank. As is stated in the attached memorandum, financial

---

[9] World Bank Annual Report, 1999, Financial Statements and Appendixes to the Annual Report Financial Statements, June 30, 2000, Notes A and C.

[10] SecM99-488 dated July 12, 1999.

assistance to non-member countries has been provided through trust fund arrangements, e.g. trust funds provided by bilateral or multilateral and other donors and administered by the Bank as a trustee, or trust funds financed from the Bank's own resources, such as from net income/surplus,[11] and administered by the Bank itself or IDA.

[11] The allocation of funds from net income or surplus would require a decision of the Board of Governors.

ANNEX

Bank Assistance to Kosovo—A Legal Analysis

Legal Memorandum by ANDRÉS RIGO
Acting Vice President and General Counsel

July 12, 1999

This memorandum addresses the question of the extent to which the Bank can assist Kosovo within the context of the Articles of Agreement and Bank practice. To this purpose, it starts with a brief analysis of the current status of Kosovo.

1. The Legal Status of Kosovo

Before the break-up of the Socialist Federal Republic of Yugoslavia (SFRY) in the early 1990s, Kosovo was a province of Serbia, the largest Republic within SFRY. Kosovo had enjoyed a significant degree of autonomy within Serbia under the 1974 SFRY constitution and the Serbian constitution of the time. An amendment of SFRY's constitution before SFRY broke up, and the subsequent Serbian constitution of 1990, restricted significantly Kosovo's autonomy. This restricted status remained when Serbia and Montenegro became the Federal Republic of Yugoslavia (FRY).

In December 1992, the Fund Executive Board found that SFRY had ceased to exist, and formal succession to membership of the SFRY was open to all its successor states provided they were able to meet specific conditions of succession set by the Fund. Subsequently (February 1993), the Bank's Board of Executive Directors also determined that SFRY as such had ceased to be a member of the Bank, as termination of Fund membership entails termination of Bank membership (unless otherwise decided by the Bank's Board of Governors in accordance with the Bank's Articles).[12] The Board further decided that SFRY's successor states would be

[12] *See* Ibrahim F.I. Shihata, *The World Bank Legal Papers* 513 (Kluwer Law Intl. 2000) (*see* ch. 20: *State Succession in the Bank—The Case of Yugoslavia* at subsection III: *Effects of the Disintegration of Yugoslavia on Bank Membership*); and Ibrahim F.I. Shihata,

allowed to succeed to SFRY's membership without new admission procedures upon the satisfaction of certain requirements, including membership in the Fund, agreement on the allocation of SFRY's shares in the Bank's capital and payments of SFRY's debt among all successor Republics, and payment of arrears on such debt or an agreed plan to pay them.[13] Subsequently, Slovenia, Croatia, the former Yugoslav Republic of Macedonia, and Bosnia and Herzegovina succeeded to membership in the Bank. FRY's succession depends on the fulfillment of the agreed requirements.

Kosovo's current status remains that of a province within a country which is not a Bank member, FRY. The peace principles agreed to by FRY, and the U.N. Security Council Resolution No. 1244 of June 10, 1999, emphasize the commitment to the territorial integrity of FRY. The U.N. Security Council Resolution establishes a temporary system of international civil and security presence in order to achieve "substantial autonomy"[14] for Kosovo. It underlines that such autonomy is to be reached "within the FRY"[15] and by "taking full account of the principles of sovereignty and territorial integrity of FRY.[16] Kosovo, therefore, must be characterized as a territory within a Bank non-member, with a yet to be determined degree of autonomy secured by international arrangements.

2. Legal Basis of Bank Assistance to Kosovo

According to the Bank's Articles of Agreement, the primary purpose of the Bank is "to assist in the reconstruction and development of territories of members.[17] The Bank is also required to use its resources and facilities "exclusively for the benefit of members.[18] While it is clear from these provisions that Bank assistance is to be

---

Matters of State Succession in the Practice of the World Bank, 12 Development and International Cooperation 7 (No.23, 1996).

[13] *See* Ibrahim F.I. Shihata, *Matters of State Succession in the Practice of the World Bank, supra* n. 12, at 16-17 and 24-25.

[14] *See* U.N. Security Council Resolution No. 1244, June 10, 1999, para. 5.

[15] *Id.*, para. 10.

[16] *Id.*, annex I to the Resolution.

[17] Article I (i) of IBRD's Articles of Agreement. Article I of IDA's Articles of Agreement contains a similar provision.

[18] Article III Section 1 (a) of IBRD's Articles of Agreement. Compare the similar provision in Article V, Section 1 (a) of IDA's Articles of Agreement.

rendered to or for the benefit of its members, we have developed approaches and mechanisms allowing the Bank, in exceptional cases, to assist non-members, while at the same time acting within the Articles' mandate.

Bank assistance to non-member countries or territories with a special status has been provided to the then Soviet Union, West Bank and Gaza, and Bosnia and Herzegovina. In all cases, the overriding consideration that ultimately led to the extension of Bank assistance was that the latter was to benefit the Bank's members, and in each case the benefits were identified and explained to the Executive Directors before the assistance was provided. The Executive Directors have the power to interpret the Articles (Article IX), and their approval to assist in these situations confirmed that in their view the assistance to be provided was of benefit to the Bank and its members. The approval by the Executive Directors of assistance to Kosovo within this framework would be required for any type of assistance, whether it is of a financial nature or is of a technical character or simply involves the administration of funds of others as trustee.

Financial assistance to non-member countries or territories with a special status has been provided through trust fund arrangements, e.g. trust funds provided by bilateral or multilateral and other donors and administered by the Bank as a trustee, or trust funds financed from the Bank's own resources, such as from net income/surplus, and administered by the Bank itself or IDA. The actual agreements providing for the assistance after establishment of the trust fund were entered into with the prospective member country,[19] or in the case of territories with a special status with special bodies designed by the territories' local authorities.[20] Given the uncertainty of the constitutional framework in Kosovo, it is too early to determine who would be, from a legal point of view, the appropriate counter-parties to agreements with the Bank.

We are keeping abreast of developments on the legal side, and we are also in consultation with the U.N., the Fund and the EBRD. We will keep you briefed.

---

[19] Thus, for example, the Resolution establishing the technical assistance trust fund for the Soviet Union referred to agreements the Bank would enter into with the USSR to provide for the general terms and conditions for technical assistance.

[20] Thus, the administrator of the trust fund for Gaza was to enter into agreements with the Palestinian Economic Council for Development and Reconstruction, the agency designated by the Palestinian Authority as the appropriate agency.

Proposed Trust Fund for the Federal Republic of Yugoslavia

Legal Note by KO-YUNG TUNG
Vice President and General Counsel

March 15, 2001

The Executive Directors of the Bank and the Association considered on March 13, 2001 the establishment of a trust fund to provide grants to the Federal Republic of Yugoslavia (FRY) to finance an emergency recovery and transition program. The proposed Trust Fund for the FRY (TFFRY) would be co-administered by the Bank and the Association, and would be funded by the transfer of a grant of $30 million from the Bank's surplus.

The Executive Directors approved the establishment of the TFFRY, subject to two conditions. First, the Executive Directors approved two clarifications to the proposed TFFRY, to be reflected in the TFFRY resolution of the Executive Directors (1) the termination of the TFFRY on the earlier of (a) by the date of approval by the Bank or the Association of the first loan or credit to the FRY and (b) 18 months after the establishment of the TFFRY, and (2) the return of any funds remaining in the TFFRY at the time of termination to the Bank's surplus.[21] Second, there was a request for confirmation by the General Counsel that establishing a trust fund to provide grants to a country both before and after it has become a member of the Bank is within the legal powers of the Bank. This Legal Note provides that confirmation.

The Bank's power to make grants to a country that span the period before membership and during membership rests, in part, on the Bank's power to provide financial assistance to a non-member country. Previous legal memoranda have confirmed that the Bank has the power to provide such assistance in cases where the Executive Directors have determined that such assistance would have benefits

---

[21] The references to membership and lending for FRY are without prejudice to the eventual decision to be made by the Executive Directors on FRY's resumption of membership.

for the members of the Bank.[22] This requirement is based on a provision of the Bank's Articles of Agreement that "the resources and the facilities of the Bank shall be used exclusively for the benefit of members."[23]

In approving the establishment of the TFFRY, the Executive Directors determined that such assistance would benefit the members of the Bank. The Executive Directors have exercised this power in the past to authorize the establishment of trust funds to provide financial assistance prior to membership in the Bank to the former Soviet Union, Bosnia and Herzegovina, West Bank/Gaza, Kosovo and East Timor. These trust funds were funded by transfers from net income or surplus, approved by the Board of Governors.[24]

The Bank may provide this financial assistance to non-members in the form of grants because of its general power to make grants, including grants to member countries.[25] The Bank's power to make grants does not derive from a specific authorization in the Articles of Agreement. Rather, this power has been found through the doctrine of implied powers, a general principle of international law applicable to international organizations. Under this principle, an international organization has the incidental powers necessary to enable it to carry out its mandate, regardless of whether these incidental powers are explicit in the constituent agreement.[26] This principle, which is implicit in the Bank's Articles, was made explicit in the subsequent Articles of Agreement for IFC, and IDA, as each of them is authorized to "exercise such other powers incidental to its operations as shall be necessary or desirable in furtherance of its purposes."[27]

---

[22] Ibrahim F.I. Shihata, *Legal memorandum concerning possible World Bank assistance to the West Bank and the Gaza Strip,* in *The World Bank Legal Papers* 537 (Kluwer Law International 2000). Ko-Yung Tung, *The Federal Republic of Yugoslavia and the Bank: Membership and Other Matters* (Oct. 12, 1999) (Note from the Vice President and General Counsel).

[23] IBRD Articles of Agreement art. III, sec. 1(a).

[24] Board of Governors' approval was required for these transfers, pursuant to Article V, Section 14(a) of the IBRD's Articles of Agreement.

[25] Ibrahim F.I. Shihata, *The Power of the Bank to Make Grants*, in *The World Bank Legal Papers*, *supra* n. 22, at 183

[26] *Id.* at 186

[27] IDA Articles of Agreement, art. V, sec. 5 (vi). IFC Articles of Agreement, art. III, sec. 6(v).

The Bank has utilized its power to make grants, out of its administrative budget and out of its net income, as far back as technical assistance grants made to member countries in 1960. In 1964, the Executive Directors approved an interpretation of the Articles of Agreement to permit the Board of Governors *to make a grant* to IDA *from net income*, noting that "the purposes of the Bank and the interests of its members would best be served by the transfer.[28] Grants out of net income, within the purposes of the Bank and serving the interests of its members, have been regularly proposed by the Executive Directors and approved by the Board of Governors since that time, and the Executive Directors have approved the provision of grants to members on several occasions.[29] Examples of such grants to members include the grants made under the Debt Reduction Facility for IDA-only countries, to eligible countries to reduce their commercial debt. Similarly, under the HIPC Trust Fund, grants have been made to members to reduce their debt to the Association. The Debt Reduction Facility and the HIPC Trust Fund were funded by the Bank, through a transfer from net income. Grants may also be made with purposes limited to one member and benefits for all members, such as the 1994 transfer from Bank surplus for emergency assistance for Rwanda.

Finally, it is noted that, in order to accomplish the stated purpose of the TFFRY (the financing of an emergency economic recovery and transition program in the FRY), the term of the TFFRY spans the time period before and after the FRY resumes membership in the Bank and the Association. This approach is consistent with that followed in the case of Bosnia and Herzegovina, where the respective trust fund was also permitted to span the period before and after membership. Grants were provided to Bosnia and Herzegovina from that trust fund prior to the resumption of lending and while the member was still in arrears.

---

[28] *Supra* n. 25.

[29] In addition to grants from its own resources, the Bank has administered numerous trust funds financed by other donors, that provide technical assistance to member countries, cofinance Bank projects and, from time to time, help countries clear arrears to the Bank.

ISLAMIC LAW ON INTEREST: THE 1999 PAKISTAN SUPREME COURT RULINGS ON *RIBA*

AKHTAR HAMID*

Interest plays a central role in Western financial systems. In contrast, Islamic law generally forbids riba or increases over the principal loan amount. In 1999 the Shariat Appellate Bench of the Supreme Court of Pakistan handed down a landmark decision through two rulings concerning the prohibition of riba. The Court defined riba in a broad sense, encompassing any gain, however slight, over the principal amount of a loan and regardless of the type or purpose of the loan. After addressing alternative financing models and other related problems, the Court laid out the changes in the legal system needed to comply with the riba prohibition and provided guidelines for the creation of a new sharia-based legal and economic framework.

Considering the length of the opinions in both the principal case (Dr. M. Aslam Khaki and others v. Syed Muhammad Hashim and others), 441 pages, and the companion case (House Building Finance Corporation v. Rana Muhammad Sharif and others), 104 pages, the opinions are not reproduced or excerpted. Instead, the following note provides a comprehensive summary of the rulings, while also giving key historical background and an overview of the principal developments in the implementation of the Court's decision.

Introduction

On December 23, 1999, the Shariat Appellate Bench of the Supreme Court of Pakistan (the Court) delivered a landmark decision through two key rulings,[1]

---

* Akhtar Hamid is lead counsel in the Middle East and North Africa/South Asia Practice Group of the Legal Vice Presidency of the World Bank. The author gratefully acknowledges the research assistance provided by Ali Awais, consultant, in the preparation of this paper.

[1] *Dr. M. Aslam Khaki and others v. Syed Muhammad Hashim and others,* Vol. I, No. 2 Shariat Law Reports 73 (Feb. 2000) (Khalil-ur-Rehman, Munir A. Sheikh, Wajihuddin

The World Bank Legal Review: Law and Justice for Development: 393-432.

Printed in the Netherlands.

upholding a 1991 Federal Shariat Court (FSC) ruling[2] that any increase, big or small, over the principal under a contract of loan or debt is *riba*[3] prohibited by the Koran, regardless of whether the loan is for a consumptive or productive purpose. In the Court's view, bank interest is riba, and so also are certain other forms of increase under a loan contract, which though not called interest are nevertheless so, such as "indexation"[4] and "mark-up."[5] In the result, the Court declared a number of interest-related fiscal and other laws, or provisions thereof, to be repugnant to the injunctions of Islam and directed that these cease to have effect from March 31, 2000. In the process, overcoming objections from some of the appellants to its jurisdiction to do so, the Court laid down guidelines and a timetable for establishing an interest-free economy and directed the government to take the necessary steps in that direction.

The Court arrived at its decision by closely examining the relevant verses of the Koran and the sayings and traditions of the Prophet (the *hadith* and the *sunna*), as well as the ancient and traditional Islamic commentaries. The Court also relied heavily on the views of contemporary Islamic scholars, economists, bankers, lawyers, and other experts, who answered questionnaires addressed to them in writing, or who appeared in person before, or otherwise made submissions to, the

---

Ahmad, Maulana Muhammad Taqi Usmani, and Mahmood A. Ghazi, JJ.) and *House Building Finance Corporation through its Executive Director v. Rana Muhammad Sharif and others,* Vol. I, No. 2 Shariat Law Reports 515 (Feb. 2000) (Maulana Muhammad Taqi Usmani, J.)

2 *Dr. Mahmood-ur-Rehman Faisal and others v. Secretary, Ministry of Law, Justice and Parliamentary Affairs, Government of Pakistan, Islamabad and other Respondents,* Pakistan Legal Decisions 1992 FSC1 (decision of Nov. 14, 1991).

3 *Riba* is generally translated into English as "usury" or "interest," but in fact has a much broader meaning under the sharia of "increase" or "gain," which is also its dictionary meaning. The root r-b-w, from which the term riba is derived, appears in the Koran twenty times (the term riba itself appearing eight times), to denote "growing," "increasing," "rising," "swelling," "raising," and being "big and great." It is also used in the sense of "hillock."

4 The practice or method of adjusting wages, pension benefits, insurance or other types of payments by linking them to commodity prices and the like to compensate for inflation.

5 A margin of profit or "mark-up" permitted to the seller, and mutually agreed between the buyer and the seller in advance, under a *bai muajjal* or sale contract. The price (including the profit) is payable on a deferred basis, either in a lump-sum or installments.

Court. Most of these hailed from within Pakistan, including a former finance minister; a former chief economist of the Ministry of Finance; representatives of the International Islamic University, Islamabad; the Faculty of Islamic and Oriental Learning, Punjab University, Lahore; the Islamic Research Council, Lahore; the Institute of Policy Studies, Islamabad; and several individuals in their capacity as prominent scholars of Islam (*ulema*), bankers, economists, chartered accountants, and senior lawyers with a special interest and expertise in Islamic financial matters. Many, however, came from overseas, including the president of the Islamic Development Bank, Jeddah, Saudi Arabia; the chief executive of the International Investment Company, Kuwait; the chief executive of Global Islamic Finance, Hong Kong & Shanghai Banking Corporation (HSBC), London; the economic advisor, Saudi Arabian Monetary Agency (SAMA), Jeddah; representatives of the King Abdul Aziz University, Jeddah; and the Al-Islamia Law Department, University of Khartoum, Sudan. The Court regarded these experts as providing it support particularly on the point that Islamic modes of financing are not only feasible, but also beneficial in helping to bring about a balanced and stable economy; and that it is no accident therefore that Islamic banks and financial institutions have been growing in the last three decades, and that, in turn Islamic banking is no longer a utopian dream.

The Court also endorsed and relied upon the reports of various committees and commissions appointed by the government from time to time to recommend ways and means of Islamicizing the economy. To name a few, these included the 1980 report of the Council of Islamic Ideology, the 1991 report of the Prime Minister's Committee on Self Reliance, and the 1997 report of the Commission for the Islamization of the Economy, all of which are discussed in later parts of this paper. The Court regarded these reports as ample proof of the substantial groundwork which has already been done to help design a strategy for the transformation of the existing financial system to an Islamic one.

This note will:

- explore some of the background against which the Court's ruling was delivered, including the events of the past two decades which had made the Court's intervention in this area inevitable;
- extract the essence from the Court's ruling, paying particular attention to: (a) the opinion of the Court as to what constitutes riba in Islam; (b) the views of the Court about the current financial system and how that system fails to measure up to what is in the Court's opinion the Islamic standard; (c) the prescriptions set out by the Court for restructuring the financial system with a view to bringing it up to that standard, including changes in the

laws, in the judicial system, in the financial institutional arrangements and the financial instruments, in the regulatory framework and generally in the way of doing business; and (d) the practical steps identified by the Court to be taken to fulfill those prescriptions, including the time-frame set out for this purpose and the various milestones to be achieved along the way; and

- highlight the Court's views on how the country's existing domestic debt should be restructured, how the country's future financing needs should be satisfied through the domestic capital market, and what should be done about the country's foreign debt.

Background

The 1980 Report of the Council of Islamic Ideology[6]

In 1980, in the discharge of one of its constitutional functions, the Council of Islamic Ideology (CII) submitted a report to the government entitled "The Elimination of Interest from the Economy" (CII Report). The CII Report contained a blueprint for the reorganization of banking practices and procedures on the basis of profit and loss sharing in accordance with the Islamic principles of joint ventures (*musharika*) and mutual investment funds (*mudaraba*). The CII Report recognized the difficulties of translating these principles into practice in their purest form, and therefore permitted the use of other, less stringent non-interest based modes of financing. The CII Report also recognized the difficulties of applying the Islamic principles to the substantial borrowings of the government from foreign governments and international financial institutions. The CII Report, therefore, provided that for the time being (i.e., until such time as foreign governments and international financial institutions are prepared to deal with the government on a basis compatible with Islamic principles or the *sharia*), foreign borrowings would have to continue on an interest basis.

---

[6] The Council is a body constituted under the constitution and charged, among other things, with compiling the injunctions of Islam for the guidance of the legislature, and recommending ways of bringing existing laws into conformity with those injunctions. It is made up of persons who are learned in Islamic principles and philosophy, and/or are familiar with the economic, political, legal or administrative problems of the country.

The Establishment of the Federal Shariat Court (FSC), 1980

In 1980, the Federal Shariat Court (FSC) was established, through constitutional amendment.[7] The FSC has jurisdiction, either of its own motion *(suo moto)* or on petition by a citizen or the government, to examine and decide whether any law or provision of law is repugnant to the injunctions of Islam. Subject to appeal to the Supreme Court (Shariat Appellate Bench (SAB)), any decision of the FSC holding any law or provision of law repugnant to the sharia takes effect on a date specified in the decision itself. And on that date, any law or provision which has been so held to be repugnant to the sharia ceases automatically to have effect to the extent of the declared repugnancy. Any court, including the Supreme Court and high courts, is prohibited from entertaining any proceedings or exercising any power or jurisdiction in respect of any matter within the FSC's jurisdiction, and a high court is bound by the decisions of the FSC. The FSC's jurisdiction was, however, subject to one restriction. Under a constitutional bar, for a period of ten years from its establishment, the FSC was precluded from examining any fiscal law or any law relating to banking or insurance practice or procedure.[8]

The Banking Reforms, 1984-88

In 1984, as a follow-up to the CII Report, the government announced that all banks and financial institutions operating in Pakistan were required to adopt and thereafter base their financing operations upon the Islamic modes of financing. The State Bank of Pakistan (SBP) was given responsibility for issuing policy directives on the introduction and implementation of the new, so-called non-interest based banking system. Accordingly, SBP issued a circular which stated that as of April 1, 1985, all finances provided by a banking company to all entities, including individuals, should be provided only on the basis of the permissible non-interest based modes of financing specified in the SBP circular. Apart from joint ventures (*musharika*) and mutual investment funds (*mudaraba*), which fell into the category of investment modes, such modes of financing included: under the category of lending modes, service charge financing and compassionate loan financing (*qarz-e-hasna);* and under the category of trade-related modes, mark-up (*bai muajja*), lease financing (*ijara*), and hire-purchase financing (*ijara wa igtana*). The SBP Circular made an exception in favor of foreign loans, which would not be

---

[7] Pakistan Const. ch. 3-A.

[8] *Id.*, art. 203-B(c).

subject to the application of the non-interest based modes of financing and would continue to be governed by their terms. References to these new financing modes were incorporated in a number of laws by amendment.

The Objectives Resolution and the Constitutional Amendment of 1985

By an amendment of 1985, a new provision[9] was added to the constitution under which the principles and provisions of the Objectives Resolution[10] set out in the constitution were declared to have become a substantive part of the constitution and to have effect accordingly. Before 1985, despite a number of attempts in that direction, the courts had refused to consider the Objectives Resolution a substantive part of the constitution and had therefore declined to enforce it as such. With the 1985 constitutional amendment however, a view began to emerge that the status of the Objectives Resolution had undergone a dramatic change and that it no longer suffered from the shortcomings which the courts had previously ascribed to it. A view was also expressed by some high court judges that, as the constitution now incorporated the Objectives Resolution as a substantive part thereof, the administration of justice according to the sharia was no longer the exclusive domain of the FSC, and that the other superior courts of the country had the authority, nay the obligation, to participate in such administration as well. There were other high court judges, however, who refused to arrogate to themselves the authority, which they believed belonged exclusively to the FSC, to strike down a law, whether co-extensive with or subservient to the constitution, which failed the test of the Objectives Resolution.[11] In any case, though inclined to pronounce interest, in all its manifestations, to be repugnant to the injunctions of Islam, they were reluctant to disallow it if the law or transaction which provided for it was protected by the constitution, the Objectives Resolution notwithstanding. In other words, though prepared to test laws on the "touchstone" of the Objectives Resolution, they refused to give the Objectives Resolution a supra constitutional status, overriding

---

9 *Id.*, art. 2-A.

10 The Objectives Resolution (Constitution of Pakistan, Annex), adopted by the first Constituent Assembly of Pakistan in 1949, declares, among other things, "that the Muslims of Pakistan are to be enabled to order their lives in the individual and collective spheres in accordance with the requirements and teachings of Islam, which would include sharia."

11 *Khar's case* (PLD 1988 Lah. 49 at 118), *Habib Bank case* (PLD 1987 Kar. 612), *Bachal Memon's case* (PLD 1987 Kar. 296 at 328-29).

the other provisions of the constitution. This controversy, which raged for some four years through 1989, left the public in confusion as to the status of riba in Pakistan's polity and economy.

The Enforcement of the 1991 Sharia Act

Two legal developments in 1990-91 had an important bearing on the future of financial and economic, including banking, transactions in the country. The first was the passage of the Enforcement of Sharia Act in June 1991. The act enabled and required the state, as represented by all three branches of the government, namely, the legislature, the executive, and the judiciary, to take measures to regulate the many and diverse aspects of life in the country, and the individual Muslim citizen, to act in the light of the sharia, which was declared to be the supreme law of the land. Under the act, the courts were obligated to interpret laws in the light of the sharia. The act required the federal government to appoint a commission to recommend ways and means of changing the existing economic system to one enunciated by Islam, particularly to oversee the process of elimination of riba from every sphere of economic activity in the shortest possible time, and to monitor progress in that direction. The act protected all international financial obligations, both existing and future, until an alternative economic system was introduced, as well as all other existing financial obligations.

The Federal Shariat Court: The Lifting of the Constitutional Bar in 1990 and the 1991 Ruling

Another important legal development in 1990-91 was the removal of the ten-year constitutional bar on the FSC's jurisdiction in respect of banking, fiscal, and other economic laws.[12] The ten years were stated to run from the date of the constitutional amendment[13] and expired on June 25, 1990, with the result that the FSC's jurisdiction in banking and fiscal matters stood restored as of June 26, 1990. Beginning soon thereafter, several petitions were filed in the FSC on behalf of

---

[12] In conferring authority on the FSC to decide whether or not any law or provision of law was repugnant to the injunctions of Islam, the 1980 Constitutional amendment had provided, that "law" for this purpose, "… does not include … until the expiration of [ten] years … any fiscal or any law relating to the levy and collection of taxes and fees or banking or insurance practice and procedure …" *Supra* n. 7.

[13] *Supra* n. 7, art. 203-B(c).

individuals, including certain members of the bar, challenging the interest-related provisions of a number of fiscal and banking laws. The FSC consolidated these petitions and disposed of them all in one voluminous ruling delivered in mid-November 1991[14].

By its ruling, the FSC declared riba in sharia to mean "an addition, however slight, over the principal," and explained that the concept covered both usury and interest; that it was not restricted to doubled and redoubled interest; that it applied to all forms of interest, whether large or small, simple or compound, doubled or redoubled; and that the Islamic injunction was not only against exorbitant or excessive but also against minimal rates of interest. The FSC also struck at certain practices which had sprung up since the 1984-85 banking reforms of allowing such increase but without calling it "interest", including indexation, sales against deferred payment (*bai-muajjal*), and mark-up as loan financing techniques. According to the FSC, the best modes of financing under the sharia were those based on profit-and-loss sharing, namely, mutual investment funds (*mudaraba*) and joint ventures (*musharika*), and mark-up and leasing were but poor and transient substitutes. As a result, the interest-related provisions of some 20 fiscal or related laws, including the Interest Act, 1839, the Negotiable Instruments Act, 1881, the Code of Civil Procedure, 1908, the State Bank of Pakistan Act, 1956, the Agricultural Development Bank Rules, 1961, the Banking Companies Ordinance, 1962, and Banking Companies (Recovery of Loans) Ordinance, 1979, were held repugnant to the injunctions of Islam, and the government, both federal and provincial, was directed to take steps to bring these laws into conformity with such injunctions. In addition, the FSC directed that all borrowing and lending stop in Pakistan and the banking system change over completely to a profit-and-loss sharing basis. The FSC also directed a halt to all borrowing and lending on an interest basis at the government level from foreign governments, international financial institutions and foreign commercial banks, and that fresh ideas be tried out for arranging funding for economically profitable projects on a profit-and-loss sharing basis.

The Report of the Prime Minister's Committee on Self Reliance, 1991

The government and others filed appeals against the 1991 FSC ruling, which was stayed and as a result remained in abeyance until late 1998, when soon after the military take-over the Shariat Appellate Bench of the supreme court finally de-

---

[14] *See supra* n. 2.

cided to take up and decide the appeals. Matters had not, however, stood completely still in the nine years or so during which this much awaited event was expected.

In 1991, a committee, called the Prime Minister's Committee on Self Reliance (the Committee), was established to assist the government in its endeavor to deal with domestic and foreign debt on an interest-free basis. In its report, the Committee recommended various ways for the government to convert its domestic debt to an Islamic basis, without imposing a real threat for the economy. The Committee proposed that intra-governmental debt be converted under a scheme mutually agreed upon at the national level; and that the government immediately stop paying interest on State Bank loans, substitute non-interest bearing paper for interest-based loans from commercial banks, and convert public savings schemes to mutual fund schemes. With respect to foreign loans, the Committee recommended a two-year preparatory period to allow the government time to renegotiate them. Domestic loans were proposed to be eliminated with effect from July 1, 1991. The Committee also proposed that a committee be formed to hold negotiations with the foreign lenders.

The Report of the Commission for the Islamization of the Economy on the Elimination of Riba, 1997

Another body that was active in the 1990's was the Commission for the Islamization of the Economy, which was established under the Enforcement of 1991 Sharia Act. This commission having first reported in that year was reconstituted as the Raja Zafarul Haq Commission in 1997 (the Commission), in which year it published its *Report on the Elimination of Riba* and a proposed draft of a *Prohibition of Riba Act,* suggesting a framework for the settlement of debt, both public and private, domestic and foreign, which attracted the rule against riba.[15] The Commission proposed that domestic private debt be given six months to be converted to the permissible modes of financing; that domestic public debt be settled by the issuance of share certificates in a mutual fund or by outright retirement through repurchase with proceeds from the privatization of public assets; and that all intergovernmental and state bank loans be made interest-free from the effective date of the proposed new act. The Commission also proposed that the federal government renegotiate all existing foreign debt on the basis of permissible modes of financing, but did not lay down any fixed timetable for the purpose.

---

[15] Proposed Prohibition of Riba Act, sec. 6.

The Shariat Appellate Bench Ruling

How Is the Court Concerned in this Matter?

Early in the proceedings, some of the religious scholars and others appearing in the case questioned the Court's power to lay down the parameters for a policy and legal framework for a riba-free financial system, as requested by the government. They argued:

- that, under the constitution, the responsibility for framing the financial, economic, and fiscal policies of the state, and for proposing the necessary legal framework to execute such policies, lies with the federal government alone;
- that, in the absence of an act to regulate the custody of the Federal Consolidated Fund[16] and the borrowing powers of the government, the federal government has complete freedom to manage the finances of the federation; and
- that the provisions of the constitution under which this freedom is protected cannot be reviewed by the Court in the light of the injunctions of Islam, as made part of the constitution under the Objectives Resolution, since it is established law that a superior court cannot use one provision of the constitution as a basis for striking down another, in the event of an apparent conflict between the two.

In other words, the Court was being asked to limit itself to its constitutional mandate of determining whether any laws or provisions thereof were repugnant to the injunctions of Islam, and to set a date or dates on which such laws or provisions thereof would cease to have effect, if found to be so repugnant.

Following an examination[17] of the relevant provisions of the constitution and the case law on the subject, the Court, however, found the actual situation to be somewhat different. The Court acknowledged that the government does indeed have the power to manage its own finances and to borrow moneys, but pointed out that the constitution mandates that this power be regulated by an act of parliament.

---

[16] "All revenues received by the Federal Government, all loans raised by that Government, and all moneys received by it in repayment of any loan, shall form part of a consolidated fund, to be known as the Federal Consolidated Fund." Pakistan Const. art. 78(1).

[17] A task which the Court had to shoulder by itself, without assistance from the government's lawyers.

In the Court's view, the mere fact that such an act has not been passed, even after all these years, should not be taken to mean that the government's powers in this area are unfettered, and completely free of scrutiny by parliament and the superior courts. The Court noted with disapproval how, taking shelter behind Government Rules of Business, the Ministry of Finance had been acting as if they were, and, by doing so, only managed to help ruin the economy and saddle the nation with a huge debt. In the Court's view, it was imperative, therefore, that such act be passed without further loss of time, so that prudent measures can be adopted to regulate the government's fiscal powers as stipulated in the constitution. The Court made it plain that such act, when passed, would be subject to scrutiny by the Court, and liable to be struck down if found to be repugnant to the injunctions of Islam. The Court stated that it therefore had a real concern and interest in indicating in advance how the financial, economic, and fiscal policies to be given effect by such (or any other?) act can be made sharia-compliant, so that the act itself does not run afoul of the Objectives Resolution, and either fail to pass through parliament or, if passed, be struck down by the Court.

The Court denied that its exercise of authority (possibly, even its obligation) to lay down the regulated guidelines amounted to invoking certain provisions of the constitution (Article 2-A, incorporating the Objectives Resolution) to strike down certain other provisions of the constitution, which it had been argued "protected" the financial powers of the government. The Court explained that, by exercising this authority, it was actually trying to discharge its duty of giving effect to the provisions of Article 2-A, which had been made an integral part of the constitution, by reading the other provisions of the constitution in "harmony" with them, it being established law that, since the constitution is an organic whole, all its provisions ought to be read in harmony with one another, so as to give effect to its "soul or spirit." In support, the Court cited authority[18] specifically on the point that the provisions of the constitution conferring jurisdiction on the Court to review laws in the light of the sharia are to be interpreted in a manner which would give full effect to the other provisions of the constitution which mandate a process of Islamization.

---

[18] *Hakim Khan and 3 others v. Government of Pakistan through Secretary Interior and others* (PLD 1992 SC 595); *The State v. Syed Qaim Ali Shah* (1992 SCMR 2192); *Zaheeruddin and others v. The State and others* (1993 SCMR 1718); *Mushtaq Ahmad Mohal and others v. The Honorable Lahore High Court, Lahore and others* (1997 SCMR 1043); *Dr. Mahmood-ur-Rahman Faisal v. Government of Pakistan through Secretary Ministry of Justice, Law and Parliamentary Affairs, Islamabad* (PLD 1994 SC 607).

What is Riba?

The jurisdictional hurdle having been surmounted, the first substantive question that the Court took up was one of defining riba, before deciding whether the country's economic and financial system is riba-based, and whether the laws supporting that system were repugnant to the injunctions of Islam. In this connection, based on a review of the relevant passages from the Koran, the relevant traditions of the Holy Prophet (*hadith and sunna*) and the available body of juristic and theological consensus *(ijma)*, the Court reached the conclusion:

- that, when applied in its lexical meaning to a contract of loan or debt, the term riba implies an increase or gain over and above the principal amount of the loan;
- that any such increase is frowned upon by the sharia, irrespective of whether it is described in the Koran (*riba-al-Koran*) or in the sunna (*riba-al-sunna);*
- that there is no difference between types of loans, the prohibition against riba applying just as much to commercial loans for productive purposes as to personal loans for consumptive purposes;
- that the concept of riba covers both usury and interest: it makes no difference, for purposes of applying the Koranic injunction against riba, whether the interest is large or small, doubled or redoubled, simple or compound; in other words, the injunction covers not only exorbitant or excessive but also minimal rates of interest; and
- that riba cannot be categorized into different types: it can take any shape or form; it can occur in Muslim and non-Muslim countries whether between Muslims, *inter se*, or between Muslims and non-Muslims; and its character does not change with the financial status of the parties.

In reaching these conclusions, the Court had to fend off a series of counter arguments put forward by the appellants. These included the following:

- that the verses of the Koran dealing with riba fall within the area of ambiguity (*mutashabihat*) because they were revealed in the last days of the life of the Holy Prophet; that he could not have had an opportunity to interpret them properly; and that therefore no hard and fast definition of riba can be found in the Koran or the sunna;
- that, insofar as the basic cause (*illat*) of the prohibition of riba is the injustice resulting from it, the focus in a given situation of alleged riba should be on whether it involves an element of such injustice; if it does, the transaction should be considered riba and therefore prohibited in every circum-

stance except in dire necessity (*haraam),* otherwise not. From this, it was argued that there is no injustice in charging an increase to a rich person who has borrowed money for productive purposes (in this connection, incidentally, a distinction can be drawn between loans for consumption purposes, which were the only type in vogue in the time of the Holy Prophet and prohibited as riba, and loans for productive purposes, which were not so in vogue and could not therefore have been prohibited); and that there is no injustice in charging an increase unless charged at an excessive rate; and

- that the Koranic prohibition of riba *(riba-al-Koran)* is limited to pre-Islamic interest practices (*riba-al-jahiliyya)*, while *riba-al-fadl*,[19] which is mentioned in the sunna *(riba-al-sunna),* is not absolutely prohibited except in dire necessity, but only inadvisable (*makrooh*).

Based on a close examination of the fairly complex works of scholarship on the subject, the Court responded to these arguments *seriatim* as follows:

- that, when looked at chronologically, the Koranic verses in question contain sufficient evidence to establish that the prohibition against riba dates back to the second year of the Islamic calendar and would not therefore be considered ambiguous or confusing (*mutashabihat*). As for a hard and fast definition of riba, the Koran had studiously and deliberately refrained from providing such a definition since to define it would be to limit and restrict its meaning; and that, in any case, as in the case of the prohibition against pork, liquor, gambling etc., a hard and fast definition is not needed because the meaning of the offending term is well known. There is, in short, no ambiguity about the meaning of the term;
- that there is a big difference between the *illat* and the *hikmat* of a particular rule: *illat* is the basic cause or feature of the transaction without which the relevant rule cannot be applied to it, whereas the *hikmat* is the underlying wisdom or philosophy taken into account by the framer in drawing up the rule or intending the benefit to be drawn from its enforcement. With respect to the rule against riba, the Koran has mentioned injustice as the underlying philosophy of the rule, but this does not mean that the rule ceases to apply if

[19] This refers to riba in the sense of the following saying of the Prophet Mohammed: "Gold for gold, silver for silver, wheat for wheat, barley for barley, date for date, salt for salt, must be equal on both sides and hand to hand. Whoever pays more or demands more (on either side) indulges in riba."

the element of injustice is lacking in a particular case. The basic cause giving rise to the rule is the excess claimed over and above the principal in a loan transaction, and if this cause is present, the application of the rule will follow, regardless of whether the underlying philosophy is or is not visible in a particular transaction. No basis can, therefore, be found in the Koranic verses dealing with riba for differentiating between, say, a consumption loan (sought by the poor and the needy to satisfy their most basic wants) and a commercial loan (sought by the affluent to finance an entrepreneurial scheme). When the Koran prohibits a transaction, it is the basic idea of the transaction and not any particular form of it which is hit by the injunction; and therefore the validity of a financial or commercial transaction depends on the intrinsic nature or substance of the transaction itself and not, say, on the financial position of the parties. In comparison, a sale is a valid transaction whereby a lawful profit is generated, and where the profit is allowed regardless of whether the purchaser is rich or poor. Nor is there any force in the contention that the prohibition of riba is confined to an excessive rate of interest. The Koran and the sunna are quite explicit on the point that any amount, however little, stipulated in addition to the principal in a loan transaction is riba, and hence prohibited; and

- that riba is riba no matter what form it takes, and there is no basis for distinguishing riba which is absolutely prohibited except in dire circumstances from riba which is only inadvisable. The practice of riba prohibited by the Koran is not confined to anything in particular; it has various forms all of which were practiced by the Arabs of the time before Islam (*jahilyya*); at times debt was created through a transaction of sale and at times through a loan; at times the increased amount was charged on a monthly basis, while the principal was to be paid at a stipulated date and sometimes it was charged along with the principal; all these forms used to be called riba because the lexical meaning of the term is "increase." With regard to *riba-al-fadl*,[20] in all probability, even in exchanges of commodities borrowed and returned after some time, the Holy Prophet wanted to prevent these from occurring in unequal quantities. The Holy Prophet, in any case, preferred the exchange of commodities for cash (sale) to the exchange of commodities for commodities (barter), because, under a barter it was not possible, except for an expert, to visualize the fair equivalent of one commodity in terms of

---

[20] *Supra* n. 19.

another, and there was therefore a risk that riba would result. That is why *riba-al-fadl,* like other forms of riba, is also prohibited in Islam. The explanation for sales against deferred payment (*bai' muajjal*), which are clearly permissible under Islam, lies in the fact that, in all probability, the Holy Prophet wished to encourage monetary transactions (even upon deferral) over barter, the latter having the potential of degenerating into a transaction tainted by riba.

How does Riba Taint the Financial System?

Is Bank Interest Riba?

In the Court's view, interest charged by banks or other financial institutions or individuals in today's times has all the elements of riba as defined under the sharia. According to the Court, such interest constitutes an increase over and above the principal amount payable under a loan contract against nothing but time; and, if the debtor under a loan contract fails to pay back the loan together with an increase over and above the principal amount at the stipulated time and wishes to obtain an extension of the period of the loan, he is required to agree to a further increase not just over and above the principal amount but over and above that amount and the amount of the first increase put together, thus leading to a doubling and redoubling of the increase. The Court regarded these as precisely the types of practices promoted under the prevailing banking system. The Court noted that, when a person borrows from a bank, a financial institution or a credit company and fails to pay back the debt at the stipulated time, he has to pay an increase at the prevalent rate, and if he fails to pay the amount (principal plus the first increase) at the second stipulated time, he has to pay a further increase calculated exclusively in terms of time. The Court considered these practices as falling under the concept of riba-al-koran, and hence un-Islamic.

The Court found no force in the appellants' argument, which was based on the concept of interest as practiced at the time of the Koranic revelations, that the position of bank interest charged on commercial or productive loans is entirely different from that of usury or riba, because in the case of interest no compulsion or coercion (*zulm*) is involved. According to the Court, the history of commercial or productive loans, which goes back some two thousand years before Christ, suggests that such loans were common in all ancient civilizations, including Arab ones, and were known at the time of the Koranic revelations. In the Court's view, the Koranic prohibition therefore applies equally to interest charged by banks or other financial institutions and individuals in modern times as it did to interest charged by institutions and individuals in the business of making commercial loans at the time of the Koranic revelations.

Nor did the Court see a case for arguing, as the appellants had attempted to argue, that modern interest-based financial and banking transactions, even if tainted by riba, should be saved under the doctrine of necessity.[21] In the Court's view, the doctrine of necessity in Islam is not an obscure concept which can be applied willy-nilly. According to the Court, its application is subject to certain criteria, expounded by Muslim jurists in the light of the Koran and the sunna, for determining the magnitude of the necessity and the extent to which a Koranic commandment can be relaxed on the basis of an emergency situation. Accordingly, the Court felt that, before deciding an issue on the basis of necessity, it must be certain that the necessity is real and not exaggerated by imaginary apprehensions, and cannot be met by any other means than committing an impermissible act. The Court characterized the appellants' apprehensions in this case as arising from ignorance of recent developments in Islamic banking and being completely unfounded. The Court noted that the appellants' argument was that commercial interest forms the backbone of modern economic activity throughout the world; that no country or its nationals can altogether avoid involvement in interest-based financial transactions; and that it would be suicidal for a country to try to banish interest altogether from domestic or foreign transactions to which it or its nationals are a party. The Court, however, regarded the emerging situation to be far more fluid than suggested by the appellants: it noted how in recent years Islamic banks and financial institutions have proliferated at rapid speed in many parts of the world, and how in certain countries interest-free banking has come to account for a sizeable proportion of the economy.[22] The Court, therefore, saw no compelling need to protect the present interest-based financial system forever or for an indefinite period, and declared that, at most, necessity can be pleaded as a grounds for allowing a reasonable time for the government to take steps to switchover to an interest-free, sharia-based financial system.

---

[21] The presence or pressure of circumstances that justify or compel a certain course of action which otherwise would be contrary to law.

[22] The Court noted that Islamic banks had grown to more than 200 across 65 countries of the world with US$ 90 billion capital (at a growth rate of 15% per annum); that, by the year 2000 the Islamic finance industry was expected to be a U.S. $ 100 billion plus business; and that 15% of Kuwait's and 5% of Malaysia's economy was based on interest-free banking.

Is Indexation Riba?

Once it had endorsed the position that, in sharia, any increase, no matter how small, over and above the principal advanced by way of a loan is riba, it was but a short step for the Court to strike at certain practices which have sprung up in recent years of allowing such increase, but without calling it "interest." One such practice, which was the focus of the Court's attention, centers around the concept of indexation, under which the lender is allowed an increase over the principal amount loaned out, which is indexed, say, to changes in the price level of commodities to hedge against inflation. Relying on previous instances of judicial approval already given to this practice,[23] some of the appellants argued in favor of indexation as a meritorious device for preserving the value of money.

The Court's view, however, was that indexation cannot be used as a substitute for interest in the present banking system. The Court found the authority for stating this:

- in the absolute unanimity in the relevant Islamic jurisprudence (*fiqh*) literature on the point that, in all cases of deferred payment, any concern with the devaluation of money should be ignored; in other words, the same amount should be paid back as was originally paid and agreed to be returned, in complete disregard of the difference in the value of money arising between the time of the loaning and the time of the repayment;
- in the fact that indexation of financial liabilities is in itself fraught with injustice and contrary to the spirit of the sharia;[24] and
- in the CII Report, which rejected indexation as a possible alternative to interest both on sharia and purely economic grounds, and which mentions how the current practice of indexing bank deposits, advances, and investment loans poses a major problem as this could amount to riba. The CII

---

[23] *See e.g. Aijaz Haroon v. Imam Durrani* (PLD 1989 Karachi 304) (in which the High Court held that indexation could be adopted as a solution to protect the purchasing power of money. The court's opinion was based in part on an early 19th century booklet written by a celebrated jurist of that time, Ibn Abidin Shami. The booklet discusses the liability of payment under situations of demonitization, debasement, fluctuation in value of the coin etc., and reproduces the opinions of earlier scholars on this issue.)

[24] The preponderance of scholarly opinion uncovered by the Court is that this practice places the burden of inflation on those who are not responsible for creating the inflationary conditions in the first place.

> Report concedes that indexation of wages and salaries, as opposed to loans, could be allowed under the sharia with some minor adjustments.

The Court was not unmindful of the fact that the issue of finding ways of combating inflation is a much bigger one. The Court exhorted Muslim economists to find ways of doing so which are sanctioned by the sharia. The Court, however, refrained from passing judgment on indexation as a general principle until more work had been done on the subject.

Are Non-Interest Based Financial Instruments Really Riba-free?

The Court also gave attention to certain other practices which have sprung up in recent years that allow an increase over and above the amount of a loan but without calling it "interest." These practices center around the so-called non-interest-based financial instruments which have been in use in the country since the banking reforms of 1984-85. In examining the relevant issues, the Court placed reliance on the findings of the CII Report, which had led up to the development of those instruments in the first place. As captured by the Court, the essence of these findings is as follows:

- that the true alternative to interest is profit and loss sharing (PLS) based on joint venture (*musharika*) and mutual investment funds arrangements (*mudaraba*);
- that there are, however, certain areas (*e.g.*, when banks deal in assets like leases) where financing on this basis is not practicable. For these areas, a technique can be adopted usually known to Islamic banks as cost-plus financing (*murabahah*);
- under murabahah, instead of advancing a loan in the form of money to a customer for financing the purchase of a commodity, the bank itself purchases the commodity directly from the market and then sells it to the customer on deferred payment basis, retaining a margin or "mark-up" (profit) added to its cost. This is not a financing in the strict sense, but rather a sale of a commodity effected in favor of the customer. Under this technique, the bank assumes the risks of the sales transaction so long as the commodity remains in its possession; and
- that this technique should, however, be used on an exceptional basis, in cases where joint venture (musharika) or mutual investment fund (mudaraba) arrangements are really not practicable. The technique is not appropriate in cases where the customer wants funds for some purpose other than purchasing a commodity.

The Court found the mark-up system prevalent in Pakistan to be in no way close to the original concept of cost-plus financing (murabahah) as set out in the CII Report. It noted with disapproval:

- how, under the prevalent mark-up system, there is no real concern with the purchase and sale of a commodity: in most cases there is no commodity involved at all in a real sense; if there is any, it is never purchased by the bank nor sold to the customer after being acquired by the bank; and
- how, in some cases, the technique is applied in the form of a buy-back arrangement, under which a commodity already owned by the customer is sold by him to the bank and simultaneously bought back by him from the bank at a higher price. This practice is a travesty of the original concept, the arrangement usually turning out to be nothing but a paper transaction in practice, with no genuine commodity being bought and sold.

The Court concluded that, since mark-up currently in vogue in the country under this arrangement is really interest in disguise, it invites all the objections to interest and cannot be saved from being declared repugnant to the injunctions of the Koran and the sunna.

The Court had no problem, however, in endorsing joint venture arrangements (musharika) as a true alternative to interest. In doing so, the Court refused to subscribe to the appellants' view that musharika has no place in a modern financial system. The appellants had expressed the fear, for instance, that depositors would not be happy about allowing their bank to risk their funds under a musharika instrument, and that there would therefore be a tendency under a musharika-based system for bank deposits to dry up. The Court thought that this would be unlikely to happen since the bank would be expected to take steps to mitigate the risk: before embarking on a venture, the bank studies the feasibility of the project for which funds are proposed to be advanced, and the funds are advanced only when the bank is completely satisfied about the project's prospects of success. In the Court's view, theoretically, the possibility of loss to a joint stock company, whose business is restricted to a limited sector of commercial activity, is much greater than the possibility of loss to a financial institution and yet the public is not discouraged from purchasing shares and investing in companies. The appellants had expressed the fear also that, under musharika financing, dishonest borrowers would be able to exploit the situation to their own advantage by falsely declaring a loss and refusing to pay a return to the financier. The Court thought that this was unlikely to happen if a well-designed system of credit rating, auditing, and punishment for wrong-doing could be implemented to discourage such behavior. The appellants had expressed the fear that, in any case, as believed by certain scholars, profit under musharika was no different from bank interest, and that a musharika-based system was at risk of degenerating into a system tainted by riba. The Court thought that this was unlikely to happen because, under musharika, the profit or loss which investors share proportionally is determined on the basis of the success or failure of the enterprise in which the investment is made and not on the basis of the time or the duration of the investment.

The Court also endorsed certain other non-interest based modes of financing, such as lease financing (*ijara*), outright sale (*salam*), and a progressive payment system tied to job description (*istisna*). The Court expressed its satisfaction with the details concerning these modes set out in the reports of various government-appointed commissions on the Islamization of the economy.[25] The Court considered these reports as constituting at least the basic groundwork for bringing about a change in the present financial system.

Are Letters of Credit and Negotiable Instruments Tainted by Riba?

With respect to the letter of credit facility of banks,[26] the Court stated that there was no objection to this from the sharia point of view, provided the service that the bank performs, namely quick and easy payment and transfer of money from one place to another, is properly compensated in terms of the sharia. According to the Court, the payment made by the bank to an importer or purchaser under a letter of credit is in the nature of debt (*qard*), and therefore subject to the rule against riba. In the Court's view, if, as is currently the case, the payment of compensation or remuneration for the service provided by the bank is related to the duration or time of the payment by the bank under the letter of credit and calculated as a percentage of the amount paid, then it amounts to riba. The Court stated that if, however, such compensation were linked to the volume or magnitude of the service, the speed of the payment and the level and credibility of the bank, then it would be a kind of service charge, a concept which has met with the approval of almost all contemporary Islamic scholars and learned institutions. The Court therefore proposed that

---

[25] CII Report 1980; Commission for Islamization of the Economy Reports on the Elimination of Riba 1991 and 1997.

[26] Letter of credit is an instrument under which the issuer (a bank), at a customer's request, agrees to honor a draft or other demand for payment made by a third party (the beneficiary), as long as the draft or demand complies with specified conditions, and regardless of whether any underlying agreement between the customer and the beneficiary is satisfied.

the State Bank of Pakistan determine flat rates of compensation for the letter of credit facility provided by banks, which could differ from transaction to transaction, but would remain fixed for a given transaction throughout the life of that transaction.

The Court, however, raised objections from a sharia point of view to the prevalent practice of discounting bills of exchange. According to the Court, a promissory note or bill of exchange represents a debt payable by the issuer to the holder, which cannot be transferred to a third party except at face value, and the discounting of a note or a bill or a check therefore amounts to a sale of a debt for a higher price, and involves the payment of increase or interest. In the Court's view, the transaction does not amount to a sale of the bank's title to a loan; owing to the involvement of the element of deferred payment, it is at best a sale of money for money. The Court concluded that, in the circumstances, the transaction is to be construed and regulated as a loan, which means that any increase ultimately earned by the bank would fall under the category of riba. The Court added that, in its view, in a truly Islamic financial market, paper representing money or debt cannot be traded, but paper evidencing the holder's ownership of tangible assets, such as a share or lease or joint venture (musharika) certificate, can be and is a viable secondary market can be developed on that basis.

How Can the Country's Financial System/Economy Be Freed from Riba?

How Can the Riba-based Domestic Debt be Eliminated?

Having established that the country's financial and economic system is tainted by riba, the Court took what it believed was the next logical step of considering how that system can be freed from this burden. The Court noted with regret that, even though there is general agreement that financial and economic management of the country be shifted to a riba-free basis, the government (especially the State Bank of Pakistan, which has primary responsibility for monitoring fiscal and monetary operations) had made no move to do so, even though it had had all the time needed for the purpose. The Court regretted particularly that the State Bank had been ignoring the recommendations made in this connection by the several expert commissions appointed by the government from time to time, even though these, together with the 1991 FSC ruling, constitute an excellent barometer for the State Bank to measure the level of general agreement and consensus on the subject in the country. The Court regarded these recommendations as constituting the basic groundwork for the reform to be carried out in this area.

With respect to private domestic debt specifically, the Court stated that this should be converted to a riba-free basis in accordance with the recommendations of the 1997 Commission.[27] The Court noted that this debt, the bulk of which is made up of borrowings by private and public sector enterprises from commercial banks and development finance institutions and some of transactions between private parties, has been contracted on the basis of one or another of the 12 non-interest based modes of financing in vogue since the reforms of 1979-85. The Court expressed some concern that, since Islamic scholars have seriously questioned the permissibility of these modes of financing (as noted in the 1997 Commission Report), the restructuring of this debt could pose problems. The Court was, however, confident that these could be easily overcome and the debt converted on the basis of the permissible financing modes illustrated in the 1997 Commission Report, and provided for in the proposed draft Prohibition of Riba Act attached thereto. The Court noted how the draft act requires domestic private parties to a debt to re-negotiate a fresh contract on the basis of one or another of the permissible modes of financing within six months of the effective date of the act.

The Court's interventions in the area of domestic public debt were prompted largely by its concern for the financial viability of the government. Mentioning the urgent need to relieve the government of the deadening weight of its domestic debt, the Court had no hesitation in agreeing with the recommendation made from time to time by government-appointed experts and commissions: that government loans obtained from the public by issuing domestic debt instruments with a fixed rate of return or profit as well as loans taken by the public from government-controlled banks should either be retired or converted to an interest-free liability, such as equity; and that, similarly, inter-governmental debt should be converted and placed on an interest-free footing.

While on the subject of domestic public debt, the Court reviewed and endorsed the relevant findings of the Prime Minister's Committee on Self Reliance, which were summed up by the Court as follows: So far as inter-governmental loans are concerned, these are rarely driven by the profit motive, and the risk to that profit is not a consideration in their settlement. The lending government should therefore have no objection to having such loans converted to some interest-free transaction, and it should be quite feasible to achieve such conversion. A rationing scheme could be adopted to decide on the future allocation of this category of loans, for which a specific proposal could easily be developed in the context of the

---

[27] *See supra* ch. 1, *The Report of the Commission for the Islamization of the Economy on the Elimination of Riba, 1997.*

recommendation of the National Finance Commission.[28] With respect to bank loans to the government, interest should no longer be paid on State Bank holdings of treasury bills; and future borrowings should continue as before but on an interest-free basis. Existing government debt with other banks should be settled by provision of new non-interest bearing government paper, redeemable by the State Bank over a five-year period. Non-bank loans to the government, which are mainly derived from public saving schemes (perhaps the most important component of domestic public debt), should be settled with some care, since these are owned by private individuals. To settle these, the government should create a mutual fund financed from the sale of its shares in selected government sponsored corporations. The mechanism of a mutual fund should be particularly effective in insulating people like small investors, widows, and retired individuals from exposure to risk.

With respect to domestic public debt, the Court also endorsed the findings of the 1997 Commission for the Islamization of the Economy set forth in its Report on the Elimination of Riba and the proposed draft Prohibition of Riba Act attached thereto. The Court noted that the proposed act in relevant part lays down: (a) that such debt should be settled by the issuance of share certificates in the amount of the debt obligations in a mutual fund or by outright retirement through the use of proceeds from the privatization of public assets, and (b) all inter-governmental and State Bank debt should be made interest-free from the effective date of the act. The Court, however, realized, and was quick to point out, that such settlement cannot take place without restructuring the financial structure of the government, fundamentally changing the formulation and conduct of its fiscal policy, and impacting key economic variables, such as growth, consumption, and savings and investment. The Court also endorsed the evaluation done by the Commission of the effect of the recommended measures on the country's balance of payments, budget, credit plan, and macroeconomic framework, and the steps that would need to be taken for their improvement.

---

[28] The president of Pakistan is authorized to constitute a National Finance Commission "… (2) … to make recommendations to the President as to … (c) the exercise by the Federal Government and the Provincial Governments of the borrowing powers conferred by the Constitution; and (d) any other matter relating to finance referred to the Commission by the President …" Pakistan Const. art. 160.

Should the Foreign Debt be Made Riba-Free?

The Court did not overlook the separate but related issue of converting the country's considerable stock of foreign debt[29] to a riba-free basis and of getting foreign lenders to deal with the country on that basis in the future. The Court had the benefit of a large body of expert opinion on the subject. The experts assisting the Court pointed to the difficulties involved in such conversion.[30] They expressed the view that Pakistan should continue to honor its interest-based foreign loan liability even if interest is declared un-Islamic, because, in Islam, it is the obligation of a Muslim to honor his past obligations, regardless of whether contracted with domestic or foreign parties.[31] Most of the experts, however, recommended that the government make every effort to renegotiate the terms of the foreign loans and to pay them back under Islamic financing modes. They insisted that the government should request foreign lenders to change the forms of contracts by replacing the existing interest-based contracts with riba-free equivalents. They explained that a switch-over of the outstanding foreign debt from an interest to an interest-free basis by mutual agreement would not constitute a repudiation of debt in violation of the Islamic principle of sanctity of obligation.

In its appearance before the Court, the Islamic Development Bank of Pakistan suggested a number of possible ways for the government to get over some of the difficulties and to facilitate the conversion process. Should the country experience difficulty in securing the liquidity required to settle its outstanding foreign debt, the government could privatize the public sector, utilizing part of the proceeds of the sale of some of the public enterprises for buying back that debt at a discount, or swapping that debt for equity in the newly privatized enterprises. A dialogue could be usefully initiated by the government with foreign financing institutions to get

---

29 As of March 1, 1999 this stood at U.S. $31.15 billion or Rs. 1610 billion at the then-current inter-bank rate.

30 Pakistan's economy has a large foreign sector comprised of exports, imports, receipts, and payments of invisibles, home remittances, other inflows including borrowings by the government, and servicing of the country's external debt. Even for maintaining a reasonable rate of economic growth, Pakistan is dependent on inflow of external resources, particularly from international financial institutions.

31 Statement by the Islamic Development Bank of Pakistan in its response to the Court on the question "how to deal with the current debt, the economic effects of borrowing and alternatives to such borrowing?"

them to appreciate the advantages of Islamic modes of financing and of making foreign financing more efficient and effective in economic development. This could be followed up with the design and issuance of Islamic financial instruments in foreign currencies, and the establishment of special funds to cater to specific types of projects, such as an infrastructure fund (for financing roads and transport, airports and seaports, power stations etc.), a leasing fund, a trade financing fund, an agriculture investment fund, a housing investment financing fund, and other project-specific funds. Financial instruments based on profit-sharing could also be effectively designed to attract venture capital as well as working capital from foreign sources. Interest-based foreign borrowing could, however, be allowed in cases of "necessity," it being left to the discretion of the sharia scholars to determine what constitutes a necessity, on the basis of a full and accurate understanding of the country's real condition.

Reliance was placed by the Court upon the 1997 Report on the Elimination of Riba to debunk the notion that an attempt by Pakistan to convert its foreign debt to an interest-free basis would meet with hostility from the international financial community. The Report mentioned that debt-equity conversions are well known to the international financial community, having been resorted to extensively in the past by countries facing foreign debt problems. The Report stated that, so long as sufficient time is allowed for removing any apprehensions that the foreign debt market may have about the proposed new sharia-based system, the market could be expected to adjust to the new system. The Report pointed out that, so far as Pakistan's trade relations are concerned, these are fairly well diversified and can be damaged only if joint action is taken by all of Pakistan's trading partners in retaliation, which was thought highly unlikely. The Report stated that to speak of the possibility of a freeze on Pakistan's reserves and other assets in other countries would be to assume a situation in which again there is hostility against Pakistan of a kind which effective diplomacy cannot defuse. The Report also pointed to the already expressed willingness of international financial institutions, such as the International Finance Corporation (IFC) and the International Monetary Fund, to provide financing on a profit- and loss-sharing basis: IFC had been particularly keen on this but had become discouraged by the government's lack of enthusiasm.

The experts assisting the Court suggested, however, that it would be prudent to proceed with some caution in this matter and to allow more time for the conversion of conventional foreign debt to Islamic foreign debt, say, a period of two years. They tried to impress upon the Court that foreign loans involve not only the sanctity of the agreements made but also the credibility of the country. If Pakistan defaults (without warning?) on interest payments to its foreign lenders, no further assistance or investment would be forthcoming. Almost every development program undertaken by Pakistan in the public or the private sector depends on foreign loans and assistance, which could be expected to dry up, if the country were to refuse to honor its past commitments. In support, the experts cited the reports of the various commissions appointed by the government from time to time on the elimination of riba, which recommended more time for the government to settle or renegotiate foreign debt,[32] unlike domestic public debt which is required to be settled or renegotiated with immediate effect. In this connection, the Court took note particularly of the 1997 Commission's recommendations, which as reflected in the Commission's proposed draft Prohibition of Riba Act, left no room for doubt that, while the government would be authorized under the act to re-negotiate existing foreign debt on the basis of permissible modes of financing, it would not be required to do so within any set time-limit.

The Court acknowledged the special nature of foreign liabilities, but declared that this cannot be used as an excuse for exempting them from the prohibition against riba indefinitely or permanently on the basis of necessity. The Court could not, however, deny that more time was needed for foreign transactions to be converted to a sharia-based system than domestic transactions. According to the Court, the doctrine of necessity was applicable to this extent only. In the Court's view, there should not be much difficulty in renegotiating the existing foreign loans on Islamic lines in the long run. According to the Court, the concern of the foreign lenders was to get a return on their loans, and not to insist on a particular form. The Court suggested therefore that asset-based loans could easily be converted to leasing arrangements; that project-related loans could be reshaped on the basis of a progressive payment scheme (*istisna*); and that, for purposes of new financing, an even wider variety of instruments was available and can be made to fit the Islamic mold. The Court added that all this would be possible only if the government itself showed a firm commitment to its Islamic obligations and a true will to implement what Islam requires.

What Does the Ruling Mean for the Current Riba-based Legal Framework?

Having equated interest and mark-up (the latter, at least in the form in which it is practiced in Pakistan) with riba, the Court undertook an examination of the laws listed below, which provide for the payment or receipt of interest in one form or another, and declared them or some of their provisions repugnant to the

---

[32] The Prime Minister's Committee on Self Reliance recommended two years, and the Commission for Islamization of the Economy on Elimination of Riba eighteen months.

injunctions of Islam. The Court directed that these laws should be repealed or amended as indicated below:

The Interest Act, 1839

The act confers power on the court to allow interest to the creditor on a debt or any ascertained sum payable and recovered through the court. This is an undefined, naked and generalized power to allow interest on a debt. The entire act is struck down and should be repealed.

The Government Savings Bank Act, 1873

The act provides for payment of "interest" on any deposit made by, or on behalf of, any minor.[33] If any increase accruing on the deposit is "interest" it cannot be allowed. If it results from a permissible mode of investment, it can be. The term "interest" appearing in the act should therefore be deleted and substituted with the phrase "sharia-compliant return."

The Negotiable Instruments Act, 1881

The Court focused on those provisions of the act that provide for the calculation and payment of a "return" on a promissory note or bill of exchange, and that evidence an obligation to pay the price under a contract of sale, or the rent under a lease agreement, or the rent under a hire-purchase agreement, or the service charge under a financing agreement.[34] Such obligation constitutes a debt, and any return on a note or bill evidencing that debt is a return on that debt and subject to all the rules relevant to a loan or debt. The provisions in question are therefore struck down to the extent that these empower the court to order payment of a return to the holder of the note or bill, over and above the original price or rent or service charge, for the period during which such price or rent or service charge remains unpaid after becoming due. Such return is calculated against time only and is nothing but interest.

Also struck down are provisions of the act which confer the right: (a) on a payer for honor of a bill of exchange to recover the amount paid by him together with interest from the original debtor; and (b) on an endorser who has paid the amount of the bill to recover that amount together with interest calculated at a certain fixed rate. The act should be amended accordingly.

---

[33] Section 10.

[34] Sections 79, 80, 114, and 117(c).

The Land Acquisition Act, 1894

The provisions of the act are struck down which provide for the court to order payment of "interest" on the compensation amount awarded for compulsory acquisition of land for the period between the taking of possession and the payment of compensation (or full compensation). [35] Such interest does not amount to compensation for deprivation of the use of the land, but is merely compensation for deprivation of the use of the money representing the fair price of that land. Such interest is awarded over and above that price, and therefore constitutes an increase on it; and is calculated at a rate fixed in advance and against only the lapse of time, without regard to the fair market rent commanded by the land during the period of the deprivation. The act should be amended accordingly.

The Civil Procedure Code, 1908

The provisions of the code are struck down which provide for the court, in suits for recovery of bank loans and public dues, to order payment of "interest" at such rate as the court deems reasonable on the principal amount for the period between the filing of the suit and the award of the decree, in addition to any interest decreed on such principal amount for any period prior to the filing of the suit, with such further "interest" at such rate as the court deems reasonable on the aggregate amount so decreed, from the date of the decree to the date of payment or such earlier date as the court thinks fit.[36] Any additional amounts awarded by the court over and above the principal amount decreed in such cases would be an increase on debt, intended not to compensate the lender/decree-holder for loss caused to him by the borrower, say, through case delaying tactics, but only to provide him a return calculated in each and every case at a fixed rate based on the opportunity cost of money; and these are therefore riba. All relevant provisions[37] of the code should be amended so as to delete all references to "interest" and to substitute other suitable terms.

---

[35] Sections 28, 32, 33, and 34.

[36] Sections 34, 34-A, 34-B(b)(c).

[37] Sections 2(12), 35(3), 144(1) and Orders XXI, Rule 11, 38, 79(3), 80(3), 93, XXXIV, Rule 2(1)(a)(i), (iii), (c)(i) and (ii), Rule 2(2), Rule 4, Rule 7 (1)(a)(i) and (iii) and (c)(i) and (ii), Rule 7(2), 11, 13(1), XXXVII, Rule 2, and XXXIX, Rule 9.

The Co-operative Societies Act, 1925

All references to "interest" should be deleted from the relevant provisions of the act, on the ground that the charging, levying, and recovery of interest are not permissible under the sharia.[38]

The Insurance Act, 1938

The provisions of the act are struck down which provide for indication by the insurer of the range of "interest" rates on its investments, the guarantee of "interest" amounts, the payment of "interest" on amounts due on liquidation of insurance policies for the period between the date the amount becomes due and the date it is paid, and other matters relevant to the calculation and payment of "interest" by or to the insurer or the insured.[39] The reference is, however, allowed to be retained in the act to the "principal and interest" guaranteed by a foreign government in respect of such government's securities in which the insurer has invested its funds to back a life insurance policy issued to a foreign national expressed in such government's currency.[40] The mere presence of this "foreign" element is sufficient grounds for making this exception.

The State Bank of Pakistan Act, 1956

The provisions of the act are struck down which provide for the purchase of bills, bonds, debentures, and other commercial paper on "interest" basis. The act would need to be amended suitably in the future to reflect the new character of these financial products once made compatible with the principles of the sharia.

The West Pakistan Money-Lenders Ordinance, 1960; The West Pakistan Money-Lenders Rules, 1965; The Punjab Money-Lenders Ordinance, 1960; The Sindh Money-Lenders Ordinance, 1960; The N.W.F.P. Money-Lenders Ordinance, 1960; and The Balochistan Money-Lenders Ordinance, 1960

Since money lending and money lenders are alien to the concept of Islamic social justice, all these laws should be removed from the statute book.

---

38 Sections 59(2)(e), 71(2), Rules 14(1)(h), 22, and 41 along with Appendixes I to IV.

39 Sections 3-BB(1)(b), 29(8)(b) and (c)(iii), 47-B, 81(2)(d).

40 Section 27(3).

The Agricultural Development Bank Rules, 1961

The provisions of the act relating to the levying, charging and recovery of "interest" on loans made by the Agricultural Development Bank should be suitably amended in the light of the Court's decision.[41]

The Banking Companies Ordinance, 1962

The provisions of the act are struck down to the extent that they empower the State Bank to give directions to banking companies about the rates of "interest" to be applied to advances, or to prohibit banking companies from giving loans on "interest" basis.

References to a "mark-up" can, however, be retained under these provisions. This would allow banks to retain the flexibility of transacting business on mark-up basis under true cost-plus financing (murabaha) or deferred payment sale (bai muajjal) arrangements, which is compatible with the principles of the sharia. It is true that such instruments are not ideal for banks and will be rarely used by them, but they will nevertheless come in handy especially in the early stages of transformation of the financial system. Instead, the provision of the act is struck down which generally prohibits banks from buying and selling goods, and which would be an obstacle not only to a true deferred payment sale (bai muajjal) transaction but also to a leasing, hire-purchase, joint venture (musharika) or mutual investment fund (mudaraba) transaction.[42] The concept of Islamic banking cannot be translated into reality, unless it is realized that banks are not meant just to deal in money and paper but that they have to base their financing on, and firmly relate it to, real business activity.

The Banking Companies Rules, 1963

The Court struck down the rule which provides for the crediting of "interest" on a banking company's foreign approved securities as well as rupee securities.[43] While such interest already realized can be retained and credited to the treasury (*baitul mal),* all future such transactions which involve interest should not be permitted.

---

[41] Rule 17(1), (2), (3).

[42] Section 9

[43] Rule 9 (2), (3).

The Banks (Nationalization) Payment of Compensation Rules, 1974

The rule providing for the calculation of interest from the date of acquisition of the shares in a nationalized bank to its annual payment and the procedure for payment is struck down. Instead of just deleting references to "interest" from the rule, a new rule should be framed on the lines indicated in the Court's decision so as to effectively enforce prohibition of interest in the future.[44]

The Banking Companies (Recovery of Loans) Ordinance, 1979

The provisions of the ordinance dealing with the payment of "interest" or "mark-up" on bank loans under court recovery[45] should be treated along the lines laid down in the Court's ruling for corresponding provisions of the Civil Procedure Code.

What Can Be Done to Institute an Economic and Legal Framework Consistent with the Injunctions of Islam? The Court's Guidelines

The Court acknowledged that it was the responsibility of the concerned organs and institutions of the state, and not of the Court, to lay down economic and monetary policies and to frame laws. Nevertheless, on the insistence of the government and taking advantage of the large body of expert opinion received by it on the issues involved, the Court went on to lay down the following guidelines for consideration by the concerned authorities and for designing and implementing an economic and legal framework consistent with the injunctions of Islam.

*On the Elimination of Deception (*gharar*),[46] Deceit, and Fraud*

It will not be enough just to establish a sharia-based economic system. The system will need to be accompanied by measures designed to meet the moral hazard arising from its actual operation and to ensure its regulation and transparency in accordance with sound and practicable norms. The interests of the small investor especially will need to be protected. Until now, small investors who have invested

---

44 Rule 9.

45 Section 8 (2)(a)(b).

46 "*Gharar*" denotes the element of deception in an exchange transaction caused either by ignorance of the goods or the price, or by a faulty description of the goods. When applied to the stock market, the concept roughly translates into "non- or partial disclosure."

in the stock market or in bank deposits have seen their savings being partially or fully eroded because of the presence of deception (gharar) or speculative practices, in the case of the stock market, or of the lack of ability of banks suffering from massive loan defaults to offer a reasonable return on deposits, in the case of bank deposits. Loopholes in the economic system that allow defaulters to get away scot-free will need to be closed. Stringent measures and regulations will therefore need to be introduced to check speculative activities in the stock market; to establish an independent body responsible for formulating and administering monetary policy, competent and powerful enough to ensure compliance with that policy and with the laws and regulations governing borrowing activity; and to put in place an expeditious legal and adjudication process for debt recovery.

All this will mean establishing an effective legal framework to eliminate deceit and fraud from the system. For this purpose, the court indicated that guidelines can be obtained, for instance, from the laws, regulations, and other measures that have been adopted by the United States to ensure good governance, fair dealing, and transparency, all elements currently missing from Pakistan's economic system. These include:

- the administration of monetary policy by the Federal Reserve Board, which is an autonomous body, outside the influence of the executive, the legislature, and the judiciary;
- the Freedom of Information Act, 1966, which enjoins all U.S. government agencies to disclose records upon request, subject to certain enumerated restrictions;
- the Privacy Act, 1974, which protects government records on U.S. citizens and lawfully admitted permanent residents;
- the maintenance of public and non-public records by the Securities and Exchange Commission, such as registration statements and reports filed by regulated corporations and individuals;
- the laws which provide for regulating trading and commerce to eliminate fraud, manipulation, and dissemination of false information, and to ensure just and equitable trading;
- the restrictions on short sales so as to regulate the use of credit for trading;
- the rules against insider trading;
- the Ethics in Government Act, 1978 and the regulations issued by the Office of Government Ethics, under which public employees are enjoined from placing personal gain above public trust; from involving themselves in situations of conflict of interest, particularly with regard to outside financial

interests or outside employment or activities; and from knowingly making unauthorized commitments or promises purporting to bind the government.

The court also referred for further guidance to some of the measures adopted by the United Kingdom, which it deemed to reflect Islamic teachings on justice, fair play, and disclosure to minimize deception (gharar), including:

- the prudential regulations and disclosure rules under the Financial Services Act, 1986 and
- the establishment of an independent Serious Fraud Office as an integral part of the criminal justice system, to investigate and prosecute serious and complex abuse and misuse of powers offenses and white collar crimes, at the behest of government departments and regulatory bodies and other organizations.

On the Uniform Development of Interdependent Sectors of the Economy (Including the Capital Market)

It will not be enough to eliminate riba just from the banking sector. All critical sectors of the economy will need to be cleansed. This will open up a variety of possible sharia-compliant sectors for the investment of savings. As a consequence of having to compete with those sectors, the banking sector will be made to feel the pressure to become sharia-compliant itself and to promote the development of sharia-compliant financial instruments. The failure of the banking sector to develop such instruments in the past is attributable to the absence of such competition, for instance, from the capital market sector, which is unregulated and inefficient. Statistics obtained from other countries, particularly the United States, speak volumes for the critical and major role played by the capital market in the economic growth of those countries. Development of the capital market sector in Pakistan will help lay a solid foundation for economic growth and the equitable distribution of wealth through regulated public participation in an important economic sector. By promoting competition with the banking sector, a sharia-compliant capital market sector will facilitate the control of unlawful conduct and the elimination of deception (gharar) from all critical sectors of the economy.

The adoption of a sharia-based debt instrument in the shape of the joint venture (musharika) certificate will lead to substantial equity funds becoming available through a well-developed capital market, thus reducing reliance on banks which promote riba. Mutual investment fund (*qirad*) certificates and diminishing musharika certificates can also be developed to help generate local funds for the infrastructure needs of provinces, municipalities and corporate bodies, thus reducing their dependence on foreign exchange borrowings.

Other Measures to Promote Transparency

No individual should be allowed to obtain utilities connections, open a bank account or obtain a loan, unless that person's credit report received from a credit bureau is clean. Credit bureaus should be non-governmental entities and their databases should be accessible to any organization on payment of a nominal fee.

No institution (corporate body or other) should be allowed to seek a loan, investment or other financing unless it has received a satisfactory credit rating from a duly licensed, independent credit rating agency. Currently, there are no effective regulations in force for third party ratings and risk assessment. Although rules have been adopted for the establishment and regulation of credit companies, these have not been successfully applied.[47] Accordingly, corporate managers do not feel compelled to take investors into confidence by sharing company information with them, nor do they feel any moral obligation to share profits with them. Under this loose regulatory framework (and especially in the absence of rules on insider trading), unscrupulous agents find it highly profitable to scam investors and creditors with the aid of limited liability laws. It is no surprise therefore that dummy companies quoted on the stock exchanges have proliferated.[48] Nor is there any reliable system of market indices developed by third parties which could be pressed into service to rout out such scams and offer the investor/creditor a modicum of protection. The Karachi Stock Exchange (KSE) 100 index is maintained by the stock exchange itself and seemingly only serves the purpose of assisting a few players in the market in luring unsuspecting investors into fraudulent schemes.

In establishing a viable legal and regulatory framework for third party rating and risk assessment in Pakistan, the court pointed to the example of the United States, particularly its credit rating system provided by one of four rating agencies (Standard & Poor, Moodys, DCR, and Fitch-IBCA). Individuals, corporations, banks and financial institutions, and even municipalities are all rated by these agencies, and their credit rating is relied upon by investors planning to invest in bonds or other instruments floated or offered for investment to the public. These agencies are duly licensed and monitored for quality by the Securities and Exchange Com-

---

[47] The Credit Rating Companies Rules, 1995 framed by the federal government under section 33 of the Securities and Exchange Ordinance, 1969.

[48] The companies listed on the Karachi Stock Exchange number 750. In comparison, the number of companies listed on the New York Stock Exchange is only five times as large, even though the U.S. economy is more than 100 times the size of that of Pakistan.

mission. This system is beefed up by market indices developed by independent third parties such as Dow Jones.[49]

Financial institutions should encourage experts, lawyers, and others to establish agencies for keeping track of defaulters so that they can be brought to book. Among other things, such agencies will facilitate service of process of the court on defaulters and trace their properties and assets, whether held under their own names or third party names, so as to facilitate recovery through execution of court decrees.

Loan recovery laws should be streamlined. Along with that, an adequate number of courts should be established, presided over by competent and honest judges. The courts will not be over-burdened, and should be assigned only that number of cases which they can dispose of within three months. Recovery proceedings will be required to be instituted within a reasonable time of the default, while the defaulter and his assets are still traceable.

Train Officers and Staff

Officers and staff of financial institutions should be educated in the essential principles of Islamic economy. They should acquire the necessary knowledge about the new financial modes and products they will be using. They should attend courses on accounting and auditing procedures conforming to the sharia.

Adapt Accounting and Auditing Procedures and Standards

Accounting and auditing procedures and standards should be developed to conform to the sharia. These have been laid down in detail in a published work on the subject.[50] This task will be carried out by the Institute of Chartered Accountants, with the assistance of State Bank and Finance Division representatives.

The Next Steps

Keeping these guidelines in view and for ease of reference, the Court summarized the measures that would need to be taken and the institutional and legal framework that would need to be provided to support a sharia-based economic system essentially as follows:

- Implement strict austerity measures to curtail government expenditures drastically and to control deficit financing.

---

49 Similar market indices have been developed in the United Kingdom (FTSE) and Japan (Nikkei).

50 Accounting and Auditing Organization for Islamic Financial Institutions, Bahrain.

- Enact federal and provincial laws to regulate the Federal Consolidated Fund and the Public Account, and to provide for the power to borrow for its purpose and scope, and its utilization, regulation and monitoring, and other ancillary matters.
- Enact laws to provide for necessary prudential measures to ensure transparency, *inter alia*, along the lines of the Freedom of Information Act, the Privacy Act, and the Ethics Regulations of the United States, and the Financial Services Act of the United Kingdom.
- Establish institutions like the U.K. Serious Fraud Office to control white collar and economic crimes.
- Establish credit rating agencies in the public sector.
- Establish a system of evaluators for scrutiny of feasibility reports.
- Establish special departments within the State Bank as follows:
  a) a sharia board for scrutinizing and evaluating the State Bank's procedures and products, and for providing guidance for successfully managing Islamic economics;
  b) a board for arranging the exchange of information among financial institutions regarding the feasibility and evaluation of projects, and the credit rating of institutions, corporations, and other entities; and
  c) a board, possibly in the shape of an Islamic Financial Service Institution, for providing technical assistance to financial institutions and banks for removing anomalies emerging in the course of practical operations, difficulties connected with financial products, and transactions between financial institutions and consumers or clients. Such institution should also work in the field of shares and investment certificates underwriting, promotion, and market making, thus helping in the activation of primary and secondary markets.

The Time Frame

The Court concluded by setting various dates for the phased transformation of the economy to a sharia-based system in accordance with the guidelines set out above. The Court directed:

- that, within one month of the Court's ruling, the federal government constitute in the State Bank of Pakistan a high level Commission for Transformation, comprised of sharia scholars and committed economists, bankers, and chartered accountants, and fully empowered to carry out, control, and supervise the process of transformation;

- that, within two months of its constitution, the Commission for Transformation prepare a strategy to evaluate, scrutinize, and implement the reports of the Commission for the Islamization of the Economy, taking into account the comments and further suggestions of the leading banks, religious scholars, and economists, as well as the State Bank and the Finance Division, and, once finalized, to send it to the Ministries of Law, Finance and Commerce, and all the banks and financial institutions for implementation.
- that, within one month of the Court's ruling, the Law Ministry form a taskforce, comprising its own officials and two sharia scholars from the Council of Islamic Ideology or from the Commission for the Islamization of the Economy:
  a) to draft a new law for the prohibition of riba and other laws as proposed in the guidelines above;
  b) to review the existing financial and other laws with a view to bringing them into conformity with the requirements of the new sharia-based financial system;
  c) to draft new laws to give legal cover to the proposed new sharia-compliant financial instruments; and
  d) to submit its recommendations to the Commission for Transformation for finalization preparatory to the promulgation of the recommended laws;
- that, within six months of the Court's ruling, all the banks and financial institutions prepare sharia-compliant model agreements and documents for major operations, and present these to the Commission for Transformation for approval prior to implementation;
- that, thereafter, all the banks and financial institutions arrange training programs and seminars to educate their staff and clients about the new financing arrangements, their requirements, and their effects;
- that all joint stock companies, mutual funds, and firms seeking financing above Rs. 5 million in the aggregate a year be required by law to subject themselves to independent rating by neutral rating agencies;[51]

[51] No time was specified in this connection. Presumably, this will be required to be done as soon the relevant law is passed.

- that, within one month of the Court's ruling, the Ministry of Finance form a task force of experts to recommend the means for converting the government's domestic debt to project-related financing, and for establishing a mutual fund to finance the government on that basis;[52]
- that domestic intra-government borrowings and borrowings of the federal government from the State Bank of Pakistan be designed on an interest-free basis;[53]
- that the federal government initiate serious efforts to relieve the nation from the burden of foreign debt as soon as possible, and to renegotiate the existing loans, and to structure future borrowings, if needed, on the basis of Islamic modes of financing;
- that the following laws being repugnant to the injunctions of Islam cease to have effect from March 31, 2000:

(a) The Interest Act, 1839.

(b) The West Pakistan Money-Lenders Ordinance, 1960.

(c) The West Pakistan Money-Lenders Rules, 1965.

(d) The Punjab Money Lenders Ordinance, 1960.

(e) The Sindh Money Lenders Ordinance, 1960.

(f) The N.W.F.P. Money Lenders Ordinance, 1960.

(g) The Balochistan Money Lenders Ordinance, 1960.

(h) Section 9 of Banking Companies Ordinance, 1962.

- that other laws or provisions thereof, to the extent that they have been declared to be repugnant to the injunctions of Islam, cease to have effect from June 30, 2001.

---

52 The Court elaborated on some of the features of this mutual fund. The units of the mutual fund would be available for purchase by the public and would be tradable in the secondary market on the basis of net asset value. The bonds under existing government savings schemes based on interest would be converted to units of the mutual fund.

53 It was not indicated whether this stipulation applied only to new borrowings or whether it also covered existing borrowings. Nor was a specific time-frame mentioned for this purpose. Presumably, action would be required to be taken on this as part of, and/or following, the transformation process.

Epilogue

The government was quick to take the initial steps mandated by the Court. The Commission for Transformation and the two task forces (one each for law and finance) were promptly constituted[54] following the Court's decision, and have been extremely busy ever since. They have designed new financial instruments[55] based on joint ventures, mutual investment funds, and lease financing, among others. They have prepared a new draft law[56] to provide legal cover for these new instruments. They have reviewed the several existing laws which the Court had struck down and, at last reports, were busy rewriting them[57] so as to conform to the injunctions of Islam.

This is not to suggest, however, that the government is going ahead pell-mell to implement the Court's decision. The Court's decision calls for a complete and profound transformation of the country's financial system. Realizing the enormity of this task, the government has decided to approach it with caution and pragmatism.[58] Last June, the government therefore applied for and won a year's reprieve from the Court for implementing the Court's decision.[59] In the course of further deliberations on the subject since then, the government has identified a

---

54 *See* Gazette of Pakistan Notification No. F.2 (1) Bkg (R&S)/99-337 (Apr. 27, 2000).

55 *See* the News (Karachi, July 19, 2000) and the Business Recorder (Karachi, Apr. 20, 2001).

56 For the complete proposed text of the Draft Prohibition of Riba Ordinance, 2001, and the comments thereon of the Commission for Transformation, see the Business Recorder (Karachi, Apr. 28, 2001).

57 For progress in this area, *see* reports in the Business Recorder (Karachi, Apr. 21, 2001 and June 24, 2001).

58 For utterances to this effect of senior government officials and other spokespersons, *see e.g.* the attorney general's submission in support of the government's application for a reprieve for implementing the Court's decision, as summed up by Sh. Riaz Ahmad, J. in his order in *United Bank Ltd. v. M/s Farooq Brothers and others* (text printed in the Business Recorder, Karachi, June 15, 2001); and the views of counsel for the commercial banks co-petitioners with the government in *United Bank Ltd. v M/s Farooq Brothers and others*, and of the Commission for Transformation, all as reported in the Business Recorder, (Karachi, June 24, 2001).

59 Order of Sh. Riaz Ahmad, J. in *United Bank Ltd. v. M/s Farooq Brothers and others* (text printed in the Business Recorder, Karachi, June 15, 2001).

number of practical difficulties[60] associated with the implementation of the Court's decision. Since these were not foreseen at the time of the Court's decision, the government contemplates seeking further guidance from the Court on how they should be addressed before the Court's decision can be implemented.[61] In this connection, the government is not unmindful of the fact that no other country has been known to institute a financial system run entirely on sharia-based principles.[62] In the government's view, any attempt to do so in Pakistan now without the benefit of prior experience could prove highly and unnecessarily disruptive of the country's existing economic order.[63] The government therefore intends, with the Court's permission, to move gradually to a sharia-based financial system, first trying out various options combining limited sharia-based banking with traditional practices during the transition.[64]

---

[60] These arise from the existence of the country's large external and domestic debt burden, which it would be difficult to continue to refinance in the absence of a sharia-based instrument for deficit financing (on this, see the statement of Dr. Ishrat Hussain, Governor, State Bank of Pakistan as reported in the Business Recorder (Karachi, May 6, 2001)) and the proceedings of an inter-ministerial meeting convened under the chairmanship of General Pervez Musharraf, President of Pakistan, to review the work of the Commission for Transformation and the Task Forces as reported in the News International and the Business Recorder (Karachi both dated Sept. 5, 2001); and from the inability of a sharia-based system to provide depositor protection against inflation, and the depreciating value and declining purchasing power of currencies (on this, see a report quoting Dr. Tariq Hassan, Adviser to the Ministry of Finance in Dawn (Karachi, Aug. 14, 2001).

[61] *See* the Business Recorder, (Karachi, Apr. 21, 2001).

[62] *See* Dr. Tariq Hassan as quoted in Dawn, (Karachi, Aug. 14, 2001).

[63] *See e.g.* the newspaper reports of the proceedings of the inter-ministerial meeting mentioned in *supra* n. 60.

[64] *Id.*; *see* an address given by Dr. Ishrat Hussain to the Karachi Chamber of Commerce and reported in the Business Today (Karachi, Sept. 13, 2001), which lists some of the options which the government is studying for a "mixed" system, including: (a) the opening of a new sharia-based bank; (b) the opening of sharia-based facilities at existing banks; and (c) the opening of new sharia-based branches of existing banks; and para. 26 of the government's Letter of Intent to the International Monetary Fund dated November 22, 2001.

THE INSTRUMENT ESTABLISHING THE WORLD BANK PROTOTYPE CARBON FUND (PCF) AND THE FIRST PCF EMISSION REDUCTIONS PURCHASE AGREEMENT

Note*

On July 20, 1999 the executive directors of the World Bank approved IBRD Resolution No. 99-1 on the establishment of a Prototype Carbon Fund. Resolution No. 99-1 was amended on May 15, 2000,[1] and March 22, 2001.[2] The resolution as amended is reproduced below.

The Prototype Carbon Fund (PCF or the Fund) is unique in that it is the first trust fund established by the World Bank which permits contributions from both the public and the private sectors and which also provides something in return. Public sector participants contribute U.S.$ 10 million; private sector participants U.S.$ 5 million. In return they will receive certificated greenhouse gas emission reductions from the projects which the Fund finances. These certificated emission reductions may be used by industrialized countries to help meet their greenhouse

---

* Note contributed by David Freestone, Chief Counsel, Environmentally and Socially Sustainable Development and International Law, Legal Vice Presidency, The World Bank. The author coordinated the legal work on the development of the Fund. For more details *see* David Freestone, *The World Bank's Prototype Carbon Fund: Mobilising New Resources for Sustainable Development* in *Liber Amicorum: Ibrahim Shihata* (K.Y. Tung and S. Schlemmer-Schulte eds., Kluwer Law International 2001).

1 Resolution No 2000-1, "On changing the terms of a Second Closing and on certain other amendments to the Instrument establishing the Prototype Carbon Fund," adopted by the Executive Directors of the International Bank for Reconstruction and Development on May 15, 2000.

2 Resolution No 2000-3, "On changing the composition of the Participants Committee and on certain other amendments to the Instrument establishing the Prototype Carbon Fund," adopted by the Executive Directors of the International Bank for Reconstruction and Development on May 22, 2001.

The World Bank Legal Review: Law and Justice for Development: 433-524.

Printed in the Netherlands.

gas emission reduction targets under the Kyoto Protocol.[3] *Each contributor will receive a share of the emission reduction generated by the total portfolio of PCF projects in proportion to the contribution that it has made.*

The Fund was designed as a closed-end fund which will be wound up at the end of 2012 – the end of the Kyoto Protocol's first commitment period unless the World Bank's Board and the participants in the Fund decide otherwise. As a prototype, the size of the Fund was initially capped at U.S.$ 150 million, but the cap was later raised to U.S.$ 180 million so that all who had expressed interest in contributing would have an opportunity to do so. In the event, after two closings the Fund stands at U.S.$ 145 million.

The first project that the Fund financed is the Liepaja Solid Waste Management Project in Latvia. The Latvia Emission Reductions Purchase Agreement is novel in a number of ways. Not only is it the first PCF project agreement, and the first detailed contract of this kind to be made public, but it also – as its name suggests – follows a new paradigm. It does not use an investment model, as developed by the Global Environment Facility Implementing Agencies, under which grant money is used to finance those specific components of an existing project which are deemed incremental. Instead the PCF, having used an independent third party to satisfy itself that its funding will be "additional" as required by the Kyoto Protocol, agrees to purchase emission reductions from the project once they have been certified by the independent third party – which in time will be the Operational Entities described by the Kyoto Protocol. Also of particular interest is the detailed emission reduction sharing arrangement (see Article II) designed to ensure that Latvia will benefit should future prices of emission reduction units rise substantially.

---

3 The Protocol to the United Nations Framework Convention on Climate Change adopted at the third conference of the parties to the United Nations framework convention on climate change in Kyoto, Japan on December 11, 1997 (available at <http://www.unfccc.de/resource/convkp.html>).

INTERNATIONAL BANK FOR RECONSTRUCTION AND DEVELOPMENT

RESOLUTION NO. 99-1

AUTHORIZING ESTABLISHMENT OF THE PROTOTYPE CARBON FUND

As Amended by Resolutions No. 2000-1[1] *and No. 2001-3*[2]

WHEREAS the International Bank for Reconstruction and Development (the "Bank") desires to promote project-based mechanisms that will help countries to reduce global concentrations of greenhouse gases and therefore minimize the adverse impacts of climate change on developing countries and countries with economies in transition;

WHEREAS in order to further that objective, the Bank desires to establish the Prototype Carbon Fund to be administered by the Bank to provide participants in the Prototype Carbon Fund with the opportunity to finance projects in developing countries and countries with economies in transition to generate greenhouse gas emission reductions which could be transferred to the participants, thereby assisting them in satisfying their obligations under the United Nations Framework Convention on Climate Change, related international agreements and domestic legislation;

---

1 Resolution No. 2000-1, "On changing the terms of a Second Closing and on certain other amendments to the Instrument establishing the Prototype Carbon Fund," approved by the Executive Directors of the International Bank for Reconstruction and Development on May 15, 2000.

2 Resolution No. 2001-3, "On changing the composition of the Participants Committee and on certain other amendments to the Instrument establishing the Prototype Carbon Fund," adopted by the Executive Directors of the International Bank for Reconstruction and Development on March 22, 2001.

NOW THEREFORE IT IS HEREBY RESOLVED AS FOLLOWS:

The Executive Directors hereby establish the Prototype Carbon Fund on the terms and conditions set forth in, and substantially in the form of, Annex I attached to this Resolution.

ANNEX I

International Bank For Reconstruction And Development

INSTRUMENT ESTABLISHING THE PROTOTYPE CARBON FUND

Table of contents

Instrument Establishing the Prototype Carbon Fund

WHEREAS:

(A) The International Bank for Reconstruction and Development desires to promote project-based mechanisms that will help countries to reduce global concentrations of greenhouse gases and therefore minimize the adverse impacts of climate change on developing countries through the establishment of a Prototype Carbon Fund to be administered by the IBRD to provide Participants in the Fund with the opportunity to provide resources to projects in developing countries and countries with economies in transition to generate greenhouse gas Emission Reductions which could be transferred to the Participants, thereby assisting them in satisfying their obligations under the United Nations Framework Convention on Climate Change and related international agreements and domestic legislation;[3]

(B) The IBRD has three strategic objectives in establishing the Fund: first, to demonstrate how project-based Emission Reductions transactions can promote and contribute to the sustainable development of developing countries and countries with economies in transition that are members of the IBRD; second, to share with the Parties to the United Nations Framework Convention on Climate Change and other interested parties knowledge gained by the Trustee and Participants in the course of the Fund's operations during the period when the guidelines, modalities and procedures that will govern project-based Emission Reduction transactions are being negotiated; and third, to demonstrate how the IBRD can work in partnership with the public and private sectors to mobilize new resources for its borrowing member countries while addressing global environmental concerns; and

(C) The IBRD is prepared to establish and administer the Prototype Carbon Fund on the terms and conditions set forth below.

NOW THEREFORE it is hereby resolved that:

---

[3] Text as amended by Resolution 2000-1.

ARTICLE I

DEFINITIONS

Section 1.1. *Definitions.* Unless the context otherwise requires, the following terms shall have the meanings set forth below:

1) "Activities Implemented Jointly" means project activities undertaken under the Activities Implemented Jointly Pilot Phase of the UNFCCC;
2) "Additional Participants" means those Participants that enter into Participation Agreements with the Trustee after the First Closing;
3) "Annex I" means Annex I of the UNFCCC;
4) "Annex I Countries" means the countries listed in Annex I of the UNFCCC and, when appropriate, in Annex B of the Kyoto Protocol;
5) "Annex B" means Annex B of the Kyoto Protocol;
6) "Article 6" means the mechanism defined in Article 6 of the Kyoto Protocol that provides for the transfer and acquisition of Emission Reduction Units between Annex I Countries;
7) "Article 12" means the mechanism (known as the Clean Development Mechanism) defined in Article 12 of the Kyoto Protocol that provides for the transfer of Certified Emission Reductions from non-Annex I Countries to Annex I Countries;
8) "Assigned Amounts" means the quantity of GHG an Annex I Country can release during the first commitment period of the Kyoto Protocol and is equal to the percentage, specified in Annex B, of an Annex I Country's aggregate anthropogenic carbon dioxide equivalent emissions of GHG in 1990, or in another base year as provided by the Kyoto Protocol, multiplied by five;
9) "Association" means the International Development Association, a member of the World Bank Group;
10) "Baseline" means the situation that would have occurred without the implementation of a Project, in particular with respect to Greenhouse Gas emissions or sequestration;
11) "Certification" means the process by which either (i) operational entities designated by the COP/MOP for the purposes of Article 12 and/or, if the UNFCCC Parties deem it appropriate, Article 6 of the Kyoto Protocol or (ii) properly qualified Independent Third Parties certify that the GHG

Reductions achieved by a Project comply with a relevant set of standards or conditions;

12) "Certified Emission Reductions" means the GHG Reductions that are achieved by an Article 12 Project and are certified by operational entities designated by the COP/MOP for the purposes of Article 12 of the Kyoto Protocol;

13) "COP/MOP" means the Conference of the Parties to the UNFCCC serving as the meeting of the Parties to the Kyoto Protocol;

14) "Developing Countries" means those countries not listed in Annex I;

15) "Economies in Transition" or "EIT" means the countries listed in Annex I or Annex B that are undergoing the process of transition to a market economy;

16) "Eligible Private Sector Participant" means any person, other than an Eligible Public Sector Participant, organized in a country Party to the UNFCCC and whose participation in the Fund has been approved by the Trustee;

17) "Eligible Public Sector Participant" means any government, agency, ministry or other official entity of a country Party to the UNFCCC and whose participation in the Fund has been approved by the Trustee;

18) "Emission Reductions" means Emission Reduction Units, Certified Emission Reductions, and, pending the adoption of the relevant guidelines, modalities and procedures under the regulatory framework of the UNFCCC and/or the Kyoto Protocol, GHG Reductions certified by Independent Third Parties as complying with a relevant set of standards or conditions;

19) "Emission Reduction Units" means the GHG Reductions achieved by an Article 6 Project that meet the conditions specified in Article 6 of the Kyoto Protocol including, if the Parties to the UNFCCC deem it appropriate, certification by operational entities designated by the COP/MOP;

20) "First Closing" means the initial closing of the Fund that is expected to occur on or about February 1, 2000, or such later date as may be determined by the Trustee in consultation with the Participants;

21) "Fund Management Committee" means the Committee comprised of the individuals selected by the President of the IBRD and which is responsible for overseeing the operations of the Fund;

22) "Fund Management Unit" means the Fund Manager and other staff selected by the Fund Manager who will perform services for the Fund on a full-time basis;

23) "Fund Manager" means the IBRD staff member selected by the President of the IBRD to head the Fund Management Unit and to act as chairperson of the Fund Management Committee;

24) "Fund Property" or "Property" means all property contributed to the Fund and all other assets, receipts and interests of the Fund;

25) "GHG Reductions" means, with respect to an Article 6 Project, the reduction of GHG emissions and the enhancement of GHG sequestration achieved by such Project and, with respect to an Article 12 Project, the reduction of GHG emissions and, if the Parties to the UNFCCC deem it appropriate, the enhancement of GHG sequestration achieved by such Project;

26) "Global Environment Facility" or "GEF" means the mechanism established by the 1994 Instrument for the Establishment of the Restructured Global Environment Facility;

27) "Greenhouse Gases" or "GHG" means the six gases listed in Annex A of the Kyoto Protocol, which are carbon dioxide, methane, nitrous oxide, hydrofluorocarbons, perfluorocarbons, and sulphur hexafluoride;

28) "High Quality Emission Reductions" means Emission Reductions of a sufficient quality so that, in the opinion of the Trustee at the time a Project is selected and designed, there will be a strong likelihood, to the extent it can be assessed, that Participants may be able to apply their share of Emission Reductions for the purpose of satisfying the requirements of the UNFCCC, related international agreements, or applicable national legislation;

29) "Host Country" means a country that is a member of the IBRD and in which a Project is located;

30) "Host Country Agreement" means an agreement entered into between the Trustee and the Host Country in respect of a Project;

31) "Host Country Committee" means the committee described in Article VII of this Instrument;

32) "Host Country Observer" means a member of the Host Country Committee who is elected to serve as a non-voting observer at a Participants' meeting or a Participants' Committee meeting;

33) "IFC" means the International Finance Corporation, a member of the World Bank Group;

34) "Independent Third Party" means an entity, such as an environmental auditing company, which is independent from the IBRD, the relevant Host Country and the relevant Project Entity;

35) "Initial Participants" means those Participants that entered into Participation Agreements with the Trustee on or before the First Closing;

36) "Instrument" means this Instrument establishing the Prototype Carbon Fund;

37) "Kyoto Protocol" or "Protocol" means the Protocol to the United Nations Framework Convention on Climate Change adopted at the Third Conference of the Parties to the United Nations Framework Convention on Climate Change in Kyoto, Japan on December 11, 1997;

38) "Letter of Endorsement" means the letter from the Host Country to the Trustee confirming that the Host Country is prepared to endorse further development of a Project;

39) "Monitoring" means activities pursuant to which the Project Entity or another person collects and records data which assess the GHG Reductions resulting from a Project pursuant to the terms of the Monitoring and Verification protocol for that Project;

40) "Participant" means any Eligible Private Sector Participant or Eligible Public Sector Participant that has signed a Participation Agreement, or any assignee thereof pursuant to the terms of this Instrument;

41) "Participants' Committee" means the committee described in Article VI of this Instrument;

42) "Participation Agreement" means an agreement between a Participant and the Trustee with respect to the Participant's contribution to, and participation in, the Fund;

43) "person" means and includes individuals, corporations, partnerships, trusts, unincorporated associations, unincorporated organizations, joint ventures and other entities, and governments and agencies and political subdivisions thereof;

44) "Private Sector Participant" means a Participant that is a person, other than a Public Sector Participant, organized in a country Party to the UNFCCC;

45) "Project" means an activity for which the Trustee has agreed to provide financing under Project Agreements, or project resources, in the form of the purchase of Emission Reductions, to Recipients under Project Agreements;[4]

46) "Project Agreement(s)" means a Host Country Agreement, or a Host Country Agreement and a Project Entity Agreement;

[4] Text as amended by Resolution 2000-1.

47) "Project Concept Note" means a brief description of a Project prepared by the Fund Management Unit that is to be presented for consideration by the Fund Management Committee and the Participants' Committee;

48) "Project Entity" means one or more persons with which the Trustee has entered into a Project Entity Agreement;

49) "Project Entity Agreement" means an agreement between the Trustee and a person defined as a Project Entity that provides, *inter alia,* for the implementation, operation and Monitoring of a Project;

50) "Project Portfolio Criteria" means the criteria specified as such in Schedule 1 to the Instrument;

51) "Project Selection Criteria" means the criteria specified as such in Schedule 1 to the Instrument;

52) "Public Sector Participant" means a Participant that is a government, agency, ministry or other official entity of a country Party to the UNFCCC;

53) "Quantified Emission Limitation or Reduction Commitment" or "QELRO" means the commitment by countries listed in Annex B to reduce Greenhouse Gas emissions by the percentage provided for in such Annex from a base year established pursuant to the Kyoto Protocol;

54) "Recipient(s)" means a Host Country, or a Host Country and a Project Entity;

55) "Second Closing" means the additional closing of the Fund that may occur on or about July 14, 2000, or such later date as may be determined by the Trustee in consultation with the Participants;[5]

56) "Third Party Project" means a Project that originates from outside the World Bank Group's project pipeline;

57) "Trustee" means the IBRD acting not in its individual or personal capacity but solely in its capacity as trustee of the Fund;

58) "Underlying Project" means a project financed by the IBRD, the IFC or a third party for which the Fund agrees to provide supplementary financing or resources through a Project;[6]

59) "UNCITRAL" means the United Nations Commission on International Trade Law;

---

[5] Text as amended by Resolution 2000-1.

[6] *Id.*

60) "United Nations Framework Convention on Climate Change" or "UNFCCC" means the United Nations Framework Convention on Climate Change adopted in New York on May 9, 1992;

61) "Validation" means the assessment by a third party of a Project design, including its Baseline, before the Project's implementation;

62) "Verification" means the periodic auditing of the data recorded by the person responsible for Monitoring to verify the amount of Emission Reductions achieved by the Project in relation to its Baseline and the Project's compliance with other relevant requirements;

63) "World Bank Group" means the International Bank for Reconstruction and Development, the International Finance Corporation, the International Development Association and the Multilateral Investment Guarantee Agency;

64) "World Bank Group Operational Policies and Procedures" means the environmental and social operational polices and procedures of the institution of the World Bank Group which conducts the environmental and social review of the Project and which are in effect at the time of such review and the operational policies and procedures of the IBRD in other areas.[7]

[7] Text inserted by Resolution 2001-3.

ARTICLE II

ESTABLISHMENT

Section 2.1. *Establishment.* The Prototype Carbon Fund is hereby established as a trust fund of the IBRD, constituted of the funds that shall from time to time be contributed in accordance with the provisions of this Instrument, and any other Fund Property. The IBRD shall be the Trustee of the Fund and in this capacity shall, as legal owner, hold in trust the Fund Property which constitutes the Fund, and manage and use the Fund Property only for the purposes of and in accordance with the provisions of this Instrument, keeping the Fund Property separate and apart from all other accounts and assets of, or administered by, the IBRD.

Section 2.2. *Trust Only.* It is the intention of the parties to this Instrument to create only the relationship of trustee and beneficiary between the Trustee and each Participant and not to create a general partnership, limited partnership, joint stock association, corporation, bailment or any form of legal relationship other than a trust. Nothing in this Instrument shall be construed so as to make the Participants, either by themselves or with the Trustee, partners or members of a joint stock association.

Section 2.3. *Authority to Enter into Participation Agreements; Maximum Size of Fund.* The Trustee may enter into Participation Agreements with Initial Participants during the period commencing on a date to be determined by the Trustee but not earlier than November 15, 1999, and ending on and including the date of the First Closing. The Trustee may, thereafter, at its discretion, enter into Participation Agreements with Additional Participants during the period commencing after the First Closing and ending on and including the date of the Second Closing; provided that the aggregate amount of contributions to be provided under all of the Participation Agreements shall not exceed U.S.$ 180 million.[8] Except as otherwise provided in this Instrument, the Trustee shall not enter into any Participation Agreements or accept any new contributions from any Participant after the Second Closing.

---

[8] Text as amended by Resolution 2000-1.

ARTICLE III

OPERATIONAL PRINCIPLES AND OPERATIONS OF THE FUND

Section 3.1. *Operational Principles.* The operational principles of the Fund are: (i) to provide resources for Projects which are intended to generate High Quality Emission Reductions; (ii) to endeavor to effect an equitable sharing between the Participants and the Host Countries of any Emission Reductions and other benefits arising from Projects; and (iii) to disseminate broadly the knowledge gained by the Trustee in the development of the Fund and the implementation of Projects.[9]

Section 3.2. *Operations of the Fund.* The Fund shall finance Projects designed to achieve GHG Reductions in return for (i) the exclusive right as against any third party, other than a person authorized under the regulatory framework of the UNFCCC and/or the Kyoto Protocol, to have an Independent Third Party certify the quality and quantity of any GHG Reductions generated by the Projects; and (ii) the right to have transferred to Participants an agreed amount of any Emission Reductions generated. The operations of the Fund may include the provision of project resources in the form of the purchase of Emission Reductions, either directly or through intermediaries.[10] The Trustee shall facilitate the processes of Validation, Verification and Certification whereby an Independent Third Party certifies the quality and quantity of any GHG Reductions achieved by the Projects in accordance with relevant standards and/or criteria to be developed under the regulatory framework of the UNFCCC and/or national laws. The Trustee shall also facilitate the transfer of an agreed amount of any Emission Reductions achieved by each Project from the Recipient to the Participants, on a pro rata basis.

Section 3.3. *Selection of Projects.* The Trustee shall select Projects in accordance with the Project Selection Criteria and with the intent, over the term of the Fund, of meeting the Project Portfolio Criteria. No material changes may be made to the Project Selection Criteria without the prior consent at a Participants' meeting of Participants holding not less than two-thirds of the votes of the Fund.

[9] Text as amended by Resolution 2000-1.

[10] Text introduced by Resolution 2000-1.

Section 3.4. *Compliance with World Bank Group Operational Policies and Procedures.*[11] The operations of the Fund shall comply with the World Bank Group Operational Policies and Procedures, except to the extent that such operational policies and procedures may be inconsistent with the guidelines, modalities and procedures adopted by the Parties to the UNFCCC regarding the procurement of services by Independent Third Parties, in which case the latter shall govern.

---

[11] Text as amended by Resolution 2001-3.

ARTICLE IV

CONTRIBUTIONS FROM PARTICIPANTS

Section 4.1. *Payment of Contributions.*[12] Each Public Sector Participant will be required to contribute US$ 10 million to the Fund and each Private Sector Participant will be required to contribute US$ 5 million to the Fund. Each Initial Participant's and Additional Participant's required contribution to the Fund will be paid at the First Closing and the Second Closing, respectively, through the issuance and delivery of a promissory note made payable to the Trustee on demand. At the First Closing and Second Closing, the Trustee will provide Participants with an anticipated schedule of demands for payment of their respective promissory notes. However, such schedule of payments will remain at the sole discretion of the Trustee, having regard to the financial requirements of the Fund including the anticipated requirements for payments to Recipients under Project Agreements. The Trustee will make demands for payment by Participants under the promissory notes on a pro-rata basis; provided, that the failure of any Participant to make any such payment when due shall not relieve any other Participant of its obligation to make its respective payment. Participants will be entitled to prepay up to the entire amount of their required contribution. No interest will be payable by Participants on any portion of the required contribution not yet demanded by the Trustee or by the Fund on any prepaid portion of the required contribution. The first payment from Initial Participants will be due within 30 days following the First Closing, and the first payment from Additional Participants and a further payment from Initial Participants, if any, will be due within 30 days following the Second Closing. The Trustee will provide Participants with at least 30 days' notice of all subsequent payment demands.

Section 4.2. *Payment of Premium.* All Participation Agreements entered into after the First Closing shall provide that the Additional Participants shall, in addition to their required contribution, pay a premium in an amount equal to 2.5% of the amount of such contribution.[13] The premium shall be payable on the same terms as the contribution. The premium shall not be taken into account in determining the Participant's interests in the Fund or in the calculation of the size of the Fund.

---

[12] Text as amended by Resolution 2000-1.

[13] *Id.*

ARTICLE V

PARTICIPANTS' MEETINGS

Section 5.1. *Participants' Meetings.* A meeting of the Participants shall be held annually, at such date and time and in such place as shall be determined by the Trustee. At each such annual meeting, the Participants may review the operations of the Fund and existing Projects to provide the Trustee with general policy and strategic guidance on the operations of the Fund and shall have the following powers and duties:

a) reviewing and approving the business plan and annual budget for the Fund for the next fiscal year;
b) reviewing and approving by a two-thirds majority of the votes of the Fund any amendments to the Project Selection Criteria or the Project Portfolio Criteria, other than amendments that in the Trustee's opinion are merely technical in nature; provided, that any such amendment shall be consistent with World Bank Group Operational Policies and Procedures in the opinion of the Trustee and otherwise be acceptable to the Trustee;[14]
c) providing general guidance to the Trustee on the selection of Projects;
d) commencing with the second annual Participants' meeting, electing the members of the Participants' Committee to serve until the next annual Participants' meeting;
e) for each of the first ten annual Participants' meetings, reviewing and, if acceptable, approving the recommendation, if any, of the Participants' Committee regarding a performance-linked payment to be paid to the Trustee for the preceding fiscal year pursuant to Section 11.3 hereof;
f) at the first annual Participants' meeting, reviewing and authorizing the payment to the IBRD of any development costs related to the Fund's establishment not presented at the organizational Participants' meeting; and
g) taking any other action that may be taken by the Participants under this Instrument.

Special meetings of the Participants may be called at any time by the Trustee for any purpose consistent with this Instrument, including without limitation voting

---

[14] Text as amended by Resolution 2001-3.

on the removal of Ineligible Participants pursuant to Section 9.2 hereof. At any such special meeting, one or more Participants may, if all of the other Participants participating in the meeting consent, participate by means of such telephone or other communications facilities as permit all Participants participating in the meeting to hear each other or participate by other electronic means, and a Participant participating in such a meeting by such means is deemed for the purposes of this Instrument to be present at that meeting.

Section 5.2. *Organizational Meeting*. The Trustee shall convene an organizational Participants' meeting within 14 days of the First Closing, at such date and time and in such place as shall be determined by the Trustee. At such organizational Participants' meeting, the Participants shall have the following powers and duties:

a) reviewing and approving the business plan and budget for the Fund for the period from the First Closing to the last day of the fiscal year of the Fund in which the organizational Participants' meeting is held;
b) electing the members of the Participants' Committee to serve for a term running from the date of the organizational Participants' meeting until the second annual Participants' meeting; and
c) reviewing and authorizing the payment to the IBRD of the development costs related to the Fund's establishment.

Section 5.3. *Notice*. The Trustee shall provide each Participant and each Host Country Observer with written notice of a Participants' meeting not less than 30 days before the date of the meeting unless such notice has been waived by the intended recipient. Such notice shall state the place, date, and time of the meeting and, in the case of a special meeting, the purpose or purposes for which the meeting is called. Notwithstanding this Section, written notice of the organizational Participants' meeting shall be given to the Participants and each Host Country Observer on the First Closing.

Section 5.4. *Voting*. Each Participant shall be entitled to one vote for each US dollar of its contribution to the Fund (exclusive of any premium paid) on each matter submitted for a vote at a meeting of the Participants. Except as otherwise provided, every matter submitted to a Participants' meeting shall be decided by the majority of the votes cast by Participants represented at such Participants' meeting.

Section 5.5. *Quorum*. Participants represented at a meeting of the Participants holding a majority of all the votes of the Fund shall constitute a quorum for the transaction of business at a Participants' meeting.

Section 5.6. *Action Without Meeting.* Action required or permitted to be taken at a Participants' meeting may be taken without a meeting if a consent in writing, setting forth the action to be so taken, has been circulated to all of the Participants and Host Country Observers and signed in one or more counterparts by Participants holding not less than two-thirds of the votes of the Fund or, in the case of an action requiring unanimous approval, by all Participants.

Section 5.7. *Proxies.* Any Participant entitled to vote at a Participants' meeting may vote by proxy if a duly executed proxy has been received by the Trustee for verification prior to the meeting.

ARTICLE VI

PARTICIPANTS' COMMITTEE

Section 6.1. *Participants' Committee.*

(a) At the organizational Participants' meeting, the Participants will establish a Participants' Committee, which shall be comprised of seven.[15] The members of the Participants' Committee shall be officers, directors, employees or officials of Participants; provided, that not more than one member shall be a representative of the same Participant. The members of the Participants' Committee shall be elected by majority vote of the votes cast at a Participants' meeting. At the organizational Participants' meeting, the Participants shall elect members of the Participants' Committee for a term running from such meeting to the date of the second annual Participants' meeting. At the second annual Participants' meeting and at each annual Participants' meeting thereafter, the Participants shall elect members of the Participants' Committee to be members until the next succeeding annual Participants' meeting. The Participants' Committee shall elect one of its members to serve as chairperson until such time as such member has ceased to be a member of the Participants' Committee or until such member's successor as chairperson has been elected.

(b) Each member of the Participants' Committee shall serve until the member's successor shall have been elected; provided, that at the time a member of the Participants' Committee ceases to be an officer, director, employee or official of a Participant, such member's term as a member of the Participants' Committee shall cease. That Participant may appoint another officer, director, employee or official of such Participant to fill any vacancy in the Participants' Committee resulting from the resignation, death or incapacity of a member that is or was an officer, director, employee or official of such Participant, failing which, after 30 days, any vacancy in the Participants' Committee shall be filled by the affirmative vote of a majority of the remaining members of the Participants' Committee. A member elected to fill such a vacancy shall be elected for the unexpired term of the member's predecessor in office. At any time, any member of the Participants'

---

[15] Text as amended by Resolution 2001-3.

Committee may be removed by the Participant for which such member is a representative and replaced with another representative of that Participant.

(c) The Participants' Committee elected at the organizational Participants' meeting shall be comprised of four members who are officials of Public Sector Participants and three members who are officers, directors or employees of Private Sector Participants. The Participants' Committee elected at the second annual Participants' meeting shall be comprised of three members who are officials of Public Sector Participants and four members who are officers, directors or employees of Private Sector Participants.[16] Thereafter, the representation of Public Sector Participants and Private Sector Participants on subsequent Participants' Committees will alternate annually between three and four members, respectively, unless the Participants shall decide unanimously to adopt an alternative procedure.[17]

Section 6.2. *Actions of the Participants' Committee*. Each member of the Participants' Committee shall be entitled to cast one vote, and a majority of the members of the Participants' Committee present at a meeting shall constitute a quorum for the transaction of business. Every matter submitted to the Participants' Committee shall be decided by the majority vote of the votes cast at the meeting; provided, that the actions referred to in Section 6.4(c) hereof shall be approved unless at least two members of the Participants' Committee object within 30 days of the presentation, by the Trustee, of the relevant Project Concept Note to the Participants.

Section 6.3. *Meetings of the Participants' Committee*. Meetings of the Participants' Committee shall be called by the chairperson or the Trustee. Each member of the Participants' Committee, each Host Country Observer and the Trustee shall be given at least 14 days' written notice of any Participants' Committee meeting unless such notice has been waived by the intended recipient. Such notice shall specify the matters to be considered and shall designate the place, date, and time of the meeting. One or more members of the Participants' Committee may, if all of the other members of the Participants' Committee participating in the meeting consent, participate in a meeting of the Participants' Committee by means of such telephone or other communications facilities as permit all members participating

[16] Text as amended by Resolution 2001-3.

[17] *Id.*

in the meeting to hear each other or participate by other electronic means, and a member of the Participants' Committee participating in such a meeting by such means is deemed for the purposes of this Instrument to be present at that meeting. No member of the Participants' Committee shall receive any compensation from the Fund for its services as such, nor shall any member of the Participants' Committee be entitled to payment or reimbursement from the Fund or Trustee for travel or other costs incurred in attending meetings of the Participants' Committee.

Section 6.4. *Powers and Duties of Participants' Committee.* The Participants' Committee shall have the following powers and duties:

a) providing general advice to the Trustee on issues regarding the operation of the Fund;
b) reviewing the operations of the Fund and advising the Trustee on the extent to which the Project Agreements negotiated and to be entered into by the Trustee accord with the Project Selection Criteria;
c) reviewing Project Concept Notes for each proposed Project in order to determine whether to object to the inclusion of such Project in the Fund's portfolio;
d) for each of the first ten years of the Fund, providing recommendations to the annual Participants' meeting regarding the making of a performance-linked payment to the Trustee pursuant to Section 11.3 of this Instrument for the preceding fiscal year of the Fund; and
e) for any fiscal year, authorizing expenditures, other than those incurred pursuant to Section 8.1(i) and Article XII of this Instrument, which exceed the total annual budget previously approved by the Participants for that fiscal year by more than 10%.

ARTICLE VII

HOST COUNTRY COMMITTEE

Section 7.1. *Host Country Committee.* The Trustee shall invite each Host Country and each potential Host Country that has signed a Letter of Endorsement or a memorandum of understanding with the Trustee with respect to the Fund to appoint a representative to serve on the Host Country Committee. Such Host Country or potential Host Country may also invite one Project Entity or potential Project Entity which is expected to implement a Project in its territory to appoint a representative to attend meetings of the Host Country Committee as a non-voting observer.

Section 7.2. *Powers of the Host Country Committee.* The Host Country Committee shall have the following powers:

a) providing advice to the Trustee, copied to the Participants, on proposed amendments to the Project Selection Criteria and Project Portfolio Criteria;
b) providing advice to the Trustee, copied to the Participants, on the composition of the Project portfolio and providing views on the consistency of the Project portfolio with the regulatory framework of the UNFCCC;
c) providing advice to the Trustee, copied to the Participants, on how to effect an equitable sharing between the Participants and the Host Countries of any Emission Reductions and other benefits arising from Projects;
d) providing advice to the Trustee, copied to the Participants, on Project implementation, including the processes of Validation, Verification and Certification; and
e) providing advice to the Trustee on the development and improvement of vehicles for the dissemination of the knowledge gained by it in the development of the Fund and the implementation of Projects.

Section 7.3. *Election of Chairperson and Host Country Observers.*

(a) At its first meeting, the Host Country Committee shall elect one of its members as chairperson of the Host Country Committee to serve as such until the chairperson's successor has been elected. The Host Country Committee shall also elect three of its members to serve as Host Country Observers at Participants' meetings and one of its members to serve as a Host Country Observer at Participants' Committee meetings, until each such member's successor has been elected. Such Host Country Observers shall be entitled to be present at all Participants' meetings or Participants' Committee meetings, as the case may be. The Host Country Observers shall receive no compensation from the Fund or Trustee for their services as such nor shall they be entitled to payment or reimbursement from the Fund or Trustee for travel or other costs incurred in attending the relevant meetings.

(b) Until such time as the initial Host Country Observers have been elected, the Trustee shall designate and invite specific members of the Host Country Committee to attend meetings of the Participants and meetings of the Participants' Committee.

Section 7.4. *Meetings of the Host Country Committee*. Meetings of the Host Country Committee shall be held at least annually, at such dates and times and in such places as shall be determined by the Trustee to permit the Host Country Committee to interact with the Participants.

Section 7.5. *Notice*. The Trustee shall provide each member of the Host Country Committee with written notice of a Host Country Committee meeting not less than 30 days before the date of the meeting unless such notice has been waived by the intended recipient. Such notice shall state the place, date and time of the meeting.

ARTICLE VIII

ADMINISTRATION

Section 8.1. *Authorization and Administration.* The administration of the Fund shall be governed by the following provisions:

a) The Trustee shall hold all Fund Property in trust for the benefit of the Participants. The Trustee shall manage and use Fund Property only for the purposes of, and in accordance with, the provisions of this Instrument, keeping it separate and apart from the assets of the IBRD, the IFC and the Association but may commingle it for investment purposes with other trust fund assets maintained by the IBRD, the IFC or the Association. At its discretion, the Trustee may at any time exchange any funds received from a Participant or any other Fund Property for one or more other currencies in order to facilitate the administration of the Fund.

b) The Trustee shall exercise the same care in the discharge of its functions under this Instrument as the IBRD exercises with respect to its own affairs and shall not have any additional obligation in respect hereof. The privileges and immunities accorded to the IBRD shall apply to the Property, archives, operations and transactions of the Fund. The obligations of the Trustee pursuant to this Instrument are not obligations of any government.

c) The Trustee is authorized to enter into Participation Agreements and accept contributions in the required amount from Participants at any time after a date to be determined by the Trustee, but not earlier than November 15, 1999, through the Second Closing, as provided in this Instrument. The Trustee shall not be authorized to recognize more than one person joining together as a joint Participant. Participation Agreements shall be in form and substance satisfactory to the Trustee. The Trustee shall use the contributions to the Fund and the income earned from the investment of such contributions pending disbursement solely for the purposes set out in this Instrument.

d) The Trustee may, at any time and with the approval of Participants holding not less than two-thirds of the votes cast at any meeting of Participants, solicit an amount of voluntary supplementary contributions from Participants. No Participant will have any obligation to contribute such additional amount. Any such voluntary supplementary contribution made by a Participant will be taken into account in determining the Participants' pro rata interests in the Fund, and the pro rata interest of a Participant may be reduced or increased depending upon the amount, if any, of such voluntary supplementary contributions. No premium (as described above) will be payable by Participants in respect of any supplementary contributions. The aggregate amount of contributions to be made to the Fund, including any voluntary supplementary contributions under this Section, will under no circumstances exceed US$ 180 million (exclusive of any premium paid by Participants).[18]

e) The Trustee is authorized to perform all acts and enter into all contracts as it shall deem necessary or desirable to accomplish the purposes of the Fund, including, without limitation, Project Agreements. Subject to the terms of this Instrument, the selection of Recipients and Projects, the preparation and negotiation of Project Agreements and the monitoring and supervision of Projects shall be the responsibility solely of the Trustee.

f) The Trustee is authorized to invest funds held by the Fund pending disbursement in such manner as it may decide. All the income from such investments shall be credited to, and used exclusively for the purposes of, the Fund. Without limiting the foregoing, the Trustee shall have the power to invest Fund Property in such securities, instruments and other obligations as are authorized investments for other trust fund assets maintained by the IBRD, the IFC or the Association or retain Fund assets in cash; from time to time to change the investments of the assets of the Fund; and to exercise any and all rights, powers and privileges of ownership or interest in respect of any and all such investments of any kind and description, including, without limitation, the right to consent and otherwise act with respect thereto, with power to designate one or more individuals, firms, associations or corporations to exercise any of said rights, powers and privileges in respect of any of said instruments. The Trustee shall not be limited to investing in obligations maturing before the possible termination of the Fund, nor shall the Trustee be limited by any law limiting the investments which may be made by fiduciaries.

g) To ensure the efficient operation of the Fund's cash management and investment transactions, the Trustee shall have the power to borrow from commercial banks and other financial institutions, for periods of up to thirty days, in any currency or currency unit.

---

[18] Text as amended by Resolution 2000-1.

h) The Trustee shall have the power to incur and pay any costs or expenses which in its opinion are necessary or desirable to carry out any of the purposes of the Fund, and to make payments from Fund Property to itself as Trustee to the extent provided in this Instrument; provided, that without the approval of the Participants' Committee, such costs or expenses, other than those incurred pursuant to Section 8.1(i) and Article XII of this Instrument, shall not exceed the total annual budget for the Fund previously approved by the Participants by more than 10%.

i) The Trustee shall have the power to collect all property due to the Fund and to pay all claims against Fund Property. The Trustee shall have the power to engage in and to prosecute, defend, compromise, abandon, or adjust, by arbitration, or otherwise, any actions, suits, proceedings, disputes, claims, and demands relating to the Fund, including without limitation those relating to Project Agreements, and out of the Property of the Fund to pay or to satisfy any debts, claims or expenses incurred in connection therewith, including those of litigation, and such power shall include without limitation the power of the Trustee to dismiss any action, suit, proceeding, dispute, claim, or demand, derivative or otherwise, brought by any person, including a Participant in its own name or the name of the Fund, whether or not the Fund or the Trustee may be named individually therein or the subject matter arises by reason of business for or on behalf of the Fund.

j) The Trustee shall have the power to: (i) employ or contract with such individuals or persons as it may deem desirable to conduct the business of the Fund; (ii) enter into joint ventures, partnerships, and any other combinations or associations; (iii) subject to the terms of this Instrument, elect and remove such officers and appoint and terminate such agents or employees of the Fund as it considers appropriate; (iv) purchase and pay for out of Fund Property, to the extent available on commercially reasonable terms, such insurance as the Trustee deems desirable to protect it, the IBRD, the Participants and any other individual or person entitled to indemnification by the Fund; and (v) make amendments to the Project Selection Criteria or Project Portfolio Criteria that in its opinion are merely technical in nature.

k) The Trustee may from time to time appoint or otherwise engage one or more banks or trust companies or other financial institutions to serve as escrow agent(s) on behalf of the Fund in respect of Fund Property that may be deposited into an escrow account pending disbursement.

l) Except as otherwise provided in this Instrument, the Trustee shall have the exclusive power to conduct the business of the Fund and carry on its operations wheresoever the Trustee deems necessary, proper or desirable in order to promote the interests of the Fund. Any determination made by the Trustee in good faith as to what is in the interests of the Fund shall be conclusive. In construing the provisions of this Instrument, the presumption shall be in favor of a grant of power to the Trustee. The enumeration of any specific power herein shall not be construed as limiting the aforesaid power. Such powers of the Trustee may be exercised without order of or resort to any court or other authority.

m) Nothing in this Instrument shall preclude the IBRD from acting for its own account and from entering into or being interested in any contract or transaction with any person, including, but not limited to, any Participant, Host Country or Project Entity, with the same rights as it would have had if it were not acting as the Trustee, and the IBRD need not account for any profit therefrom.

n) Any power, duty or discretion to be exercised by the Trustee pursuant to the terms of this Instrument shall, unless otherwise provided, be exercised by the Trustee in its sole discretion.

Section 8.2. *Project Validation, Verification and Certification of Greenhouse Gas Reductions.* The Trustee may from time to time enter into one or more contracts with persons for such services, and on such terms and conditions, as the Trustee shall consider appropriate with respect to Project Validation, as well as for Verification and Certification of GHG Reductions. Without limiting the foregoing, such services may include:

a) Validation of the Project's design, primarily on the basis of the Project Appraisal Document and other relevant documentation prepared during Project development;

b) Verification of GHG Reductions and of Project compliance with relevant requirements specified in the Project Entity Agreements;

c) Certification of GHG Reductions by operational entities designated by the Parties to the UNFCCC or, pending the adoption of the relevant guidelines, modalities and procedures, by an Independent Third Party; and

d) Submission of periodic reports to the Trustee concerning (i) actions recommended to be taken by the Trustee or the Recipient to address problems relating to Project specifications, criteria or objectives; (ii) risks that may materialize in future Verification periods; and (iii) any suggested means of improving Project performance.

Section 8.3. *Administrative Services.* The Trustee may from time to time contract with one or more persons (including with related persons such as the IBRD) for goods, services, and personnel whereby such persons will provide to the Trustee or to the Fund, goods, services or administrative personnel on such terms and conditions as the Trustee may determine.

Section 8.4. *Registrar, Transfer Agent and/or Custodian Services.* The Trustee may from time to time engage one or more persons to act as registrar, transfer agent and/or custodian on behalf of the Fund in respect of Fund Property, instruments evidencing entitlement to Emission Reductions, or other interests of the Participants, on such terms and conditions as the Trustee may determine.

Section 8.5. *Parties to Contract.* Any payment, transaction or contract which is authorized under this Instrument may be made or entered into, as the case may be, with any person, and the validity of any such payment, transaction or contract shall not be affected by reason of the existence of any relationship between the Trustee and any such person; nor shall any person holding such relationship be liable merely by reason of such relationship for any loss or expense to the Fund under or by reason of said payment, transaction or contract or accountable for any profit realized directly or indirectly therefrom.

Section 8.6. *Limits on Trustee's Powers.* Notwithstanding any other provision of this Instrument, the Trustee shall not:

a) incur any costs or expenses, other than those incurred pursuant to Section 8.1(i) and Article XII of this Instrument, for the account of the Fund in any fiscal year or thereafter which exceed the total annual budget previously approved by the Participants by more than 10%, excluding development costs reimbursable under Section 11.2, without the approval of the Participants' Committee; or

b) commit Fund Property to the preparation of a Project unless the Trustee has presented a Project Concept Note to the Participants' Committee and less than two members of the Participants' Committee have objected to the preparation of the Project within 30 days thereafter.

Section 8.7. *Fund Management Committee.* The Trustee shall establish a Fund Management Committee comprised of five members, consisting of the Fund Manager and four other members of the IBRD's management, who shall be selected by the President of the IBRD. The Fund Manager will chair and coordinate the business of the Fund Management Committee, including its meetings and decision-making schedules. The Fund Management Committee shall be responsible for overseeing the operations of the Fund, and it shall also (i) approve each Project proposal prior to the Participants' Committee review of such Project; (ii) review and decide whether to proceed with a Project after due consideration of comments received by any Participants after the Participants' Committee review; (iii) review and, if acceptable, approve each Project Agreement following its negotiation by the Trustee with the Host Country and Project Entity, but prior to its execution; (iv) approve each business plan and annual budget for the Fund prior to their submission to the Participants at their annual meeting; (v) approve expenses for the account of the Fund which exceed the total annual budget previously approved by the Participants by more than 10% of that budget, if deemed necessary for the continuation of the Fund's operations; and (vi) supervise the knowledge-sharing activities of the Fund in furtherance of the Fund's knowledge dissemination principle set forth in Section 3.1(iii) of this Instrument.

Section 8.8. *Fund Management Unit.* A Fund Management Unit shall be established by the Trustee. The Fund Manager shall head the Fund Management Unit as the chief executive officer and shall have overall responsibility for the day-to-day operations of the Fund, including, without limitation: (i) overseeing the operations of the Fund Management Unit, including the selection of its staff; (ii) representing the Fund's interests at international fora and maintaining contact with Participants and Recipients; (iii) overseeing the selection of Projects, reviewing Projects during their appraisal, implementation and operation, and negotiating Project Agreements; (iv) ensuring compliance with Project Selection Criteria and Project Portfolio Criteria; (v) seeking to ensure consistency, to the extent possible, of the Fund's operations with the regulatory framework of the UNFCCC and the World Bank Group Operational Policies and Procedures;[19] and (vi) collecting, organizing, managing, and disseminating the knowledge and information obtained by the Trustee in the course of its operation of the Fund.

---

[19] Text as amended by Resolution 2001-3.

ARTICLE IX

DEFAULT AND REMOVAL OF PARTICIPANTS

Section 9.1. *Default in Paying Installment.*

(a) If, after demanded by the Trustee, a Participant (the "Defaulting Participant") fails to pay any installment of a contribution (or any part thereof) when due and such failure continues for 15 days, the Trustee shall notify the Defaulting Participant and the other Participants of such default. If, after 30 days from such notification, the Defaulting Participant fails to pay such amount in full, the Trustee will so notify the other Participants. Any of the other Participants may, between 15 and 30 days following such notice from the Trustee, notify the Trustee that it intends to purchase the Defaulting Participant's interest in the Fund. If only one Participant so notifies the trustee, the Trustee shall notify such Participant that it may purchase the Defaulting Participant's interest in the Fund by making payment (i) to the Defaulting Participant of an amount equal to 50% of the fair market value (as determined by an independent third party selected by the Trustee) of the Defaulting Participant's pro rata interest in the Fund (the "Purchase Price"), less any expenses incurred by the Trustee or the Fund in connection with the sale, and (ii) to the Trustee of the amount of the unpaid installment due to the Fund from the Defaulting Participant.

(b) If more than one Participant notifies the Trustee of an intention to purchase the Defaulting Participant's interest in the Fund, then the Trustee shall so notify each such Participant that elects to purchase a portion of the Defaulting Participant's interest in the Fund, and each such Participant may purchase that portion of the Defaulting Participant's interest that corresponds to the electing Participant's proportion of the interest of all the electing Participants' interests in the Fund.

(c) If no Participant notifies the Trustee of an intention to purchase the Defaulting Participant's interest in the Fund, the Trustee may arrange for a private sale of such interest to a person acceptable to the Trustee.

(d) The Defaulting Participant shall receive from the proceeds of the sale an amount equal to the lesser of the sale proceeds or the Purchase Price, less any expenses incurred by the Trustee or the Fund in connection with the sale. Upon disposition of the Defaulting Participant's interest as described above, the Defaulting Participant shall be deemed to have transferred to the purchaser(s) all of its rights and interest in the Fund, including without limitation, any further distributions of Fund Property which it is entitled to receive, and the Trustee shall consent to such transfer.

(e) If there is no sale of a Defaulting Participant's interest in the Fund within 90 days following the default of such Defaulting Participant, such Defaulting Participant shall thereupon, without any further notice or action by the Trustee, be deemed to have forfeited all of its rights and interest in the Fund, including, without limitation, the right to further distributions of Fund Property which it is entitled to receive, and such rights and interest shall thereupon, without any further notice or action by the Trustee, be cancelled.

Section 9.2. *Removal of Ineligible Participants.*

(a) If, following the development by the Parties to the UNFCCC and/or the Kyoto Protocol of criteria for the financing of Article 6 or Article 12 Projects or for the transfer of Emission Reductions, in the opinion of the Trustee the continued participation of any Participant (the "Ineligible Participant") will prevent the transfer to the Participants of Emission Reductions which are capable of being credited towards Annex I Countries' QELROs and/or prevents the Fund from financing Article 6 or Article 12 Projects, the Trustee, having obtained approval of a two-thirds majority of the votes of the Fund, exclusive of the Ineligible Participant, may require the removal of the Ineligible Participant from the Fund and shall notify the Participants of such decision. Any of the other Participants may, between 15 and 30 days following such notice from the Trustee, notify the Trustee that it intends to purchase the Ineligible Participant's interest in the Fund. If only one Participant so notifies the Trustee, the Trustee shall notify such Participant that it may purchase the Ineligible Participant's interest in the Fund by making payment to the Ineligible Participant of an amount equal to the fair market value (as determined by an independent third party selected by the Trustee) of the Ineligible Participant's pro rata share of the Fund (the "Purchase Price").

(b) If more than one Participant notifies the Trustee of its intention to purchase the Ineligible Participant's interest in the Fund, then the Trustee will so notify each such Participant that does elect to purchase a portion of the Ineligible Participant's interest and each such Participant may purchase that portion of the Ineligible Participant's interest that corresponds to the electing Participants' proportion of the interest of all the electing Participants' interest in the Fund.

(c) If no Participant notifies the Trustee of an intention to purchase the Ineligible Participant's interest in the Fund, the Trustee may arrange for a private sale of such interest to a purchaser acceptable to the Trustee.

(d) The Ineligible Participant shall receive from the proceeds of a sale referred to in Section 9.2(b) or (c) above an amount equal to the lesser of the Purchase Price or the amount realized from such sale less the costs of such sale, as determined by the Trustee. The Ineligible Participant shall be deemed to have transferred to the purchaser(s) all of its rights and interest in the Fund, including any further distributions of Fund Property which it is entitled to receive, and the Trustee shall consent to such transfer.

(e) If there is no sale of an Ineligible Participant's interest in the Fund within 90 days following notice from the Trustee of the removal of the Ineligible Participant, the Trustee shall redeem the Ineligible Participant's interest in the Fund upon payment, out of then available Fund resources, of an amount equal to the Purchase Price (or a part thereof) as provided below. In the event that there are then insufficient available Fund resources to make such payment in full, the Purchase Price (or any part thereof remaining unpaid) shall be paid out of the proceeds of the next succeeding drawdown of the remaining Participants' funding obligations, in which case the Ineligible Participant shall be entitled to receive interest (at the prevailing rate as determined by the Trustee) on the Purchase Price remaining unpaid from the date of redemption of the Ineligible Participant's interest to the date payment is made. If there is no sale of an Ineligible Participant's interest as described above or if, within 120 days following notice from the Trustee of the removal of the Ineligible Participant, the Trustee determines that there are then insufficient available Fund resources and insufficient further funding obligations of the remaining Participants to pay the Purchase Price, such Ineligible Participant shall, without any further notice or action by the Trustee, be deemed to have forfeited all of its rights and interest in the Fund, including, without limitation, the right to Emission Reductions and any further distribution of Fund assets which it is entitled to receive, and such rights and interest shall be cancelled.

ARTICLE X

FISCAL YEAR; RECORDS AND REPORTS

Section 10.1. *Fiscal Year*. The fiscal year of the Fund shall be the same as the fiscal year of the IBRD, which runs from July 1 to June 30 of the following year.

Section 10.2. *Business Plan; Annual Budget*. The Trustee shall prepare a business plan which shall include a proposed budget for the operation of the Fund for each fiscal year and submit such proposed business plan and budget to the Participants for their consideration at the annual Participants' meeting no later than 30 days prior to the commencement of such fiscal year, except that the business plan and budget to be submitted to the Participants at the organizational Participants' meeting shall be provided to the Participants at the First Closing.

Section 10.3. *Financial Statements*. The Trustee shall maintain separate record and ledger accounts in respect of the Fund. Within 90 days of each – March 31, June 30, September 30 and December 31 – the Trustee shall prepare financial statements with respect to the Fund and forward a copy to each of the Participants. The annual financial statements shall be audited financial statements. The Trustee shall cause such annual financial statement to be audited by the same auditors as are engaged by the IBRD from time to time and shall send a copy of the auditors' report to each of the Participants.

Section 10.4. *Reports to Participants*. The Trustee shall within 90 days of each June 30 and December 31 prepare a report on the operation of the Fund for the preceding six-month period and send a copy to each of the Participants. Each such report shall contain a Project status report, including a cash flow, cost analysis and disbursement schedule for the Projects, and information on any changes to the structure or operations of the Fund resulting from decisions of the Participants at the preceding annual Participants' Meeting. Each such Participants' report shall be accompanied by a statement of account for each Participant evidencing such Participant's share of Fund Property.

Section 10.5. *Other Documentation*. To the extent consistent with the IBRD's, the IFC's or a Third Party Project sponsor's policies, as applicable, with respect to disclosure of information, the Trustee shall provide the Participants with copies of all final documents prepared or received by the Trustee with respect to each Project (including, without limitation, project concept notes, project concept documents, project appraisal documents, validation reports, and verification reports) and, from time to time as warranted, in the Trustee's discretion, with information on good practices and lessons of experience learned by the Trustee from the development and operation of the Fund, including, without limitation, methodological research and procedures for Validation and Verification. The Trustee shall prepare and keep updated a specific "Project Information Document" for each Project which shall be made publicly available through IBRD's Public Information Center. The Trustee will report to the UNFCCC Secretariat on Projects in accordance with reporting requirements established by the Parties to UNFCCC as and when such requirements are established.

ARTICLE XI

EXPENSES AND FEES

Section 11.1. *Expenses*. Fund Property shall be used by the Trustee to pay or reimburse it or any other person, including the IBRD and the IFC, for all costs and expenses incurred in the administration of the Fund, including without limitation: (i) all costs incurred in connection with the appraisal, selection, and supervision of Projects; (ii) costs of office space and facilities, equipment, and supplies and services, including, without limitation, the cost of utility services; (iii) communication expenses, including, without limitation, mailing, telephone, and facsimile expenses; (iv) salaries, benefits, travel, accommodation, and subsistence expenses of all personnel performing services in respect of the Fund, including, without limitation, those incidental to the appraisal, selection and supervision of Projects; (v) expenses for documentary and other relevant requirements, including fees relating to the UNFCCC and/or the Kyoto Protocol, project approval and validation, verification and certification processes; (vi) any payments required in connection with Article 12 Projects and, if the Parties to the UNFCCC deem it appropriate, in connection with Article 6 Projects; (vii) any compensation and expenses of any consultant, agent, adviser, contractor or subcontractor engaged by the Trustee for the Fund; (viii) costs of any insurance policies obtained in connection with, or on behalf of, the Fund, Participants or other persons; (ix) costs of legal, accounting and auditing services provided in respect of the Fund; and (x) public relations and representation costs.

Section 11.2. *Fund Development Costs*. Upon presentation to the Participants at the organizational meeting or a subsequent annual meeting of the Participants of an itemized statement thereof, Fund Property shall also be used by the Trustee to reimburse the IBRD for 80% of all costs and expenses incurred by the IBRD prior to the First Closing of the Fund in relation to the development of the Fund, including, without limitation: (i) the salaries and benefits of personnel of the IBRD; (ii) the travel, accommodation, and subsistence expenses of personnel of the IBRD; (iii) compensation and expenses of any consultant, adviser, contractor, subcontractor, or auditor retained by the IBRD, including, without limitation, legal advisers, and (iv) costs and expenses associated with the preparation of all legal documentation in respect to the formation and operation of the Fund; provided however, that the aggregate amount of Fund Property so used for such purposes shall not exceed U.S.$ 2 million, and the amount of Fund Property to be so used shall be paid to the IBRD in five equal annual installments. In addition to the foregoing, Fund Property may also be used by the Trustee to reimburse the IBRD for all costs and expenses incurred by the IBRD prior to the First Closing of the Fund in relation to the identification, preparation and appraisal of proposed Projects, provided the IBRD has obtained the express agreement of Participants therefor.

Section 11.3. *Performance-linked Payment.* During each of the first ten years of the Fund's operations, the IBRD may be entitled to receive a performance-linked payment of up to U.S.$ 100,000, payable annually as soon as practicable after June 30 of each fiscal year, based upon the performance of the Fund during the preceding fiscal year. The amount of this payment, if any, to be paid to the Trustee for any fiscal year shall be determined by the Participants at their discretion at the annual Participants' meeting taking into account performance indicators determined by the Participants, including, without limitation, the number and quality of the Projects developed, compliance with the Project Selection Criteria and Project Portfolio Criteria, and the cost effectiveness of the Trustee's management of the Fund.

ARTICLE XII

INDEMNIFICATION

Section 12.1. *Indemnification of Trustee and IBRD*. The Trustee, the IBRD, and any person who is, or has been, an officer, employee or agent of the Trustee, the IBRD or the Fund (each an "Indemnified Party") shall be indemnified out of Fund Property against any loss, liability, cost, claim, action, demand or expense (including, but not limited to, all reasonable costs, charges, and expenses paid or incurred in disputing or defending any of the foregoing) which any Indemnified Party may incur or which may be made against any of them arising out of or in connection with the Fund's activities (including, without limitation, any such claims arising from Participants' actions or failure to act pursuant to this Instrument), except as may result from the Trustee's gross negligence or willful misconduct.

Section 12.2. *Indemnification of Participants*. The Trustee will indemnify, out of Fund Property only, each of the Participants against any loss, liability, cost, claim, action, demand or expense (including, but not limited to, all reasonable costs, charges, and expenses paid or incurred in disputing or defending any of the foregoing) which a Participant may incur or which may be made against a Participant arising out of or in connection with the Fund's activities, except as may result from its gross negligence or willful misconduct.

Section 12.3. *No Waiver of Privileges and Immunities*. Nothing in this Instrument shall be considered to be a waiver of any privileges and immunities of the Trustee, the IBRD, or where applicable, the Participants or their respective officers, employees or agents, under the Articles of Agreement of the IBRD or any applicable law, all of which are expressly reserved.

Section 12.4. *No Personal Liability*. Neither the Trustee, the IBRD and the Participants nor any officer, employee or agent of any of the foregoing shall be subject to any personal liability whatsoever to any third party in connection with the activities of the Fund, and all such third parties shall look solely to Fund Property for satisfaction of claims of any nature arising in connection with Fund activities. Every written obligation, contract, instrument, certificate or undertaking made or issued by the Trustee shall recite that the same is executed or made by it not personally or in its individual capacity, but as Trustee of the Fund under this Instrument, and that the obligations of the Fund under any such instrument are not binding upon the Trustee or any of the Participants, personally or in their respective individual capacities, but bind only the Fund, and may contain any further recital which the Trustee may deem appropriate, but the omission of such recital shall not affect the validity of such obligation, contract, instrument, certificate or undertaking and shall not operate to bind or obligate the Trustee or the Participants personally or in their respective individual capacities.

Section 12.5. *No Duty of Investigation.* No individual or person dealing with the Trustee or any officer, employee or agent of the Trustee or the Fund shall be bound to make any inquiry concerning the validity of any transaction purported to be made by the Trustee or by said officer, employee or agent or be liable for the application of money or property paid, loaned to or delivered to or on the order of the Trustee or of said officer, employee or agent. Every obligation, contract, instrument, certificate or undertaking, and every other act or thing whatsoever executed in connection with the Fund, shall be conclusively presumed to have been executed or done by the executors thereof only in their capacity as officers, employees or agents of the Trustee or the Fund.

Section 12.6. *Reliance on Experts.* The Trustee and each officer and employee of the Trustee or the Fund shall, in the performance of its duties, be fully and completely justified and protected with regard to any act or any failure to act resulting from reliance in good faith upon the books of account or other records of the Fund, upon an opinion of counsel, or upon reports made to the Trustee or the Fund by any of its officers or employees or by any accountant, auditor, appraiser or other expert or consultant selected with reasonable care by the Trustee or by any officer, employee or agent of the Trustee or the Fund.

ARTICLE XIII

INTERESTS IN AND LEGAL OWNERSHIP OF EMISSION REDUCTIONS; DISTRIBUTIONS TO PARTICIPANTS

Section 13.1. *Adaptability to the Requirements of the UNFCCC.* In recognition that the regulatory framework of the UNFCCC and/or the Kyoto Protocol relating to the ownership, holding, and transfer of Emission Reductions is still under development, and to maximize the likelihood that the Fund may achieve its stated objectives, the Trustee will endeavor to ensure that the contractual arrangements entered into among the Trustee, Participants, Host Countries, Project Entities, and other parties will be structured flexibly so as to enable them to conform with the guidelines, modalities, and procedures of the regulatory framework of the UNFCCC and/or the Kyoto Protocol if, when and as they are developed.

Section 13.2. *Statements of Accounts.* At the request of a Participant, the Trustee will produce a statement of account confirming the number of Emission Reductions to which a Participant is entitled. Such statement will reflect the Trustee's records indicating the total number of Emission Reductions to which the Participants are entitled and the Participant's pro rata share thereof. The Trustee may also send such statements of account to Participants from time to time in the absence of requests.

Section 13.3. *Distributions Subject to UNFCCC Requirements.* Subject to such guidelines, modalities and procedures as may be determined by the parties to the UNFCCC and/or the Kyoto Protocol, it is the intent of the parties to this Instrument that Project Agreements shall provide for Emission Reductions to be transferred from Recipients to or to the order of the Participants. Subject to such procedures as may be determined by the parties to the UNFCCC and/or the Kyoto Protocol, the Trustee shall, at the request of Participants, make all reasonable efforts to ensure that the Emission Reductions generated by the Projects will be capable of being credited towards Annex I Countries' QELROs. If, for any of the Participants, it is not possible to ensure that Emission Reductions generated by the Projects will be credited towards Annex I Countries' QELROs, the Trustee will seek to provide, or to cause others to provide, the necessary documentation to establish the Participants' entitlement to such Emission Reductions. Notwithstanding any other provision of this Instrument, none of the IBRD, the Trustee or the Fund assumes any responsibility for the right of Participants to receive Emission Reductions under the UNFCCC, any other applicable law or otherwise or for the right of

Participants to use Emission Reductions to fulfill any obligation to which the Participant may be subject under the UNFCCC, any other applicable law or otherwise.

Section 13.4. *Withdrawal.* No Participant shall have the right to withdraw any part of its contribution to the Fund or to receive any distributions from the Fund except as provided in this Instrument.

ARTICLE XIV

ASSIGNMENT OF PARTICIPANTS' INTERESTS

Section 14.1. *Assignment of Participants' Interests.* A Participant may assign all, but not part, of its interest in the Fund or any of its rights under the Participation Agreement or this Instrument to an Eligible Private Sector Participant or an Eligible Public Sector Participant with the prior written consent of the Trustee, such consent not to be unreasonably withheld, provided that such assignee agrees, in form and substance acceptable to the Trustee, to be bound by the terms of this Instrument and the Participation Agreement entered into between the Trustee and the assignor Participant.

ARTICLE XV

DURATION; TERMINATION OF THE FUND; AMENDMENT

Section 15.1. *Duration.* Except as otherwise provided in this Article XV, the Fund shall terminate on December 31, 2012. The Participants may, by unanimous vote, decide to continue the business of the Fund after December 31, 2012 on such terms as they may determine, provided, that the Trustee will continue to serve as trustee only if the Executive Directors of the IBRD have expressly agreed to the extension and to the terms of such extension.

Section 15.2. *Termination of the Fund.*

(a) The Fund may be terminated before December 31, 2012 by (i) the resolution of Participants passed at a Participants' meeting by not less than a two-thirds majority of the votes cast at such meeting; or (ii) a unanimous consent in writing, setting forth the action to be taken, circulated to, and signed by all of the Participants.

(b) The Fund shall terminate if, as of the First Closing, (i) the Trustee has not entered into Participation Agreements providing in the aggregate for contributions to the Fund from Participants of at least U.S.$ 60 million, or (ii) the Trustee determines that the group of Participants that have entered into Participation Agreements is not sufficiently diverse to achieve one of the IBRD's strategic objectives in establishing the Fund, namely working in partnership with the public and private sectors to mobilize new resources for the IBRD's borrowing member countries while addressing global environmental concerns.

(c) The Fund shall also terminate upon the resignation of the IBRD as Trustee of the Fund.

(d) Upon the termination of the Fund:

i) the Trustee shall carry on no business for the Fund except for the purpose of winding up its affairs;

ii) the Trustee shall proceed to wind up the affairs of the Fund, and all of the powers of the Trustee under this Instrument shall continue until the affairs of the Fund shall have been wound up; and

iii) after paying or adequately providing for the payment of all liabilities, and upon receipt of such releases, indemnities, and refunding agreements as it may deem necessary for its protection, the Trustee shall distribute the remaining Fund Property in cash or in kind, or partly each, among the Participants according to their respective rights; notwithstanding the foregoing, in the event the remaining Fund Property includes the right to purchase Emission Reductions to be generated after the termination date of the Fund, the Trustee shall, subject to any applicable restrictions under international law, national law or otherwise, including regulations under the UNFCCC and/or the Kyoto Protocol, endeavor to make such arrangements as are necessary to effect a transfer of such rights to or to the order of the Participants, but shall not have any liability to the Participants if it is unable to do so.

Section 15.3. *Amendment Procedures.* This Instrument may only be amended by the Executive Directors of the IBRD with the prior unanimous consent of Participants. Notwithstanding the foregoing, this Instrument may be amended by the Trustee without prior notice to or consent from any Participant if such amendment is (i) to supply any omission, or cure, correct or supplement any manifest error or ambiguous, defective or inconsistent provision hereof, or (ii) for any other purpose which does not adversely affect the rights of any Participant; provided, that all Participants are notified of any such amendment within 15 days after the effective date of such amendment.

Section 15.4. *Further Assurances.* Upon the request of the Trustee, each of the Participants shall do, execute, acknowledge, and deliver or cause to be done, executed, acknowledged or delivered all such further acts, deeds, documents, instruments, assignments, transfers, conveyances, powers of attorney, and assurances as may be necessary or desirable to effect the purpose of this Instrument and carry out its provisions.

ARTICLE XVI

APPROVAL AND AUTHORIZATION

Section 16.1. *Approval.* By entering into a Participation Agreement, a Participant shall be deemed to have approved the Projects for the purposes of Article 6 and 12 of the Kyoto Protocol.

Section 16.2. *Authorization.* By entering into a Participation Agreement, a Participant that is entitled to authorize legal entities to participate, under its responsibility, in actions leading to the generation, transfer or acquisition of Emission Reductions shall be deemed to have expressly authorized the Trustee to act on its behalf in this respect.

ARTICLE XVII

CONFLICTS OF INTEREST

Section 17.1. *Trustee Withdrawal from Dispute or Claim.* In order to avoid any potential conflict of interest between the IBRD and the Trustee, and notwithstanding any other provision of this Instrument, the Trustee shall not have any obligation to prosecute, defend, compromise, negotiate, abandon or adjust, by arbitration, or otherwise, any action, suit, proceeding, dispute, claim or demand or any default or potential default by a Host Country or Project Entity under a Project Agreement (collectively a "dispute") in any way relating to any Project Agreement. If the Trustee determines that it will refrain from taking any such action, the Trustee shall so notify the Participants and the Trustee and the Participants shall use their best efforts to endeavor to agree to satisfactory arrangements for dealing with such dispute including the assignment and transfer of all or part of the Trustee's rights and obligations under the relevant Project Agreement to the Participants or to a third party acting on their behalf. The Trustee shall have no liability to the Participants as a result of the Trustee's determination to refrain from taking any such action in respect of a dispute or as a result of the failure of the Trustee and the Participants to reach such satisfactory arrangements in a timely manner or otherwise.

Section 17.2. *Participant Disclosure of Competing Interests.* Prior to the Participants' Committee's review of the relevant Project Concept Note, a Participant which participates, or which has affiliates or employees which participate individually and/or collectively, in funds or other investment vehicles having objectives and policies similar to those of the Fund which, as a result, may compete with the Fund for investment opportunities, supplies of raw materials, government franchises, customers or otherwise ("Other Ventures"), or a Participant or its affiliate or employee which has an interest in an Underlying Project, shall fully disclose such interest in Other Ventures or in an Underlying Project to the Trustee. If the Trustee determines that such participation or interest is such that the Participant should not participate in the Participants' Committee's deliberations on whether or not to object to the Project subject to this conflict or potential conflict of interest, it shall advise the Participant making the disclosure to recuse itself from the Participants' Committee's deliberations with respect to that Project. If the Participant disagrees with the Trustee's determination, it shall advise the Participants' Committee of the conflict or potential conflict, and the Participants' Committee (excluding the Participant making the disclosure) will decide whether such Participant should be permitted to participate in the Committee's deliberations on the Project concerned. The failure of a Participant to disclose such participation or interest in an Underlying Project or Other Venture in a timely manner will constitute a breach of this Instrument by such Participant, and the Trustee shall determine what remedies to exercise after consultation with the other Participants.

ARTICLE XVIII

ARBITRATION; EXERCISE OF REMEDIES

Section 18.1. *Validity*. The rights and obligations of the Trustee and the Participants with respect to the Fund shall be valid and enforceable in accordance with the terms of this Instrument and any agreement between the Trustee and the Participants. Neither the Trustee nor any Participant shall be entitled in any proceeding to assert any claim that any provision of this Instrument or such agreement is invalid or unenforceable because of any provision of the charter or constitutive documents of the Participant or the Articles of Agreement of the IBRD.

Section 18.2. *Arbitration*. Any dispute between the Trustee and a Participant arising out of or relating to this Instrument or such Participant's Participation Agreement shall be settled by arbitration in accordance with the UNCITRAL Arbitration Rules as at present in force. The number of arbitrators shall be three. The appointing authority shall be the Secretary-General of the Permanent Court of Arbitration at The Hague. In the event of a conflict between the UNCITRAL Arbitration Rules and the terms of this Instrument or of the Participation Agreement, the terms of the Instrument and Participation Agreement shall prevail.

Section 18.3. *Delays*. No delay in exercising, or failure to exercise, any right, power or remedy accruing to any party under this Instrument or any agreement between the Trustee and a Participant, whether or not upon any default, shall impair any such right, power or remedy or be construed to be a waiver thereof or an acquiescence in such default. No action of such party in respect of any default, or any acquiescence by it in any default, shall affect or impair any right, power or remedy of such party in respect of any other or subsequent default.

SCHEDULE 1

PROJECT SELECTION CRITERIA

and

PROJECT PORTFOLIO CRITERIA

Project Selection Criteria. The Trustee shall select Projects in accordance with the following Project Selection Criteria:

a) *Consistency with UNFCCC and/or the Kyoto Protocol.* The Trustee shall ensure that Projects comply with all current guidelines, modalities, and procedures adopted by the Parties to the UNFCCC and/or the Kyoto Protocol, as well as all future guidelines, modalities, and procedures when adopted, in particular those pertaining to sustainable development and additionality.

b) *Consistency with Relevant National Criteria.* The Trustee shall seek to ensure that the Projects' designs are compatible with and supportive of the national environment and development priorities of the Host Countries. In addition, the Projects and the transfer of Emission Reductions should be consistent with the rules and criteria adopted by Host Countries regarding Article 6 and Article 12 Projects.

c) *Consistency with the IBRD's Country Assistance Strategy.* The Trustee will seek to ensure that Projects are designed to be consistent with, and supportive of, the then current Country Assistance Strategy of the IBRD for the Host Country and the Host Country's own development objectives.

d) *Complementarity with GEF.* The Trustee shall seek to ensure that Projects are complementary to the GEF and do not compete with the GEF's long-term operational program nor with its short-term response measures. In furtherance of this criterion, potential Projects will be reviewed by the Secretariat of the GEF to determine their GEF eligibility. Only if it is determined that a potential Project will not receive GEF financing will the Fund Manager consider including it as a Fund Project.

e) *Achievement of National and Local Environmental Benefits.* The Trustee shall seek to ensure that Projects provide at least the same level of national and local environmental benefits as the Underlying Projects.

f) *Consistency with the Fund's Strategic Objectives and Operating Principles.* The Trustee shall seek to select Projects with a view to achieving the strategic objectives and operational principles of the Fund as set forth in the Instrument.

g) *Consistency with the General Guidance Provided by Participants.* The Trustee shall seek to ensure that Projects comply with the general guidance provided by Participants at their meetings.

h) *Additional Characteristics of Projects.* The Trustee shall seek to ensure that Projects are selected to mitigate various types of risk. Projects should generally entail manageable technological risk. The technology to be used in a Project should be commercially available, have been demonstrated in a commercial context, and be subject to customary commercial performance guarantees. The technical competence in the Host Country to manage this technology should be established in the course of Project appraisal. Projected Emission Reductions over the life of the Project should be predictable and should involve an acceptable level of uncertainty. GHG Reductions should also be amenable to standardized validation and verification processes with existing methodologies.

Project Portfolio Criteria. The Trustee will develop a Project portfolio with the intention that during the term of the Fund:

a) a broad balance will be achieved in the number of Projects undertaken in Economies in Transition and in Developing Countries and that, notwithstanding potential Projects identified prior to the establishment of the Fund, emphasis should be directed initially to the development of Projects in Developing Countries;

b) a major emphasis should be directed at development of Projects in the area of renewable energy technology such as, but not limited to, geothermal, wind, solar, and small hydro energy;

c) no less than approximately 2% nor more than approximately 10% of the Fund's assets should be invested in any one Project;

d) no more than approximately 20% of the Fund's assets should be invested in Projects in the same Host Country;

e) no more than approximately 10% of the Fund's assets should be invested in land-use sector Projects. Further, unless the Parties to the UNFCCC deem it appropriate, no such Project shall be located in a Developing Country; and

f) no more than approximately 25% of the Fund's assets should be invested in Projects using the same technology.

TF024104

PROTOTYPE CARBON FUND EMISSION REDUCTIONS PURCHASE AGREEMENT

(Liepaja Solid Waste Management Project)

by and between

REPUBLIC OF LATVIA

and

INTERNATIONAL BANK FOR RECONSTRUCTION AND DEVELOPMENT, AS TRUSTEE OF THE PROTOTYPE CARBON FUND

Dated December 19, 2000

TABLE OF CONTENTS

TF024104

PROTOTYPE CARBON FUND EMISSION REDUCTIONS PURCHASE AGREEMENT

This PROTOTYPE CARBON FUND EMISSION REDUCTIONS PURCHASE AGREEMENT (the "Agreement"), dated December 19, 2000, is entered into by and between the REPUBLIC OF LATVIA (the "Host Country") and the INTERNATIONAL BANK FOR RECONSTRUCTION AND DEVELOPMENT ("IBRD"), not in its individual capacity but as trustee of the Prototype Carbon Fund (the "PCF") pursuant to the Instrument (in such capacity the "Trustee").

WHEREAS:

(A) Pursuant to Resolution No. 99-1 of the Executive Directors of the IBRD dated 20 July 1999, the Prototype Carbon Fund was established for the purposes of (i) demonstrating how project-based transactions in Greenhouse Gas emission reductions can contribute to the sustainable development of developing countries and countries with economies in transition; (ii) sharing the knowledge gained in the course of the PCF's operations with all interested parties; and (iii) demonstrating how the IBRD can work in partnership with the public and private sectors to mobilize new resources for its borrowing member countries while addressing global environmental concerns;

(B) the Host Country has ratified the United Nations Framework Convention on Climate Change (the "UNFCCC") on 23 February 1995, and signed on 14 December 1998 the Protocol that was adopted at the Third Conference of the Parties to the UNFCCC in Kyoto, Japan on 11 December 1997 (the "Kyoto Protocol");

(C) the Host Country, through a letter dated 21 September 1998 from its Ministry of Environmental Protection and Regional Development has endorsed the development of the project defined in Section 1.01 of this Agreement (the "Project") for the purpose of Article 6 of the Kyoto Protocol, and has committed itself to render such assistance as may be necessary in the registration of the Emission Reductions generated by the Project for the purposes of the UNFCCC;

(D) the Baseline and design of the Project has been Validated as set forth in the Validation Report, and the Project is expected to provide a reduction in Greenhouse Gas emissions by sources, that is additional to any that would otherwise occur;

(E) the Project will be carried out by Liepajas RAS, Ltd., a non-profit limited liability company established on February 24, 2000 under the laws of the Republic of Latvia (the "Project Entity"), with the Host Country's assistance;

(F) the Host Country intends to contract from IBRD a loan in a principal amount equal to U.S.$ 2,220,000 to finance a portion of the costs of the Project on the terms and conditions set forth in an agreement (the "Loan Agreement") to be entered into between the Host Country and IBRD;

(G) the Host Country intends to contract from Nordic Investment Bank a loan in a principal amount equivalent to U.S.$ 1,500,000 to assist in financing part of the Project on the terms and conditions set forth in an agreement (the "NIB Loan Agreement") to be entered into between the Host Country and Nordic Investment Bank;

(H) the Host Country intends to contract from the European Union a grant in Euro in an amount equivalent to U.S.$ 4,860,000 to assist in financing the Project on the terms and conditions set forth in an agreement (the "EU Financing Memorandum") to be entered into between the Host Country and European Union;

(I) the Host Country intends to contract from the Swedish International Development Agency a grant in Swedish Krone in an amount equivalent to approximately U.S.$ 1,180,000 to assist in financing the Project on the terms and conditions set forth in an agreement (the "SIDA Grant Agreement") to be entered into between the Host Country and the Swedish International Development Agency; and

(J) the Host Country, having satisfied itself as to the feasibility and priority of the Project wishes to sell, and the Trustee, based inter alia on the foregoing, wishes to purchase, upon the terms and conditions set forth in this Agreement, Emission Reductions achieved by the Project;

NOW THEREFORE the Parties hereto hereby agree as follows:

ARTICLE I

Definitions; Interpretation; Headings; Schedules

Section 1.01 Definitions

Unless the context otherwise requires, the following capitalized terms shall have the following meanings wherever used in this Agreement and its preamble:

(i) "Additional Emission Reductions" or "AERs" means any and all Emission Reductions generated by the Project during the period from 1 January 2013 to the Project Termination Date, as well as any and all Emission Reductions generated before that period over and above the Total MERs;

(ii) "Advance Payment" means the advance granted by the Trustee to the Host Country pursuant to the letter of agreement dated December 18, 2000, signed on behalf of the Trustee and on behalf of the Host Country;

(iii) "Assigned Amount" means the quantity of Greenhouse Gases that the Host Country can release in accordance with the Kyoto Protocol, during the first quantified emission limitation and reduction commitment period of that protocol;

(iv) "Baseline" means the situation as described in the Validation Report, that would have occurred without the implementation of the Project, in particular with respect to GHG emissions;

(v) "Certification" means the process by which either (i) if the Parties to the UNFCCC deem it appropriate, an operational entity designated by the COP/MOP for the purposes of Article 6 or in absence thereof (ii) an Independent Third Party appointed by the Trustee, certifies that the reductions in GHG emissions generated by the Project comply with the relevant standards and conditions of the UNFCCC and the Kyoto Protocol as reflected in the Monitoring and Verification Protocol;

(vi) "Commercial Operations" shall have the meaning ascribed thereto in *Schedule 1* to this Agreement, as such schedule may be amended from time to time by agreement between the Trustee and the Host Country;

(vii) "COP/MOP" means the Conference of the Parties to the UNFCCC serving as the meeting of the Parties to the Kyoto Protocol;

(viii) "Development and Construction Phase" means the phase of the Project described in part A of Schedule 1 to this Agreement;

(ix) "Effective Date" means the date on which this Agreement shall be effective as provided in Section 10.03 of this Agreement;

(x) "Emission Reductions," or "ERs" means reductions in emissions of Greenhouse Gases generated by the Project in excess of the applicable Baseline that have successfully undergone Certification;

(xi) "EU Financing Memorandum" shall have the meaning ascribed thereto in the preamble to this Agreement;

(xii) "Euro" shall mean the lawful currency of the member states of the European Union that adopt the single currency in accordance with the Treaty establishing the European Community, as amended by the Treaty on European Union;

(xiii) "Final Payment" shall have the meaning ascribed thereto in Section 2.02(b);

(xiv) "First Payment" shall have the meaning ascribed thereto in Section 2.02(b);

(xv) "Greenhouse Gases" or "GHG" means the six gases listed in Annex A to the Kyoto Protocol, which are carbon dioxide, methane, nitrous oxide, hydrofluorocarbons, perfluorocarbons, and sulphur hexafluoride;

(xvi) "Host Country" shall have the meaning ascribed thereto in the preamble to this Agreement;

(xvii) "IBRD" shall have the meaning ascribed thereto in the preamble to this Agreement;

(xviii) "Independent Third Party" means an entity, such as an environmental auditing company, which is independent from the Trustee, the Host Country and the Project Entity;

(xix) "Initial Verification" shall have the meaning ascribed thereto in Section 5.02(a)(vi) of this Agreement;

(xx) "Instrument" means the Instrument establishing the Prototype Carbon Fund as approved by the Executive Directors of the IBRD on 20 July 1999 by Resolution No. 99-1, as may be amended from time to time;

(xxi) "Kyoto Protocol" shall have the meaning ascribed thereto in the preamble to this Agreement;

(xxii) "LIBOR" means, in respect of any period for which interest is payable, the London interbank offered rate for six-month deposits in U.S. Dollars, expressed as a percentage per annum, that appears on the Relevant Telerate Page as of 11:00 a.m., London time, on the LIBOR Reset Date for said interest period. If such rate does not appear on the Relevant Telerate Page, the Trustee shall request the principal London office of each of four major banks to provide a quotation of the rate at which it offers six-month deposits in U.S. Dollars to leading banks in the London interbank market at approximately 11:00 a.m. London time on the LIBOR Reset Date for said interest period. If at least two such quotations are provided, the rate in respect of said interest period shall be the arithmetic mean (as determined by the Trustee) of the quotations. If less than two quotations are provided as requested, the rate in respect of said interest period shall be the arithmetic mean (as determined by the Trustee) of the rates quoted by four major banks selected by the Trustee in the principal financial center for U.S. Dollars, at approximately 11:00 a.m. in said financial center, on the LIBOR Reset Date for said interest period for loans in U.S. Dollars to leading banks for a period of six months. If less than two of the banks so selected are quoting such rates, LIBOR in respect of said interest period shall be equal to LIBOR in effect for the interest period immediately preceding that period;

(xxiii) "LIBOR Reset Date" means the day two London Banking Days prior to the first day of the relevant period on which interest becomes payable;

(xxiv) "Lien" includes mortgages, pledges, charges, privileges and priorities of any kind;

(xxv) "Loan Agreement" shall have the meaning ascribed thereto in the preamble to this Agreement;

(xxvi) "London Banking Day" means any day on which commercial banks are open for general business (including dealings in foreign exchange and currency deposits) in London;

(xxvii) "Milestone Payment" shall have the meaning ascribed thereto in Section 2.02(b);

(xxviii) "Minimum Emission Reductions" or "MERs" means with respect to any year in the schedule set forth in Section 2.03, the minimum amount of Emission Reductions to be generated by the Project and delivered by the Host Country during such year in accordance with that schedule;

(xxix) "Monitoring" means activities pursuant to which the Project Entity or another person collects and records data assessing the reductions in emissions of Greenhouse Gases resulting from the Project pursuant to the terms of the Monitoring and Verification Protocol;

(xxx) "Monitoring and Verification Protocol" means the set of requirements incorporated in *Schedule 4* to this Agreement, as such schedule may be amended from time to time in accordance with Section 9.06;

(xxxi) "NIB Loan Agreement" shall have the meaning ascribed thereto in the preamble to this Agreement;

(xxxii) "Parties" means the Host County and the Trustee, and each of them shall be individually referred to as a "Party";

(xxxiii) "PCF" or "Prototype Carbon Fund" shall have the meaning ascribed thereto in the preamble to this Agreement;

(xxxiv) "PCF Participants" means any or all of the eligible private sector participants or eligible public sector participants that have entered into a participation agreement under the terms of the Instrument, or any assignee thereof pursuant to the terms of the Instrument;

(xxxv) "Project" means the project as described in *Schedule 1*, relating to the development, financing construction, ownership, operation and maintenance of a solid waste management project in Liepaja, Latvia, and all activities in connection therewith, as the description thereof may be amended from time to time by agreement between the Trustee and the Host Country;

(xxxvi) "Project Entity" shall have the meaning ascribed thereto in the preamble to this Agreement;

(xxxvii) "Project Termination Date" means 31 December 2020;

(xxxviii) "Purchase Account" means the account established with the Trustee on behalf of the PCF for the purposes of this Agreement from which the Trustee is entitled to withdraw funds from time to time in order to effect the payments required hereunder;

(xxxiv) "Purchase Price" shall have the meaning ascribed thereto in Section 2.02(a);

(xl) "Relevant Telerate Page" means the display page designated on the Dow Jones Telerate Service as the page for the purpose of displaying LIBOR for deposits in U.S. Dollars (or such other page as may replace such page on such service, or such other service as may be selected by the Trustee as the information vendor, for the purpose of displaying rates or prices comparable to LIBOR);

(xli) "SIDA Grant Agreement" shall have the meaning ascribed thereto in the preamble to this Agreement;

(xlii) "Subsidiary Agreement" shall have the meaning ascribed thereto in Section 5.02;

(xliii) "Swedish Krone" means the lawful currency of the Kingdom of Sweden;

(xliv) "Total Minimum Emission Reductions" or "Total MERs" shall have the meaning ascribed thereto in Section 2.03;

(xlv) "Trustee" shall have the meaning ascribed thereto in the preamble to this Agreement;

(xlvi) "UNFCCC" shall have the meaning ascribed thereto in the preamble to this Agreement;

(xlvii) "U.S. Dollars" and "U.S.$" each means the lawful currency of the United States of America;

(xlviii) "Validation" or "Validated" means the assessment by an Independent Third Party of the Project design, including its Baseline, before the implementation of the Project;

(xlix) "Validation Report" means the report set forth in *Schedule 3* to this agreement, prepared by an Independent Third Party;

(l) "Verification" or "Verified" means the auditing from time to time by an Independent Third Party of the data recorded by the person responsible for Monitoring to verify the amount of Emission Reductions achieved by the Project in relation to its Baseline and the requirements of the Monitoring and Verification Protocol; and

(li) "Verification Report" means a report prepared by an Independent Third Party pursuant to a Verification, which reports the findings of the Verification process and, inter alia, states the amount of reductions in emission of Greenhouse Gases that have been found to have been generated.

Section 1.02 Interpretation; Headings; Schedules

(a) The terms of this Agreement shall be interpreted in a manner that is consistent with the UNFCCC, the Kyoto Protocol, and any decisions, guidelines, modalities, and procedures adopted under the foregoing, and the Instrument, as such instruments may be amended or supplemented from time to time.

(b) All terms defined herein have the meanings assigned to them herein for all purposes, and such meanings are equally applicable to both the singular and plural forms of the terms defined. "Include" "includes" and "including" shall be deemed to be followed by "without limitation" whether or not they are in fact followed by such words or words of like import. "Writing," "written," and comparable terms refer to printing, typing, lithography and other means of reproducing words in a visible form. Any instrument or law defined or referred to herein means such instrument or law as from time to time amended, modified or supplemented, including (in the case of instruments) by waiver or consent and (in the case of any law) by succession of comparable successor laws and includes (in the case of instruments) references to all attachments thereto and instruments incorporated therein. References to a person are, unless the context otherwise requires, also to its successors and assigns. Any term defined herein by reference to any instrument or law has such meaning whether or not such instrument or law is in effect. "Shall" and "will" have equal force and effect. "Hereof," "herein," "hereunder," and comparable terms refer to the entire instrument in which such terms are used and not to any particular article, Section, or other subdivision thereof or attachment thereto. References in an instrument to "Article," "Section," or another subdivision or to an attachment are, unless the context otherwise requires, to an article, Section or subdivision of, or an attachment to, such instrument. References to any gender include, unless the context otherwise requires, references to all genders, and references to the singular include, unless the context otherwise requires, references to the plural and vice versa.

(c) The headings of the Articles and Sections are inserted for convenience of reference only and shall be ignored in construing this Agreement.

(d) The Schedules to this Agreement are an integral part thereof.

ARTICLE II

Sale, Generation and Delivery of Emission Reductions

Section 2.01 Sale of Emission Reductions

Subject to the terms and conditions set forth in this Agreement, and in consideration for the Purchase Price to be paid by the Trustee pursuant to Section 2.02, the Host Country hereby sells, assigns, and transfers to the Trustee, free and clear of any Lien, and the Trustee hereby accepts in trust on behalf of the PCF Participants, all rights, title, and interests in and to (i) all of the Minimum Emission Reductions generated by the Project until such time as the Total Minimum Emission Reductions have been delivered as required pursuant to Section 2.03, and (ii) such portions of the Additional Emission Reductions generated by the Project as required to be delivered to the Trustee pursuant to Section 2.04 below. All Greenhouse Gas emission reductions sold, assigned, and transferred hereunder shall be subject to Verification and Certification, and shall be delivered to the Trustee, in accordance with Section 2.05 hereof.

Section 2.02 Purchase Price; Payments and Notification

(a) Subject to the terms and conditions set forth in this Agreement, the Trustee shall pay the Host Country a total purchase price (the "Purchase Price") of U.S.$ 2,477,000, from which shall be retained by the Trustee (1) certain costs incurred by the Trustee in connection with this Agreement and the Project and equal to U.S.$ 201,000; (2) an administrative fee of U.S.$ 25,000, and (3) the Advance Payment equal to U.S.$ 595,000.

(b) Upon effectiveness of this Agreement the amount of the Purchase Price shall be credited to the Purchase Account by the Trustee, to be transferred by the Trustee from that account in installments as follows; an amount equal to U.S.$ 821,000 shall be transferred from that account to be retained by the Trustee in satisfaction for the items listed in subparagraphs (1), (2) and (3) of paragraph (a) of this Section; thereafter, the Trustee shall make five (5) payments to the Host Country (each such payment a "Milestone Payment," and collectively, the "Milestone Payments") upon the achievement by the Project of certain specified milestones, as set forth in the payment schedule provided in *Schedule 2* hereto; the Trustee shall make a final payment to the Host Country (the "Final Payment") following the delivery to the Trustee of the Total Minimum Emission Reductions in accordance with Section 2.03

of this Agreement. Each of the foregoing payments shall be made in accordance with the following provisions:

(i) *Administrative fee and costs incurred.* Following the Effective Date, the Trustee shall be entitled at its discretion to withdraw from the Purchase Account and pay to itself an amount equal to U.S.$ 226,000 for the administrative fee and the costs incurred as set out in paragraph (a) of this Section;

(ii) *Repayment of Advance Payment.* After the Effective Date, the Trustee shall, on behalf of the Host Country, withdraw from the Purchase Account and pay to itself the amount required to repay the amount of the Advance Payment withdrawn and outstanding as of such date;

(iii) *Milestone Payments.* Upon the achievement of each of the five (5) milestones set forth in *Schedule 2*, the Host Country shall deliver to the Trustee written notice thereof accompanied by any evidence or proof of such milestone (including the report of any independent engineer retained for the Project) which the Trustee shall be free to verify within a period of ninety (90) days of such written notice. Within thirty (30) days of such written notice, or, if the Trustee chooses to verify, within thirty (30) days of the verification of such milestone, the Trustee shall withdraw from the Purchase Account and effect payment to the Host Country of an amount corresponding to the Milestone Payment required in respect of such milestone as set forth in *Schedule 2*. In the event the Trustee finds that the relevant milestone has not been met or if the Trustee is unable to verify such milestone, it shall promptly notify the Host Country thereof in writing; and

(iv) *Final Payment.* Upon delivery of the Total Minimum Emission Reductions as required pursuant to Section 2.03, the Trustee shall withdraw from the Purchase Account and effect payment to the Host Country of an amount equal to the Final Payment as required pursuant to this Section 2.02(b) and Schedule 2.

(c) The Trustee shall make all payments in U.S. Dollars via wire transfer into such account as the Host Country shall designate.

(d) In consideration for the administrative fee to be received pursuant to Section 2.02 (b)(i) and subject to the terms and conditions set forth in this Agreement, the Trustee shall pay for all costs incurred in connection with Validation, Initial Verification, Verification and Certification of MERs and of its portion of AERs in accordance with Section 2.04, and Project supervision by the Trustee.

Section 2.03 Minimum Emission Reductions

Unless the Trustee and the Host Country agree otherwise, the Host Country shall be required to deliver to the Trustee minimum amounts of Emission Reductions in accordance with the provisions of this Section 2.03.

(a) *Total MERs.* The total amount of Emission Reductions delivered to the Trustee must reflect, at a minimum, a total reduction of GHG emissions of no less than 105,800 metric tonnes of carbon equivalent emissions (such amount, the "Total Minimum Emission Reductions" or "Total MERs"). Generation and delivery of the Total MERs shall be completed on or prior to 1 January 2013. The Total MERs shall be generated and delivered to the Trustee in accordance with the requirements of paragraph (b) below.

(b) *Annual MERs.* Other than as permitted pursuant to paragraph (c) below or as otherwise agreed by the Trustee, the Host Country shall (until such time as the Total MERs have been delivered) deliver to the Trustee, in respect of each calendar year listed in the following schedule, any and all Emission Reductions generated by the Project during such year provided that the Emission Reductions delivered for any such year shall be in an amount no less than the Minimum Emission Reductions for such year set forth in this schedule:

Calendar Year	*Minimum Emission Reductions to be Delivered (in metric tonnes of carbon equivalent emissions)*
2002	4,800
2003	6,700
2004	8,400
2005	9,700
2006	10,100
2007	10,500
2008	11,000
2009	11,000
2010	11,100
2011	11,200
2012	11,300
Total MERs	**105,800**

(c) *Make-up of MERs Shortfalls*. In the event the Host Country fails to deliver the quantity of Minimum Emission Reductions for any given calendar year as set forth in paragraph (b) above, the Host Country shall be required to make-up the shortfall over the course of the following calendar year or such later period as acceptable to the Trustee in its sole discretion; *provided however*, that the Host Country shall not be permitted to deliver any make-up quantities of MERs beyond 31 December 2012, and all MERs for prior years shall be delivered to Trustee in full by such date, unless otherwise permitted in writing by the Trustee. Any Emissions Reductions delivered as make-up quantities after 31 December 2012 shall be in addition to the portion of Additional Emission Reductions generated by the Project and required to be delivered to the Trustee pursuant to Section 2.04.

(d) *ERs in excess of the Total MERs*. For the avoidance of doubt, any ERs generated in excess of the Total MERs due in accordance with paragraph (a) above shall be considered AERs and be delivered in accordance with Section 2.04.

Section 2.04 Additional Emissions Reductions

(a) Additional Emission Reductions

The Host Country shall deliver to the Trustee 50% of all Additional Emission Reductions generated by the Project, provided that, the average market price for Emission Reductions applicable to the period for which any such Additional Emissions Reductions are being delivered is not more than U.S.$ 25 per metric tonne of carbon equivalent emissions. In the event the market price is determined to be more than U.S.$ 25 per metric tonne of carbon equivalent emissions pursuant to the provisions of Section 2.04(b) below, the Host Country shall deliver to the Trustee the percentage of the Additional Emission Reductions generated by the Project in respect of such period corresponding to the applicable price as set forth in the table below:

Market Price (U.S.$ per Metric Tonne of Carbon Equivalent Emissions)	*Trustee's Portion of the Additional Emission Reductions*
25 and below	50%
Between 26 and 50	45%
Between 51 and 75	40%
Between 76 and 80	35%
Between 81 and 95	30%
Over 95	25%

(b) Determination of Market Price

For any period for which Additional Emissions Reductions are to be delivered, the Host Country shall have the right to file with the Trustee a claim that the applicable market price for such period is above U.S.$ 25 per metric tonne of carbon equivalent emissions; provided that such a claim is delivered to the Trustee prior to the Verification and Certification of Additional Emission Reductions for such period in accordance with the procedures established under Section 2.05. Such a claim must specify the market price that the Host Country believes is accurate for the period in question and provide the basis for such belief.

(i) *No Dispute*. If the Trustee agrees with the Host Country on the applicable market price, the Host Country shall deliver to the Trustee the percentage of the Additional Emission Reductions generated by the Project during such period corresponding to such price as set forth in the table in Section 2.04(a) above.

(ii) *Dispute*. If the Trustee disagrees with the Host Country's claim, the Host Country shall (1) deliver to the Trustee the percentage of the Additional Emission Reductions generated by the Project during such period as set forth in the table in Section 2.04(a) above based on the applicable market price asserted in the Host Country's claim and (2) place the remaining portion of Additional Emission Reductions in dispute in escrow in accordance with escrow arrangements agreed upon with the Trustee until the applicable price for such period is determined in accordance with the procedures in paragraph (iii) below. Upon such determination of the applicable price, the Additional Emission Reductions held in escrow shall be delivered to the appropriate Party based on the applicable price so determined.

(iii) *Dispute Resolution.* If the Trustee disagrees with the Host Country's claim:

(1) *Consultation.* The Trustee shall respond to the Host Country's claim in writing within fifteen (15) days of receipt of such claim and, in any event, shall, over the course of the thirty (30) days following the receipt of such claim, consult or negotiate with the Host Country to arrive at a mutually agreed upon applicable price;

(2) *Mediation or Expert Determination.* In the event such consultations do not lead to a mutually agreed upon price, the Parties shall refer the matter to a mutually agreed upon third party mediator or third party expert that, in the case of a mediator, shall attempt to mediate the dispute and (failing a settlement) shall be required to issue its determination as to the applicable price, and, in the case of an expert, shall determine the applicable price based on its own expertise or market research. In all events (unless agreed by the Parties), the determination of the mediator or expert shall be issued by no later than the date thirty (30) days following the date the dispute was submitted to such mediator or expert. Subject to the provisions of sub-paragraph (iii)(3) below, the Parties agree to accept the determination of the mediator or expert;

(3) *Arbitration.* In the event the Parties cannot agree upon a mediator or expert, or if, within fifteen (15) days after the issuance of the determination of the mediator or expert, one Party notifies the other that it does not accept that determination, then either Party may submit the matter to arbitration in accordance with the provisions of Section 9.03;

(4) *Cost of Mediation or Expert Determination.* The Parties shall share equally the cost of the mediator or expert.

Section 2.05 Verification and Certification of Emissions Reductions

(a) The Greenhouse Gas emission reductions generated by the Project shall be subject to Verification in accordance with the Monitoring and Verification Protocol, and be subject to periodic Certification at intervals to be determined by the Trustee.

(b) Following each Verification the Trustee shall instruct the Independent Third Party performing the Verification to issue a Verification Report that includes inter alia: (i) a statement of the amount of verified and certified Greenhouse Gas emission reductions the Project has generated in the relevant period, and (ii) such other matters as may be required by the UNFCCC or Kyoto Protocol.

ARTICLE III

Representations and Warranties

Section 3.01 Representations and Warranties of Host Country

The Host Country represents and warrants, as of the date of this Agreement, that:

(a) It has all requisite legal power and authority to execute this Agreement and to carry out the terms, conditions and provisions hereof. All corporate, legislative, administrative or other governmental action required to authorize the execution, delivery and performance by the Host Country of this Agreement and the transactions contemplated hereby have been duly taken and are in full force and effect. This Agreement constitutes the valid, legal, and binding obligation of the Host Country, enforceable in accordance with the terms hereof. There are no actions, suits or proceedings pending or, to the Host Country's knowledge, threatened, against or affecting the Host Country before any court or administrative body or arbitral tribunal which might materially adversely affect the ability of the Host Country to meet and carry out its obligations under this Agreement. The execution, delivery, and performance of this Agreement by the Host Country will not contravene any provision of, or constitute a default under, any other agreement, treaty, or instrument to which it is party or subject, or by which it or its property may be bound;

(b) It has all rights, title, and interest in and to all of the Emission Reductions to be generated by the Project, and that such Emission Reductions have not been sold, assigned or transferred to any party (other than hereunder), or otherwise subjected to any Lien;

(c) It is in compliance with its relevant obligations under the UNFCCC, the Kyoto Protocol, and any decisions, modalities, guidelines, and procedures adopted thereunder;

(d) It is not prevented pursuant to the relevant provisions of the UNFCCC or the Kyoto Protocol from transferring Emission Reductions required to be transferred hereunder; and

(e) It hereby approves the Project for the purposes of Article 6 of the Kyoto Protocol and authorizes the Trustee (and as appropriate the PCF Participants) to participate, under its responsibility, in actions leading to the generation, transfer or acquisition of Emission Reductions and emission reduction units from the Project, and agrees to take whatever steps may be required under the UNFCCC and Kyoto Protocol for these purposes.

ARTICLE IV

Obligations of the Trustee

Section 4.01 Obligations of the Trustee

The Trustee hereby covenants and agrees that it shall:

(a) Pay the installments of the Purchase Price as set out in this Agreement;

(b) Arrange for Initial Verification in accordance with this Agreement in a timely manner;

(c) Arrange for Verification and Certification in accordance with this Agreement in a timely manner; in particular with respect to GHG emission reductions generated by the Project in years where MERs constitute a milestone for a Milestone Payment;

(d) Fully cooperate with the Host Country and any Independent Third Party to ensure proper Verification, Certification, transfer, and delivery of Greenhouse Gas emission reductions in accordance with the UNFCCC, the Kyoto Protocol, and any decisions, guidelines, modalities, and procedures adopted under those agreements; and

(e) Carry out its other obligations set forth in this Agreement.

ARTICLE V

Obligations of the Host Country

Section 5.01 Obligations Related to the Project

The Host Country hereby covenants and agrees that it shall:

(a) Use its good offices to enable the Project Entity to develop, finance, construct, own, operate, insure, and maintain the Project with due diligence, speed, and efficiency so as to generate the maximum number of Emission Reductions. To this end, the Host Country shall take all necessary action including the provision, granting or issuance, as applicable, of facilities, services, permits, licenses, consents, authorizations and (during the Development and Construction Phase) of funds and other resources, necessary or appropriate to enable the Project Entity to perform such obligations, and shall refrain from, prohibit, or prevent any action that would prevent or interfere with such performance;

(b) Fully cooperate with the Trustee, the PCF Participants and any Independent Third Party to ensure proper certification of Greenhouse Gas emission reductions in accordance with the UNFCCC, the Kyoto Protocol, and any decisions, guidelines, modalities, and procedures adopted under those agreements and transfer to the order of the Trustee of the emission reductions thus certified;

(c) Take such action as is reasonable and appropriate to enable the Project Entity to secure a suitable site and all easements required for the Project;

(d) Not sell, assign, or transfer to any party, or otherwise subject to any Lien, the Emission Reductions generated by the Project and sold, assigned, and transferred to the Trustee hereunder; and

(e) Upon notice by the Trustee, grant any validator, verifier, and certifier, any staff or other authorized representative of the Trustee, and any accredited representatives of any PCF Participants, unlimited, and unrestricted access to its territory for the purposes of this Agreement.

Section 5.02 Subsidiary Agreement between Host Country and Project Entity

(a) The Host Country shall enter into a subsidiary agreement with the Project Entity under terms and conditions that shall have been agreed by the Trustee prior to its conclusion (the such Subsidiary Agreement to provide, inter alia, that:

(i) The Project Entity shall carry out the Project with due diligence and efficiency and in conformity with appropriate administrative, financial, engineering and environmental practices, and shall, provide or cause to be provided, promptly as needed, fund, facilities and other resources required for the Project;

(ii) The Project entity shall at all times operate and maintain its plant, machinery, equipment, and other property, and from time to time, promptly as needed, make all necessary repairs and renewals thereof, all in accordance with sounds engineering, financial and environmental practices;

(iii) The Project Entity shall satisfy any obligations in respect of applications for all licenses, permits, consents, and authorizations required to implement the Project, and the Host Country shall support and use all reasonable efforts to expedite the Project Entity's applications for the same;

(iv) The Project Entity shall obtain, and the Host Country shall take such action as is reasonable and appropriate to enable the Project Entity to obtain, adequate supplies of water, utilities, materials, and equipment, and procure the necessary transportation arrangements for the transport of all materials and equipment necessary to develop, construct, operate, and maintain the Project;

(v) The Project Entity shall obtain and maintain at all times such insurance and in such amounts as satisfactory to the Trustee;

(vi) Upon Project completion and prior to the commencement of Commercial Operations, the Project shall be subject to initial verification by an Independent Third Party acceptable to the Trustee, in order to allow the Trustee to assess whether the Project as constructed by the Project Entity complies with the specifications of design and construction, and the provisions of the Monitoring and Verification Protocol ("Initial Verification");

(vii) The Project Entity shall install, operate, and maintain the facilities and equipment necessary for gathering all such data as may be required by the Monitoring and Verification Protocol and necessary for the purposes of Verification and Certification. The Project Entity shall gather such data, provide it to the Trustee, allow the Trustee to divulge it at its sole discretion, and provide it to such other persons as the Trustee at its sole discretion may designate;

(viii) Following commencement of Commercial Operations, the Project shall be subject to periodic Verification, in accordance with the Monitoring and Verification Protocol, by an Independent Third Party acceptable to and contracted by the Trustee;

(ix) The Project Entity, upon notice by the Trustee, shall: *(i)* grant any validator, verifier, and certifier, any staff or other authorized representative of the Trustee, and any accredited representatives of any PCF Participants, unlimited and unrestricted access to the Project, the Project site, and information and data pertaining to the abatement of GHG emissions; and *(ii)* allow and facilitate the performance by the Independent Third Party verifier of all tests or other procedures necessary for the aforementioned verification processes; and

(x) The Host Country has all rights, title, and interest in and to any and all Emission Reductions generated by the Project, and that such Emission Reductions shall not be sold, assigned, or transferred to any party, or otherwise subject to any Lien, in a manner inconsistent with the Host Country's obligations under this Agreement.

(b) The Host Country shall exercise its rights under the Subsidiary Agreement in such a manner as to protect the interests of the Host Country and the Trustee and to accomplish the purposes of this Agreement so as to maximize the generation of Emission Reductions from the Project and, except as the Trustee shall otherwise agree in writing, the Host Country shall not assign, amend, abrogate, or waive the Subsidiary Agreement or any provision thereof.

Section 5.03 Compliance with UNFCCC and Kyoto Protocol

The Host Country shall continue to be in good standing with the UNFCCC, the Kyoto Protocol and any decisions, guidelines, modalities, and procedures adopted under those agreements. To this effect, the Host Country specifically covenants that:

(a) It will continue to maintain itself in compliance with its obligations under the UNFCCC, the Kyoto Protocol, and the decisions, modalities, guidelines and procedures adopted under that regulatory framework. In particular, but without limitation to the foregoing, it shall ensure compliance with its obligations under Articles 4 and 12 of the UNFCCC and Articles 3, paragraphs 1 and 2, and Articles 5, 7 and 10 of the Kyoto Protocol; and

(b) It shall ensure that during the life of the Project it does not by its own acts or omissions prevent itself from transferring the agreed amount of Total Minimum Emission Reductions generated by the Project.

ARTICLE VI

Events of Default by the Host Country; Remedies

Section 6.01 Events of Default

(a) Each of the following events shall constitute an event of default on the part of the Host Country:

(i) The EU Financing Memorandum shall have failed to become effective by November 1, 2001, or on such later date as the Trustee may agree; provided however that the provisions of this paragraph shall not apply if the Host Country establishes to the satisfaction of the Trustee that adequate funds for the Project are available to the Host Country from other sources on terms and conditions consistent with the obligations of the Host Country under this Agreement.

(ii) The occurrence of an event of default under the Loan Agreement or any other grant, loan, or agreement made or entered for the purpose of financing the Project.

(iii) The suspension, cancellation, acceleration prior to the agreed maturity thereof or termination in whole or in part, of the Loan Agreement or any other agreement or instrument providing for a grant or loan for the purpose of financing the Project, *provided that*, with respect to any grant or loan pursuant to an agreement or instrument *other than* the Loan Agreement, the foregoing shall not constitute an event of default if the Host Country establishes to the satisfaction of the Trustee that such suspension, cancellation, acceleration, or termination is not caused by the failure of the Host Country or Project Entity to perform any of its obligations under such agreement or instrument, and adequate funds for the Project are available to the Host Country or Project Entity from other sources on terms and conditions consistent with its obligations under this Agreement.

(iv) Changes in the ownership structure of Project Entity in a manner that detrimentally affects its ability to carry out the Project in the reasonable opinion of Trustee.

(v) The dissolution, disestablishment, liquidation, insolvency, or bankruptcy (voluntary or involuntary) of the Project Entity.

(vi) Failure of the Project Entity to enter or obtain in a timely manner (as reasonably determined by the Trustee), or any default under, any material contract, permit, consent, or license relating to the ownership, development, construction, operation, or maintenance of the Project (or any portion thereof) that, in the reasonable opinion of the Trustee, would materially adversely affect the ability of the Host Country to perform its obligations hereunder.

(vii) Any delay in Project construction such as to make it improbable in the reasonable opinion of the Trustee that the Total Minimum Emission Reductions would be generated before 1 January 2013.

(viii) Any suspension for any reason of the Project's construction prior to the completion, if no other arrangements reasonably satisfactory to the Trustee shall have been made to ensure the timely completion of the Project and the attainment of its objectives.

(ix) Failure of either the Host Country or the Project Entity to comply with their respective obligations under the Subsidiary Agreement or any other agreement between the Host Country and Project Entity.

(x) Failure of the Host Country to ratify the Kyoto Protocol within 180 days of its entry into force.

(xi) Withdrawal, or the delivery of written notice for withdrawal, of the Host Country from the UNFCCC or the Kyoto Protocol, or the exclusion of the Host Country from Annex I to the UNFCCC, or Annex B to the Kyoto Protocol.

(xii) Breach of any representation, warranty, covenant, or agreement of the Host Country provided under this Agreement, other than failure to deliver the Minimum Emission Reductions due per calendar year as set forth in the schedule in Section 2.03.

(xiii) Failure of the Host Country to deliver for three (3) consecutive calendar years the Minimum Emission Reductions due pursuant to Section 2.03, provided that the cumulative amount of MERs delivered in the three years in question is at least 30% short of the cumulative amount of MERs that the Host Country was required to deliver in that three year period.

(xiv) Failure of the Host Country to deliver for five consecutive calendar years the Minimum Emission Reductions due pursuant to Section 2.03 of this Agreement, provided that the cumulative amount of MERs delivered in the five years in question is at least 15% short of the cumulative amount of MERs that the Host Country was required to deliver in that five-year period.

(xv) Non-delivery by the Host Country of the Total MERs prior to 1 January 2013 or on such other date as permitted in writing by the Trustee.

(xvi) The authorization or undertaking by any person or entity of an investment in the territory of the Host Country that is, in the reasonable opinion of the Trustee, inconsistent with the provisions of this Agreement, and shall make it improbable for its objectives to be attained.

(xvii) The occurrence of any other event or circumstance that, in the reasonable opinion of the Trustee, materially adversely affects the ability of the Host Country to perform its obligations hereunder.

(b) The event set forth in subparagraph (xv) of paragraph (a) of this Section, shall not constitute an event of default in case the Trustee fails to pay within thirty (30) days of the notice set forth in Section 7.03 (a) of this Agreement any portion of the Purchase price due, and such failure causes such a delay in the Project's Development and Construction Phase that generation of the Total MERs before 1 January 2013 becomes unlikely; Host Country shall have the right to file with the Trustee a claim that the Schedule of Minimum Emission Reductions To Be Delivered set forth in Section 2.03 of this Agreement, is to be adjusted. Such a claim must specify the amounts of MERs per calendar year and Total MERs that the Host Country believes are appropriate and provide the basis for such belief.

(i) *No Dispute.* If the Trustee agrees with the Host Country on the said amounts and years, the schedule set forth in Section 2.03 of this Agreement shall be adjusted accordingly.

(ii) *Dispute Resolution.* If the Trustee disagrees with the Host Country's claim:

(A) *Consultation.* The Trustee shall respond to the Host Country's claim in writing within fifteen (15) days of receipt of such claim and, in any event, shall, over the course of the thirty (30) days following the receipt of such claim, consult or negotiate with the Host Country to arrive at a mutually agreed upon applicable amounts of MERs per calendar year and Total MERs;

(B) *Mediation or Expert Determination.* In the event such consultations do not lead to a mutually agreed upon amounts of MERs per calendar year and Total MERs, the Parties shall refer the matter to a mutually agreed upon third party mediator or third party expert that, in the case of a mediator, shall attempt to mediate the dispute and (failing a settlement) shall be required to issue its determination as to the applicable price, and, in the case of an expert, shall determine the applicable price based on its own expertise or market research. In all events (unless agreed by the Parties), the determination of the mediator or expert shall be issued by no later than the date thirty (30) days following the date the dispute was submitted to such mediator or expert. Subject to the provisions of Section 6.01 (b)(iii)(C) below, the Parties agree to accept the determination of the mediator or expert;

(C) *Arbitration.* In the event the Parties cannot agree upon a mediator or expert, or if, within fifteen (15) days after the issuance of the determination of the mediator or expert, one Party notifies the other that it does not accept that determination, then either Party may submit the matter to arbitration in accordance with the provisions of Sections 9.03;

(D) *Cost of Mediation or Expert Determination.* The Parties shall share equally the cost of the mediator or expert.

Section 6.02 Notice and Cure

(a) Upon the occurrence of any of the events of default specified under Section 6.01, the Trustee shall deliver to the Host Country a notice of default, specifying with particularity the occurrence, event, or condition upon which the notice is based.

(b) Other than with respect to the events or occurrences specified under Sections 6.01(xi) (for which no cure period shall apply), the Host Country shall have sixty (60) days following the delivery of a notice of default to cure the defaults specified in such notice, *provided that*, the parties may mutually agree to extend the time for such cure. The Host Country's failure to demonstrate to the satisfaction of the Trustee that all such defaults have been cured within the sixty day period, or such other period as mutually agreed, shall give rise to the Trustee's right to pursue the remedies set forth in Section 6.03.

Section 6.03 Remedies

Upon the occurrence of any event of default under Section 6.01 and the failure of the Host Country to cure such default as provided under Section 6.02, the Trustee may elect to exercise any one or more rights provided hereunder. In addition, the Trustee shall be entitled to pursue all other rights or remedies provided under applicable law; such rights or remedies shall be cumulative and may be exercised concurrently or successively. The selection of any one or more rights or remedies shall not operate as a waiver of any other rights or remedies.

(a) If any event of default occurs during the period prior to the start of Commercial Operations of the Project, then the Trustee may terminate this Agreement upon notice to the Host Country, and require the Host Country to repay the Trustee, within ninety (90) days of such request, any portions of the Purchase Price already paid plus interest on any such amounts at the rate of LIBOR plus 0.55% from the dates such portions of the Purchase Price were delivered to the Host Country to the dates such amounts are repaid to the Trustee.

(b) If any event of default occurs after the start of Commercial Operations of the Project, then the Trustee may, upon a notice to the Host Country, terminate this Agreement and require the Host Country to repay the Trustee, within ninety (90) days of such request, an amount that shall be equal to:

$$\frac{\text{Total MERs} - \text{MERs actually delivered}}{\text{Total MERs}} \quad \text{x} \quad \text{Purchase Price}$$

plus interest on any such amounts so calculated at a rate equal to LIBOR plus 0.55% from the dates such amounts were delivered to the Host Country to the dates such amounts are repaid to the Trustee.

ARTICLE VII

Events of Default by the Trustee; Remedies

Section 7.01 Events of Default by Trustee

Each of the following events shall constitute an event of default on the part of the Trustee:

(a) Failure to pay installments of the Purchase Price in accordance with this Agreement.

(b) Failure to arrange for Initial Verification, Verification and Certification in accordance with this Agreement in a timely manner; in particular with respect to GHG emission reductions generated by the Project in years where MERs constitute a milestone for a Milestone Payment.

(c) Failure to cooperate with the Host Country and any Independent Third Party to ensure proper Verification, Certification, transfer, and delivery of Greenhouse Gas emission reductions in accordance with the UNFCCC, the Kyoto Protocol, and any decisions, guidelines, modalities, and procedures adopted under those agreements.

Section 7.02 Notice and Cure

(a) Upon occurrence of any of the events specified under Section 7.01, the Host Country shall deliver to the Trustee a notice of default, specifying with particularity the occurrence, event, or condition upon which the notice is based.

(b) The Trustee shall have thirty (30) days following the delivery of a notice of default to cure the defaults specified in such notice, provided that the Parties may mutually agree to extend the time for such cure. The Trustee's failure to demonstrate to the satisfaction of the Host Country that all such defaults have been cured within the thirty day period, or such other period as mutually agreed, shall give rise to the Host Country's right to pursue the remedies set forth in Section 7.03.

Section 7.03 Remedies

(a) Upon the occurrence of any event of default under paragraph (a) of Section 7.01 and the failure of the Trustee to cure such default as provided under Section 7.02, the Host Country may upon notice to the Trustee, require the Trustee to pay within ninety (90) days of such request any portion of the

Purchase Price due, plus interest on any such amounts at the rate of LIBOR plus 0.55%, from the dates such portion were due to the dates such amounts are paid to the Host Country.

(b) Upon the occurrence of any event of default under paragraphs (b), (c) or (d) of Section 7.01 and the failure of the Trustee to cure such default as provided under Section 7.02, the Host Country may, upon notice to the Trustee, suspend delivery of ERs, until such time as Trustee shall have resumed it's obligations under said paragraphs, upon which delivery by the Host Country of any amounts of ERs for which delivery was suspended, shall be made in full.

ARTICLE VIII

Cooperation and Information

Section 8.01 Cooperation and Information

The Host Country and Trustee shall cooperate fully to assure that the purposes of this Agreement will be accomplished. To that end, the Host Country and Trustee shall:

(a) from time to time, at the request of any one of them, exchange views with regard to the progress of the Project, the purpose of this Agreement and their respective obligations under this Agreement; and furnish to the other Party all such information related thereto as it shall reasonably request; and

(b) promptly inform each other of any condition which interferes with, or threatens to interfere with, the matters referred to in paragraph (a) above.

Section 8.02 Treatment of information and release of information

Each Party to this Agreement shall be allowed to disclose or divulge non-proprietary information regarding the Project to third parties. The Parties shall keep each other informed of any such disclosure.

ARTICLE IX

Miscellaneous Provisions

Section 9.01 Enforceability

The rights and obligations of the Host Country and the Trustee under this Agreement shall be valid and enforceable in accordance with their terms notwithstanding the law of any state or political subdivision thereof to the contrary. Neither the Host Country nor the Trustee shall be entitled in any proceeding arising out of or relating to this Agreement to assert any claim that any provision of this Agreement is invalid or unenforceable because of any provision contained in the Instrument.

Section 9.02 Failure to Exercise Rights

No delay in exercising, or omission to exercise, any right, power, or remedy accruing to any party under this Agreement shall impair any such right, power, or remedy or be construed to be a waiver thereof. No action of such party in respect of any default or any acquiescence by it in default, shall affect or impair any right, power, or remedy of such party in respect of any other or subsequent default.

Section 9.03 Arbitration

Without prejudice to the provisions of Sections 2.04(b)(ii), 2.04(b)(iii) and 6.01(b)(ii), any dispute between the Parties arising out of or relating to this Agreement shall be finally settled by arbitration in accordance with the UNCITRAL Arbitration Rules as at present in force. The number of arbitrators shall be three. The appointing authority shall be the Secretary-General of the Permanent Count of Arbitration at The Hague. The language to be used in the arbitral proceedings shall be English.

Section 9.04 Revalidation of Baseline

(a) The Trustee and Host Country may each require and arrange for re-Validation of the Baseline, each at its own expense, provided that the Independent Third Party that is to perform such re-Validation and the methodology to be utilized in such re-Validation, is subject to prior written approval by the Trustee.

(b) In the event that re-Validation of the Baseline is required by any decisions, guidelines, modalities, and procedures to be adopted under the regulatory framework of the UNFCCC or the Kyoto Protocol, the Trustee, at its own expense, shall arrange for such re-Validation.

Section 9.05 Amendments to Monitoring and Verification Protocol

The Trustee has the right to introduce amendments to the Monitoring and Verification Protocol (i) when such amendments are necessary to reflect any guidelines for Monitoring, Verification and reporting that may be elaborated by the Parties to the UNFCCC; (ii) when such amendments appear warranted by concerns identified by the Independent Third Party; or (iii) in the event that a re-Validation of the Baseline leads to an outcome which is substantially different from that in the Validation Report.

Section 9.06 Amendments to the Agreement

Except as otherwise provided herein, this Agreement may not be amended except by a written agreement executed by Trustee and the Host Country.

Section 9.07 IBRD Capacity; Non-Recourse; Privileges and Immunities

(a) This Agreement is entered into by the IBRD, not personally or in its individual capacity, but as trustee of the PCF pursuant to the Instrument. The obligations of the PCF under this Agreement are not binding upon the IBRD or any of the PCF Participants, personally or in their respective individual capacities, but bind only the PCF.

(b) The Host Country agrees to look solely to the assets of the PCF for the enforcement of any obligations, claims, or liabilities under or in connection with this Agreement or the Project, as neither the Trustee, IBRD, any of its affiliated entities, the PCF Participants, other beneficiaries of the PCF, nor any of their respective officers, directors, employees, partners, members, or shareholders, assume or shall be subject to any personal liability for any of the obligations, claims, or liabilities entered into, or incurred hereunder, on behalf of PCF.

(c) Nothing in this Agreement shall be considered to be a waiver of any privileges and immunities of the IBRD, the Trustee, or, where applicable, the PCF Participants or their respective officers, employees, representatives or agents, under the Articles of Agreement of IBRD or any applicable law. All such privileges and immunities are expressly reserved.

Section 9.08 Notices

Any notice communication, request, or correspondence required or permitted under the terms of this Agreement shall be in writing, in the English language (it being understood that any such communication in a language other than English shall be of no force and effect), and shall be delivered personally, or via courier, mail, or facsimile to the address and telecopier numbers provided below.

For the Host Country:

Ministry of Finance

1 Smilsu Street
Riga, LV-1919
Republic of Latvia

Telex: 871 161 299
Facsimile: 371 7095 503

For the Trustee:

Prototype Carbon Fund

1818 H Street, N.W.
Washington, D.C. 20433
United States of America

Cable address: INTBAFRAD, Washington, D.C.
Telex: 248423 (MCI) or 64145 (MCI)
Facsimile: (202) 477-6391

Section 9.09 Execution in counterparts; Language

This Agreement shall be executed in two counterparts in the English language, each of which shall be an original.

Section 9.10 Action on behalf of the Host Country or Trustee

(a) For the purposes of Section 9.10(b) the Minister of Finance of the Host Country is hereby designated as representative of the Host Country and the Vice President of Environmentally and Socially Sustainable Development is hereby designated as representative of the Trustee.

(b) Any action required or permitted to be taken, and any documents required or permitted to be executed, pursuant to this Agreement on behalf of the

Host Country (or Trustee) may be taken or executed by the representative of the Host Country (or Trustee) designated in this Agreement for the purposes of this Section or any person thereunto authorized in writing by such representative. Any modification or amplification of the provisions of this Agreement may be agreed to on behalf of the Host Country (or Trustee) by written instrument executed on behalf of the Host Country (or Trustee) by the representative so designated or any person thereunto authorized in writing by such representative; provided that, in the opinion of such representative, such modification or amplification is reasonable in the circumstances and will not substantially increase the obligations of the Host Country (or Trustee) under this Agreement. The Host Country (or Trustee) may accept the execution by such representative or other person of any such instrument as conclusive evidence that in the opinion of such representative any modification or amplification of the provisions of this Agreement effected by such instrument is reasonable in the circumstances and will not substantially increase the obligations of the Host Country (or Trustee) thereunder.

Section 9.11 Evidence of Authority

The Parties shall furnish to each other sufficient evidence of the authority of the person of persons who will, on their behalf, take any action to execute any documents required or permitted to be taken or executed by the respective Parties under this Agreement, and the authenticated specimen signature of each such person.

ARTICLE X

Effective Date; Expiration; Earlier Termination

Section 10.01 Conditions Precedent to Effectiveness of this Agreement

This Agreement shall become effective on the date evidence satisfactory to the Trustee shall have been furnished to the Trustee demonstrating that:

(a) The execution and delivery of this Agreement on behalf of the Host Country has been duly authorized or ratified by all necessary governmental and corporate action and, upon execution and delivery, this Agreement shall constitute the legal, valid, binding, and enforceable obligation of each Party hereto;

(b) The Loan Agreement the NIB Loan Agreement, the SIDA Grant Agreement have been executed and delivered, and all conditions precedent (other than the effectiveness of this Agreement) to their effectiveness and to the right of the Host Country to effect draws thereunder, have been fulfilled;

(c) the Subsidiary Agreement has been executed and delivered, and all conditions precedent to its effectiveness, other than the effectiveness of this Agreement, have been fulfilled; and

(d) The Host Country has notified the Secretariat of the UNFCCC, in a manner satisfactory to the Trustee, of this Agreement and of its intention to debit its Assigned Amount in the amount of at least the Total MERs.

Section 10.02 Legal Opinions or Certificates

As part of the evidence to be furnished pursuant to Section 10.01, there shall be furnished to the Trustee opinions satisfactory to the Trustee of counsel acceptable to the Trustee or, if the Trustee shall so request, a certificate satisfactory to the Trustee of a competent official of the Host Country demonstrating that:

(a) This Agreement has been duly authorized or ratified by, and executed and delivered on behalf of the Host Country, and is a legal, valid and binding obligation of the Host Country enforceable in accordance with its terms;

(b) The Loan Agreement, the NIB Loan Agreement, and the SIDA Grant Agreement have been duly authorized or ratified by the Host Country, and each is a legal, valid and binding obligation of the parties thereto enforceable in accordance with its terms;

(c) The Subsidiary Agreement has been duly authorized or ratified by the Host Country and the Project Entity and is a legal, valid and binding obligation of the Host Country and Project Entity enforceable in accordance with its terms; and

(d) The Host Country has duly notified the Secretariat of the UNFCCC of this Agreement and of its intention to debit its Assigned Amount in the amount of at least the Total MERs.

Section 10.03 Effective Date; Expiration

This Agreement shall enter into effect on the date upon which the Trustee delivers to the Host Country notice of its acceptance of the evidence required by Section 10.01, and, unless otherwise earlier terminated in accordance with the provisions hereof, shall continue in full force and effect until the Project Termination Date.

Section 10.04 Termination of this Agreement for Failure to Become Effective

If this Agreement shall not have entered into effect by ninety (90) days after the date of this Agreement, this Agreement and all obligations of the Parties hereunder shall terminate, unless the Trustee, in its sole discretion after consideration of the reasons for the delay, shall establish a later date for the purposes of this Section. The Trustee shall promptly notify the Host Country of such later date.

Section 10.05 Assignment

(a) The Host Country may not assign, delegate, or revoke its rights or obligations under this Agreement to any party without the prior written consent of the Trustee, such consent not to be unreasonably withheld. Any such purported assignment without such consent shall be deemed ineffective and void.

(b) The Trustee may assign all or a part of its rights and obligations under this Agreement at any time to any one or more parties, and in the event of such assignment, the Host Country shall continue to perform its obligations hereunder for the benefit of such assignee(s), it being understood that any reference to the Trustee; or the PCF, or the PCF Participants herein, shall, following such assignment, be deemed to be a reference to such assignee(s). The Trustee shall promptly notify the Host Country of such assignment.

IN WITNESS WHEREOF, the parties hereto have caused this Agreement to be duly executed as of the date first above written.

REPUBLIC OF LATVIA

_____________/s/______________________

By: Gundars Berzins

Title: Minister of Finance

INTERNATIONAL BANK FOR RECONSTRUCTION AND DEVELOPMENT, AS TRUSTEE OF THE PROTOTYPE CARBON FUND

_____________/s/______________________

By: Basil Kavalski

Title: Acting Vice President, Europe and Central Asia

SCHEDULE 1

Description of the Project

The objective of the Project is to generate Greenhouse Gas emission reductions through maximum collection and utilization of landfill gas in Liepaja City and Liepaja Region.

The Project consists of the following parts, subject to such modifications thereof as the Host Country and the Trustee may agree upon from time to time to achieve such objectives:

Part A: Development and Construction Phase

1. Remediation and closure of selected existing dumpsites through separation of surface water coverage and/or re-vegetation, according to the condition of each site.
2. Improvement of site operation through establishment of: (a) a sorting line for separation of recyclable materials; (b) separate storage areas for recyclable and hazardous materials treatment plant for collected leachate; and (c) automated transportation system between cells and special equipment to treat sludge.
3. Shredding equipment for pretreatment of waste before transport to the energy cells, installation of energy cells and a landfill gas collection system.
4. Installation of a power generator, running on landfill gas, of about 1 megawatt capacity at Grobina and of about 0.3 megawatts capacity at Skede.
5. Establishment of waste collection points in each municipality in Liepaja Region to assure the efficient transport of waste to the regional disposal site, and provision of vehicles for transportation.
6. Provision of the detailed design, including technical specifications, bill of quantities, and all necessary drawings for project implementation and bidding documents.

Part B: Commercial Operations Phase

Operation of the Project after Initial Verification until the Project Termination Date during which there shall be (1) collection of landfill gas (LFG) containing about 50 percent methane, and (2) use of captured methane to generate electricity.

SCHEDULE 2

Schedule of payments (in '000 U.S.$)

	Fiscal Year (starting July 1)	*Amount ('000 U.S.$)*	
SUMS TO BE RETAINED BY TRUSTEE			
*** following the Effective Date**			
1. costs incurred by Trustee	FY01*	201	
2. administrative fee	FY01*	25	
3. Advance Payment	FY01*	595	15-Jan-01
Sub Total		821	31-Mar-01
MILESTONE PAYMENTS			
1. Award of contract for remediaton of Skede waste disposal site	FY02	585	
2. Installation of gas pumping station and power generation equipment at Grobina	FY03	372	1-Jul-02
3. Delivery of MERs for calendar year 2003	FY04	22	1-Jul-03
4. Delivery of MERs for calendar year 2004	FY05	280	1-Jul-04
5. Delivery of MERs for calendar year 2005	FY06	147	1-Jul-05
			31-Dec-12
FINAL PAYMENT (upon delivery of Total MERs)	FY13	250	
Total PURCHASE PRICE		2477	

SCHEDULE 3

Validation Report

WORLD BANK

VALIDATION OF THE LIEPAJA REGIONAL SOLID WASTE MANAGEMENT PROJECT

Summary

DNV[23] has validated the Greenhouse gas components (methane capture and electricity generation) of the PCF financed Liepaja Regional Solid Waste Management Project. The report describes the methods employed for validating the project, presents a validation protocol as the main tool for a transparent verification of the project design, and concludes with a validation opinion.

The Liepaja validation, the first of a series of possible PCF investments, has been performed in the absence of clearly agreed criteria and methodologies for auditing of such projects. Also, the modalities and procedures for JI projects under the Kyoto Protocol have not yet been agreed. This validation should thus be seen as a first step in developing clear and transparent procedures and methods of validating PCF projects. This is in line with the learning objective of the PCF.

The methods used to estimate and monitor emissions and emission reductions have been found to be acceptable, and when applied correctly, are likely to generate the GHG reductions to be expected from the project. The validation has not attempted to quantify the emission reductions expected from the project.

In the opinion of DNV and based on our identified requirements for PCF investments, JI projects and those of the host country, the project design, including the baseline and the Monitoring and Verification Protocol, meets all the requirements necessary to qualify for financing by the PCF.

---

20 Det Norske Veritas.

ETHICAL NORMS FOR THE JUDICIAL BRANCH OF THE REPUBLIC OF GUATEMALA

Note*

Following the signing of Guatemala's historic peace accords in December 1996, the country undertook to design a major reform of its judicial branch. It was realized that the success of the judiciary would hinge on its ability to serve the people, on the incorporation of the spirit of ethics and fairness into its judicial body, and on the furtherance of that body's professional development.

In response to this challenge, and as part of its medium-term modernization plan, the Guatemalan judicial branch selected a group of justices and technical professionals from a wide range of institutions and organizations to take part in a series of workshops focused on developing a code of ethics. These included the Guatemalan Institute of Magistrates, the Guatemalan Association of Judges and Magistrates, circuit judges, the Modernization Unit of the Guatemalan Judiciary, and representatives from the international development assistance community. Discussions centered not only on technical content but also, and perhaps more importantly, on transformation of the judicial mindset. The historical circumstances dictated the overall framework for the effort: the fundamental need for the application of integrity and fairness in both the comportment of the judge and in the interpretation of the law.

In working out the structure and content of the code, a large number of public and private sector ethics codes were consulted. Among the codes applicable to judiciaries and other public entities, sources from many different countries were used, including the United States, Mexico, Colombia, Argentina, Barbados, and the Dominican Republic, as well as the United Nation's Basic Principles on the Independence of the Judiciary. The private sector codes that were consulted included those of entities like the National Publishers Association of Guatemala, Proctor & Gamble USA, and El Economista (Mexican newspaper).

---

* Note contributed by Waleed Malik, Senior Public Sector Management Specialist, World Bank. The author gratefully acknowledges the invaluable assistance of Justices Carlos Esteban Larios Ochaita and Barreda Valenzuela of the Guatemalan Supreme Court of Justice.

The World Bank Legal Review: Law and Justice for Development: 525-539.

Printed in the Netherlands.

The code of ethics that resulted from the effort is reproduced in its entirety below. It is included here as a recent example of how one country's judiciary that is serious about tackling issues of integrity and public trust resolved the difficult questions that arise in the crafting of a new code of ethics. Also included is the official introduction by Magistrate Dr. Barreda Valenzuela, who spearheaded the effort and whose comments demonstrate eloquently the wider societal context in which the document needs to be seen and its importance appreciated.

Introduction

Supreme Court Agreement No.7-2001, "Ethical Norms for the Judicial Branch of the Republic of Guatemala", is the product of a collective effort by the Magistrates' Institute, the Association of Judges and Magistrates of the Judicial Branch and of members of civil society who participated in the workshops held over the past year.

The Supreme Court of Justice dedicated a number of extraordinary plenary sessions to considering the Draft Agreement and benefited from the collaboration and support of Dr. Roberto Brenes.

To all those who contributed their constructive criticism and disinterested comments during this process, I extend my sincere thanks. They enlarged the original scope of the project and contributed to the adoption, on March 21, 2001, of the first legal body of ethical norms in Guatemala's history ever to be adopted by a state institution.

Agreement No.7-2001 will serve as a basis for workshops and seminars to be offered throughout Guatemala over the coming years to ensure that all judicial branch civil servants take up the mantle of integrity and arm themselves with rectitude, honor, loyalty, and prudence. The overriding goal of this project is to achieve justice, by ensuring that the constitution is rigorously applied and that human rights are respected, thereby contributing to building the lasting peace that Guatemalans so desire.

Well aware that the judicial branch is not an island unto itself, but rather part of a system, we join forces with other government institutions in the fight against corruption with the publication of these norms and activities to promote their application in every court in the land.

Dr. Edgardo Daniel Barreda Valenzuela

Magistrate X

Supreme Court of Justice

Supreme Court of Justice

ETHICAL NORMS FOR THE JUDICIAL BRANCH

AGREEMENT NO.7-2001

THE SUPREME COURT OF JUSTICE

RECOGNIZING that the Supreme Court of Justice has a duty to ensure the fulfillment of its obligations to impart justice and to preserve and strengthen democracy.

CONSCIOUS that magistrates, judges, civil servants, auxiliary and administrative support staff are an essential part of the administration of justice, that they must serve the community and that their functions must therefore be carried out in accordance with clear ethical and moral norms requiring each and every one of them to act with: honor, probity, decorum, prudence, rectitude, loyalty, respect, independence, impartiality, veracity, efficiency, solidarity and dignity in all matters, demonstrating exemplary conduct, honesty and good faith in every one of their actions.

EMPOWERED by paragraph (f) of article 54 of the Judicial Branch Act,

HAS AGREED on the following:

ETHICAL NORMS FOR THE JUDICIAL BRANCH OF THE REPUBLIC OF GUATEMALA

CHAPTER I – DEFINITIONS AND SCOPE OF APPLICATION

Article 1 – Scope of application

These norms will apply to the acts of all judges, civil servants and employees of the Guatemalan Judicial Branch, subject to provisions of other applicable norms.

Article 2 – Binding nature

The norms set out in this Agreement are binding on all Judicial Branch personnel whenever they apply. The bodies established by the Judicial Career Act and the Act Respecting the Judicial Branch Civil Service must, within their respective areas of competence, ensure strict compliance with these norms and, where necessary, impose appropriate sanctions in cases of a violation in accordance with the aforementioned laws.

Article 3 – Definitions

For the purposes of this Agreement, the following definitions apply:

a) Judge: Any civil servant elected to the position of magistrate or appointed to the position of judge.
b) Employee: all auxiliary judicial personnel and all administrative and technical support staff.
c) *A quo:* a judge or tribunal whose decision may be appealed.
d) *Ad quem:* a judge or tribunal to whom a party has appealed the decision of a lower tribunal.
e) *Sub judice:* a case in process, pending judicial resolution.

CHAPTER II – ESSENTIAL VALUES AND ETHICAL PRINCIPLES FOR THE ADMINISTRATION OF JUSTICE

Article 4 – Fundamental values

It is the State's duty to carry out the administration of justice, thereby providing an essential public service oriented toward resolving conflicts in a manner that preserves peace and the stability of the democratic system, as well as protecting human rights and the security of its citizens. This service must be of the highest quality and efficiency, taking into account each of the values and propositions set out in the second paragraph of the Preamble to this Agreement.

Article 5 – Guiding principles of integrity and independence

In exercising their function, judges must ensure that they conduct themselves with integrity and independence in their sensitive functions, thereby contributing to strengthening respect for, and confidence in, the judiciary.

Article 6 – Moderation and self-evaluation

All those who administer justice must use moderation in exercising the powers attributed to them, keeping in mind their personal responsibility for every action they take. Thus, they must continuously evaluate their own beliefs and convictions, while maintaining absolute respect for those of their colleagues when they form part of a bench together.

Article 7 – Justification for and reasoning in judicial decisions

In fulfilling his or her duty to justify judicial decisions, the judge must not limit him or herself to citing the applicable legislation, especially where the decision relates to the substantial issues of the case. Rather, the judge must respond to the arguments and pleadings advanced by the parties so as to ensure that the decision appears reasonable and well founded to them.

Article 8 – Duty of transparency

In order to guarantee transparency, every judicial civil servant must record in writing, and permit publication of, all actions taken, subject to exceptions to the duty of public disclosure established by law.

Article 9 – Duty of secrecy

The judge has a duty of secrecy with respect to matters *sub judice* when the law so provides or, in the absence of applicable provisions, when the judge is of the view that the legitimate rights or interests of one of the parties to the case might be affected, or where it is clear that it is not in the public interest to publish the information. Similarly, a judge who is a member of a panel must safeguard the secrecy of all tribunal deliberations.

Article 10 – Limitations on judicial independence

Judicial independence is subject only to the Political Constitution of the Republic of Guatemala, to the laws of the land and to the fundamental values and principles contained therein.

Article 11 – Advancing the rule of law

Without prejudice to the fulfillment of their duties, judges shall participate in and promote activities oriented toward improving and strengthening the rule of law, the administration of justice and respect for human rights.

CHAPTER III – FUNCTIONS, RELATIONSHIPS AND DISCIPLINE

Article 12 – Qualities required of judges in the exercise of their substantive judicial functions

The proper exercise of judicial functions requires the judge to be hard working, prudent, serene, impartial and meticulous. The judge must be devoted to the study of the law, constantly updating his or her knowledge of the law and engaging in continuing education whenever possible. The judge must be diligent at all times.

Article 13 – Updating knowledge and continuing education

Judicial civil servants must commit themselves to modernizing and improving the administration of their courts and of the legal system.

Article 14 – Minimizing formal requirements.

Judges must keep to a minimum any formal requirements that would prevent the resolution of matters within their jurisdiction. Provided there is no legal prohibition on doing so, judges must promote reconciliation between the parties, or at the very least, seek to mitigate hostility between them.

In accordance with the principle of effective judicial tutelage, a judge shall only reject submissions made to him or her due to a failure to comply with formal requirements where those requirements are clearly established by law and where the defect therefore cannot be rectified.

Article 15 – Personal relationships

Persons who administer justice must maintain professional and cooperative relationships among themselves and among the staff they employ, in order to achieve the efficient administration of justice.

The conduct of persons who administer justice must be governed by the principles of mutual respect, cordiality and professional cooperation, without regard to hierarchical status.

Persons who administer justice shall avoid making unfounded or unnecessary criticisms that would diminish the prestige of their fellow judges. They shall ensure that their conduct as judicial professionals conforms to these ethical norms and is exemplary both in their personal lives and in the exercise of their professional functions.

Article 16 – Respect for, and availability to, parties and citizens

Judges shall make themselves available to parties and their lawyers and maintain a respectful attitude toward them, while ensuring that their contact with parties and their lawyers does not create the perception that there exists any privileged relationship between them or that they are acting outside of their professional relationship.

This same attitude must be maintained in dealings with all citizens, demonstrating the consideration and respect owed to every person.

Article 17 – Reporting improper acts

When judges, or other civil servants or employees of the judicial branch, become aware of any improper or dishonest act by a colleague or by a lawyer, they must take appropriate actions to ensure that proper proceedings are carried out.

Article 18 – Basic duties of civil servants and employees of the judicial branch

The following are the basic duties and conduct required of civil servants and employees of the judicial branch:

a) To carry out with maximum diligence any services required of them, ensuring that their work is carried out in a punctual fashion and abstaining from any acts or omissions that would cause the services provided to be suspended or to function poorly.

b) To safeguard documents and information in their charge, by preventing the misuse, removal, destruction, concealment or failure to use documents or information.

c) To conduct themselves properly in all aspects of their employment, treating with respect, diligence, impartiality, and honesty all people with whom they come into contact, whether they be parties, the public or other civil servants.

d) To abstain from any offense, misappropriation or abuse of authority.

e) To refuse to accept or receive, either directly or indirectly, any present, gift, offer or promise in exchange for carrying out their duties or for abstaining from carrying out their duties. It is also prohibited for civil servants and employees to accept, in the conduct of their duties, any gift, employment, position or commission for themselves, their spouses or their relatives, offered by any natural or legal person whose professional, commercial or industrial activities are directly linked to the civil servant or employee's work, or are subject to a proceeding, or are regulated or supervised by the civil servant or employee.

f) To abstain from intervening or participating without cause in the selection, appointment, designation, contracting, promotion, suspension, dismissal, relocation, elevation, compulsory retirement or punishment of any civil servant or employee where there exists a personal interest in the outcome – either due to a family or business relationship – or where an advantage or benefit may be derived for the civil servant or employee or for his or her spouse or relatives.

g) To carry out their job without seeking benefits additional to the salary and other legal entitlements provided by the judicial branch for the exercise of their functions.

h) Superiors must act in accordance with the rules of good conduct toward their staff. Similarly, all civil servants and employees must maintain a respectful attitude toward their superiors.

Article 19 – Special duties for persons exercising substantive judicial functions

In addition to the duties outlined above and others established in these ethical norms applying to persons exercising substantive judicial functions, the following are also basic duties for those who exercise substantive judicial functions:

a) To ensure that no attacks are made on the dignity of, and respect owed to tribunals.

b) To take all necessary measures to prohibit improper conduct in the administration of justice, whether it be by lawyers, prosecutors, civil servants or employees of the tribunal or by any other person.

c) To act with prudence.

d) To ensure that judicial proceedings and the conduct of the tribunal are carried out in a disciplined, solemn and respectful environment and to ensure that no employee or person be allowed to disturb the order which must govern in court.

e) To treat lawyers and all other persons who come before the tribunal with courtesy.

f) To ensure that experts, arbitrators, trustees and others who provide assistance to the court are selected based on their knowledge of the subject-matter at hand and are competent, impartial and honorable.

CHAPTER IV – IMPARTIALITY AND INDEPENDENCE

Article 20 – Impartiality

Every judge must be impartial and conduct him or herself in such a way as to exclude any appearance that he or she is susceptible to the influence of other persons, groups or parties, or to the influence of public opinion, considerations of popularity or notoriety, or to any other improper motive. Every judge shall remain conscious that his or her only task is to impart justice in accordance with the applicable law, with total equanimity and without regard for any criticism of his or her work.

Every judge must impart justice freely, subject only to the law and the principles that sustain it, impervious to any emotional considerations that might influence his or her decision.

Article 21 – Respect for dignity and equality

Every judge must respect the dignity of human beings and recognize their right to equality, without discrimination on the basis of sex, culture, ideology, race, religion, language, nationality, personal or socioeconomic status.

Each judge must make every effort to become aware of, and eventually overcome, his or her own cultural prejudices based on origins or training, particularly if these may have a negative impact on the full appreciation and weighing of the facts or in the interpretation of the law.

Article 22 – Rejection of pressure

Every judge must reject any pressure, influence or request of any type that is made for the illegitimate purpose of affecting the time required or the method used to resolve the cases under his or her consideration. In order to prevent such situations from arising, the judge shall refuse invitations and requests to hold private meetings with parties outside of the exercise of his or her functions. The judge must avoid direct ties to political parties, to unions or to business organizations that might influence the exercise of his or her duties or tarnish his or her image as independent and impartial.

In carrying out his or her duties, the judge must avoid acts or attitudes that in any way give the impression that his or her social, business or family relationships or friendships have an influence on his or her decisions.

Article 23 – Employee impartiality

Every employee exercising or assisting with judicial functions must act impartially in carrying out his or her duties.

Judges must monitor fulfillment of this duty by employees under their authority.

Article 24 – Limits on hierarchical relationships

The *ad quem* shall not intervene, interfere or seek to influence the *a quo* in any cases heard by the *a quo* or in the decisions made thereby, since the only opportunity for review is by way of appeal or by other recourse available to the parties.

Article 25 – Abstention from intervention

Every judge must abstain from intervening in a judicial proceeding where he or she is the object of a recusation proceeding made in accordance with the provisions of the Judicial Branch Act or, more generally, in any case where the judge is of the opinion that he or she may be influenced by factors that would compromise his or her impartiality.

CHAPTER V – PROHIBITED POLITICAL ACTIVITIES, OBLIGATIONS AND PRIVATE MEETINGS

Article 26 – Independence and political activities

Judges must protect and promote their own independence and that of the judicial branch as a means of maintaining the necessary balance in a democratic system. For this reason, no judge may participate in the political process, without prejudice to his or her right to vote, right to hold personal opinions on political matters and duty to exercise functions governed by electoral laws and regulations.

Article 27 – Political activities of civil servants and employees

It is the judge's duty to ensure that other civil servants and employees of the tribunal or tribunals under his or her authority do not engage in political activity that would bring the image and impartiality of the judicial branch into disrepute.

Article 28 – Application of the duty to act with diligence

Judges shall intervene in the conduct of proceedings to avoid unjustified delays, to clarify any matters outstanding and to prevent injustice.

Article 29 – The judge as guarantor of the right to due process

Every judge shall remain aware of the fact that he or she is not simply an arbiter or moderator of a debate, but rather the guarantor of respect for the right to fair process and, in this respect, that the judge in general has an obligation of result, rather than of mere respect or non-interference.

Article 30 – Prohibition on reprisals for the exercise of a right

During all proceedings, and especially at the moment of sentencing, the judge shall not allow the exercise of the right to due process to influence his or her state of mind. On the contrary, the judge must ensure that this right is exercised in accordance with all guarantees.

Article 31 – Private meetings with parties

Judges shall ensure that private meetings with parties or their lawyers, or communications or arguments made by the same, do not contravene the principles of procedural fairness and equality, nor do they lead to the denial of the right to full and fair defense of one of the parties. Judges shall take special care to ensure that the impartiality of their judgment is not impaired.

CHAPTER VI – CONDUCT DURING TRIALS

Article 32 – Consideration and respect as general duty

Judges' integrity and the severity required of them in certain cases shall never go beyond the bounds of respect and consideration for the parties involved in the proceeding. In particular, the judge must remain conscious of the need to limit the publicity of proceedings in cases where intimacy, modesty or human suffering demand it, provided that this does not give rise to a risk of prejudicing a just outcome or the rights involved.

Article 33 – Duty of consideration and courtesy

Every judge shall be considerate and respectful toward the parties and their lawyers. Judges must conduct themselves in the same manner with witnesses, experts, trustees, civil servants of the tribunal and any other person appearing before them.

Similarly, judges shall ensure that all employees of the tribunal, lawyers and any other persons appearing before them act in the same manner.

Article 34 – Punctuality and delays

Every judge must be punctual in carrying out his or her duties, recognizing the value of time for lawyers, litigants, witnesses, parties and all others appearing before him or her.

All judges shall take necessary measures to avoid situations in which the parties, their lawyers or any other person mentioned in the last paragraph cause unjustified delays in the litigation. Judges shall remain diligent in processing the matters submitted to them for their consideration.

CHAPTER VII – INFLUENCE AND COMMUNITY RELATIONS

Article 35 – Conflicts of interest

No judge shall use his or her position to further the success of his or her private business or for personal benefit.

Article 36 –Undue influence in judicial proceedings

Every judge must avoid all conduct or behavior that, for his or her personal benefit or the benefit of third parties, would exert undue influence over the judgment of any other judge in acting his or her judicial capacity.

Article 37 – Decorum and conduct in public

Judges must be scrupulous in avoiding any acts that might reasonably give the appearance that his or her social, business or family relationships or friendships have an influence on his or her judicial decisions.

Article 38 – Discussion and explanation to the public of judicial acts

Any judge may make statements, whether directly or through the specialized office of the judicial branch, provided that they do not in any way divulge in advance his or her views on matters pending resolution.

Similarly, every judge shall ensure that civil servants and employees under his or her authority conduct themselves in the same fashion.

Article 39 – Statements to the media

Judges who offer statements to the media must take great care to ensure that the statements are objective and do not compromise their duty of impartiality.

With respect to the decisions made by a judge, no limitation may be placed on the right to freedom of expression or the right to access to information except for any law that provides otherwise.

CHAPTER VIII – FINAL PROVISIONS

Article 40 – Other norms

The norms established in the present Agreement do not exclude the observance of other ethical norms designed to achieve upstanding human conduct.

Article 41 – Entry into force

This Agreement shall enter into force thirty days from its publication in the Official Gazette.

Made in the Palace of Justice, in Guatemala City, this twenty-first of March 2001.

Members of the Supreme Court of Justice

President	Justice Hugo Leonel Maúl Figueroa (2000-2001)
Magistrate I	Justice José Rolando Quesada Fernández
Magistrate II	Justice Héctor Aníbal De León Velasco
Magistrate III	Justice Otto Marroquín Guerra
Magistrate IV	Justice Alfonso Carrillo Castillo
Magistrate V	Justice Amanda Ramírez de Arias
Magistrate VI	Justice Carlos Alfonso Alvarez-Lobos V.
Magistrate VIII	Justice Marieliz Lucero Sibley
Magistrate IX	Justice Carlos Esteban Larios Ochaita
Magistrate X	Justice Edgardo Daniel Barreda Valenzuela
Magistrate XI	Justice Napoleón Gutiérrez Vargas
Magistrate XII	Justice Gerardo Alberto Hurtado Flores
Magistrate XIII	Justice Roderico Pineda Sánchez

THE RIGHT TO HOUSING

Government of the Republic of South Africa and Others v. Grootboom and Others, 2000 (11) BCLR 1169 (CC)

Note*

The needs for adequate shelter worldwide are immense. There are an estimated 100 million homeless individuals in our world, and over one billion people lack decent shelter. However, resource constraints impose severe limitations on the capacity of central and local governments to provide for all needs when markets and other private efforts fail. In recognition of this reality, constitutional and legislative requirements with respect to housing typically contain provisions tempering the state's obligations with considerations of reasonableness and financial and other resource availability. As a result, the right to housing, as well as other social and economic rights, pose special problems of implementation and enforceability, especially in poor countries. It is sometimes argued that these rights are not justiciable at all.

The Constitutional Court of South Africa was squarely confronted with these issues in the Grootboom case. Mrs. Irene Grootboom, the lead plaintiff (respondent before the Constitutional Court), and her companions in misery (390 adults and 510 children) were living in conditions of severe hardship while waiting to be allocated subsidized housing. Their wait was likely to last several years. Living, as characterized by the Court, in intolerable conditions, the respondents took matters in their own hands, invaded private property earmarked for low-cost housing, and set up their shacks. Within the year they were forcibly evicted by the municipality and, facing homelessness, found temporary shelter on the municipality's sports field and petitioned the judiciary for relief. The Cape of Good Hope High Court ordered the authorities to provide the children and their parents with shelter, and the authorities, representing national as well as local government, appealed.

---

* Editor's note.

The World Bank Legal Review: Law and Justice for Development: 541-570.

Printed in the Netherlands.

The Constitutional Court found for respondents but set aside the High Court's order. It based its ruling on the constitutional right of access to adequate housing, rather than, as the High Court had done, on the constitutional provision for the shelter of children. It found that the authorities had failed to meet the constitutional requirement that the state must take reasonable legislative and other measures, within its available resources, to achieve the progressive realization of the right to have access to adequate housing. The fact that the relevant governmental housing programs did not include provision for "relief of people who have no access to land, no roof over their heads, and who are living in intolerable conditions or crisis situations" was critical in the Court's reasoning. Consequently, the Court directed the state to fashion and implement, within its available resources, a comprehensive and coordinated program that includes reasonable measures for the relief of people so situated and that will progressively realize the right of access to adequate housing.

It should be noted that in crafting the order as it did, the Court did not grant respondents the relief they had requested, namely the provision of adequate temporary shelter pending the allocation of more permanent accommodations. It did not decide who exactly was entitled under its ruling to reasonable measures for relief, nor what those measures should consist of. Rather, the Court directed the authorities to devise and carry out a plan that left for executive decision the precise manner in which competing priorities and resource constraints would be resolved. To help ensure that its order would yield effective results, the Court appointed the South African Human Rights Commission to monitor the state's implementation of its obligations in accordance with the provisions of the judgment.

In reaching this result, the Court proceeded on the basis of constitutional analysis, interpreting the relevant provisions contextually, with due regard to precedent, and against the social and historical backdrop of the country. While Grootboom is squarely a case of constitutional jurisprudence, the Court duly noted the South African constitutional command that when interpreting the Bill of Rights, a court must consider international law as an interpretive tool, and that this includes "nonbinding as well as binding [public international] law." Even though South Africa was not a party to the International Covenant on Economic, Social and Cultural Rights, the Court discussed its corresponding provisions and, in particular, noted with approval the interpretation by the United Nations Committee on Economic, Social and Cultural Rights of the "progressive realization" standard of the Covenant, which also appears in Section 26(2) of the constitution, and which it adopted. The Grootboom case is a landmark in the jurisprudence of social rights. The main portions of the Constitutional Court's judgment are set forth below.

CONSTITUTIONAL COURT OF SOUTH AFRICA

Case CCT 11/00

THE GOVERNMENT OF THE REPUBLIC OF SOUTH AFRICA	First Appellant
THE PREMIER OF THE PROVINCE OF THE WESTERN CAPE	Second Appellant
CAPE METROPOLITAN COUNCIL	Third Appellant
OOSTENBERG MUNICIPALITY	Fourth Appellant

versus

IRENE GROOTBOOM AND OTHERS	Respondents

Heard on : 11 May 2000

Decided on : 4 October 2000

JUDGMENT *

YACOOB J:

A. Introduction

[1] The people of South Africa are committed to the attainment of social justice and the improvement of the quality of life for everyone. The Preamble to our Constitution records this commitment. The Constitution declares the founding values of our society to be "[h]uman dignity, the achievement of equality and the advancement of human rights and freedoms."[1] This case grapples with the realization of these aspirations for it concerns the state's constitutional obligations in relation to housing: a constitutional issue of fundamental importance to the development of South Africa's new constitutional order.

[2] The issues here remind us of the intolerable conditions under which many of our people are still living. The respondents are but a fraction of them. It is also a reminder that unless the plight of these communities is alleviated, people may be tempted to take the law into their own hands in order to escape these conditions. The case brings home the harsh reality that the Constitution's promise of dignity and equality for all remains for many a distant dream. People should not be impelled by intolerable living conditions to resort to land invasions. Self-help of this kind cannot be tolerated, for the unavailability of land suitable for housing development is a key factor in the fight against the country's housing shortage.

[3] The group of people with whom we are concerned in these proceedings lived in appalling conditions, decided to move out and illegally occupied someone else's land. They were evicted and left homeless. The root cause of their problems is the intolerable conditions under which they were living while waiting in the queue for their turn to be allocated low-cost housing. They are the people whose constitutional rights have to be determined in this case.

---

* The court's judgment appears here in excerpted form. The full opinion is available at <http://www.concourt.gov.za>.

1 See section 1(a) of the Constitution.

[4] Mrs Irene Grootboom and the other respondents[2] were rendered homeless as a result of their eviction from their informal homes situated on private land earmarked for formal low-cost housing. They applied to the Cape of Good Hope High Court (the High Court) for an order requiring government to provide them with adequate basic shelter or housing until they obtained permanent accommodation and were granted certain relief.[3] The appellants were ordered to provide the respondents who were children and their parents with shelter. The judgment provisionally concluded that "tents, portable latrines and a regular supply of water (albeit transported) would constitute the bare minimum."[4] The appellants who represent all spheres of government responsible for housing[5] challenge the correctness of that order.

[5] At the hearing of this matter an offer was made by the appellants to ameliorate the immediate crisis situation in which the respondents were living. The offer was accepted by the respondents. This meant that the matter was not as urgent as it otherwise would have been. However some four months after argument, the respondents made an urgent application to this Court in which they revealed that the appellants had failed to comply with the terms of their offer. That application was set down for 21 September 2000. On that day the Court, after communication with the parties, crafted an order putting the municipality on terms to provide certain rudimentary services.

. . .

---

2 The respondents are 510 children and 390 adults. Mrs Irene Grootboom, the first respondent, brought the application before the High Court on behalf of all the respondents.

3 The judgment of Davis J in which Comrie J concurred is reported as *Grootboom v Oostenberg Municipality and Others* 2000 (3) BCLR 277 (C).

4 *Id.* at 293A.

5 The first appellant is the Government of the Republic of South Africa (the national government); the second is the Premier of the Province of the Western Cape representing the Western Cape Provincial Government (the Western Cape government); the third appellant, the Cape Metropolitan Council (the Cape Metro) is the supervisory tier of local government in the area; and the fourth appellant is the Oostenberg Municipality (the municipality) which is a further tier of local government. All the appellants are organs of government.

. . .

[7] Mrs Grootboom and most of the other respondents previously lived in an informal squatter settlement called Wallacedene. It lies on the edge of the municipal area of Oostenberg, which in turn is on the eastern fringe of the Cape Metro. The conditions under which most of the residents of Wallacedene lived were lamentable. A quarter of the households of Wallacedene had no income at all, and more than two thirds earned less than R500 per month.[8] About half the population were children; all lived in shacks. They had no water, sewage or refuse removal services and only 5% of the shacks had electricity. The area is partly waterlogged and lies dangerously close to a main thoroughfare. Mrs Grootboom lived with her family and her sister's family in a shack about twenty metres square.

[8] Many had applied for subsidised low-cost housing from the municipality and had been on the waiting list for as long as seven years. Despite numerous enquiries from the municipality no definite answer was given. Clearly it was going to be a long wait. Faced with the prospect of remaining in intolerable conditions indefinitely, the respondents began to move out of Wallacedene at the end of September 1998. They put up their shacks and shelters on vacant land that was privately owned and had been earmarked for low-cost housing. They called the land "New Rust."

[9] They did not have the consent of the owner and on 8 December 1998 he obtained an ejectment order against them in the magistrates' court. The order was served on the occupants but they remained in occupation beyond the date by which they had been ordered to vacate. Mrs Grootboom says they had nowhere else to go: their former sites in Wallacedene had been filled by others. The eviction proceedings were renewed in March 1999. The respondents' attorneys in this case were appointed by the magistrate to represent them on the return day of the provisional order of eviction. Negotiations resulted in the grant of an order requiring the occupants to vacate New Rust and authorising the sheriff to evict them and to dismantle and remove any of their structures remaining on the land on 19 May 1999. The magistrate also directed that the parties and the municipality mediate to identify alternative land for the permanent or temporary occupation of the New Rust residents.

[10] … [O]n 18 May 1999, at the beginning of the cold, windy and rainy Cape winter, the respondents were forcibly evicted at the municipality's expense. This

---

[8] The figures appear from a needs assessment of the Wallacedene community compiled in December 1997 on behalf of the municipality.

…

was done prematurely and inhumanely: reminiscent of apartheid-style evictions. The respondents' homes were bulldozed and burnt and their possessions destroyed. Many of the residents who were not there could not even salvage their personal belongings.

[11] The respondents went and sheltered on the Wallacedene sports field under such temporary structures as they could muster. Within a week the winter rains started and the plastic sheeting they had erected afforded scant protection. The next day the respondents' attorney wrote to the municipality describing the intolerable conditions under which his clients were living and demanded that the municipality meet its constitutional obligations and provide temporary accommodation to the respondents. The respondents were not satisfied with the response of the municipality[10] and launched an urgent application in the High Court on 31 May 1999. As indicated above, the High Court granted relief to the respondents and the appellants now appeal against that relief.

...

B. The case in the High Court

[13] Mrs Grootboom and the other respondents applied for an order directing the appellants forthwith to provide:

(i) adequate basic temporary shelter or housing to the respondents and their children pending their obtaining permanent accommodation;

(ii) or basic nutrition, shelter, healthcare and social services to the respondents who are children.[11]

The respondents based their claim on two constitutional provisions. First, on section 26 of the Constitution which provides that everyone has the right of access to adequate housing. Section 26(2) imposes an obligation upon the state to take reasonable legislative and other measures to ensure the progressive realisation of this

---

[10] The municipality responded on 27 May 1999 stating that it had supplied food and shelter at the Wallacedene Community Hall to the respondents and that it was approaching Western Cape government for assistance to resolve the problem. The respondents, however, considered that the Community Hall provided inadequate shelter as it could only house 80 people.

[11] Above n 3 at 280F-G.

right within its available resources. The section is fully considered later in this judgment. The second basis for their claim was section 28(1)(c) of the Constitution which provides that children have the right to shelter.

[14] After conducting an inspection *in loco*, Josman AJ ordered that, pending the final determination of the application, temporary accommodation be provided for those of the respondents who were children and for one parent of each child who required supervision. Appellants furnished comprehensive answering affidavits to demonstrate that the state housing programme complied with their constitutional obligations. On the return day, the matter came before two judges. The High Court judgment consists of two separate parts. The first, under the heading "Housing" considered the claim in terms of section 26 of the Constitution. On this part of the claim the High Court concluded:

> "In short [appellants] are faced with a massive shortage in available housing and an extremely constrained budget. Furthermore in terms of the pressing demands and scarce resources [appellants] had implemented a housing programme in an attempt to maximise available resources to redress the housing shortage. For this reason it could not be said that [appellants] had not taken reasonable legislative and other measures within its available resources to achieve the progressive realisation of the right to have access to adequate housing."[12]

The court rejected an argument that the right of access to adequate housing under section 26 included a minimum core entitlement to shelter in terms of which the state was obliged to provide some form of shelter pending implementation of the programme to provide adequate housing. This submission was based on the provisions of certain international instruments that are discussed later.[13]

[15] The second part of the judgment addressed the claim of the children for shelter in terms of section 28(1)(c). The court reasoned that the parents bore the primary obligation to provide shelter for their children, but that section 28(1)(c) imposed an obligation on the state to provide that shelter if parents could not. It went on to say that the shelter to be provided according to this obligation was a significantly more rudimentary form of protection from the elements than is provided by a house and falls short of adequate housing. The court concluded that:

---

[12] Above n 3 at 285A-B.

[13] The International Covenant on Economic, Social and Cultural Rights, and the general comments issued by the United Nations Committee on Social and Economic Rights.

"an order which enforces a child's right to shelter should take account of the need of the child to be accompanied by his or her parent. Such an approach would be in accordance with the spirit and purport of section 28 as a whole."

[16] In the result the court ordered as follows:

"(2) It is declared, in terms of section 28 of the Constitution that;

(a) the applicant children are entitled to be provided with shelter by the appropriate organ or department of state;

(b) the applicant parents are entitled to be accommodated with their children in the aforegoing shelter; and

(c) the appropriate organ or department of state is obliged to provide the applicant children, and their accompanying parents, with such shelter until such time as the parents are able to shelter their own children; ..."

...

C. Argument in this Court

...

[18] Written argument submitted on behalf of the appellants and the respondents concentrated on the meaning and import of the shelter component and the obligations imposed upon the state by section 28(1)(c). The written argument filed on behalf of the *amici* sought to broaden the issues by contending that all the respondents, including those of the adult respondents without children, were entitled to shelter by reason of the minimum core obligation incurred by the state in terms of section 26 of the Constitution. It was further contended on behalf of the *amici* that the children's right to shelter had been included in section 28(1)(c) to place the right of children to this minimum core beyond doubt. Respondents' counsel filed further written contentions in which they supported and adopted these submissions. No objection was taken to the issues having been thus broadened.

D. The relevant constitutional provisions and their justiciability

[19] The key constitutional provisions at issue in this case are section 26 and section 28(1)(c). Section 26 provides:

"(1) Everyone has the right to have access to adequate housing.

(2) The state must take reasonable legislative and other measures, within its available resources, to achieve the progressive realisation of this right.

(3) No one may be evicted from their home, or have their home demolished, without an order of court made after considering all the relevant circumstances. No legislation may permit arbitrary evictions."

Section 28(1)(c) provides:

"(1) Every child has the right –

...

(c) to basic nutrition, shelter, basic health care services and social services".

These rights need to be considered in the context of the cluster of socio-economic rights enshrined in the Constitution. They entrench the right of access to land,[15] to adequate housing and to health care, food, water and social security.[16] They also protect the rights of the child[17] and the right to education.[18]

[20] While the justiciability of socio-economic rights has been the subject of considerable jurisprudential and political debate,[19] the issue of whether socio-economic

---

[15] Section 25(5) provides:

"The state must take reasonable legislative and other measures, within its available resources, to foster conditions which enable citizens to gain access to land on an equitable basis."

...

[16] [Citation omitted]

[17] Section 28 provides:

"(1) Every child has the right –

...

(b) to family care or parental care, or to appropriate alternative care when removed from the family environment;

(c) to basic nutrition, shelter, basic health care services and social services;

...

[18] [Citation omitted]

[19] Haysom "Constitutionalism, Majoritarian Democracy and Socio-Economic Rights" (1992) 8 *SA Journal of Human Rights* at 451; Mureinik "Beyond a Charter of Luxuries: Economic Rights in the Constitution" (1992) 8 *SA Journal of Human Rights* at 464; Davis "The Case Against the Inclusion of Socio-Economic Demands in a Bill of Rights

rights are justiciable at all in South Africa has been put beyond question by the text of our Constitution as construed in the Certification judgment.[20] During the certification proceedings before this Court, it was contended that they were not justiciable and should therefore not have been included in the text of the new Constitution. In response to this argument, this Court held:

> "[T]hese rights are, at least to some extent, justiciable. As we have stated in the previous paragraph, many of the civil and political rights entrenched in the [constitutional text before this Court for certification in that case] will give rise to similar budgetary implications without compromising their justiciability. The fact that socio-economic rights will almost inevitably give rise to such implications does not seem to us to be a bar to their justiciability. At the very minimum, socio-economic rights can be negatively protected from improper invasion."

Socio-economic rights are expressly included in the Bill of Rights; they cannot be said to exist on paper only. Section 7(2) of the Constitution requires the state "to respect, protect, promote and fulfil the rights in the Bill of Rights" and the courts are constitutionally bound to ensure that they are protected and fulfilled. The question is therefore not whether socio-economic rights are justiciable under our Constitution, but how to enforce them in a given case.[21] This is a very difficult issue

---

Except as Directive Principles" (1992) 8 *SA Journal of Human Rights* at 475; Liebenberg "Social and Economic Rights: A Critical Challenge" in Liebenberg (ed) *The Constitution of South Africa from a Gender Perspective* (The Community Law Centre at the University of the Western Cape in association with David Philip Publishers, Cape Town 1995) at 79; Corder *et al A Charter For Social Justice: A contribution to the South African Bill of Rights debate* (University of Cape Town, Cape Town 1992) at 18; Scott and Macklem "Constitutional Ropes of Sand or Justiciable Guarantees? Social Rights in a New South African Constitution" (1992) 141 *University of Pennsylvania Law Review* at 1; De Villiers "Social and Economic Rights" in van Wyk, Dugard, De Villiers and Davis (eds) *Rights and Constitutionalism: The New South African Legal Order* (Juta, Cape Town, 1994) at 599; South African Law Commission *Final Report on Group and Human Rights* (Project 58, October 1994) at 179.

[20] *Ex Parte Chairperson of the Constitutional Assembly: In Re Certification of the Constitution of the Republic of South Africa, 1996* 1996 (4) SA 744; 1996 (10) BCLR 1253 (CC) at para 78.

[21] Section 38 of the Constitution empowers the Court to grant appropriate relief for the infringement of any right entrenched in the Bill of Rights.

which must be carefully explored on a case-by-case basis. To address the challenge raised in the present case, it is necessary first to consider the terms and context of the relevant constitutional provisions and their application to the circumstances of this case. Although the judgment of the High Court in favour of the appellants was based on the right to shelter (section 28(1)(c) of the Constitution), it is appropriate to consider the provisions of section 26 first so as to facilitate a contextual evaluation of section 28(1)(c).

E. Obligations imposed upon the state by section 26

i) Approach to interpretation

[21] Like all the other rights in Chapter 2 of the Constitution (which contains the Bill of Rights), section 26 must be construed in its context. The section has been carefully crafted. It contains three subsections. The first confers a general right of access to adequate housing. The second establishes and delimits the scope of the positive obligation imposed upon the state to promote access to adequate housing and has three key elements. The state is obliged: (a) to take reasonable legislative and other measures; (b) within its available resources; (c) to achieve the progressive realisation of this right. These elements are discussed later. The third subsection provides protection against arbitrary evictions.

[22] Interpreting a right in its context requires the consideration of two types of context. On the one hand, rights must be understood in their textual setting. This will require a consideration of Chapter 2 and the Constitution as a whole. On the other hand, rights must also be understood in their social and historical context.

[23] Our Constitution entrenches both civil and political rights and social and economic rights. All the rights in our Bill of Rights are inter-related and mutually supporting. There can be no doubt that human dignity, freedom and equality, the foundational values of our society, are denied those who have no food, clothing or shelter. Affording socio-economic rights to all people therefore enables them to enjoy the other rights enshrined in Chapter 2. The realisation of these rights is also key to the advancement of race and gender equality and the evolution of a society in which men and women are equally able to achieve their full potential.

[24] The right of access to adequate housing cannot be seen in isolation. There is a close relationship between it and the other socio-economic rights. Socio-economic rights must all be read together in the setting of the Constitution as a whole. The state is obliged to take positive action to meet the needs of those living in extreme conditions of poverty, homelessness or intolerable housing. Their interconnected-

ness needs to be taken into account in interpreting the socio-economic rights, and, in particular, in determining whether the state has met its obligations in terms of them.

[25] Rights also need to be interpreted and understood in their social and historical context. The right to be free from unfair discrimination, for example, must be understood against our legacy of deep social inequality.[22] The context in which the Bill of Rights is to be interpreted was described by Chaskalson P in *Soobramoney*:[23]

> "We live in a society in which there are great disparities in wealth. Millions of people are living in deplorable conditions and in great poverty. There is a high level of unemployment, inadequate social security, and many do not have access to clean water or to adequate health services. These conditions already existed when the Constitution was adopted and a commitment to address them, and to transform our society into one in which there will be human dignity, freedom and equality, lies at the heart of our new constitutional order. For as long as these conditions continue to exist that aspiration will have a hollow ring."[24]

ii) The relevant international law and its impact

[26] During argument, considerable weight was attached to the value of international law in interpreting section 26 of our Constitution. Section 39 of the Constitution[25] obliges a court to consider international law as a tool to interpretation of

---

[22] See, for example, *Brink v Kitshoff NO* 1996 (4) SA 197 (CC); 1996 (6) BCLR 752 (CC); *Prinsloo v Van der Linde and Another* 1997 (3) SA 1012 (CC); 1997 (6) BCLR 759 (CC). For an application of this type of contextual interpretation, see also *S v Makwanyane and Another* 1995 (3) SA 391 (CC), 1995 (6) BCLR 665 (CC); *Shabalala and Others v Attorney-General, Transvaal and Another* 1996 (1) SA 725 (CC); 1995 (12) BCLR 1593 (CC).

[23] *Soobramoney v Minister of Health, KwaZulu-Natal* 1998 (1) SA 765 (CC); 1997 (12) BCLR 1696 (CC) at para 8.

[24] See also the comments of Mahomed DP in *Azanian Peoples Organisation (AZAPO) and Others v President of the Republic of South Africa and Others* 1996 (4) SA 671 (CC); 1996 (8) BCLR 1015 (CC) at para 43, albeit in a different context.

[25] Section 39 of the Constitution provides:

"(1) When interpreting the Bill of Rights, a court, tribunal or forum –

the Bill of Rights. In *Makwanyane*[26] Chaskalson P, in the context of section 35(1) of the interim Constitution,[27] said:

> "... public international law would include non-binding as well as binding law. They may both be used under the section as tools of interpretation. International agreements and customary international law accordingly provide a framework within which [the Bill of Rights] can be evaluated and understood, and for that purpose, decisions of tribunals dealing with comparable instruments, such as the United Nations Committee on Human Rights, the Inter-American Commission on Human Rights, the Inter-American Court of Human Rights, the European Commission on Human Rights, and the European Court of Human Rights, and, in appropriate cases, reports of specialised agencies such as the International Labour Organisation, may provide guidance as to the correct interpretation of particular provisions of [the Bill of Rights]." (Footnotes omitted)

The relevant international law can be a guide to interpretation but the weight to be attached to any particular principle or rule of international law will vary. However,

---

(a) must promote the values that underlie an open and democratic society based on human dignity, equality and freedom;

(b) must consider international law; and

(c) may consider foreign law.

(2) When interpreting any legislation, and when developing the common law or customary law, every court, tribunal or forum must promote the spirit, purport and objects of the Bill of Rights.

(3) The Bill of Rights does not deny the existence of any other rights or freedoms that are recognised or conferred by common law, customary law or legislation, to the extent that they are consistent with the Bill."

26 *S v Makwanyane and Another* above n 22 at para 35.

27 Section 35(1) of the interim Constitution provides:

"In interpreting the provisions of this Chapter a court of law shall promote the values which underlie an open and democratic society based on freedom and equality and shall, where applicable, have regard to public international law applicable to the protection of the rights entrenched in this Chapter, and may have regard to comparable foreign case law."

where the relevant principle of international law binds South Africa,[28] it may be directly applicable.

[27] The *amici* submitted that the International Covenant on Economic, Social and Cultural Rights (the Covenant)[29] is of significance in understanding the positive obligations created by the socio-economic rights in the Constitution. Article 11.1 of the Covenant provides:

> "The States Parties to the present Covenant recognize the right of everyone to an adequate standard of living for himself and his family, including adequate food, clothing and housing, and to the continuous improvement of living conditions. The States Parties will take appropriate steps to ensure the realization of this right, recognizing to this effect the essential importance of international co-operation based on free consent."

This Article must be read with Article 2.1 which provides:

> "Each State Party to the present Covenant undertakes to take steps, individually and through international assistance and co-operation, especially economic and technical, to the maximum of its available resources, with a view to achieving progressively the full realization of the rights recognized in the present Covenant by all appropriate means, including particularly the adoption of legislative measures."

[28] The differences between the relevant provisions of the Covenant and our Constitution are significant in determining the extent to which the provisions of the Covenant may be a guide to an interpretation of section 26. These differences, in so far as they relate to housing, are:

(a) The Covenant provides for a *right to adequate housing* while section 26 provides for the *right of access* to adequate housing.

(b) The Covenant obliges states parties to take *appropriate* steps which must include legislation while the Constitution obliges the South African state to take *reasonable* legislative and other measures.

---

[28] See sections 231-235 of the Constitution which regulate the application of international law in detail.

[29] The Covenant was signed by South Africa on 3 October 1994 but has as yet not been ratified.

[29] The obligations undertaken by states parties to the Covenant are monitored by the United Nations Committee on Economic, Social and Cultural Rights (the committee).[30] The *amici* relied on the relevant general comments issued by the committee concerning the interpretation and application of the Covenant, and argued that these general comments constitute a significant guide to the interpretation of section 26. In particular they argued that in interpreting this section, we should adopt an approach similar to that taken by the committee in paragraph 10 of general comment 3 issued in 1990, in which the committee found that socio-economic rights contain a minimum core:

> "10. On the basis of the extensive experience gained by the Committee, as well as by the body that preceded it, over a period of more than a decade of examining States parties' reports the Committee is of the view that minimum core obligation to ensure the satisfaction of, at the very least, minimum essential levels of each of the rights is incumbent upon every State party. Thus, for example, a State party in which any significant number of individuals is deprived of essential foodstuffs, of essential primary health care, of basic shelter and housing, or of the most basic forms of education, is *prima facie*, failing to discharge its obligations under the Covenant. If the Covenant were to be read in such a way as not to establish such a minimum core obligation, it would be largely deprived of its raison d'etre. By the same token, it must be noted that any assessment as to whether a State has discharged its minimum core obligation must also take account of resource constraints applying within the country concerned. Article 2(1) obligates each State party to take the necessary steps "to the maximum of its available resources." In order for a State party to be able to attribute its failure to meet at least its minimum core obligations to a lack of available resources it must demonstrate that every effort has been made to use all resources that are at its disposition in an effort to satisfy, as a matter of priority, those minimum obligations.

[30] It is clear from this extract that the committee considers that every state party is bound to fulfill a minimum core obligation by ensuring the satisfaction of a minimum essential level of the socio-economic rights, including the right to

---

[30] The committee consists of eighteen independent experts. Its purpose is to assist the United Nations Economic and Social Council to carry out its responsibilities relating to the implementation of the Covenant. See Craven *The International Covenant on Economic, Social and Cultural Rights* (Clarendon, Oxford 1995) at 1 and 42.

adequate housing. Accordingly, a state in which a significant number of individuals is deprived of basic shelter and housing is regarded as *prima facie* in breach of its obligations under the Covenant. A state party must demonstrate that every effort has been made to use all the resources at its disposal to satisfy the minimum core of the right. However, it is to be noted that the general comment does not specify precisely what that minimum core is.

[31] The concept of minimum core obligation was developed by the committee to describe the minimum expected of a state in order to comply with its obligation under the Covenant. It is the floor beneath which the conduct of the state must not drop if there is to be compliance with the obligation. Each right has a "minimum essential level" that must be satisfied by the states parties. The committee developed this concept based on "extensive experience gained by [it] . . . over a period of more than a decade of examining States parties' reports." The general comment is based on reports furnished by the reporting states and the general comment is therefore largely descriptive of how the states have complied with their obligations under the Covenant. The committee has also used the general comment "as a means of developing a common understanding of the norms by establishing a prescriptive definition."[31] Minimum core obligation is determined generally by having regard to the needs of the most vulnerable group that is entitled to the protection of the right in question. It is in this context that the concept of minimum core obligation must be understood in international law.

[32] It is not possible to determine the minimum threshold for the progressive realisation of the right of access to adequate housing without first identifying the needs and opportunities for the enjoyment of such a right. These will vary according to factors such as income, unemployment, availability of land and poverty. The differences between city and rural communities will also determine the needs and opportunities for the enjoyment of this right. Variations ultimately depend on the economic and social history and circumstances of a country. All this illustrates the complexity of the task of determining a minimum core obligation for the progressive realisation of the right of access to adequate housing without having the requisite information on the needs and the opportunities for the enjoyment of this right. The committee developed the concept of minimum core over many years of examining reports by reporting states. This Court does not have comparable information.

---

[31] *Id.* at 91.

[33] The determination of a minimum core in the context of "the right to have access to adequate housing" presents difficult questions. This is so because the needs in the context of access to adequate housing are diverse: there are those who need land; others need both land and houses; yet others need financial assistance. There are difficult questions relating to the definition of minimum core in the context of a right to have access to adequate housing, in particular whether the minimum core obligation should be defined generally or with regard to specific groups of people. As will appear from the discussion below, the real question in terms of our Constitution is whether the measures taken by the state to realise the right afforded by section 26 are reasonable. There may be cases where it may be possible and appropriate to have regard to the content of a minimum core obligation to determine whether the measures taken by the state are reasonable. However, even if it were appropriate to do so, it could not be done unless sufficient information is placed before a court to enable it to determine the minimum core in any given context. In this case, we do not have sufficient information to determine what would comprise the minimum core obligation in the context of our Constitution. It is not in any event necessary to decide whether it is appropriate for a court to determine in the first instance the minimum core content of a right.

iii) Analysis of section 26

[34] I consider the meaning and scope of section 26 in its context. Its provisions are repeated for convenience:

> "(1) Everyone has the right to have access to adequate housing.
>
> (2) The state must take reasonable legislative and other measures, within its available resources, to achieve the progressive realisation of this right.
>
> (3) No one may be evicted from their home, or have their home demolished, without an order of court made after considering all the relevant circumstances. No legislation may permit arbitrary evictions."

Subsections (1) and (2) are related and must be read together. Subsection (1) aims at delineating the scope of the right. It is a right of everyone including children. Although the subsection does not expressly say so, there is, at the very least, a negative obligation placed upon the state and all other entities and persons to desist from preventing or impairing the right of access to adequate housing.[32] The

[32] See, in this regard, the Certification judgment, above para 20.

negative right is further spelt out in subsection (3) which prohibits arbitrary evictions. Access to housing could also be promoted if steps are taken to make the rural areas of our country more viable so as to limit the inexorable migration of people from rural to urban areas in search of jobs.

[35] The right delineated in section 26(1) is a right of "access to adequate housing" as distinct from the right to adequate housing encapsulated in the Covenant. This difference is significant. It recognises that housing entails more than bricks and mortar. It requires available land, appropriate services such as the provision of water and the removal of sewage and the financing of all of these, including the building of the house itself. For a person to have access to adequate housing all of these conditions need to be met: there must be land, there must be services, there must be a dwelling. Access to land for the purpose of housing is therefore included in the right of access to adequate housing in section 26. A right of access to adequate housing also suggests that it is not only the state who is responsible for the provision of houses, but that other agents within our society, including individuals themselves, must be enabled by legislative and other measures to provide housing. The state must create the conditions for access to adequate housing for people at all economic levels of our society. State policy dealing with housing must therefore take account of different economic levels in our society.

[36] In this regard, there is a difference between the position of those who can afford to pay for housing, even if it is only basic though adequate housing, and those who cannot. For those who can afford to pay for adequate housing, the state's primary obligation lies in unlocking the system, providing access to housing stock and a legislative framework to facilitate self-built houses through planning laws and access to finance. Issues of development and social welfare are raised in respect of those who cannot afford to provide themselves with housing. State policy needs to address both these groups. The poor are particularly vulnerable and their needs require special attention. It is in this context that the relationship between sections 26 and 27 and the other socio-economic rights is most apparent. If under section 27 the state has in place programmes to provide adequate social assistance to those who are otherwise unable to support themselves and their dependants, that would be relevant to the state's obligations in respect of other socio-economic rights.

[37] The state's obligation to provide access to adequate housing depends on context, and may differ from province to province, from city to city, from rural to urban areas and from person to person. Some may need access to land and no more; some may need access to land and building materials; some may need

access to finance; some may need access to services such as water, sewage, electricity and roads. What might be appropriate in a rural area where people live together in communities engaging in subsistence farming may not be appropriate in an urban area where people are looking for employment and a place to live.

[38] Subsection (2) speaks to the positive obligation imposed upon the state. It requires the state to devise a comprehensive and workable plan to meet its obligations in terms of the subsection. However subsection (2) also makes it clear that the obligation imposed upon the state is not an absolute or unqualified one. The extent of the state's obligation is defined by three key elements that are considered separately: (a) the obligation to "take reasonable legislative and other measures"; (b) "to achieve the progressive realisation" of the right; and (c) "within available resources."

Reasonable legislative and other measures

[39] What constitutes reasonable legislative and other measures must be determined in the light of the fact that the Constitution creates different spheres of government: national government, provincial government and local government.[33]

...

[40] ... Each sphere of government must accept responsibility for the implementation of particular parts of the programme but the national sphere of government must assume responsibility for ensuring that laws, policies, programmes and strategies are adequate to meet the state's section 26 obligations. ...

[41] The measures must establish a coherent public housing programme directed towards the progressive realisation of the right of access to adequate housing within the state's available means. The programme must be capable of facilitating the realisation of the right. The precise contours and content of the measures to be adopted are primarily a matter for the legislature and the executive. They must, however, ensure that the measures they adopt are reasonable. In any challenge based on section 26 in which it is argued that the state has failed to meet the positive obligations imposed upon it by section 26(2), the question will be whether the legislative and other measures taken by the state are reasonable. A court considering reasonableness will not enquire whether other more desirable or favourable

---

33 See Chapter 3 of the Constitution.

...

measures could have been adopted, or whether public money could have been better spent. The question would be whether the measures that have been adopted are reasonable. It is necessary to recognise that a wide range of possible measures could be adopted by the state to meet its obligations. Many of these would meet the requirement of reasonableness. Once it is shown that the measures do so, this requirement is met.

[42] The state is required to take reasonable legislative *and* other measures. Legislative measures by themselves are not likely to constitute constitutional compliance. Mere legislation is not enough. The state is obliged to act to achieve the intended result, and the legislative measures will invariably have to be supported by appropriate, well-directed policies and programmes implemented by the executive. These policies and programmes must be reasonable both in their conception and their implementation. The formulation of a programme is only the first stage in meeting the state's obligations. The programme must also be reasonably implemented. An otherwise reasonable programme that is not implemented reasonably will not constitute compliance with the state's obligations.

[43] In determining whether a set of measures is reasonable, it will be necessary to consider housing problems in their social, economic and historical context and to consider the capacity of institutions responsible for implementing the programme. The programme must be balanced and flexible and make appropriate provision for attention to housing crises and to short, medium and long term needs. A programme that excludes a significant segment of society cannot be said to be reasonable. Conditions do not remain static and therefore the programme will require continuous review.

[44] Reasonableness must also be understood in the context of the Bill of Rights as a whole. The right of access to adequate housing is entrenched because we value human beings and want to ensure that they are afforded their basic human needs. A society must seek to ensure that the basic necessities of life are provided to all if it is to be a society based on human dignity, freedom and equality. To be reasonable, measures cannot leave out of account the degree and extent of the denial of the right they endeavour to realise. Those whose needs are the most urgent and whose ability to enjoy all rights therefore is most in peril, must not be ignored by the measures aimed at achieving realisation of the right. It may not be sufficient to meet the test of reasonableness to show that the measures are capable of achieving a statistical advance in the realisation of the right. Furthermore, the Constitution requires that everyone must be treated with care and concern. If the measures,

though statistically successful, fail to respond to the needs of those most desperate, they may not pass the test.

Progressive realisation of the right

[45] The extent and content of the obligation consist in what must be achieved, that is, "the progressive realisation of this right." It links subsections (1) and (2) by making it quite clear that the right referred to is the right of access to adequate housing. The term "progressive realisation" shows that it was contemplated that the right could not be realised immediately. But the goal of the Constitution is that the basic needs of all in our society be effectively met and the requirement of progressive realisation means that the state must take steps to achieve this goal. It means that accessibility should be progressively facilitated: legal, administrative, operational and financial hurdles should be examined and, where possible, lowered over time. Housing must be made more accessible not only to a larger number of people but to a wider range of people as time progresses. The phrase is taken from international law and Article 2.1 of the Covenant in particular.[39] The committee has helpfully analysed this requirement in the context of housing as follows:

> "Nevertheless, the fact that realization over time, or in other words progressively, is foreseen under the Covenant should not be misinterpreted as depriving the obligation of all meaningful content. It is on the one hand a necessary flexibility device, reflecting the realities of the real world and the difficulties involved for any country in ensuring full realization of economic, social and cultural rights. On the other hand, the phrase must be read in the light of the overall objective, indeed the raison d'être, of the Covenant which is to establish clear obligations for States parties in respect of the full realization of the rights in question. It thus imposes an obligation to move as expeditiously and effectively as possible towards that goal. Moreover, any deliberately retrogressive measures in that regard would require the most careful consideration and would need to be fully justified by reference to the totality of the rights provided for in the Covenant and in the context of the full use of the maximum available resources."[40]

Although the committee's analysis is intended to explain the scope of states parties' obligations under the Covenant, it is also helpful in plumbing the meaning of

---

[39] The text of Article 2.1 appears at para 27 above.

[40] Para 9 of general comment 3, 1990.

"progressive realisation" in the context of our Constitution. The meaning ascribed to the phrase is in harmony with the context in which the phrase is used in our Constitution and there is no reason not to accept that it bears the same meaning in the Constitution as in the document from which it was so clearly derived.

Within available resources

[46] The third defining aspect of the obligation to take the requisite measures is that the obligation does not require the state to do more than its available resources permit. This means that both the content of the obligation in relation to the rate at which it is achieved as well as the reasonableness of the measures employed to achieve the result are governed by the availability of resources. Section 26 does not expect more of the state than is achievable within its available resources. As Chaskalson P said in *Soobramoney*:[41]

> "What is apparent from these provisions is that the obligations imposed on the State by ss 26 and 27 in regard to access to housing, health care, food, water, and social security are dependent upon the resources available for such purposes, and that the corresponding rights themselves are limited by reason of the lack of resources. Given this lack of resources and the significant demands on them that have already been referred to, an unqualified obligation to meet these needs would not presently be capable of being fulfilled."

There is a balance between goal and means. The measures must be calculated to attain the goal expeditiously and effectively but the availability of resources is an important factor in determining what is reasonable.

F. Description and evaluation of the state housing programme

...

[51] It emerges from the general principles read together with the functions of national, provincial and local government that the concept of housing development as defined is central to the Act. Housing development, as defined, seeks to provide citizens and permanent residents with access to permanent residential structures with secure tenure ensuring internal and external privacy and to provide

---

[41] See n 23 above at para 11.

...

adequate protection against the elements. What is more, it endeavours to ensure convenient access to economic opportunities and to health, educational and social amenities. All the policy documents before the Court are postulated on the need for housing development as defined. This is the central thrust of the housing development policy.

[52] The definition of housing development as well as the general principles that are set out do not contemplate the provision of housing that falls short of the definition of housing development in the Act. In other words there is no express provision to facilitate access to temporary relief for people who have no access to land, no roof over their heads, for people who are living in intolerable conditions and for people who are in crisis because of natural disasters such as floods and fires, or because their homes are under threat of demolition. These are people in desperate need. Their immediate need can be met by relief short of housing which fulfils the requisite standards of durability, habitability and stability encompassed by the definition of housing development in the Act.

[53] What has been done in execution of this programme is a major achievement. Large sums of money have been spent and a significant number of houses has been built.[47] Considerable thought, energy, resources and expertise have been and continue to be devoted to the process of effective housing delivery. It is a programme that is aimed at achieving the progressive realisation of the right of access to adequate housing.

[54] A question that nevertheless must be answered is whether the measures adopted are reasonable within the meaning of section 26 of the Constitution. Allocation of responsibilities and functions has been coherently and comprehensively addressed. The programme is not haphazard but represents a systematic response to a pressing social need. It takes account of the housing shortage in South Africa by seeking to build a large number of homes for those in need of better housing. The programme applies throughout South Africa and although there have been difficulties of implementation in some areas, the evidence suggests that the state is actively seeking to combat these difficulties.

...

---

[47] Some 362 160 houses were built or under construction between March 1994 and September 1997, while an overall total of some 637 190 subsidies had been allocated for projects in various stages of planning or development by October 1997.

[56] This Court must decide whether the nationwide housing programme is sufficiently flexible to respond to those in desperate need in our society and to cater appropriately for immediate and short-term requirements. This must be done in the context of the scope of the housing problem that must be addressed. This case is concerned with the situation in the Cape Metro and the municipality and the circumstances that prevailed there are therefore presented.

[57] The housing shortage in the Cape Metro is acute. About 206 000 housing units are required and up to 25 000 housing opportunities are required in Oostenberg itself. Shack counts in the Cape Metro in general and in the area of the municipality in particular reveal an inordinate problem. 28 300 shacks were counted in the Cape Metro in January 1993. This number had grown to 59 854 in 1996 and to 72 140 by 1998. Shacks in this area increased by 111 percent during the period 1993 to 1996 and by 21 percent from then until 1998. There were 2121 shacks in the area of the municipality in 1993, 5701 (an increase of 168 percent) in 1996 and 7546 (an increase of 32 percent) in 1998. These are the results of a study commissioned by the Cape Metro.

[58] The study concludes that the municipality "is the most critical local authority in terms of informal settlement shack growth at this point in time", this despite the fact that, according to an affidavit by a representative of the municipality, 10 577 houses had been completed by 1997. The scope of the problem is perhaps most sharply illustrated by this: about 22 000 houses are built in the Western Cape each year while demand grows at a rate of 20 000 family units per year. The backlog is therefore likely to be reduced, resources permitting and, on the basis of the figures in this study, only by 2 000 houses a year.

[59] The housing situation is desperate. The problem is compounded by rampant unemployment and poverty. As was pointed out earlier in this judgment, a quarter of the households in Wallacedene had no income at all, and more than two-thirds earned less than R500-00 per month during 1997. As stated above, many of the families living in Wallacedene are living in intolerable conditions. In some cases, their shacks are permanently flooded during the winter rains, others are severely overcrowded and some are perilously close to busy roads. There is no suggestion that Wallacedene is unusual in this respect. It is these conditions which ultimately forced the respondents to leave their homes there.

[60] The Cape Metro has realized that this desperate situation requires government action that is different in nature from that encompassed by the housing development policy described earlier in this judgment.

...

[61] The Cape Metro land programme was formulated by the Cape Metro specifically "to assist the metropolitan local councils to manage the settlement of families in crisis." Important features of this programme are its recognition of (i) the absence of provision for people living in crisis conditions; (ii) the unacceptability of having families living in crisis conditions; (iii) the consequent risk of land invasions; and (iv) the gap between the supply and demand of housing resulting in a delivery crisis. Crucially, the programme acknowledges that its beneficiaries are families who are to be evicted, those who are in a crisis situation in an existing area such as in a flood-line, families located on strategic land and families from backyard shacks or on the waiting list who are in crisis situations. Its primary objective is the rapid release of land for these families in crisis, with services to be upgraded progressively.

. . .

[63] Section 26 requires that the legislative and other measures adopted by the state are reasonable. To determine whether the nationwide housing programme as applied in the Cape Metro is reasonable within the meaning [of] the section, one must consider whether the absence of a component catering for those in desperate need is reasonable in the circumstances. It is common cause that, except for the Cape Metro land programme, there is no provision in the nationwide housing programme as applied within the Cape Metro for people in desperate need.

[64] Counsel for the appellants supported the nationwide housing programme and resisted the notion that provision of relief for people in desperate need was appropriate in it. Counsel also submitted that section 26 did not require the provision of this relief. Indeed, the contention was that provision for people in desperate need would detract significantly from integrated housing development as defined in the Act. The housing development policy as set out in the Act is in itself laudable. It has medium and long term objectives that cannot be criticised. But the question is whether a housing programme that leaves out of account the immediate amelioration of the circumstances of those in crisis can meet the test of reasonableness established by the section.

[65] The absence of this component may have been acceptable if the nationwide housing programme would result in affordable houses for most people within a reasonably short time. However the scale of the problem is such that this simply cannot happen. Each individual housing project could be expected to take years and the provision of houses for all in the area of the municipality and in the Cape Metro is likely to take a long time indeed. The desperate will be consigned to their fate for the foreseeable future unless some temporary measures exist as an integral

part of the nationwide housing programme. Housing authorities are understandably unable to say when housing will become available to these desperate people. The result is that people in desperate need are left without any form of assistance with no end in sight. Not only are the immediate crises not met. The consequent pressure on existing settlements inevitably results in land invasions by the desperate thereby frustrating the attainment of the medium and long term objectives of the nationwide housing programme. That is one of the main reasons why the Cape Metro land programme was adopted.

[66] The national government bears the overall responsibility for ensuring that the state complies with the obligations imposed upon it by section 26. The nationwide housing programme falls short of obligations imposed upon national government to the extent that it fails to recognise that the state must provide for relief for those in desperate need. They are not to be ignored in the interests of an overall programme focused on medium and long-term objectives. It is essential that a reasonable part of the national housing budget be devoted to this, but the precise allocation is for national government to decide in the first instance.

[67] This case is concerned with the Cape Metro and the municipality. The former has realised that this need has not been fulfilled and has put in place its land programme in an effort to fulfil it. This programme, on the face of it, meets the obligation which the state has towards people in the position of the respondents in the Cape Metro. Indeed, the *amicus* accepted that this programme "would cater precisely for the needs of people such as the respondents, and, in an appropriate and sustainable manner." However, as with legislative measures, the existence of the programme is a starting point only. What remains is the implementation of the programme by taking all reasonable steps that are necessary to initiate and sustain it. And it must be implemented with due regard to the urgency of the situations it is intended to address.

[68] Effective implementation requires at least adequate budgetary support by national government. This, in turn, requires recognition of the obligation to meet immediate needs in the nationwide housing programme. Recognition of such needs in the nationwide housing programme requires it to plan, budget and monitor the fulfilment of immediate needs and the management of crises. This must ensure that a significant number of desperate people in need are afforded relief, though not all of them need receive it immediately. Such planning too will require proper co-operation between the different spheres of government.

[69] In conclusion it has been established in this case that as of the date of the launch of this application, the state was not meeting the obligation imposed upon

it by section 26(2) of the Constitution in the area of the Cape Metro. In particular, the programmes adopted by the state fell short of the requirements of section 26(2) in that no provision was made for relief to the categories of people in desperate need identified earlier. I come later to the order that should flow from this conclusion.

. . .

H. Evaluation of the conduct of the appellants towards the respondents

. . .

[92] This judgment must not be understood as approving any practice of land invasion for the purpose of coercing a state structure into providing housing on a preferential basis to those who participate in any exercise of this kind. Land invasion is inimical to the systematic provision of adequate housing on a planned basis. It may well be that the decision of a state structure, faced with the difficulty of repeated land invasions, not to provide housing in response to those invasions, would be reasonable. Reasonableness must be determined on the facts of each case.

I. Summary and conclusion

[93] This case shows the desperation of hundreds of thousands of people living in deplorable conditions throughout the country. The Constitution obliges the state to act positively to ameliorate these conditions. The obligation is to provide access to housing, health-care, sufficient food and water, and social security to those unable to support themselves and their dependants. The state must also foster conditions to enable citizens to gain access to land on an equitable basis. Those in need have a corresponding right to demand that this be done.

[94] I am conscious that it is an extremely difficult task for the state to meet these obligations in the conditions that prevail in our country. This is recognized by the Constitution which expressly provides that the state is not obliged to go beyond available resources or to realise these rights immediately. I stress however, that despite all these qualifications, these are rights, and the Constitution obliges the state to give effect to them. This is an obligation that courts can, and in appropriate circumstances, must enforce.

[95] Neither section 26 nor section 28 entitles the respondents to claim shelter or housing immediately upon demand. The High Court order ought therefore not to have been made. However, section 26 does oblige the state to devise and implement a coherent, co-ordinated programme designed to meet its section 26 obliga-

tions. The programme that has been adopted and was in force in the Cape Metro at the time that this application was brought, fell short of the obligations imposed upon the state by section 26(2) in that it failed to provide for any form of relief to those desperately in need of access to housing.

[96] In the light of the conclusions I have reached, it is necessary and appropriate to make a declaratory order. The order requires the state to act to meet the obligation imposed upon it by section 26(2) of the Constitution. This includes the obligation to devise, fund, implement and supervise measures to provide relief to those in desperate need.

[97] The Human Rights Commission is an *amicus* in this case. Section 184 (1) (c) of the Constitution places a duty on the Commission to "monitor and assess the observance of human rights in the Republic." Subsections (2) (a) and (b) give the Commission the power:

"(a) to investigate and to report on the observance of human rights;

(b) to take steps to secure appropriate redress where human right have been violated."

Counsel for the Commission indicated during argument that the Commission had the duty and was prepared to monitor and report on the compliance by the state of its section 26 obligations. In the circumstances, the Commission will monitor and, if necessary, report in terms of these powers on the efforts made by the state to comply with its section 26 obligations in accordance with this judgment.

. . .

J. The Order

[99] The following order is made:

1. The appeal is allowed in part.
2. The order of the Cape of Good Hope High Court is set aside and the following is substituted for it:

   It is declared that:

   (a) Section 26(2) of the Constitution requires the state to devise and implement within its available resources a comprehensive and coordinated programme progressively to realise the right of access to adequate housing.

   (b) The programme must include reasonable measures such as, but not necessarily limited to, those contemplated in the Accelerated Managed Land

Settlement Programme, to provide relief for people who have no access to land, no roof over their heads, and who are living in intolerable conditions or crisis situations.

(c) As at the date of the launch of this application, the state housing programme in the area of the Cape Metropolitan Council fell short of compliance with the requirements in paragraph (b), in that it failed to make reasonable provision within its available resources for people in the Cape Metropolitan area with no access to land, no roof over their heads, and who were living in intolerable conditions or crisis situations.

3. There is no order as to costs.

Chaskalson P, Langa DP, Goldstone J, Kriegler J, Madala J, Mokgoro J, Ngcobo J, O'Regan J, Sachs J and Cameron AJ concur in the judgment of Yacoob J.

AGREEMENT ESTABLISHING THE AFRICAN TRADE INSURANCE AGENCY

Note*

January 20, 2001 marked a milestone in Africa's ongoing efforts to alleviate poverty through sustainable, private sector-led economic growth, for it was on that date that the Agreement Establishing the African Trade Insurance Agency (Agreement) came into effect.

An initiative of the Common Market for Southern and Eastern Africa (COMESA), the establishment of the African Trade Insurance Agency (ATI) seeks to address a severe constraint upon private sector development in Africa: the dearth of financing for viable, short- and medium-term commercial transactions within the region and with third countries. Such limited access to capital is due, in part, to a perception of the high risk in the region as a whole, and in individual countries within the region.

Recognizing the importance of COMESA's proposal, and drawing upon experience acquired in projects in which it had helped establish political risk guarantee and insurance facilities in several Eastern European countries, the International Development Association worked with COMESA in the early stages to develop the concept and the design of the project implementation entity. Ultimately, it was decided that a regional approach, using a common, multilateral implementing agency (ATI), would be most suitable. A country-by-country approach was rejected as it would not have permitted the pooling and diversification of risk or the realization of operating costs' economies of scale, and also to enhance the credibility of ATI in the eyes of the private sector, by placing it beyond the direct control of the individual governments whose political risks it sought to cover.

---

* Note contributed by Mark Walker, Lead Counsel, Cofinancing and Project Finance Practice Group, Legal Vice Presidency, World Bank. The author acted as principal legal advisor to the International Development Association in the Regional Trade Facilitation Project.

The World Bank Legal Review: Law and Justice for Development: 571-611.

Printed in the Netherlands.

Under COMESA's leadership, the process from conception to realization was reached in a little over a year, a remarkable achievement and a shining example of international cooperation: the Agreement was adopted at the Summit of Heads of State and Government of COMESA on May 18, 2000 and recommended for signature. Open to participation by all African states, Burundi, Kenya, and Uganda signed the Agreement at the summit, and by January 2001 Malawi, Rwanda, and Zambia had also signed. These six countries subsequently ratified the Agreement and paid their initial capital contribution to the African Trade Insurance Agency, thus becoming ATI's founding members at the first meeting of ATI's General Assembly held in Nairobi, Kenya on February 19 and 20, 2001. A seventh country, Tanzania, has since also signed and ratified the Agreement, and other African countries have also expressed an interest in membership.

Technical assistance and institutional support for ATI's creation was financed by the European Union, the Government of Japan, as well as the World Bank's Institutional Development Fund. In addition, the International Development Association provided credits to ATI and its initial seven member countries totaling U.S.$110 million equivalent. Furthermore, and significantly, in December 2001 ATI concluded arrangements with a leading global insurance company that will allow ATI to offer trade credit insurance (which provides protection to exporters against a buyer's credit risk) in addition to the political risk insurance it could already offer. As a result, ATI now has the ability to be a "one-stop shop" for full-covering, comprehensive trade insurance.

The African Trade Insurance Agency, the continent's only pan-African export credit and political risk agency, officially launched its operations in August 2001.

AGREEMENT ESTABLISHING THE AFRICAN TRADE INSURANCE AGENCY

TABLE OF CONTENTS

PREAMBLE

THE PARTIES TO THE PRESENT AGREEMENT,

COGNIZANT of the fact that lack of adequate political, non-commercial and commercial risk insurance is a significant impediment to the availability of finance for investments in Africa and the expansion of African foreign trade and intra-Africa trade,

ACKNOWLEDGING previous multilateral efforts made by African States towards regional economic integration through co-operation in trade liberalization and development so as to attain sustainable growth, promote economic activity and create an enabling environment for foreign trade, as well as cross-border and domestic investments,

RECALLING the economic objectives and aims of the Charter of the Organization of African Unity and the Treaty Establishing the African Economic Community and the other several African Treaties on regional economic integration, including the Treaty Establishing the Common Market for Eastern and Southern Africa, the Treaty Establishing the Southern African Development Community and the Treaty Establishing the Economic Community of West African States,

RECOGNIZING the significant role played by both the private sector and multilateral development institutions in trade, investments and other productive activities in Africa,

DESIROUS of the economic and social benefits, more particularly poverty reduction, which increased partnership among African States, multilateral development institutions and the private sector regarding trade, investments and other productive activities, would bring to African peoples,

CONVINCED that the establishment of an African trade insurance agency would increase the availability of financial resources for trade, investments and other productive activities and reduce the cost of trade finance in Africa by mitigating the associated political, non-commercial and commercial risks,

HAVE HEREBY AGREED AS FOLLOWS:

ARTICLE 1

Interpretation

1. General

(a) Any reference to this Agreement shall include any amendments or modifications thereto as may be made thereunder after the date on which this Agreement enters into force.

(b) Words signifying the singular number only shall include the plural number and vice versa. Words importing the masculine gender include the feminine gender.

(c) The use of headings in this Agreement is for convenience of reference only. The headings do not confer any special meaning or emphasis whatsoever and this Agreement is to be read in its entirety. This Agreement is divided into Articles, paragraphs, sub-paragraphs and clauses, in hierarchical order.

2. Definitions

Except where the context otherwise requires, the following terms shall have the following meanings:

"African State" means any State which is, or which is qualified to become, a member of the Organization of African Unity;

"Agency" means the African Trade Insurance Agency established under paragraph 1 of Article 2 of this Agreement;

"Body" means an International Development Financial Institution or a Regional Economic Organization;

"Body Corporate" means a body corporate duly established or registered under the laws of a Participating State or in any other State;

"Depository" means the Secretary-General of the Organization of African Unity or such other Person to whom the power to act as depository may be delegated pursuant to paragraph 1 of Article 29 of this Agreement;

"Eligible Risks" means the risks eligible for coverage under policies of insurance, coinsurance and reinsurance, or under contracts of guarantee issued or supported by the Agency, as may be determined by the Agency from time to time;

"Financial Year" means, in respect of the Agency, the period between the first day of the month of January and the last day of the month of December in each calendar year or such other period as may be determined by the General Assembly;

"Founding Member" means an African State which signs this Agreement prior to the date upon which it enters into force;

"General Assembly" means the General Assembly referred to in Article 10 of this Agreement;

"International Development Financial Institution" means a multilateral organization or institution constituted by sovereign States to facilitate the financing of projects and programs to promote economic and social development within the territories of its members;

"Member" means an African State, Body or Body Corporate party to this Agreement;

"Participating State" means an African State party to this Agreement;

"Person" means a natural or a legal person, and includes an International Development Financial Institution and a Regional Economic Organization;

"Regional Economic Organization" means a multilateral organization or institution constituted by sovereign States of a given region upon which those member States have conferred competence in respect of matters relating to economic and social development within the region;

"State" means any state or grouping of states, and includes a Participating State.

ARTICLE 2

Establishment

1. Establishment

There is established an institution to be known as the African Trade Insurance Agency.

2. Autonomy

The Agency shall be autonomous and shall enjoy administrative and financial independence in the discharge of its functions.

ARTICLE 3

Legal Capacity

1. International Character

The Agency shall possess international legal personality.

2. Corporate Character

The Agency shall be deemed to be a legally constituted body corporate with perpetual succession and a common seal under the national laws of each of the Participating States.

3. Legal Capacity

The Agency shall possess full juridical personality and, in particular, the legal capacity to:

(a) institute and be a party to judicial and other legal or administrative proceedings;

(b) acquire and dispose of any property by any means;

(c) enter into contracts and conclude agreements;

(d) borrow funds in the manner that the Board of Directors, guided by sound and prudent financial principles, may consider appropriate to achieve its object and purpose;

(e) open and maintain accounts in any bank or other financial institution, in a Participating State or elsewhere, in domestic or foreign currency;

(f) accept gifts, grants, donations or benefactions from any Person;

(g) act as an agent for any Participating State or Person or authorize any Person to act as its agent;

(h) take such steps and do all such things as may appear to it necessary or desirable to protect its interests; and

(i) generally do all such things as are incidental or conducive to the attainment of its object and purpose, the exercise of its powers and the conduct of its business as are conferred or prescribed by this Agreement.

ARTICLE 4

Object and Purpose

1. Object and Purpose

The object and purpose of the Agency are to facilitate, encourage and develop the provision of, or the support for, insurance, including coinsurance and reinsurance, guarantees, and other financial instruments and services, for purposes of trade, investments and other productive activities in Africa in supplement to those which may be offered by the private sector, or in cooperation with the private sector.

The Agency shall be guided in all its decisions by the provisions of the preceding paragraph.

2. Functions

To serve its object and purpose, the Agency shall:

(a) facilitate the development of trade, investments and other productive activities in Africa through the provision of, or support for, insurance, coinsurance, reinsurance or guarantees against political, non-commercial and commercial risks;

(b) establish and administer, on behalf and with the concurrence of Participating States, whether jointly or severally, insurance, coinsurance, reinsurance or guarantee schemes and facilities for promoting trade, investments and other productive activities in Africa;

(c) mobilize financial resources necessary or useful to achieve its object and purpose; and

(d) undertake such other activities and provide such other services as it may consider incidental or conducive to the attainment of its object and purpose.

3. National Legislative and Administrative Action

Each Participating State shall, within a reasonable period, take all legislative action under its national law and all administrative measures necessary to enable the Agency to fully and effectively fulfill its object, purpose and functions. To this end, each Participating State shall promptly inform the Agency in writing of the specific action which it has taken for the aforementioned purpose.

ARTICLE 5

Membership

1. Membership

(a) Membership in the Agency shall be open to:

(i) African States or any public entity nominated or designated by any such African State; and

(ii) such other Bodies or Bodies Corporate as may become Members upon the approval of the General Assembly.

(b) Membership in the Agency shall be acquired upon:

(i) signature and ratification of this Agreement in the case of a Founding Member;

(ii) depositing an instrument of accession to this Agreement in the case of an African State which is not a Founding Member; or

(iii) executing and depositing with the Depository a letter of acceptance of the provisions of this Agreement in the case of a Body or a Body Corporate, subject to a prior decision of the General Assembly pursuant to Article 11, clause 2(b)(i) to admit such Body or Body Corporate.

(c) Membership in the Agency may be held in:

(i) the name of a Participating State;

(ii) the name of a public entity nominated or designated and empowered to that effect by a Participating State; or

(iii) the official or corporate name of a participating Body or Body Corporate.

2. Separate Memberships

Nothing in this Article shall be deemed to restrict the ability of a Participating State, or a Body or Body Corporate based or established in that Participating State, to acquire and hold separate memberships in the Agency.

Provided where membership is held in the name of a Participating State, the concerned Participating State shall not nominate or designate a public entity to hold its membership.

3. State Guarantee for Public Entity

Where a Participating State has nominated or designated a public entity under clauses 1(a)(i) and 1(c)(ii) of this Article to be a Member of the Agency, that Participating State shall be a guarantor, as principal and not merely as a surety, of all the obligations of such public entity towards the Agency.

ARTICLE 6

Authorized Capital Stock and Allocation of Shares

1. Authorized Capital Stock

The Agency shall have an open-ended capital stock based on an initial authorized nominal capital stock of Four Million United States Dollars (US Dollars 4,000,000) divided into Forty (40) shares having a par value of One Hundred Thousand United States Dollars (US Dollars 100,000) each, which shall be available for subscription by Members.

2. Classes of Shares

Shares of the Agency shall be divided into three classes as follows:

(a) Class "A" shares, which shall be offered, allotted and issued to Participating States or their nominated or designated public entities on a one share per Member basis;

(b) Class "B" shares which shall be offered, allotted and issued to Participating States on such terms and conditions as the Board of Directors may determine; and

(c) Class "C" shares which shall be offered, allotted and issued to Bodies or Bodies Corporate on such terms and conditions as the Board of Directors may determine.

3. Division of Class "B" Shares of the Authorized Capital Stock into Paid-In and Callable Shares

Class "B" shares of the authorized capital stock of the Agency shall be divided into paid-in shares and callable shares, in such proportion as the Board of Directors may determine.

4. Increase of Authorized Capital Stock

The initial authorized nominal capital stock and any subsequent authorized capital stock of the Agency may be increased by a two-thirds majority resolution of the General Assembly. Any increase of the authorized capital stock of the Agency shall comply with the relevant provisions of this Agreement.

5. Limitation of Members' Liability

(a) The liability of the Members holding Class "B" shares or Class "C" shares shall be limited to the unpaid portion, if any, of their respective shares.

(b) No Member shall be liable for the obligations of the Agency by reason of its membership in the Agency.

6. Shares not to be Pledged or Encumbered

A Member shall not pledge or cause to be encumbered in any manner whatsoever the shares of the Agency's capital stock. Any pledge or other encumbrance made in contravention of this paragraph shall be null and void *ab initio*.

ARTICLE 7

Subscriptions

1. Determination of Subscriptions

Subject to this Agreement, the Board of Directors shall determine the allotment and subscription of shares of the capital stock of the Agency by Members.

2. Payment of Subscriptions for Class "A" Shares by Participating States

Payment for Class "A" shares subscribed by a Participating State shall be made in United States Dollars or in any convertible currency acceptable to the Agency at the rate of exchange then prevailing, as determined by the Board of Directors, within sixty days of depositing an instrument of ratification with the Depository, in the case of a Founding Member, and within sixty days of depositing an instrument of accession with the Depository, in the case of a Participating State other than a Founding Member.

3. Payment of Subscriptions for Class "B" Shares by Participating States

Payment for such portion of the Class "B" shares subscribed by a Participating State which the Board of Directors has determined be paid in shall be made upon subscription in United States Dollars or in any convertible currency acceptable to the Agency at the rate of exchange then prevailing, as determined by the Board of Directors.

4. Payment of Subscriptions for Class "C" Shares by Bodies or Bodies Corporate

Payment for Class "C" shares subscribed by a Body or Body Corporate shall be made in United States Dollars or in any convertible currency acceptable to the Agency at the rate of exchange then prevailing, as determined by the Board of Directors, within sixty days of depositing a letter of acceptance of this Agreement, in the case of a Body or Body Corporate, with the Depository.

5. Payment of Subscriptions Following Increase of Authorized Capital Stock

The requirements of Article 7, paragraphs 2, 3 and 4 of this Agreement shall apply with the necessary modifications to any shares allotted and issued following an increase in the authorized capital stock of the Agency.

6. Regulation of Shares

Calls on shares, matters relating to share registers and certificates, the Agency's lien on shares, the transfer of shares and other matters related to shares shall be regulated by the Board of Directors in accordance with the provisions of the rules and regulations made by the General Assembly pursuant to this Agreement.

ARTICLE 8

Operations

1. General

(a) The resources and the facilities of the Agency shall be used exclusively to achieve the object, purpose and functions specified in Article 4, paragraphs 1 and 2 of this Agreement.

(b) To this end, the Agency shall operate in accordance with the provisions of this Agreement and the rules and regulations, including internal operational procedures, made pursuant to this Agreement.

2. Risk Insurance and Procedures

(a) Subject to such rules and regulations as the General Assembly shall adopt, the terms and conditions of policies of insurance, coinsurance and reinsurance or contracts of guarantee issued or supported by the Agency shall each be in a form approved by the Board of Directors, including provisions regarding Eligible Risks, transactions eligible for support and Persons eligible for insurance or guarantees.

(b) The Agency shall, subject to the rules and procedures adopted by the General Assembly and guidance received from the Board of Directors, have the power to conclude insurance, co-insurance, reinsurance and guarantee transactions.

(c) The Board of Directors shall establish and periodically review the rates of premiums, fees and other charges, if any, applicable to each policy of insurance, coinsurance and reinsurance, and each contract of guarantee, issued or supported by the Agency.

3. Political Interference Prohibited

The Agency, its officers and staff shall not interfere in the political affairs of any Participating State; nor shall they be influenced in their decisions by the political character of the Participating State or States concerned.

ARTICLE 9

Financial Provisions

1. Financial Management

(a) The Agency shall carry out its activities in accordance with sound business and prudent financial management practices with a view to maintaining under all circumstances its ability to meet its financial obligations.

(b) The Agency shall allocate its net income to reserves until such reserves reach ten times the subscribed capital stock of the Agency. After the reserves of the Agency have reached the prescribed level, the General Assembly shall decide whether, and to what extent, the Agency's net income shall be allocated to reserves, be distributed to the Agency's Members or be used otherwise. Any distribution of net income to the Agency's Members shall be made in proportion to the share of each Member in the capital stock of the Agency.

(c) The Agency may invest funds not immediately needed in its operations or funds held by it for pensions in such investments as the Board of Directors may approve from time to time, provided that such investments shall:

(i) not be speculative in nature;

(ii) be such that the capital thereof is not susceptible to depreciation or otherwise at risk of loss; and

(iii) be liquid in nature so as to ensure that funds are available to meet the financial obligations of the Agency.

2. Budget

The Managing Director shall prepare an annual budget of revenues and expenditures of the Agency for approval by the Board of Directors.

3. Accounts

The Agency shall publish an annual report which shall include statements of its accounts, as audited by independent external auditors. The Agency shall circulate to Members at appropriate intervals a summary statement of its financial position and a profit and loss statement showing the results of its operations.

ARTICLE 10

Organization and Management

The Agency shall have a General Assembly, a Board of Directors, and such other organs as the General Assembly may determine. It shall also have a Managing Director and such other officers and staff as the Board of Directors may determine are necessary for the Agency to carry out its functions efficiently.

ARTICLE 11

General Assembly

1. Composition

Every Member of the Agency shall be a member of the General Assembly. Each Member of the Agency shall appoint one representative and one alternate to the General Assembly.

2. Functions and Powers

(a) Subject to the provisions of this Agreement, all the powers of the Agency shall be vested in the General Assembly.

(b) In addition to the other functions and powers set out and conferred upon it by this Agreement, the General Assembly shall have the power to:

(i) admit new members and, in the case of Bodies or Bodies Corporate, determine the conditions of their admission;

(ii) determine the remuneration of the Directors;

(iii) appoint and remove, on the recommendation of the Board of Directors, the Managing Director and determine his remuneration and terms and conditions of service, including disciplinary rules relating to the Managing Director;

(iv) appoint the external auditors of the Agency and determine their mandate and remuneration;

(v) consider, approve or reject the annual accounts of the Agency;

(vi) subject to Article 9, sub-paragraph 1(b) of this Agreement, determine and authorize, on the recommendation of the Board of Directors, the allocation and distribution of net income;

(vii) suspend or terminate the operations of the Agency and determine the distribution of the assets of the Agency in the event of dissolution;

(viii) consider and determine any matter which the Board of Directors may refer to it;

(ix) generally provide guidance to the Board of Directors in the discharge of its functions; and

(x) perform such other functions and exercise such other powers as may be incidental or conducive to the discharge of any of the functions or exercise of any of the powers provided under this Agreement.

3. Delegation of Powers

(a) Subject to this Agreement, the General Assembly may, by resolution, either generally or in any particular case, delegate to the Board of Directors the exercise of any of its powers or the performance of any of its functions under this Agreement with the exception of the powers and functions set out in paragraph 2 of this Article.

(b) The General Assembly shall retain full power to exercise authority over any matter delegated to the Board of Directors under sub-paragraph 3(a) of this Article.

4. Chairman of the General Assembly

The Chairman of the General Assembly shall be elected from among the members representing the Participating States.

5. Meetings

The General Assembly shall meet at least once in every Financial Year and may hold extraordinary meetings at the request of any Member, provided that such a request is supported by at least one-third of the Members. All meetings of the General Assembly shall be held at the interim or permanent headquarters of the Agency.

6. Quorum

For the purposes of transacting any business under this Agreement, fifty percent of the Members plus one shall constitute the quorum for a meeting of the General Assembly .

7. Voting

(a) Each fully paid up Class "A" share held by a Participating State shall carry one vote at any meeting of the General Assembly.

(b) Class "B" shares shall not carry any right to vote at any meeting of the General Assembly.

(c) Except as provided under sub-paragraph (e) of this paragraph 7 and Article 12, clause (1)(a)(ii) of this Agreement, Class "C" shares shall not carry any right to vote at any meeting of the General Assembly.

(d) Save as expressly provided by this Agreement, all decisions of the General Assembly shall be by simple majority of the Participating States present and voting.

(e) Class "C" shares shall be entitled to vote in respect of the matters set forth under clauses (2)(b)(iv) and (v) of this Article at the meeting of the General Assembly where these matters are to be determined.

8. Rules, Regulations and Procedure

Subject to this Agreement, the General Assembly is hereby empowered, either on its own motion or on the recommendation of the Board of Directors, to make rules and regulations prescribing for matters that are required or permitted by this Agreement to be prescribed or are necessary or convenient to be prescribed for giving full effect to the provisions of this Agreement, including, without limiting the generality of the foregoing, its own procedure.

ARTICLE 12

Board Of Directors

1. Composition

(a) The Board of Directors shall comprise:

(i) six Directors, three of whom shall be from the private sector, elected by Members of the Agency holding fully paid up Class "A" shares; and

(ii) one Director elected by Members of the Agency holding fully paid up Class "C" shares.

(b) The Board of Directors shall elect a Chairman from among the Directors appointed under clause 1(a)(i) of this Article.

(c) The Members of the Agency holding fully paid up Class "A" shares shall have the power to remove a Director elected under Article 12, clause (1)(a)(i). The Members holding fully paid up Class "C" shares shall have the power to remove a Director elected under Article 12, clause (1)(a)(ii).

(d) The Chairman, the other Directors and their Alternates shall be elected immediately prior to the annual meeting of the General Assembly.

(e) The Chairman, the other Directors and their Alternates shall hold office for a term of three years and shall be eligible for reappointment for only one further term of three years after the initial appointment.

(f) An Alternate Director shall have full power to act for the Director to whom he is an Alternate, if such Director is not present. Any Alternate Director may participate in meetings of the Board of Directors but may vote only in the absence of the Director to whom he is an Alternate.

2. Qualifications of Directors

The Chairman, the other Directors and their Alternates shall be persons with internationally recognized qualifications and extensive practical experience in at least one of the following fields: insurance; trade finance and banking; commercial law; and economics.

3. Disqualification of Directors

(a) No person shall be appointed as the Chairman, a Director or an Alternate if the person:

(i) does not have the qualifications prescribed by paragraph 2 of this Article;

(ii) has been convicted of any offence in which dishonesty is an element, or of any offence for which he is sentenced to a term of imprisonment without the option of a fine; or

(iii) has been declared financially insolvent or bankrupt by a court of competent jurisdiction.

(b) No person shall continue in office as the Chairman, a Director or an Alternate if the person:

(i) is unable to perform the functions of his office by virtue of mental or physical infirmity;

(ii) is declared financially insolvent or bankrupt by a court of competent jurisdiction;

(iii) is convicted of any offence in which dishonesty is an element, or of any offence for which he is sentenced to a term of imprisonment without the option of a fine;

(iv) is absent without valid reason from three consecutive meetings of the Board of which he or she has received notice and without the consent of the Chairman; or

(v) fails to comply with the requirements of paragraph 8 of this Article.

4. Functions and Powers

(a) The Board of Directors shall be responsible for managing the business and general operations of the Agency, and for this purpose shall discharge all the functions and exercise all the powers conferred upon it under this Agreement or delegated to it by the General Assembly.

(b) Without limiting the generality of sub-paragraph 4(a) of this Article, the Board of Directors shall have the power to:

(i) suspend the Managing Director for a period up to three months and make appropriate recommendations to the General Assembly;

(ii) administer the organization's structure and determine the qualifications and responsibilities attaching to all posts within the Agency;

(iii) control, supervise and administer the property and other assets of the Agency in such manner as best promotes the object and purpose for which the Agency is established;

(iv) approve the annual budget of revenues and expenditures of the Agency prepared by the Managing Director;

(v) cause to be kept all proper books and records of accounts of the income, expenditure and assets of the Agency;

(vi) cause to be prepared and submitted to the General Assembly, within a period of three months from the end of each Financial Year, annual accounts of the Agency together with a statement of the income and expenditure of the Agency during the year in reference and a statement of the assets and liabilities of the Agency on the last day of the year in reference;

(vii) consider and approve the annual report of the Agency prepared by the Managing Director; and

(viii) provide secretarial services to the General Assembly and any other services that the General Assembly may require.

5. Meetings

The Board of Directors shall meet as often and in such places within Africa as the business of the Agency may require, but not less than two times in any Financial Year. The Managing Director shall attend the meetings of the Board of Directors, but shall have no vote in respect of any matter before the Board of Directors.

6. Quorum

The quorum for the transaction of any business by the Board of Directors shall be four members including the person presiding.

7. Voting

(a) Each Director shall have one vote.

(b) All decisions of the Board of Directors shall be by resolution passed by a majority of the Directors present and voting. In the case of an equality of votes, the Chairman shall have a casting vote.

8. Disclosure of Personal Interest

A member of the Board of Directors who has a direct or indirect personal interest in a matter being considered or to be considered by the Board of Directors shall, as soon as possible after the relevant facts concerning the matter have come to his knowledge, disclose the nature of his interest to the Board of Directors, and shall not be present during any deliberations on the matter by the Board of Directors or vote on such matter. Any disclosure under this paragraph shall be recorded in the minutes of the meeting in question.

9. Procedure

Subject to this Agreement and any general directives of the General Assembly, the Board of Directors shall regulate its own procedure.

ARTICLE 13

Managing Director

1. Qualifications of the Managing Director

The Managing Director shall be a person of integrity and of the highest competence with internationally recognized qualifications and extensive practical experience in at least one of the following fields: insurance, banking, or trade finance.

2. Conduct of the Managing Director

The Managing Director shall not, while in office, engage in any activities that in the opinion of the Board of Directors are incompatible with his office in the Agency.

3. Responsibilities of the Managing Director

(a) The Managing Director shall be the chief executive officer of the Agency and shall, subject to this Agreement, be responsible to the Board of Directors for the day-to-day management of the affairs of the Agency.

(b) The Managing Director shall be responsible for the appointment, discipline and dismissal of all staff members of the Agency, in accordance with regulations prescribed by the Board of Directors. The Managing Director shall ensure the highest standards of efficiency, technical competence and integrity of the staff of the Agency, who shall also be required to refrain from engaging in any activities that in the opinion of the Managing Director are incompatible with their functions.

(c) The Agency shall, in the exercise of its legal personality, be represented by the Managing Director.

(d) The Managing Director shall perform such functions as are conferred by this Agreement and such additional duties as the Board of Directors may direct.

4. Tenure of Office for the Managing Director

The Managing Director shall hold office for a term of four years and shall be eligible for reappointment for only one further term of four years after the initial appointment.

5. Independence

The Managing Director, the officers and staff of the Agency, in the discharge of their functions, owe their duty exclusively to the Agency and shall neither seek, nor receive instructions in regard to the discharge thereof from any authority external to the Agency. Each Member shall respect the international character of this duty and shall refrain from any action to influence the Managing Director, the officers or the staff in the discharge of their functions.

6. Disqualification

The provisions of Article 12, paragraph 3 regarding disqualification of Directors shall, with the necessary modifications, apply to the Managing Director.

ARTICLE 14

Permanent Headquarters and Offices

1. Permanent Headquarters

(a) The permanent headquarters of the Agency shall be located within the territory of a Participating State selected by the General Assembly.

(b) Any transfer of the permanent headquarters temporarily to the territory of another Participating State shall not constitute a removal thereof unless there is an express decision by the General Assembly to that effect.

(c) The Participating State hosting the permanent headquarters shall recognize its extraterritoriality. The permanent headquarters shall be inviolable.

2. Headquarters Agreement

The Participating State selected by the General Assembly to host the permanent headquarters of the Agency shall, as soon as practicable following notification of its selection and, in any event, within thirty days of such notification, conclude a headquarters agreement with the Agency, and take all necessary measures to render the headquarters agreement effective.

3. Branch or Representative Offices

(a) In discharging its functions under this Agreement, the Agency may establish branch or representative offices in any country, whether or not that country is a Participating State, as the Board of Directors may deem necessary for the fulfillment of the Agency's object and purpose.

(b) A Participating State in whose territory a branch or representative office of the Agency is located shall, as soon as practicable following notification of the decision to locate a branch or representative office in its territory, conclude appropriate agreements with the Agency in respect of such branch or representative office, taking into account the provisions of Article 15 of this Agreement.

ARTICLE 15

Immunities, Exemptions and Privileges

1. Immunities, Exemptions and Privileges

Each Participating State shall take all legislative action and all administrative measures under its national laws necessary to enable the Agency to fully and effectively fulfil its object and purpose, and to carry out the functions entrusted to it. To this end, each Participating State shall accord to the Agency, in its territory, the status, immunities, exemptions and privileges set forth in this Agreement, and shall promptly inform the Agency in writing of the specific action which it has taken for that purpose.

2. Immunity of Property and Assets

The property and other assets of the Agency, wherever located and by whomsoever held, shall be immune from:

(a) search, requisition, confiscation, expropriation, nationalization or any other forms of seizure, taking or foreclosure by executive or legislative action; and

(b) seizure, attachment or execution before the delivery of final judgement or award against the Agency in any proceedings.

3. Immunity of Archives

The archives of the Agency and, in general, all documents belonging to, or held by it shall be inviolable and immune from seizure wherever they may be located, except that the immunity provided for in this paragraph 3 shall not extend to documents required to be produced in the course of judicial or arbitral proceedings to which the Agency is a party or proceedings arising out of transactions concluded by the Agency.

4. Freedom from Restrictions

(a) To the extent necessary to fulfill the object and purpose of the Agency and carry out its functions, each Participating State shall waive, and refrain from imposing, any administrative, financial or other regulatory restrictions that would hinder in any manner the efficient functioning of the Agency or impair its operations.

(b) To this end, the Agency, its property, other assets, operations and activities shall be free from restrictions, regulations, supervision or controls, moratoria and other legislative, executive, administrative and monetary restrictions of any nature.

5. Freedom from Taxation

(a) The Agency, its property, other assets, income, and its operations and transactions, shall be exempt from all taxation.

(b) The Agency, and its receiving, fiscal and paying agents, shall also be exempt from any obligation relating to, or liability for, the payment, withholding or collection of any tax or duty.

(c) Articles imported and exported by the Agency for official purposes shall be exempt from all custom duties and other levies, and from prohibitions and restrictions on imports and exports.

(d) The exemptions hereby granted shall be applied without prejudice to the right of the Participating States to tax their legal persons in the manner each Participating State deems appropriate.

6. Privilege for Communications

Official communications of the Agency shall be accorded by each Participating State the same treatment it accords to the official communications of other international institutions of which it is a member.

7. Waiver of Immunities, Exemptions and Privileges of the Agency

The immunities, exemptions and privileges granted to the Agency in this Agreement are in the interest and for the benefit of the Agency. The Board of Directors may waive, to such extent and upon such conditions as it may determine, such immunities, exemptions and privileges in cases where such waiver would, in its opinion, further the interests of the Agency.

8. Personal Immunities, Exemptions and Privileges

All Directors, Alternates, the Managing Director, and staff of the Agency shall enjoy within and with respect to Participating States the following immunities, exemptions and privileges:

(a) immunity from legal process of any kind in respect of words spoken or written, and of acts performed, by them in their official capacity, such immunity to continue notwithstanding that the persons concerned may have ceased to be officials of the Agency;

(b) immunity from seizure of their personal and official baggage;

(c) exemption from taxation in respect of the salaries, emoluments, indemnities and pensions paid to them by the Agency for services past and present or in connection with their service to the Agency;

(d) exemption from any form of taxation on income derived by them from sources outside a Participating State;

(e) exemption, with respect to themselves, their spouses, their dependent relatives and other members of their households from immigration restrictions and alien registration requirements and national service obligations, and the same facilities as regards exchange regulations as are accorded by each Participating State to representatives, officials and employees of comparable rank of other states or international organizations;

(f) freedom to acquire or maintain within a host Participating State or elsewhere foreign securities, foreign currency accounts, and other movables and the right to take or transfer the same out of a host Participating State through authorized channels without prohibition or restriction;

(g) the same protection and repatriation facilities with respect to themselves, their spouses, their dependant relatives and other members of their households as are accorded in time of national or international crisis to members having comparable rank of the missions accredited to the concerned Participating State; and

(h) immunity from personal arrest or detention, except that this immunity shall not apply to civil liability arising from a road traffic accident or to a traffic offence.

9. Representatives, Experts, Consultants and others

The representatives of Members to a meeting of or convened by the Agency, technical experts or advisors (other than officials of the Agency) performing missions authorized by or serving on committees or other subsidiary organs of, or consulting at its request in any way with the Agency, shall, while exercising their functions within a Participating State, enjoy the following immunities, exemptions and privileges:

(a) immunity in respect of themselves, their spouses, their dependent children and other members of their households from personal arrest or detention and from seizure of their personal and official baggage;

(b) immunity from legal process of any kind with respect to words spoken or written, and of acts done, by them in the performance of their official functions, such immunity to continue notwithstanding that the persons concerned may no longer be employed on missions or serving on committees of, or acting as consultants for the Agency, or may no longer be present at the permanent headquarters or attending meetings convened by the Agency;

(c) inviolability for all papers and documents relating to the business or functions of the Agency;

(d) exemption with respect to themselves, their spouses, their dependent children and other members of their households from immigration restrictions, alien registration requirements and national service obligations;

(e) the same protection and repatriation facilities with respect to themselves, their spouses, their dependent relatives and other members of their households as are accorded in time of national or international crises to members, having comparable rank, of the staffs of chiefs of diplomatic missions accredited to a host Participating State;

(f) the same privileges with respect to currency and exchange restrictions as are accorded to representatives of foreign Governments on temporary official missions; and

(g) the same exemptions from taxes and customs duties, including exemption from income tax in respect of emoluments received by them for services rendered in performing services past and present for or on behalf of the Agency, as are accorded to representatives of foreign Governments on temporary official missions, save that the relief allowed from customs and excise duties shall be limited to goods imported as part of their personal baggage.

10. Waiver of Personal Immunities

The Managing Director shall have the right and duty to waive the immunity of any officer, employee, representative, expert, advisor, or consultant of the Agency in cases where in his opinion the immunity would impede the course of justice and can be waived without prejudice to the interests of the Agency. In similar circumstances and under the same conditions, the Board of Directors shall have the right and duty to waive the immunity of the Managing Director of the Agency.

11. Nationals of Participating States

Nothing in this Article shall be construed as requiring any Participating State to accord any of the immunities, privileges, or exemptions provided for under paragraphs 8 and 9 of this Article to any of its nationals.

ARTICLE 16

Legal Process and Regime

1. Actions Against the Agency

Actions may be brought against the Agency only in a court of competent jurisdiction in the territory of a Participating State in which the Agency has its permanent headquarters or an office, or in the territory of a Participating State or non-member State where it has appointed an agent for the purpose of accepting service or notice of process, or has otherwise agreed to be sued. No such action against the Agency may be brought:

(a) by a Member or a former Member of the Agency or persons acting for, or deriving claims from, a Member or a former Member; or

(b) in respect of personnel matters.

2. National Treatment

Participating States shall ensure that parties suing the Agency within their territories have right of access to judicial and administrative proceedings, including redress and remedy, under conditions at least equal to that afforded their nationals or permanent residents.

ARTICLE 17

Relations with other Organizations and Institutions

1. Co-operation

Subject to approval by the General Assembly, the Agency may, in furtherance of its object and purpose, and within the limits of its functions as set forth in this Agreement, cooperate with private and public organizations or institutions of national, regional or international character engaged in the fields of development, insurance, coinsurance and reinsurance. Without limiting the generality of the foregoing, the Agency may cooperate with the African Development Bank, the African Export-Import Bank, the Eastern and Southern Africa Trade and Development Bank, the PTA Re-insurance Company (ZEP-Re), the International Bank for Reconstruction and Development, the International Development Association, the International Finance Corporation, the Multilateral Investment Guarantee Agency and the International Center for the Settlement of Investment Disputes.

2. Agreements of Co-operation

For the purposes of paragraph 1 of this Article, the Agency may, with the approval of the Board of Directors, conclude agreements of co-operation with the organizations or institutions aforementioned or approved thereunder.

3. Delegation of Non-core Functions

The Agency may, on a competitive basis and with the approval of the Board of Directors, entrust some of its non-core functions to private or public organizations or institutions. In this respect the Agency shall formally appoint the concerned organization or institution by way of a written agreement.

ARTICLE 18

Inauguration and Commencement of Operations

1. First General Assembly

Within sixty days from the date upon which this Agreement enters into force, the Depository shall convene the First General Assembly of the Agency to be held at a venue within the territory of a Participating State.

2. Functions and Powers of the First General Assembly

The First General Assembly shall:

(a) consider and ratify, as appropriate, any actions, appointments, commitments and decisions made by the Founding Members or Depository in preparation for the inauguration of the Agency;

(b) decide where the permanent headquarters of the Agency shall be situated and in the event that a final decision cannot be reached, decide where an interim headquarters shall be situated;

(c) appoint a date on which the interim headquarters agreement shall be concluded in the event that a final decision cannot be reached on a permanent headquarters;

(d) appoint the Managing Director of the Agency; and

(e) appoint a date on which the Board of Directors of the Agency will hold their first meeting and indicate the nature of business to be conducted thereat, including the appointment of the key management staff of the Agency.

3. Appointment of the First Directors

The Members of the Agency holding fully paid up Class “A” shares shall, immediately prior to the First General Assembly, elect six Directors, as provided for under Article 12, clause (1)(a)(i) of this Agreement. Notwithstanding sub-paragraph 1(e) of Article 12, two of the first three Directors from the private sector and their Alternates and one of the other Directors and his Alternate appointed under clauses 1(a)(i) and (ii) of Article 12 by the First General Assembly shall be appointed for a term of two years only. The Directors and their Alternates appointed to succeed such Directors and Alternates shall hold office for a term of three years and shall be eligible for reappointment for only one further term of three years after the initial appointment.

4. Commencement of Operations

The Agency shall commence operations on a date appointed by the Board of Directors following:

(a) conclusion of an interim or permanent headquarters agreement;

(b) appointment of a Managing Director and key management staff; and

(c) confirmation by the Chairman that the minimum financial requirements of the Agency have been met.

ARTICLE 19

Suspension or Termination of Operations

1. Duration of Agreement

This Agreement shall have indefinite duration.

2. Suspension of Operations

(a) The Board of Directors may, whenever it deems it justified, suspend the issuance of new policies of insurance, coinsurance and reinsurance, or new contracts of guarantee, or suspend the provision of new support for such policies or contracts, for a specified period.

(b) In an emergency, the Board of Directors may suspend all activities of the Agency for a period not exceeding the duration of such emergency, provided that necessary arrangements shall be made for the protection of the interests of the Agency and of third parties.

(c) The decision to suspend operations shall have no effect on the obligations of the Members under this Agreement or on the obligations of the Agency towards holders of an insurance, coinsurance or reinsurance policy or a contract of guarantee or towards third parties.

3. Termination of Operations

Notwithstanding the provisions of paragraph 1 of this Article, the General Assembly, by resolution approved by a vote of not less than two-thirds of the Participating States holding fully paid up Class "A" shares, may decide to terminate operations and to liquidate the Agency.

4. Cessation of Activities

Upon decision of the General Assembly to terminate operations taken in accordance with the provisions of paragraph 3 of this Article, the Agency shall forthwith cease all activities, except those incidental to the orderly realization, conservation and preservation of its property and other assets and the settlement of its obligations. Until final settlement and distribution of property and other assets, the Agency shall remain in existence and all rights and obligations of Members under this Agreement shall continue unimpaired, including, without limitation, the liability of Members for uncalled subscriptions to shares of the capital stock of the Agency.

5. Discharge of Liabilities

No distribution of property or other assets shall be made to Members until all liabilities to holders of insurance, coinsurance and reinsurance policies and to holders of contracts of guarantee and other creditors shall have been discharged or provided for and until the General Assembly shall have decided to make such distribution. No Member shall be entitled to share in the property or assets of the Agency unless that Member has settled all outstanding claims by the Agency against it.

6. Distribution of Assets

Subject to the preceding paragraphs of this Article, the property and other assets of the Agency shall be distributed amongst its Members in accordance with the rules and regulations made by the General Assembly. Every distribution of property and other assets shall be made at such times as the General Assembly shall determine and in such manner as it shall consider fair and equitable.

ARTICLE 20

Settlement of Disputes

1. Disputes Avoidance

Participating States shall fully comply with their obligations as stipulated herein and shall endeavour to avoid disputes.

2. Settlement of Disputes between Participating States

(a) Participating States shall settle disputes concerning the interpretation or application of this Agreement by peaceful means, such as by negotiation, enquiry, mediation, conciliation, resort to regional agencies or arrangements, or by any other peaceful means of their own choice.

(b) If the Participating States parties to a dispute do not reach an agreement on a solution or on a dispute settlement arrangement within six months following the notification by one party to another and the Board of Directors that a dispute exists, the dispute shall, at the request of one of the parties, be submitted for final decision to arbitration as follows:

(i) the tribunal shall consist of an odd number of arbitrators; each party nominating a single arbitrator and the nominated arbitrators appointing the Chairperson of the tribunal who shall not be from amongst the nominated arbitrators. Where the Chairperson of the tribunal has not been appointed within sixty days of receipt of notice of arbitration, the said Chairperson shall be appointed by the Secretary General of the Organization of African Unity at the request of any party to the dispute. The arbitral tribunal shall regulate its own procedure with the Chairperson having full power to settle all questions of procedure where the arbitrators are in disagreement with respect thereto. An award rendered by the majority of the arbitrators shall be final and binding on the parties to the dispute; or

(ii) the parties may refer the matter to the Court of Justice of the Common Market for Eastern and Southern Africa for arbitration in accordance with Article 28(a) of the Treaty Establishing the Common Market for Eastern and Southern Africa.

3. Settlement of Disputes Between Participating States, other Members and the Agency

Where the dispute is between a Participating State and a Member other than another Participating State or between Members other than Participating States, or between a Member or Members and the Agency, the dispute shall be referred to arbitration as provided for under sub-paragraph 2(b)(i) of this Article.

ARTICLE 21

Supplementary Agreements

1. Supplementary Agreements Between Participating States

Participating States may enter into multilateral agreements that supplement this Agreement.

2. Supplementary Agreements Between Members and the Agency

A Member or a group of Members, may enter into agreements with the Agency to the extent necessary to achieve the object and purpose of this Agreement.

ARTICLE 22

Amendments

1. Proposals for Amendments

Any Participating State may propose amendments to this Agreement. The text of any such proposed amendment shall be submitted to the Chairman of the General Assembly, who shall provide a copy to the Board of Directors. The Chairman of the General Assembly shall transmit the proposed amendment within one month to all the Members with a specific request that each Member indicates whether or not an extraordinary meeting of the Participating States should be convened to consider the proposed amendment.

2. Adoption of Amendments

At the request of one-third of the Participating States, the Chairman of the General Assembly shall call an extraordinary meeting of the Participating States to consider the proposed amendment. The Participating States shall make every effort to reach agreement on any proposed amendment by consensus. If all efforts at reaching a consensus have been exhausted, and no agreement reached, the amendment shall as a last resort be adopted by a two-thirds majority vote of the Participating States who are present and voting at the extraordinary meeting. The adopted amendment shall be communicated by the Chairman of the General Assembly, who shall circulate it to all Participating States and other Members. For purposes of this Article "present and voting" means Participating States present and casting an affirmative or negative vote.

3. Entry into Force of Amendments

Amendments shall enter into force for all Members fifteen days after the date of communication by the Chairman.

ARTICLE 23

Signature

This Agreement shall be open for signature from the eighteenth (18th) day of May, 2000.

ARTICLE 24

Ratification

This Agreement shall be subject to ratification by Founding Members. Instruments of ratification shall be deposited with the Depository.

ARTICLE 25

Accession or Acceptance

1. Accession

This Agreement shall be open for accession by African States after its entry into force. Instruments of accession shall be deposited with the Depository.

2. Acceptance

(a) This Agreement shall be open for acceptance by International Development Financial Institutions, Regional Economic Organizations and Bodies Corporate. Letters of acceptance of the provisions of this Agreement shall be executed and deposited with the Depository.

(b) In their letters of acceptance, International Development Financial Institutions and Regional Economic Organizations shall declare the extent of their competence with respect to the matters governed by this Agreement.

(c) Any International Development Financial Institution or Regional Economic Organization which becomes party to this Agreement without any of its member states being party shall be bound by all the obligations under this Agreement. In the case of such organizations, one or more of whose member states is party to this Agreement, the organization and its member states shall decide on their respective responsibilities for the performance of their obligations under this Agreement. In such cases, the organization and the member states shall not be entitled to exercise rights under this Agreement concurrently.

ARTICLE 26

Entry into Force

1. Entry into Force on Ratification

This Agreement shall enter into force on the fifteenth day after the deposit of the third instrument of ratification.

2. Entry into Force on Accession

For each African State that accedes to this Agreement after the date upon which it shall have entered into force, this Agreement shall enter into force on the fifteenth day after the deposit by such African State of its instrument of accession.

3. Entry into Force on Acceptance

For each International Development Financial Institution, Regional Economic Organization and Body Corporate that accepts this Agreement after the date upon which it shall have entered into force, this Agreement shall enter into force on the fifteenth day after the deposit by such International Development Financial Institution, Regional Economic Organization and Body Corporate of its letter of acceptance.

4. Failure of Agreement to Enter into Force

If this Agreement shall not have entered into force within two years after its opening for signature, the Depository shall convene a conference of interested Participating States to determine the future course of action.

ARTICLE 27

Reservations

No reservations may be made to this Agreement.

ARTICLE 28

Suspension and Withdrawal from Membership

1. Suspension from Membership

(a) If it appears to the General Assembly, on the recommendation of the Board of Directors, that a Member fails to fulfil any of its obligations to the Agency, that Member may be suspended by resolution of the General Assembly approved by a vote representing not less than two-thirds of the total Class "A" voting power of the Members of the Agency.

(b) The decision to suspend a Member shall be subject to review by the General Assembly at any time. The General Assembly may rescind the suspension by the same majority as provided in paragraph 1 of this Article.

(c) A Member so suspended shall automatically cease to be Member of the Agency from the date of suspension. While under suspension, a Member shall not be entitled to exercise any rights under this Agreement, except the right of withdrawal, but shall remain subject to all obligations.

2. Withdrawal from Membership

(a) At any time after three years from the date on which this Agreement has entered into force for a Participating State, International Development Financial Institution, Regional Economic Organization or Body Corporate, that Member may withdraw from this Agreement by giving written notification to the Depository.

(b) Any such withdrawal shall become effective upon the expiry of one calendar year from the date on which the written notification of intention to withdraw was received by the Depository, or on such later date as may be specified in the notification of the withdrawal.

3. Effects of Suspension or Withdrawal from Membership

Save as provided under paragraph 1(c) of this Article, suspension or withdrawal from membership in the Agency and the effects that this may have on existing liabilities and the rights and duties that will survive such suspension or withdrawal from membership shall be determined in accordance with the rules and regulations made by the General Assembly.

ARTICLE 29

Depository

1. Name of Depository

The Secretary-General of the Organization of African Unity shall be the Depository of this Agreement. The Depositary shall have the power to delegate its power to another Body based in Africa.

2. Functions and Powers of the Depository

In addition to its other functions under this Agreement, the Depository shall:

(a) upon the request of any African State, arrange for signature of this Agreement before its entry into force;

(b) pronounce this Agreement to have entered into force;

(c) register this Agreement with the Secretariat of the United Nations in accordance with Article 102 of the Charter of the United Nations; and

(d) notify all Participating States, and, upon the entry into force of this Agreement, International Development Financial Institutions and Regional Economic Organizations, the Bodies Corporate and the Agency, as appropriate, of the following:

(i) signatures of this Agreement;

(ii) deposits of instruments of ratification, accession and acceptance of this Agreement;

(iii) the date on which any amendment to this Agreement enters into force; and

(iv) any suspension or withdrawal of a Member from this Agreement and the Agency.

ARTICLE 30

Authentic Texts

The original of this Agreement, of which the English and French texts are equally authentic, shall be deposited with the Secretary-General of the Organization of African Unity. The original of this Agreement shall be translated into Arabic, Portuguese and Spanish, which, following their authentication, shall be regarded as equally authentic to the English and French texts, and shall be deposited with the Secretary-General of the Organization of African Unity.

DONE at Grand Bay in the Republic of Mauritius on the Eighteenth Day of May in the Year 2000.

IN FAITH WHEREOF the undersigned have placed their signatures at the end of this Agreement.

- The President of the Republic of Angola
- The President of the Republic of Burundi
- The President of the Federal Islamic Republic of the Comoros
- The President of the Democratic Republic of Congo
- The President of the Republic of Djibouti
- The President of the Arab Republic of Egypt
- The President of the State of Eritrea
- The Prime Minister of the Federal Democratic Republic of Ethiopia
- The President of the Republic of Kenya
- The President of the Republic of Madagascar
- The President of the Republic of Malawi
- The Prime Minister of the Republic of Mauritius
- The President of the Republic of Namibia
- The President of the Republic of Rwanda

- The President of the Republic of Seychelles
- The President of the Republic of Sudan
- His Majesty the King of the Kingdom of Swaziland
- The President of the United Republic of Tanzania
- The President of the Republic of Uganda
- The President of the Republic of Zambia
- The President of the Republic of Zimbabwe

RECENT REPORTS

CHINA AND THE KNOWLEDGE ECONOMY: SEIZING THE 21ST CENTURY

Excerpts from Chapter 4: Updating Economic Incentives and Institutions

Note

In October 2001 the World Bank Institute and the World Bank's East Asia and Pacific Region jointly published a major new study: China and the Knowledge Economy: Seizing the 21st Century.[1] *The study reviews the acute challenges faced by China in the face of the knowledge and information revolution, and recommends seven priority actions for moving the country toward a knowledge economy. The very first of these recommendations is: "Pursue reform of the economic incentive and institutional regime through the rule of law and its enforcement, property rights, a clearer regulatory framework, stronger economic competition, and extracting political influences from business management."*[2] *In view of the prime importance attached to the rule of law and legal reform for building a knowledge economy, the relevant chapter is excerpted below.*[3]

---

1 Carl J. Dahlman and Jean-Eric Aubert, *China and the Knowledge Economy – Seizing the 21st Century* (The World Bank 2001).

2 *Id.* at xxv.

3 *Id.*, ch. 4, *Updating Economic Incentives and Institutions.* Some text, all tables, and all boxes have been omitted. Notes have been reformatted. Editorial changes are indicated by square brackets.

The World Bank Legal Review: Law and Justice for Development: 615-625.

Printed in the Netherlands.

ESTABLISHING A MORE FORMAL AND TRANSPARENT RULE OF LAW

The legal system in China is extraordinarily complex, often unclear, and sometimes even contradictory. This uncertainty seems to result principally from the many uncoordinated legal initiatives of the different levels of government – central, provincial, and local – and the various government ministries, each with specific responsibilities and administrative territories. A complicated grid has developed, leading to an accumulation of legal and bureaucratic regulations. … Additional problems include corruption, weak enforcement mechanisms, inadequately trained (and underpaid) judges, and long consensus efforts to unite administrative players with contradictory interests. This penalizes entrepreneurs, particularly those not plugged into power networks and foreigners unfamiliar with the legal and administrative climate.

…

Moreover, several important legal pillars of a market economy are still lacking. Property rights are still undefined in many areas. Unclear rules for the ownership of state enterprises impede their restructuring. Competition and anti-monopoly laws are incomplete. Many laws affecting the financial sector, such as bankruptcy and the regulation of financial institutions, are also ineffective. So are laws to provide adequate social safety nets, consumer protection, and environmental regulations.

The highest Chinese institutions, such as the National People's Congress and the State Council, should initiate appropriate policy measures to address these barriers. Needed are adjustments to laws, auditing or hearing procedures for preparing those adjustments, and providing the financial and human resources to implement laws and regulations.

Clarifying and enforcing the law are of utmost importance. These mechanisms require informed and diligent prosecutors, well-established courts, cataloging of and adherence to precedents from prior decisions, and imposing stiff penalties. China has traditionally paid little attention to the rule of law in the western sense. The predictable and equitable application of the law has not been fully integrated into Chinese practice. Some areas for further development:

- Creating transparent, stable, and predictable legislative processes;
- Enhancing public understanding of the law;
- Improving access to legal advice to protect the rights and obligations of parties to economic transactions;

- Solidifying public confidence in the fairness of dispute resolution mechanisms; and
- Ensuring that the government, as well as individual enterprises, is accountable to the law.

INTELLECTUAL PROPERTY RIGHTS

Special attention also needs to be paid to the development of appropriate incentives for knowledge creation, valuation, and protection. Urgent action is needed on widely spread copying practices, which are problematic not only for foreign enterprises, but also for an increasing number of domestic ones, notably the new technology-based firms. A series of laws were recently passed to update the intellectual property rights regime in China to place it on par with those of industrial countries.[4] However, serious problems of enforcement remain, requiring multi-pronged actions that include education and awareness campaigns, recruitment and training of appropriate human resources, streamlining of the judicial and administrative procedures, and strengthening of penalties. Intellectual property rights issues in certain sectors, such as pharmaceuticals, where there are major areas of friction with foreign companies, should receive the greatest attention. The counterfeiting practices that plague not only foreign investors,[5] but also many domestic producers, should be energetically combated with vigilant monitoring and penalties. Chinese authorities are well aware of most of these issues and stronger enforcement actions are being taken on trademarks and copyrights; however, enforcement on patent legislation is lagging behind. This area will need to be strengthened, particularly as China moves to more sophisticated technologies and upgrades its own technology development and patenting mechanisms.

---

[4] The law on employee inventors is particularly progressive. It gives employees a fairly substantial financial reward for their inventions, either when enterprises exploit them or when the employees establish their own firms to commercialize their inventions. These incentives have been neglected in Western countries, despite having played a decisive role in building the competitive strengths of a number of industrialized nations, notably Germany between the two world wars.

[5] Foreign investors have constituted a coalition against counterfeiting (CAC), grouping major firms from Europe, North America, and Asia. The coalition has listed the many cases and problems encountered in the current situation and has transmitted detailed complaints to the Chinese government.

However, China should also participate in the global discussion addressing the evolving international agreements on intellectual property rights. Many new and complex issues, particularly in biogenetics and software, with important implications for China are being opened as the technological base evolves. China should actively represent its interests in the formulation of these agreements. It can also play an important leadership role in representing the interests of other developing countries in this complex area.

STRENGTHENING COMPETITION AND REGULATORY FRAMEWORKS

Establishing effective regulation is a complex, arduous, and never-ending task. Even in the most advanced countries, continual tweaking ensures that the economic system encourages competition and equality, yet discourages rent-seeking and fraudulent activity. But guiding economic participants to interact effectively through capable regulation still is much less demanding than controlling all economic activity through exchanges forced by government.

TRADE

One key to creating stronger incentives to make effective use of knowledge for development is fostering more competition in the economy. The conditions of economic competition in China are still poor – still strongly affected by monopolies, opaque procurement policies, protected markets, and inter-provincial barriers to trade. Rent seeking and inefficient management of public funds put a drag on GDP that ranges anywhere from 5.1% to 7.2% a year.[6] Competitive pressure is the best incentive for improving management, encouraging innovation, and spurring economic growth. China's admission into the WTO will help promote these changes, by placing great pressure to restructure activities and profit from China's international comparative advantages. But even more reform is needed, and the government is establishing appropriate rules and standards in under-administered sectors, while taking action to deregulate sectors in which it has too much control.

Another area requiring attention is the array of administrative and other obstacles to the free flow of goods and services among Chinese provinces. By joining

---

6 Angang Hu, *Corruption and Anti-Corruption Strategies in China* (Carnegie Endowment for International Peace 2001) (study for the Center for China Study, Chinese Academy of Sciences, Tsinghua University).

the WTO China is going to reap even greater gains from international specialization. But many tariff and nontariff barriers to internal trade defeat the potential of China's large internal market for realizing economies of scale and scope. Taking advantage of a large market at home is a big part of the reason the United States was so well positioned to expand to international markets. It is also the main force driving the European Union and many other regional trading arrangements. The Chinese government should remove internal trade barriers to take full advantage of its large market.

COMPETITION AND REGULATIONS

Market-supporting institutions [in the fields of fair trade and anti-monopoly] should also be strengthened to maintain discipline among large domestic monopolists, as well as the multinationals that will be entering many sectors. Both have the potential to abuse superior technologies, creating insurmountable first mover advantages and monopoly power in such sectors as telecommunications, finance, distribution, and marketing. Small and medium enterprises and independent new start-ups, perhaps the most significant prospective vehicles for growth in China, are particularly vulnerable to predatory behavior. Administrative, industrial, financial, and geographic restrictions hinder their development – restrictions that need to be gradually eliminated.[7]

In addition, the government has to put in place appropriate regulations to deal with safety, standards, and environmental regulation. In the environmental area it also needs to strengthen market mechanisms to internalize some of the costs of using the environment.

...

[7] As a result of vague criteria for official review, administrators have great discretion. For example, the partnership law gives officers the power to evaluate whether the relationship fits the "fairness and equity" criteria. The wholly individual owned enterprise law requires enterprise owners to prove their business ability to the officers. Successful registration partially depends on the judgment of the officers. For restrictions to entry, the central government stipulates that access to certain industries be restricted; as a result, private firms face restrictions on license for 15 types of businesses. These include such industries as copper, steel, polyethylene products, aviation, power, automobile manufacturing, financial services, and radio and audio products.

INFORMATION COLLECTION AND DISSEMINATION

More generally, the government has to promote better collection and dissemination of information. This should start with improving the collection of statistics on socioeconomic activities, which can be used to track economic performance as well as social development. It should also include stronger requirements for the disclosure of financial information by firms and organizations (including government) to promote greater transparency and accountability. Finally, it should also include the promotion of specialized institutions to analyze and disseminate information, such as credit-rating agencies; testing and quality control, and product evaluation agencies.

TAXATION

Tax collection in China is also underdeveloped. The tax revenue of the central and provincial governments is just 14% of GNP, less than half the average for OECD countries. The government is forced to finance a large part of its spending through off-budget funds, including those from the banks. Under the command economy, China had a very simple taxation system for enterprises and individuals. But with the transition to a socialist market economy, the tax system has become more complex. Authorities at all levels have far too much latitude to manipulate the tax code. To promote economic activity, they have established many tax incentives to try to attract firms, stimulate innovation, and promote other economic activity. The result: inconsistent, inefficient tax collection, contributing to the government's deepening financial difficulties.

Improving tax collection would also be important to fund government programs to improve social safety nets and social spending to deal with problems of equity and inequality across provinces.

The central authorities, … should establish a precise list of useful incentives that foster the promotion of a knowledge-based economy without being a drag on revenues, potentially establishing some order in the muddled array of arrangements that currently exist. Establishing functional incentives that promote innovation will be more beneficial than those that endorse specific sectors or industries. Specific recommendations include providing rebates for researchers or overseas Chinese who create enterprises … and supporting the development of nonprofit organizations – essential for technical training and knowledge diffusion.

EXPANDING THE PRIVATE SECTOR

China's growth has been based on first restructuring agriculture and then moving people out of agriculture and into industry, including SOEs, TVEs, and foreign enterprises. China is now in the middle of a dramatic transformation from a command economy to a socialist market economy. The number of workers in state-owned enterprises plunged from 112 million in 1995 to 86 in 1999, and those in collective urban enterprises from 32 million to 17, for declines of 23% and 46% in just four years. Meanwhile the number in the private enterprises – broadly defined to include enterprises fully registered as private plus some sort of shareholding companies – rose from 13 million to 32 million, and the self-employed from 46 million to 62 million. The private sector (private plus self-employed) shot up from 59 million to 94 million employees (59%) in just four years!

This recent transformation has set the stage for unleashing one of China's greatest assets – the tremendous entrepreneurial capability of its people. Although people in China are remarkably resourceful, they have had difficulty establishing themselves as visible private entrepreneurs. But despite the unclear legal and regulatory environments,[8] entrepreneurs have found ingenious informal ways of overcoming bureaucratic hurdles in order to survive. Informality has allowed private enterprises to respond flexibly to changing policies and regulations and react nimbly to new market opportunities, while diversifying risk and avoiding excessive taxation, regulation, and competition.

Informality, however, has its limits, especially for firms growing in size and complexity. Employment in private enterprises, more narrowly defined, was only 17 million at the end of 1999 – only 1.5 million of 8 million enterprises, with sales of 720 billion yuan, or slightly less than 10% of China's 7.7 trillion yuan economy in 1998 ... Large, mature companies are often unfocused with limited management capacity and have difficulty in attracting funding and technical skills.

[Following] the 15th Party Congress held in September 1997, the private sector was recognized in a constitutional amendment. The amendment provides greater assurance of a better policy environment for private firms. It should also encourage more formalization of enterprises, creating conditions that would increase the capacity of domestic firms to withstand the foreign competition from joining the WTO. But these actions are not enough. Clarifying the current functional

---

[8] There are not even very clear statistics on the size of the private sector, because of the bias until very recently against even acknowledging the private sector.

definitions, including the distinction between public and private enterprises, and determining the governance structures and incentive regimes that pertain to each are essential to establish greater transparency and to reward effort fairly.

The next major step will be explicitly recognizing private property. The current lack of clarity and fear of possible appropriation by the state are still disincentives for Chinese people to fully apply themselves, expand their businesses, and innovate – thus hampering economic growth. While this action might seem inconsistent with socialist theory, it seems compatible with the "one country, two systems" arrangement in Hong Kong and Macao.

PROMOTING SMALL AND MEDIUM ENTERPRISES

In addition to establishing a legal basis for private property, the government should undertake proactive strategies to help the development of small and medium-size enterprises in all sectors, from agriculture to services:

- Drastically reducing the many regulatory hurdles for establishing and operating new private enterprises.
- Ensuring that small- and medium-size enterprises have access to bank credit.
- Promoting informal lending schemes to small start-up businesses, such as group lending and special micro-venture schemes.
- Providing small and medium enterprises access to market and technical information.
- Developing formal and informal basic business and accounting skill training aimed at small and medium enterprises.
- Strengthening university and continuing education offerings relating to business and entrepreneurial skills.
- Drawing on extensive global experience on small and medium enterprise support programs, adapting the most relevant to the Chinese context.

...

The Chinese government should encourage private enterprise within service industries. Due to past policy biases, China does not yet have a well-developed service sector, so the potential for growth is huge in such industries as financial and insurance services, management and technical consulting, call centers, law, sales, marketing, advertising, public relations, accounting, computer programming, travel, and tourism. Service industries are knowledge and labor-intensive, and therefore are particularly necessary for the transition to a knowledge-based society. Productivity gains made in service sector industries not only benefit the service industries themselves, but benefits also trickle down through other sectors, including manufacturing and agriculture, leading to huge productivity and efficiency gains in all segments of the economy.

REFORMING THE STATE-OWNED ENTERPRISES

Still employing almost 90 million people and accounting for more than 60% of government revenues, SOEs play a major role in the Chinese economy, and their transformation is the most challenging industrial policy problem faced by any government in the world. A majority of these enterprises are experiencing difficulties and will be forced to lay off large numbers of employees to survive. The proposed reforms are not that the state should get out of the production process entirely, but that it should get out of sectors that are not strategic, or those in which it does not have a comparative advantage. In some sectors SOEs are demonstrating fairly competitive capabilities, allowing them to successfully enter difficult world markets. These successful ventures could stay in state hands as long as they do not receive special financial or regulatory treatment, or garner other unfair advantages over non-state owned competitors.

To make the SOEs more efficient and productive, a three-pronged approach is recommended:

- First, a reform of the corporate governance structure is necessary. As long as the government appoints the top managers, the SOEs will only respond to their bosses within the government instead of reacting to the needs of the market, leading to corruption, rent-seeking, and resistance to change, risk, and innovation. SOEs should be given more autonomy with elected managers and independent boards of directors, while government representatives, whatever their level, should be separated from business decisions.
- Second, social services should be unbundled. SOEs are burdened by obligations to provide housing, kindergarten, pension plans, and other social service functions. This unbundling will require the rapid establishment of a social security system as well as other safety nets.
- Third, asset ownership should be resolved. Assets now belong to the state and can therefore not be freely used, sold, or transformed by enterprise management. As long as this remains unresolved, the climate for innovation and increased competitiveness in SOEs will remain poor.

A concerted effort should facilitate the spinoff or creation of small private enterprises from bankrupt and other state enterprises. For both, the issue of the ownership of state assets is critical. For bankrupt state enterprises it is important to have efficient ways to redeploy their assets to productive use. For existing enterprises it is important to have them shed noncore activities and to contract out services that private firms can provide more efficiently. This can help absorb the labor and support the development and growth of an efficient service sector.

. . .

STRENGTHENING THE FINANCIAL SECTOR

. . .

In summary, in today's competitive global environment, China must develop a much larger and more efficient financial market. Some of the specific actions include:

- Reducing the use of the banking system to finance special policy programs or to bail out failing enterprises. These should be financed as direct fiscal outlays of the treasury in order to have greater transparency on government expenditures and to avoid contaminating and constraining the banking system.
- Strengthening supervision of the banking system, accounting practices, and loan classifications.
- Training bank managers and loan officers more thoroughly in project analysis and portfolio management so that they can allocate credit to the projects with the best returns, and monitor the performance of their loan portfolios.
- Using foreign financial institutions to provide innovative new products and better management practices.
- Developing an effective stock market with appropriate disclosure rules and safeguards against insider trading as well as effective governance of the traded firms and the financial intermediaries.
- Developing the venture capital market, critical to finance entrepreneurs with new ideas who do not have tangible collateral required by bankers.
- Implementing appropriate bankruptcy legislation and procedures to be able to re-deploy the productive assets of failed enterprises to new economic uses.
- Developing an effective insurance market to help companies and individuals deal with risk.

More fundamentally, China needs a substantially overhauled system offering a broader array of products and services to a wider range of customer segments, particularly those in the private sector. The government so far has been more focused on the providers of the financial services than on the users, which is not surprising as it is virtually the only provider of such services. However, the government should be playing a different role. Rather than providing all the services itself, it should be establishing the infrastructure (laws, information, incentive focused regulation and supervision) necessary to allow a competitive, innovative, and prudently managed financial sector to develop. Besides the problems of conflict of interest between its role as main provider and that of developer, facilitator and guarantor, an additional problem is the lack of accountability for financial sector reform and development within the government itself. Therefore, the government needs to rethink the way it approaches financial sector development, creating an overreaching infrastructure to drive a comprehensive reform program.

PRINCIPLES AND GUIDELINES FOR EFFECTIVE INSOLVENCY AND CREDITOR RIGHTS SYSTEMS

Note

In April 2001, the World Bank's Board of Executive Directors reviewed the report Principles and Guidelines for Effective Insolvency and Creditor Rights Systems[1] *and endorsed it as the basis for further work. The report was also considered by the Development Committee, which welcomed its contribution to the international financial architecture and encouraged the further development of the Principles and Guidelines in close consultation with borrowing member countries and partner institutions.*[2]

Effective insolvency and creditor rights systems are indispensable to the working of any market economy and contribute materially to the stability and efficiency of a country's financial system. The report, the result of a truly multinational effort,[3] *presents a distillation of international best practice and is intended to guide systemic reform in developing and transition economies. A further report on the Principles and Guidelines, including comparative law materials, will be published in the World Bank's Law, Justice, and Development Series. In the meantime, in order to bring the Principles and Guidelines to the attention of a wider international audience, the executive summary of the report and the principles are set forth below.*

---

1 An updated version of the report is available at <www.worldbank.org/gild>.

2 The Development Committee is a joint committee of the Boards of Governors of the International Bank for Reconstruction and Development and the International Monetary Fund. The communiqué of its April 30, 2001 meeting is available at <http://lnts022/dcs/devcom.nsf>.

3 *See* para. 2 and note 2 of the Introduction and Executive Summary *infra* for the list of organizations who collaborated in the drafting of the *Principles and Guidelines* and for the international consultative process that was followed in the preparation of the report.

The World Bank Legal Review: Law and Justice for Development: 627-645.

Printed in the Netherlands.

Introduction and Executive Summary

1. Since the 1997-98 financial crisis in emerging markets, considerable progress has been made in identifying the components of the global financial system and in articulating and applying standards and assessment methodologies for core system elements. The Principles and Guidelines for Effective Insolvency and Creditor Rights Systems contributes to that effort as an important milestone in promoting international consensus on a uniform framework to assess the effectiveness of insolvency and creditor rights systems, offering guidance to policymakers on the policy choices needed to strengthen them.

2. The principles in Principles and Guidelines were developed against the backdrop of earlier and ongoing initiatives to promote cross-border cooperation on multi-jurisdictional insolvencies, modernization of national insolvency and secured transactions laws, and development of principles for out-of-court corporate workouts.[1] The principles draw on common themes and policy choices of those initiatives and on the views of staff, insolvency experts and participants in regional workshops sponsored by the Bank and its partner organizations.[2] The consultative process on the Principles and Guidelines has been among the most extensive of its kind, involving more than 70 international experts as members of the Bank's Task Force and working groups, and with regional participation by more than 700 public and private sector specialists from approximately 75 mostly developing countries. The Bank also included papers and consultative drafts on its website to obtain feedback from the international community.[3]

---

1 The Addendum to this paper contains a brief survey of the leading initiatives in these fields. [EN: omitted in this presentation.]

2 The *Principles and Guidelines* report was prepared by Bank staff in collaboration with the African Development Bank, Asian Development Bank, European Bank for Reconstruction and Development, Inter-American Development Bank, International Finance Corporation, International Monetary Fund, Organisation for Economic Co-operation and Development, United Nations Commission on International Trade Law, INSOL International, and International Bar Association (Committee J).

3 The papers can be accessed in the Best Practice directory on the Global Insolvency Law Database at <http://www.worldbank.org/gild>.

Role of Insolvency and Creditor Rights Systems

3. There are two dimensions to the global financial system. On the one hand, national financial systems operate autonomously and respond to domestic needs. On the other, national systems are tied to and interact daily with the systems of their trading partners. Insolvency and creditor rights systems lie at the juncture of this duality.

4. The country dimension. National systems depend on a range of structural, institutional, social and human foundations to make a modern market economy work. There are as many combinations of these variables as there are countries, though regional similarities have created common customs and legal traditions. The principles espoused in the report embody several underlying propositions:

- Effective systems respond to national needs and problems. As such, these systems must be rooted in the country's broader cultural, economic, legal and social context.
- Transparency, accountability and predictability are fundamental to sound credit relationships. Capital and credit, in their myriad forms, are the lifeblood of modern commerce. Investment and availability of credit are predicated on both perceptions and the reality of risks. Competition in credit delivery is handicapped by lack of access to accurate information on credit risk and by unpredictable legal mechanisms for debt enforcement.
- Legal and institutional mechanisms must align incentives and disincentives across a broad spectrum of market-based systems – commercial, corporate, financial and social. This calls for an integrated approach to reform, taking into account a wide range of laws and policies in the design of insolvency and creditor rights systems.

5. The international dimension. New methods of commerce, communication and technology are constantly reshaping national markets and redefining notions of property rights. Businesses routinely transcend national boundaries and have access to new types of credit. Credit and investment risks are measured by complex formulas, and capital moves from one market to the next at the tap of a computer key. Capital flows are driven by public perceptions and investor confidence in local markets. Effective insolvency and creditor rights systems play an important role in creating and maintaining the confidence of both domestic and foreign investors.

The Principles

6. The Principles and Guidelines emphasize contextual, integrated solutions and the policy choices involved in developing those solutions.[4] The principles are a distillation of international best practice in the design of insolvency and creditor rights systems. Adapting international best practices to the realities of developing countries, however, requires an understanding of the market environments in which these systems operate. The challenges include weak or unclear social protection mechanisms, weak financial institutions and capital markets, ineffective corporate governance and uncompetitive businesses, and ineffective laws and institutions. These obstacles pose enormous challenges to the adoption of systems that address the needs of developing countries while keeping pace with global trends and international best practices. The application of the principles in this paper at the country level will be influenced by domestic policy choices and by the comparative strengths (or weaknesses) of laws and institutions.

7. The Principles and Guidelines highlights the relationship between the cost and flow of credit (including secured credit) and the laws and institutions that recognize and enforce credit agreements (sections 1 and 2). It also outlines key features and policy choices relating to the legal framework for corporate insolvency and the informal framework for consensual debt workouts (section 3), which must be implemented within sound institutional and regulatory frameworks (section 4). The principles have broader application beyond creditor rights and corporate insolvency regimes, as well. The ability of financial institutions to adopt effective credit practices to resolve or liquidate non-performing loans depends on having reliable and predictable legal mechanisms that provide a means for more accurately pricing recovery and enforcement costs. Where non-performing assets or other factors jeopardize the viability of a bank, or where economic conditions create systemic crises, these conditions raise issues that deserve special consideration. Annexes I and II to the Principles and Guidelines contain a discussion of issues relevant to bank exit and restructuring strategies and management of systemic financial crises, areas in which the Bank will continue to collaborate with the Fund and the international community to develop principles.

---

[4] Effective systems rest on details as well as broad principles. The Bank is preparing a companion technical paper with more detailed guidelines on aspects of this paper. Other organizations, specifically UNCITRAL (in collaboration with INSOL International and Committee J of the International Bar Association), are also developing guidelines to help legislators design effective insolvency laws.

Following is brief summary of the key elements of the Principles and Guidelines:

8. Role of enforcement systems. A modern, credit-based economy requires predictable, transparent and affordable enforcement of both unsecured and secured credit claims by efficient mechanisms outside of insolvency, as well as a sound insolvency system. These systems must be designed to work in harmony. Commerce is a system of commercial relationships predicated on express or implied contractual agreements between an enterprise and a wide range of creditors and constituencies. Although commercial transactions have become increasingly complex as more sophisticated techniques are developed for pricing and managing risks, the basic rights governing these relationships and the procedures for enforcing these rights have not changed much. These rights enable parties to rely on contractual agreements, fostering confidence that fuels investment, lending and commerce. Conversely, uncertainty about the enforceability of contractual rights increases the cost of credit to compensate for the increased risk of nonperformance or, in severe cases, leads to credit tightening.

9. Legal framework for creditor rights. A regularized system of credit should be supported by mechanisms that provide efficient, transparent and reliable methods for recovering debt, including seizure and sale of immovable and movable assets and sale or collection of intangible assets, such as debt owed to the debtor by third parties. An efficient system for enforcing debt claims is crucial to a functioning credit system, especially for unsecured credit. A creditor's ability to take possession of a debtor's property and to sell it to satisfy the debt is the simplest, most effective means of ensuring prompt payment. It is far more effective than the threat of an insolvency proceeding, which often requires a level of proof and a prospect of procedural delay that in all but extreme cases make it not credible to debtors as leverage for payment.

10. While much credit is unsecured and requires an effective enforcement system, an effective system for secured rights is especially important in developing countries. Secured credit plays an important role in industrial countries, notwithstanding the range of sources and types of financing available through both debt and equity markets. In some cases equity markets can provide cheaper and more attractive financing. But developing countries offer fewer options, and equity markets are typically less mature than debt markets. As a result most financing is in the form of debt. In markets with fewer options and higher risks, lenders routinely require security to reduce the risk of nonperformance and insolvency.

11. Legal framework for secured lending. The legal framework should provide for the creation, recognition and enforcement of security interests in all types of assets

– movable and immovable, tangible and intangible, including inventories, receivables, proceeds and future property, and on a global basis, including both possessory and non-possessory interests. The law should encompass any or all of a debtor's obligations to a creditor, present or future and between all types of persons. In addition, it should provide for effective notice and registration rules to be adapted to all types of property, and clear rules of priority on competing claims or interests in the same assets.

12. Legal framework for corporate insolvency. Though approaches vary, effective insolvency systems should aim to:

- Integrate with a country's broader legal and commercial systems.
- Maximize the value of a firm's assets by providing an option to reorganize.
- Strike a careful balance between liquidation and reorganization.
- Provide for equitable treatment of similarly situated creditors, including similarly situated foreign and domestic creditors.
- Provide for timely, efficient and impartial resolution of insolvencies.
- Prevent the premature dismemberment of the debtor's assets by individual creditors.
- Provide a transparent procedure that contains incentives for gathering and dispensing information.
- Recognize existing creditor rights and respect the priority of claims with a predictable and established process.
- Establish a framework for cross-border insolvencies, with recognition of foreign proceedings.

13. Where an enterprise is not viable, the main thrust of the law should be swift and efficient liquidation to maximize recoveries for the benefit of creditors. Liquidations can include the preservation and sale of the business, as distinct from the legal entity. On the other hand, where an enterprise is viable, meaning it can be rehabilitated, its assets are often more valuable if retained in a rehabilitated business than if sold in a liquidation. The rescue of a business preserves jobs, provides creditors with a greater return based on higher going concern values of the enterprise, potentially produces a return for owners and obtains for the country the fruits of the rehabilitated enterprise. The rescue of a business should be promoted through formal and informal procedures. Rehabilitation should permit quick and easy access to the process, protect all those involved, permit the negotiation of a commercial plan, enable a majority of creditors in favor of a plan or other course of action to bind all other creditors (subject to appropriate protections) and pro-

vide for supervision to ensure that the process is not subject to abuse. Modern rescue procedures typically address a wide range of commercial expectations in dynamic markets. Though such laws may not be susceptible to precise formulas, modern systems generally rely on design features to achieve the objectives outlined above.

14. Framework for informal corporate workouts. Corporate workouts should be supported by an environment that encourages participants to restore an enterprise to financial viability. Informal workouts are negotiated in the "shadow of the law." Accordingly, the enabling environment must include clear laws and procedures that require disclosure of or access to timely and accurate financial information on the distressed enterprise; encourage lending to, investment in or recapitalization of viable distressed enterprises; support a broad range of restructuring activities, such as debt write-offs, reschedulings, restructurings and debt-equity conversions; and provide favorable or neutral tax treatment for restructurings.

15. A country's financial sector (possibly with help from the central bank or finance ministry) should promote an informal out-of-court process for dealing with cases of corporate financial difficulty in which banks and other financial institutions have a significant exposure – especially in markets where enterprise insolvency is systemic. An informal process is far more likely to be sustained where there are adequate creditor remedies and insolvency laws.

16. Implementation of the insolvency system. Strong institutions and regulations are crucial to an effective insolvency system. The insolvency framework has three main elements: the institutions responsible for insolvency proceedings, the operational system through which cases and decisions are processed and the requirements needed to preserve the integrity of those institutions – recognizing that the integrity of the insolvency system is the linchpin for its success. A number of fundamental principles influence the design and maintenance of the institutions and participants with authority over insolvency proceedings.

17. Ongoing efforts. Substantial progress has been made in identifying links between the corporate insolvency and creditor rights systems and bank insolvency (and restructuring) and financial crisis, and the policy issues affecting the treatment of the later. Over the coming months the Bank in collaboration with the Fund and others will engage the international community in a dialogue on principles pertaining to bank and systemic insolvency. In addition, the Bank will continue to work with its partner institutions, including UNCITRAL, on the implementation of more technical guidelines based on the principles.

18. Next Steps. The Bank will carry out a series of pilot country assessments in FY2001-02 in connection with the program to develop Reports on the Observance of Standards and Codes (ROSC), using a common template based on the principles. The criteria for the selection of countries will include regional and legal diversity and levels of financial system development. The assessments would be carried out by Bank staff supported by experts from other institutions. The assessments are expected to provide valuable inputs to future Financial Sector Assessments, Country Assistance Strategies and other Bank economic and sector work, and to eventually help governments prioritize reform needs and build capacity. The Bank will also continue to collaborate with the International Monetary Fund and other organizations on the future development of complementary principles related to bank insolvency and restructuring and systemic insolvency.

The Principles

Legal Framework for Creditor Rights

Principle 1 Compatible Enforcement Systems

Principle 2 Enforcement of Unsecured Rights

Principle 3 Security Interest Legislation

Principle 4 Recording and Registration of Secured Rights

Principle 5 Enforcement of Secured Rights

Legal Framework for Insolvency

Principle 6 Key Objectives and Policies

Principle 7 Director and Officer Liability

Principle 8 Liquidation and Rehabilitation

Principle 9 Commencement: Applicability and Accessibility

Principle 10 Commencement: Moratoriums and Suspension of Proceedings

Principle 11 Governance: Management

Principle 12 Governance: Creditors and the Creditors Committee

Principle 13 Administration: Collection, Preservation, Disposition of Property

Principle 14 Administration: Treatment of Contractual Obligations

Principle 15 Administration: Fraudulent or Preferential Transactions

Principle 16 Claims Resolution: Treatment of Stakeholder Rights and Priorities

Features Pertaining to Corporate Rehabilitation

Principle 17 Design Features of Rehabilitation Statutes

Principle 18 Administration: Stabilizing and Sustaining Business Operations

Principle 19 Information: Access and Disclosure

Principle 20 Plan: Formulation, Consideration and Voting

Principle 21 Plan: Approval of Plan

Principle 22 Plan: Implementation and Amendment

Principle 23 Plan: Discharge and Binding Effects

Principle 24 International Considerations

Informal Corporate Workouts and Restructuring

Principle 25 Enabling Legislative Framework

Principle 26 Informal Workout Procedures

Implementation of the Insolvency System (Institutional & Regulatory Frameworks)

Principle 27 Role of Courts

Principle 28 Performance Standards of the Court; Qualification and Training of Judges

Principle 29 Court Organization

Principle 30 Transparency and Accountability

Principle 31 Judicial Decision Making and Enforcement

Principle 32 Integrity of the Court

Principle 33 Integrity of Participants

Principle 34 Role of Regulatory or Supervisory Bodies

Principle 35 Competence and Integrity of Insolvency Administrators

The Principles

Legal Framework for Creditor Rights

Principle 1 – Compatible Enforcement Systems

A modern credit-based economy requires predictable, transparent and affordable enforcement of both unsecured and secured credit claims by efficient mechanisms outside of insolvency, as well as a sound insolvency system. These systems must be designed to work in harmony.

Principle 2 – Enforcement of Unsecured Rights

A regularized system of credit should be supported by mechanisms that provide efficient, transparent, reliable and predictable methods for recovering debt, including seizure and sale of immovable and movable assets and sale or collection of intangible assets such as debts owed to the debtor by third parties.

Principle 3 – Security Interest Legislation

The legal framework should provide for the creation, recognition, and enforcement of security interests in movable and immovable (real) property, arising by agreement or operation of law. The law should provide for the following features:

- Security interests in all types of assets, movable and immovable, tangible and intangible, including inventory, receivables, and proceeds; future or after-acquired property, and on a global basis; and based on both possessory and non-possessory interests;
- Security interests related to any or all of a debtor's obligations to a creditor, present or future, and between all types of persons;
- Methods of notice that will sufficiently publicize the existence of security interests to creditors, purchasers, and the public generally at the lowest possible cost;
- Clear rules of priority governing competing claims or interests in the same assets, eliminating or reducing priorities over security interests as much as possible.

Principle 4 – Recording and Registration of Secured Rights

There should be an efficient and cost-effective means of publicizing secured interests in movable and immovable assets, with registration being the principal and strongly preferred method. Access to the registry should be inexpensive and open to all for both recording and search.

Principle 5 – Enforcement of Secured Rights

Enforcement systems should provide efficient, inexpensive, transparent and predictable methods for enforcing a security interest in property. Enforcement procedures should provide for prompt realization of the rights obtained in secured assets, ensuring the maximum possible recovery of asset values based on market values. Both nonjudicial and judicial enforcement methods should be considered

Legal Framework for Corporate Insolvency

Principle 6 – Key Objectives and Policies

Though country approaches vary, effective insolvency systems should aim to:

- Integrate with a country's broader legal and commercial systems.
- Maximize the value of a firm's assets by providing an option to reorganize.
- Strike a careful balance between liquidation and reorganization.
- Provide for equitable treatment of similarly situated creditors, including similarly situated foreign and domestic creditors.
- Provide for timely, efficient and impartial resolution of insolvencies.
- Prevent the premature dismemberment of a debtor's assets by individual creditors seeking quick judgments.
- Provide a transparent procedure that contains incentives for gathering and dispensing information.
- Recognize existing creditor rights and respect the priority of claims with a predictable and established process.
- Establish a framework for cross-border insolvencies, with recognition of foreign proceedings.

Principle 7 – Director and Officer Liability

Director and officer liability for decisions detrimental to creditors made when an enterprise is insolvent should promote responsible corporate behavior while fostering reasonable risk taking. At a minimum, standards should address conduct based on knowledge of or reckless disregard for the adverse consequences to creditors.

Principle 8 – Liquidation and Rehabilitation

An insolvency law should provide both for efficient liquidation of nonviable businesses and those where liquidation is likely to produce a greater return to creditors, and for rehabilitation of viable businesses. Where circumstances justify it, the system should allow for easy conversion of proceedings from one procedure to another.

Principle 9 – Commencement: Applicability and Accessibility

A. The insolvency process should apply to all enterprises or corporate entities except financial institutions and insurance corporations, which should be dealt with through a separate law or through special provisions in the insolvency law. State-owned corporations should be subject to the same insolvency law as private corporations.

B. Debtors should have easy access to the insolvency system upon showing proof of basic criteria (insolvency or financial difficulty). A declaration to that effect may be provided by the debtor through its board of directors or management. Creditor access should be conditioned on showing proof of insolvency by presumption where there is clear evidence that the debtor failed to pay a matured debt (perhaps of a minimum amount).

C. The preferred test for insolvency should be the debtor's inability to pay debts as they come due – known as the liquidity test. A balance sheet test may be used as an alternative secondary test, but should not replace the liquidity test. The filing of an application to commence a proceeding should automatically prohibit the debtor's transfer, sale or disposition of assets or parts of the business without court approval, except to the extent necessary to operate the business.

Principle 10 – Commencement: Moratoriums and Suspension of Proceedings

A. The commencement of bankruptcy should prohibit the unauthorized disposition of the debtor's assets and suspend actions by creditors to enforce their rights or remedies against the debtor or the debtor's assets. The injunctive relief (stay) should be as wide and all embracing as possible, extending to an interest in property used, occupied or in the possession of the debtor.

B. To maximize the value of asset recoveries, a stay on enforcement actions by secured creditors should be imposed for a limited period in a liquidation proceeding to enable higher recovery of assets by sale of the entire business or its productive units, and in a rehabilitation proceeding where the collateral is needed for the rehabilitation.

Principle 11 – Governance: Management

A. In liquidation proceedings, management should be replaced by a qualified court-appointed official (administrator) with broad authority to administer the estate in the interest of creditors. Control of the estate should be surrendered immediately to the administrator except where management has been authorized to retain control over the company, in which case the law should impose the same duties on management as on the administrator. In creditor-initiated filings, where circumstances warrant, an interim administrator with reduced duties should be appointed to monitor the business to ensure that creditor interests are protected.

B. There are two preferred approaches in a rehabilitation proceeding: exclusive control of the proceeding by an independent administrator or supervision of management by an impartial and independent administrator or supervisor. Under the second option complete power should be shifted to the administrator if management proves incompetent or negligent or has engaged in fraud or other misbehavior. Similarly, independent administrators or supervisors should be held to the same standard of accountability to creditors and the court and should be subject to removal for incompetence, negligence, fraud or other wrongful conduct.

Principle 12 – Governance: Creditors and the Creditors' Committee

Creditor interests should be safeguarded by establishing a creditors committee that enables creditors to actively participate in the insolvency process and that allows the committee to monitor the process to ensure fairness and integrity. The committee should be consulted on non-routine matters in the case and have the ability to be heard on key decisions in the proceedings (such as matters involving dispositions of assets outside the normal course of business). The committee should serve as a conduit for processing and distributing relevant information to other creditors and for organizing creditors to decide on critical issues. The law should provide for such things as a general creditors assembly for major decisions, to appoint the creditors committee and to determine the committee's membership, quorum and voting rules, powers and the conduct of meetings. In rehabilitation proceedings, the creditors should be entitled to select an independent administrator or supervisor of their choice, provided the person meets the qualifications for serving in this capacity in the specific case.

Principle 13 – Administration: Collection, Preservation, Disposition of Property

The law should provide for the collection, preservation and disposition of all property belonging to the debtor, including property obtained after the commencement of the case. Immediate steps should be taken or allowed to preserve and protect the debtor's assets and business. The law should provide a flexible and transparent system for disposing of assets efficiently and at maximum values. Where necessary, the law should allow for sales free and clear of security interests, charges or other encumbrances, subject to preserving the priority of interests in the proceeds from the assets disposed.

Principle 14 – Administration: Treatment of Contractual Obligations

The law should allow for interference with contractual obligations that are not fully performed to the extent necessary to achieve the objectives of the insolvency process, whether to enforce, cancel or assign contracts, except where there is a compelling commercial, public or social interest in upholding the contractual rights of the counter-party to the contract (as with swap agreements).

Principle 15 – Administration: Fraudulent or Preferential Transactions

The law should provide for the avoidance or cancellation of pre-bankruptcy fraudulent and preferential transactions completed when the enterprise was insolvent or that resulted in its insolvency. The suspect period prior to bankruptcy, during which payments are presumed to be preferential and may be set aside, should normally be short to avoid disrupting normal commercial and credit relations. The suspect period may be longer in the case of gifts or where the person receiving the transfer is closely related to the debtor or its owners.

Principle 16 – Claims Resolution: Treatment of Stakeholder Rights and Priorities

A. The rights and priorities of creditors established prior to insolvency under commercial laws should be upheld in an insolvency case to preserve the legitimate expectations of creditors and encourage greater predictability in commercial relationships. Deviations from this general rule should occur only where necessary to promote other compelling policies, such as the policy supporting rehabilitation or to maximize the estate's value. Rules of priority should support incentives for creditors to manage credit efficiently.

B. The bankruptcy law should recognize the priority of secured creditors in their collateral. Where the rights of secured creditors are impaired to promote a legitimate bankruptcy policy, the interests of these creditors in their collateral should be protected to avoid a loss or deterioration in the economic value of their interest at the commencement of the case. Distributions to secured creditors from the proceeds of their collateral should be made as promptly as possible after realization of proceeds from the sale. In cases where the stay applies to secured creditors, it should be of limited specified duration, strike a proper balance between creditor protection and insolvency objectives, and provide for the possibility of orders being made on the application of affected creditors or other persons for relief from the stay.

C. Following distributions to secured creditors and payment of claims related to costs and expenses of administration, proceeds available for distribution should be distributed pari passu to remaining creditors unless there are compelling reasons to justify giving preferential status to a particular debt. Public interests generally should not be given precedence over private rights. The number of priority classes should be kept to a minimum.

Features Pertaining to Corporate Rehabilitation

Principle 17 – Design Features of Rehabilitation Statutes

To be commercially and economically effective, the law should establish rehabilitation procedures that permit quick and easy access to the process, provide sufficient protection for all those involved in the process, provide a structure that permits the negotiation of a commercial plan, enable a majority of creditors in favor of a plan or other course of action to bind all other creditors by the democratic exercise of voting rights (subject to appropriate minority protections and the protection of class rights) and provide for judicial or other supervision to ensure that the process is not subject to manipulation or abuse.

Principle 18 – Administration: Stabilizing and Sustaining Business Operations

The law should provide for a commercially sound form of priority funding for the ongoing and urgent business needs of a debtor during the rescue process, subject to appropriate safeguards.

Principle 19 – Information: Access and Disclosure

The law should require the provision of relevant information on the debtor. It should also provide for independent comment on and analysis of that information. Directors of a debtor corporation should be required to attend meetings of creditors. Provision should be made for the possible examination of directors and other persons with knowledge of the debtor's affairs, who may be compelled to give information to the court and administrator.

Principle 20 – Plan: Formulation, Consideration and Voting

The law should not prescribe the nature of a plan except in terms of fundamental requirements and to prevent commercial abuse. The law may provide for classes of creditors for voting purposes. Voting rights should be determined by amount of debt. An appropriate majority of creditors should be required to approve a plan. Special provision should be made to limit the voting rights of insiders. The effect of a majority vote should be to bind all creditors.

Principle 21 – Plan: Approval of Plan

The law should establish clear criteria for plan approval based on fairness to similar creditors, recognition of relative priorities and majority acceptance. The law should also provide for approval over the rejection of minority creditors if the plan complies with rules of fairness and offers the opposing creditors or classes an amount equal to or greater than would be received under a liquidation proceeding. Some provision for possible adjournment of a plan decision meeting should be made, but under strict time limits. If a plan is not approved, the debtor should automatically be liquidated.

Principle 22 – Plan: Implementation and Amendment

The law should provide a means for monitoring effective implementation of the plan, requiring the debtor to make periodic reports to the court on the status of implementation and progress during the plan period. A plan should be capable of amendment (by vote of the creditors) if it is in the interests of the creditors. The law should provide for the possible termination of a plan and for the debtor to be liquidated.

Principle 23 – Discharge and Binding Effects

To ensure that the rehabilitated enterprise has the best chance of succeeding, the law should provide for a discharge or alteration of debts and claims that have been discharged or otherwise altered under the plan. Where approval of the plan has been procured by fraud, the plan should be subject to challenge, reconsidered or set aside.

Principle 24 – International Considerations

Insolvency proceedings may have international aspects, and insolvency laws should provide for rules of jurisdiction, recognition of foreign judgments, cooperation and assistance among courts in different countries, and choice of law.

Informal Corporate Workouts and Restructurings

Principle 25 – Enabling Legislative Framework

Corporate workouts and restructurings should be supported by an enabling environment that encourages participants to engage in consensual arrangements designed to restore an enterprise to financial viability. An enabling environment includes laws and procedures that require disclosure of or ensure access to timely, reliable and accurate financial information on the distressed enterprise; encourage lending to, investment in or recapitalization of viable financially distressed enterprises; support a broad range of restructuring activities, such as debt writeoffs, reschedulings, restructurings and debt- equity conversions; and provide favorable or neutral tax treatment for restructurings.

Principle 26 – Informal Workout Procedures

A country's financial sector (possibly with the informal endorsement and assistance of the central bank or finance ministry) should promote the development of a code of conduct on an informal out-of-court process for dealing with cases of corporate financial difficulty in which banks and other financial institutions have a significant exposure – especially in markets where enterprise insolvency has reached systemic levels. An informal process is far more likely to be sustained where there are adequate creditor remedy and insolvency laws. The informal process may produce a formal rescue, which should be able to quickly process a packaged plan produced by the informal process. The formal process may work better if it enables creditors and debtors to use informal techniques.

Implementation of the Insolvency System

Principle 27 – Role of Courts

Bankruptcy cases should be overseen and disposed of by an independent court or competent authority and assigned, where practical, to judges with specialized bankruptcy expertise. Significant benefits can be gained by creating specialized bankruptcy courts.

The law should provide for a court or other tribunal to have a general, non-intrusive, supervisory role in the rehabilitation process. The court/tribunal or regulatory authority should be obliged to accept the decision reached by the creditors that a plan be approved or that the debtor be liquidated.

Principle 28 – Performance Standards of the Court, Qualification and Training of Judges

Standards should be adopted to measure the competence, performance and services of a bankruptcy court. These standards should serve as a basis for evaluating and improving courts. They should be enforced by adequate qualification criteria as well as training and continuing education for judges.

Principle 29 – Court Organization

The court should be organized so that all interested parties – including the administrator, the debtor and all creditors – are dealt with fairly, objectively and transparently. To the extent possible, publicly available court operating rules, case practice and case management regulations should govern the court and other participants in the process. The court's internal operations should allocate responsibility and authority to maximize resource use. To the degree feasible the court should institutionalize, streamline and standardize court practices and procedures.

Principle 30 – Transparency and Accountability

An insolvency system should be based on transparency and accountability. Rules should ensure ready access to court records, court hearings, debtor and financial data and other public information.

Principle 31 – Judicial Decision making and Enforcement

Judicial decision making should encourage consensual resolution among parties where possible and otherwise undertake timely adjudication of issues with a view to reinforcing predictability in the system through consistent application of the law. The court must have clear authority and effective methods of enforcing its judgments.

Principle 32 – Integrity of the Court

Court operations and decisions should be based on firm rules and regulations to avoid corruption and undue influence. The court must be free of conflicts of interest, bias and lapses in judicial ethics, objectivity and impartiality.

Principle 33 – Integrity of Participants

Persons involved in a bankruptcy proceeding must be subject to rules and court orders designed to prevent fraud, other illegal activity or abuse of the bankruptcy system. In addition, the bankruptcy court must be vested with appropriate powers to deal with illegal activity or abusive conduct that does not constitute criminal activity.

Principle 34 – Role of Regulatory or Supervisory Bodies

The body or bodies responsible for regulating or supervising insolvency administrators should be independent of individual administrators and should set standards that reflect the requirements of the legislation and public expectations of fairness, impartiality, transparency and accountability.

Principle 35 – Competence and Integrity of Insolvency Administrators

Insolvency administrators should be competent to exercise the powers given to them and should act with integrity, impartiality and independence.

INFORMATION FOR AUTHORS

Authors are invited to submit manuscripts for consideration to the *Review.* All works should be original and preferably between 50 and 100 double-spaced pages (including footnotes) in length. The *Review* follows *The Chicago Manual of Style* as modified by *The World Bank Publications Style Guide*; the spelling and usage authority is *Webster's Third New International Dictionary* (Unabridged). All footnotes should provide complete citation information and preferably be formatted in accordance with the *ALWD Citation Manual.* Detailed submission guidelines and copyright assignment forms are available at <http://www.worldbank.org/legal/publications.html>.

INDEX